Prosecution of Core Crimes in Ethiopia

International Criminal Law Series

Founding Editor
M. Cherif Bassiouni
Editor-in-Chief
William Schabas, Professor of International Law, Department of Law, Middlesex University; Professor of International Criminal Law and Human Rights, Leiden University; Honorary Chairman, Irish Centre for Human Rights, National University of Ireland, Galway; Canada/Ireland

Editorial Board

Kai Ambos, Judge at the Kosovo Specialist Chambers (KSC), The Hague; Professor of Law and Head, Department for Foreign and International Criminal Law, Georg August Universität; Gottingen, Germany

Mahnoush Arsanjani, Member, Institut de Droit International; former Director, Codification Division, United Nations Office of Legal Affairs, Iran

M. Cherif Bassiouni, Distinguished Research Professor of Law Emeritus, President Emeritus, International Human Rights Law Institute, DePaul University College of Law; Honorary President, International Institute of Higher Studies in Criminal Sciences; Honorary President, Association Internationale de Droit Pénal; Chicago, USA/Egypt

Mohamed Chande Othman, Chief Justice, Court of Appeal of Tanzania; Dodoma, Tanzania

Eric David, Professor of Law, Free University of Brussels, Faculty of Law, Brussels, Belgium

Mireille Delmas-Marty, Professor of Comparative Legal Studies and Internationalisation of Law, Collège de France; former Professor of Criminal Law, University of Paris; Paris, France

Adama Dieng, UN Secretary-General's Special Adviser on the Prevention of Genocide; former Registrar, International Criminal Tribunal for Rwanda; former Secretary General, International Commission of Jurists, Senegal

Mark Drumbl, Class of 1975 Alumni Professor of Law, Director, Transnational Law Institute, Washington and Lee University School of Law, USA

Chile Eboe-Osuji, Judge, Trial Division, International Criminal Court; former Legal Adviser to the High Commissioner for Human Rights, Office of the High Commissioner for Human Rights, Nigeria

Geoff Gilbert, Professor of Law and Head of the School of Law, University of Essex, Colchester UK

Philippe Kirsch, Ad hoc Judge, International Court of Justice; former President, International Criminal Court; Ambassador (Ret.) and former Legal Advisor, Ministry of Foreign Affairs of Canada; Sallèles d'Aude, Belgium/Canada

André Klip, Professor of Law, Department of Criminal Law and Criminology, Faculty of Law, Maastricht University; Maastricht, The Netherlands

Errki Kourula, Former Judge and President of the Appeals Division, International Criminal Court; The Hague, Finland

Motoo Noguchi, Chair of the Board of Directors, ICC Trust Fund for Victims; Ambassador for International Judicial Cooperation, MOFA; Former UN International Judge, ECCC, Japan

Diane Orentlicher, Professor of International Law, Co-Director, Center for Human Rights and Humanitarian Law, Washington College of Law, American University; Washington, USA

Fausto Pocar, Judge and former President, International Criminal Tribunal for the Former Yugoslavia; President, International Institute of Humanitarian Law; Professor of International Law Emeritus, University of Milan; Italy

Leila Nadya Sadat, Henry H. Oberschelp Professor of Law, Director, Whitney R. Harris World Law Institute, Washington University School of Law; Alexis de Tocqueville Distinguished Fulbright Chair, University of Cergy-Pontoise; St. Louis, France/USA

Michael Scharf, Dean and John Deaver Drinko-Baker & Hostetlier Professor of Law, Director, Frederick K. Cox International Law Center, Case Western Reserve University School of Law; Cleveland, USA

Ulrich Sieber, Professor of Criminal Law, Director, Max Plank Institute for Foreign and International Criminal Law, University of Freiburg; Freiburg, Germany

Goran Sluiter, Professor of Law, Department of Criminal Law and Criminal Procedure, Faculty of Law, University of Amsterdam; Amsterdam, The Netherlands

Françoise Tulkens, Former Vice-President, European Court of Human Rights; Strasbourg, France

Xuimei Wang, Professor of International Criminal Law, College for Criminal Law Science, Beijing Normal University; Executive Director, ICC Project Office; Beijing, China

Christine van den Wyngaert, Judge, International Criminal Court; former Judge, International Criminal Tribunal for the Former Yugoslavia; former *Ad hoc* Judge, International Court of Justice, Belgium

Gert Vermeulen, Professor of Criminal Law, Director, Research Group Drug Policy, Criminal Policy and International Crime, Ghent University; Extraordinary Professor of Evidence Law, Maastricht University; Ghent, Belgium

Giuliana Ziccardi Capaldo, Professor of International Law, Faculty of Law, University of Salerno; Salerno, Italy

VOLUME 15

Prosecution of Core Crimes in Ethiopia

Domestic Practice vis-à-vis International Standards

By

Tadesse Simie Metekia

BRILL
NIJHOFF

LEIDEN | BOSTON

Library of Congress Cataloging-in-Publication Data

Names: Metekia, Tadesse Simie, 1984- author.
Title: Prosecution of core crimes in Ethiopia : domestic practice
  vis-à-vis international standards / by Tadesse Simie Metekia.
Description: Leiden, The Netherlands : Koninklijke Brill NV, [2021] |
  Series: International criminal law series, 2213-2724 ; volume 15 | Based
  on author's thesis (doctoral - Rijksuniversiteit Groningen, 2020). |
  Includes bibliographical references and index.
Identifiers: LCCN 2021000329 (print) | LCCN 2021000330 (ebook) |
  ISBN 9789004447257 (hardback) | ISBN 9789004447264 (ebook)
Subjects: LCSH: Criminal law–Ethiopia. | Prosecution–Ethiopia. |
  International crimes–Law and legislation–Ethiopia.
Classification: LCC KRP3800 .M48 2021 (print) | LCC KRP3800 (ebook) |
  DDC 345.63/05042–dc23
LC record available at https://lccn.loc.gov/2021000329
LC ebook record available at https://lccn.loc.gov/2021000330

Typeface for the Latin, Greek, and Cyrillic scripts: "Brill". See and download: brill.com/brill-typeface.

ISSN 2213-2724
ISBN 978-90-04-44725-7 (hardback)
ISBN 978-90-04-44726-4 (e-book)

Copyright 2021 by Koninklijke Brill NV, Leiden, The Netherlands.
Koninklijke Brill NV incorporates the imprints Brill, Brill Hes & De Graaf, Brill Nijhoff, Brill Rodopi, Brill Sense, Hotei Publishing, mentis Verlag, Verlag Ferdinand Schöningh and Wilhelm Fink Verlag.
All rights reserved. No part of this publication may be reproduced, translated, stored in a retrieval system, or transmitted in any form or by any means, electronic, mechanical, photocopying, recording or otherwise, without prior written permission from the publisher. Requests for re-use and/or translations must be addressed to Koninklijke Brill NV via brill.com or copyright.com.

This book is printed on acid-free paper and produced in a sustainable manner.

In loving memory of a dear friend, Belay Gezahegn Kassa

Contents

Acknowledgments XI
List of Tables XIII
Abbreviations XIV

1 **Introduction** 1
   1.1   Ethiopia's Involvement with International Crimes: A Prelude   1
   1.2   Statement of the Problem   6
   1.3   Central Questions of the Book   14
   1.4   Review of the Literature   15
   1.5   Methodology   20
   1.6   Scope of the Book   29
   1.7   Structure of the Book   32

PART 1
The Setting in Motion of Prosecutions of Core Crimes in Ethiopia

2 **The Decision to Prosecute Core Crimes**
   Contexts and Contents   43
   2.1   Introduction   43
   2.2   Amnestying or Prosecuting the *Dergue*: The Choice of the TGE   46
   2.3   The Scope of the Decision to Prosecute: 'Heinous and Horrendous' Criminal Acts   62
   2.4   The Decision to Prosecute: Removing Latent Impediments   76
   2.5   Conclusion   88

3 **The Decisions to Prosecute**
   Possible Motivations   90
   3.1   Introduction   90
   3.2   The TGE's Conviction to Uphold a Duty to Prosecute   94
   3.3   The Absence of Actual or Perceived Adversary   109
   3.4   Perpetrators' Lack of Remorse and Apology   114
   3.5   The TGE's Intention to Use Prosecution for Political Legitimacy   122

3.6 Post-TGE Decisions to Prosecute Core Crimes: The Persistence of Political Considerations   129
3.7 Conclusion   137

4 The Decisions to Prosecute
Who Should Be Brought to Justice?   139
4.1 Introduction   139
4.2 Delineating Prosecutorial Scope: The Notion of Unjustified Selectivity   140
4.3 The Issue of Fugitive Offenders: Trial *in Absentia* / Trial by Default   170
4.4 Conclusion   185

PART 2
Ethiopian Core Crimes Trials: Applicable Laws, Crimes, and Punishment

5 The Crime of Genocide in Ethiopian Law   189
5.1 Introduction   189
5.2 The Early Ethiopian Ratification of the Genocide Convention   191
5.3 Incorporating the Crime of Genocide into Ethiopian Law   194
5.4 Evolution of the Ethiopian Law on Genocide   208
5.5 The Status of the Genocide Convention in the Ethiopian Legal System   219
5.6 Conclusion: The Duality of Laws Applicable to the Crime of Genocide in Ethiopia   231

6 The Crime of Genocide in Ethiopian Trials
Elements of the Crime   236
6.1 Introduction   236
6.2 Material Element: Protected Groups   239
6.3 *Actus Reus* of Genocide: Underlying Offenses   251
6.4 Mental Element of Genocide   271
6.5 Conclusion: Undiscussed Genocides   305

7 War Crimes in Ethiopia
Law and Practice   308
7.1 Introduction   308

7.2   Early Efforts to Punish War Crimes in Ethiopia: The UNWCC and the EWCC   313
7.3   War Crimes Law in Ethiopia and the Serious Violations of IHL Yardstick   321
7.4   Neutrality of the Ethiopian War Crimes Provisions: The Abolition of the Distinction between Armed Conflicts   327
7.5   The Scope of War Crimes in Ethiopian Law: Interpretative and Direct Application of IHL   334
7.6   Individual Acts of War Crimes: Ethiopian Law *vis-à-vis* the ICC Statute   348
7.7   War Crimes in Ethiopian Practice: The *Legesse Asfaw et al.* Case   353
7.8   The Absence of More War Crimes Trials: Why Only *Legesse Asfaw Et al.*?   366
7.9   Conclusion   370

8 Punishment and Sentencing of Core Crimes in Ethiopia   373
8.1   Introduction   373
8.2   Applicable Penalties for Core Crimes under Ethiopian Law: Principal and Secondary   378
8.3   Changes in Applicable Penalties and the Principle of *Lex Mitior*   399
8.4   Sentencing Rationales   403
8.5   Factors in Sentence Determination: Aggravation and Mitigation   407
8.6   Multiplicity of Convicts and the Problem of Individualization of Punishment   427
8.7   Conclusion   429

9 Conclusion
Trying Core Crimes with Political Ambition and Judicial Ineptness   431
9.1   Findings in Part 1 Prosecuting Core Crimes through Political Emphasis and Indifference   432
9.2   Findings in Part 2 Duality of the Applicable Law and Singularity of the Jurisprudence   439
9.3   Final Remarks: Legacy of Trials That Did Not Mirror ICL Standards   447

List of Cases   450
List of Laws   466
Bibliography   475
Index   498

Acknowledgments

This Book is a result of a PhD thesis defended on 20 February 2020 at the University of Groningen in the Netherlands. I am forever indebted to my promoter, Professor Caroline Fournet, for her years of guidance and support including during the time of publishing this book. It was her extremely understanding and unceasingly encouraging supervision that helped me continue working on the research even when the process took longer than planned.

I also wish to thank my second supervisor, Professor Alette Smeulers, whose insightful comments has greatly benefited this book. The inspiration to publish this book also came from comments and encouragements I received from Professor William Schabas, Professor Anja Matwijkiw, Professor Hein Wolswijk, Professor Marcel Brus, Professor Panos Merkouris, Professor Michael Bohlander, and Professor Harmen van der Wilt, members of the examining and *cum laude* committee of my PhD thesis.

Extended and multiple stays in Ethiopia and the Netherlands to carry out this research were made possible by generous funding from the University of Groningen's Ubbo Emmius Scholarship and the Department of Criminal Law and Criminology, the Civil Society Scholars Award of the Open Society Foundation, and Jimma University in Ethiopia. A special thank you to Professor Berend Keulen for making the initial arrangements for my research.

Too many friends encouraged and assisted me with various aspects of my research. Special gratitude is reserved for Dr. Fitsum Tiche. Blen Shimengus's support merits special mention. I am also grateful to Dr. Abera Kaney, Solomon Awuraris, Feven Mekonnen, Abay Addis, Sineshaw Abate, Ermyas Admasu, Rahel Tassew, Wagari Negassa, Ayaantu Dereje, Muluken Getachew, Milkessa Chimdessa, Balewgize Seleshi, Abraham Wondimu, Dr. Wondwessen Melaku, Dr. Tekabe Legesse, and my uncle, Birhanu Legesse. I wish to thank my many colleagues at the University of Groningen, but particularly Suzanne Schot, Yves Sezirahiga, Professor Kai Lindenberg, Professor Ward Ferdinandusse, and Dr. Willem Geelhoed. Several of my colleagues at Jimma University understood the challenges of conducting research with intermittent access to the internet and frustrating data collection process. I am grateful to Seyoum Adugna, Kibrome Mekonnen, Azeb Belachew, and Dr. Adula Bekele, whose support helped me to focus on the research.

Financial support by Groningen Graduate School of Law enabled me to travel to all of the regional and federal courts that have tried the core crimes in Ethiopia. Nonetheless, I could not have accessed the unpublished judicial decisions without the help of Belay Gezahegn and Bisrat Mulugeta from Hawassa,

Birhanu Korsa, Birhanu Beyene, and Dr. Mahammud Abdulahi from Harar, Birtukan Haile from Mekelle, Melkamu Aboma from Bahir Dar. My deepest thanks go to Lincoln Enu (Kiyya) and Natnael Aklilu (Beka), who relentlessly visited the archives of the Federal High Court in Addis Ababa for more than a year in search of misplaced genocide and war crimes case files. Special gratitude to Aklilu Beyene, Professor Edward Kissi, Dr. Biruk Haile, Dr. Jacob Weibel, Dr. Thijs Bouwknegt, Hirut Abebe Jiri, Judge Melaku Kassaye, Amanuel Yigezu, Behailu Bekele, Behailu Woldeyehuannes, and Yonas Tariku for sending me information and materials that I could not have otherwise found. I also had the rare chance of discussing some of the issues in this book with one of the prosecutors in the *Dergue* trials, Mr. Yosef Kiros, Deputy-Chief SPO.

To complement the process of data collection, I have set up a website, the Ethiopian Criminal Law Network, http://www.ethcriminallawnetwork.com, which aims at serving as a comprehensive database of laws, documents, and cases on Ethiopian criminal law. Most of the court cases referred to in this book are now available on the website. I am greatly indebted to Dr. Taye Tolu who took the time to build this website. I also thank the personnel of Brill Publishing, in particular Fem Eggers and Lindy Melman, for their support and reliable professionalism.

I would be surprised if I find the right words to express, even remotely, my love and respect for my Mom and Dad, and my siblings: Mesi, Demoz, Alex, and Asu. Their endless love and unfailing support is matchless.

Tables

1   Summary of the Ethiopian Trials   13
2   Summary of Ethiopian laws on major omissions and additions to the Convention's definition of genocide   218
3   Genocide trials in Ethiopia   236
4   Brief comparison of war crimes in the ICC Statute and FDRE Criminal Code   349
5   Summary of number of persons indicted, convicted, and acquitted on charges of genocide and war crimes   374
6   Summary of sentences imposed for genocide and war crimes   376
7   Penalties applicable to core crimes: Ethiopian law *vis-à-vis* the Statutes of the ICC and UNICTs   380
8   Penalties for Core Crimes under the Penal Code and the Criminal Code   400

Abbreviations

AESM	All Ethiopian Socialist Movement
AHC	African Human Rights Commission
ASC	Amhara Supreme Court
CAT	Convention Against Torture
CODEF	Coalition Democratic Ethiopia Forces
CRID	Central Revolutionary Investigation Department
CUD	Coalition for Unity and Democracy
ECHR	European Convention on Human Rights
ECtHR	European Court of Human Rights
EDU	Ethiopian Democratic Union
EPLF	Eritrean Liberation Front
EPRA	Ethiopian Peoples' Revolutionary Army
EPRDF	Ethiopian Peoples' Revolutionary Democratic Front
EPRP	Ethiopian People's Revolutionary Party
ETv	Ethiopian Television
EWCC	Ethiopian War Crimes Commission
FDRE	Federal Democratic Republic of Ethiopia
FHC	Federal High Court
FSC	Federal Supreme Court
FSC CB	Federal Supreme Court Cassation Bench
HoF	House of Federations (Ethiopia)
HPR	House of Peoples' Representatives (Ethiopia)
HRC	Human Rights Committee
HSC	Harari Supreme Court
HUDAS	Higher Urban Dwellers Associations
IACtHR	Inter-American Court of Human Rights
ICC	International Criminal Court
ICCPR	International Covenant on Civil and Political Rights
ICL	International Criminal Law
ICTR	International Criminal Tribunal for Rwanda
ICTY	International Criminal Tribunal for Former Yugoslavia
IHL	International Humanitarian Law
ILC	International Law Commission
IMT	International Military Tribunal
OLF	Oromo Liberation Front
ONLF	Ogaden National Liberation Front
OSC	Oromia Supreme Court

LIST OF ABBREVIATIONS

PDRE	Peoples' Democratic Republic of Ethiopia
PFSIU	Public Force Special Investigation Unit
POMOA	Provisional Office for Mass Organizations Affairs
PSPC	Public Security Protection Committee
RIU	Revolutionary Information Unit
RPPO	Regular Public Prosecutors' Office
RTS	Rape Trauma Syndrome
SCSL	Special Court for Sierra Leone
SNNPRS SC	Southern Nations Nationalities and Peoples' Regional State Supreme Court
SPO	Special Prosecutors' Office
TGE	Transitional Government of Ethiopia
TPDM	Tigray Peoples' Democratic Movement
TPLF	Tigray Peoples' Liberation Front
TSC	Tigray Supreme Court
UDHR	Universal Declaration of Human Rights
UN	United Nations
UNGA	United Nations General Assembly
UNICTS	United Nations International Criminal Tribunals
UNSC	United Nations Security Council
UNWCC	United Nations War Crimes Commission
VCLT	Vienna Convention on the Law of Treaties

CHAPTER 1

Introduction

1.1 Ethiopia's Involvement with International Crimes: A Prelude

Ethiopia, the oldest independent state in Africa that was never colonized, has a complex and duplicitous record with respect to issues involving the prosecution of international core crimes such as crimes against humanity, war crimes and genocide.[1] There are ample indicators that might have made Ethiopia appear, internationally, as a nation devoted to ensuring international peace and justice. It has for instance contributed to the creation and enforcement of an international criminal law regime as evidenced by, *inter alia*, its declaration of adherence to the London Agreement of 1945 for the Prosecution and Punishment of the Major War Criminals of the European Axis,[2] its efforts to initiate international judicial actions to denounce colonial atrocities committed outside its frontiers,[3] and being one of the pioneers in, and even an

---

1   In this book, the expressions 'core crimes' and 'international crimes' are used interchangeably. The crime of aggression, although recently included within the ambit of the International Criminal Court's jurisdiction and which could therefor also be qualified as a core crime, is here being left aside since it falls outside the Ethiopian context as it is not discussed by its courts.

2   United Nations, Agreement for the prosecution and punishment of the major war criminals of the European Axis (London Agreement), 82 U.N.T.C. 280, *entered into force* 8 August 1945. In addition to the principal signatories to the Agreement, the four major allied powers, Ethiopia and eighteen other countries showed their support to the agreement, by adherence in accordance with Article 5. For details, see The London Agreement of 8 August 1945, available at <https://treaties.un.org/pages/showDetails.aspx?objid=0800000280157a2a2> accessed 10 March 2019.

   Ethiopia's declaration of adherence to the London Agreement, as the only African State, seems to have been prompted by the fact that it had a belligerent status during the Second World War. In 1942, soon after the Italian occupation of Ethiopia came to an end with the latter regaining its independence, Ethiopia declared that, in support of what it called 'the fight for the liberation of the world', a state of war existed between itself and the Axis powers. See the Declaration of War Proclamation, Proclamation No. 33/1942, Preamble, para.1, and Article 2. For details of the second Italo-Ethiopian war, see C. Paoletti, *A military history of Italy* (Westport: Praeger Security International, 2008) 151–161.

3   For instance, in the 1960s, and thus years before the United Nations adopted the Apartheid Convention, Ethiopia, acting in concert with Liberia, instituted proceedings before the International Court of Justice for violations of the League of Nations' Mandate for South West Africa by the Government of the Union of South Africa. See International Court of Justice, South West Africa Cases: *Ethiopia v. South Africa and Liberia v. South*

exceptionally consistent contributor to, international and regional peacekeeping and peace enforcement missions.⁴

Ethiopia has acceded to and ratified a number of international treaties relevant to the field of international crimes and justice⁵ – the Rome Statute of the International Criminal Court (ICC) being a significant exception.⁶ Notably, it is

---

Africa, Second Phase, 1966, available at<https://www.icj-cij.org/files/case-related/46/046-19660718-JUD-01-00-EN.pdf> accessed 11 March 2019.

4 Ethiopia's involvement in peacekeeping operations was initiated during the second half of the 20th century as a troop contributor to a United Nations Joint Command in the Korean War of 1950–1953. See <https://history.state.gov/milestones/1945–1952/korean-war-2> accessed 20 March 2019. 'We love universal liberty' is the motto based on which Ethiopia's commitment to participate in peacekeeping operations appears to have been established. See the Memorial of the Korean War, Establishment Decree of 1952 (Ethiopia), Decree No. 12/ 1952. Currently, the country has the leading peacekeeping profile in Africa, and it is the fourth largest troop contributor to UN peacekeeping operations on the globe. For a detailed record on Ethiopia's peacekeeping profile, see <http://www.providingforpeacekeeping.org/2014 /04/03/contributor-profile-Ethiopia/> accessed 20 March 2019. Furthermore, in relation to the 1994 genocide in Rwanda, it is reported that only Ethiopia offered a unit ready for immediate service in the United Nations Assistance Mission in Rwanda, while the Security Council was unable to take a tangible decision. See W. Schabas, *Genocide in International Law* (2nd ed., Cambridge: Cambridge University Press, 2009) 549.

5 For the complete list of International Humanitarian Law (IHL) instruments and related conventions that Ethiopia acceded to or ratified, See <https://ihl-databases.icrc.org/applic/ihl/ihl.nsf/vwTreatiesByCountrySelected.xsp?xp_countrySelected=ET> accessed 20 March 2019. However, Ethiopia is not yet a signatory to the following human rights treaties: Slavery, Servitude, Forced Labor and Similar Institutions and Practices Convention of 1926 (Slavery Convention of 1926), 60 L.N.T.S. 253, *entered into force* 9 March 1927, International Convention for the Protection of All Persons from Enforced Disappearance, Human Rights Council, Report to the General Assembly on the First Session of the Human Rights Council, at 32, U.N. Doc. A/HRC/1/L.10 (2006); International Convention on the Protection of the Rights of All Migrant Workers and Members of Their Families, G.A. res. 45/158, annex, 45 U.N. GAOR Supp. (No. 49A) at 262, U.N. Doc. A/45/49 (1990), *entered into force* 1 July 2003. For more on treaty ratification status of Ethiopia, see <https://tbinternet.ohchr.org/_layouts/TreatyBodyExternal/Treaty.aspx> accessed 21 March 2019.

6 Rome Statute of the International Criminal Court U.N. Doc. 2187 U.N.T.S. 90, *entered into force* 1 July 2002. Apparently, there is no indication towards a possibility that Ethiopia may accede to the Rome Statute. The Federal Democratic Republic of Ethiopia (FDRE) has not made an official statement regarding why it is not yet ready to join the ICC. The clearest Ethiopian position towards the ICC is so far limited to statements expressed in relation to recent issues on Africa's relationship with the ICC. In his remarks, the Minister for Foreign Affairs of Ethiopia, at the 15th Extraordinary Session of the Executive Council of the African Union (AU) in October 2013, stated, 'We should not allow the ICC to continue to treat Africa and Africans in a condescending manner'. See <https://www.reuters.com/article/us-africa-icc/african-union-runs-critical-eye-over-icc-idUSBRE99A0BS20131011> accessed 18 March 2019. See also the African Union Decision on Africa's Relationship with the International Criminal Court (ICC) in which Ethiopia actively participated, Ext/Assembly/

INTRODUCTION 3

not only the first country in the world to have ratified the first UN human rights treaty, the Genocide Convention,[7] but it also has incorporated the offense of genocide into its Penal Code of 1957.[8] The same Penal Code, repealed in 2004 by the Federal Republic of Ethiopia (FDRE) Criminal Code,[9] could be mentioned as one of the very few in the world which criminalized the grave breaches of the Geneva Conventions[10] as such.[11] In fact, the incorporation of the grave breaches into the Ethiopian legal system represents a rare instance of domestic criminalization in the sense that its timing antedates even the ratification of the relevant conventions by Ethiopia, which only materialized over a decade after the entry into force of the Penal Code.[12]

AU/Dec.1 (Oct.2013), available at <https://www.legal-tools.org/en/browse/record/edad86/> accessed 20 March 2019. During this Extraordinary Session of the Assembly of the African Union, the Ethiopian Prime Minister, apparently in his capacity as a chairperson of the AU, expressly stated that Africa objected to the ICC process that has degenerated from fighting impunity into 'some kind of race-hunting'. See Reuters, available at: <http://www.reuters.com/article/2013/05/27/us-africa-icc-idUSBRE94Q0F620130527> accessed 18 March 2019.

7   Convention on the Prevention and Punishment of the Crime of Genocide, 78 U.N.T.S. 277, *entered into force* 12 January 1951 [Hereinafter: the Genocide Convention]. Ethiopia was also among the 19 States that signed the Convention on 11 December 1948. According to Edward Kissi, the fact that Ethiopia was a victim of the use of poison gas against civilians perpetrated by Italy under Benito Mussolini in 1935–36 might have created a sensitivity to become among the first nations to ratify the Genocide Convention. See E. Kissi, *Revolution and Genocide in Ethiopia and Cambodia*, (Lanham: Lexington Books, 2006) 98. It could also be because treaty ratification in Ethiopia was, during the relevant time, a non-time-consuming process, as discussed in Chapters 4 and 5 of this work.

8   The Penal Code of the Empire of Ethiopia of 1957, Proclamation No. 158/1957, Extraordinary Issue No. 1, of 1957 of the Negarit Gazeta, 23 July 1957, *entered into force* 5 May 1958 [Hereinafter: the Penal Code of 1957], Article 281.

9   The Criminal Code of the Federal Democratic Republic of Ethiopia, Proclamation No. 414/2004 *entered into force* 9 May 2005 [FDRE Criminal Code].

10 Geneva Convention for the Amelioration of the Condition of the Wounded and Sick in Armed Forces in the Field, 75 U.N.T.S. 31, *entered into force* 21 October 1950 [Hereinafter: Geneva Convention I]; Geneva Convention for the Amelioration of the Condition of Wounded, Sick and Shipwrecked Members of Armed Forces at Sea, 75 U.N.T.S. 85, *entered into force* 21 October 1950 [Hereinafter: Geneva Convention II]; Geneva Convention relative to the Treatment of Prisoners of War, 75 U.N.T.S. 135, *entered into force* 21 October 1950 [Hereinafter: Geneva Convention III]; Geneva Convention relative to the Protection of Civilian Persons in Time of War, 75 U.N.T.S. 287, *entered into force* 21 October 1950 [Hereinafter: Geneva Convention IV].

11 See the Penal Code of 1957, Articles 282–295. See also R. van Elst, 'Implementing Universal Jurisdiction Over Grave Breaches of the Geneva Conventions', (2000) 13(1) *Leiden Journal of International Law* 815–854, 825–828. For details, see Chapter 7.

12 Ethiopia ratified the Geneva Conventions only in 1969. The early incorporation of the grave breaches in the Ethiopian Penal Code is attributable to a personal initiative taken

These progressive steps notwithstanding, many mass atrocities were committed in Ethiopia. It is a country that has never managed to bring about a peaceful and orderly society. Its internal history reveals that the country has constantly gone through periods of violence which grow into situations that claimed the lives of thousands, and even hundreds of thousands, of its people.[13] For centuries, both before and after unification,[14] Ethiopians have witnessed extreme forms of violence that were de-emphasized and largely shunned from official narratives of their country's history.[15] Generations have been successively left to nurture the haunting traumatic memories of recurring calamities and atrocities instead of being offered any sort of remedy, be it in the form of restorative or retributive justice.

---

by the Penal Code's drafter, Professor Jean Graven, who was also a member of the drafting committees of the Geneva Conventions of 1949.

13 Usually, histories are often contested with countless versions emerging to either deliberately obscure or to genuinely establish the past. However, there appears to be no disagreement among historians and writers regarding Ethiopia's history of darkness. See for instance, Babile Tola who writes, '…violence has almost always been the media of government-people relations in Ethiopia. The Country's history is filled with numerous pages and chapters of repressions and massacres perpetrated by those in power against the people'. B.Tola, *To kill the Generation: The Red Terror in Ethiopia* (2nd ed., Washington DC: Free Ethiopian Press, 1989) 3. Professor Baharu Zewde, a renowned historian, regards Tola's statements as a 'simplistic rendering of Ethiopia's past', only to reiterate a statement of a similar nature, namely, that 'the history of the country is replete with wars and acts of violence'. See B. Zewde, 'The history of the Red Terror: Contexts and Consequences' in K. Tronvoll *et al.* (eds.), *The Ethiopian Red Terror Trials: Transitional Justice Challenged* (Martlesham: James Currey, 2009) 17–32, 20. Not only conflicts and wars but also widespread drought and famine, that claimed hundreds of thousands of lives of Ethiopians over and over again, depict the darkest pages in Ethiopian history. See B. Zewde, *A History of Modern Ethiopia: 1855–1991* (2nd edn., Oxford: James Currey Ltd, 2001) 71–72; D. Woldegiorgis, *Red Tears: War, Famine and Revolution in Ethiopia* (Trenton, The Red Sea Press, 1989) 121–142.

14 Ethiopia's north and south were unified after prolonged military expeditions between 1889 and 1913. See in general Zewde, *A History of Modern Ethiopia, supra* note 13, 60–71. In terms of geographic boundary, the country took its current shape between 1896–1908 by treaties signed between Ethiopia and the three major colonial powers in Africa (Italy, France and Great Britain). For details on this, see T. Haile-Selassie, *The Ethiopian Revolution 1974–1991: From a Monarchical Autocracy to a Military Oligarchy* (London: Kegan Paul International, 1997) 30–32.

15 The origins and history of Ethiopia as a nation state are highly disputed. An officially suggested impartial version of how the country emerged and evolved as a nation-state is not available. The construction of the country around a single culture that existed for thousands of years was criticized and considered as unrepresentative of the more than 84 largely distinct ethnic groups in the country. See in general C. Clapham, 'Re-writing Ethiopian History' (2002) 18(1) *Annales d'Éthiopie* 37–54.

INTRODUCTION

On 8 August 1992, however, Ethiopia managed to change the course of its history. On this date, the Transitional Government of Ethiopia (TGE), established in 1991,[16] reached an unprecedented policy decision to bring to trial those responsible for the atrocities that had befallen the country from 1974 to 1991,[17] for the purpose of which a Special Prosecutor's Office (SPO)[18] was established. The 17 years under the *Dergue*[19] regime[20] arguably represent one of the bleakest periods in the modern history of Ethiopia.[21] During this period, tens of thousands of Ethiopia's best educated were selectively killed, thousands were systematically tortured, injured, jailed or forcefully disappeared, peasants were starved and forcefully relocated, and hundreds of thousands died because of malnutrition and disease.[22] Although there is no official statement

16 The TGE was established in 1991 for a period of two years. However, subsequent extensions were made to the transitional period that led the TGE to last until 1995. See Transitional Period Charter of Ethiopia: Proclamation No.1/1991, *entered into force on* 22 July 1991 [Hereinafter: Transitional Charter of Ethiopia].

17 The policy decision to prosecute was promulgated as a law. See Proclamation Establishing the Office of the Special Prosecutor: Proclamation No. 22/1991, *entered into force* 8 August 1992. [Hereinafter: the SPO Proclamation]. This decision was unprecedented from a local point of view in the sense that it was the first and only instance in which Ethiopia decided to hold thousands of its citizens to account for violations of human rights, despite the existence of several examples of similar atrocities that took place in the context of the countless conflicts and forceful regime changes in the country's history. For a brief account of atrocities and conflicts in the period commonly referred to as modern Ethiopia (from 1885 to 1991), see Zewde, *A History of Modern Ethiopia, supra* note 13, 27–80.

18 Recently, some writers have referred to the SPO as 'the SPP' (Special Public Prosecutor). See M.T. Tessema, *Prosecution of Politicide in Ethiopia: The Red-Terror Trials* (The Hague: Asser Printing Press, 2018), 5. The use of 'the SPP' might imply that there was just a one-person special public prosecutor while in reality what was established by the TGE was an office composed of several prosecutors including the Chief and the Deputy-Chief Special Prosecutors. See The SPO Proclamation, *supra* note 17, Article 3.

19 The '*Dergue*' is an Amharic word '**ደርግ**' with Geez origins, which in its literal and original meaning denotes 'Committee/Council', though it now appears to be devoid of its original meaning and confined to indicating the heinous nature of the provisional administration council (a Council of Armed Forces, Police and Territorial Army) that ruled the country from 1974–1991. Various literatures spell '*Dergue*' as '*Derg*'. The choice to adopt the former spelling in this book is solely to conform with the spelling used in legal documents such as the SPO Proclamation.

20 The Mengistu regime came to power in 1974 through a military revolution that dethroned Emperor Haileselassie and instead established a provisional military government. See Provisional Military Government Establishment Proclamation, Proclamation No. 1 of 1974, *entered into force* 12 September 1974 [Hereinafter: PMGE Proclamation].

21 See A. Kebede, 'The Social Origins of Military Dictatorship in Ethiopia' (2010)26 (3)*Journal of Developing Societies* 295–327, 295.

22 See R. Prouveze and N. Brenaz, 'International and domestic prosecutions' in M.C. Bassiouni (ed.), *The Pursuit of International Criminal Justice, Vol. I: A World Study on*

regarding the number of victims, some have estimated that the *Dergue* regime took the lives of as many as 725,000 Ethiopians[23] while others put the estimate close to 2,000,000.[24]

1.2 Statement of the Problem

Following the TGE's decision to prosecute, 5,119 members and affiliates of the *Dergue* regime[25] were brought to trial before both federal and state courts.[26] As

---

Conflicts, Victimization, and Post-Conflict Justice (Antwerp: Intersentia, 2010) 386–387; See Human Rights Watch, 'Evil Days: 30 Years of War and Famine in Ethiopia' (Report of African Watch, September 1991) 1, available at <https://www.hrw.org/sites/default/files/reports/Ethiopia919.pdf> accessed 20 March 2019. [Hereinafter: Thirty Years of Evil Days]; Y. Santamaria, 'Afro communism: Ethiopia, Angola, and Mozambique' in M. Kramer (ed.), *The Black Book of Communism: Crimes, Terror, Repression* (Cambridge: Harvard University Press, 1999) 683–704.

23 According to African Watch Report, 500,000 'famine deaths' occurred between just 1982 and 1986 while the regime caused between 225,000 and 317,000 deaths through human rights violations. See Thirty Years of Evil Days, *supra* note 22, 172.

24 See P. Milkias, 'Mengistu Haile Mariam: Profile of a Dictator' (1994) 4 (1) *Ethiopian Review* 57–59, 57.

25 See the FDRE House of Peoples' Representatives, *Completion Report of the Special Prosecutor's Office* (7 February 2010) 11.

26 Since 1995, Ethiopia has adopted a dual judicial structure: Federal and State courts, each having three-tiered structure. At the federal level, the country has a supreme court, high courts, and first instance courts. The supreme federal judicial authority is vested in the federal Supreme Court, which also embodies a cassation bench with a power to rule over any final court decision containing a basic error of law. Nevertheless, the Federal Supreme Court does not have the power to interpret the Federal Constitution – that power is in the hands of the House of Federation, one of the two federal houses that is composed of 'representatives of nations, nationalities and peoples'. See Constitution of the Federal Democratic Republic of Ethiopia, Proclamation No. 1/1995, Articles 62, 78, 79, and 80 [Hereinafter: FDRE Constitution].

Although federal courts are usually established in Addis Ababa and Dire Dawa, the two cities under the administration of the federal government, they may hold circuit hearings in regional administrations on matters falling under their jurisdiction. See Federal Courts Amendment Proclamation, Proclamation No. 254/2001, Article 7. Besides, the Constitution allows for the nationwide establishment of federal courts, whenever deemed necessary. See FDRE Constitution, Article 78 (2).

At the state level too, the Constitution provides for the establishment of three levels of courts. Accordingly, each of the nine states has a supreme court, high courts, and first-instance courts. See ibid., Article 78 (3). An appeal can be lodged against the decision of the State Supreme Court to the FSC. An appeal against the decision of a regional supreme court's Cassation Bench can be taken to FSC's Cassation Bench (FSC CB), making the latter the highest judicial authority in the country. See FDRE Constitution, Article 80(3).

experts had already estimated, the SPO process took a very long time and was completed in 2010.[27] Most of the defendants were found guilty of perpetrating various offenses including core crimes.[28] The leader of the *Dergue,* Colonel Mengistu Hailemariam, colloquially dubbed as 'the butcher of Addis',[29] was tried in absentia and sentenced to death for masterminding and ordering acts of killing against members of political opposition groups, qualified as 'crimes against humanity and genocide' pursuant to Articles 281 of the Penal Code of 1957.[30]

A separate and exclusive court of appeal does not exist in either system. Higher courts have appellate jurisdiction over judgments of lower courts. Supreme courts both at the federal and regional levels have the final appellate power over, respectively, state and federal matters. See the FDRE Constitution, Article 80(1) and (2). Appeals are by and large limited to sentences and judgments of trial courts. Unlike international practice, Ethiopian law and practice on criminal procedure do not seem to be allowing for interlocutory appeals, except when an appeal concerns the right to bail. See Criminal Procedure Code of Ethiopia. Article 184.

As regards core crimes discussed in this book, it was the FHC that was considered to have the primary jurisdiction, although there was no clear law to that end. Regional supreme courts had, therefore, exercised jurisdiction over core crimes pursuant to the delegation principle, in which the FHC delegates its jurisdictional power to the regional supreme court of the *locus delict.* See FDRE Constitution, Article 80(2). In the Ethiopian core crimes trials, the FSC exercised appellate jurisdiction over judgments of the FHC and all other regional courts.

27 See, for instance, Ins Resource Information Center, 'Profile Series: Ethiopia, Update on Political Conditions (PR/ETH/94.001)' United States Department of Justice (December 1994) 5, available at: <http://hrlibrary.umn.edu/ins/ethiop94.pdf> accessed 20 March 2019.

28 The international crimes for which the *Dergue* stood trial included: *i*) crimes against humanity and genocide pursuant to Article 281 of the Penal Code of 1957, *ii*) war crimes against the civilian population pursuant to article 282 of the Penal Code, and *iii*) provocation and preparation to committing, permitting or supporting of acts that constitute of genocide and war crimes in violation of article 286 of the Penal Code.

Domestic crimes on the other hand included: murder (Article 522 of the Penal Code), grave willful injury (Article 538 of the Penal Code), unlawful arrest or detention (Article 416 of the Penal Code), abuse of power (Article 414 of the Penal Code), aggravated property damage (Article 654 of the Penal Code), and rape (Article 589 of the Penal Code).

29 Apparently, the reference to Mengistu as a 'butcher' was made in 1999 by the late Ethiopian prime minister Meles Zenawi (1991–2012) in a speech made at Lomé to convince the African leaders that the African Union (AU) should not move its headquarters from Addis Ababa, the capital of Ethiopia. According to Zenawi, '[i]nternally, Mengistu was a *butcher*; but, on the issue of Africa, [he] was as solid as [emperor] Haileselassie was'. [emphasis added] The speech is available at: <https://www.youtube.com/watch?v=09aHxYbWA0c> accessed 20 March 2019.

30 See FSC, SPO v. *Colonel Mengistu Hailemariam et al.,* (Appeal Judgment), 26 May 2008, File No. 30181.

The *Dergue* trials, often mistakenly referred to as 'the Red-Terror trials',[31] were the first but not the last time Ethiopia prosecuted core crimes. Absent any official reference to the trials as such, the expression Red-Terror trials appears to have been derived from the situation christened 'Red-Terror' in the late 1970's, which, arguably, signified a climax of infernal atrocities that the *Dergue* unleashed against the Ethiopia people, not least in the urban areas.[32] Referring to the *Dergue* trials as the Red-Terror trials is problematic. It unjustifiably diminishes the scope of the trials in terms of victims, nature of the crimes, and the SPO's temporal scope.[33] Furthermore, such a reference seems to have overlooked the fact that the SPO has actually prosecuted crimes perpetrated

---

31 Nearly all commentators have referred to the trials conducted by the SPO as 'Red-Terror trials'. See the Review of the Literature below (Section 1.4). Some have attempted to provide an operational definition of the Red-Terror trials by limiting the scope of these trials to a single case involving the top-officials of the *Dergue* regime, namely *Mengistu et al.* See A. Allo and B. Tesfaye, 'Spectacles of illegality: mapping Ethiopia's show trials' 13 *African Identities* (2015) 279–296.

32 Nonetheless, some authors have insisted on referring to the *Dergue* trials as the Red-Terror trials, for unclear reasons. See e.g., G.A. Aneme, 'Apology and trials: The case of the Red Terror trials in Ethiopia' (2006) 6(1) *African Human Rights Law Journal* 64–84; Tessema, *Prosecution of Politicide in Ethiopia, supra* note 18, 5. Although authors and organizations disagree as to the start date of the Red-Terror period, the fact that it intensified and ended in the late 1970s has not been disputed. For details on this, see Chapter 4, sub-section 4.2.1.2.1.1. For general discussions on genealogical aspects of the Red-Terror, see M. Tegegn, 'Mengistu's Red Terror' (2012) 10(3) *African Identities* 249–263; P. Toggia, 'The Revolutionary Endgame of Political Power: The Genealogy of 'Red Terror' in Ethiopia' (2012) 10(3) *African Identities* 265–280; Tessema, *Prosecution of Politicide in Ethiopia, supra* note 18, 36–49. For relevant remarks in the case law, see FHC, SPO v. *Hailu Burrayyu Sima et al.,* (Trial Judgment, 31 October 205), File No. 03119, 86.

33 The SPO was established to prosecute crimes committed throughout the regime, with no selectivity as to the place and time of commission. See The SPO Proclamation, *supra* note 17, preamble, para 4. As far as temporal jurisdiction is concerned, the SPO's jurisdiction covered the period between and including 1974 and 1991. See for instance, FHC, SPO v. *Teshome Bayyu et al.,* (Sentencing Judgment), 22 January 2009, File No. 07415,15. This was in fact the intention of the TGE, as evidenced by the inclusion in the SPO Proclamation of a provision on non-applicability of statute of limitations in relation to both international and domestic crimes committed during the *Dergue* regime. See the discussion in Chapter 2, sub-section 2.3.1.

The fact that the scope of the *Dergue* crimes is not limited to the Red-Terror violence will be elaborated, in particular, in Chapter 4 in relation to perpetrators, victims and offenses. As can be inferred from a discussion in Chapter 6, sub-section 6.4.1, the Red-Terror was not the only campaign of violence orchestrated and implemented by the *Dergue*. Furthermore, the Red-Terror was itself commonly misperceived as a violence that targeted only the Ethiopian People's Revolutionary Party (EPRP). As such, referring to the *Dergue* trials as the Red-Terror trials would amount to furthering the mockery of the other victims. Interestingly, the SPO emphasized that:

INTRODUCTION 9

in post-Red-Terror period, including those committed as recently as 1989 and 1990.³⁴

Besides the *Dergue* trials, Ethiopia prosecuted core crimes on three occasions. These were related to crimes committed in post-*Dergue* Ethiopia between 2002 and 2008, and in the contexts of post-election violence and inter-ethnic conflicts. More specifically, the second occasion of prosecution of core crimes were the *Anuak-Nuwer* trials, when persons responsible for committing genocide against an ethnic group were brought to justice in 2004. This represents the first ever Ethiopian prosecution of genocidal attacks directed solely against members of an ethnic group.³⁵ In this incident, which goes back to 26 July 2002, acts of killing were perpetrated against 32 South-Sudanese

---

Indisputably, 'Red-Terror' refers to the period 1977/78 where the *Dergue's* atrocious acts reached their climax. Red-Terror was a designation given by the *Dergue* to its own acts of encroachment. Nonetheless, it is a mistake to consider either that the atrocities committed during the *Dergue* occurred only during the Red-Terror period or that the EPRP was the only victim of the Red-Terror.

See Special Prosecutor's Office, *Dem Yazele Dossie: Begizeyawi Wotaderawi Dergue Weyem Mengist Abalat Benetsuhan Zegoch Laye Yetefetsem Wenjel Zegeba* (Addis Ababa: Far-East Trading P.L.C., 2010). [Hereinafter: *Dem Yazele Dossie*] 122. Translation by the author. The original (Amharic) version reads:

ቀይሽብር 1970 የደርግ የጭፍጨፋ ተግባር ማሪያ ላይ የደረሰበት ወቅት መገለጫ መሆኑ አይካድም። ቀይሽብር በአንድ ወቅት የጊዜያዊ ወታደራዊ አስተዳደር ደርግ ወይም መንግስት ለገፋ ተግባር በቀይ ሽብር ወቅት የተፈጸመው ብቻ ነበር ወይም የቀይ ሽብር ሠላባ ኢሕአፓ ብቻ ነው ብሎ ማሰብ ስህተት ነው።

34 Let alone the whole *Dergue* trials, even the *Mengistu et al.* case, which is commonly cited by those commentators who refer to the trials as the Red-Terror trials, was not only about the crimes committed during the Red-Terror. In this case, the SPO prosecuted the *Dergue's* top-officials for acts of genocide that they allegedly planned and orchestrated between 1974 and 1983. See FSC, *SPO v. Colonel Mengistu Hailemariam et al.,* (Revised Indictment of 28 November 1995), File No. 1/87, 11.

Furthermore, referring to the *Dergue* trials as the Red-Terror trials may involve the risk of excluding the SPO's war crimes case, which was concerned with a situation unrelated to the Red-Terror campaign. See FHC, *SPO v. Legesse Asfaw et al.,* (Trial Judgment), 4 March 2008, File No. 03116. See also Chapter 4, sub-section 4.2.1.2.1.2. As will be discussed further in Chapter 7, *Legesse Asfaw et al* has dealt with war crimes perpetrated between 1983 and 1988. See in particular Chapter 7, section 7.7.

For some of the SPO cases that have dealt with crimes committed in 1989 and 1990, that is over a decade after the Red-Terror period ended, see ASC, *SPO v. Dagnenet Ayalew et al.,* (Indictment), 23 December 1997. File No. 13/90, 6–9; FHC, *SPO v. Getahun Zenebe Woldeselassie et al.,* (Revised Indictment), 16 June 1999, File No. 962/89, 3–7; FHC, *SPO v. Teshome Kebede* et al., (Indictment), 23 December 1997, File No. 931/89, 2; FHC, *SPO v. Tesfaye Belayeneh* et al., (Indictment), 23 December 1997, File No. 934/89, 2; FHC, *SPO v. Colonel Tesfaye Woldeselassie Eshetie et al.,* (Indictment), 8 October 2000, File No. 206/93, 8–9.

35 For a criticism of the *Anuak-Nuwer* trials based on the absence of 'ethnic' group in the list of groups protected by the Ethiopian law on genocide, see Chapter 6, section 6.2.

refugees identified as belonging to the *Nuwer* ethnic group, a group that also inhabits parts of the regional state of *Gambella* in Ethiopia.[36] Trials were held from 2004 to 2005, and the Federal High Court (FHC) of Ethiopia found the defendants – police officers, security guards, and soldiers belonging to the *Anuak* ethnic group – guilty of committing genocide in violation of Article 281 of the Penal Code of 1957.[37]

In November 2005, the third instance of prosecution of core crimes emerged before the FHC. These are the CUD trials; trials involving an opposition coalition used to be known as Coalition for Unity and Democracy (CUD) and its members for attempt to commit genocide in relation to a post-election conflict that erupted, mainly, in Addis Ababa and some parts of the country in early 2005.[38] The coalition parties of the CUD and other juridical persons[39] as well as party leaders and several affiliated physical persons were prosecuted in the main trial for attempting to commit genocide against members of the *Tigrian* ethnic group, as well as against members of the ruling political party, the Ethiopian Peoples' Revolutionary Democratic Front (EPRDF).[40] In a separate trial, low-ranking affiliates of the CUD were prosecuted for perpetrating an act of genocide against members identified both as Tigre in terms of ethnicity and EPRDF in terms of political affiliation.[41] The prosecution was conducted on the basis of the FDRE Criminal Code's Article 269, which deals with the crime of genocide under Ethiopian law. The CUD trials ended in September 2008 with the FHC acquitting the defendants of the attempted genocide charge in the

---

36   FHC, *Federal Prosecutor* v. *Gure Uchala Ugira et al.*, (Judgment), 25 March 2005, File No. 31855.

37   See ibid. See also FSC, *Federal Prosecutor* v. *Ikok Abuna Abong*, (Decision),18 July 2005, File No. FSC 19523/97.

38   See FHC, *Federal Prosecutor* v. *Hailu Shawul et al.*, (Trial Ruling), 3 May 2007, File No. 43246/97. The CUD trials were conducted following the post-election conflict that erupted in May and June 2005 after the CUD, the largest opposition coalition at the time, refused to accept election results by alleging that it had been robbed of outright victory due to widespread government fraud. For a detailed account of the context, see Amnesty International, 'Justice Under Fire: Trials of opposition leaders, journalists and human rights defenders in Ethiopia' (Amnesty International Report, 29 July 2011) 7–10, available at: <https://www.amnesty.org/en/documents/AFR25/002/2011/en/> accessed 23 March 2019.

39   For details, see Chapter 2, Section 2.2.1.

40   See *Shawul et al., supra* note 38.

41   See FHC, *Federal Prosecutor* v. *Berehene Kehassaye Woldeselassie et al.*, (Judgment), 19 April 2007, File No. 45671/99; FHC, *Federal Prosecutor* v. *Kifle Tigneh et al.*, (Trial Ruling), 16 April 2007, File No. 44562/99.

main trial, and entering a conviction for treason instead of genocide in the separate trial.[42]

The fourth, and so far last, instance of core crimes prosecution in Ethiopia is the *Oromo – Gumuz* trials. These trials were conducted from 2008 to 2010 in relation to the crime of genocide committed in violation of Article 269 of the FDRE Criminal Code. The *Oromo-Gumuz* genocide occurred in the context of a conflict that took place in May 2008 between members of the ethnic *Oromo* and those of the ethnic *Gumuz* in western Ethiopia, across the boarders shared by the regional States of the Benishangul-Gumuz and of Oromia. According to two majority decisions of the FHC, it was held that, during the conflict, the defendants, members of the Gumuz ethnic group, had committed genocide against those they identified as belonging to the Oromo ethnic group[43] – and *vice versa*.[44]

Of these four instances, the *Dergue* trials denote the first instance of national prosecution of core crimes not only in Ethiopia but also in Africa, and are as such among the pioneer examples in the global history of national prosecution of international crimes – following WWII-related prosecutions in Israel,[45] Germany,[46]

---

42   The emphasis of the CUD trials was in fact not on the prosecution of the crime of attempted genocide or genocide, but of crimes such as outrages against the constitution or the constitutional order (Article 238), obstruction of the exercise of constitutional powers (Article 239), armed rising or civil war (Articles 240 and 258), attack on the political or territorial integrity of the State (Article 241), impairment of the defensive power of the State (Articles 247 and 258), and high treason (Articles 248 and 258).

43   See FHC, *Prosecutor* v. *Tadesse Jewanie Mengesha et al.*, (Trial Judgment), 24 August 2009, File No. 70996; FHC, *Prosecutor* v. *Tesfaye Neno Loya et al.*, (Trial Judgment, 30 April 2009), File No. 74796.

44   See FHC, *Prosecutor* v. *Aliyu Yusufe Ibrahim et al.*, (Trial Judgment), 6 September 2009, File No. 71000. In addition to the offense of genocide, the *Oromo-Gumuz* trials prosecuted crimes such as aggravated homicide (Article 539), rape (Article 620), aggravated robbery (Article 671), and aggravated damage to property (Article 690), all of which are based on the 2004 FDRE Criminal Code.

45   In 1961, Israel prosecuted Adolf Eichmann whom the District Court of Jerusalem found guilty of committing, among others, crimes against the Jewish People, crimes against humanity, and war crimes. See District Court of Jerusalem, *Attorney General* v. *Adolf Eichmann*, Criminal Case No. 40/61, Judgment, 11 December 1961, para. 244, available at <http://www.legal-tools.org/uploads/tx_ltpdb/Eichmann_Judgement_11-12-1961.pdf> accessed 10 February 2019.

46   Of the two Germanys before the reunification, only East Germany prosecuted Nazi era crimes as war crimes and crimes against humanity based on the Nuremberg Statute. In 1963, for instance, Dr. Hans Globke was convicted in absentia by the then German Democratic Republic for war crimes and crimes against humanity. See A. Mikaberidze, *Atrocities, Massacres, and War Crimes, Vol I: an Encyclopedia* (Santa Barbara: ABC-CLIO, 2013) 204–206.

France,⁴⁷ and other prosecutions in Romania,⁴⁸ and Bolivia.⁴⁹ The distinctiveness of the *Dergue* trials is further illustrated by the fact that Ethiopian courts have managed to prosecute over 5,000 individuals belonging to an ousted regime; reason for which the trials have been characterized by some as the African Nuremberg – though the Nuremberg trials were international rather than national prosecutions.⁵⁰ Some commentators have regarded the *Dergue* trials as the first instance of national prosecution conducted on the basis of duty to prosecute core crimes,⁵¹ while others have invoked the trials as an illustration of the crystallization of such a duty in general international law.⁵²

In West Germany, in the most popular trials conducted in Frankfurt from 1963–1965 (the Auschwitz Trials), Nazi crimes were prosecuted as murder instead of crimes against humanity due to the strict application of the principle of legality under the 1871 German Penal Code. For a detailed account, see R. Wittmann, *Beyond Justice: The Auschwitz Trial* (Cambridge: Harvard University Press, 2005) 15–53.

47   In France, Klaus Barbie was found guilty of crimes against humanity in 1987 while, in 1994, Paul Touvier was convicted of complicity in crimes against humanity perpetrated during the Second World War under the auspices of the government of Vichy France. For a detailed analysis of these prosecutions, see C. Fournet, *Genocide and Crimes Against Humanity: Misconception and Confusion in French Law and Practice* (Oxford: Hart Publishing, 2013) 11–47.

48   In 1989 and 1990, former Romanian President Nicolae Ceausescu, his wife Elen Ceausescu and other persons stood trial for genocide in relation to crimes committed during the revolution in Timisoara. For details, see J.B. Quigley, *The Genocide Convention: An International Law Analysis* (Farnham: Ashgate Publishing Ltd., 2006) 38–39.

49   In 1993, Bolivia concluded a decade long prosecution against General García Meza and his associates for genocide involving the extermination of the leadership of the Movement of the Revolutionary Left. See ibid., 39–41.

50   See J. Ryle, 'An African Nuremberg: Letter from Ethiopia' *The New Yorker* (2 October 1995), available at <http://www.newyorker.com/magazine/1995/10/02/an-african-nuremberg> accessed 23 March 2019.

51   For an explicit qualification of Ethiopia as the country that based its decision to prosecute the *Dergue* on the duty to prosecute international crimes, see A. Novak, *Comparative Executive Clemency: The Constitutional Pardon Power and the Prerogative of Mercy in Global Perspective* (New York: Routledge, 2016) 14; E. Kwakwa, 'Governance, Development and Population displacement in Africa: A call for Action' (1995) 3 (1) *African Yearbook of International Law* 17–52, 42; J.V. Mayfield, 'The Prosecution of War Crimes and Respect for Human Rights: Ethiopia's Balancing Act' (1995) 9 (1) *Emory International Law Journal* 553–594, 570; R. Cryer, *Prosecuting International Crimes: Selectivity and the International Criminal Law Regime* (Cambridge: Cambridge University Press, 2005) 108.

52   See W.N. Ferdinandusse, *Direct Application of International Law in National Courts* (The Hague: T.M.C. Asser Press, 2006) 195.

TABLE 1   Summary of the Ethiopian Trials

Trials	Core Crimes Tried			Special Mechanism	Courts Involved	
	Genocide		War Crimes		First-Instance	Appellate
	Targeted Groups	Inchoate Offenses				
Dergue (1992–2010)	Political[53]	Conspiracy Incitement	against civilian population	SPO	FHC & State Supreme Courts[54]	FSC
Anuak-Nuwer (2004–2005)	Ethnic	N/A	N/A	N/A	FHC	FSC
CUD (2005–2008)	Ethnic Political	Attempt	N/A	N/A	FHC	FSC
Oromo-Gumuz (2008–2010)	Ethnic	N/A	N/A	N/A	FHC	FSC

N/A – not applicable

The table above summarizes the category of core crimes prosecuted and the domestic institutions involved in each of the trials.

---

53 As will be examined in different parts of this book, Ethiopian law proscribes genocide of political groups, which does not qualify as genocide under international law.

54 These are: *i*) the Supreme Court of the Amhara Regional State (in Bahirdar and Dessie), *ii*) the Supreme Court of Harari Regional State (in Harar), *iii*) the Supreme Court of Oromia Regional State (in Assela and Jimma), *iv*) the Supreme Court of the Regional State of Southern Nations, Nationalities and People (in Hawassa), and *v*) the Supreme Court of Tigray Regional State (in Mekelle). Although the initial plan included the prosecution of about 149 defendants from the Somali region by the Supreme Court of the Somali Regional State, the cases were moved to the nearby Supreme Court of the Harari Regional State due to administrative problems. See Trial Observation and Information Project (TOIP), *Ethiopia's Red Terror Trials: Africa's First War Tribunal* (Consolidated Summary and Reports from Trial Observations made from 1996–1999, Compiled by NIHR's Project, 2000) 2. [Hereinafter: TOIP Ethiopia: Consolidated Summary and Reports].

Nonetheless, no significant study exists on these instances of national prosecution of core crimes, and a broad range of issues pertinent to the field of substantive international criminal law (ICL) in Ethiopia remains unexamined.[55] As perplexing as it may be, none of the last three prosecutions were exposed to national, let alone international, academic scrutiny, not even in *Amharic*, the language of core crimes trials in Ethiopia. Literally, no report, let alone academic work, exists in relation to the *Anuak-Nuwer* trials and the *Oromo-Gumuz* trials – not even by Amnesty International, an organization that however managed to compile a report on some of the CUD trials.[56]

The CUD cases have garnered some degree of international and national media attention, although the focus was mainly on issues concerning free and fair elections in 2005. With the exception of very brief reports by Amnesty International[57] and the U.S. Department of State,[58] there was no discussion on the category of the prosecuted offenses, in particular with respect to core crimes. Besides, the CUD trials were often dismissed altogether as *political trials*, a situation that could partly explain the absence of studies on substantive criminal law issues that Ethiopian courts might have deliberated upon in these cases.[59]

1.3 Central Questions of the Book

This book undertakes a thorough investigation of the legal and judicial situation of Ethiopia within the broader frame of international criminal law (ICL). By taking into account the fact that core crimes are defined by ICL, as elaborated in section 1.5 below, the book focuses on discussing the similarities and differences between Ethiopian law and practice regarding core crimes and the applicable rules and standards of ICL.[60] As such, the main questions of this book are:

---

55 For a detailed discussion, see the Review of the Literature below, Section 1.4.
56 See Amnesty International, *Justice under Fire: Trials of Opposition Leaders, Journalists and Human Rights Defenders in Ethiopia* (2011), available at <https://www.amnesty.org/en/documents/AFR25/002/2011/en/> accessed 20 March 2019.
57 Ibid.
58 See U.S. Department of State, Bureau of Democracy, Human Rights, and Labor, *2006 Country Reports on Human Rights Practices: Ethiopia* (6 March 2006), available at <https://www.state.gov/j/drl/rls/hrrpt/2006/78734.htm> accessed 15 March 2019.
59 For instance, see Allo and Tesfaye, 'Spectacles of illegality: mapping Ethiopia's show trials', *supra* note 31, 286–287.
60 As for the contemporary ICL standards and their temporal application to Ethiopian trials in the context of a comparative analysis this book undertakes, see below section 1.5.

i) How does the criminal justice system of Ethiopia provide for the prosecution of core crimes?
ii) Were prosecutions of core crimes in Ethiopia in line with standards of ICL? If not, which deviations and/or deficits exist (both in law and in practice) in comparison with ICL standards?

1.4 Review of the Literature

Ethiopia's prosecution of core crimes, though it began a quarter of a century ago, still calls for a comprehensive academic scrutiny. The state of scholarship on the Ethiopian trials could generally be described by a lack of critical and comprehensive analysis. Of the four trials which are central to the discussion in this book, only the *Dergue* trials have been exposed to some level of academic scrutiny, as noted above. The following paragraphs, therefore, provide a review of the available literature in relation to the *Dergue* trials only.

Studies on the crimes and the trials of the *Dergue* can be categorized into three major parts. In *the first category* are those studies with a primary focus on the social and political context in which the crimes were perpetrated during the *Dergue* regime. It is to be noted that among a handful of literature that has attempted to address the context in which crimes were committed during the entire 17 years of the regime, only a few have embodied some level of acceptable scholarly rigor.[61] Most of the literature in this category is limited to what is commonly referred to as the Red-Terror era.[62] As such, the existing scholarship has shown a near-complete disregard for crimes committed outside the context of the Red-Terror. As a result, both formal and colloquial expressions have been doing the damage of reducing the scope of the *Dergue* crimes to the Red-Terror crimes.[63]

Even then, only very few studies have succeeded in undertaking a critical analysis of the context in which the Red-Terror era crimes were perpetrated.[64]

---

61 Selected works include: A. Tiruneh, *The Ethiopian Revolution, 1974–1987: A transformation from aristocratic to a totalitarian autocracy* (Cambridge: Cambridge University Press, 1993); Zewde, *A History of Modern Ethiopia*, supra note 13; C. Clapham, Transformation and Continuity in Revolutionary Ethiopia (Cambridge: Cambridge University Press, 1989); G. Tereke, *The Ethiopian Revolution: War in the Horn of Africa* (New Haven: Yale University Press, 2009); Haile-Selassie, *The Ethiopian Revolution 1974–1991, supra* note 14.
62 See *supra* note 32.
63 See *supra* notes 33 and 34. The fact that the scope of the *Dergue* crimes was not limited to the Red-Terror violence will be elaborated further in different parts of this book.
64 See in this regard, M. Kebede, 'The Civilian left and the Radicalization of the *Dergue*' (2008) 24 (2) *Journal of Developing Societies* 159–182; J. Abbink, 'The impact of violence: The

As Jacob Wiebel noted in an essay written in 2012, the state of scholarship on the Red-Terror is 'burdened with bias, limited scope and a reproduction of the polemics, accusations and justifications of the time'.[65] The scholarship remains underdeveloped and written only in English. Recent additions come mostly in the form of unrepentant memoirs, written in Amharic by individuals who had held the highest positions of power in the *Dergue* government, some of whom served long-term prison sentences for the crimes perpetrated while they were in power.[66]

The second category of the scholarship on the crimes and the trials of the *Dergue* covers studies conducted from the perspective of transitional justice. This category focuses in particular on issues related to the initial stage of the transition from the *Dergue* regime to a new political order, and the manner in which the TGE reached its decision to bring to trial the whole leadership of the defunct regime. A review of the rather scant literature in this category reveals that the actual focus of the existing studies has mostly been on the implications and achievability of this decision.[67] Some writers have insistently

---

Ethiopian 'Red terror' as a Social Phenomenon' in P.J. Bräunlein and A. Lauser (eds.), *Kriegund Frieden: Ethnologische Perspektiven* (Bremen: Kea-Edition, 1995) 129–145; G. Tereke, The Red Terror in Ethiopia: A Historical Aberration, (2008) 24 (2) *Journal of Developing Societies* 183–206; Zewde, 'The History of the Red Terror: Contexts and Consequences', *supra* note 13, 17–32. See also, on the early stages of the 1974 revolution, J. Markakis and A. Nega, *Class and Revolution in Ethiopia* (Nottingham: Spokesman Books, 1978); F. Halliday and M. Maxine, *The Ethiopian Revolution* (London: NLB, 1981); Toggia, 'The revolutionary endgame of political power', *supra* note 32, 265–280.

65 See J. Wiebel, ' The State of Scholarship on the Ethiopian Red Terror' in ERTDRC, *Documenting the Red Terror: Bearing Witness to Ethiopia's Lost Generations* (Ottawa: ERT-DRC North America Inc, 2012) 89–96.

66 The memoirs include: F. Desta, *Abiyotuna Tizitaye* [*my Reminiscences of the Revolution*] (Los Angeles: Tsehai Publishers, 2015); F. Wogederes, *Egnana Abiyotu* [*We and the Revolution*] (Los Angeles: Tsehai Publishers, 2014). For memoirs written by members of opposing political parties, such as the Ethiopian People's Revolutionary Party (EPRP), see H. Teffera, *Tower in the Sky* (Addis Ababa: Addis Ababa University Press, 2012). For recent scholarly works, see B. Zewde, *The Quest for Socialist Utopia: The Ethiopian Student Movement, c. 1960–1974* (Oxford: James Currey, 2014); G. Prunier, 'The Ethiopian Revolution and the Derg Regime' in G. Prunier and E. Ficquet, (eds.), *Understanding Contemporary Ethiopia: Monarchy, Revolution and the Legacy of Meles Zenawi* (Oxford: Oxford University Press, 2015), 209–232; J. Abbink, 'The Ethiopian Revolution after 40 Years (1974–2014): Plan B in Progress? (2015) 31 (3) *Journal of Developing Societies* 333–357; J. Wiebel, 'Let the Red Terror Intensify': political violence, governance and society in urban Ethiopia, 1976–78' (2015) 48 (1) *International Journal of African Historical Studies*, 13–30.

67 See Aneme, 'Apology and trials: The case of the Red Terror trials in Ethiopia' *supra* note 32, 74; D.S. Reta, 'National Prosecution and Transitional Justice: the case of Ethiopia, (PhD Dissertation, University of Warwick School of Law, 2014) 143–255; J. Sarkin 'Transitional Justice and the Prosecution Model: The Experience of Ethiopia' (1999) 2(1) *Journal of*

argued in favor of reconciliation instead of prosecution, even if the overall trial process was already halfway to completion.[68] Others have touched upon issues related to the legitimacy and fairness of the process of transition and its impact on the decision to prosecute.[69]

At the same time, commentators have noted the fact that, despite its unique standing, the domestic process in Ethiopia was 'unable to attract a variety of international scholars from the broad field of transitional justice studies'.[70] Reasons for this are uncertain but the result was incomplete research. And indeed, two main shortcomings hinder the comprehensiveness of the literature in this category. The first is that it fails to discuss and link the context in which the TGE was established with the decision to prosecute. The literature does not elaborate on why and how the decision to prosecute was reached. The second is that the literature lacks a component of legal analysis. There is almost no examination of issues relating to the (un)justifiability and scope of the decision to prosecute from the perspective of international or national law.

The third category of the literature on the crimes and trials of the *Dergue* refers to those scholarly works that have dealt directly with the trial process and its outcomes. These are works that have undertaken an analysis of the law and of the findings of Ethiopian courts with respect to crimes committed during the *Dergue* regime. Although a full-fledged work is nonexistent, some commentators have discussed specific cases from these trials. The discussions have however largely focused on issues related to procedural safeguards and fundamental guarantees, not least on the right of the accused to speedy trial and access to a defense counsel.[71]

    Law, Democracy and Development 253–266, 256–264. See also the relevant chapters in K. Tronvoll *et al.* (eds.) *The Ethiopian Red Terror Trials*, *supra* note 13, 1–10, 68–84, 98–115.

68   See M. Redae, 'The Ethiopian Genocide Trial' (2002) 1(1) *Ethiopian Law Review* 1–26, 18–26.

69   D. Haile, *Accountability for Crimes of the Past and the Challenges of Criminal Prosecution: The Case of Ethiopia* (Leuven: Leuven University Press, 2000) 30–33; K. Tronvoll, 'A Quest for Justice or the Construction of Political Legitimacy?' in K. Tronvoll *et al.* (eds.), *The Ethiopian Red Terror Trials*, *supra* note 13, 84–97. E.V. Huyssteen, 'Building State & Nation Justice, Reconciliation & Democratization in Ethiopia & South Africa' in K. Tronvoll *et al.* (eds.), *The Ethiopian Red Terror Trials*, *supra* note 13, 98–115.

70   See K. Tronvoll *et al.*, 'The Context of Transitional Justice in Ethiopia' in K. Tronvoll *et al.*(eds.), *The Ethiopian Red Terror Trials, supra* note 13, 10.

71   F. Elgesem and G.A. Aneme, 'The Rights of the Accused: a Human Rights Appraisal' in K. Tronvoll *et al.* (eds.), *The Ethiopian Red Terror Trials*, *supra* note 13, 33–50; Haile, *Accountability for Crimes of the Past and the Challenges of Criminal Prosecution*, *supra* note 69, 30–33; Mayfield, 'the Prosecution of War Crimes and Respect for Human Rights', *supra* note 51, 559–591; W.L. Kidane, 'The Ethiopian Red Terror Trials' in M.C. Bassiouni (ed.), *Post-Conflict Justice* (Ardsley: Transnational Publishers, 2001) 667–694.

From the perspective of substantive ICL, the nature and the legal characterization of the crimes for which the *Dergue* stood trial, and issues related to individual criminal responsibility or a lack thereof, have been largely left unstudied. Frew Tiba appears to be the only scholar that has managed to bring the Ethiopian experience to the attention of ICL scholars through his article, 'the Mengistu Genocide Trial in Ethiopia', published in 2007 in the *Journal of International Criminal Justice*.[72] Tiba's succinct analysis of the law and the practice however focuses only on some aspects of the Mengistu trial, which is also the case in his other articles.[73]

In addition, three comparative studies were undertaken in which the *Dergue* crimes and their prosecution were compared to apparently similar crimes committed elsewhere. In 1998, Yakob Hailemariam wrote an article in which he juxtaposed the FHC to the International Criminal Tribunal for Rwanda (ICTR).[74] The analysis focused largely on the two institutions' structural and financial capacity to prosecute core crimes while at the same time ensuring respect for the rights of the accused. The only Ethiopian institution that was discussed in this work was the FHC, leaving aside the trials conducted in five regional supreme courts.

In 2004 and 2006 respectively, Edward Kissi published an article on similarities and differences among genocides perpetrated in Ethiopia under the Mengistu regime, in Cambodia under the *Khmer Rouge* regime, and in Rwanda in 1994,[75] and a book on genocide in Ethiopia and Cambodia.[76] Kissi's studies are limited to a comparison of the ideological and social intricacies behind the eras of violence in these countries. As such, neither the article nor the book discuss the relevant law and practice in relation to genocide in Ethiopia, except for a brief mention of the definition of genocide under the Penal Code of 1957.[77]

---

72 F.K. Tiba, 'The Mengistu Genocide Trial in Ethiopia' (2007) 5 (1) *Journal of International Criminal Justice* 513, 517–526. Kidane, 'The Ethiopia 'Red Terror' Trials' *supra* note 71, 671–682.

73 See F.K. Tiba, 'The Trial of Mengistu and other Derg Members for Genocide, Torture and Summary Executions in Ethiopia' in C. Murungu and B. Japhet (eds.), *Prosecuting International Crimes in Africa* (Pretoria: Pretoria University Law Press, 2011) 168–173; F.K. Tiba, 'Mass Trials and Modes of Criminal Responsibility for International Crimes: The Case of Ethiopia' in K.J. Heller and G. Simpson (eds.), *The Hidden Histories of War Crimes Trials* (Oxford: Oxford University Press, 2013) 306–326.

74 Y. Hailemariam, 'The Quest for Justice and Reconciliation: The International Criminal Tribunal for Rwanda and the Ethiopian High Court' (1999) 22(1) *Hastings International and Comparative Law Review*, 667–745, 689–745.

75 E. Kissi, 'Rwanda, Ethiopia and Cambodia: links, fault lines and complexities in a comparative study of genocide' (2004) 6 (1) *Journal of Genocide Research* 115–133.

76 Kissi, *Revolution and Genocide in Ethiopia and Cambodia, supra* note 7.

77 See ibid., 98–106.

In 2013, Jackson Maogoto wrote a book chapter on the Turkish and Ethiopian experiences in relation to prosecuting core crimes using domestic courts.[78] The purpose of this study, which attempted to compare experiences that are separated by about eight decades, is not clear. Apparently, it is based on an assumption that both the Turkish and the Ethiopian trials have 'used the extant Penal Codes to prosecute international crimes'.[79] Yet, this study appears to have certain limits. Firstly, the discussion seems to be showing a total disregard for the notion of domestic prosecution of core crimes and its link to the concept of ICL as developed after WWII. Secondly, the Ethiopian experience is only succinctly dealt with[80] and the work thus does not 'delve into the nuances of the trials',[81] thereby not solving the issue, also identified by the author, that the Ethiopian trials are understudied and hidden.

In 2018, Mareshet Tessema published a relatively comprehensive study on the trials of the *Dergue* entitled *Prosecution of Politicide in Ethiopia: The Red-Terror Trials*.[82] The book, which is the result of a PhD research, discusses the prosecution of genocide against political groups (politicide) including the manner in which the decision to prosecute the *Dergue* was reached by the TGE through the establishment of the SPO.[83] Interestingly, Tessema produced a lengthy survey of Ethiopian laws on core crimes – perhaps, his work is the first of its kind in this regard.[84] Nonetheless, his examination of the *Dergue* trials (to which he refers to as the Red-Terror trials) focuses almost exclusively on the Mengistu trial. Albeit fundamental for its analysis of information recorded in the literature dealing with the political history of the country during the *Dergue*, his research leaves aside the war crimes trials and the vast majority of genocide cases prosecuted by the SPO before federal and regional courts.[85]

To conclude, the existing scholarly works are not as numerous and as dense as one could expect, given the aforementioned unique qualifications of these trials. Overall, the existing literature on the *Dergue* trials is only big on title and low on substance. This problem finds an explanation in the fact that the cases are

---

78 J.N. Maogoto, 'Reading the Shadows of History: The Turkish and Ethiopian 'Internationalized' Domestic Crime Trials' in K.J. Heller and G. Simpson (eds.), *The Hidden Histories of War Crimes Trials* (Oxford: Oxford University Press, 2013) 290–305.
79 See ibid., 291.
80 Of a fifteen-page long discussion, only four deal with Ethiopian aspects, out of which only two provide general information on the law and practice in Ethiopia. See ibid., 300–304.
81 Ibid.
82 See Tessema, *Prosecution of Politicide in Ethiopia, supra* note18.
83 Ibid., Chapter 4.
84 Ibid., Chapter 3.
85 Ibid., Chapter 5.

not readily available because Ethiopia lacks official gazettes that publicize court judgments,[86] as already noted by commentators who attempted to include a more elaborated discussion on Ethiopian trials.[87] In addition, a language barrier, in particular with respect to international commentators, might have isolated the Ethiopian trials from being exposed to a comprehensive critique.[88]

Regardless, there is a strong interest among scholars to investigate the Ethiopian cases. Notably, the *Dergue* trials have caught the attention of several scholars in the field of national prosecution of core crimes. In fact, as mentioned above and as studied in this book, the Ethiopian cases are unique and could offer significant lessons to the global effort to fight against impunity for core crimes, which any comprehensive study on national prosecutions of core crimes cannot afford to disregard. That is, apparently, why the major studies in the field of ICL are compelled to make at least a hearsay-based reference to the *Dergue* trials and the Ethiopian laws on core crimes.

1.5 Methodology

This book employs a method of international comparative analysis focused on analyzing the features of Ethiopian law and practice in comparison with the rules and practices operating in the international arena. This in-depth analysis necessarily implies a full engagement with the existing literature on the issue of domestic application of international criminal law as well as a meticulous exploration of the relevant norms and case law – at the international and Ethiopian levels. Since the focus of the discussion in this book is limited to answering whether the prosecution of core international crimes in Ethiopia is in line with international standards, the comparative method only implies the analysis of other domestic cases in a restricted manner namely, when it is relevant to do so to address and answer the central questions of the book.

The comparative approach allows to exhaustively address and answer the questions raised in this book by reflecting on the differences and similarities

---

86 It is only in 2005 that a law was enacted to impose on the Federal Supreme Court an obligation to publish binding decisions of its cassation bench. See Federal Courts Proclamation Re-Amendment Proclamation, Proclamation No. 454/2005, Article 2 (1), para. 2.
87 See M.C. Bassiouni, *International Criminal Law: International Enforcement* (3rd ed., Leiden: Martinus Nijhoff Publishers, 2008) 311; Ferdinandusse, *Direct Application of International Law in National Courts*, *supra* note 52, 70–71. For challenges regarding the accessibility of Ethiopian laws and cases, see below the discussion under the methodology of this book (Section 1.5).
88 See on this, Tiba, 'Mass Trials and Modes of Criminal Responsibility for International Crimes', *supra* note 73, 310–311.

between international criminal law standards and the law and practice of national prosecutions in Ethiopia. The comparative analysis is based on the fact that there exists a functional equivalence between national and international prosecutions of core crimes in the sense that both systems deal with the enforcement of international law rules that define core crimes. The assertion that the law that governs the prohibition of core crimes has its source in international treaties and custom has a firm existence in the relevant doctrine,[89] to which several

---

[89] In this regard, Robert Cryer asserted that, '...the fundamental point to understand about [core crimes] is that the locus of the criminal prohibition is not the domestic, but the international legal order'. See R. Cryer, 'The Doctrinal Foundations of International Criminal Law' in M.C. Bassiouni (ed.), *International Criminal Law, Vol I: Sources, Subjects, and Contents* (3rd ed., Leiden: Martinus Nijhoff Publishers, 2008), 107–128, 108 [Emphasis added]. See also B. Broomhall, *International Justice and the International Criminal Court: Between Sovereignty and the Rule of Law* (Oxford: Oxford University Press, 2003) 9–10; A. Cassese *et al.* (eds.), *Cassese's International Criminal Law* (Oxford: Oxford University Press, 2013) 9–18; D. Akande, 'Sources of International Criminal Law' in A. Cassese, (ed.) *The Oxford Companion to International Criminal Justice*' (Oxford: Oxford University Press, 2009) 41–53; D. Luban, 'Fairness to Rightness: Jurisdictional, Legality, and the Legitimacy of International Criminal Law' in S. Besson and J. Tasioulas (eds.) *The Philosophy of International Law* (Oxford: Oxford University Press, 2010) 570–588, 572; G. Werle and F. Jessberger, *Principles of International Criminal Law* (3rd ed., Oxford: Oxford University Press, 2014) 56–72; H. Thirlway, *The Sources of International Law* (Oxford: Oxford University Press, 2014) 195–197; F. Jessberger, 'International v. National Prosecution of International Crimes' in A. Cassese, (ed.) *The Oxford Companion to International Criminal Justice*' (Oxford: Oxford University Press, 2009) 208–216; K. Ambos, *Treatise on International Criminal Law, Vol I: Foundations and General Part* (Oxford: Oxford University Press, 2013) 65; M.C. Bassiouni, 'The Discipline of international Criminal Law' in M.C. Bassiouni (ed.), *International Criminal Law, Vol I: Sources, Subjects, and Contents* (3rd ed., Leiden: Martinus Nijhoff Publishers, 2008) 1–17; R. Cryer *et al.*, *Introduction to International Criminal Law and Procedure* (2nd ed., Cambridge: Cambridge University Press, 2010) 9–13; R. O'Keefe, *International Criminal Law* (Oxford: Oxford University Press, 2015) 54; V.D. Degan, 'On the Sources of International Criminal Law' (2005) 4(1) *Chinese Journal of International Law* 45–83, 54.

The law that criminalizes a 'widespread or systematic attack against a civilian population', therefore, crimes against humanity, is simply not of a domestic origin, but originates from customary international law. For a survey of national laws on crimes against humanity before WWI, an instance generally accepted as having caused the emergence of 'crimes against humanity' as a legal concept, see M.C. Bassiouni, *Crimes Against Humanity: Historical Evolution and Contemporary Application* (Cambridge: Cambridge University Press, 2011) 651–659.

With regards to war crimes too, there are underlying offenses that ordinary penal provisions do not usually cover. See van Elst, 'Implementing Universal Jurisdiction Over Grave Breaches of the Geneva Conventions' *supra* note 11, 827–828; who states that in most cases the ordinary penal provisions do not normally cover the grave breaches such as the willful deprivation of protected persons of the right to fair trial, and inhumane treatment. According to the Revised ICRC Commentary, 'grave breaches such as compelling a protected person or a prisoner of war to serve in the forces of a hostile power (Geneva

national[90] and international[91] courts concur.

>Convention III, Article 129) or the unlawful deportation or transfer of a protected person (Geneva Convention IV, Article 146) are 'specific and uniquely related to armed conflict'. See ICRC, *Commentary on the First Geneva Convention: Convention (I) for the Amelioration of the Condition of the Wounded and Sick in Armed Forces in the Field*, 2nd edition, 2016, para 2848, *fn*. 73, available at <https://ihl-databases.icrc.org/ihl/full/GCI-commentary> accessed 26 September 2019. Besides, ordinary criminal law provisions are deemed unable to capture and reflect the international nature and consequence of war crimes. See A. Clapham *et al*, *The 1949 Geneva Conventions: A Commentary* (Oxford: Oxford University Press, 2014) 657–659; A.M.L. Rosa, *Preventing and Repressing International Crimes: Towards an "Integrated" Approach Based on Domestic Practice: Report of the Third Universal Meeting of National Committees for the Implementation of International Humanitarian Law*, Volume I (Geneva, International Committee of the Red Cross, 2014) 31–32; Ferdinandusse, *Direct application of International Criminal Law in National Courts*, *supra* note 52, 206–207; K. Dörmann and R. Geiß 'The Implementation of Grave Breaches into Domestic Legal Orders' (2009) 7 (1) *Journal of International Criminal Justice* 703, 715–716.
>   By the time the Genocide Convention was adopted, for example, some nations and organizations opined that the Convention contained offenses that are not different from those already proscribed in municipal legal systems. As Robinson noted, however, there was no offense in domestic legal orders that had, as its (essential) elements, the 'intent to destroy' and victims' membership to the 'protected groups'. N. Robinson, *The Genocide Convention: A Commentary* (New York: Institute of Jewish Affairs, 1960) 32–33. It was also stated that the American Bar Association opined that what the Convention made international crimes that were traditionally domestic crimes. See ibid., 32. According to Schabas, Belgium, Egypt, Ecuador, Greece, Iraq, Iceland, India, Norway, Pakistan, Senegal, Ukraine, and Bahrain considered that their domestic law had already criminalized the crime of genocide. See W. Schabas, *Genocide in International Law: The Crime of Crimes* (2nd ed., Cambridge: Cambridge University Press, 2009) 407–08. Some of those states have now changed their position as a result of membership to the ICC. See B. Saul, 'The Implementation of the Genocide Convention at the National Level' in P. Gaeta (ed.), *The UN Genocide Convention: A Commentary* (Oxford: Oxford University Press, 2009) 66.

90 As stated by the Canadian Supreme Court in *R.* v. *Finta*, 'war crime or crimes against humanity is not the same as domestic offence. [...] there are fundamentally important additional elements involved in a war crime or a crime against humanity'. *Regina* v. *Finta*, (Canada Sup. Ct. 24 March 1994), 1 S.C.R. 701 706. However, it is to be noted that with respect to the crime of genocide, 'Canada considered a provision for genocide unnecessary except with respect to 'advocating genocide''. See Schabas, *Genocide in International Law* 408. Further, the fact that the very nature of core crimes transcends the municipal legal system's ambit has been acknowledged by the French Court of Cassation in the *Barbie* case: the Court reiterated the statement of the *Chambre d'Accusation* of the Lyon Court of Appeal that, '...by reason of their nature, crimes against humanity ... do not simply fall within the scope of the French municipal law but are subject to an international criminal order to which the notions of frontiers and extradition rules arising therefrom are completely foreign'. See *Fédération Nationale de Déportés et Internés Résistants et Patriotes And Others* v. *Barbie*, 78 International Law Reports 125, 130 (Cass. crim.1983).

91 The uniqueness of genocide as compared to ordinary crimes was also emphasized by the ICTR, which, in denying the prosecutor's request for the referral of Michel Bagaragaza to

The analysis in this book is not based on the assumption that each and every aspect of international criminal law is superior to that of national criminal law relating to core international crimes. Consequently, when there is a difference between the two, further analyses are made to determine whether the national prosecution can – in a given instance – justifiably adopt an approach that does not conform to what has been established by international criminal law.

With respect to establishing the manner in which ICL provides for standards relating to the core crimes, the analysis in this book fully engages with the relevant international norms and case law. In doing so, the book employs a method of literature and legal analysis. Academic legal works (monographs and academic articles) addressing the relevant norms of ICL are used. The Rome Statute of the ICC is relied upon owing to the fact that it is the most comprehensive manifestation of contemporary standards of ICL, save the fact that the Statute may not always be congruous with ICL standards.[92] Where relevant, works engaging with international humanitarian law and international human rights law are also used. Legal sources such as treaties, customary international law, and general principles of law are studied in order to show the relevant standards of ICL applicable to the prosecution of core crimes.

International case law is used to highlight how international and human rights courts and tribunals have interpreted and applied ICL rules governing various aspects of core crimes. In this regard, the book consulted databases of international and regional courts/tribunals such as the International Criminal Tribunal for Former Yugoslavia (ICTY), the ICTR, the ICC, the Special Court for Sierra Leone (SCSL), the Inter-American Court of Human Rights (IACtHR) and the European Court of Human Rights (ECtHR).

Norway, stated that the legal values protected by the offense of genocide and murder are different. See ICTR, *Prosecutor* v. *Bagaragaza*, Appeals Chamber, (Decision on Rule 11 *bis* Appeal), 30 August 2006, Case No. ICTR-05-86-AR11bis, paras 17–18.

92 On the (in)consistency of the ICC Statute with ICL, see A. Cassese, 'The Statute of the International Criminal Court: Some Preliminary Reflections' (1999) 10(1) *European Journal of International Law* 144–171, 150–153; Cassese *et al.* (eds.), *Cassese's International Criminal Law, supra* note 86, 79–83, 105–108,129–130; T.E. Davies, 'How the Rome Statute Weakens the International Prohibition on Incitement to Genocide' (2009) 22 (2) *Harvard Human Rights Journal* 245–270, 269–270. See also, K. Dörmann, 'War crimes under the Rome Statute of the International Criminal Court, with a Special Focus on the Negotiations on the Elements of Crimes' (2003) 7(1) *Max Planck Yearbook of United Nations Law* 342–407, 348.

The fact that international criminal courts and tribunals were not yet established at the time Ethiopia reached the decision to prosecute the *Dergue* in 1992 might raise concerns regarding the methodology employed in this book and prompt the question of the accuracy of analyzing Ethiopian trials using ICL standards that were not in place when the decision to prosecute in Ethiopia was taken and implemented. Nevertheless, such concerns are actually not relevant as this book does not see international courts and tribunals as being superior to Ethiopian courts. Besides, the Ethiopian trials were conducted around the same time, if not completed after, international criminal courts and tribunals were prosecuting core crimes. It is true that the initial indictment in the Dergue's *Mengistu et al.* case was filed on 25 October 1994,[93] which was just a few months after the establishment of the ICTY[94] and two weeks before that of the ICTR.[95] Yet, the pioneering aspect of the Ethiopian cases did not go beyond some of the initial indictments, as the trials were significantly delayed. For example, the ICTR's *Akayesu* judgment[96] antedates Ethiopia's first genocide judgment in *Gereme Debele*.[97] The most significant ruling[98] and judgment[99] in the *Dergue* trials came out only on, respectively, 23 January

---

93 FHC, SPO v. *Colonel Mengistu Hailemariam et al.*, (Indictment), 25 October 1994, File No. 1/87.

94 The ICTY was established on 25 May 1993 pursuant to Security Council Resolution No. 827. See S/RES/827 (1993), 25 May 1993.

95 The ICTR was established on 8 November 1994 pursuant to Security Council Resolution No 955. See S/RES/955 (1994), 8 November 1994.

96 ICTR, *Prosecutor v. Akayesu*, Trial Chamber, (Judgment), 2 September 1998, ICTR-96-4-T.

97 FHC, SPO v. *Geremew Debele*, (Trial Judgment), 8 February 1999, File No. 952/89.

98 In Ethiopian criminal procedure, 'ruling' refers to the stage in a trial whereby courts make a determination as to whether the case against the accused has been established in the prosecution's evidence. See Criminal Procedure Code of Ethiopia, Proclamation No. 185 of 1961, *entered into force* 2 February 1962, Articles 141 and 142. In this book, this stage is referred to as 'Trial Ruling', and it is different from a ruling that courts enter in relation to preliminary objections, which is referred to in this book as 'Ruling on Preliminary Objections'. See ibid., Article 131.

99 Often, there are three kinds of judgments in Ethiopian trials: *i*) trial judgment by a trial court, that is the court with first instance jurisdiction (these are, for the purpose of core crimes, the Federal High Court (FHC) and the Regional Supreme Courts); *ii*) sentencing judgment by a trial court, which is often rendered in a separate hearing after the judgment; and *iii*) appeals judgment by a court with appellate jurisdiction, (which is the Federal Supreme Court (FSC) as far as core crimes are concerned). This book refers to these judgments as, respectively, 'Trial Judgment', 'Trial Sentencing Judgment', and 'Appeals Judgment'.

INTRODUCTION

2003[100] and 11 December 2006[101] – that is, years after most of the significant judgments were rendered by the ICTY and ICTR; after the SCSL's Trial Chamber had delivered two of its judgments;[102] and after the ICC became fully operational.[103] The other trials – the CUD, *Anuak-Nuwer*, and the *Oromo-Gumuz* trials –were conducted between 2005 and 2010.[104] As far as war crimes trials are concerned, the ICTY's *Tadić* judgment[105] had entered international jurisprudence over a decade before the FHC reached its judgment in *Legesse Asfaw et al.*, the only war crimes case prosecuted by the SPO.[106]

In order to fully address the question of the manner in which the Ethiopian criminal justice system provides for the prosecution of core international crimes, this study uses the dual method of literature analysis and analysis of legal materials. For the book to be authoritative, it is necessary to exhaustively analyze the relevant literature on the four instances of core crimes trials in Ethiopia. It is important to note that all of the four instances of prosecution of core crimes in Ethiopia were conducted without a prior independent and impartial investigation, be it by a local or an international commission of experts. This leaves the book to fully depend on available scholarship, in particular with respect to issues related to the context in which the core crimes were perpetrated. In addition to scholarly works, reports and policy papers by international organizations such as the International Committee of the Red Cross

---

100 See FHC, SPO v. *Colonel Mengistu Hailemariam et al.,* (Trial Ruling), 23 January 2003, File No. 1/87.

101 See FHC, SPO v. *Colonel Mengistu Hailemariam et al.,* (Trial Judgment), 12 December 2006, File No. 1/87. As discussed in Chapter 6, this case is the most significant, in particular in relation to understanding genocidal *mens rea* under the Penal Code of 1957. See Chapter 6, Section 6.3.

102 The Trial Chamber of the Special Court for Sierra Leone had already passed judgments in the CDF and AFRC cases. See SCSL, *Prosecutor v. Fofana et al.,* Trial Chamber, (Judgment), 2 August 2007, SCSL-04-14-T; SCSL, *Prosecutor v. Brima et al.,* Trial Chamber, (Judgment), 20 June 2007, SCL-04-16-T.

103 The ICC became operational on 1 July 2002, the date of entry into force of its Rome Statute. By 2007, investigations were already opened in situations such as the Democratic Republic of Congo (June 2004), Uganda (July 2004), Darfur, Sudan (June 2005), and the Central African Republic (May 2007). See information available at: <https://www.icc-cpi.int/pages/situations.aspx> accessed 24 May 2019. Moreover, Pre-Trial Chamber I already confirmed the charges against Lubanga in early 2007. See ICC, *Prosecutor v. Lubanga*, Pre-Trial Chamber I, (Decision on the Confirmation of Charges), 29 January 2007, ICC-01/04-01/06.

104 See *supra* notes 35–44.

105 ICTY, *Prosecutor v. Tadić*, Trial Chamber, (Judgment), 7 May 1997, IT-94-1.

106 See *Legesse Asfaw et al., supra* note 34.

(ICRC), and non-governmental organizations, such as Amnesty International and Human Rights Watch, are used.

As its central method, this book is predominantly based on the analysis of the domestic legal materials (the law and the practice), which it examines in their Amharic (authoritative) versions.[107] The analysis of the law and practice required extensive empirical research namely, the collection and analysis of data collected in Ethiopia. This could be regarded as the most important – and most difficult – part of the research in this book, given the inaccessibility of both judicial decisions and most of the relevant

---

107   One of the commonly cited shortcomings of studies conducted on Ethiopian trials is that they do not engage with the law in its (original) Ethiopian language. Amharic, the official language of Ethiopia when the Penal Code of 1957 was promulgated and the working language of its federal government since 1991, is the language used to incorporate core crimes into the Ethiopian legal system. It was, in fact, in 1942 that Ethiopia promulgated into law that a law shall be published in the official gazette in Amharic and English languages. See Administration of Justice Proclamation, Proclamation 1/1942, Article 22. Nonetheless, it was only in 1995 that a clear legislation as to which version should be treated as authoritative was promulgated. See Federal Negarit Gazeta Establishment Proclamation, Proclamation No. 3/1995, Article 2(4), which reads, 'the Federal Negarit Gazeta shall be published in both the Amharic and English Languages; in case of discrepancy between the two versions the Amharic shall prevail'.

Regarding the laws before 1995, the absence of a clear provision determining an authoritative version of legislation is perplexing, given that it was a discrepancy between the Amharic and foreign (Italian) version of a law that triggered a dispute between Italy and Ethiopia, which culminated in the battle of Adwa in 1896. See 'Treaty of Wuchale: Italy-Ethiopia[1889]' available at: <https://www.britannica.com/event/Treaty-of-Wichale> accessed 28 September 2019.

Nonetheless, there is no legal basis in Ethiopian law to use the English version of legislation when the Amharic text reads differently. To the contrary, it could be argued that there was a sort of unwritten law in Ethiopia that the Amharic version had been the authoritative version of the law. Amharic served as the Official Language of the country while English was never regarded as the second official language in Ethiopia. The laws promulgated by the Emperor as well as those passed by Parliament (both during the Emperor and the *Dergue*) were considered by those authorities in their Amharic versions.

From a practical point of view too, the analysis of Ethiopian trials should be based on the Amharic, not the English, version of the applicable laws, because the former has always been the language of core crimes trials in Ethiopia. Furthermore, Amharic has been expressly regarded as the authoritative version of the Penal Code in the *Dergue* trials. See for instance FHC, SPO v. *Colonel Mengistu Hailemariam et al.*, (Ruling on Preliminary Objections), 10 October 1995, File No. 1/87, 119. See also Chapter 5, section 5.1.

Accordingly, this book refers to – and quotes – the English version of Ethiopian laws only when it is not inconsistent with the Amharic version of the laws. When the Amharic version of a legislation is used owing to its authoritative status, this is accompanied with an unofficial English translation by the author.

INTRODUCTION 27

domestic legislation. This process required a rigorous work of data collection as detailed below.

As noted above, in all of the four instances, judgments of Ethiopian courts have largely remained unreported except for the redacted versions of the cases of SPO v. *Mengistu et al*, from the *Dergue* trials, and of *Federal Prosecutor v. Engineer Hailu Shawul et al,* from the CUD trials, which were made available to the public only in Amharic and only in a hard copy published in September 2008 by the FHC.[108] In the same year, the Hareri Supreme Court (HSC), a regional supreme court that adjudicated the *Dergue* crimes committed in the then Harergie province, published extracts from its judgments in the cases of SPO v. *Amanshoa Gebrewolde*[109] and of SPO v. *Colonel Zelleke Beyene*.[110] However, these extracts are too incomplete to be relied upon as a source in a comprehensive analysis.[111]

Concerning legislation, Ethiopian laws are not officially available online. In particular, the inaccessibility, even in a hard copy format, of the pre-1991 Ethiopian laws has posed a challenge to the process of data collection. Another challenge in this regard is the untraceability of explanatory notes or *travaux préparatoires* of fundamental pieces of legislation, such as the Penal Code of 1957.[112]

Two important steps have been taken in order to solve the challenges related to data collection so that the book could be as authoritative as possible. The first step required travelling to the record and file offices of each

---

108 See ፌዴራል ከፍተኛ ፍርድ ቤት፣ ልዩ ዐቃቤ ሕግ በእነ ኮሎኔል መንግስቱ ሃይለማርያም ላይ ያቀረበው ክስ እና የፌዴራል ከፍተኛ ፍርድቤት ውሳኔ [*The SPO's Indictment Against Colonel Mengistu Hailemaraim et al. and the Judgment, the Federal High Court*] Addis Ababa, 2008; ፌዴራል ከፍኛ ፍርድ ቤት፣ ፌዴራል ዐቃቢ ሕግ በእነ ኢንጂነር ሐይሉ ሻዉል ላይ ያቀረበው ክስና የፌዴራል ከፍተኛ ፍርድ ቤት ውሳኔ [*The Federal Prosecutor's Indictment Against Engineer Hailu Shawul et al. and the Judgment, the Federal High Court*], Addis Ababa, 2008. It should be noted here that in referring to the case of *Colonel Mengistu Hailemariam et al.*, the book uses the published version of the case, which is,including the indictment, 492 pages and easier to read as compared to its 1028 pages long handwritten version.

109 See HSC, SPO v. *Amanshoa Gebrewolde et al.*, (Trial Judgment), 2 February 2004, File No.4/90/1.

110 See HSC, SPO v. *Colonel Zelleke Beyene et al.*, (Trial Judgment), 5 May 2004, File No. 2/95 (00252).

111 The extracts were published in Harari Supreme Court, *Yemilinium Leyu Metsehet* [Millennium Extraordinary Magazine] (Harar: Harari Supreme Court, 2008) 27, 59, 66.

112 Efforts made by the author to locate explanatory notes or *travaux préparatoires* for Ethiopian laws codified in 1950s and 1960s were not successful. Because the codes were solely prepared by individual experts from foreign countries without actual discussion and debate, it is possible that there in fact exist no such documents.

of the Ethiopian courts that have adjudicated core crimes to collect the relevant documents. In addition to the Federal High and Supreme Courts, five regional supreme courts have adjudicated the core crimes committed during the *Dergue* regime.[113]

Collecting judicial decisions related to the *Dergue* trials (128 trial decisions out of approximately 300 and 280 FSC appeals decisions) from all of the concerned courts took approximately four months. Nonetheless, locating some of the decisions of the trial courts required even more time as files were often misplaced or moved from their alleged original locations. In particular, the trial court's decision on war crimes, i.e. the case of *Legesse Asfaw et al.,* was collected after frequent visits to the FHC were made in a process that lasted for more than a year and half. Cases relating to the CUD trials (all three decisions), the *Anuak-Nuwer* trials (one trial decision and one appeals decision) and the *Oromo-Gumuz* trials (all three trial decisions and 99 appeals decisions)[114] were all collected from the Federal High and Supreme Courts in Addis Ababa. No regional court has adjudicated these cases. Not all of these decisions are cited in this book due to the fact that, as noted when relevant, most trial decisions lack explanation and discussion. Likewise, the majority of the FSC appeals decisions are not expressly cited because, as mentioned notably in Chapters 6 and 8, the FSC very often dismissed the appeal by merely stating that there was no ground to revise the lower court's decision.

The search for relevant legislation enacted since 1930, the year Ethiopia started using written penal laws, was conducted mainly in Addis Ababa and in Jimma. In Addis Ababa, although the library of the House of People's Representatives maintains a collection of the old laws and documents that were not destroyed during the military transition in May 1991, the library grants only very limited permission to photocopy or scan its collections. As a result, only a few documents were collected from this library. Instead, legislation was collected from the Research and Documentation Office of the Federal Supreme Court in Addis Ababa, the Ethiopian National Archives and Library in Addis Ababa, and the Library of Jimma Zone High Court in Jimma.

The second step that was taken to overcome challenges related to data collection was to set up a website, the Ethiopian Criminal Law Network,

---

113   See *supra* note 54.
114   The number of cases on appeal before the FSC was higher than the number of cases before trial courts because nearly all of the core crimes cases were multi-defendant cases – this created the possibility of multiple and separate appeals against a single trial judgment. For instance, all of the 99 appeals in the Oromo-Gumuz cases were lodged against the FHC judgment in the case of *Mengesha et al.,* which had 147 defendants.

http://www.ethcriminalawnetwork.com, to serve as a comprehensive database of laws, documents, and cases on Ethiopian criminal law. In addition to making documents collected for this study accessible to anyone interested, the website aims at creating a network of researchers and academics, and serves as a common database where documents that are in the hands of some individuals and organizations can be uploaded and accessed by others.

The website benefited this book by ensuring accessibility of laws and documents that might not have been collected during the data collection stage, as it was impossible to foresee and collect at once all of the documents that were relevant for the research conducted in this book. As such, the website helped to generate as many sources as possible and to keep track of some periodic documents such as the cassation decisions of the Federal Supreme Court, which, due to their legally binding status, are very relevant for the interpretation of existing laws.[115] In addition to data collection, the website serves as a data verification portal so that anyone interested in checking the validity of the facts, arguments, and outputs of this research will be able to cross-check them with documents uploaded on the website. To this end, most of the domestic materials used in this book have been uploaded on the website.

Finally, the study employed a key informant interview as a means of data collection in order to substantiate the information gathered through the methods mentioned above. This was in particular aimed at acquiring in-depth details regarding the work of the SPO. In that respect, the author conducted a face to face interview with Mr. Yosef Kiros, who was purposively selected owing to his extensive experience and expertise on the manner in which the SPO prosecuted the *Dergue*. He was indeed Deputy-Chief SPO, the longest-serving SPO prosecutor, and the lead prosecutor in the most significant *Dergue* trials such as *Mengistu et al.* and *Legesse Asfaw et al.* His availability and willingness to discuss the work of the SPO for the purposes of this study made his input – to which, where relevant, the book refers to – was thus paramount to further the understanding of the functioning of, and the challenges faced by, the SPO in fulfilling the aims for which it had been established.

1.6   Scope of the Book

This book is limited to the analysis of instances of Ethiopian domestic prosecutions of core crimes that are already completed. As pointed out above, this

---

115   See Federal Courts Proclamation Re-Amendment, *supra* note 86, Article 2 (1), para. 1.

book discusses these prosecutions in comparison with standards of ICL. Issues regarding potential prosecutions or absence of prosecution for core crimes, though important, are not discussed in the book. Hence, whether Ethiopia, by failing to investigate and prosecute other allegations of core crimes,[116] has been in breach of its international obligation to prosecute, or whether the alleged instances really do constitute instances of perpetration of core crimes are questions beyond the scope of this book.

Furthermore, all of the four instances of prosecution of core crimes that this book examines were under the jurisdiction of federal courts.[117] In fact, it is not fully clear whether State/regional courts have jurisdiction over core crimes. There is no accessible information on regional courts and it therefore cannot be authoritatively affirmed that there were, or were not, any cases related to core crimes;[118] this is a limitation to the study conducted in this book but one that could not be avoided.

---

116 This however does not mean that there are no other allegations related to the perpetration of international crimes in contemporary Ethiopia. Notable allegations include: 1) the *Anuak* Situation which represents the continued commission of international crimes against the *Anuak* communities in South West Ethiopia allegedly by Ethiopian National Defense Force (ENDF) since 2003; see Targeting the *Anuak*, Human Rights Watch, available at: <http://www.hrw.org /reports /2005/03/23/targeting-*Anuak*> accessed 20 March 2019; 2) the Ogaden conflict in which alleged commissions of war crimes and crimes against humanity by the ENDF have been reported; see Human Rights Watch, Collective Punishment: War Crimes and Crimes against Humanity in the Ogaden area of Ethiopia's Somali Region, 13 June 2008, available at: <http://www.hrw.org/node/62176> accessed 20 March 2019; 3) The eviction and deportation of members of the Amhara ethnic group from the *Benishangul-Gumuz* regional states have been widely portrayed as an act of ethnic-cleansing; see B.A. Taye, 'Ethnic Cleansing in Ethiopia', (2018) 50 (1) *Journal of Peace Research* 77–104, 85; 4) A widespread and systematic attack against the members of ethnic *Oromos* as reported by different organizations such as Amnesty International; see for instance, Amnesty International, 'Because I am *Oromo*: Sweeping repression in the Oromia region of Ethiopia' (Amnesty International Report, 27 October 2014), available at: <https://www.amnesty.org/en/documents/afr25/006/2014/en/> accessed 20 March 2019.

117 Regional courts adjudicated core crimes in the *Dergue* trials owing to a jurisdictional power delegated by the FHC pursuant to Article 78(2) of the FDRE Constitution. See *supra* note 26.

118 Inquiries made by the author as to whether regional courts have prosecuted core crimes could not receive a reliable answer, which could perhaps be due to the fact that regional courts lack computerized database or even an adequate file management system. There is no official or central database in Ethiopia that could be used to locate and access judgments of the regional courts. Although there are limited online platforms claiming to offer access to court cases, they tend to focus only on reproducing those cases that are published by the FSC CB in Addis Ababa.

INTRODUCTION   31

From a substantive point of view, this book focuses on issues related to how Ethiopia reached a decision to prosecute and the manner in which defendants were tried for allegedly perpetrating international crimes committed in Ethiopia. In relation to the analysis of the actual prosecutions, the book deals mainly with the substantive aspects of the crimes involved and the punishment applied, as discussed below under section 1.7. As such, discussion on the rules of evidence, standards of proof, individual criminal responsibility or participation in the commission of international crimes is not part of the book, unless considered relevant to further elucidate the analysis of the definition of crimes and punishment.

It is also important to note that there are foreign trials involving crimes committed in Ethiopia during the *Dergue* regime. The Netherlands convicted Eshetu Alemu for war crimes in relation to acts committed in the late 1970s in the then Gojam Province in Ethiopia.[119] In the U.S., Kalbessa Negawo, an Ethiopian fugitive, was prosecuted based on the Alien Tort Claims Act for having participated in the violence that occurred during the Red-Terror period.[120] Besides, the U.S. has been prosecuting Ethiopian fugitives for violating immigration laws by concealing their involvement in the *Dergue* era violence.[121] Nonetheless, these foreign trials are not going to be discussed in this book except when found to be important to clarify a certain point. This is because

---

119 Eshetu Alemu was a chairperson of the *Dergue's* revolutionary operations coordinating committee and its permanent representative in the then Gojjam province. See District Court of The Hague, *Prosecutor* v. *Eshetu Alemu*, Judgment, 15 December 2017, (ECLI:N-L:RBDHA:2017:14782).For an unofficial English translation of the case, see <https://uitspraken.rechtspraak.nl/inziendocument?id=ECLI:NL:RBDHA:2017:16383> accessed 28 September 2019.

120 In 1990, while the *Dergue* was still in power in Ethiopia, Negawo stood trial in the US in connection with acts of torture committed during the *Dergue* regime. United States District Court, Georgia, Atlanta Division *Abebe-Jiri* v. *Negewo*, (20 August 1993) Case No. 1:90-CV-2010-GET, N.D, paras 5–7. The decision was affirmed on appeal: *Abebe-Jiri* v. *Negewo*, United States Court of Appeal, Eleventh Circuit (No. 93–9133) 10 January 1996. The United States Federal Supreme Court denied his petition for writ of certiorari. See *Abebe-Jiri* v. *Negewo*, 519 U.S. 830, 117 S.Ct. 96 (Mem), 136 L.Ed.2d 51, 65 USLW 3258; *Negewo* v. *Chertoff*, United States District Court, S.D. Alabama, Northern Division. January 5, 2007, Civil Action No. 06-00631-WS-C (2007 WL 38336), paras 1- 5.

121 See District Court for the District of Colorado, *United States* v. *Worku*, (27 May 2014) D.C. No. 1:12-CR-00346-JLK-1. More recently, the Eastern District Court of Virginia sentenced Mergia Negussie Habteyes to 37 months of imprisonment for fraudulently obtaining citizenship through a series of lies, including failure to disclose participation in persecution during Red-Terror. See <https://www.justice.gov/opa/pr/ethiopian-human-rights-abuser-sentenced-fraudulently-obtaining-us-citizenship-admitted-series> accessed 28 September 2019.

the book, as noted above, aims at undertaking an international – vertical – comparative analysis as opposed to a horizontal analysis, that is, an analysis of Ethiopian trials with those conducted in other countries.

Finally, as noted in Table 1 above, Ethiopian courts have tried perpetrators for inchoate forms of genocide such as attempt, complicity, conspiracy, and incitement. Nonetheless, the survey of the jurisprudence reveals that no discernable discussion of the inchoate offenses took place during the trials. Although the first charge brought by the SPO in *Mengistu et al.* against top former officials of the *Dergue* referred to 'provocation and preparation' to commit genocide,[122] both the ruling[123] and the judgment[124] in this case predominantly focused on the crime of genocide in the second count of the SPO's indictment.[125] As a result, the analysis of Ethiopian jurisprudence in Part 2 of this book is limited to the crime of genocide itself, and does not include the inchoate offenses.

1.7 Structure of the Book

In order to address its central questions in a clear and comprehensive manner, the book is structured into two parts. The first part deals with issues related to the *setting in motion of the prosecution of core crimes* while the second part focuses on issues pertinent to the stage of *actual prosecution* of core crimes.[126] Most importantly, this structure is adopted as a result of the nature of national prosecutions of core crimes in general and of the Ethiopian prosecutions in particular, as will be explained below.

National prosecutions of core crimes usually involve a process that is different from both national prosecutions of domestic crimes[127] and prosecutions

---

122 See FHC, SPO v. *Colonel Mengistu Hailemariam et al.*, (Revised Indictment), 28 November 1995, File No. 1/87, count 1. For details of the charge, see Tessema, *Prosecution of Politicide in Ethiopia, supra* note 18, 179–181.
123 *Colonel Mengistu Hailemariam et al.*, (Trial Ruling), *supra* note 100.
124 *Colonel Mengistu Hailemariam et al.*, (Trial Judgment), *supra* note 101.
125 *Colonel Mengistu Hailemariam et al.*, (Revised Indictment), *supra* note 122, count 2.
126 The phrases 'process of prosecution' or 'process of national prosecution of core crimes' here refer to all judicial/prosecutorial activities that take place from the moment the decision to prosecute is taken until the end of the trial and the final judgment.
127 Compared to the process of national prosecution of domestic crimes, the stage of the setting in motion of prosecution of core crimes by national courts is an additional stage; one of the reasons for such an additional phase may be found in the prosecuting state's legal system itself, which is usually dimly familiar, if not entirely unfamiliar, with the notion of core crimes and with their prosecution. This lack of familiarity may cause undue delays, notably if the state embarks on such a process for the first time.

of international crimes by international institutions involving international judges, be they *ad hoc* or permanent. Indeed, unlike national courts, both the ICTY and the ICTR were innovative designs equipped and enabled to operate in an international arena, disconnected from the legal and territorial influence of the relevant countries in which the core crimes had been or were being committed. Also established for the sole purpose of prosecuting international crimes, the ICC benefits from a permanent vocation and has been conceived as a regular judicial organ with almost everything, in terms of applicable rules and infrastructure, in place to guarantee such prosecutions. By contrast, national prosecutions of international crimes by domestic judges involve the use of domestic institutions and of existing legal systems, which generally need to be updated and revitalized in the period that follows the announcement of the decision to prosecute and that precedes the filing of the initial indictment. As such, the phase of the setting in motion of national prosecutions of core crimes is, to put it briefly, a preparatory stage in which the prosecuting state complements its decision or willingness to prosecute with the adoption of measures necessary to enable the actual bringing to trial of those responsible for perpetrating core crimes.

With respect to the stage of the setting in motion of national prosecutions of core crimes, it appears that, due to the novelty and complexity of the process that ensues, a decision to prosecute core crimes does not necessarily guarantee that prosecutions will actually follow. In this respect, it is worth noting that under the complementarity principle of the Rome Statute, a state may still be regarded as unwilling by the court despite its official announcement of its willingness to prosecute international crimes.[128] The fact that, in the eyes of international law, a mere policy decision to prosecute is not a sufficient indication of a commitment to bring perpetrators to justice can also be inferred from decisions of other courts.

---

128 Even in clear cases of announcement of a state's willingness to prosecute core crimes, it could still be possible that the state does not fully intend to bring to trial those responsible for the perpetration of international crimes and is thus 'unwilling' according to the ICC Statute. As emphasized by the OTP, 'the existence of general institutional deficiencies (political subordination of investigative, prosecutorial or judicial branch), procedural irregularities indicating a lack of willingness to genuinely investigate or prosecute, or unwillingness of one or more of the state functionaries such as the military, the executive, the judiciary or the investigative or due to selective willingness' may lead the State into being considered as unwilling. See Office of the Prosecutor, *The principle of complementarity in practice* (informal expert paper), available at: <https://www.icc-cpi.int/NR/rdonlyres/20BB4494-70F9-4698-8E30-907F631453ED/281984/complementarity.pdf> accessed 20 March 2019.

As indicated by the ECtHR in *M.C*,[129] *Nachova*,[130] *Timurtas*,[131] *Kuznetsov*,[132] and *Tepe*,[133] the process of bringing perpetrators to justice shall be accompanied with measures ensuring its 'effectiveness' such as through undertaking proper and thorough investigation.[134] The IACtHR followed a similar approach to assess whether a state has complied with the obligation to investigate and prosecute crimes as enshrined under Article 1 (1) of the American Convention on Human Rights (ACHR).[135] In *Velásquez-Rodríguez* v. *Honduras*, the Court underlined that a state that prosecutes human rights violations shall conduct investigations in a 'serious manner and not as mere formality preordained to be ineffective'.[136] The Court has ever since stressed the importance of this statement in various related cases.[137]

---

129 ECtHR, *M.C.* v. *Bulgaria*, (Judgment), 4 December 2003, Application No. 39272/98, para 153.

130 ECtHR, *Nachova and others* v. *Bulgaria*, (Judgment), 6 July 2005, Applications Nos. 43577/98 and 43579/98, paras 110–113.

131 ECtHR, *Timurtas* v. *Turkey*, (Judgment, Merits and Just Satisfaction), 13 June 2000, Application No. 23531/94, paras 88 and 110.

132 ECtHR, *Kuznetsov* v. *Ukraine*, (Judgment, Merits and Just Satisfaction), 29 April 2003, Application No. 39042/97, para. 106.

133 ECtHR, *Tepe* v. *Turkey*, (Judgment, Merits and Just Satisfaction), 9 May 2003, Application No. 27244/95, paras 181–182.

134 For details, see W.A. Schabas and M.M. El Zeidy, 'Article 17: Issues of Admissibility' in O. Triffterer and K. Ambos (eds.), *The Rome Statute of the International Criminal Court: A Commentary* (3rd. ed., Munich: C.H. Beck – Hart – Nomos, 2015), 781–831, 818–820.

135 American Convention on Human Rights, O.A.S. Treaty Series No. 36, 1144 U.N.T.S. 123, *entered into force* July 18, 1978, *reprinted in* Basic Documents Pertaining to Human Rights in the Inter-American System, OEA/Ser.L.V/II.82 doc.6 rev.1 at 25 (1992). For the existence under the ACHR of an obligation to prosecute human rights violations, see IACtHR, *Luis Alfredo Almonacid Arellano et al.* v. *Chile*, (Judgment, Preliminary Objections, Merits, Reparations and Costs), 26 September 2006, Report No. 44/02, Case No. 12.057, para. 110. See also IACtHR, *Velásquez-Rodríguez* v. *Honduras*, (Judgment), 29 July 1988, Series C No. 4, para. 166.

136 See *Velásquez-Rodríguez* v. *Honduras, supra* note 135, para. 177. See also IACtHR, *El Amparo* v. *Venezuela*, (Judgment, Reparations), 14 September 1996, Series C No. 28, para. 61, where the court stated that the obligation to prosecute a violation of human rights is 'an obligation that must be discharged seriously and not as a mere formality'.

137 IACtHR, *Cantoral-Benavides* v. *Peru*, (Judgment, Reparations and Costs), 3 December 2001, Series. C No.88, para. 69; IACtHR, *Cesti Hurtado* v. *Peru*, (Judgment, Reparation and Costs), 31 May 2001, Series. C No. 86, para. 62; IACtHR, *Villagrán-Morales et al. (The Street Children)* v. *Guatemala*, (Judgment, Reparations and Costs), 26 May 2001, Series. C No. 63, para. 100; IACtHR, *Trujillo-Oroza* v. *Bolivia*, (Judgment, Reparations and Costs), 27 February 2002, Series C No. 92, para. 100; IACtHR *Myrna Mack Chang* v. *Guatemala*, (Judgment, Merits, Reparations and Costs), 25 November 2003, Series C No. 101, para. 153.

Hence, a national prosecution of international crimes demands a lot more than just a declaration of willingness or a decision to investigate and prosecute core crimes. It requires the setting in motion of the process of prosecution, which comprises the adoption of a series of complex reforms to the prosecuting state's own legal system. This is the case notably if the state embarks on the prosecution of core crimes for the first time. This process of equipping and enabling the national legal system requires identifying and removing impediments that may hinder the existing legal system from commencing, or continuing with, the prosecution of core crimes.

This preparatory stage is not to be overlooked, if only because domestic legal and/or institutional impediments may seriously jeopardize, if not altogether impede, prosecutions of core crimes at the national level. As noted by the UN Human Rights Committee (HRC)[138] as well as by the IACtHR, unless these impediments are removed, the whole process of national prosecution of human rights violations cannot attain its due effect.[139] Institutional impediments relate to the nature of the resources invested and the ability of the state institutions to cope with prosecuting large-scale crimes. In particular, a lack of necessary personnel, judges, investigators, prosecutors as well as, most importantly, bleak prospects of capacity improvement will more often than not lead to ineffective, if not altogether inexistent, prosecutions. It is therefore vital that the prosecuting state explores possible solutions and alternatives to reduce any infrastructural impediments hindering the prosecution of core crimes at the national level.

---

138   According to the Human Rights Committee, impediments to the establishment of legal responsibility for human rights violations such as amnesties, official status, immunities and indemnities, unreasonably short period of statutory limitations should be removed. See Human Rights Committee, General Comment 31, Nature of the General Legal Obligation on States Parties to the Covenant, U.N. Doc. CCPR/C/21/Rev.1/Add.13 (2004), para. 18.

139   The stringency of the obligation to prosecute was displayed in several cases in which the IACtHR ordered states to remove *de facto* and *de jure* impediments to prosecution such as amnesty, extinguishment, statute of limitations, and other measures designed to eliminate responsibility. See *Luis Alfredo Almonacid Arellano et al. v. Chile, supra* note 135, paras 113–114, 119,151–153; IACtHR, *Baldeón-García v. Perú*, (Judgment, Merits, Reparations, and Costs), 6 April 2006, Series C No. 147, para. 201; IACtHR, *Blanco-Romero et al. v. Venezuela*, (Judgment, Merits, Reparations and Costs), 28 November 2005, Series C No. 138, para. 98; *Myrna Mack Chang v. Guatemala, supra* note 137, para. 153; IACtHR, *Ituango Massacres v. Colombia*, (Judgment on Preliminary Objections, Merits, Reparations and Costs), 1 July 2006, Series C No. 148, para. 402; IACtHR, *Mapiripán Massacre v. Colombia*, (Judgment, Merits, Reparations, and Costs), 5 September 2005, Series C No. 134, para 237; IACtHR, *The Massacres of El Mozote and Nearby Places v. El Salvador*, (Judgment, Merits, Reparations, and Costs), 25 October 2012, Series C No. 252, para 300.

Legal impediments to the prosecution of core crimes such as amnesty laws, statute of limitations, immunities, and the *ne bis in idem* principle hinder actual prosecutions from kicking off, or only allow them to partially kick off.[140] Laws on jurisdictions or on prosecutorial scope may contain stipulations that lead to an unjustified selectivity of crimes and/or perpetrators to be prosecuted. This problem is admittedly increased in the case of a total absence of laws addressing issues highly relevant to the prosecution of international crimes (such as modes of criminal liability, grounds excluding criminal liability, and elements of crimes).

Accordingly, in setting the prosecutions in motion, the prosecuting state attempts – or should attempt – to eliminate the legal impediments by enacting entirely new legislation or amending and repealing the old one, or by providing for provisions that allow domestic courts to directly apply the applicable rules of ICL. This process has often raised serious concerns in relation to the principle of legality. Studies indicate that states have, more often than not, prosecuted acts that could constitute core crimes as ordinary crimes and, therefore, relied largely on their own municipal laws.[141] In some other states, courts have blocked prosecutions involving core crimes on the ground that there existed no domestic legislation before or at the time of the commission of the relevant conduct.[142] However, as will be discussed further in Chapter 7,

---

140   See Office of the Prosecutor, *The principle of complementarity in practice*, supra note 128. See also Cassese *et al.* (eds.), *Cassese's International Criminal Law*, supra note 89, 309.

141   For copious examples, see Ferdinandusse, *Direct Application of International Criminal Law in National Courts*, supra note 52, 18–21, 205–206; W. Ferdinandusse, 'The Prosecution of Grave Breaches in National Courts' (2009) 7 (1) *Journal of International Criminal Justice* 723–741, 729–734.

142   In Senegal, the recently completed criminal trial of Hissène Habré was initially rejected by both the Chambre d'accusation de la Cour d'appel de Dakar (on 4 July 2000) and the Cour de Cassation of Senegal (on 20 March 2001) on the ground that such a prosecution would violate a constitutional provision on the principle of legality, for there was no domestic provision that incorporated the relevant international crimes. For details, including on the misinterpretation of the non-retroactivity principle by the Court of Justice of the Economic Community of West African States (ECOWAS Court), see V. Spiga, Non-retroactivity of Criminal Law: A New Chapter in the Hissène Habré Saga' (2011) 9(1) *Journal of International Criminal Justice* 5–23.

See also the decision of the ECOWAS Court of Justice in *Habré v. Senegal*, which, based on the non-retroactivity principle, stated that only an *ad hoc* tribunal, *but not a domestic court*, is entitled to prosecute international crimes that are not prohibited by a domestic law at the time of their commission. See Court of Justice ECOWAS, *Hissein Habré v. Republic of Senegal*, Judgment No: ECW/CCJ /Jud/06/10 of 18 November 2010) General Role No. ECW/CCJ/App/07/08, paras 58–61. An unofficial English translation of the case by Human Rights Watch is available at: <http://www.asser.nl/upload/documents/20120419T034816-Habre%20Ecowa%202010.pdf> accessed 20 March 2019.

INTRODUCTION

regional and international organs and courts such as the HRC,[143] the ECtHR,[144] the IACtHR,[145] the ICTY,[146] the ICTR,[147] and the Special Tribunal for Lebanon (STL)[148] do not regard domestic provisions on the principle of legality as relevant to reject domestic or international prosecutions of core crimes as long as the crimes were, at the time when they were committed, sufficiently defined in international law.

In addition to the foregoing discussion, the context in which Ethiopia embarked on the prosecution of core crimes imposes the structuring of this book into two parts. As noted above, this book is concerned with the analysis of four instances of prosecution of core crimes in Ethiopia. Of these, the *Dergue* trials, which are the first of their kind, also represent a case of large-scale prosecution of core crimes conducted within a post-conflict legal system. This fact indicates that, at the time the TGE decided to prosecute the core crimes in 1992, it is possible that the Ethiopian legal system was not prepared

---

> In Spain, the non-retroactivity principle lies at the heart of the controversies that occurred in relation to the *Historical Memory* case regarding disappearances during the repression from 17 July 1936 to 31 December 1951. Both Baltasar Garzón, the *Audiencia Nacional's* investigative judge, and the Supreme Court, refused to qualify as crimes against humanity the enforced disappearances perpetrated during the period in question. The refusal was based on the absence of domestic legislation on crimes against humanity at the time the acts were allegedly committed and on the fact that the 2004's Article 607*bis* of the Spanish Penal Code, which introduced crimes against humanity, could not be applied retroactively. See S. S. i Linares, 'Francoism Facing Justice: Enforced Disappearances before Spanish Courts' (2013), 11 (1) *Journal of International Criminal Justice* 463–483, 468–469.

143 HRC, *David Michael Nicholas v. Australia*, Communication No. 1080/2002, U.N. Doc. CCPR/C/80/D/1080/2002 (2004), para. 7.5; HRC, *Klaus Dieter Baumgarten v. Germany*, Communication No. 960/2000, U.N. Doc. CCPR/C/78/D/960/2000 (2003), para. 9.3.

144 See ECtHR, *Kononov v. Latvia*, (Judgment), 17 May 2010, Application no. 36376/04, para. 238; ECtHR, *Korbely v. Hungary*, Grand Chamber, (Judgment), 19 September 2008, Application No. 9174/02, paras 73–76; EctHR, *Šimšić v. Bosnia and Herzegovina*, (Judgment), 10 April 2012, Application no. 51552/10, para. 24.

145 According to the Court, 'the State may not invoke ....the non-retroactivity of criminal law... to decline its duty to investigate and punish those responsible [for international crimes]' *Luis Alfredo Almonacid Arellano et al. v. Chile, supra* note 135, para. 151.

146 See ICTY, *Prosecutor v. Hadžihasanović*, Trial Chamber, (Judgment), 15 March 2006, IT-01-47-AR72, para. 34; ICTY, *Prosecutor v. Milutinović et al.*, Appeals Chamber, (Decision on Dragoljub Ojdanić's Motion Challenging Jurisdiction – Joint Criminal Enterprise), 21 May 2003, IT-99-37-AR72, para. 42.

147 See ICTR, *Prosecutor v. Nahimana et al.*, Appeals Chamber, (Judgment), 28 November 2007, ICTR-99-52-A, paras 988, *fn.* 2264.

148 STL, *Unnamed defendants v. the Prosecutor*, Appeals Chamber, (Interlocutory on the Applicable Law: Terrorism, Conspiracy, Homicide, Perpetration, Cumulative Charging), 16 February 2011, STL-11-01/I/AC/R176bis, paras 135–136.

to deal with the prosecution of core crimes at all, let alone to such a large scale. It is thus essential to firstly deal with the analysis of the initial stage of the process of prosecution of core crimes in Ethiopia, before directly discussing the manner in which Ethiopian courts have interpreted and applied the laws applicable to core crimes.

Part 1 investigates in detail the manner in which the prosecutions were set in motion and the steps taken to identify and clear away impediments – be them legal, political or structural – in order to bring those responsible to justice. As such, it contributes to answering the question: 'how does the criminal justice system of Ethiopia provide for the prosecution of core crimes?' This part focuses on whether the Ethiopian legal system (in both practical and legal aspects) was, from the standpoint of ICL, adequately prepared for the purpose of prosecuting those responsible for perpetrating core crimes – and it is divided into three chapters.

Chapter 2 examines the contextual background and the contents of the TGE's decision to prosecute core crimes. It emphasizes the extent to which amnesty was rejected both *de jure* and *de facto*. It also provides a preliminary analysis of the crimes for which a decision to prosecute was reached. The issue of statute of limitations and the question of immunity of state officials are examined under this chapter. It analyzes whether and, if so, how this particular decision to prosecute attempted to remove possible impediments to prosecutions.

Chapter 3 focuses on the analysis of grounds that may trigger prosecution of core crimes in Ethiopia. It examines possible motives behind the decisions to prosecute core crimes committed during the *Dergue* regime as well as those perpetrated in the post-*Dergue* Ethiopia. It establishes, from the analysis of the law and of the practice, Ethiopia's general approach towards the prosecution of core crimes, and discusses whether this approach was/is compatible with ICL standards or not.

Chapter 4 deals with the manner in which the preparatory stage of the prosecutions in Ethiopia removed, or attempted to remove, political and practical impediments related to the actual bringing to trial of those implicated in the perpetration of core crimes. This chapter examines who, among those involved in the commission of core crimes, was prosecuted and who was not, and why. Using ICL standards as a comparison yardstick, this chapter examines the issue of personal jurisdiction, as well as the efforts and remedies proposed regarding dealing with fugitive offenders.

Part 2 appraises the extent to which Ethiopian prosecutions were conducted in compliance with ICL standards. This part directly relates to the central question of the book: 'were prosecutions of core crimes in Ethiopia in line with standards of ICL?' The objective of this part is to study, in comparison with the relevant rules and standards of ICL, consistency and deviations that might exist in Ethiopian law and practice regarding core crimes. In particular, it extensively examines judgments rendered by Ethiopian courts in all of the four instances of prosecution of core crimes. A critical examination of the manner in which Ethiopian courts understood and interpreted the relevant law on core crimes is conducted. Where a deviation is pointed out, a further in-depth analysis is carried out in order to examine whether it could be regarded as a deficiency of the domestic system or as a case of acceptable divergence between the municipal and the international systems.[149] To this end, this part of the book is divided into four separate chapters.

Chapters 5, 6, and 7 analyze the available substantive laws of, respectively, genocide and war crimes as the only core crimes adjudicated by Ethipian courts and the manner in which they were applied by these courts. The analysis of the crime of genocide is divided into two chapters (5 and 6). Chapter 5 discusses the domestication of the international crime of genocide into the Ethiopian legal system. Chapter 6 examines the trials and the manner in which Ethiopian courts have interpreted and applied the elements of genocide. Chapter 7 deals with war crimes in Ethiopia, both in terms of the law and of the practice.

The analysis in Part 2 of this book engages in a meticulous examination of Ethiopian law and practice pertaining to the elements of these core crimes. Where, for whatever reason, judicial reasoning is non-existent in relation to one or more core crimes, the chapters compare and contrast the relevant domestic laws on the elements of core crimes with the corresponding rules of ICL.

Chapter 8 examines the law of sanctions for core crimes and their enforcement in the Ethiopian context. It explores the available penalties, the purpose of punishment, the actual penalties imposed on those found guilty of committing core crimes, and the manner of their enforcement. The analysis under this chapter aims at studying whether the sentencing factors as well as the theories

---

149 In distinguishing between divergence and deficiency, this books takes into account the fact that ICL is an incomplete and evolving body of law, because of which the application of rules of municipal criminal law becomes not only an essential but also an inevitable component in the national prosecutions of core crimes. Municipal law in particular serves to interpret ambiguous international rules or to fill gaps in ICL in the form of general principles of law. See for instance, ICC Statute, Article 21(1) (c); M.M. Deguzman, 'Article 21: Applicable Law' in O. Triffterer and K. Ambos (eds.), *The Rome Statute of the International Criminal Court: A Commentary* (3rd. ed., Munich: C.H. Beck – Hart – Nomos, 2015) 932–948, 942–45.

and objectives of punishment used by domestic courts coincide with the international approach in force at the time of the trials.

This book concludes that prosecutions of core crimes in Ethiopia were conducted, on several aspects, in a manner that is inconsistent with applicable standards of ICL. The analysis in Part 1 of the book indicates that, while it removed some of the legal impediments to core crimes' prosecution, Ethiopia also left other legal, political, and institutional impediments to persist throughout the trials. This in turn gave way for some of the deficiencies pointed out in Part 2 of the book.

The findings in Part 2 reveal that there are a number of issues on which Ethiopian law and practice questionably diverge from international standards. Not only the manner in which Ethiopian courts interpreted the applicable laws was problematic but also the laws applied in the prosecutions possessed inherent – yet arguably fixable – deficiencies.

PART 1

*The Setting in Motion of Prosecutions
of Core Crimes in Ethiopia*

∴

CHAPTER 2

The Decision to Prosecute Core Crimes
Contexts and Contents

2.1 Introduction

At the end of every conflict, of any nature and scale, the question of what is to be done with those responsible for the crimes committed during the conflict arises. A state may respond in different ways: by granting a blanket amnesty, by holding at least a number of those responsible accountable, or by adopting an approach that combines both amnesty and prosecution. Transitional governments may find competing justifications to opt for or against prosecuting past crimes.[1] Compared to prosecution, amnesty happens more regularly, even where international crimes are concerned.[2] Since amnesty can be *de jure* or *de facto*,[3] it may co-exist with a decision to prosecute without even being noticed.

There are however strong scholarly opinions which advocate for the rejection of amnesties based on philosophical and legal grounds, in particular when core crimes have been committed.[4] The 1948 Genocide Convention and the 1949 Geneva Conventions clearly stipulate that a state party must prosecute when, respectively, genocide and grave breaches of the Geneva Conventions have been committed.[5] In time, the UN has also revised its position regarding

---

1   See D.F. Orentlicher, 'The Duty to Prosecute Human Rights Violations of a Prior Regime' (1991)100(8) *The Yale Law Journal Company* 2537–2615.
2   Pursuant to Mallinder's study on the practice of states in introducing amnesties, of the close to 500 amnesty laws introduced since the end of the Second World War and until 2008, only 19 per cent excluded crimes under international law. See L. Mallinder, *Amnesty, Human Rights and Political Transitions: Bridging the Peace and Justice Divide* (Portland: Hart Publishing, 2008) 121.
3   See ibid., 3.
4   See A. Cassese, 'Reflections on International Criminal Justice' (1998) 61(1) *Modern Law Review* 1–10; B. Chigara, *Amnesty in International Law: The Legality under International Law of National Amnesty Laws*, (London: Longman, 2002) 1–21; M.C. Bassiouni 'International Crimes: Jus Cogens and Obliagtio Erga Omnes' (1996) 59(4) *Law and Contemporary Problems*, 63–74; F.Z. Ntoubandi, *Amnesty for Crimes against Humanity under International Law* (Leiden: Martinus Nijhoff Publishers 2007); K. Henrard, 'The Viability of National Amnesties in View of the Increasing Recognition of Individual Criminal Responsibility at International Law' (1999) 8 (1) *Michigan State University-DCL Journal of International Law* 595–650.
5   This will be further discussed in Chapter 3, sub-section 3.2.1.

amnesties involving core crimes – a change in stance witnessed in relation to the Lomé Accord of 7 July 1999 which was agreed upon immediately after the establishment of the icc in 1998,[6] although the Rome Statute of the icc itself does not contain a clear stipulation regarding amnesty.[7] The obligation to bring perpetrators to justice is not one of result,[8] in the sense that the state does not have to be successful in actually holding the prosecution. It is however necessary to have genuinely tried. As a decision to prosecute core crimes can therefore not in itself be considered a sufficient indicator of a commitment to prosecute such crimes, a state needs to have really made an effort to actually get the case to court and to take all necessary measures to ensure that the envisaged prosecution would be carried out in compliance with icl standards.[9]

With respect to the subject of this book – the Ethiopian cases – it is clear that Ethiopia *chose* to bring to justice those responsible for core crimes perpetrated in the aforementioned trilogy of conflicts, which ultimately resulted in the *Dergue* trial, the *Anuak-Nuwer* trials, the CUD trials, and the *Oromo-Gumuz* trials. What is less clear is how the decision to prosecute core crimes was reached as well as the scope of the prosecutions it had envisioned.[10] Unfortunately, the existing literature has failed to offer an explanation on these issues. This chapter, thus, undertakes a close scrutiny of the context and the practice in order to identify the details of the decisions to prosecute. The question as to why the decision to prosecute was reached, which requires an examination of the possible motives behind this decision, is addressed in Chapter 3.

Each of the four instances of Ethiopian prosecutions of international crimes took place in a different social, political, and legal context. A decision to

---

6   For a detailed account of the position of the UN on amnesties, see M. Freeman, *Necessary Evils: Amnesties and the search for justice* (Cambridge: Cambridge University Press, 2009) 88–106. See also Mallinder, *Amnesty, Human Rights and Political Transitions, supra* note 2, 122.

7   Even though the issue of amnesty is not explicitly addressed in the Rome Statute of the ICC, national amnesties are considered to be falling within the scope of Article 17(1) or (2) of the Statute. See T. Ongen and C. Wyngaert, 'Ne bis in idem Principle, Including the Issue of Amnesty' in A. Cassese *et al.* (eds.), *The Rome Statute of the International Criminal Court, Volume I: A Commentary* (Oxford: Oxford University Press 2002) 705–729, 726–727.

8   The obligation to bring perpetrators to justice 'does not impose a requirement that a State must necessarily succeed in locating and prosecuting perpetrators', see ECtHR, *Tepe* v. *Turkey*, (Judgment, Merits and Just Satisfaction), 9 May 2003, Application No. 27244/95, para. 177.

9   See Chapter 1, section 1.7.

10 Ethiopia reached a decision to prosecute core crimes explicitly and for the first time in relation to the *Dergue* era atrocities. As will be discussed, each of the *Anuak-Nuwer*, the CUD, and the *Oromo-Gumuz* trials were conducted like any other trial of domestic crimes without involving any official announcement to prosecute or any similar significant policy decision.

prosecute or to grant an amnesty often takes into consideration political interests and the power balance among the parties involved. The latter depends on the political stability in the country in question. The Ethiopian situations could be divided into two general categories. The first category refers to the prosecution of the *Dergue* era crimes, which took place following a lengthy civil war that brought about a political transition in the country. As will be discussed later, the *Dergue* trials were initiated while the country was under a transitional government and in a situation of increased internal tensions; a context that usually makes it hard to choose between amnesty and prosecution.[11] The second category encompasses the remaining three instances of prosecution of core crimes, all of which were committed in conflicts that triggered neither a change of government nor lead to a significant political and structural reform.

Owing to the complexity of the decision to prosecute the *Dergue* era atrocities, this Chapter focuses on the discussion of the initial circumstances related to this decision, which is why the title of this Chapter is phrased using the singular noun, decision. As such, the decisions in the other three core crimes trials, namely the *Anuak-Nuwer*, the CUD, and the *Oromo-Gumuz* trials will be discussed in subsequent chapters. In line with this division, this chapter is structured around four sections. Section 2.2 deals with the analysis of the response that the TGE, a government established in 1991 following the fall of the *Dergue* regime,[12] took regarding crimes committed during the regime it had just replaced. This section analyzes in detail the context in which the decision to prosecute was reached and its scope as regards amnesty. Section 2.3 discusses the scope of the planned prosecution of the crimes allegedly perpetrated during the *Dergue* regime. Section 2.4. examines whether the decision to prosecute was accompanied with measures necessary to remove possible impediments to its implementation. Specifically, this section discusses issues such as statutory limitations and immunity from prosecution that might have resulted from the application of extant laws.

---

11   See Chigara, *Amnesty in International Law, supra* note 4, 1. Nevertheless, studies show that the practice of amnesty began (and is still practiced until recently) in relation to situations of international armed conflicts as opposed to contexts of transitional justice resulting from internal armed conflicts. See Ntoubandi, *Amnesty for Crimes against Humanity under International Law, supra* note 4, 15–21. The factors behind the decision to prosecute will be discussed in detail in Chapter 3.

12   The Transitional Government of Ethiopia was established in 1991 for a period of two years. However, subsequent extensions were made to the transitional period that led the TGE to last until 1995.

2.2 Amnestying or Prosecuting the *Dergue*: The Choice of the TGE

In 1991, an unconstitutional change of government took place in Ethiopia for the second time in less than two decades.[13] In May that year, the Ethiopian People's Democratic Revolutionary Front (EPRDF)[14], the main rebel coalition, controlled the capital, Addis Ababa, after defeating the *Dergue* forces. This marked the coming to an end of a 17 year long bloody civil war in Ethiopia.[15] A controversial transitional government (the TGE)[16] headed by the EPRDF was established in July 1991 pledging to bring democracy to the country.[17] As is usually the case with post-conflict political transitions, the TGE was faced with numerous challenges and options that were to be preferred or precluded in order to shape the future of the country.

Prior to the establishment of the TGE, i.e. from May to July 1991, the EPRDF arrested thousands of individuals, members, and affiliates of the deposed

---

13   Here, the first unconstitutional change of government refers to the 1974 military revolution that ended the monarchical regime of Emperor Haileselassie and brought to power the *Dergue* regime.

14   At this time, the EPRDF was headed mainly by the Tigray Liberation Front (TPLF) and composed of two other ethno-nationalist People's Democratic Organizations (PDOs) established by the TPLF in the final days of the civil war. These were the Oromo Peoples Democratic Organization (OPDO) and the Ethiopian People's Democratic Movement (EPDM), which later changed its name to Amhara National Democratic Movement (ANDM). See A. Berhe, *A Political History of the Tigray People's Liberation Front (1975–1991): Revolt, Ideology and Mobilisation in Ethiopia* (PhD Dissertation, Vrijie Universiteit Amsterdam, 2009), 230.

15   The Ethiopian civil war is commonly referred to as having lasted for 17 years. This can be true as long as this reference is made only in relation to the *Dergue* that coexisted with a civil war throughout the 17 years of its regime. In reality, the Eritrean Peoples' Liberation Front (EPLF) initiated the civil war in Ethiopia in 1961; since Eritrea was part of Ethiopia until it secured its independence in 1991, the actual duration of the Ethiopian civil war is 30 years. See Human Rights Watch, 'Evil Days: 30 Years of War and Famine in Ethiopia' (Report of African Watch, September 1991) 1, available at <https://www.hrw.org/sites/default/files/reports/Ethiopia919.pdf> accessed 28 September 2019 [Hereinafter: Thirty Years of Evil Days].

16   In addition to the EPRDF's dominating role in its establishment, the controversial nature of the TGE lies in the fact that it was perceived as composed of political parties that do not fully represent diverse interests and groups in the country, as will be pointed out in different parts of this chapter.

17   See G.A. Lewthwaite, 'Rebels pledge democracy in Ethiopia: U.S.-brokered talks end in agreement after fall of capital' *The Baltimore Sun* (London, 29 May 1991), available at: <http://Articles.baltimoresun.com/1991-05-29/news/1991149072_1_addis-ababa-ethiopians-eprdf> accessed 28 September 2019.

regime.[18] The need to look back at the past and devise an appropriate course of action with respect to those allegedly responsible for the atrocities that befell the country from 1974 to 1991 was, presumably, a pressing issue for the TGE. A closer scrutiny of the historical context reveals that the issue regarding how to respond to the atrocities perpetrated during the *Dergue* regime was for the first time raised at the Conference held in London at the end of May 1991, which was immediately before the *Dergue*'s final fall. In August 1992, the TGE issued the SPO Proclamation that announced a decision to hold accountable those responsible for crimes committed during the *Dergue* era. The following developments discuss in detail, and step by step, the evolution the TGE's decision to prosecute the *Dergue* era atrocities.

2.2.1 The London Conference: An Attempt to Negotiate Amnesty

During most parts of the conflict, the Ethiopian civil war was devoid of any chance of peace negotiations among the warring parties. Bipartisan negotiations and preliminary talks only began in 1989. Talks were held in Atlanta from 9 to19 September 1989 between the *Dergue* and the Eritrean Liberation Front (EPLF)[19] and again in Nairobi from 20 to 29 November 1989.[20] There were also talks in Rome from 12 to18 December 1990 between the *Dergue* and the Tigray Liberation Front (TPLF)[21] and in Sanaa from 1 to 21 April 1990 between the *Dergue* and the Eritrean Liberation Front (ELF).[22] None of these talks was successful. According to Ottway, the negotiations were initiated in an unpromising time, and a shift in the character of the conflicts together with an absence of a political culture of compromise rendered them fruitless.[23]

---

18 Approximately 2000 suspects associated with the *Dergue* regime were detained soon after the fall down of the regime, which started as early as May 1991. See Human Rights Watch, 'Ethiopia: Reckoning under the Law' (Human rights Watch, 1 December) 19, available at: <https://www.hrw.org/report/1994/12/01/ethiopia-reckoning-under-law> accessed 28 September 2019.

19 J. Cohen, *Intervening in Africa: Superpower Peacemaking in a Troubled Continent* (New York: St. Martin's Press LL.C., 2000), 26–27.

20 See Ethiopian News Agency, 'Peace Talks Resume' 1989 (13) (2) *Quarterly Yekatit* 8.

21 See 'Giving Peace a Chance' 1990 (13) (3) *Quarterly Yekatit* 5–6.

22 See 'The Search for Lasting Peace' 1990 (13) (4) *Quarterly Yekatit* 6–8.

23 See M. Ottway, 'Eritrea and Ethiopia: negotiations in a transitional conflict' in W. Zartman (ed.), *Elusive Peace: Negotiating an End to Civil Wars*, (Washington DC: Brookings Institution Press, 1995) 103–120, 104–115. See also A.P. Micheau, 'The 1991 Transitional Charter of Ethiopia: A New Application of the Self-Determination Principle' 1996 (28) 2 *Case Western Reserve Journal of International Law* 367–394, 378.

It was only in May 1991, following the end of the cold war and the withdrawal of Soviet military advisers from Ethiopia,[24] that the U.S., pursuant to an alleged request from Colonel Mengistu Hailemariam, the president of the then Peoples' Democratic Republic of Ethiopia (PDRE),[25] brokered a multiparty peace talks. The peace talks, initially scheduled for 15 May 1991, had to be postponed twice to give precedence to the airlifting of more than 20,000 *Falashas* (Ethiopian Jews) to Israel and were finally held in London from 26 to 28 May 1991.[26]

The London Conference was the only major conference organized after the Ethiopian civil war with the aim to forge the country's peaceful transition from the communist dictatorial regime to a new political order. Nevertheless, the conference was widely criticized for its inadequate timing as it was held on the brink of the fall of Addis Ababa, the country's capital city, into the hands of the rebel forces. Even if, unlike the bipartisan talks of the previous years, the London Conference had hoped to involve all of the well-known groups, as well as lesser-known ones, that were operating in Ethiopia, in the end only the *Dergue*, the EPLF, the TPLF, and the Oromo Liberation Front (OLF) were invited.[27] Involvement in the armed struggle against the *Dergue* was arguably the criterion used to selectively invite the opposition groups to the peace talks.[28]

According to Teferra Hailesellasie, the then Ethiopian Ambassador to Britain and member of the *Dergue* delegation to the London Conference, the *Dergue* came up with a proposal for establishing a provisional government.[29] The *Dergue*'s terms of reference for the intended provisional government included, among others, the granting of an amnesty to party and government functionaries as well as to those it referred to as 'the insurgents' (the EPLF, the TPLF, and the OLF).[30]

24   The Soviet troops had been withdrawn from Ethiopia as of early February 1990. See D.H. Shinn and T.P. Ofcansky, *Historical Dictionary of Ethiopia* (Lanham: Scarecrow Press, 2013) xxviii. See also Cohen, *Intervening in Africa, supra* note 19, 36–37.
25   See Cohen, *Intervening in Africa, supra* note 19, 45.
26   Ibid., 46–47.
27   Some of the parties that were not invited to the London Conference included: Ethiopian People's Revolutionary Party (EPRP); All Ethiopian Socialist Movement (AESM); the Coalition of Democratic Ethiopian Forces (CODEF); and the Ogaden National Liberation Front (ONLF).
28   See T. Haile-Selassie, *The Ethiopian Revolution 1974–1991: From a Monarchical Autocracy to a Military Oligarchy* (London: Kegan Paul International, 1997) 313.
29   Ibid.
30   Ibid., 314.

At this stage, the amnesty provision proposed by the *Dergue* appeared to be of a transitory nature. As recorded in a book recently published by Tesfaye Dinka, the *Dergue*'s interim prime minister following Colonel Mengistu Hailemariam's escape to Zimbabwe on 8 May 1991 and head of the *Dergue* delegation to the London Conference, the proposed amnesty was intended to 'enable free and fair participation, *during the transition*, in political campaigning and elections by all groups'.[31] As such, so it seems, the *Dergue*'s initial request for amnesty was not aimed at curtailing criminal accountability indefinitely, but only at delaying the issue of accountability so that it could be addressed at the end of the transitional period by a democratically elected government.

As reported by Dinka, the proposed terms of reference were not entirely objectionable to Mr. Herman Cohen, the chairperson of the peace talks and then U.S. Assistant Secretary of State for African Affairs. The amnesty question was apparently not a matter of priority for the U.S. government, as it was rather overwhelmingly interested in ensuring that the outgoing government would not emphasize the question of proportion of representation in the would-be transitional government and that a 'special package' could be arranged for Eritrea.[32] Hence, the proposal regarding amnesty was neither explicitly dismissed nor supported by Mr. Cohen. As further noted by Dinka, a proposed agreement drafted by the U.S. government did not mention whether the provisional government that would be established as early as 1 June 1991 should consider amnesty, as suggested by him, during the talks.[33] Rather, in what seemed to be recommending a mixed approach combining prosecution and amnesty, Mr. Cohen stated, under Article 5 of his proposal, that 'all parties to the agreement pledge to conduct their activities in the spirit of *reconciliation* and justice and the rule of law for all Ethiopians'.[34]

Cognizant of the fact that the U.S. government was far from taking a clear stance regarding the subject of amnesty, the *Dergue*'s counter-proposal interpreted the use of the term 'reconciliation' in Mr. Cohen's proposal only as prompting that 'all parties to the agreement shall refrain from all acts of

---

31   T. Dinka, *Ethiopia during the Derg Years: An Inside Account* (Los Angeles: Tsehai Publishers: 2016) 266.
32   Ibid. [Emphasis added]. See also G. Metaferia, *Ethiopia and the United States: History, Diplomacy, and Analysis* (New York: Algora Publishing, 2009) 77–80.
33   An alleged copy of the proposed agreement of the U.S. government was reproduced in Haile-Selassie's book under the caption 'the proposed agreement of the U.S. government, London, 27 May 1991'. See Haile-Selassie, *the Ethiopian Revolution, supra* note 28, 315–316.
34   Ibid.

reprisal'.[35] It was also evident from the proposals that Mr. Dinka himself was actively engaged in drafting an agreement containing an amnesty clause that would explicitly enable his government to circumvent accountability. Moreover, perhaps out of distrusting the rebel forces, he wanted an amnesty agreement to be reached then and there in front of an international audience, as an assurance that it would not be subjected to a revengeful revocation by the incoming government. Accordingly, under Article 9 of its counter proposal, the *Dergue* formulated a more elaborated amnesty clause, which read:

> A general amnesty shall come into force on the day of the cessation of hostilities. Such amnesty shall be extended to government and party officials, as well as to members of all opposition forces. The amnesty shall be irrevocably and internationally guaranteed.[36]

However, neither the *Dergue's* amnesty proposal nor the revised terms it proposed for the establishment of a provisional government were debated. The talks were interrupted when the *Dergue* withdrew its delegation from the Conference following Mr. Cohen's suggestion to the representative of the TPLF to move its army and take control of the capital, Addis Ababa.[37] The U.S. justified encouraging the TPLF's entry into Addis Ababa by its willingness to spare the city from a blood-shed similar to what had happened in Monrovia and Mogadishu the preceding year.[38] As alleged by Mr. Cohen, the U.S. action might also have been prompted by the fact that they lacked the power to force the TPLF to stay out of the city indefinitely.[39]

As the circumstances of the time indicate, and even before the *Dergue* withdrew, there were no peace talks but only isolated consultations conducted by the U.S. with the Ethiopian participants.[40] The participants never sat in a conference room together, and there is no clear evidence that Mr. Dinka's proposal

---

35   An alleged copy of the PDRE delegation's counter-proposal was reproduced in Haile-Selassie's book under a caption 'the counter-proposal of the PDRE Delegation, London, 28 May 1991'. See Article 10 of the counter proposal in Haile-Selassie, *The Ethiopian Revolution, supra* note 28, 317.
36   Ibid.
37   Cohen, *Intervening in Africa, supra* note 19, 53; Dinka, *Ethiopia During the Derg Years, supra* note 31, 269–70.
38   Ibid. See also T. Lyons, 'The Transition in Ethiopia' (1991) 127 (1) *CSIS Africa Notes* 1–8, 5.
39   Ibid.
40   See Metaferia, *Ethiopia and the United States, supra* note 32, 80; Lyons, 'The Transition in Ethiopia' *supra* note 38, 5. See also. Dinka, *Ethiopia during the Derg Years, supra* note 31, 270.

and/or counter proposal were ever presented to any of the three insurgent delegations. Talks however did not cease upon the *Dergue*'s withdrawal from the Conference and the U.S. continued its bilateral consultations with the remaining three forces. The decision to continue the consultations was prompted by the U.S. view that the *Dergue*'s absence was of zero impact on the country's transition,[41] and that, as Mr. Cohen conceded, the U.S. interest in convening the peace talks had little to do with a peaceful transition of the country.[42]

Two days later, on 28 May 1991, Mr. Cohen gave a press statement summarizing the consultations in London, even if they concluded without having forged a tangible agreement among the parties.[43] The press statement contained a list of recommendations made by the U.S. Government on three main topics: the establishment of a transitional government, the situation in Addis Ababa, and the facilitation of international relief efforts.[44] With respect to the issue of accountability of those responsible for the *Dergue* era atrocities, Mr. Cohen suggested that a broadly representative transitional government should be quickly established to assume all legal and political responsibility and should also 'consider an appropriate amnesty or indemnity for past acts not consisting violations of the law of war or human rights'.[45]

---

41   Cohen, *Intervening in Africa, supra* note 19, 54.
42   From the circumstances, it is clear that in convening the London Conference, the U.S. were interested in getting rid of the pro-Soviet government, in regaining the *Kagnew* Station in the Eritrean highlands that served as an important U.S. communication facility in the region, in arranging for the departure of 20,000 *Falashas* (Ethiopian Jews), and in pushing away the incoming force from its pro-communist ideology. See Cohen, *Intervening in Africa, supra* note 19, 19–47. As such, and given the fact that the U.S. had prior communication with the opposition fronts in Ethiopia, it was more likely than not that the U.S. had a complete picture of the status of the parties and of the situation in Addis Ababa and in the whole country. See ibid., 17, 19, 57. For a contrary view contending that the U.S. had no complete picture of the reality on the ground, see G. Tereke, *The Ethiopian Revolution: War in the Horn of Africa* (New Haven: Yale University Press, 2009) 310.
43   Haile-Selassie, *The Ethiopian Revolution, supra* note 28, 320.
44   Ibid.
45   He also added that 'any person accused of such offences should be afforded due process of law'. See Cohen, *Intervening in Africa, supra* note 19, 53. On this issue, Haile-Selassie's record holds a more elaborated version and contains the phrase 'international human rights' instead of 'human rights'. It also includes a recommendation on the manner in which accused persons should be tried. See Haile-Selassie, *The Ethiopian Revolution, supra* note 28, 321, which states that the transitional government shall:
consider an appropriate amnesty or indemnity for past acts not consisting violations of the law of war or *international* human rights. Any person accused of such offences should be afforded due process of law in accordance with international norms, and all procedures should be open to observers from internationally recognized organizations.

On the same day, an allegedly joint statement of the EPLF, the TPLF and the OLF was released for the press. From its content, it is clear that the statement was an assertion of the TPLF's political prominence in that it was made the sole state power pending the establishment of the transitional government.[46] The brief joint statement did not mention any plan or agreement on how to address the issue of accountability for crimes committed during the civil war, nor was it pointed out in the separate press statements released by the TPLF and the EPLF later that day.[47]

The fact that, of all the recommendations made by the U.S. government, only the amnesty issue was left out in the joint and separate press statements of the insurgents indicates that the incoming government was not yet ready to make the issue a priority. Besides, it is even doubtful that Mr. Cohen's call for the prosecution of violations of the law of war and international human rights was something more than just a political pretense, since, as admitted a decade later, the U.S. was at the time involved in finding a safe haven for Mengistu Hailemariam in Zimbabwe.[48]

At this stage, and unlike the conclusion reached by Stan and Nedelsky,[49] the TPLF lacked a clear policy direction concerning whether to prosecute or to grant amnesty for crimes of the past, as was further displayed in interviews its leaders gave to journalists in London. In one interview, the TPLF hinted that

---

46 For the details of the press conference, see Haile-Selassie, *The Ethiopian Revolution, supra* note 28, 322. The OLF was not mentioned in any way, and nor is there any mention that it delivered its own press conference. Reportedly, the OLF expressed misgivings over the obscurity of the London Conference and of the manner in which the EPRDF was made a leader of the interim government. See ibid., 326. According to Dimma Noggo Sarbo, an OLF delegate to the London Conference, it was due to the U.S. dishonesty that the EPRDF entered Addis Ababa and assumed state power. See D.N. Sarbo, *Contested Legitimacy: Coercion and the State in Ethiopia* (PhD Dissertation, University of Tennessee, 2009) 151–153.

47 For the press statements of the EPLF and EPRDF, See Haile-Selassie, *The Ethiopian Revolution, supra* note 28, 323.

48 See BBC News, 'US admits helping Mengistu escape' (The BBC, 22 December 1991), available at: <http://news.bbc.co.uk/2/hi/africa/575405.stm> accessed 28 September 2019. The fact that Assistant Secretary of State Herman Cohen pressured Mengistu to resign and arranged for his exile in Zimbabwe was in fact already noted in a research conducted under the auspices of the Library of Congress in July 1991. See, E.J. Keller, 'Government and Politics' in T.P. Ofcansky and L. Berry (eds.), *Ethiopia: A Country Study* (Washington, D.C.: Federal Research Division Library of Congress, 1991) 207–266, 263. According to Keller, securing a safe passage for Mengistu Hailemariam was widely regarded as essential, in order to successfully conduct the London talks. See ibid.

49 L. Stan and N. Nedelsky (eds.), *Encyclopaedia of Transitional Justice: Volume II.* (Cambridge: University Press, 2013) 169.

the *Dergue* officials 'might be brought to justice'.[50] In another, it mentioned a possibility of involving some members of the outgoing government who were not tainted with crimes of the past in the new provisional government.[51] Most importantly, it was also stated that the TPLF did not rule out a blanket amnesty in case the general public would want to grant one.[52]

In general, what appears to be obvious from the review of all of the press statements and interviews heard in relation to the London Conference is that the rebel groups failed to come to an agreement on most of the issues raised during the talks. The only agreement that was reached in London was that a follow-up conference would be convened in Addis Ababa no later than 1 July 1991 to discuss the details of the transitional period. The following section addresses the Addis Ababa Conference and its aftermath with the view of exploring and analyzing developments regarding prosecuting or amnestying the *Dergue* era crimes.

2.2.2 *The Addis Ababa Conference and the Transitional Charter: Nation's Wounds Heal through a 'Just-Peace'*

As promised in London, a national conference, dubbed 'Peace and Democracy Transitional Conference of Ethiopia', was held in Addis Ababa from 1 to 5 July 1991. It was attended by Worker's Representatives, Addis Ababa University, and 27 seven mostly ethnic-based liberation fronts, most of which were 'created by the EPRDF for the occasion'.[53] The Conference approved the establishment of the TGE following the formation of a Transitional Period Council of Representatives, which allocated the majority of its seats to the EPRDF (a group that was headed by the TPLF).[54] Even though several members of the

---

50   See Lewthwaite, 'Rebels pledge democracy in Ethiopia', *supra* note 17.

51   See 'Ethiopian rebels pledge democratic rule', *The Stanford Daily* (London, 29 May 1991), available at: <http://stanforddailyarchive.com/cgi-bin/stanford?a=d&d=stanford19910529-01.2.19&e=-------en-20--1--txt-txIN-------> accessed 20 March 2019.

52   See B. Harden, 'Rebel leaders Pledges Coalition Government, then Free Elections' The Washington Post (Washington DC, 29 May 1991), available at: <https://www.washingtonpost.com/archive/politics/1991/05/29/rebel-leader-pledges-coalition-government-then-free-elections/a5818143-9397-470d-a1b2-b44e28e9e98d/> accessed 20 March 2019.

53   See Berhe, *A Political History of the Tigray People's Liberation Front*, *supra* note14, 335; A. Tesfaye, *Political Power and Ethnic Federalism: The struggle for Democracy in Ethiopia* (Lanham: University Press of America, 2002) 77; T. M. Vestal, *Ethiopia: A Post-Cold War African State* (Westport: Preager Publishers, 1999) 7.

54   At the Conference, a Transitional Period Council of Representatives of a total of 87 members was established. The EPRDF took 32 out of the 87 seats of the Transitional Period Council of Representatives, while the OLF was given 12. The remaining 43 seats were allotted to the other 22 parties. See Tesfaye, *Political Power and Ethnic Federalism*, *supra* note 53, 77–78. See also S. Vaughan, 'The Addis Ababa Transitional Conference of July 1991: Its

unseated government were already detained in May and June 1991,[55] the Addis Ababa Conference did not come up with a plan to either bring them to justice or offer them an amnesty.

The possibility of discussing how to respond to the crimes perpetrated by the previous regime had in fact died before the beginning of the Conference, which could be due for two main reasons. Firstly, long-standing groups such as the Ethiopian People's Revolutionary Party (EPRP), All Ethiopian Socialist Movement (AESM),[56] and the Coalition of Democratic Ethiopian Forces (CODEF) were excluded from the Conference for they had ideological differences with the EPRDF and also because – the AESM and CODEF in particular – were suspected of having collaborated with the *Dergue* regime.[57] Had they participated in the Conference, the EPRP, given that it was allegedly the primary target and victim of the *Dergue*'s notorious Red-Terror campaign from 1974 to 1978,[58] could have raised the question of the accountability of the *Dergue* while the AESM and the CODEF could have requested an amnesty from accountability for wrongdoings that might have resulted from their involvement with the regime. Secondly, the EPRDF's TPLF was overwhelmingly occupied with avoiding concerns regarding Eritrea's secession and with instilling its ethnonationalist agenda, without which its survival was endangered.[59] As a result, there was simply no room to discuss the *Dergue* and its atrocities.

The Addis Ababa Conference was tailored in a manner that made it entirely focused on discussing and approving a Charter, drafted after the London Conference, by the TPLF and the OLF in the deserts of Eritrea under the auspices of the EPLF.[60] Thus, the issues that the Conference was held to discuss were only those delineated under the 20 articles of the draft Charter. Most

Origins, History and Significance' (1994) 54 (1) *Occasional Papers, Edinburgh University Centre of African Studies 1994*, 1–79, 5.

55 African Watch, 'Ethiopia, Waiting for Justice: Shortcomings in Establishing the Rule of Law' (Human Rights Watch, 8 May 1992), available at: <http://www.refworld.org/docid/45cc5f472.html> accessed 20 March 2019. See also, SPO, 'Report of the Office of the Special Prosecutor 1994: The Special Prosecution Process of War Criminals and Human Rights Violation in Ethiopia' in N.J. Kritz (ed.), *Transitional Justice: How emerging democracies reckon with former regimes; Laws, Rulings and Reports* (Washington DC: United States Institute of Peace Press, 1995) 559. [Hereinafter: the SPO Report (1994)].
56 AESM is widely known by its Amharic acronym, MElSON.
57 A. Tesfaye, *Political Power and Ethnic Federalism, supra* note 53, 74.
58 This will be further discussed in Chapter 3.
59 Berhe, *A Political History of the Tigray People's Liberation Front, supra* note 14, 334.
60 See L. Lata, The *Ethiopian State at the Crossroads: Decolonization and Democratization or Disintegration* (Lawrenceville: Red Sea Press, 1999) 14; Vaughan, 'The Addis Ababa Transitional Conference of July 1991', *supra* note 54, 38.

important was that the aim of the organizers was to get the Charter approved as drafted; the EPRDF was practically not willing to hear amendments to its Charter, so much so that some of the participants had to agree to the terms of the Charter under the threat of being expelled from the Conference.[61] Consequently, the Conference adopted the Transitional Period Charter as drafted, and established the TGE.[62] The Charter was given legal force to serve as the supreme law of the land (an interim constitution) for the duration of the transitional period.[63]

None of the provisions of the Charter however addressed the issue of prosecuting or giving amnesty to those responsible for the crimes from which the country was yet to revive. The only provision that pondered a concept somehow closer to the issue at hand was the third paragraph of the Charter's preamble, which read:

> peace and stability as essential conditions of development require the end of all hostilities, the *healing of wounds caused by conflicts* and the establishment and maintenance of good neighborliness and co-operation.[64]

Ethiopia was a severely wounded nation; there was no question that the wounds had to heal for the country to have a future. The Charter spoke of 'healing of wounds' as *conditio sine qua non* to bring 'peace and stability', which are required in order to attain a further end, namely, a 'development'.[65] What the Charter did not contemplate in clear terms was a mechanism based on which the TGE should strive to heal Ethiopia's wounds caused by those who had perpetrated atrocities against the people.

Nevertheless, a settled approach that could automatically be adopted in order to bring the nation's wounds into healing exists neither in theory nor in practice. Some scholarly opinions advocate the view that prosecution, and only prosecution, brings true healing to the wounds of a nation.[66] Experiences of countries that have dealt with atrocities of a similar nature indicate the presence of a firm belief that a nation's wounds would heal through adopting

---

61   Berhe, *A Political History of the Tigray People's Liberation Front*, supra note 14, 337.
62   Transitional Period Charter of Ethiopia: Proclamation No.1/1991, *entered into force on* 22 July 1991, Article 6. [Hereinafter the Transitional Charter of Ethiopia].
63   Ibid., Article 18.
64   Ibid., Preamble, para. 3. [Emphasis added].
65   Ibid.
66   See J. Van Dyke, 'The Fundamental Human Right to Prosecution and Compensation' (2000–2001) 29 *Denver Journal of international Law and Policy* 77–100.

a transitional justice approach that introduces amnesty or an approach that combines both amnesty and prosecution.

With respect to introducing amnesty as a prerequisite to creating lasting peace by healing the wounds of a nation, vivid explanations and justifications were specified in the practices of other states, both before and after Ethiopia's encounter with the issue. Such justifications and explanations are to be found, for instance, in the Philippines's Presidential Decree 1754 of 1980,[67] in the establishment of South Africa's Truth and Reconciliation Commission (TRC) as explained by the Constitutional Court in the AZAPO judgment,[68] and in the series of accords reached in Abidjan,[69] Conakry,[70] and, finally, in Lomé[71] to end the civil war and establish Sierra Leone's TRC.

It has also been argued that adopting reconciliatory measures or truth commissions, in addition to prosecution, helps to heal a nation's wounds and

---

67 See Presidential Decree No. 1754 (Philippines): A Decree Prescribing a Condition for Amnesty (Manila, issued on 24 December 1980), available at: <http://www.lawphil.net/statutes/presdecs/pd1980/pd_1754_1980.html> accessed 20 March 2019. Pursuant to paragraph 3 of its Preamble, the Decree stated:
> to heal and bind the nation's wounds and prevent such from becoming permanent and festering afflictions upon the Filipino nation's unity and harmony, and thereby establish a clean, fresh and unscarred start for all Filipinos, united in one sustained effort to rebuild their nation, all thoughts of recrimination should be laid to rest.

68 See *Azanian People's Organization (AZAPO) and Others v. President of the Republic of South Africa and Others* (CCT17/96) [1996] ZACC 16; 1996 (8) BCLR 1015; 1996 (4) SA 672, 25 July 1996, para. 17, which reads: the country begins the long and necessary process of *healing the wounds of the past*, transforming anger and grief into a mature understanding and creating the emotional and structural climate essential for the 'reconciliation and reconstruction' which informs the very difficult and sometimes painful objectives of the amnesty articulated in the epilogue. [Emphasis added].

69 Peace Agreement between the Government of the Republic of Sierra Leone and the Revolutionary United Front of Sierra Leone (RUF/SL), done in Abidjan on 30 November 1996, Article 15, available at: <http://www.sierra-leone.org/abidjanaccord.html> accessed 22 March 2019.

70 ECOWAS Six Month Peace Plan for Sierra Leone, 23 October 1997–22 APRIL 1998, Conakry Accord, 23 October 1997, Article 8, available at: <http://www.incore.ulst.ac.uk/services/cds/agreements/pdf/serria1.pdf> accessed 20 March 2019.

71 Peace Agreement between the Government of Sierra Leone and the Revolutionary United Front of Sierra Leone, issued in Lomé, 3 June 1999, Article XXVI. Available at: <http://www.sierra-leone.org/lomeaccord.html> accessed 20 March 2019. According to Article XXVI, which deals with the issue of human rights violations:
> A Truth and Reconciliation Commission shall be established to address impunity, break the cycle of violence, provide a forum for both the victims and perpetrators of human rights violations to tell their story, get a clear picture of the past in order to facilitate genuine healing and reconciliation.

restore long lasting peace and stability. For instance, the UN Security Council, in referring the Darfur situation to the ICC, stated that it

> emphasizes the need to promote healing and reconciliation and encourages in this respect the creation of institutions, involving all sectors of Sudanese society, such as truth and/or reconciliation commissions, in order to complement judicial processes and thereby reinforce the efforts to restore long lasting peace.[72]

For its part, the EPRDF's Charter, in a terminology that seems to add further complexity to the matter, mentions 'just-peace', as a kind of peace towards the achievement of which the TGE should strive.[73] A closer reading of the Charter indicates that the attainment of just-peace requires the healing of wounds caused by the long and bloody civil war.[74] Nonetheless, the Charter did not define or illustrate just-peace. It also failed to shed light on how Ethiopia's wounds would heal. The Addis Ababa Conference did not discuss these issues.

So far, only Leenco Lata, the then OLF representative who participated both in drafting the Charter and in discussing it at the Addis Ababa Conference, wrote about the Charter's notion of 'just-peace'. Lata juxtaposed just-peace with a kind of peace that had reigned in all previous regimes in Ethiopia and which he referred to as 'unjust peace' – a phenomenon that resulted from the old regimes', as he put it, 'habit of equating governmental will with peace and stability'.[75] According to him, therefore, all institutions of repression installed by previous regimes to enforce an 'unjust peace' must be abolished in order to introduce and establish a just-peace.[76]

Lata did not specify whether the act of dismantling the institutions of repression, which was in fact also mentioned by the Charter,[77] included bringing to justice those who had installed these institutions. His discussion was

---

72 See UN Security Council Resolution 1593 (31 March 2005) UN Doc S/RES/1593, para. 5. The Security Council did not mention what it really meant by the need to implant institutions of reconciliation in order to heal the country and bring stability, and in particular whether truth and reconciliation approaches may include the offering of amnesty to selected perpetrators.
73 The Transitional Period Charter, Preamble, para. 4.
74 Ibid., paras 3–4.
75 L. Lata, 'The Making and Un-making of Ethiopia's Transitional Charter', Paper presented on the thirty-seventh annual meeting of the African Studies Association (No. 1994:105, Toronto: November 1994) 1–25, 6.
76 Ibid.
77 See The Transitional Period Charter, Preamble, para. 4.

nevertheless not aimed at providing first-hand information on the Charter's concept of just-peace. Rather, as it was written after his party decided to stay away from the TGE, its focus was on the justifiability of future resistance against undemocratic regimes by all means in case 'unjust peace' reigned in the country instead of the one emphatically promised by the Charter.[78]

The truth is that the notion of just-peace is not as obvious as the Charter might have believed it to be. Several experts regarded just-peace as peace through justice, that is, through the upholding and implementation of existing international legal norms. Insofar as, as it will be discussed in Chapter 3, existing international legal norms at the time of the Charter already envisaged a duty to prosecute, it may be submitted here that the just-peace envisaged by the Transitional Charter required the bringing to trial of those allegedly responsible for the crimes committed during the *Dergue* regime.

Allan and Keller, on the other hand, reject the above notion of just-peace because it poses difficulties in the process of solving conflicts.[79] According to them, just-peace is a result of a series of process that involves putting opposing parties through requirements referred to as *thin recognition* (recognizing each other's autonomous existence), *thick recognition* (understanding each other's core identities), *renouncement* (making concessions), and *rule* (specifying terms of agreement).[80] Central to their illustration of just-peace is the need to solve conflicts such as civil wars by involving parties with a different status, culture, history, and identity.[81] Following this notion of just-peace, it is more likely for amnesties to be offered for the sake of restoring peace.

However, Allen and Keller examined the notion of just-peace in the context of the need to end conflicts and emphasized the necessity of bringing to the negotiating table parties that possess some sort of a bargaining power. As such, the relevance of their notion of just-peace to the case at hand is doubtful because the conflict in Ethiopia had already ended. Indeed, by the time the Transitional Charter was drafted, the civil war was already over and the *Dergue* was no longer in a position to make demands or negotiate peace, as will be discussed in Chapter 3.

Be that as it may, it should be noted that the preceding paragraphs are not meant to conclude that the Charter was totally devoid of a hint as to how to heal

---

78   Ibid. From the overall context of his paper, the point Lata was trying to make was that the decision of the OLF to continue in an armed struggle against the EPRDF was as justified as the previous struggles against unjust peace.
79   P. Allen and A. Keller, 'The Concept of a Just Peace, or Achieving Peace Through Recognition, Renouncement, and Rule' in P. Allen and A. Keller (eds.), *What Is Just Peace?* (Oxford: Oxford University Press, 2006) 197–215, 212.
80   Ibid., 195–209.
81   Ibid., 212.

wounds and instore just-peace, but to emphasize its lack of any clear proposal as to what to do with those responsible for crimes of the past. Apart from that, the Charter did actually attempt to propose, in a generalized way, a mechanism in which wounds heal, just-peace reigns, the country becomes stable, and development becomes real – aspirations which, according to the Charter, were to be achieved through 'the proclamation of a democratic order'.[82] This was envisaged as a system that safeguards the rights and interests of the deprived citizens through the establishment of a democratic government elected by, and accountable to, the people.[83] To achieve this, the Charter underscored the need to draft and adopt a new constitution, on the basis of which members of the 'National Assembly' would be elected to replace the TGE.[84] Although the initial plan was to establish the said 'democratic order' within a maximum of two and a half years after the establishment of the TGE,[85] the latter did not give way to the former until 1995.

In sum, the Charter failed to address the question of accountability for crimes committed during the *Dergue* regime. As one may point out, the only scenario that it clearly established was that the *Dergue* officials detained by the EPRDF were not to be subjected to summary execution by the TGE. Such action was unequivocally proscribed pursuant to Article 1 of the Charter.[86] In this regard, it appears that the Charter aimed at alerting the TGE not to repeat the history of the 1974 revolution, in which the *Dergue* summarily executed 59 senior officials of the Haileselassie regime.[87] In reality, however, given the prevalent extrajudicial executions that were being carried out by the army and the Peace and Stability Committees (PSCs),[88] nothing was yet guaranteed by the TGE.[89]

---

[82] See the Transitional Period Charter of Ethiopia, Preamble, para. 4: 'for the fulfilment of the aforementioned conditions and for the reign of a just peace, the proclamation of a democratic order is a categorical imperative'.

[83] Ibid.

[84] Ibid., Articles 11 and 12.

[85] Ibid., Article 12.

[86] According to Article 1 of the Charter, the Universal Declaration of Human Rights (UDHR) was, for the first time in Ethiopian history, made part of the supreme law of the land for the period of the transition.

[87] See FHC, SPO v. *Colonel Mengistu Hailemariam et al.*, (Revised Indictment), 28 November 1995, File No.1/87, 10.

[88] Peace and Stability Committees (PSCs) refer to committees of civilians tasked with carrying out police activities in their neighborhood – a measure required as the country was without a functioning police force for almost a year after the EPRDF took control of the country. See Human Rights Watch, 'World Report 1993: Ethiopia', available at: <https://www.refworld.org/docid/467fca5dc.html> accessed 28 September 2019.

[89] Human Rights Watch, *Ethiopia: Waiting For Justice: Shortcomings in Establishing the Rule of Law*, 8 May 1992, 4, available at: <https://www.refworld.org/docid/45cc5f472.html>

2.2.3 *The Decision to Prosecute the* Dergue: *The Establishment of the* SPO

For more than a year after its formation, the TGE was generally silent on the fate of the more than 2000 *Dergue* officials it had detained. In particular, an independent investigation, which could have been carried out by setting up specialized bodies such as a commission of inquiry, into the *Dergue* era violence never occurred. The silence was unexpectedly broken on 8 August 1992, the date on which the TGE established the Office of the Special Prosecutor (SPO) to prosecute crimes committed during the *Dergue* regime. The relevant part of the Proclamation announced the decision to prosecute in the following terms:

> [I]n view of the fact that the historical mission of the Ethiopian People's Revolutionary Democratic Front [EPRDF] has been accomplished, it is essential that higher officials of the WPE [Workers Party of Ethiopia] and members of the security and armed forces who have been detained at the time of the EPRDF assumed control of the country and thereafter and who are suspected of having committed offences, as well as representatives of urban dwellers associations and peasant associations, and other persons who have associated with the commission of said offenses, must be brought to trial.[90]

In doing so, the TGE took a path in which it chose prosecution not only over summary executions but also over amnesty. Its decision was fundamentally different from the choices made earlier, for instance, by Argentina[91] and Chile[92]

---

accessed 25 May 2019.The prevalence of extra-judicial killings was also implied in Amnesty International's 1991 report. See Amnesty International, 'Ethiopia: End of an Era of Brutal Repression – A New Chance for Human Rights' (Amnesty International, 18 June 1991) 48, available at: <https://www.amnesty.org/en/documents/afr25/005/1991/en/> accessed 28 September 2019.

90 Ibid., Preamble, para. 4.
91 For a detailed discussion on the choices made in Argentina regarding the crimes committed between 1976 and 1982, see P. Engstrom and G. Pereira, 'From Amnesty to Accountability: Ebb and Flow in the Search for Justice in Argentina' in F. Lessa and L.A. Payne (eds.), *Amnesty in the Age of Human Rights Accountability: Ccomparative and International Perspectives* (Cambridge: Cambridge University Press, 2012) 97–122.
92 See Supreme Decree No.355 (Chile): Creation of the Commission on Truth and Reconciliation, (Santiago, 25 April 1990) available at: <http://www.usip.org/sites/default/files/file/resources/collections/commissions/Chile90-Charter.pdf> accessed 28 September 2019. According to the first paragraph of the Decree's preamble, the TRC was established considering 'that the moral conscience of the nation demands that the truth about grave violations of human rights committed in [Chile] between September 11 1973 and March 11, 1990 be brought to trial'.

and, later, by Sierra Leone and South Africa, which included a provision on amnesty and on the establishment of TRCs to establish the whole truth and, as noted above, heal the wounds.

However, the SPO was also responsible for establishing the historical truth regarding the atrocities committed during the *Dergue* regime. According to paragraph 5 of the preamble of the SPO Proclamation, the SPO was responsible for 'recording for posterity the brutal offenses and the embezzlement of property perpetrated against the people of Ethiopia', since such a task was, as the Proclamation added, demanded by the 'interest of just historical obligation'.[93] This was generally understood as the second mandate of the SPO.

Some have suggested that the SPO was mandated with competing responsibilities.[94] Implicit in their concern was that the SPO's responsibility to record the whole truth might require devising a working mechanism, which could, drawing from the experiences of other states, involve establishing a TRC.[95] This could be a valid concern, because recording and establishing the whole truth may require a resort to a process that ensures genuine participation of the actual parties (victims and perpetrators) in telling and identifying the truth. Usually, unless there is some kind of mechanism that guarantees non-prosecution such as offering an amnesty, perpetrators are hardly willing to tell the truth about their crimes, as can be inferred from the experiences of the TRCs in South Africa[96] and Sierra Leone.[97]

In the absence of any guidance in the Proclamation, the SPO seems to have understood its second mandate in terms of documenting and reporting a 'judicial truth' i.e. a truth that is uncovered through judicial proceedings. The SPO's interpretation of its mandate appears to be plausible. Given that promising non-prosecution in the form of an amnesty was off the table, the TGE must

---

93 See Proclamation Establishing the Office of the Special Prosecutor: Proclamation No. 22/1991, *entered into force* 8 August 1992, Preamble, para. 5. [Hereinafter: SPO Proclamation].
94 See SPO Report (1994), *supra* note 54, 559.
95 See the experiences of Chile, South Africa, and Sierra Leone mentioned above.
96 This fact was highlighted by the Constitutional Court of South Africa in the AZAPO judgment. See *Azanian People's Organization (AZAPO) and Others v. President of the Republic of South Africa and Others*, *supra* note 68, para. 24.
97 In Sierra Leone, the final report of the TRC concluded that 'some people were reluctant to participate in the truth-telling process out of fear of prosecution by the Special Court for Sierra Leone', which it regarded as 'one of the unfortunate costs of the parallel and simultaneous existence [of the TRC and the SCSL]'. See The Sierra Leone Truth and Reconciliation Commission, *Witness to Truth: Final Report, Volume III b* (2004), available at: <http://www.sierraleonetrc.org/index.php/view-the-final-report/download-table-of-contents/volume-three-b> accessed 20 June 2018, 378.

have aimed to reach the truth through judicial proceedings. Nevertheless, the truth-reporting task itself was later on dropped as the SPO focused on prosecution alone.[98] *Dem Yazele Dossie* (literally, 'blood-soaked dossier') is the only report that the SPO published for public access just before its closure in 2010.[99] Even then, the report offered a highly selective presentation of crimes committed only by the highest-ranking *Dergue* officials.

2.3 The Scope of the Decision to Prosecute: 'Heinous and Horrendous' Criminal Acts

The SPO Proclamation did not refer to the legal characterization of crimes in relation to which the decision to prosecute was reached. Under the second preambular paragraph of the Proclamation, the crimes for the prosecution of which the SPO was established were referred to as *'heinous and horrendous criminal acts* which occupy a special chapter in the history of the people of Ethiopia …'.[100] Paragraph one of the Preamble stated that 'the *Dergue* regime has deprived the people of Ethiopia of its human and political rights and subjected it to gross oppression'.[101] According to the third paragraph of the Preamble, the *Dergue* regime 'impoverished the economy of the country by illegally confiscating and destroying the property of the people as well as by misappropriating public and state property'.[102] None of the remaining provisions of the Proclamation contains a clear description of the crimes to be prosecuted by the SPO.

The following sections discuss the SPO's subject-matter jurisdiction with the view of identifying whether the crimes it was established to prosecute and/or has prosecuted were domestic crimes or could also be qualified as international crimes. In doing so, it analyzes both the law and the practice of the SPO.

---

98 See P. Hayner, 'Past Truths, Present Dangers: The Role of Official Truth Seeking in Conflict Resolution and Prevention' in P. Stern and D. Druckman (eds.), *International Conflict Resolution after the Cold War* (Washington DC.: National Academy Press, 2000) 338–382, 349.

99 See Special Prosecutor's Office, *Dem Yazele Dossie: Begizeyawi Wotaderawi Dergue Weyem Mengist Abalat Benetsuhan Zegoch Laye Yetefetsem Wenjel Zegeba* (Addis Ababa: Far-East Trading P.L.C., 2010) [Hereinafter: *Dem Yazele Dossie*].

100 SPO Proclamation, Preamble, para 2. [Emphasis added].

101 Ibid., Preamble, para. 1.

102 Ibid., Preamble, para. 2.

2.3.1 'Heinous and Horrendous' Criminal Acts: International or Domestic Crimes?

The SPO Proclamation fails to explain whether the expression 'heinous and horrendous' criminal acts refer to international or domestic crimes, or to both. International crimes are, by all accounts, heinous and horrendous, provided that these terms were employed to imply the 'gravity' of the offenses, as also alluded to by the third paragraph of the Preamble of the Rome Statute.[103] If such terms are understood as referring to the gravity of the offenses, they contain an element of ambiguity when taken in the Ethiopian context insofar as various categories of domestic crimes also fall in the category of grave crimes.

Under Ethiopian law, a grave crime is generally one that entails a severe penalty. The Penal Code of 1957, the criminal law that was in force from 1958 to 2005, on the basis of which the SPO prosecuted the *Dergue*, prescribes *rigorous imprisonment* 'only to offenses of a very grave nature'.[104] Rigorous imprisonment ranges from a period of one year to life, and is accompanied with more severe conditions of imprisonment[105] as compared to simple imprisonment, which is generally for a period of ten days up to three years.[106] Consequently, a number of purely domestic crimes satisfy the gravity requirement if defined by reference to the severity of the penalty.

Another criminal legislation used in the *Dergue* trials which may be relevant to explain the concept of grave crimes in Ethiopia is the Special Penal Code (SPC) of 1974 (revised in 1981)[107] – promulgated to supplement (not to repeal) the Penal Code of 1957.[108] Enacted immediately after the coming to power of the *Dergue*, the SPC was meant to adapt to the new political order 'criminal laws relating to *grave offenses*'[109] and, in particular, to provide severe penalties

---

103 According to O'Keefe however defining international crimes in terms of 'gravity' is a misconception. See R. O'Keefe, *International Criminal Law* (Oxford: Oxford University Press, 2015), 57–59.
104 See The Penal Code of 1957 of Ethiopia, Article 107. A similar provision is included in the FDRE Criminal Code, which came into force in 2005 by repealing the Penal Code of 1957, and which served as the applicable law in the CUD trials and the *Oromo-Gumuz* trials. See the FDRE Criminal Code, Article 108.
105 Ibid.
106 The Penal Code of 1957, Article 105; FDRE Criminal Code, Article 106.
107 The Special Penal Code, Proclamation No. 8 of 1974 *entered into force* 16 November 1974; The Revised Special Penal Code, Proclamation No. 214/1981 *entered into force* 5 November 1981. The SPC played only a marginal role in the prosecution of the *Dergue* era crimes. The SPO did not frame its charges based on the SPC, although the courts have occasionally referred to it. See for instance, FSC, *Melaku Rufael* v. *SPO*, Appeals Chamber, (Judgment), 2 August 2004, File No. 13241.
108 The Special Penal Code of 1974, Article 2(2).
109 Ibid., Preamble, para. 2.

to grave crimes which were deemed as receiving too light a penalty under the Penal Code of 1957.[110] The analysis of the SPC reveals that the code identified some offenses as 'exceptionally grave', in relation to which it imposed the sentences of life imprisonment or death. Nevertheless, none of the SPC's exceptionally grave offenses were international crimes.

Capital punishment has always been one of the applicable penalties in Ethiopian criminal law; its an analysis may thus help to further clarify the concept of grave crimes. Although this was not clearly stated in the Penal Code of 1957, it is generally understood in Ethiopian law that capital punishment is reserved for 'serious criminal offenses'.[111] The Penal Code contained about 30 capital crimes, of which only five were international crimes.[112]

A further assessment of some other Ethiopian laws applicable during the *Dergue* regime shows that core crimes have not been typical examples of grave or serious offenses. For instance, in referring to the gravest of all crimes in Ethiopia, the PDRE Constitution of 1987, the last Constitution before the establishment of the SPO, did not mention genocide or war crimes, but *treason*

---

110 Ibid., Preamble, para. 8.
111 This can be inferred from Article 15 of the FDRE Constitution, which deals with the right to life. The provision stated that only *serious criminal offenses* entail death penalty. Looking back to the *travaux préparatoires* of the Constitution, members of the constitutional commission had debated over choosing an adequate label for crimes that would entail death penalty and specifically over using the English expression 'grave crimes' or 'exceptionally grave crimes'. The commission finally adopted the phrase 'serious criminal offences' which appeared in the final version of the Constitution. See 'The Minutes of the 84th Ordinary Session of the Constitutional Committee (24 February 1994)' in The Constitutional Commission, 'Minutes, Vol. II: Ordinary Sessions No 51- No 88 held from 2 November 1993 to 3 April 1994' (Addis Ababa: FDRE House of Federations, available at the library of the FDRE House of People's representatives) 197–198.
112 The same is true for the FDRE Criminal Code. Regarding international crimes incurring death penalty, see Penal Code of 1957, Article 281 (Genocide; Crimes against Humanity), Article 282 (War Crimes against the Civilian Population), Article 287(dereliction of duty towards the enemy), Article 288 (Use of Illegal Means of Combat), and Article 290 (Breach of Armistice or Peace Treaty).

Other death penalty provisions in the Penal Code include Articles 248–253 (Outrages against the Emperor, the Constitution or the State), Articles 259–266, 268, 270 (Offences against the External Security and the Defensive Power of the State), Article 300 (Desertion), Article 310 (Breach of Military Duty: Insult or Threats to, or Assault upon, a Superior Officer), Article 312 (Mutiny), Article 316 (Breaches of Guard Duty), Article 324 (Demoralization of Troops), Article 333 (Attack on a Member of the Armed Forces while on Active Duty), Article 522 (Aggravated Homicide- Homicide in the First Degree), Article 527 (Infanticide), and Article 637 (Aggravated Robbery).

against the motherland,[113] a crime defined under several provisions both in the Penal Code of 1957 and in the SPC.[114]

Turning to other jurisdictions, the expression 'heinous crimes' is apparently not a preferred usage to denote a certain category of offenses. Where it is used, it refers to various offenses that generally entail severe penalties. In India, for instance, heinous offenses are those offenses for which the minimum punishment is seven years,[115] while under the criminal law of the Philippines heinous crimes generally refer to offenses punishable by death.[116] Under the laws of Brazil[117] Colombia,[118] or Pakistan[119] the expression 'heinous offense' contains a non-exhaustive list of crimes generally considered severe, with the list growing from time to time. The Constitution of Angola defines 'heinous offenses', which it interchangeably uses with 'repugnant offenses', as constituted by genocide, crimes against humanity and other crimes stipulated as such in law.[120] Hence, the use of the phrase 'heinous and horrendous criminal acts' does not denote a precise category of criminal offenses.

Some commentators also noted the problematic nature of the SPO Proclamation in defining the subject-matter jurisdiction of the SPO. For instance, Hailemariam argued that 'as far as the Proclamation is concerned, those officials targeted for prosecution could be charged with crimes ranging from petty theft to genocide and crimes against humanity'.[121] However, it is more plausible to consider that offenses under the Penal Code's law of petty

---

113   See PDRE Constitution, Article 53.
114   Since there was no crime exactly labeled as 'treason against the mother land', the Constitution was therefore referring to offences known as treason under Articles 262, 263, and 264 of the Penal Code of 1957, and those later elaborated by the Revised Special Penal Code of 1981 under its Articles 1–7.
115   See The Juvenile Justice (Care and Protection of children) Act of India, 2015, Article 33.
116   The Constitution of the Republic of Philippines, section 19 (1) available at: <http://www.gov.ph/constitutions/1987-constitution/> accessed 28 September 2019.
117   Brazil's Constitution of 1988 with Amendments through 2014, section XLIII. available at: <https://www.constituteproject.org/constitution/Brazil_2014.pdf> accessed 28 September 2019.
118   Colombia's Constitution of 1991 with Amendments through 2005, Transitory Article 30, available at: <https://www.constituteproject.org/constitution/Colombia_2005.pdf> accessed 28 September 2019.
119   Pakistan 1973 (reinst. 2002, rev. 2015), Article 212B, available at: <https://www.constituteproject.org/constitution/Pakistan_2015?lang=en> accessed 11 January 2019.
120   Constitution of Angola 2010, Article 61, Article 129(e), available at: <https://www.constituteproject.org/constitution/Angola_2010?lang=en> accessed 28 September 2019.
121   See Y. Hailemariam, 'The Quest for Justice and Reconciliation: The international Criminal Tribunal for Rwanda and the Ethiopian High Court' (1999)22(1) *Hastings International and Comparative Law Review*, 667–745, 692.

offenses such as petty theft (Article 806) could not fall under the SPO's jurisdiction, because petty offenses are by no standard heinous and horrendous criminal acts.

2.3.2 The Reason behind the 'Heinous and Horrendous' Formulation: The Absence of a Commission of Inquiry

The vagueness of the SPO Proclamation in stating the nature of the crimes did put the decision taken by the EPRDF in a blur. When seen in comparison with the constitutive instruments of several post-conflict criminal tribunals that have spelled out, either in general or in specific terms, the alleged offenses over which the tribunals would exercise jurisdiction,[122] the SPO Proclamation might appear to be a poorly drafted piece of legislation. The fact that it was a pioneer instrument enacted at a time when there was no relevant instrument that could have served as its model could explain the flaws in the SPO Proclamation.

The Proclamation's incompleteness in specifiying the crimes for which the SPO was established might also find its answer hidden in the fact that a preliminary investigation was never conducted before the SPO was established;

---

122   See for example, Statute of the International Tribunal for the Prosecution of Persons Responsible for Serious Violations of International Humanitarian Law Committed in the Territory of the Former Yugoslavia since 1991, U.N. Doc. S/25704 at 36, annex (1993) and S/25704/Add.1 (1993), adopted by Security Council on 25 May 1993, U.N. Doc. S/RES/827 (1993), Articles 2–5 [Hereinafter the ICTY Statute]; Statute of the International Tribunal for Rwanda, adopted by S.C. Res. 955, U.N. SCOR, 49th Sess., 3453d mtg. at 3, U.N. Doc. S/RES/955 (1994), 33 I.L.M. 1598, 1600 (1994), Articles 2–4 [Hereinafter the ICTR Statute]; UN Security Council, Statute of the Special Court for Sierra Leone, 16 January 2002, Articles 2–5, available at: <http://www.refworld.org/docid/3dda29f94.html> accessed 11 November 2018 [Hereinafter the SCSL Statute]; Law on the Establishment of the Extraordinary Chambers in the Courts of Cambodia, with inclusion of amendments as promulgated on 27 October 2004 (NS/RKM/1004/006), Articles 3–8, available at: <https://www.eccc.gov.kh/sites/default/files/legal-documents/KR_Law_as_amended_27_Oct_2004_Eng.pdf> accessed 28 September 2019 [Hereinafter: the ECCC Statute]; Statute of the Extraordinary African Chambers within Senegalese judicial system for the prosecution of international crimes committed on the territory of the Republic of Chad during the period from 7 June 1982 to 1 December 1990, available at: <http://legal.au.int/en/sites/default/files/Agreement%20AU-Senegal%20establish ing%20AEC-english_0.pdf> accessed 1 January 2019, Articles 4–8 [Hereinafter: the EAC Statute]; UNTAET Regulation No. 2000/15 on the Establishment of Panels with Exclusive Jurisdiction over Serious Criminal Offences, Articles 4–9, available at: <https://www.legal-tools.org/doc/c082f8/> accessed 28 September 2019 [Hereinafter the ET-SPSC Statute]; The Statute of the Iraqi Special Tribunal, issued 10 December 2003, Articles 10–14, available at: <https://www.legal-tools.org/uploads/tx_ltpdb/Iraq_IST_Statute__2003__E__01_03.pdf> accessed 28 September 2019, [Hereinafter: the IST Statute].

an important step that is commonly undertaken prior to establishing post-conflict judicial organs. It is true that the SPO antedated the establishment of international commission of inquiries, as set up in East-Timor,[123] Former Yugoslavia,[124] Rwanda,[125] Lebanon,[126] and Cambodia,[127] and Ethiopia thus had

---

[123] In East Timor, fact-finding missions were carried out separately by the Indonesian government and the UN. An International Commission of Inquiry was established by the UN on 27 September 1999. See United Nations High Commissioner for Human Rights, Situation of human rights in East Timor: Commission on Human Rights resolution 1999/S-4/1 (adopted at its fourth special session), 27 September 1999, available at: <http://www.unhchr.ch/Huridocda/Huridoca.nsf/(Symbol)/E.CN.4.RES.1999.S-4.1.En?Opendocument> accessed 28 September 2019. A few days earlier, on 22 September 1999, an independent Fact-Finding Commission for Post-Ballot Human Rights Violations in East Timor (Komisi Penyelidik Pelanggaran Hak Asasi Manusia di Timor Timur (KPP- HAM)) was established by the Indonesian National Commission on Human Rights (Komnas HAM).

[124] A Commission of Experts was established on 16 November 1992 pursuant to Security Council resolution 780 (1992) to examine reported violations of international humanitarian law in the former Yugoslavia. See Security Council, Resolution 780(1992) Adopted by the Security Council at its 3119th meeting on 6 October 1991, S/RES/780(1992), available at: <http://www.un.org/en/ga/search/view_doc.asp?symbol=S/RES/780(1992)> accessed 28 September 2019.

[125] On 1 July 1994, an Impartial Commission of Experts was established pursuant to Security Council resolution 935 (1994) to examine and analyze information derived from investigations, with a view to providing the Secretary-General with its conclusions on the evidence of grave violations of international humanitarian law committed in the territory of Rwanda, including the evidence of possible acts of genocide. See Security Council, Resolution 935(1994) Adopted by the Security Council at its 3400th meeting on 1 July 1994, S/RES/935(1994), available at: <https://www.refworld.org/docid/3b00f16034.html> accessed 28 September 2019.

[126] Following the assassination of the former Prime Minister of Lebanon, Rafiq Hariri, along with 22 others, in Beirut on 14 February 2005, an International Independent Investigation Commission (IIIC) was established by Security Council resolution 1595 (2005) of 7 April 2005. The IIIC was established to assist the Lebanese authorities in their investigation of all aspects of the incident. See UN Security Council, Security Council Resolution 1595 (2005) on Lebanon, adopted by the Security Council at its 5160th meeting on 7 April 2005, S/RES/1595 (2005) available at: <https://unispal.un.org/DPA/DPR/unispal.nsf/0/AAF6AAC927E83BEE85256FDD0050FCFA> accessed 28 September 2019.

[127] The UN General Assembly, in its resolution 52/135, requested the Secretary-General to examine the possibility of appointing a group of experts to evaluate the existing evidence and propose further measures in relation to a series of violations in Cambodia that took place between 17 April 1975 and 7 January 1994. See Resolution Adopted by the General Assembly [on the report of the Third Committee (A/52/644/Add.2)] Resolution 52/135, Situation of Human Rights in Cambodia, adopted on 27 February 1998, A/RES/52/135, available at: <http://www.unakrt-online.org/content/resolution-52135-adopted-general-assembly> accessed 28 September 2019. Following the resolution, the Secretary-General, Kofi-Annan, appointed a fact-finding mission commonly known as the UN Group of Experts for Cambodia. The mandate of the Group of Experts included: (1) to evaluate

no international model to follow. Yet, it may also be noted that other states, such as Argentina, established commissions of enquiries years before the international trend and in fcat years before the SPO Proclamation was enacted in Ethiopia.[128] Be that as it may, it had no commission of experts assigned to evaluate available evidence and determine the nature of the crimes perpetrated during the *Dergue* regime.

As noted by the SPO itself, the absence of a prior inquiry into the abuses of the Mengistu regime posed challenges to the successful accomplishment of responsibilities as emanating from the Proclamation. According to Mr. Girma Wakjira, the Chief Special Prosecutor,

> Ethiopia and the Office of Special Prosecutor were at a distinct disadvantage to other similarly situated countries. In Argentina, an extensive government sponsored study was done before anyone was arrested and tried. Ethiopia's unique circumstances lead to the arrest of almost two thousand people before [the establishment of] the Transitional Government of Ethiopia even has developed a clear policy on the past.[129]

Due to the sheer magnitude of the conflicts and atrocities reported from the period 1974–1991, establishing a commission of inquiry, national or international, at least in consultation with the UN, should have crossed the minds of the TGE officials before establishing the SPO. In fact, the need to establish a commission of inquiry was brought to the attention of the TGE in September 1991 by African Watch and Amnesty International. African Watch in particular urged the TGE to establish a national human rights commission, a permanent and independent body, alongside an *ad hoc* commission of inquiry that would

---

the existing evidence and determine the nature of the crimes committed; (2) to assess the feasibility of bringing Khmer Rouge leaders to justice; and (3) to explore options for trials before international or domestic courts. See S. Ratner, 'The United Nations Group of Experts for Cambodia' (1991) 93(4) *The American Journal of International Law* 948–953.

128   In December 1984, Argentina established the National Commission on the Disappeared (Comisión Nacional sobre la Desaparición de Personas, CONADEP) with a mandate to investigate the disappearances of people between 1976 and 1983 and uncover the facts involved in those cases, including the locations of the bodies. See Decree No. 187/83, 15 December 1983 (Decreto 187, 15 diciembre 1983), reprinted in Anales de Legislación Argentina (1984), Tomo XLIV-A, LA LEY, 137–138.

129   See D. Haile, *Accountability for Crimes of the Past and the Challenges of Criminal Prosecution: The Case of Ethiopia* (Leuven: Leuven University Press, 2000), 35 *citing* the Special Prosecutors Office, Intervention by Mr. Girma Wakjira, Chief Special Prosecutor of the Transitional Government of Ethiopia at the Plenary Session of the UN's Human Rights Commission (17 February 1994) 4.

investigate the causes of famine as it was considered that famine was closely associated to abuses of human rights during the *Dergue* regime.[130] Likewise, Amnesty International called for the urgent establishment of an impartial and independent commission of inquiry to clarify alleged offenses of torture and enforced disappearances.[131]

Most importantly, by failing to establish a commission of inquiry to investigate past abuses, the TGE ignored a relevant previous example of such a commission.[132] The 1974 Commission of Inquiry, established on the eve of the 1974 revolution, could indeed be regarded as a relevant domestic experience as it concerned the investigation of crimes committed by officials of a previous regime.[133] This instance signifies that establishing a commission of inquiry was not an entirely foreign experience to the Ethiopian legal system, although the *Dergue* had begun committing atrocities, such as the summary execution of officials of the Haileselassie regime, and disregarded the ongoing inquiry of the Commission, which it soon dissolved.[134]

What is more perplexing is the fact that, aside from the issue of establishing a commission of experts, there is no evidence that the drafting of the SPO Proclamation went through a rigorous debate.[135] In the absence of a prior

---

130   Thirty Years of Evil Days, *supra* note 15, 377–379.
131   See Amnesty International, 'Ethiopia: End of an Era of Brutal Repression', *supra* note 89, 47.
132   With regards to an inquiry commission established to look into the 2005 post-election violence, see Chapter 4, Section 4.2.2.
133   See the Commission of Inquiry Establishment Proclamation, Proclamation No. 326 of 1974, *entered into force* 12 July 1974. For details on the composition of the commission of inquiry, see Haile-Selassie, *The Ethiopian Revolution 1974–1991*, *supra* note 28, 103–105. For a detailed background of the commission of inquiry, see B. Shimeles, 'Ye 1966tu Mermari Komisiyon Anesase, Kenewune ena Keziya Yekesemenew' 2009 (5) 2 *Wonber- Alemayehu Haile Memorial Foundations Periodical* 3–24.
134   The execution of the 59 officials took place on 4 November 1974. See *Colonel Mengistu Hailemariam et al.,* (Revised Indictment), *supra* note 87, 7–8. In fact, the work of the 1974 Commission of Inquiry was not completed when it was dissolved on 10 November 1975 on the ground that the remaining task could be undertaken by the 'regular investigation machineries of the government'. See the Commission of Inquiry Establishment Proclamation Repealing Proclamation, Proclamation No. 61 of 1975 *entered into force* 10 November 1975, Preamble, para. 2.
135   Noticeably, the Proclamation reflected the absence of rigorous debate and adequate attention –even a mediocre understanding of the relevant laws and of the situation could have produced a proclamation with better clarity. Perhaps the EPRDF was overwhelmingly preoccupied with, as some suggested, the making and un-making of transitional political power aimed at self-aggrandizement. See, for instance, Lata 'The Making and un-making of the Transitional Charter of Ethiopia', *supra* note 75, 10–15; A.G. Selassie,

investigation by a commission of inquiry, subjecting the drafting process to a rigorous debate among experts could have solved the vagueness of the Proclamation on the nature of the crimes to be prosecuted.[136] In drafting the SPO Proclamation, the TGE did not invite international experts, although the SPO process was later assisted by renowned scholars in the field of ICL, such as Professor Cherif Bassiouni, as will be touched up on in other parts of this book.[137]

2.3.3 The SPO's Interpretation of the 'Heinous and Horrendous' Formulation: International and Domestic Crimes

Despite the easily noticeable vagueness of the 'heinous and horrendous' formulation, the SPO Proclamation was never amended; and there exists no record of any other form of effort made by the TGE to clarify the crimes for which the SPO was established. No reference is included in other laws that could help understand the subject-matter jurisdiction of the SPO. For example, Proclamation No. 40 of 1993, a law which established a restructured court system as well as jurisdiction of courts over various categories of crimes, stated that central courts shall exercise jurisdiction over 'offences falling under the competence of the SPO as indicated under the SPO Proclamation', where the latter declared nothing in clear terms.[138]

As such, the precise question regarding what falls inside or outside the scope of the SPO's jurisdiction *ratione materiae*, remained unanswered not only by the SPO Proclamation but also by other relevant domestic laws. Apparently, the only viable option was for the SPO to define its own subject-matter jurisdiction. In this regard, it is important to note that the SPO, unlike a regular prosecutor in the Ethiopian legal system, had both investigative and prosecutorial powers;[139] a duality which might have given the office an autonomy to decide on its subject-matter jurisdiction.

'Ethiopia: Problems and Prospects for Democracy' 1992(1)1 *William and Mary Bill of Rights Journal* 205–226, 213–221.

136 In that respect, it should be noted that the drafting of the Statutes of several international tribunals have involved diverse groups of international experts. The Statute of the Iraqi Supreme Tribunal (IST) could be a good example as its drafting process is believed to have benefited from months of debates among lawyers from the UK, US, other experts outside Iraq, and the Coalition Provisional Authority (CPA). M.A. Newton, 'The Iraqi High Criminal Court: Controversy and Contributions'(2006) 88 (862) *International Review of the Red Cross* 399–425, 409.

137 See in particular, Chapter 5, section 5.3.

138 See Central Courts Establishment Proclamation, No. 40/1993, Article 27.

139 See SPO Proclamation, Article 6.

The precise nature and content of the SPO's subject-matter jurisdiction came to be known two years after its establishment in October 1994 when it filed its first indictment against 106 members and high-ranking officials of the *Dergue*.[140] This indictment, which covers crimes committed in several parts of the country under 211 counts and could be regarded as representative of all other indictments brought by the SPO in terms of the crimes involved, interpreted the Proclamation's reference to 'the heinous and horrendous offenses' as referring to both international[141] and domestic crimes.

As for *international crimes,* the SPO identified: i) the crime of genocide pursuant to Article 281 of the Penal Code,[142] ii) war crimes against the civilian population pursuant to Article 282 of the Penal Code,[143] and iii) provocation and preparation to committing, permitting or supporting of acts that constitute genocide and war crimes in violation of Article 286 of the Penal Code.[144] Crimes against humanity were mentioned in the indictments in a more generic manner and as identical to the crime of genocide; an equalization due to a misconception in Ethiopian law regarding the two crimes, as will be discussed further under Chapter 4 of this book. Besides, by genocide, the SPO refers to genocide against political groups, often coined by social scientists as *politicide*.[145] It should also be noted that the SPO often refers to core crimes as 'crimes against humanity' instead of international crimes, which could be due to the ambiguity pertaining to the notion of international crimes in the Ethiopian legal system.[146]

The *domestic crimes* on the other hand included: murder (Article 522 of the Penal Code),[147] grave willful injury (Article 538 of the Penal Code),[148] unlawful

---

140 See *Colonel Mengistu Hailemariam et al.,* (Revised Indictment), *supra* note 87, 7–8. In the revised indictment, the SPO decreased the number of defendants from 106 to 73. See ibid., (Revised Indictment, 28 October 1995).

141 In Ethiopian laws, international crimes or core crimes are referred to as 'offences against the law of nations' or 'crimes in violation of international law'. See respectively, the Penal Code of 1957, Book III, Title II; the FDRE Criminal Code, Book III, Title II.

142 *Colonel Mengistu Hailemariam et al.,* (Revised Indictment), *supra* note 87, 7–8.

143 See FHC, SPO v. *Legesse Asfaw et al.,* (Indictment), 3 May 2001, File No. 03116.

144 As noted in Chapter 1, provocation and preparation to commit, permit or support acts of genocide was the first ever charge brought by the SPO against the *Dergue* officials (106 individuals). See *Colonel Mengistu Hailemariam et al.,* (Revised Indictment), *supra* note 87, Count 1.

145 See B. Harff and T.R Gurr, 'Victims of the State: Genocides, Politicides and Group Repression since 1945' (1989)1(1) *International Review of Victimology* 23–41.

146 This is discussed in detail in Chapter 5.

147 See *Colonel Mengistu Hailemariam et al.,* (Revised Indictment), *supra* note 87.

148 Ibid.

arrest or detention (Article 416 of the Penal Code),[149] abuse of power (Article 414 of the Penal Code),[150] aggravated property damage (Article 654 of the Penal Code),[151] and rape (Article 589 of the Penal Code).[152]

It appears from its overall practice that the SPO was interested in the prosecution of international crimes. Most of the indictments listed international crimes as their main charges while ordinary crimes were included in the alternative charges. Reports and communications released by the SPO prior to the filing of the initial indictment in *Mengistu et al.* had consistently demonstrated the Office's particular interest in the prosecution of international crimes. For instance, in a report to the UN human rights commission, the SPO explicitly stated that,

> [t]he crimes committed by the former regime were not only crimes against the victims and the Ethiopian people, in many cases they were crimes against humanity – crimes that the international community has a particular interest to prevent, to investigate and to punish.[153]

The SPO's approach of charging almost all of its defendants with international crimes was however challenged. Defendants in the case of *SPO v. General Solomon Negussie et al.* raised a preliminary objection regarding a mismatch between the details of the offense and the provision of the Penal Code of 1957 used in the charge[154] and argued that the SPO had attempted to give international characteristics to an ordinary crime.[155]

The objection was dismissed by the court, which deemed convincing the SPO's response. In responding to the preliminary objection, the SPO stated that the offenses for which the defendants stood trial were essentially of an international nature, because they fulfilled the following three conditions:

---

149 Ibid.
150 See ibid. The crime of abuse of power as mentioned in the case was used as an offence referring to what the Proclamation considered as misappropriation of public funds.
151 See, for instance, OSC, SPO v. *Brigadier General Tedela Desta et al.*, (Initial Indictment), 20 September 1999, File No. 28/85.
152 See the Special Prosecution Office, 'Annual Report to the House of Peoples' Representatives of Ethiopia' (Addis Ababa, 04 February 2010) 10. [Hereinafter: SPO's Annual Report to the HPR (2010)].
153 Letter dated 28 January 1994 from the Permanent Representative of the Transitional Government of Ethiopia to the United Nations Office in Geneva addressed to the Assistant Secretary-General for Human Rights, E/CN.4/1994/103, 4.
154 HSC, SPO v. *General Solomon Negussie et al.*, (Defendants preliminary objection to the indictment), 3 December 1999, File No. 04/1990.
155 Ibid., 12.

i) the crimes were state sponsored and their perpetration was accompanied with a state plan or policy; *ii*) the crimes resulted in a large number of victims; iii) besides the death and injury inflicted to the people, international peace had been continuously threatened through the causing of the destruction of one or more of the racial, religious, and other groups, the infliction of a suffering of grave nature on human kind, and the armed conflict which ensued as a result.[156]

In relation to the domestic crimes, in the case of SPO v. *Basha Bekele Fasil and Abera Lemma,* the Federal High Court (FHC) dismissed a charge on aggravated homicide on the ground that it did not fall within the scope of Article 6 of the SPO Proclamation.[157] The Federal Supreme Court (FSC) upheld the FHC's decision by declaring that the SPO had no jurisdiction over purely domestic crimes.[158] Although the SPO argued that 'there was nothing in its proclamation that limited its subject-matter jurisdiction to genocide and other politically motivated crimes',[159] the FSC asserted that Article 6 authorized the prosecution of domestic crimes only if they were perpetrated: *i*) in relation to the crime of genocide; or *ii*) as a result of the perpetrator's abuse of position of authority.[160]

While the second reasoning of the FSC is in line with the invoked provision, the first is however not clear. Article 6 does not contain a legal characterization of the crimes to be prosecuted by the SPO. The Proclamation referred to the subject-matter jurisdiction of the SPO through the expression 'heinous and horrendous' criminal acts, which, as discussed above, could be

---

156 Ibid., 4. Translation by the author. The original (Amharic) version reads:
ሀ) ወንጀሉ የተፈፀመዉ በመንግስት ድጋፍና በመንግስት ተግባርና መረሃ ግብር በመሆኑ
ለ) በአጠቃላይ በወንጀሉ ተግባር ከፍተኛ ቁጥር ያላቸው ሰዎች ተጎጂ መሆናቸው
ሐ) በዉንጀሎቹ ዲርጊቶች ምክንያት የሰዎች መሞትና መጎዳት ብቻ ሳይሆን ከተለያየ ዘር፣ ሃይማኖት ፣ አስተሳሰብ ወዘተ መካከል አንዱ ውይም ሌላኛው አንዲጠፋ በማድረግ ፣ በአጠቃላይ የሰው ልጅ ላይ የሚደርስው ጉዳት ከፍተኛ መሆኑና፣ በእነዚህ ምክንቶች ሰላም ታዉክ ጦርናቶች በማስካት ፣ የአለምን ሰላም ሲያዉኩ የቆዩ መሆኑ ነው፡፡
157 FHC, SPO v. *Basha Bekele Fasil and Abera Lemma,* (Trial Ruling), 3 June 1999, File No. 263/1989. Article 6 of the SPO Proclamation reads:
The [SPO] shall, in accordance with the law, have the power to conduct investigation and institute proceedings in espect of any person having committed or responsible for the commission of an offence by abusing his position in the party, the government or mass organization under the *Dergue*-WPE regime.
158 FSC, SPO v. *Basha Bekele Fasil and Abera Lemma,* (Appeals Judgment), 26 October 1999, File No. 4166/92.
159 Ibid., 2–3. Translation by the author. The original (Amharic) version reads.
160 In this regard, the SPO claimed that it was not given sufficient time to establish that the defendants had committed aggravated homicide by abusing their official position. See ibid.

interpreted as comprising both international and domestic crimes. As such, the Proclamation contained no specific reference to the crime of genocide. The Court did not explain its reasoning further, and why it referred to genocide alone while excluding the other two core crimes, i.e. crimes against humanity and war crimes, remains unanswered.

Be that as it may, neither the preceding nor the subsequent *Dergue* trials conformed to the FSC's judgment in the case at hand. As for the core crimes, and although the large majority of the SPO indictments comprised genocide as a principal offense,[161] the SPO also prosecuted war crimes, as will be discussed in Chapter 4.[162] As for the importance of the position of authority of the defendants, international crimes were prosecuted by the SPO even when the defendants had no position of authority in the *Dergue* administration as required by Article 6. The same was also the case with respect to domestic crimes. As will be discussed further in Chapter 3, the SPO's process targeted all sorts of individuals including personal informants, associates, and chauffeur.

In the large majority of its cases, the SPO prosecuted domestic crimes mainly as alternative charges to genocide. There were also instances in which it prosecuted domestic crimes as independent and additional charges.[163] Yet, some of the SPO cases have dealt exclusively with purely domestic crimes committed with no apparent political motivation and without any connection to genocide or war crimes. In this respect, the cases of *SPO v. Aman Gobena et al.*[164] and *SPO v. Abdulekadir Mohammed Burka*[165] may stand out, notably because several defendants were sentenced to death for committing *aggravated homicide* in violation of Article 522 of the Penal Code of 1957.[166]

At this juncture, it is worth pointing out that there are crimes that the SPO did not prosecute, unlike what has been considered to be the case by NGOs,

---

161　In *Mengistu et al.*, the highest-ranking *Dergue* officials stood trial for one more principal offense, namely, conspiracy to commit genocide in violation of Article 286 of the Penal Code of 1957. See *Colonel Mengistu Hailemariam et al.*, (Revised Indictment), *supra* note 87, count 1, 6.

162　In relation to war crimes, See FHC, *SPO v. Legesse Asfaw et al.*, (Trial Judgment) 4 March 2008, File No. 03116.

163　See ibid. For example, counts 210 (unlawful arrest and detention) and 211 (abuse of power) were independent charges as ordinary crimes.

164　OSC, *SPO v. Aman Gobena et al.*, (Trial Judgment), 11 April 2000, File No. 8/92.

165　FHC, *SPO v. Abdulekadir Mohammed Burka*, (Trial Judgment), 8 July 2004, File No. 17011.

166　OSC, *SPO v. Aman Gobena et al.*, (Sentencing Judgment), 23 April 2002, File No. 8/92, 7–9; FHC, *SPO v. Abdulekadir Mohammed Burka*, (Sentencing Judgment),13 July 2004, File No. 17011, 4.

media outlets, and even some writers.[167] For instance, torture and crimes against humanity are often cited as crimes prosecuted by the SPO while no single SPO case has dealt with these crimes.

The misconception that the SPO prosecuted torture[168] might have resulted from mistaking the offense of torture for the other two injury-related crimes included in most of the SPO indictments: 'grave willful injury' (Article 538 of the Penal Code) and 'serious injury to the physical or mental health of members of the group' (Article 281(a) of the Penal Code). These crimes are not identical to torture. Torture, as understood under international law and as defined in the Convention against Torture,[169] requires the *purpose* and *state official* elements,[170] which are not necessary to establish the SPO's injury-related offenses, as it will be discussed in detail in Chapter 4 of this book.

Contrary to what some writers have suggested, the *Dergue* trials were not trials for crimes against humanity,[171] which have never been proscribed in Ethiopian laws. The confusion appears to have resulted from the fact that the

---

167 Various authors and commentators have added several other crimes to the list of crimes perpetrated by the *Dergue* and prosecuted by the SPO. Among the crimes commonly referred to are: crimes against humanity, forced disappearance, starvation, forced relocation and movement of people. Some have suggested some kind of vague offences such as Red Terror, and misuse of humanitarian aid and policy. See for instance, H. Tsadik, 'Prosecuting the past – affecting the future: the Ethiopian Transitional Justice Trials' (A SIDA Minor Field Study, Department of Peace and Conflict Research Uppsala University, 2007), 16 available at: <https://www.pcr.uu.se/digitalAssets/654/c_654492-l_1-k_mfs_tsadic.pdf> accessed 24 March 2019.
168 See for instance, F.K. 'The Trial of Mengistu and other Derg Members for Genocide, Torture and Summary Executions in Ethiopia' in C. Murungu and B. Japhet (eds.), *Prosecuting International Crimes in Africa* (Pretoria: Pretoria University Law Press, 2011) 163–184; F.K.Tiba, 'Mass Trials and Modes of Criminal Responsibility for International Crimes: The Case of Ethiopia' in K.J. Heller and G. Simpson (eds.), *The Hidden Histories of War Crimes Trials* (Oxford: Oxford University Press, 2013) 306–326, 307.
169 Convention against Torture and Other Cruel, Inhuman or Degrading Treatment or Punishment, G.A. res. 39/46, [annex, 39 U.N. GAOR Supp. (No. 51) at 197, U.N. Doc`. A/39/51 (1984)], *entered into force* 26 June 1987.
170 For a brief discussion of the elements of torture, see A. Cassese et al., *Cassese's International Criminal Law* (3rd edn., Oxford: Oxford University Press, 2013), 132–135.
171 See F. Elgesem and G.A. Aneme, 'The Rights of the Accused: a Human Rights Appraisal', in K. Tronvoll et al. (eds.), *The Ethiopian Red Terror Trials: Transitional Justice Challenged* (Suffolk: James Curry, 2009), 33–50, 48; M.C. Bassiouni, *Crimes Against Humanity: Historical Evolution and Contemporary Application* (Cambridge: Cambridge University Press, 2011) 707; S. Vaughan, 'The Role of the Special Prosecutor's Office' in K. Tronvoll et al. (eds.), *The Ethiopian Red Terror Trials: Transitional Justice Challenged* (Suffolk: James Curry, 2009) 51–67; W.L. Kidane, 'The Ethiopia 'Red Terror Trials' in M.C. Bassiouni (ed.), *Post-Conflict Justice* (Ardsley: Transnational Publishers, 2001) 667–694, 668.

caption of Article 281 of the Penal Code, the main provision that the SPO used to prosecute the *Dergue*, amalgamated genocide with crimes against humanity. However, this Article, as was also explained by the FHC in *Mengistu et al.*, only criminalized genocide.[172]

2.4 The Decision to Prosecute: Removing Latent Impediments

A decision to prosecute core crimes, as noted in Chapter 1, should go beyond a mere expression of interest. In addition to outlawing amnesty, which the TGE's decision did (as discussed above), a state is required to take measures to remove other impediments that may interfere with the effective implementation of its decision to prosecute.[173] In that respect, the fact that the decision to prosecute the *Dergue* was the first of its kind in Ethiopia could rise the question whether Ethiopian law was equipped to regulate the complex issues of international criminal law. In fact, unlike what is commonly the case in post-conflict judicial organs that have dealt with international crimes, the SPO was not established with a separate statute determining the applicable substantive and procedural laws. As stated in the SPO Proclamation, the applicable laws were those in existence at the time the SPO was established.[174] As noted above, it was the SPO itself that carried out investigations and determinations as to the nature and type of the crimes it then prosecuted.

In line with this mandate and the applicable law, the applicability of statutory limitations may appear as a potential impediment to prosecution, given that the temporal scope of the decision to prosecute covers crimes committed as far as two decades before the establishment of the SPO. Immunity laws could also be regarded as potential impediments because the commission of the alleged crimes have involved the entire state apparatus and the highest-ranking government officials. The following paragraphs discuss how Ethiopia has addressed these issues and whether its decision to

---

172   FHC, *SPO* v. *Colonel Mengistu Hailemariam et al.*, (Ruling on Preliminary Objections), 10 October 1995, File No. 1/87, 104–105. See also, Chapter 5, sub-section 5.3.2.
173   See Chapter 1, section 1.7.
174   SPO Proclamation, Article 7(1). According to this provision, existing 'laws concerning criminal investigation and institution of criminal proceedings as well as laws applicable to the ordinary prosecutors shall also apply to the activities undertaken by the [SPO]'. For a more elaborated discussion on the applicable law, see Chapter 6, section 6.1.

prosecute international crimes was accompanied with the removal of potential impediments.

2.4.1 *Statutory Limitations*

By the time the TGE's decision to prosecute was reached, Ethiopia, a non-state party to the Convention on the Non-Applicability of Statutory Limitations to War Crimes and Crimes Against Humanity,[175] had already prescribed statutory limitations with respect to all kinds of crimes. Article 226 of the Penal Code, which contained a list of periods upon the expiry of which a prosecution or criminal action shall be deemed barred, stated that a criminal action may be brought within 25 years from the date of the commission of crimes that are punishable by death or life imprisonment. These included genocide, war crimes, and the ordinary crime of aggravated homicide (murder).[176] As of August 1992, that is when the SPO Proclamation announced the TGE's decision to prosecute crimes committed between 1974 and 1991, the *Dergue's* first criminal conduct, namely, the mass execution of 59 officials of the Haileselassie regime, was already 18 years old.[177] Based on the law in force at the time, that period could have barred the prosecution of offenses that were punishable with a rigorous imprisonment of up to ten years.[178]

Interestingly, however, the TGE's decision to prosecute the *Dergue* era crimes was complemented by the inclusion in the SPO Proclamation of a

---

175 Convention on the Non-Applicability of Statutory Limitations to War Crimes and CrimesAgainst Humanity, G.A. res. 2391 (XXIII), annex, 23 U.N. gaor Supp. (No. 18) at 40, U.N. Doc. A/7218 (1968), *entered into force* 11 November P1970.

176 See The Penal Code of 1957, Article 226. This provision sets a limitation period for all crimes by dividing them into six categories based on range of penalty of imprisonment. It reads:
 the limitation period of a criminal action shall be:
 (a) of twenty-five years for offences punishable with death or rigorous imprisonment for life;
 (b) of twenty years for offences punishable with rigorous imprisonment exceeding ten years but not exceeding twenty-five years;
 (c) of fifteen years for offences punishable with rigorous imprisonment exceeding five years but not exceeding ten years;
 (d) of ten years for offences punishable with rigorous imprisonment not exceeding five years;
 (e) of five years for offences punishable with simple imprisonment exceeding one year;
 (f) of three years for offences punishable with simple imprisonment not exceeding one year, or with fine only.

177 See *Colonel Mengistu Hailamarima et al.,* (Revised Indictment) *supra* note 87, 12–14.

178 See the Penal Code of 1957, Article 226(d). See also FDRE Criminal Code, Article 217.

provision that removed the statutory limitations provided under the Penal Code. According to Article 7(2) of the Proclamation,

> the provision concerning the limitations of criminal actions and the time limit for the submission of criminal charges, evidence and pleading to charges shall not be applicable to proceedings instituted by the [SPO].[179]

Symptomatically, this provision could be seen as proof that the decision to prosecute was more than just a declaration of interest as it provided for the removal of one of the traditional impediments to prosecution.

Yet, the provision had limited practical significance. Firstly, the SPO Proclamation's clause on the inapplicability of statutory limitations was specific to the SPO proceedings as it was meant to apply to crimes committed during the *Dergue* and only to those over which the SPO had jurisdiction to prosecute. Due to this status as a situation and office specific law, this clause was not meant to govern similar crimes when prosecuted by other organs such as the Office of the Regular Public Prosecutor (RPPO).[180] In that sense, Ethiopian law did not recognize the inapplicability of statutory limitations for core crimes until the coming into force of the FDRE Constitution in 1995, which states, in its Article 28 that the 'criminal liability of persons who commit 'crimes against humanity', so defined by international agreements ratified by Ethiopia and by other laws of Ethiopia 'such as genocide, summary executions, forcible disappearances or [and] torture shall not be barred by statute of limitation'.[181] Arguably, war crimes are also covered under this provision as they fall within the category of crimes referred to as 'crimes against humanity' in Ethiopian law.[182]

Secondly, the relevance of Article 7(2) of the SPO Proclamation in the *Dergue* trials was strongly debated. In several of the SPO cases, the defendants objected to the charge on the ground that the crimes were barred by statutes of limitations and that Article 7(2) of the SPO Proclamation could not apply retroactively to remove the Penal Code's period of limitation. As far as international crimes were concerned, the objection was raised in *Mengistu et al.* in relation to the first charge that dealt with incitement to commit genocide, as it was punishable by a maximum of five years of imprisonment.[183] The SPO

---

179 SPO Proclamation, Article 7(1).
180 For the relationship between the SPO and the RPPO as regards crimes committed during the *Dergue*, see Chapter 4, sub-section 4.2.2.4.
181 See the FDRE Constitution, Article 28. Emphasis added.
182 This is discussed further in Chapter 5, Section 5.2.
183 See *Colonel Mengistu Hailemariam et al.*, (Ruling on Preliminary Objections), *supra* note 172, 99. The objection did not relate to the second charge, on the crime of genocide, as the

responded to the objection of the defendants by stating that statutory limitations were removed pursuant to Article 7(2) of its Proclamation and Article 28 of the FDRE Constitution.[184] In *Mengistu et al.*, the SPO alleged that the crimes were committed in a period that allowed for a complete absence of criminal accountability and that such a reality should be considered as an exception to the counting of a period of limitation.[185] It also argued that since the crimes were committed in a continuous manner from 1974 to 1991, the period of limitation shall be deemed to have started running from the time the commission of the crimes came to end in May 1991, when the regime was ousted by force.[186]

In rejecting the defendants' objection, the FHC in *Mengistu et al.* recited the last two arguments mentioned by the SPO. The Court stated:

> Nonetheless, pursuant to Article 282 (2) of the Penal Code the period of limitation shall begin to run from the day on which criminal activities have ceased, if they were pursued over a period of time. The SPO has indicted the defendants for committing crimes mentioned in the indictment during the period in which they had established a provisional military government, under which they organized themselves in general assembly, standing committee, and sub committees. As it was clear that, from the circumstances that existed during that period, there was no authority that could have brought criminal proceedings against these defendants for crimes committed while they were in power, it cannot be said that the ordinary period of limitation has run its course pursuant to Article 226 of the Penal Code.[187]

---

period of limitations set for this crime was 25 years. The SPO's first indictment of October 1994 in *Mengistu et al.* was filed exactly 20 years after the first alleged genocidal mass executions took place in October 1974. See FHC, SPO v. *Colonel Mengistu Hailemariam et al.*, (Indictment), 25 October 1994, File No. 1/87, 12–14. However, the FSC have concluded in 2008 that the Dergue's first mass-executions did not constitute genocide. See Chapter 6, section 6.4.

184 See *Colonel Mengistu Hailemariam et al.*, (Ruling on Preliminary Objections), *supra* note 172, 99.
185 See ibid., 100.
186 Ibid., 101.
187 Ibid., 98–99. Translation by the author. The original (Amharic) version reads,

ነገር ግን፣ በወንጀለኛ መቅጫ ሕግ ቁጥር 282/2 መሠረት ይርጋው መቆጠር የሚጀምረው ጥፋተኛ በማራዘም ሲፈጸም የነበረውን ጥፋት ካመነበት ቀን ጀምሮ ነው። የልዩ ዐቃቤ ሕግ በተከሳሾቹ ላይ ያቀረበው የጊዜያዊ ወታዳራዊ አስተዳደር መንግስት አጽቁመው በጠቅላላ ጉባኤ በቋሚ ኮሚቴና በንዑሳን ኮሚቴነት ተዋቅረው በነበር ጊዜ በክሱ የተመለከቱትን ወንጀሎች ፈጽመዋል በማለት በመሆኑ በነበረው ተጨባጭ ሁኔታም ቢሆን ተከሳሾቹ ከሥልጣን ከወረዱበት ጊዜ በክሱ የተመለከቱትን ወንጀሎች ፈጽመዋል

The second part of the ruling, which was based on the absence of criminal accountability during the *Dergue* regime, was however indefensible and superfluously contradictory. It was wrong, because the absence of any possibility to institute proceedings during the *Dergue* regime against the *Dergue* officials could not have, in the eyes of the law, interrupted or suspended the running of the relevant period of limitation. Pursuant to Article 229(1) of the Penal Code, a period of limitation runs irrespective of any act the offender might volitionally undertake to prevent the institution or continuation of criminal prosecution.[188] It was superfluous, because it had no contribution to the first part of the ruling, which was based on the fact that the crimes for which the *Dergue* stood trial came to an end in 1991. Moreover, the second part of the ruling contradicted the first part. In the second part, the Court specified that the period of limitation was suspended while it had already stated in the first part that the period of limitation did not start running until the cessation of the commission of crimes in 1991. Furthermore, there was no comment in the ruling regarding the (in)applicability of Article 7(2) of the SPO Proclamation or of Article 28 of the Constitution to the issue at hand.

2.4.2 *Immunity from Prosecution*

Unlike the case of statutory limitations, the issue of immunity from prosecution was not expressly dealt with in the SPO Proclamation. Given that the TGE's decision to prosecute aimed at prosecuting the top-ranking officials of the *Dergue* regime, it could have been essential for the Proclamation to address the potential question of immunity from prosecution, unless the legislator believed that Ethiopian law never recognized immunity from prosecution. The following sub-sections explore this particular issue by examining the Ethiopian legal framework and, then, the trials.

2.4.2.1   A Survey of Ethiopian Laws on Immunity

Previously, the monarchical system that ended in 1974 used to grant absolute immunity for the emperor.[189] The absolute nature of the immunity of a king was traditionally illustrated in expressions like **ንጉስ አይከሰስ ሰማይ አይታረስ**, which loosely translates into: *not suable a king is; not plowable the sky is.* Immunity

---

በማለት በእንርሱ ላይ ማንም ሰው ክስ ለማቅረብ እንደማይችል ግልጽ ስለነበር በክሱ የተጠቀሱት የወንጀል አደራጎቶች በመ/ሕ/ቁ/226 በመደበኛ የክስ አቀራረብ ይርጋ አቆጣጠር ላይ ተመስርቶ ክሱ በይርጋ ቀሪ ይሆናል ማለት የሚቻል አይደለም። ስለሆነም የተከሳሾች ጠበቆች ክሱ በይርጋ ሊተገድ ይገባዋል በማለት የቀረቡትን የመቃወሚያ ክርክር አልተቀበልነውም።

188 See also the FDRE Criminal Code, Article 220(2).
189 See the 1931 Constitution of Ethiopia, Article 5.

from prosecution was regarded to be the divine right of the king, and of the king only: it was thus not extendable to members of the royal family.[190] The 1955 Revised Constitution of Ethiopia, the first and last constitution to contain express provisions on the personal immunity of the emperor, stated that such an immunity emanated from the 'sacred person, inviolable dignity, and indisputable powers' of the Emperor.[191]

Today, Ethiopian law recognizes personal immunities as protected under public international law.[192] However, an Ethiopian enjoying immunity from prosecution in a foreign country cannot invoke it to object to charges brought in Ethiopia for crimes committed abroad.[193] As a result, a member of the Ethiopian diplomatic or consular service or an Ethiopian official or agent who cannot be prosecuted at the place of commission of the crime(s) could still be prosecuted in Ethiopia, except for petty offenses.[194]

With respect to immunity *ratione materiae*, all of the constitutions enacted in the history of Ethiopia, with the exception of the 1931 Constitution and the 1991 Transitional Period Charter (interim Constitution), contained a provision granting immunity from prosecution to members of Parliament. Under the – current – FDRE Constitution, members of the two Federal Houses, namely the House of Peoples' Representatives (HoPR)[195] and the House of Federation (HoF),[196] cannot be prosecuted except in the case of *flagrante delicto* involving *serious crimes*.[197] This immunity is however a conditional one and criminal prosecution can be instituted against a member of the Federal Houses upon obtaining permission from the concerned House.[198] The rationale behind the adoption of functional immunity is to ensure that members of Parliament execute their functions without fear of interference from the executive or the judiciary. As noted by the 1994 Constitutional Commission, the objective of

---

190 See P. Graven, *An Introduction to Ethiopian Penal Law: Arts.1–84 Penal Code* (Addis Ababa: Faculty of Law of Haile Selassie University 1, 1965) 13–14.
191 See the 1955 Revised Constitution of Ethiopia, Articles 4, 5, and 62(2).
192 See FDRE Criminal Code, Articles 4 and 11(2); The Criminal Procedure Code of Ethiopia, Article 39 (1) (c).
193 See FDRE Criminal Code, Article 14.
194 Ibid.
195 See FDRE Constitution, Article 54(6).
196 Ibid., Article 63(2).
197 See ibid. The English version of the provision does not make any reference to the category of crimes in relation to which immunity could be revoked, it merely states that the member of the two Houses may not be prosecuted except in the case of *flagrante delicto*. The Amharic version however expressly states that the immunity could only be revoked if the member of Parliament is apprehended in *flagrante delicto* for a serious criminal offense.
198 See ibid.

this immunity is only to protect the function of the Federal Houses, but not to absolve any member of the Houses from criminal responsibility for either simple or grave crimes.[199]

The FDRE Constitution adopted, using similar terms to those of the 1955 Revised Constitution[200] and of the 1987 PDRE Constitution,[201] an absolute immunity in relation to a vote a member of a Federal House casts or opinion he/she expresses in the House.[202] The immunity applies only with regards to acts committed when the Federal Houses are in session.[203] The rationales for the adoption of this absolute immunity are: *i*) the need to ensure constructive debates, opinions, and criticisms through the application of unlimited freedom of expression; *ii*) the presumption that members of the Federal Houses do not engage in disseminating unfounded defamatory rumors against the reputation of individuals and organizations, or inflammatory statements that can incite a war or disturb a peace; and *iii*) the need to guarantee that if such statements are made, there would always be a chance to prevent them from reaching the public's ears.[204]

The Criminal Code extended the ambit of functional immunity, notably in relation to offences against honor.[205] In addition to members of the two Federal Houses, members of the executive and of the judiciary are granted immunity from prosecution, as long as the conducts are limited to offences against honor as proscribed by Articles 607–610 of the Criminal Code. This immunity is available only where the crime is committed in conformity with and in the regular discharge of duties.[206]

As an exception, an Ethiopian enjoying immunity under municipal laws can still be prosecuted if caught in *flagrante*. This exception has been understood as referring to a person arrested while attempting to commit, committing, or immediately after having committed the crime, and while running away from the crime scene.[207] In addition, an immunity may be revoked by a subsequent decision of the relevant organ of the government.[208]

---

199 See the 1994 Constitutional Commission, *The FDRE Constitution: Explanatory Note*, (unpublished, available at the Library of the FDRE House of People's Representatives), 118.
200 See the 1955 Revised Constitution of Ethiopia, Article 62(1).
201 See the 1987 PDRE Constitution, Article 73.
202 See the FDRE Constitution, Articles 54(5) and 63(1).
203 See ibid.
204 See the 1994 Constitutional Commission, *The FDRE Constitution: Explanatory Note*, supra note 199, 114.
205 See FDRE Criminal Code, Article 611, the Penal Code of 1957, Article 578.
206 See ibid.
207 See the 1994 Constitutional Commission, *The FDRE Constitution: Explanatory Note*, supra note 199, 113.
208 Ibid.

With respect to core crimes, Ethiopian laws do not provide any exception based on the nature of the crimes. However, the applicability of immunity from prosecution in Ethiopia varies based on the nationality of the suspect, and on whether he/she is a foreigner or an Ethiopian. The prosecution of a foreigner suspected of having committed core crimes, either in Ethiopia or abroad, depends on the principles of public international law applicable to immunities. Customary international law recognizes immunity from prosecution for core crimes of an incumbent head of State.[209] Accordingly, any foreigner, except an incumbent head of state, suspected of committing core crimes can be prosecuted in Ethiopia.

A relevant practical illustration involves former President Omar al-Bashir of Sudan, against whom the ICC issued an arrest warrant while he was in office.[210] President al-Bashir visited Ethiopia on several occasions predominantly to attend the African Union (AU) summits at its Headquarters in Addis Ababa, for the purpose of which heads of states enjoy immunity from arrest under the AU General Convention on the Priviliges and Immuniteies.[211] In 2012, for instance, an AU summit was moved to Ethiopia with the specific purpose of enabling President al-Bashir's attendance. Malawi, where the AU summit was initially due to take place, had declared that, as a State party to the Rome Statute, it would arrest him should he attend the summit in Lilongwe.[212] In addition to being a State not party to the Rome Statute, Ethiopia has never enterd an *ad hoc* arrangement or an agreement with the court under Article 87(5) of the Statute.[213] As such, it may not have an obligation to cooperate with the court

---

209 See Cassese *et al.* (eds.), *Cassese's International Criminal Law, supra* note 170, 322–325. For the ICJ's reasoning in relation to immunity from prosecution of incumbent Ministers for Foreign Affairs, see ICJ, Case Concerning the Arrest Warrant of 11 April 2000 (*Democratic Republic of the Congo* v. *Belgium*) Judgment, 14 February 2002, para. 55. The Court stated that,
   It has been unable to deduce ... that there exists under customary international law any form of exception to the rule according immunity from criminal jurisdiction and inviolability to incumbent Ministers for Foreign Affairs, where they are suspected of having committed war crimes or crimes against humanity.

210 See ICC, *The Prosecutor* v. *Omar Hassan Ahmad Al Bashir*, (Warrant of Arrest for Omar Hassan Ahmad Al Bashir, Pre-Trial Chamber I, 4 March 2009), ICC-02/05-01/09-1; ICC, *The Prosecutor* v. *Omar Hassan Ahmad Al Bashir*, (Second Warrant of Arrest for Omar Hassan Ahmad Al Bashir, Pre-Trial Chamber I,11 July 2010) ICC-02/05-01/09-1.

211 See General Convention on the Privileges and Immunities of the Organization of African Unity, CAB/LEG/24.2/13, *entered into force* 25 October 1965, Article v.

212 See BBC News, 'Ethiopia to Host Africa Union Summit after Omar al-Bashir Malawi Row' (12 June 2012), available at: <http://www.bbc.co.uk/news/world-africa-18407396> accessed 28 December 2016.

213 For details on the implication of a third State's cooperation with the ICC based on arrangments made under Article 87(5) of the Statute, see C. Kreß and K. Prost, 'Article 87' in

in arresting a sitting head of state in pursuance of an arrest warrant issued by the ICC.

In some intstances, Ethiopia appeared strongly opposed to the idea of prosecuting a sitting head of State using international courts – a position that could be inferred from statements made by its officials in relation to the Kenya-ICC feud involving Kenya's President Uhuru Kenyatta. Speaking at the AU conference held in Addis Ababa in 2013, the Ethiopian Foreign Minister stated: 'we underscored that sitting heads of state and governments should not be prosecuted while in office'.[214] However, such political stances might have emanated from a failure to fully realize the status of the said immunity in international law. Although customary international law recognizes immunity of heads of State, States can agree in a treaty, as they did in relation to the Rome Statute, not to recognize it anymore.[215] What is more important is that, on the one hand, the notion of immunity of heads of state under customary international law does not negate treaty provision that allow for exception to the notion. On the other, as the ICJ noted in the *Arrest Warrant* decision, the availability of such a provision in a treaty or statutes of international criminal tribunals does not imply the existance of an exception in customary international law allowing for prosecution of incumbent heads of state by national courts.[216]

2.4.2.2   The Practice: Immunity of Heads of State and the *Dergue* Trials

Of the four instances of Ethiopian trials that this book is dealing with, only the *Dergue* trials have raised the question of immunity for acts accomplished in an official capacity. This issue was particularly acute in *Mengistu et al.*, which involved the prosecution of high-ranking government officials.

In *Mengistu et al.*, the counsel for the defendants raised an objection to the SPO indictment mentioning that the defendants – all of the 73 high-ranking *Dergue* officials – were heads of State at the time the alleged crimes were committed. According to this objection, the head of the State, unlike the rest of the individuals living in the terrirtoy of the concerned state, is not required

---

O. Triffterer and K. Ambos (eds), *The Rome Statute of the International Criminal Court: A Commentary* (3rd ed., München: C.H.Beck.Hart.Namos, 2016) 2029–2031.

214   See A. Maasho and E. Blair, 'Africans Tell ICC: Heads of State Should not be Tried' (Reuters, World News, 11 October 2013) available at: <http://www.reuters.com/article/us-africa-icc-idUSBRE99A0YT20131011> accessed 28 December 2016.

215   See Rome Statute of the International Criminal Court U.N. Doc. 2187 U.N.T.S. 90, *entered into force* 1 July 2002, Article 27. See also Cassese *et al.* (eds.), *Cassese's International Criminal Law, supra* note 170, 322–326.

216   See ICJ, *Democratic Republic of the Congo v. Belgium, supra* note 209, para. 75.

THE DECISION TO PROSECUTE CORE CRIMES: CONTEXTS AND CONTENTS 85

to respect laws it enacts including those proscribing acts such as murder.[217] In fact, the objection used the singular marker 'a head of state' (ርዕሰ ብሔር), in order to indicate that all of the *Dergue* officials had such a status collectively and indivisibly.[218] This reference mirrors the remarks of Proclamation No. 2 of 1974, which declared the *Dergue* as the head of the State and of the Government.[219]

In support of the objection, the defense counsels cited the 1955 Revised Constitution under the auspices of which the Penal Code of 1957 was enacted.[220] This Constitution was, however, never enforced during the *Dergue* regime for it was suspended as the first official act of the *Dergue* in 1974.[221] They also invoked international law but only in general terms advancing that, even if it was true that the defendants had issued political decisions to murder individuals, international law did not regard such acts as punishable as long as they were committed in the defendants' capacity as heads of State.[222]

The SPO, which argued that the defendants did not have the status of a 'head of state',[223] considered the objection baseless, 'both in the eyes of the law and morality'.[224] The SPO's argument against the objection is based mainly on international law and State practice. With regards to the former, it argued that international agreements since 1919, and numerous United Nations human rights treaties since, have established that a head of State is as prosecutable as any other individual.[225] The SPO substantiated its argument by listing several treaties and quoting their relevant provisions.[226] The Statutes of international criminal tribunals, except that of the ICC, were also quoted to show the irrelevance of official capacity for the prosecution of the crimes for which the *Dergue* stood trial.[227] Nevertheless, the argument did not specifically elaborate

---

217 *Colonel Mengistu Hailemariam et al.*, (Ruling on Preliminary Objections), *supra* note 172, 22.
218 Ibid.
219 See Definitions of Power of Provisional Military Administration Council and of its Chairman, Proclamation No.2 /1974, *entered into force* 15 September 1974, Articles 2 and 3.
220 Ibid.
221 See Provisional Military Government Establishment Proclamation, Proclamation No.1 of 1974, *entered into force* 12 September 1974, Article 5.
222 See *Colonel Mengistu Hailemariam et al.*, (Ruling on Preliminary Objections), *supra* note 172, 22.
223 See M.T. Tessema, *Prosecution of Politicide in Ethiopia: The Red-Terror Trials*, (The Hague: Asser Printing Press, 2018),187–188.
224 See *Colonel Mengistu Hailemariam et al.*, (Ruling on Preliminary Objections), *supra* note 172, 24.
225 See ibid.
226 See ibid. See also *Dem Yazele Dossie*, *supra* note 99, 147–152.
227 See ibid. See also *Dem Yazele Dossie*, *supra* note 99, 150.

on the relationship between immunity and the nature of the crimes under consideration.

With respect to State practice, the SPO asserted that 'heads of states were prosecuted in countries such as Mali, Malawi, Argentina, Bolivia, France, and Greece'.[228] These examples were not discussed in detail, not least in relation to the category of crimes for which the said prosecutions were conducted and to how these prosecutions could justify prosecuting the *Dergue* leaders in Ethiopia. What the SPO was trying to establish by citing these foreign domestic prosecutions remains unclear: was it implying the existence of a norm of customary international law revoking the immunity of heads of States? Or was it merely asserting that Ethiopia would not be the first State to prosecute its former heads of State?

In ruling on the question of immunity, the FHC looked into both national and international laws. With respect to national laws, the Court used as a point of reference Article 4 of the Penal Code of 1957, which dealt with the principle of equality before the law:

> no difference in the treatment of offenders may be made except as provided by this Code and are derived from immunities sanctioned by public international and constitutional law[229]

The Court rightly noted that Article 4 of the Penal Code could be set aside only upon the availability of a pre-existing international or domestic law that *expressly* granted immunity to certain offenders.[230] It went on to state that 'no Ethiopian law, currently in force or in force at the time when the defendants were in political power, has granted immunity from prosecution to heads of State'.[231]

This however calls for a series of remarks. In stating that there was no law susceptible of granting immunity to the defendants, the Court overlooked the 1987 PDRE Constitution, which stated, under Article 75, that 'no people's deputy [a member of the Parliament] shall be arrested or prosecuted without the permission of the National Shengo [the Parliament]'. All of the 73 defendants in *Mengistu et al.* were members of the National Shengo, and therefore enjoyed

---

228 *Colonel Mengistu Hailemariam et al.*, (Ruling on Preliminary Objections), *supra* note 172, 23.
229 See the Penal Code of 1957, Article 4, para 2.
230 See *Colonel Mengistu Hailemariam et al.*, (Ruling on Preliminary Objections), *supra* note 172, 25.
231 Ibid., 23–25.

immunity from prosecution, pursuant to Article 75 of the PDRE Constitution, for the crimes perpetrated from 1987 to 1991, i.e. when the Constitution was in force before being repealed and replaced altogether by the 1991 Transitional Charter. The Court should have discussed whether this constitutional immunity could have been invoked as a valid defense against a post-conflict prosecution initiated by a new government that came to power by suspending the very law that granted the immunity in question.

Turning to international law, the Court invoked three instruments: the Nuremberg Charter, the Universal Declaration of Human Rights (UDHR), and the Genocide Convention.[232] Relying on these instruments, the Court stated, 'the defendants did not produce in evidence any legislation that had granted them immunity from criminal accountability for crimes they have committed. Even if they were to produce one, a law granting immunity from prosecution for genocide would not have been regarded as acceptable in the light of international law'.[233] Although this is an interesting development in terms of direct application of international law in Ethiopian courts, the Court however failed to explain how these international instruments, and notably the Nuremberg Charter and the UDHR, were relevant to the case at hand.

It is true that Ethiopia is one of the 20 States that immediately expressed adherence to the London Agreement of 1945, thus accepting the provisions of the Nuremberg Charter in relation to the prosecution of the major war criminals of WWII. Nevertheless, it is not clear how this instrument could be used in relation to the *Dergue* defendants. Likewise, except mentioning that Article 7 of the UDHR contains a principle similar to the one provided under Article 4 of the Penal Code of 1957 (equality before the law), the Court failed to explain how this obliged States not to recognize the immunity of heads of States.

Article IV of the Genocide Convention, which the Court also invoked in its ruling, states that 'persons committing genocide or any of the other acts enumerated in article III shall be punished, whether they are constitutionally responsible rulers, public officials or private individuals'.[234] The Court claimed that by ratifying the Genocide Convention even before the coming to power of the *Dergue*, Ethiopia had already incorporated into its domestic law the fact

---

232   Ibid.
233   Ibid,. 26. Translation by the author. The original (Amharic) version reads,
      እናዚህ ተከሳሾች ከሚፈጽሙት የወንጀል አዲራጎት ከተጠያቂነት ነጻ ሊሆኑ እንዳሚችሉ በሕግ የተሰጣቸው ልዩ መብት ስለመኖሩ በማስረጃነት አላቀረቡም ። ቢቀርብ ኖሮ እንኳን በዘር ማጥፋት ወንጀል ከመከሰስ ነጻ የሚያደርግ ህግ መኖሩ ከዓለም አቀፍ ሕግ ድንጋጌ አኳያ ተቀበይነት ሊኖረው አይችልም ነበር።
234   Convention on the Prevention and Punishment of the Crime of Genocide, 78 U.N.T.S. 277, *entered into force* 12 January 1951, Article IV.

that there would not be any form of immunity for those accused of committing the crime of genocide.[235] It here seems that the Court simply reiterated the SPO's argument against the defendants' preliminary objection[236] and omitted to consider that the Genocide Convention had not been formally incorporated within the Ethiopian domestic legal system, as will be further discussed in Chapter 4.

Regardless, the FHC made several direct references to the Genocide Convention in a manner that treated the Convention as constituting part of domestic law.[237] Yet, as discussed in Chapter 3, the problem remains that the crime for which the *Dergue* stood trial (genocide against political groups) is different from what the Genocide Convention prohibits as genocide.[238] In other words, the Court applied the Convention to an issue involving a crime that is not covered by it, thereby raising concerns as to the *bien-fondé* of its reasoning.[239]

2.5 Conclusion

The details of the TGE's decision to prosecute, as discussed in this chapter, indicate that amnesty was entirely rejected, although attempts were unsuccessfully made to introduce it. The context in which the decision to prosecute was reached by the TGE lacked sufficient publicity and the question of how to respond to the past crimes was not raised in some significant gatherings such as the Addis Ababa Conference in July 1991. It is also difficult to state whether the decision to prosecute was a result of discussions among the relevant stakeholders in Ethiopia. It was also not clear from the decision as to why it was the only choice that the TGE had to make, as will be discussed further in Chapter 3.

Although it is commendable that the TGE decided for the first time in Ethiopia to bring perpetrators of core crimes to justice in a manner discussed in this chapter, the decision was not preceded by an independent inquiry into the crimes. This resulted in an ambiguous reference to the crimes allegedly

---

235 See *Colonel Mengistu Hailemariam et al.*, (Ruling on Preliminary Objections), *supra* note 172, 25.
236 See ibid.,19.
237 See ibid., 47.
238 See Chapter 3, sub-section 3.2.1.1.
239 In the same ruling, the Court discussed genocide against political groups and acknowledged that the Convention offers a narrow protection compared to Article 281 of the Penal Code of 1957. See *Colonel Mengistu Hailemariam et al.*, (Ruling on Preliminary Objections), *supra* note 172, 82. See also Chapter 5, section 5.5.

committed in the past. This, coupled with the fact that the drafting of the SPO Proclamation did not involve experts in ICL, meant that the TGE did not have a well-thought-out plan to prosecute the *Dergue*. The lack of sufficient preparation and focus to prosecute was also visible from the lack of efforts to remove latent impediments to the prosecution of core crimes; a lack of efforts which prompts the question as to why the decision to prosecute was reached in the first place.

CHAPTER 3

The Decisions to Prosecute
Possible Motivations

3.1 Introduction

The TGE's landmark decision to bring the *Dergue* to justice has not been celebrated by everyone and several scholars have criticized the decision. Some have questioned the entire decision as a reversal of a centuries-old tradition of reconciliation and forgiveness in Ethiopia.[1] Such suggestions however appear erroneous. Rather than a tradition of reconciliation or forgiveness, it seems that the pre-1991 Ethiopian tradition was much more one of not offering any form of justice with respect to several large-scale atrocities alleged to have been perpetrated against the civilian population.[2]

Perhaps more convincingly, many others – while not criticizing the decision itself – have questioned the scope of the decision. The TGE's aim to bring a large number of offenders to trial, irrespective of their status and level of involvement, caused some eyebrows to raise, mainly because it was believed that the country was not yet ready to embark on such a large-scale prosecution. Genuine concerns were expressed regarding the reasons why the TGE had not envisaged selective prosecutions, which would have focused on bringing to trial only those allegedly bearing the highest responsibility for the crimes that took place.

---

1 The most striking essay in this regard was written by Charles Schaefer, who based his argument on the magnanimity shown by Emperor Minilik towards Italian PoWs in the aftermath of the battle of Adwa, 1896. See C. Schaefer, 'The Red Terror Trials Versus Traditions of Restorative Justice' in K. Tronvoll *et al.* (eds.), *The Ethiopian Red Terror Trials: Transitional Justice Challenged* (Martlesham: James Currey, 2009) 68–83. Nonetheless, Scheafer's argument could be seen as too swiftly equalizing a mere act of monarchical clemency with reconciliation and societal forgiveness.

2 One may point out instances such as the massacre of Muslims in Wallo during the reign of Emperor Yehuannes, the Massacre of Catholic Christians in Gonder under Emperor Suseneyous, the massacre of Ormos in Arsi by armed forces of Emperor Minilik. In those instances, the perpetrators did not reconcile with the victims, and the nation did not undergo a healing process, which is perhaps why contemporary political debates and disputes in Ethiopia revolve, in part, around issues of past injustices. See M. Bulcha, 'Genocidal Violence in the Making of Nation and State in Ethiopia' (2005) 9 (2) *African Sociological Review* 1–54; P.B. Henz, *Layers of Time: A history of Ethiopia* (New York: Palgrave, 2000) 95–102.

While the decision can be applauded as a progressive step in the fight against impunity for international crimes, it also seems fair to suggest that it might have been too ambitious. Admittedly, in remarks made a decade after the decision to prosecute was reached, the late Prime Minister Melese Zenaw, who was also the President of the TGE at the time of the decision, stated, 'I think we sort of swallowed more than we could chew'.[3] This assertion indeed holds some truth.

Firstly, the capacity of Ethiopia as to its infrastructure was problematic as by the time the decision to prosecute was reached, the country had an almost collapsing judicial infrastructure, which was not even able to adequately address day-to-day disputes during the transitional period. The country only had one law school established in 1963,[4] and it was reported that many experienced judges had fled the country during the Mengistu regime due to fear of persecution.[5] As also recognized by the EPRDF, the impartiality of the remaining judges and lawyers was highly doubtful due to their prior affiliation with the ousted regime.[6] Logically therefore, deciding to prosecute the atrocities of the past while simultaneously trying to maintain law and order in a volatile transitional period entailed the taking of a significant risk of rebuilding the country on shaky grounds.

It should also be pointed out here that, compared to the UN International Criminal Tribunals (ICTR and ICTY), the tasks and responsibilities that the SPO was about to embark upon were not smaller in scope and complexity but the resources were. For instance, Haile-Mariam, who compared the SPO, which had only 30 prosecutors two years after its establishment,[7] with resources put

---

3   See K. Tronvoll, 'The Quest for Justice or the Construction of Political Legitimacy: The Political Anatomy for the Red Terror Trials' in K. Tronvoll *et al.* (eds.), *The Ethiopian Red Terror Trials: Transitional Justice Challenged* (Martlesham: James Currey, 2009) 84–95, 92.
4   See Addis Ababa University School of Law: An Overview, available at: <http://www.aau.edu.et/clgs/academics/school-of-law/overview/> accessed 28 September 2019.
5   See Human Rights Watch, 'Ethiopia: Reckoning under the Law' (Human rights Watch, 1 December), 19, available at: <https://www.hrw.org/report/1994/12/01/ethiopia-reckoning-under-law> accessed 28 September 2019 [Hereinafter: Human Rights Watch, 'Ethiopia: Reckoning under the Law'].
6   For instance, Article 5 (3) of the SPO Proclamation states that a member of the SPO must be an Ethiopian citizen who was not a member of the Workers Party of Ethiopia (the *Dergue*) and its security forces. African Watch was however concerned by the fact that former *Dergue* members were being debarred, as a category, from serving in the judiciary. See Human Rights Watch, 'Ethiopia: Waiting For Justice: Shortcomings in Establishing the Rule of Law', 8 May 1992, 18, available at: <https://www.refworld.org/docid/45cc5f472.html> accessed 28 September 2019.
7   Y. Haile-Mariam, 'The Quest for Justice and Reconciliation: The International Criminal Tribunal for Rwanda and the Ethiopian High Court' (1998–1999) 22(1) *Hastings*

together for the ICTR concluded that trying to compare the two 'is like trying to compare the weight of an elephant with that of a mouse, the scale tipping heavily in favour of the ICTR'.[8] Besides, material and financial resources that are necessary to carry out large-scale investigations were non-existent and there was at the time a bleak prospect of improvement due to acute and pervasive poverty in the country. Simply because in such a poor country every single penny supposedly counts, it was unlikely for the TGE to have miscalculated the costs of prosecuting thousands of people for crimes committed over a very long period of time.

Secondly, and most importantly, the TGE's decision to prosecute a large number of alleged offenders was made against an explicit warning from Human Rights Watch (HRW), an international organization that was also a pioneer in advocating for the establishment of an international tribunal for 'grave breaches' committed in the former Yugoslavia.[9] In its report released in September 1991, following the arrest of the *Dergue* officials, HRW, addressing both the TGE and the Provisional Government of Eritrea, stated that:

> It is important that the desire to bring as many as possible of those principally responsible for gross abuses to court should not lead to the adoption of a lower standard of proof, or the abrogation of due process. A few prosecutions of those with the highest level of responsibility for the most grave abuses, conducted according to internationally-recognized standards, are more important than many conducted against lesser offenders according to lower standards.[10]

International and Comparative Law Review 667–745, 726. In fact, Ethiopia had to request for material, expert, and financial assistance from the international community to mitigate some of the challeneges the SPO was facing. For details of international assistance acquired by the SPO from countries such as Canada, Norway, the Netherlands, Denmark, US/Carter Center as well as from numerous NGOs, see SPO, 'Report of the Office of the Special Prosecutor 1994: The Special Prosecution Process of War Criminals and Human Rights Violation in Ethiopia' in N.J. Kritz (ed.), *Transitional Justice: How emerging democracies reckon with former regimes; Laws, Rulings and Reports* (Washington DC: United States Institute of Peace Press, 1995), 559–575, 571–572. [Hereinafter: SPO Report (1994)].

8   See Haile-Mariam, 'The Quest for Justice and Reconciliation', supra note 7, 726.
9   Human Rights Watch, 'War Crimes in Bosnia Herzegovina' (Report of Helsinki Watch, August 1992) 1,17,190, available at: <https://www.hrw.org/reports/pdfs/y/yugoslav/yugo.928/yugo928full.pdf> accessed 28 September 2019.
10 See Human Rights Watch, 'Evil Days: 30 Years of War and Famine in Ethiopia' (Report of African Watch, September 1991) 376, available at <https://www.hrw.org/sites/default/files/reports/Ethiopia919.pdf> accessed 20 March 2019.

Yet, apart from advising that a particular focus should be given to bringing to trial only the 'Big-Fish' – an approach followed during the Nuremberg trials, and later to a certain extent at the ICTY and the ICTR,[11] and more expressly at the SCSL[12] – HRW did not specify whether amnesty should be introduced with respect to low-level offenders. Nevertheless, if Ethiopia had focused exclusively on the 'Big-Fish', the process would have naturally resulted in a *de facto* amnesty of all the others. Unlike the cases of Rwanda and the Former Yugoslavia where – in time – two court systems, international and national, were put to operation with each focusing on different categories of defendants, Ethiopia only had its own fragile judicial system at its disposal.

There was no explanation accompanying the SPO Proclamation as to why prosecution – and only prosecution – was considered by the TGE as an 'essential' course of action.[13] This decision begs critical scrutiny, notably since it pre-dated the development of the contemporary international criminal justice system from which many international criminal law standards could be derived and was thus taken with no international guidance.

According to Haile, the legacy of the past, the circumstances of the transition, the balance of power, and the international context at the time of the transition were among the factors that led to the decision to prosecute.[14] For Allo and Tesfaye, as well as Tronvoll, the key driver behind the prosecution of the *Dergue* was the current regime's pursuit for political legitimacy.[15] The TGE and the SPO provided a sort of *ex post facto* justification that the decision was

---

11 Both at the ICTY and at the ICTR, the sole targeting of the 'big fish' developed gradually, although the Statutes did not insinuate any kind of selectivity in prosecuting alleged criminals. Regarding the manner in which the ICTY was made to focus on those bearing the greatest responsibility, see A. Cassese, 'The ICTY: A Living and Vital Reality' (2004) 2 (1) *Journal of International Criminal Justice* 585–597, 588–89; C. del Ponte, 'Prosecuting the Individuals Bearing the Highest Level of Responsibility', (2004) 2 (1) *Journal of International Criminal Justice*, 516–519.

12 UN Security Council, *Statute of the Special Court for Sierra Leone*, 16 January 2002, available at <http://www.refworld.org/docid/3dda29f94.html> accessed 21 March 2019 [Hereinafter the SCSL Statute]. According to Article 1(1) of the SCSL Statute, 'The Special Court shall, except as provided in subparagraph (2), have the power to prosecute persons who bear the greatest responsibility for serious violations of international humanitarian law...'.

13 See SPO Proclamation, para 4.

14 See D. Haile, *Accountability for Crimes of the Past and the Challenges of Criminal Prosecution: The Case of Ethiopia* (Leuven: Leuven University Press, 2000) 30–33. The forthcoming analysis will touch up on these points either directly or indirectly.

15 See Tronvoll, 'The Quest for Justice or the Construction of Political Legitimacy', *supra* note 3, 94; See A. Allo and B. Tesfaye, 'Spectacles of illegality: mapping Ethiopia's show trials' 13 *African Identities* (2015) 279–296, 286–287.

reached in order to respond to Ethiopia's obligation to prosecute.[16] Ultimately, multiple motivations might have significantly affected the two-fold decision to prosecute and to deny amnesty. Save the possible role of several other obscure motivations in the process of the decision-making, the following four factors are worth considering to elucidate why the TGE decided the way it did. These are:

i. The TGE's conviction to uphold a duty to prosecute.
ii. The absence of actual or perceived adversary.
iii. The defendants' lack of remorse and apology.
iv. The TGE's intention to use prosecution for political legitimacy.

The following sections (3.2–3.5) provide an in-depth analysis of these possible motivations behind the TGE's decision to prosecute *Dergue* era crimes. Section 3.6. discusses similar issues but in the post-transitional government of Ethiopia. As will be discussed further in this book, compared to the transitional period and the period before that, the political situation in Ethiopia became relatively stable after 1995, although the country's stability did not prevent international crimes from being perpetrated.[17] In that respect, this section focuses on providing an explanation as to how and why Ethiopia embarked on a process of prosecuting core crimes perpetrated in connection with the *Anuak-Nuwer*, the CUD, and the *Oromo-Gumuz* conflicts.

3.2 The TGE's Conviction to Uphold a Duty to Prosecute

Prior to the TGE's decision to prosecute, international organizations had argued that there was an international duty to prosecute the crimes committed in Ethiopia.[18] Nevertheless, the SPO Proclamation never explained the legal

---

16 See below, sub-section 3.2.2.
17 This is not to suggest that Ethiopia was turned into a democratic state after the period of transition. 'Political stability' is used here to refer to a situation characterized by the absence of violence. For details on the concept and meaning of political stability, see K.M. Dowding and R. Kimber, 'The Meaning and Use of 'Political Stability' (1983) 11(1) *European Journal of Political Research* 229–243.
18 Amnesty International and Human Rights Watch both called upon the EPRDF and the TGE to comply with their international obligation and bring to trial those responsible for brutal offenses during the *Dergue* era. See Human Rights Watch 'Evil Days', *supra* note 10, 374; See Amnesty International, 'Ethiopia: End of an Era of Brutal Repression – A New Chance for Human Rights' (Amnesty International, 18 June 1991), 46–48, available at: <https://www.amnesty.org/en/documents/afr25/005/1991/en/> accessed 20 March 2019.

basis for the decision to prosecute crimes committed during the past regime. It appeared that the TGE gradually started presenting its decision to prosecute as a means of showing its commitment to uphold international as well as national obligations to bring to trial those responsible for committing core crimes. According to the SPO itself,

> implicit in the decision to prosecute was the acceptance of the TGE of its *international* and *national* legal obligations to investigate and bring to justice those responsible for *Dergue*-era crimes.[19]

However, the nature of the international or national obligation on which the TGE allegedly based its decision to prosecute was never fully explained. This begs the question of whether there indeed was an obligation for the TGE to prosecute those crimes; question which is discussed in the following sections.

3.2.1 *The TGE's International Obligation to Prosecute the SPO's Core Crimes*

Neither the notion of ICL, in general, nor the scope of the obligation to prosecute, in particular, is concerned with crimes of a purely domestic nature. Accordingly, in assessing whether the TGE was indeed under an international obligation to prosecute the *Dergue* era crimes, the following section discusses only the international crimes identified as such by the SPO, namely, genocide and related offenses as well as war crimes.

3.2.1.1 Genocide

For two of the SPO-crimes, namely, genocide and provocation and preparation to commit, permit or support acts of genocide, the FHC stated in *Mengistu et al.* that Ethiopia had both an *obligation* and a *right* to prosecute these crimes using its own courts.[20] The statement was made as part of a response to a preliminary objection raised by the defendants claiming that an international tribunal like the one in Nuremberg should adjudicate their case.[21] As a result, the court's analysis focused on Ethiopia's sovereign right to prosecute international crimes using its own courts, and consequently did not elaborate on the issue of the nature and source of Ethiopia's obligation to prosecute these crimes.

---

19 SPO Report (1994), *supra* note 7, 559.
20 See FHC, SPO v. *Colonel Mengistu Hailemariam et al.*, (Ruling on Preliminary Objections), 10 October 1995, File No. 1/87 77.
21 Ibid.

On its part, the SPO underlined in its final report that 'neither the government of Ethiopia nor any other party had the right to amnesty or pardon crimes involving genocide or mass destruction'.[22] Besides, in a report discussing the extradition of Mengistu Hailemariam from Zimbabwe to Ethiopia in order to be tried for genocide, the SPO implied that the Genocide Convention imposed on the TGE an obligation to prosecute genocide.[23] Several writers have opined, in conformity with the SPO's assertion, that the obligation to bring to trial those allegedly involved in the commission of the crime of genocide emanated from the Genocide Convention, which Ethiopia had ratified some twenty-five years before the *Dergue* took control of the country.[24]

It is true that the Genocide Convention imposes a duty to prosecute pursuant to its Article VI.[25] This Article states that 'persons charged with genocide or any of the other acts enumerated in article III shall be tried by a competent tribunal of the State in the territory of which the act was committed...' Article VI restricts the scope of the duty to prosecute genocide in the sense that a state party may consider that such a duty does not exist when the

---

22   This was primarily argued by the SPO to indicate that it was the right of the victims to grant or not to grant amnesty for atrocities committed against them. See Special Prosecutor's Office, *Dem Yazele Dossie: Begizeyawi Wetaderawi Dergue Weyem Mengist Abalat Benetsuhan Zegoch Laye Yetefetseme Wenjel Zegeba* (Addis Ababa: Far-East Trading P.L.C., 2010), 168. Translation by the author. The original (Amharic) version reads:
የኢትዮጵያ መንግስት ወይም ሌላ ማናቸውም ወገን የዘር ማጥፋት ወይም የጅምላ ጭፍጨፋ ወንጀሎችን አስመልክቶ ምህረት ወይም ይቅርታ የማድረግ ሥልጣን የለዉም።.

23   SPO Report (1994), *supra* note 7, 569–570. The SPO's reference to the Genocide Convention in its report of 1994 was however aimed at indicating and emphasizing the existence for Zimbabwe of a duty to extradite col. Mengistu Hailemariam to Ethiopia.

24   See D.S. Reta, *National Prosecution and Transitional Justice: The Case of Ethiopia*, (PhD Dissertation, University of Warwick School of Law, 2014), 101; G.A. Aneme, 'Apology and trials: The case of the Red Terror trials in Ethiopia' (2006) 6(1) *African Human Rights Law Journal* 64–84, 75; Haile-Mariam 'The Quest for Justice and Reconciliation', *supra* note 7, 703–704; J. Sarkin 'Transitional justice and the prosecution model: The experience of Ethiopia' (1999) 2(1) *Journal of Law, Democracy and Development* 253–266, 259; J.V. Mayfield, 'The Prosecution of War Crimes and Respect for Human Rights: Ethiopia's Balancing Act' (1995) 9 (1) *Emory International Law Journal* 553-594,570; Human Rights Watch, 'Ethiopia: Reckoning under the Law', *supra* note 5, 14; Report of the Office of the Special Prosecutor 'The Special Prosecution Process of War Criminals and Human Rights Violation in Ethiopia', *supra* note 21, 570.

25   The duty to prosecute an act of genocide emanates from Article IV of the Genocide Convention. See also C.J. Tams et.al., *Convention on the Prevention and Punishment of the Crime of Genocide: A Commentary* (Munich: C. H. Beck, 2014) 198–199. Articles I and VI of the Genocide Convention are also relevant. Article I, which imposes the duty to punish, is considered to be an introductory clause whose scope is determined by the other two Articles, IV and VI. See ibid., 43–45.

crime was committed outside its territory. This exception is not relevant as far as the Ethiopian situation is concerned since virtually all of the crimes the SPO wanted to prosecute were perpetrated in the territory of Ethiopia by and against its own nationals.[26]

Nevertheless, it is tricky to consider that the TGE was under an obligation to prosecute the *Dergue* era genocide. As will be discussed in more depth in Chapter 4, the contents of the domestic law applied in the SPO cases and the nature of the conducts considered by the SPO as constituting the crime of genocide differs from what is qualified as such by the Genocide Convention. This is notably the case in relation to the protected groups. While the Convention qualifies certain crimes against a limited number of groups (ethnic, racial, national and religious) as genocide, the SPO also used the qualification of genocide for acts perpetrated against certain political groups. Even further, the SPO stated explicitly that there was no genocidal policy that targeted in any form members of groups other than those established on the basis of political affiliation. In the SPO's own words,

> the *Dergue* did not kill a single boy based on which [ethnic, racial, national or religious] group the boy belonged or based on the kind of school the boy went to, but only because of the boy's alleged affiliation to certain political groups such as the EDU [Ethiopian Democratic Union] and the EPRP.[27]

What the SPO considered as genocide was therefore 'an act of destroying members of political groups', which pursuant to Article 281 of the Penal Code of 1957 was indeed qualified as a crime of genocide in Ethiopia.[28] Consequently, the

---

26 The only exception in which the SPO identified and prosecuted crimes committed outside Ethiopia is to be found in the case of *SPO v. Colonel Tesfaye Woldeselassie Eshete*, which involved the prosecution of offences committed in Italy (Rome), Germany (Berlin), and Eritrea (Asmara and Massawa). See FHC, *SPO v. Colonel Tesfaye Woldeselassie Eshete*, (Revised Indictment), 09 November 2000, File No. 268/85, 10–11, 28–30.

27 Translation by the author. See Ethiopian Television, Documentary: findings of human rights abuse during Red Terror era – Part 1 (ETV Documentary part 2, 2010), available at: <http://www.ethiotube.net/video/8194/documentary-findings-of-human-rights-abuses-during-red-terror-era-part-2> accessed 22 September 2015. See also, for instance, FHC, *SPO v. Colonel Mengistu Hailemariam et al.,* (Revised Indictment), 28 November 1995, File No. 1/87. There was no single charge of genocide on racial, religious, ethnic and national groups. See *Dem Yazele Dossie, supra* note 22, 137. A full account of the nature of the genocide that took place, and was prosecuted, in Ethiopia is provided under Chapter 4.

28 The chapeau of Article 281 of the Penal Code states that a crime of genocide takes place when a person commits, organizes, orders, or engages in the prohibited acts '...with intent

validity of the assertion that the Genocide Convention imposed on the TGE a duty to prosecute the *Dergue* era crimes depends on whether the Convention imposes such an obligation only with respect to acts conventionally qualified as genocide or whether this obligation extends to crimes domestic law characterizes as such, in this case to the destruction of political groups, which is commonly referred to as *politicide*.[29]

It is important to note that, unlike general human rights treaties such as the International Covenant on Civil and Political Rights (ICCPR) and the European Convention on Human Rights (ECHR),[30] the Genocide Convention is a specific treaty exclusively concerned with the prevention and punishment of genocide. Owing to the specificity of the Convention, and in accordance with the textual meaning of Article VI, the obligation to prosecute that emanates from the Convention is limited to the prosecution of acts of genocide defined as such by the Convention, that is to the prosecution of acts directed against a selective list of protected groups.

Indeed, the obligation to prosecute genocide only operates in relation to the four groups (racial, ethnic, national and religious) explicitly mentioned by the Convention. Given that political groups are not among the protected groups, the only possibility of deriving from the Convention an obligation for States Parties to prosecute genocide against political groups is if such prosecution can be undertaken on the basis of the Convention. That may be the case provided that the international rules of treaty interpretation support the inclusion of political groups in the Convention's list of protected groups. If that fails to be the case, it seems absurd to consider that an obligation to prosecute emanates from a specific treaty like the Genocide Convention for an act that cannot be prosecuted on the basis of that treaty.

---

to destroy, in whole or in part, a national, ethnic, racial, religious or political group ..., whether in time of war or in time of peace'.

29   See however, Aneme 'Apology and trials' *supra* note 24, 74; Haile-Mariam 'The Quest for Justice and Reconciliation', *supra* note 7, 704, *fn*.179. Hailemariam appears to have noted the expansive definition of genocide in Ethiopian law but still insists that the Genocide Convention imposes an obligation to prosecute not only on Ethiopia but also on other countries where some of the *Dergue* officials took refuge. For the opposite view that the Penal Code sufficiently covered the concept of genocide as proscribed under the Genocide Convention and that the obligation to prosecute genocide emanated from the Genocide Convention, see Reta, *National Prosecution and Transitional Justice: The Case of Ethiopia, supra* note 24, 100.

30   Convention for the Protection of Human Rights and Fundamental Freedoms, 213 U.N.T.S. 222, *entered into force* 3 September 1953, *as amended by* Protocols Nos 3, 5, 8, and 11 *which entered into force* on 21 September 1970, 20 December 1971, 1 January 1990, and 1 November 1998 respectively.

Turning to the issue of whether the prosecution of politicide can be undertaken on the basis of the Genocide Convention, it should, first of all, be noted that the Convention contains an exhaustive list of groups, i.e. it only protects the four groups it specifically enumerates.[31] In addition, the exclusion of political groups from the Convention's list of protected groups was a controversial but nevertheless deliberate decision. It was deleted for political reasons and one may not find a firm philosophical or legal justification for the decision which was merely taken in order to reach a compromise.[32]

It is true that several States, including Ethiopia, have expanded the scope of the conventional definition of genocide with respect to the protected groups.[33] This is not *per se* problematic. As noted by the FHC in *SPO v. Mengistu et al.*[34] and, more recently, by the ECtHR in *Vasiliauskas v. Lithuania*, providing for a broader concept of genocide in domestic legislation and applying an expanded definition is not prohibited by the Genocide Convention.[35] This is however different from invoking the Convention to justify the prosecution of acts not covered by it. According to the ECtHR,

> the fact that certain States decided later to criminalise genocide of a political group in their domestic laws does not, as such, alter the reality that the text of the 1948 Convention did not do so.[36]

Any attempt to justify prosecuting genocide directed against political groups by either including political groups within one of the groups already protected in the Genocide Convention or invoking customary international law is hardly convincing. In relation to the 1998 rulings of the Spanish National Audience in the *Augusto Pinochet* case, which interpreted the Convention's definition of genocide as encompassing political groups and all other groups,[37] Schabas

---

31   For a detailed discussion on this, see Chapter 5, section 5.5.
32   Ibid.
33   For the list of States which have extended their domestic provision on genocide to include political groups, see D. L. Nersessian, *Genocide and Political Groups* (Oxford: Oxford University Press, 2010) 269.
34   See *Colonel Mengistu Hailemariam et al.*, (Ruling on Preliminary Objections), *supra* note 20, 110.
35   ECtHR, *Vasiliauskas v. Lithuania,* Grand Chamber, (Judgment), 20 October 2015, Application no. 35343/05, paras 181, 184.
36   Ibid., para. 170.
37   W.A. Schabas, *Genocide in International Law: The Crime of Crimes* (2nd ed., Cambridge: Cambridge University Press, 2009) 170–171. For the *Pinochet* case, see Audiencia Nacional, Auto de la Sala de lo Penal de la Audiencia Nacional confirmando la jurisdicción de España para conocer de los crímenes de genocidio y terrorismo cometidos

explained that the view that customary international law has already broadened the ambit of genocide regarding protected groups is not more than just a 'wishful thinking of some commentators'.[38] One should also bear in mind that, in determining the absence in customary international law of a broader definition of genocide that would protect political groups, the ECtHR's reasoning in *Vasiliauskas v. Lithuania* is based mainly on the fact that all subsequent international instruments (including the 1998 ICC Statute) contain a *verbatim* copy of the Convention's definition of genocide.[39] This overwhelmingly indicates that genocide against political groups is not recognized under customary international law.

Further, because political groups are not protected by the Genocide Convention, invoking this Convention as the law applicable to prosecute genocide against these groups may constitute a violation of the *nullum crimen sine lege* principle, unless, as was the case in Ethiopia, the prosecution is conducted based on – the more extensive – domestic criminal legislation. In support of this point, one may refer again to the ECtHR's decision in *Vasiliauskas v. Lithuania* where the Grand Chamber found that the Lithuanian courts, which had prosecuted political genocide based on the Genocide Convention and interpreted the Convention's terms 'national' or 'ethnic' as encompassing 'partisans' and political groups, had erred in their reasoning, resulting in a violation of Article 7 of the ECHR.[40]

In sum, prosecuting the *Dergue* for genocide against political groups is justified based on the provision of the penal code. Yet, the SPO's assertion in relation to the duty to prosecute is problematic. Invoking the obligation that emanates from the Genocide Convention as the source of the TGE's decision to prosecute politicide amounts to arguing that the Convention applies to matters that fall outside of its scope. Such an argument may not be justified based on the text of the Convention which has exhaustively enumerated the groups it protected for the purpose of genocide.

3.2.1.2 War Crimes

With respect to war crimes against the civilian population as defined by Article 282 of the penal code,[41] it has been widely argued that the TGE's obligation

---

durante la dictadura chilena, (5 November 1998), Case 173/98, available at : <www.derechos.org/nizkor/chile/juicio/audi.html> accessed 12 July 2017.

38 Ibid., 17.
39 *Vasiliauskas v. Lithuania, supra* note 35, para. 175.
40 Ibid., paras 182–186.
41 Article 282 of the Penal Code reads:Whosoever, in time of war, armed conflict or occupation, organizes, orders or engages in, against the civilian population and in violation of

to prosecute resulted from the 1949 Geneva Conventions.[42] There is no doubt that international humanitarian law imposes on all contracting states a duty to prosecute war crimes even when, unlike the approach followed by the Genocide Convention, the crimes were entirely perpetrated outside their respective territory. The duty to prosecute war crimes now exists with respect to the vast majority of States in the world as the Geneva Conventions have received extensive ratification.[43] That duty is nevertheless limited to the 'grave breaches' which, according to the text of the Conventions, can only occur in the context of an international armed conflict as delineated in Article 2 common to the Conventions.[44]

---

the rules of public international law and of international humanitarian conventions: (a) killings, torture or inhuman treatment, including biological experiments, or any other acts involving dire suffering or bodily harm, or injury to mental or physical health; or (b))willful reduction to starvation, destitution or general ruination through the depreciation, counterfeiting or systematic debasement of the currency; or (c) the compulsory movement or dispersion of the population, its systematic deportation, transfer or detention in concentration camps or forced labour camps; or (d) forcible enlistment in the enemy's armed forces, intelligence services or administration; or (e) denationalization or forcible religious conversion; or (f) compulsion to acts of prostitution, debauchery or rape; or (g) measures of intimidation or terror, the taking of hostages or the imposition of collective punishments or reprisals; or (h) the confiscation of estates, the destruction or appropriation of property, the imposition of unlawful or arbitrary taxes or levies, or of taxes or levies disproportionate to the requirements of strict military necessity, is punishable with rigorous imprisonment from five years to life, or, in cases of exceptional gravity, with death.

42 SPO Report (1994), *supra* note 7, 569–570; T.S. Engelschøin, 'Ethiopia: War Crimes and Violations of Human Rights' [1995] 34(9) *Military Law and Law of War Review* 9–32, 14–15; Aneme, 'Apology and Trial: The Case of the Red-Terror Trials in Ethiopia', *supra* note 24, 75; Haile-Mariam, 'The Quest for Justice and Reconciliation', *supra* note 7, 750; Sarkin, 'Transitional justice and the prosecution model', *supra* note 24, 59; Mayfield, 'The Prosecution of War Crimes and Respect for Human Rights', *supra* note 24, 570; Human Rights Watch 'Ethiopia: Reckoning under the Law', *supra* note 5, 14; Reta, *National Prosecution and Transitional Justice: The Case of Ethiopia, supra* note 24, 99–100.

43 There are currently 196 state parties to the 1949 Geneva Conventions. See <https://www.icrc.org/applic/ihl/ihl.nsf/States.xsp?xp_viewStates=XPages_NORMStatesParties&xp_treatySelected=365> accessed 28 September 2019.

44 See Geneva Convention relative to the Protection of Civilian Persons in Time of War, 75 U.N.T.S. 287, *entered into force* 21 October 1950, Articles 146–148; Geneva Convention relative to the Treatment of Prisoners of War, 75 U.N.T.S. 135, *entered into force* 21 October 1950, Articles 129–131; Geneva Convention for the Amelioration of the Condition of Wounded, Sick and Shipwrecked Members of Armed Forces at Sea, 75 U.N.T.S. 85, *entered into force* 21 October 1950, Articles 49–50; and Geneva Convention for the Amelioration of the Condition of the Wounded and Sick in Armed Forces in the Field, 75 U.N.T.S. 31, *entered into force* 21 October 1950, Articles 49–50.

Commendably, and as will be discussed further in other parts of this book,[45] the Penal Code of 1957, in its war crimes provisions, did not distinguish the elements of crimes, the degree of culpability, and the penalty clauses based on the international or non-international nature of the conflict to which the crimes were linked.[46] Perhaps because of this, the parties in the *Dergue* trials did not dispute the context in which the violations of Article 282 had occurred, and the courts did not have to put themselves through the task of classifying the conflicts into international or non-international.[47]

Nonetheless, the manner in which the SPO applied Article 282 to its case against the *Dergue* officials revealed that the crime was committed in the context of a civil war. The episode prosecuted by the SPO as a violation of Article 282 happened in the 1980s when the *Dergue* war planes bombed undefended localities (Hawzien, Chila, and Wukro towns in northern Ethiopia) killing up to a total of 10,000 civilians, as detailed in Chapter 7.[48] Based on IHL, the incidents would constitute a violation of Article 3 common to the Geneva Conventions – not only in terms of the nature of the conflict[49] but also with regards to the nature of the prohibited acts.[50]

---

45 See Chapter 7.
46 The chapeau of 'war crimes against civilian population' under Article 282 of the Penal Code reads: 'Whosoever, in time of war, armed conflict or occupation, orders or engages in, against the civilian population and in violation of the rules of public international law and of international humanitarian conventions'.
47 For details, see Chapter 7, section 7.4.
48 See *Dem Yazele Dossie*, *supra* note 22, 432–433. The SPO reported that it was not possible to substantiate with evidence other allegations of war crimes committed during the *Dergue* regime. See however Chapter 7, section 7.8.
49 Neither the substantiated nor the unsubstantiated allegations of war crimes mentioned by the SPO happened outside the context of an internal armed conflict. The nature of the conflict falls within the definition of non-international armed conflict as it was a 'protracted armed violence between governmental authorities and organized armed groups'. For the definition of non-international armed conflicts envisaged by common Article 3, see ICTY, *Prosecutor* v. *Tadić*, Appeals Chamber, (Decision on the defense motion for interlocutory appeal on jurisdiction), 2 October 1995), IT-94-1-AR72, para. 70. On the contrary, Mehari Redae argued that the atrocities in Ethiopia, in particular during the period of the Red-Terror, were committed in a situation that did not even qualify as an armed conflict. See M. Redae, 'The Ethiopian Genocide Trial' (2002) 1(1) *Ethiopian Law Review* 1–26, 18. Although a conflict of international character was notably fought between Ethiopia and Somalia from 1977–1978 – commonly known as the Ogden War or the Ethio-Somali War – the SPO was not established to investigate possible violations that may have occurred during this war. A full account of the nature of the armed conflicts and the alleged crimes is presented in Chapter 7.
50 In this regard, it should be noted that, in terms of prohibited conducts, Article 282 of the Penal Code is broader than the Common Article 3 prohibitions since it also includes

However, at the time of the *Dergue* trials, violations of Article 3 common to the Geneva Conventions had not yet been qualified as offenses entailing an obligation to prosecute: it was only in 1995 that, pursuant to the decision of the ICTY Appeals Chamber in the *Tadić* case, the scope of such violations as war crimes was for the first time explained by a criminal court.[51] No matter how one may sympathize with the victims of violations of common Article 3 and emphasize the unfairness of discriminating between similar crimes solely based on the nature of the conflict,[52] the Geneva Conventions were not ambiguous regarding the non-existence of an obligation to prosecute war crimes perpetrated in non-international armed conflicts.

Aside from common Article 3, the Second Additional Protocol to the Geneva Conventions (AP II)[53] was also cited to infer Ethiopia's obligation to prosecute war crimes committed during the *Dergue* regime.[54] Yet, AP II – an instrument that has been referred to as the first real legal instrument for the protection of victims of non-international armed conflicts[55] – did not impose on state parties an obligation to prosecute. And even if it had, it was only ratified by the TGE two years *after* the decision to prosecute was publicized.[56]

---

grave breaches. However, in the Hawzien, Chila, and Wukro incidents, the SPO charged the defendants with acts that were prohibited both under Article 282 (a) of the penal code and Article 3(a) common to the Geneva Conventions, namely 'violence to life and person, in particular murder of all kinds, mutilation, cruel treatment and torture'. See FHC, SPO v. *Legesse Asfaw et al.*, (Judgment), 4 February 2008, File No. 03116. See also Chapter 7, section 7.7.

51 See *Tadić*, *supra* note 49, paras 81–85.
52 See P. Akhavan, 'Universal Repression of Crimes Against Humanity' in L.N. Sadat (ed.,) *Forging a Convention for Crimes Against Humanity* (Cambridge: Cambridge University Press, 2011) 28–42, 29.
53 Protocol Additional to the Geneva Conventions of 12 August 1949, and Relating to the Protection of Victims of Non-International Armed Conflicts (Protocol II), 1125 U.N.T.S. 609, *entered into force* 7 December 1978.
54 See T Engelschøin, 'Ethiopia: War Crimes and Violations of Human Rights' *supra* note 42, 15. He argues that, even if Ethiopia had not ratified the 1977 Additional Protocols by the time the SPO was established, the binding nature of the Protocols emanated from the fact that they were already regarded as part of customary international law. This position is however debatable.
55 See AP II, Preamble, para. 3. The Protocol was needed to ensure a better protection for the victims of armed conflicts not of an international character. See also S.S. Junod, 'Commentary on Protocol II' in Sandoz and others (eds.), *Commentary on the Additional Protocols of 8 June 1977 to the Geneva Conventions of 12 August 1949* (Leiden: Martinus Nijhoff Publishers, 1987) 1320, para. 4337.
56 Ethiopia ratified AP II on 9 July 1994, about two years after the establishment of the SPO. See <https://www.icrc.org/applic/ihl/ihl.nsf/vwTreatiesByCountrySelected.xsp?xp_countrySelected=ET&nv=4>, accessed 25 March 2019.

Furthermore, even if the Rome Statute of the ICC does envisage the crystallization of an obligation to prosecute certain war crimes committed in non-international armed conflicts,[57] this development fails to be relevant to examine the TGE's decision to prosecute the *Dergue*, because: *i*) Ethiopia is not party to the Rome Statute, and *ii*) most importantly, the TGE's decision to prosecute antedates the signing and entry into force of the Rome Statute by almost a decade. There was thus no international obligation that could have compelled the TGE to prosecute war crimes committed during the *Dergue* regime.

3.2.2   *The TGE's National Obligation to Prosecute the SPO Crimes*

The SPO contended that:

> the TGE's decision to bring to trial those responsible for the atrocities – a decision which it carried out notably by designating an investigative body and by establishing an impartial judiciary – *was a response to* an obligation under international law and *its national law*.[58]

The SPO did not specify the alleged national law that prescribed the duty to prosecute the *Dergue* era crimes; in fact, it did not indicate whether it was a duty to prosecute or a duty to designate an investigative body and an impartial judiciary that was enacted in the alleged national law. In a report published immediately after the establishment of the SPO, African Watch identified four domestic pieces of legislation that it considered as declaring Ethiopia's duty to prosecute the *Dergue* era crimes. According to the report,

> Ethiopian law has recognized a duty to prosecute crimes against humanity by, for example, the incorporation of "offences Against the Law of Nations" in Article 281 and the following of the Penal Code of 1957. The TGE has recognized its duties under these international human rights standards [the Genocide Convention, the Torture Convention, and the Geneva Conventions] in the wording of the Transitional Charter, in the

---

57   For details on the status of common Article 3 violations under the Rome Statute of the ICC, see M. Bothe, 'War Crimes' in Cassese and others (eds.), *The Rome Statute of the International Criminal Court: A Commentary* (Oxford: Oxford University Press, 2002) 417–424.

58   *Dem Yazele Dossie*, *supra* note 22, 168. Translation by the author. The original (Amharic) version reads:
የኢትዮጵያ የሽግር መንግስት ያደረገው ቢኖር አንደ መንግስትነቱ ዓለምዓቀፍና አገር አቀፍ የሕግ...ግዴታውን ለመወጣት መርማሪ አካል መሰየም ነጻ ፍርድ ቤት ማቋቋም ነው።.

plans to incorporate protection of human rights in the new constitution, and in the proclamation establishing the Special Prosecutor's Office.[59]

According to African Watch, therefore, the fact that a particular conduct is proscribed under national penal legislation implies the materialization of a duty to prosecute the perpetration of that particular conduct. Indeed, domestic criminalization is crucial; even where a state unequivocally accepts a duty to prosecute, the absence of prior domestic criminalization undoubtedly poses a challenge to bring those responsible to trial due to the non-retroactivity aspect of the principle of legality.[60] Nonetheless, as far as Ethiopian law is concerned, domestic criminalization is not necessarily an indicator of a commitment to bring offenders to trial. For the following two reasons, a criminal proscription in Ethiopia should not be understood as connoting something more than the making of an option available for the state to prosecute a criminal transgression.

Firstly, as is the case with several other states, Ethiopian criminal law recognizes the application of 'the principle of opportunity' whereby the public prosecutor may refuse to pursue prosecution on grounds of interests of justice, despite the availability of sufficient evidence to go forward with a case.[61] This form of refusal, unlike other forms of refusal of prosecution on grounds such as the offense being subject to pardon or amnesty, only requires the existence of an order of the Ministry of Justice to that effect.[62] In fact, such a prosecutorial discretion not to institute a proceeding is absolute, in the sense that it is not to be subjected to judicial review, as opposed to other forms of refusal where the interested party could contest a decision not to prosecute before a court of law.[63] As a result, the existence of domestic criminalization does not, by and of itself, establish a duty to prosecute in Ethiopian law.

---

59 Human Rights Watch, 'Ethiopia: Reckoning Under the Law', *supra* note 5, 14. Emphasis added.

60 For further discussion, see Chapter 7, section 7.5.2.

61 See The Criminal Procedure Code Proclamation, Extraordinary Issue No. 1 of 1961: Proclamation No.185/1961 *entered into force* 2 November 1961 [Hereinafter the Criminal Procedure Code of Ethiopia], Article 42(1)(d), which states, 'no proceedings shall be instituted where he public prosecutor is instructed not to institute proceedings in the public interest by the Minister [of Justice] by order under his hand'. For similar provisions in other jurisdictions, see, for instance, The Dutch Code of Criminal Procedure, Articles 67 (2) and 242 (2), Unofficial English translation available at<http://www.ejtn.eu/PageFiles/6533/2014%20seminars/Omsenie/WetboekvanStrafvordering_ENG_PV.pdf accessed 28 September 2019.

62 See the Criminal Procedure Code of Ethiopia, Article 41(1)(c).

63 A refusal to prosecute may also result in cases where the public prosecutor is of the opinion that there is not sufficient evidence to justify a conviction, or there is no possibility of

Secondly, the concept of a national obligation to prosecute seems in general to lack a firm and sustainable binding nature. It establishes itself on a fragile expectation: if a national law forbids amnesty from being introduced with respect to a certain category of crimes, the state will *a fortiori* have a duty to prosecute the excluded crimes at all times. If this expectation might be legally convincing, it is however politically frail. The national law forbidding amnesty is an ordinary law and, as such, is easily amendable. And even in the unlikely case that such law had constitutional status, in a period of post-conflict transition, the constitution itself is not immune from amendment or repeal.[64] This holds very true for Ethiopia, where no constitution survived through successive regimes due to the longstanding custom that a particular regime shall either have no constitution at all or forge its own unique – and ephemeral – constitution.[65]

Still, for the purposes of the study conducted in this book, it is important to identify whether there was a national obligation to prosecute enshrined in domestic legislation, on which the TGE's decision might have been based. As mentioned above, commentators who argued that the TGE was under a national obligation to prosecute have cited four national pieces of legislation in support of their claim: the Penal Code of 1957, the Transitional Period Charter, the SPO Proclamation, and the 1995 FDRE Constitution.

Yet, the only legislation worth considering here is the Penal Code of 1957, which was not only in force at the time the decision to prosecute was reached but was also the main substantive law used by the SPO to prosecute the *Dergue* era crimes.[66] The other three national laws are not to be discussed

---

finding the accused and the case is one which may not be tried in his absence. See ibid., Article 41 (1)(a) and (b). An interested party that disagrees with the prosecutor's refusal to prosecute may apply to court 'for an order that the public prosecutor institutes proceedings'. See ibid., Article 44 (2).

64 See M. Brandat, *Constitutional Assistance in Post-Conflict Countries: The UN Experience: Cambodia, East Timor & Afghanistan* (June 2005), United Nations Development Program, 1, available at: <https://www.agora-parl.org/sites/default/files/Constitutional%20Assistance%20in%20Post-Conflict%20Countries.pdf> accessed 25 March 2019.

65 The first Constitution in Ethiopia was promulgated in 1931. It was revised and replaced by the 1955 Constitution mainly to accommodate issues related to Eritrea's confederation. Following the 1974's regime change, the 1955 Constitution was suspended. The *Dergue* ruled the country without constitution until 1987 when it drafted the People's Democratic Republic of Ethiopia's Constitution. In 1991, the TGE enacted a Transitional Charter and the 1987 Constitution became in applicable. In 1994, the FDRE enacted its own Constitution, which is applicable to date.

66 The SPO's use of the Penal Code as the only applicable law to prosecute the *Dergue* era crimes is discussed further under Chapters 5 and 7.

here, because: *i*) the Transitional Period Charter did not, as discussed above, impose any form of obligation to prosecute the *Dergue* era crimes;[67] *ii*) the SPO Proclamation was enacted only to announce the decision to prosecute, not to impose an obligation to prosecute; and *iii*) the 1995 FDRE Constitution did not exist at the time the decision to prosecute was reached.

The enactment of the Penal Code of 1957 was undertaken with the aim of fundamentally reforming the Ethiopian criminal justice system. By repealing the 1930 Penal Code together with all of its amendments,[68] the Penal Code was promulgated as the only comprehensive substantive criminal legislation. As regards prosecution and punishment, the principle that 'punishment cannot be avoided since it acts as a deterrent to crimes' served as a basis for the code.[69] This, however, did not imply an obligation to prosecute each and every violation of the Penal Code's provisions.

First of all, it should be noted that it could not have been possible for the Penal Code to impose an obligation to prosecute. This is mainly because it was enacted under the auspices of the 1955 Revised Constitution,[70] which had already reserved for the Emperor a power to grant amnesty to offenders, and thus rendered the prosecution of alleged criminals optional.[71] Second of all, the Penal Code expressly recognized that prosecution, though normal under normal circumstances, may not be pursued for pragmatic reasons. According Article 240 (1) of the Penal Code,

> an amnesty may be granted in respect to certain offences or certain classes of offenders, either absolutely or subject to certain conditions or obligations by the appropriate constitutional authority when circumstances seem to indicate that such a measure is expedient.[72]

This Article is the first of its kind as neither the 1955 Revised Constitution nor any other pre-existing legislation contained as explicit and detailed an amnesty provision.[73] More significantly, the Article was given unrestricted

---

67 See the discussion Chapter 2, sub-section 2.2.2.
68 The Penal Code of 1957, Preamble, para. 3.
69 Ibid., Preface, v.
70 See ibid., Preface, para. 8.
71 See 1955 Revised Constitution of Ethiopia, *entered in to force* 2 November 1955, Article 35.
72 The Penal Code of 1957, Article 240 (1).
73 Under the 1930 Penal Code, the first criminal law legislation in Ethiopia, amnesty was not indicated as one of the factors that discontinue prosecution and penalty. See the Penal Code of the Empire of Ethiopia 1930, *entered into force* September 1930. The code, under its Articles 145–151, mentioned only the death of the defendant and the expiry of a period of limitation as reasons for which the prosecutor shall not proceed with a case. The

scope as regards the type of crimes which could lead to an amnesty. An alleged or actual perpetrator could thus be granted amnesty irrespective of the domestic or international nature of the perpetrated crime. This can be inferred from the absence of a provision in the Penal Code, or in any other applicable law, excluding certain categories of crimes from being subjected to amnesty.

Amnesty, as understood by the Penal Code, applies to both pre- and post-prosecution stages: it could be granted to bar or discontinue a prosecution or to put an end to the enforcement of a sentence. In the latter's sense, amnesty served as means to commute a sentence and appeared similar to pardon.[74] However, unlike pardon, amnesty cancels the sentence as well as all its other consequences under criminal law and renders the conviction non- existent.[75] In relation to this, it is important to note that, pursuant to Article 119 of the Penal Code, amnesty also cancels a death sentence: put differently, all capital offenses – including core crimes – may potentially lead to an amnesty.

Moreover, the *Dergue* regime increased the reach of the Penal Code's amnesty provisions by enacting legislation and issuing decrees. If it revoked amnesties which had been granted by the Haileselassie regime through the Special Court Establishment Proclamation of 1981,[76] it however retained the amnesty provisions of the Penal Code,[77] applicable to offenses under the jurisdiction of the Special Court.[78] As a result, the Penal Code of 1957's amnesty provisions were extended to cover offenses under the Revised Special Penal Code of 1981.[79] In practice too, the *Dergue* regime granted amnesty on more than one occasion; it issued specific decrees in 1975,[80]

---

general nature of the criminal justice system as could be inferred from various aspects of the code, in particular the issues of instituting criminal proceedings or imposing penalties, were however highly dependent on imperial discretions.

74 See the Penal Code of 1957, Article 239.
75 See ibid., Article 240(2).
76 A Proclamation to Provide for the Establishment of a Special Court: Proclamation No.215/1981.
77 Moreover, from the reading of Article 240 (2) of the Penal Code in conjunction with Articles 42(c) and 130(c) of the Criminal Procedure Code of Ethiopia, it is clear that amnesty could be granted at any time – before, during or after a trial.
78 Proclamation No.215/1981, *supra* note 71, Article 17.
79 The Revised Special Penal Code, Proclamation No 241/1981 *entered into force* 8 September 1981.
80 The 1975 Amnesty Proclamation (A proclamation to provide for the granting of amnesty to outlaws who have committed homicide and other offences, Proclamation No.29/1975, *entered into force* 4 February 1975) granted amnesty for every Ethiopian hiding in the villages, bushes or towns who had committed homicide, robbery or other offenses. See ibid., Article 2. The proclamation attached a condition to the amnesty that the person

1980,[81] and 1989,[82] which amnestied wide-ranging categories of grave offenses.[83]

In sum, even though core crimes were never *de jure* amnestied in Ethiopia, probably because there was no formal allegation concerning their perpetration, they were never given a special status as far as amnesty or prosecution was concerned. In light of the foregoing, the argument that the Penal Code imposed an obligation on the TGE to bring to trial those responsible for the SPO-crimes is therefore unconvincing. Although criminalization implies that a state may, under ordinary circumstances, prosecute offenses, the Penal Code did not contain a provision that imposed a duty to prosecute on the TGE either expressly or in any other way such as through declaring that the SPO-crimes were not to be subjected to amnesty.

3.3 The Absence of Actual or Perceived Adversary

This section argues that one of the reasons that encouraged the TGE to bring to trial officials and affiliates of the *Dergue* regime could be the fact that the officials of the deposed regime were not in a position to negotiate terms of the transition, as discussed above in relation to the intricacies of the London Conference. In addition to that, members and sympathizers of the *Dergue*

---

granted amnesty shall engage in peaceful occupation and reconcile with his victims (private opponents) with the cooperation of elders in accordance with the custom and usage applicable. Ibid., Articles 3 and 4.

81   The 1980 Proclamation for Repatriation of Ethiopian Refugees in the Republic of Djibouti, Proclamation No. 183/1980, exempted all Ethiopian refugees in Djibouti from prosecution for any crime committed by them for political purposes before they had left Ethiopia or prior to the date of their return to Ethiopia. Ibid., Article 6.

82   See High Commissioner for the Implementation of the National Peace Call Establishment Decree, Council of State Special Decree No.8/1989, *entered into force* 25 February 1989. The whole idea of the national peace call was to provide amnesty in exchange for resumption of 'normal life'. The High Commissioner for national peace call was established to facilitate conditions for peace and to receive citizens resuming 'normal life'. See ibid., Preamble, paras 3 and 4.

83   For instance, the crime of 'treason against the mother land' was amnestied during the later period of the *Dergue* regime. In 1989, the Council of State issued a special decree to announce a peace call to those it referred to as 'Ethiopians roaming in the desert and in foreign lands with destructive missions in mind'. Given the circumstances of the time, the decree was referring to those participating in war of liberation against the state. At the time, engaging in an armed activity against the state constituted an act of treason against the mother land pursuant to Article 2 of the Revised Special Penal Code.

regime were viewed by the incoming powers as incapable of posing a threat to the peace and longevity of the new political order.

In several countries, various forms of amnesties have been introduced as a response to curb actual or potential protests against the state.[84] In cases involving a regime change, the bargaining power of the parties that participated at the peace talks leading to the establishment of a transitional government determines the likelihood of employing amnesty or prosecution. The more powerful the out-going government is the more likely amnesties are introduced in its favour. In Chile, for instance, General Augusto Pinochet Ugarte, under whose control the military power remained until 1990, explicitly warned the new government not to ignore the 1978 amnesty[85] and 'not to touch a single hair of a single soldier'.[86] Likewise, in Argentina, where the shift in power balances played a significant role in shaping the country's search for justice, the military actively resisted accountability by enacting a blanket self-amnesty law for crimes committed between1973–1982.[87] This amnesty was eventually lifted by the Supreme Court in 2005 on the ground that it violated international law, which, according to the Court, has precedence over national law.[88]

With respect to Ethiopia's situation, the fact that the *Dergue*, a regime that once had the most powerful military in sub-Saharan Africa,[89] became not more than a disintegrated and harmless power was noted even before the beginning of the London peace talks.[90] In particular, the incoming powers, notably

---

84   L. Mallinder, 'Exploring the Practice of States in Introducing Amnesties, Study submitted for the International Conference 'Building a Future on Peace and Justice', (Nuremberg, 25–27 June 2007), ii.

85   Decree Law 2.191 of April 1978 (Chile).

86   See SPO Report (1994), *supra* note 7, 454.

87   For a detailed discussion, see P. Engstrom and G. Pereira, 'From Amnesty to Accountability: Ebb and Flow in the Search for Justice in Argentina' in F. Lessa and L.A. Payne (eds.), *Amnesty in the Age of Human Rights Accountability: Comparative and International Perspectives* (Cambridge: Cambridge University Press, 2012) 97–122.

88   See Ch.A.E. Bakker, 'A Full Stop to Amnesty in Argentina: The Simón Case' 2005 (3) *Journal of International Criminal Justice* 1106–1120, 1111–1113.

89   See N. Colletta *et al.*, 'Case Studies in War-to-Peace Transition: the Demobilization and Reintegration of Ex-Combatants in Ethiopia, Namibia, and Uganda' The World Bank (Washington, D.C.: 30 June 1996) 27, available at: <http://documents.worldbank.org/curated/en/1996/06/696461/case-studies-war-to-peace-transition-demobilization-reintegration-ex-combatants-ethiopia-namibia-uganda> accessed 28 March 2019.

90   See *The New York Times* reporting the views that 'a Western diplomat predicted that the Government and guerrillas would attend the London talks, and that Addis Ababa would have little left to bargain with'. C Krauss, 'Ethiopia's Dictator Flees: Officials Seeking U.S. Help', *The New York Times*, 22 May 1991, available at: <<http://www.nytimes.com/1991/05/22/world/ethiopia-s-dictator-flees-officials-seeking-us-help.html?pagewanted=all> accessed 20 March 2019.

the EPRDF, were confident that the *Dergue* was facing a complete defeat and would therefore not pose a challenge to the political transition. For instance, at the end of the London peace talks, Mr. Melese Zenawi, the leader of the EPRDF and of the TPLF, was quoted saying, in reference to Mr. Tesfaye Dinka, that 'the government represented nothing'.[91]

The turning point for the *Dergue*'s military collapse seems to be Colonel Mengistu's abrupt departure to Zimbabwe, which caused the army to disintegrate and army-generals to flee.[92] The final shift in the balance of power that enabled the rebel forces to dominate both the military and the politics of the country ensued a unilateral ceasefire declared by General Tesfaye Geberekidan, the acting president following Mengistu's departure.[93] A week earlier, on 23 May 1991, the rebel forces had already rejected Geberekidan's call to start a joint ceasefire and his plea to establish an interim-government.[94] The unilateral ceasefire occurred in the midst of the London talks, and there was literally no army under *Dergue*'s control by the time the rebel forces moved to capture Addis Ababa.[95]

On top of that, it was very shortly after Addis Ababa was under their control that the EPRDF, together with the EPLF and the OLF, demobilized the whole army of the *Dergue*. This was accomplished even before the EPRDF issued a directive ordering members and officials of the *Dergue* to turn themselves in.[96] As mentioned above, it was also before the establishment of the TGE that thousands of the *Dergue*'s ex-soldiers were arrested and detained.

---

91 See, B Harden, 'Rebel leaders Pledges Coalition Government, then Free Elections', *The Washington Post*, 29 May 1991, available at: <https://www.washingtonpost.com/archive/politics/1991/05/29/rebel-leader-pledges-coalition-government-then-free-elections/a5818143-9397-470d-a1b2-b44e28e9e98d/> accessed 25 March 2019. In reference to Mr. Dinka's protest against the peace talks it was reported that this protest, however, did not appear to bother either the rebels or the Americans. Cohen said the boycott meant nothing to the progress of the talks because rebels hold all the power. Meles said Dinka 'represented nothing'.

92 See T. Haile-Selassie, *The Ethiopian Revolution 1974–1991: From a Monarchical Autocracy to a Military Oligarchy* (London: Kegan Paul International, 1997), 328; G. Tereke, *The Ethiopian Revolution: War in the Horn of Africa* (New Haven: Yale University Press, 2009), 309–312.

93 Ibid.

94 See 'Ethiopian President Asks for Cease-Fire', *The Stanford Daily*, 23 May 1991, available at: <http://stanforddailyarchive.com/cgi-bin/stanford?a=d&d=stanford19910523-01.2.16> accessed 25 March 2019.

95 See Haile-Selassie, *The Ethiopian Revolution*, supra note 92, 328; Tereke, *The Ethiopian Revolution: War in the Horn of Africa*, supra note 92, 309–312.

96 See Colletta *et al.*, 'Case Studies in War-to-Peace Transition' supra note 89, 27–34. See also W.L. Kidane, 'The Ethiopia 'Red Terror' Trials' in M.C. Bassiouni (ed.), *Post-Conflict Justice* (Ardsley: Transnational Publishers, 2001) 667–694, 671.

Even though some low-level protests by pro-*Dergue* civilians were seen mainly in Addis Ababa at the beginning of the EPRDF's rule,[97] a directive was soon issued and the situation was put under control by the provisional government. Consequently, all sorts of demonstrations were officially and successfully banned throughout the country until 12 August 1991.[98] Thus, threats from the military as well as from its civilian supporters, if any, were well under control. As a result, there was no one from the deposed regime to re-raise the amnesty issue that Mr. Tesfaye Dinka had attempted to negotiate in London.[99]

It is true that threats, either actual or perceived, may take various forms, and, besides the ability to organize and manage a military or civilian protest, power may be defined in reference to the capacity to control and direct the economy of a given country. Where a certain group substantially controls the economy, there is a possibility for that group to negotiate terms of post-conflict transition, including amnesty. For instance, the introduction of amnesty within South Africa's TRC was partly needed so as not to endanger the economic interests of the country, because the country's 'overwhelming economic power resided in a few major business groupings with huge bargaining power vis-à-vis the state'.[100]

However, such a scenario did not occur in Ethiopia due to *Dergue's* adoption of socialism, the political and economic ideology implemented by the regime as a groundwork to transform the country into communism. Pursuant to legislation issued in particular between 1974 and 1975, such as Proclamations No.

---

97 A.G. Selassie, 'Ethiopia: Problems and Prospects for Democracy' (1992) (1) *William & Mary Bill of Rights Journal* 205–226, 212. According to Amnesty International's report, over 20,000 suspected government opponents were arrested in 1991 and 1992 and remained in detention without charge or trial, without observance of legal formalities or safeguards, and in many cases *incommunicado*. See Amnesty International, 'Ethiopia: Report of 1994' (Amnesty International, January 1994), available at: <http://www.refworld.org/docid/3ae6a9f512.html> accessed 25 March 2019.

98 See Selassie, 'Ethiopia: Problems and Prospects for Democracy', *supra* note 97, 212.

99 In a similar vein, Human Rights Watch argued that the fact that the Mengistu regime and its army were completely defeated and did not appear to pose a military threat to the new government may be the most important factor in favor of the decision to prosecute. See Human Rights Watch, 'Ethiopia: Reckoning under the Law', *supra* note 5, 42.

100 See for instance, *Report of Truth and Reconciliation Commission of South Africa, V. IV* (1998), para. 48, available at <http://www.justice.gov.za/trc/report/finalreport/Volume%204.pdf> accessed 28 September 2019. See also B. Hamber and S. Kibble, *From Truth to Transformation: The Truth and Reconciliation Commission in South Africa*, Catholic Institute for International Relations, February 1999, available at: <http://www.csvr.org.za/publications/1714-from-truth-to-transformation-the-truth-and-reconciliation-commission-in-south-africa> accessed 28 September 2019.

26/1974,[101] No. 31/1975,[102] and No. 47/1975,[103] the 'broad masses', to borrow the expression used by the *Dergue* to refer to itself, gained ownership and control of the means of production and distribution. This made both the military power[104] and the State's economy to indivisibly rest in the hands of the same entity, the *Dergue*. However, as soon as the *Dergue* officials were militarily defeated, they lost every sort of control they had over the economy of the country. As a result, by 1991, the *Dergue* was left with neither real nor perceived economic power that it could have used as a leverage to pressure the TGE into granting an amnesty.[105]

That the *Dergue*'s total loss of power helped the TGE opt for a decision to prosecute was also reflected in statements made during the trial process. In the form of a preliminary objection to the charges brought against them, the *Dergue* officials questioned the legitimacy of the TGE's decision to prosecute on the basis that it was not good for the future of the country.[106] The defendants argued that Ethiopia should have taken a lesson from South Africa, a country to which they referred as 'too busy to hate'.[107] The SPO responded that 'South Africa accepted national reconciliation because Nelson Mandela was pressured into it by white army-generals', indicating it as a missing scenario in Ethiopia's transition where the decision to prosecute was a result of a shift in a balance of power.[108]

---

101   Government Ownership and Control of the Means of Production Proclamation, Proclamation No. 26 of 1974, *entered into force,* 7 February 1975.
102   Public Ownership of Rural Lands Proclamation, Proclamation No. 31 of 1975, *entered into force,* 4 March 1975.
103   Government Ownership of Urban Lands and Extra Houses Proclamation: Proclamation No. 47/1975, *entered into force,* 7 August 1975.
104   In 1974, the *Dergue* assumed power as a provisional military government established pursuant to Proclamation No. 1/1974. See Provisional Military Government Establishment Proclamation, Proclamation No. 1 of 1974, *entered into force,* 12 September 1974. Even though there was an indication that a civilian government would be established, the military managed to hold on to power until its total demise in 1991.
105   For a comparison of the South African and Ethiopian experiences in relation to the influence of the economic power of the incoming and the outgoing governments on deciding between reconciliation and prosecution, see E. van Huyssteen, 'Building State & Nation: Justice, Reconciliation & Democratization in Ethiopia & South Africa' in K. Tronvoll *et al.* (eds.), *The Ethiopian Red Terror Trials: Transitional Justice Challenged* (Martlesham: James Currey, 2009) 98–115, 101–102.
106   TSC, SPO v. *Colonel Ayanaw Mengistie et al.,* (Ruling on Preliminary Objections), 23 November 1999, File No. 3/90, 9.
107   Ibid.
108   Ibid., 11.

For the SPO, the absence of any adversary is apparently among the few factors without which the decision to prosecute could not have been reached and implemented. In its final summary of the overall trial process, the SPO wrote, by comparing Ethiopia's experience with that of other (unnamed) countries,

> A popular support, the availability of relevant law, and *the complete removal of the civilian and military institutions of the Dergue administration,* had created a favourable condition for the implementation of the aforementioned laudable decision [to prosecute]. This was not the case for several other countries.[109]

3.4 Perpetrators' Lack of Remorse and Apology

It was reported that some of the *Dergue* officials interned by the TGE requested the government of Ethiopia to adopt an approach of national reconciliation that would have offered amnesty instead of prosecution.[110] According to the request,

> there is and will be nothing one can do to bring back the dead to life, there should be a national reconciliation. A magnanimous decision by the government is a better choice so that wounds heal and resentments fade away.[111]

The government did not attend to their request. The SPO, in explaining why it was denied, stated that 'the request is simply a question misplaced'.[112] It also added that such a suggestion violated the rights of the victims and allowed

---

109   See *Dem Yazele Dossie, supra* note 22, 439. Emphasis added. Translation by the author. The original (Amharic) version reads:
ከላይ ለተጠቀሰው የሚመሰገን ዉሳኔ ተፈፃሚነት የሕዝብ ድጋፍ፤ አግባብነት ያለው ሕግ ማኖርና የደርግ መንግስት የሲቪልን የጦር ተቋም ፍፁም መወገድ አመቺ ሁኔታን ፈጠሩ። ይህ የበዙ አገሮች መልካም አጋጣሚ አልነበረም።.

110   Ibid., 167.

111   See ibid. Translation by the Author. The original (Amharic) version reads: ምንም ብናደርግ የሞቱትን መልሰን ስለማናገኛቸው ብሔራዊ እርቅ መደረግ አለበት። ደም እንዲደርቅ ቂም እንዲፋቅ ልብ ሰፊነት ያካተተ የመንግስት ዉሳኔ የተሻለ አማራጭ ነው The context and exact time of this request were not mentioned in the record of the SPO. It is however possible to assume that this was done after the decision to prosecute was already announced as there appears no evidence of similar communications while the defendants were in detention. See also the discussion at the end of this section.

112   Ibid.

for the crimes and the perpetrators to remain concealed.[113] In a manner that seems to be suggesting that the choice between prosecution and amnesty was entirely made by the victims, the SPO explained,

> neither the government of Ethiopia nor any other party had the right to amnesty or pardon crimes involving genocide or mass destruction. Such a right belonged to the victims. The defendants could not recognize this, even today. Thousands of victims from the central and regional levels in the country had, by organizing themselves and others into anti-Red-Terror committees, demanded that the government designates an investigating organ and establishes a tribunal in order to bring to trial the officials of the *Dergue* responsible for committing gross violations of human rights. No one shall be able to open this right of the victims to negotiation.[114]

These statements have described the government as a mere facilitator of conditions through which citizens exercise their rights to deny or grant amnesty, which is an interesting concept. The fact that the rights of the victims were deemed non-negotiable acknowledges the idea that the government could only introduce amnesty when the actual victims approved the importance of such a measure.[115] This actually fits into one of the theoretical reasons suggested against the introduction of amnesty for international crimes. According to Ben Chigara, who argues against amnesty from the perspective of justice as fairness, as asserted by Rawls, neither the ousted nor the incoming government 'have ownership of victims' personal rights'.[116] In

---

113   Ibid.
114   Ibid., 168. Translation by the author. The original (Amharic) version reads:
      የኢትዮጵያ መንግስት ወይም ሌላ ማናቸውም ወገን የዘር ማጥፋት ወይም የጅምላ ጭፍጨፋ ወንጀሎችን አስመልክቶ ምህረት ወይም ይቅርታ የማድረግ ሥልጣን የለዉም። ይህ መብት ያለው ከተጎጂዎች ጋር ነው። ይህንን ግን ተከሳሾች ዛሬም ከግምት ዉስጥ ሊያስገቡላቸው አልቻሉም። በብዙ ሺዎች ይሚቆጠሩ ተጎጂዎች ከመአከል አስከ ክልል በጸረ ቀይ ሽብር ኮሚቴነት ትደራጅተው ይሰበአዊ መብት ረገጣ የፈጸሙ የቀድሞ ባለስልጣኖች ሁሉ ለፍርድ አንዲቀርቡ መርማሪ አካልና ፍርድ ቤት አንዲቾቾም ሲጠይቁ ቆይተዋል። በዚህ ተጎጂዎች መብት ማንም ተደራዳሪ ሊያሆን አይችልም።.
115   For possible functions of amnesty, see Lessa and Payne (eds.), *Amnesty in the Age of Human Rights Accountability*, supra note 87, 4. For the argument on amnesty as a lesser evil, see M. Freman, *Necessary Evils: Amnesties and a Search for Justice* (Cambridge: Cambridge University Press, 2009) 23.
116   Chigara's argument refers by extension to Locke, Rousseau, and Kant, as well as to the philosophy of property rights of victims as advocated by Macpherson, Jankélévitch and Asmal. See B. Chigara, *Amnesty in International Law: The Legality under International Law of National Amnesty Laws*, (London: Longman, 2002), 4–5, 12–14.

emphasizing the rights of the victims, the SPO was asserting just that: neither the *Dergue* nor the TGE had a right to introduce amnesty. Besides, as could be seen from practices of countries such as South Africa, an amnesty introduced after a thorough debate among numerous political and community representatives may result in public discontent and the process could ultimately lack popular support.[117]

A closer look into the matter nonetheless reveals that the emphasis given to victims' right was just window dressing. Firstly, the SPO's claim that victims from every corner of the country had asked for prosecution and were opposed to amnesty was hardly true. As Reta's doctoral study on the transitional justice of Ethiopia unveiled, there was no public participation and support behind the TGE's decision to prosecute; it was the EPRDF that formulated the choice without properly seeking a public or victims' opinion on the matter.[118] Haile also noted that there was no direct or indirect communication of opinion on this issue from the public to the TGE (either in the form of a referendum or of a political debate).[119] According to a study recently conducted by Conley, the participation of victims in Ethiopia's transitional period politics was limited to scattered gathering of mourners which aimed more at finding the whereabouts of the dead or disappeared victims.[120]

Secondly, and most importantly, it appears that the TGE rejected the request for amnesty and national reconciliation because it perceived the alleged perpetrators as *unapologetic* and *unremorseful*. The *Dergue*, according to the SPO, did not acknowledge that the victims possess the right to have the perpetrators punished in accordance with the law.[121] The crux of the matter is that the SPO's emphasis was on the defendants' failure to mention and recognize the rights of the victims, but not *per se* on the rights of the victims. It appears that the

---

117 For objections to South Africa's decision to grant amnesties under the TRC scheme, see L.S. Graybill, 'Pursuit of Truth and Reconciliation in South Africa' (1998) 45(1) *Africa Today* 103–133, 114–116; R.A. Wilson, *The Politics of Truth and Reconciliation in South Africa – Legitimizing the Post-Apartheid State* (Cambridge: Cambridge University Press, 2001) 19–23; J.L. Gibson, 'The Truth about Truth and Reconciliation in South Africa' (2005)26(4)*International Political Science Review* 341–361, 348–350.

118 See Reta, *National Prosecution and Transitional Justice: The Case of Ethiopia*, supra note 24, 186–7. It is however stated that there were demands by some of the victims and their families who organized anti-Red-Terror campaigns to ask the government to bring the perpetrators to justice. Ibid. See also, Haile, *Accountability for Crimes of the Past and the Challenges of Criminal Prosecution*, supra note 14, 59–60.

119 Ibid., 59–60.

120 See B. Conley, *Memory from the Margins: Ethiopia's Red Terror Martyrs Memorial Museum* (Gewerbestrasse: Palgrave Macmillan, 2019) 85.

121 *Dem Yazele Dossie*, supra note 22, 168.

government was filled with indignation at the defendants' disingenuous and trivializing remarks, referring to the situation as the 'dead is dead' and suggesting reconciliation on the ground that the living can do nothing to bring the dead back to life.[122]

There is evidence to indicate that, had it felt that the defendants were truly apologetic and regretful of the crimes they had allegedly committed, the government could have considered the granting of an amnesty. To begin with, the potential advantage of a national reconciliation process in healing the wounds of the nation was never disputed. On the contrary, the TGE manifested an inherent inclination towards amnesty and reconciliation. For instance, in addition to the aforementioned statement the EPRDF made at the end of the London Conference, which left amnesty open for consideration,[123] the prime minister's comment in relation to the Rwandan genocide appears to be supporting reconciliation over prosecution:

> revenge would be as backward and primitive as genocide itself ... you are expected to forgive and not forget. You should forgive in the interest of national reconciliation, in the interest of future generations. What you see there...is your past, do not let it cloud your future.[124]

In what further supports the point that it was the *Dergue*'s alleged unwillingness to apologize to the survivors and their families that made the government retreat from considering reconciliation over prosecution, the SPO stated,

> reconciliation begins with apology. It is the wrongdoer that has to apologize. The wrongdoer must admit his wrongs and find forgiveness from his victims. In this regard, our culture is precise. The rest is hypocrisy.[125]

---

122   Ibid., 167.
123   See Harden, 'Rebel leaders Pledges Coalition Government, then Free Elections', *supra* note 91. The EPRDF leader did not rule out a blanket amnesty if Ethiopian voters wanted to grant one.
124   See *Colonel Ayanaw Mengistie et al.*, (Ruling on Preliminary Objections),*supra* note 106, 7. See also H. Tsadik, 'Prosecuting the past- affecting the future: the Ethiopian Transitional Justice Trials' (A SIDA Minor Field Study, Department of Peace and Conflict Research Uppsala University, 2007), 28 available at: <https://www.pcr.uu.se/digitalAssets/654/c_654492-l_1-k_mfs_tsadic.pdf> accessed 24 March 2019.
125   Ibid., p. 168. Emphasis added. Translation by the Author. The original (Amharic) version reads: አርቅ ከይቅርታ ይጀምራል። ይቅርታ የሚጠይቀው አጥፊ ነው። አጥፊ አጥፊነቱን አምኖ የበደለውን ሰው ይቅርታ ማግኘት አለበት። በዚህ በኩል ባህላችን ግልጽ ነው። ሌላዉ ሽፍጥ ነው።.

The same reason was invoked to justify why Ethiopia, unlike South Africa where amnesty was included as an option when perpetrators tell the full truth,[126] opted for prosecution only instead of reconciliation and amnesty. As reported in a minor field study conducted in 2007, the Federal Ombudsman commented,

> the world sees the South African Truth Commission as an example [of successful transitional justice], but it would not work for Ethiopians. The background of the Ethiopian people has to be taken into consideration; it has to be useful in your context. In the Ethiopian context, you never tell the truth if not coerced.[127]

The statement that Ethiopians 'never tell the truth unless coerced' is overly simplistic, if not outrageous. Nonetheless, the Ombudsman's concern is understandable in the sense that truth telling is essential for the process of national reconciliation to succeed. In that regard, the concept of truth seems to have more than a perceived relevance. As Gibson's study established, truth has indeed contributed to reconciliation in South Africa.[128]

In fact, in the context in which it was made, the above statement may be interpreted as referring only to the *Dergue* and its perceived lack of remorse. The SPO and other government officials were not alone in perceiving the *Dergue* as such and several scholars shared this perception. In this regard, one may mention Beharu Zewde, renowned scholar on Ethiopian history, Germachew Alemu, legal scholar, and Alemayehu G. Mariam, professor of political science and persistent online critic of Ethiopian politics. All of them agree on the fact that the *Dergue* lacked remorse, and even failed to sincerely acknowledge the atrocities that had befallen Ethiopia during its administration.[129]

---

126   See South Africa, 'Report of The Truth and Reconciliation Commission: Minority Position'(TRC, Vol 5, 29 October 1998) 443–444 available at:<http://www.justice.gov.za/trc/report/finalreport/Volume5.pdf> accessed 30 May 2019. See also Wilson, *The Politics of Truth and Reconciliation in South Africa,* supra note 117, 19–23.

127   Tsadik, 'Prosecuting the past-affecting the future: The Ethiopian Transitional Justice Trials', *supra* note 124, 28. Emphasis in the original.

128   J.L. Gibson, 'Overcoming apartheid: can truth reconcile a divided nation?' (2010) 31(2) *South African Journal of Political Studies* 129–155.

129   See Aneme, 'Apology and Trial: The Case of the Red-Terror Trials in Ethiopia', *supra* note 24, 81–84; A.G. Mariam, 'Ethiopia: Remember the 24th of November 1974' (ECADF, 30 November 2014), available at: <http://almariam.com/2014/11/30/ethiopia-remember-the-24th-of-november-1974/> accessed 15 December 2015; B. Zewde, 'The history of the Red Terror: Contexts and Consequences' in K. Tronvoll *et al.* (eds.), *The Ethiopian Red Terror Trials: Transitional Justice Challenged* (Martlesham: James Currey, 2009) 17–32, 21.

The perpetrators' refusal to acknowledge the pain they caused might be a reason to prosecute them, since, as Cohen explained, victims need such acknowledgment, even when everybody already knows what really happened.[130] Yet, the validity of the assertion that the *Dergue's* lack of remorse might have pushed the TGE towards adopting prosecution, should be inspected from both conceptual and practical perspectives.

From a conceptual point of view, a lack of remorse and apology is a deal-breaker in the Ethiopian context, without which it could be difficult to successfully negotiate and adopt a process that could heal societal wounds and bring about reintegration through reconciliation. In this regard, the traditional methods of dispute resolutions developed by the various communities in Ethiopia may offer a good explanation, although their scope and specifics remain mostly unstudied, or insufficiently studied. As can be inferred from traditional dispute resolution mechanisms and institutions such as *gereb*,[131] *gudegambela*,[132] *guma*,[133] *Luba basa* and *Harma Hodha*,[134]

---

[130] S. Cohen, 'State crimes of previous regimes: knowledge, accountability, and the policing of the past, Law and Social Inquiry' (1995) 20(1) *Law and Social Inquiry* 7–50. 12–22.

[131] *Gereb* is a traditional institution of inter-ethnic conflict resolution developed in northern and north eastern Ethiopia by the Afar jointly with the neighboring Tigray community. For a detailed account, See K.T. Reda, 'Conflict and alternative dispute resolution among the Afar pastoralists of Ethiopia' (2011) 3(3) *African Journal of History and Culture* 38–47.

[132] As practiced by the Kembata society in southern Ethiopia, *gudagambela* is known as a traditional mechanism of dispute resolution in which inter-clan conflicts are resolved on the basis of purification of a curse from the offender and reconciliation of conflicting parties. See A. Mengesha *et al.*, 'Indigenous Conflict Resolution Mechanisms among the Kembata Society' (2015) 3(2) *American Journal of Educational Research* 225–242.

[133] The Oromos are mostly known for their tradition of *guma*, a practice of settling blood feuds between *warra-gumaa* (parties at conflict) as a mechanism of restoring *nagaa* (peace), which is understood by the society in terms of an orderly universe (not only that of human beings) and societal (not merely of individual) well-being. See D. Gemechu, 'Conflict and Conflict Resolution among Waliso Oromo of Eastern Macha: the Case of the Guma' (PhD Dissertation, Addis Ababa University, 2007); H. Tusso, 'Indigenous Processes of Conflict Resolution in Oromo Society' in I.W. Zartman (ed.,) *Traditional Cures for Modern Conflicts: African Conflict "Medicine"* (London: Lynne Rienner Publishers, 2000) 79–93; T. Keneni, 'Exploring Gumaa as an Indispensable Psycho-Social Method of Conflict Resolution and Justice Administration' (2013) 13(1) *African Journal on Conflict Resolution* 37–58. For definition and concept of *nagaa* (peace), see M. Aguilar, 'The Nagaa Boorana: Contemporary Discussions on Ritual and Political Diversity' (2008) 15(1) *Journal of Oromo Studies* 181–202.

[134] See E. Tsegaw, 'Luba Basa & Harma Hodha: Traditional Mechanisms of Conflict Resolution in Metekkel, Ethiopia' (Asien-Afrika-Institut, Universität Hamburg, Germany, 2004) available at: <http://www.justiciarestaurativa.org/mount/www.restorativejustice.org/Articlesdb/Articles/4657> accessed 30 May 2019. The traditional mechanism of conflict resolution in Metekele have been shared among inhabitants with diverse ethnic

michu,[135] and *shimglena*,[136] reconciliation involves truth telling, apology, and forgiveness, the conclusion of which in most cases ends with a sort of ritual performance of feasting and oath taking as a symbol of restoration of peace and harmony and an assurance to refrain from vengeance.

The Ethiopian traditional philosophies to peace and reconciliation share various similarities with the concepts used in other places to either justify a choice of amnesty and reconciliation over prosecution or to adopt an approach that combines amnesty with prosecution. The *ubuntu* ideology in South Africa,[137]

---

backgrounds such as Gumuz, Shina sha, Amara, Oromo, and Agaw. Allegedly, these institutions are intra as well as inter-ethnic conflict resolution principles and are widely applied in many parts of Ethiopia; they can even meet demands outside Africa. See ibid.

135   As known in the Gumuz community of western Ethiopia, the notion of *michu* (which literally means friendship) governs conflict resolution with the objective of restoring peace and uniting the conflicting parties. See L.J. Myers and D.H. Shinn, 'Appreciating Traditional forms of Healing Conflict in Africa' (2010) 2(1) *Black Diaspora Review* 2–13, 7. The concept of *michu* as a basis and mechanism of conflict resolution is also common among the Oromos. See Keneni, 'Exploring Gumaa as an Indispensable Psycho-Social Method of Conflict Resolution and Justice Administration', *supra* note 133, 38.

136   The Amhara communities in Ethiopia maintain widespread practices of *Shimglena*, a form of conflict mediation by elders that emphasizes forgetting and forgiving. See E.L. Enyew, 'Ethiopian customary dispute resolution mechanisms: forms of restorative justice?' (2014) 14(1) *African Journal on Conflict Resolution* 125–154, 144. *Shimglena* does not involve an undertaking of ritual procedure, and it now appears to be in practice in most places in Ethiopia.

137   *Ubuntu*, commonly portrayed as 'I am because you are', is considered as the basis for the law that established the TRC in South Africa. See Promotion of National Unity and Reconciliation Act 34 of 1995 (SA), para 4. The importance of *Ubuntu* in relation to the approach of amnesty and reconciliation was also pointed out in the report of the TRC, in which it was stated that:
the provisions for amnesty in the interim Constitution came at the very end of the negotiations [...] They moved us away from strife and towards understanding, towards forgiveness (by the state) and away from vengeance. They endorsed our reconciliation and national unity after decades, centuries of strife. So, we are faced with a paradox: The disclosure of sometimes horrendous deeds, crimes, gross violations of human rights, committed with political motive under an old order, to be followed by a joyous reintegration into society within a new order of the perpetrator of those self-same deeds. This is seeing both the deed and the doer and severing them from each other. This is part of restorative justice. This is part of the spirit of *Ubuntu*. It is part of the restoration of the organism that is our nation South Africa.

See South Africa, 'Report of The Truth and Reconciliation Commission: Minority Position'(TRC, Vol 5, 29 October 1998) 443–444 available at:<http://www.justice.gov.za/trc/report/finalreport/Volume5.pdf> accessed 30 May 2019. The concept of *Ubuntu* and its relation to the principle of restorative justice adopted by the TRC has been described to be vague and complex. See, CBN Gade, 'Restorative Justice and the South African Truth and Reconciliation Process' (2013) 32 (1) *South African Journal of Philosophy* 11–35.

the notion of 'forgive and forget' that existed in North America and Europe,[138] and traditions like *Kpande yia, ii yia* in Sierra Leone[139] have been regarded as evidence for the fact that contemporary approaches and practices of truth and reconciliation have mostly evolved from the relevant society's indigenous wisdoms in conflict resolution. Admitting guilt and asking for forgiveness are the most important elements in these traditional approaches to conflict resolutions, although, in the case of South Africa's TRC, apology was not made a legal requirement to grant amnesty.[140] Appreciating the full notions of reconciliation as defined in the Ethiopian society requires the wrongdoers to plead guilty and demand apology more than it requires the victims to embrace the reality that the dead are dead and will never come back.

From a practical point of view, however, the assertion that the decision to prosecute was reached due to the *Dergue's* perceived lack of remorse is questionable. In particular, there is no evidence that members of the *Dergue* were given a chance to acknowledge their participation in the atrocities that took place during the time they were in power. What is known is, as pointed out in Chapter 2, that about 2000 individuals belonging to the *Dergue* government were arrested and detained by the EPRDF forces immediately between May and July, even before the TGE was established. They were still behind bars when the decision to prosecute was reached by the TGE in August 1992. As also pointed out above, because the *Dergue* was not perceived as capable of posing any challenge to the transition, there was no need for a negotiated transition between the victors and the vanquished. In that sense, it is not clear if and how the *Dergue's* unwillingness to ask for forgiveness was established before the decision to prosecute was reached.

Quite to the contrary, existing evidence suggests that members of the *Dergue* had in fact shown willingness to apologize to the Ethiopian public for crimes

---

138 R. Shaw, 'Rethinking Truth and Reconciliation Commissions: Lessons from Sierra Leone' (United States Institute for Peace Special Reports, Washington DC, 2005) 7 available at: <https://www.usip.org/publications/2005/02/rethinking-truth-and-reconciliation-commissions-lessons-sierra-leone> accessed 30 May 2019. However, according to Shaw, alternative and incommensurable understandings of the healing powers of forgetting have been displaced and discredited through the expanding dominance of a memory culture that prioritizes remembering over forgetting.

139 According to Alie, '*Kpande yia, ii yia*,' which literally means 'when a gun is fired, it is fired', appears to be a saying in the Mende community of Sierra Leone that suggests that one must look to the future with the view of reconciling. See J. Alie, 'Reconciliation and traditional justice: tradition-based practices of the Kpaa Mende in Sierra Leone' in L. Huyse and M. Salter (eds.), *Traditional Justice and Reconciliation after Violent Conflict: Learning from African Experiences* (Stockholm: International IDEA, 2008) 145.

140 See Wilson, *The Politics of Truth and Reconciliation in South Africa, supra* note 117, 24.

committed during the time they were in power; a willingness which might also be inferred from the statements quoted above at the outset of this section. Even further, members of the *Dergue* mentioned their willingness to apologize by asking for national reconciliation instead of prosecution on multiple occasions and, arguably, whenever they had the chance. Such willingness was mentioned in their preliminary objections to the charges, as recorded in several cases, including *Mengistu et al.*[141] In that regard, it should be highlighted here that in Ethiopian criminal trials, the stage of preliminary objection is the first encounter for a suspect to address the court.[142] Put differently, by mentioning their willingness at this stage of the proceedings, the suspects used the first chance they found to do so. Whether their undertaking was sincere is another issue and, although a genuine apology may be required to reach a decision to establish a process of national reconciliation that may include amnesty, the argument that the decision to prosecute the *Dergue* was reached due to its unwillingness to apologize to the victims is not entirely convincing. Evidence does not seem to be available to indicate whether reconciliation was considered as an option by the TGE before the decision to prosecute was reached or whether the detained members of the *Dergue* were in a position to communicate their (un)willingness to apologize. No relevant discussions were held between victims and perpetrators, or between victims and victors, or still between victors and vanquished. In fact, the limited evidence that is available suggests that members of the *Dergue* expressed willingness to apologize, although this was done after charges were already brought against them.

3.5 The TGE's Intention to Use Prosecution for Political Legitimacy

In writing on why the Dergue were put on trial, Tronvoll noted that the Dergue trials were designed to serve as rituals to disconnect the current regime from the past and 'to define a new starting point – a year zero – for democracy',[143] although they were dwarfed into representing a repressive continuity.[144] Allo and Tesfaye reasoned in similar terms, arguing that the Dergue trials represented the beginning of a series of 'juridico-political' engagements aimed at

---

141   See for instance, *Colonel Mengistu Hailemariam et al.*, (Ruling on Preliminary Objections), *supra* note 20, 86.
142   See the Criminal Procedure Code of Ethiopia, Article 129.
143   See Tronvoll, 'The Quest for Justice or the Construction of Political Legitimacy', *supra* note 3, 13.
144   Ibid., 94–96.

'legitimizing and rationalizing politics of repression and elimination' that had been ongoing in Ethiopia.[145]

These authors' assertions are plausible and well grounded. Nonetheless, their underlying analyses do not give a separate treatment to the context in which the decision to prosecute the Dergue was reached. The authors focused not on the background of the decision to prosecute, but on the legitimacy and legacy of the trials, although they assess the decision to prosecute in retrospect based on Ethiopia's contemporary political realities and on the current government's alleged human rights violations. As Allo and Tesfaye's discussion is aimed at analysing several high-profile trials in aggregate, the Dergue trials do not appear to be holding a unique position, which is perhaps why their discussion does not include the context of transition and its possible role in shaping the decision to prosecute.[146]

Examining the decision that brought the Dergue to justice based on current political and policy directions in Ethiopia is however not erroneous, not only because the present may explain the past, but also because those groups and individuals who were in charge of making policy decisions during the transitional period are still holding the same official positions. However, the question whether the tge's decision to prosecute the Dergue was made in order to garner political legitimacy could – and arguably should – also be discussed from the perspective of the context in which the transition took place.

As noted in the foregoing, it is more likely that the decision to prosecute the *Dergue* era atrocities was taken without popular participation. Undoubtedly, a government elected by the people did not take this decision, simply because there was no popular government at the time. It is also doubtful that the decision was made by the TGE because, by then, the TGE was in reality almost disintegrated.[147] Tellingly, the SPO Proclamation made no reference to the TGE. It

---

145 Allo and Tesfaye, 'Spectacles of Illegality: Mapping Ethiopia's Show Trials' *supra* note 15, 279, 286.
146 See ibid., 283*ff*.
147 It is on 23 June 1992, thus two months before the SPO was established, that the OLF had to leave due to what it considered as 'the absence of a level playing field for all political parties in the country'. See A. Kefale, *Federalism and Ethnic Conflict in Ethiopia: A Comparative Regional Study* (New York: Routledge, 2013) 25–26; A. Matsuoka and J. Sorenson, *Ghosts and Shadows: Construction of Identity and Community in an African Diaspora* (Toronto: University of Toronto Press, 2001) 43; L. Lata, 'The Making and Unmaking of Ethiopia's Transitional Charter', Paper presented on the thirty-seventh annual meeting of the African Studies Association (Toronto: November 1994), 6. The remaining four non-EPRDF parties were expelled by the EPRDF from the council of representatives in 1993. See U.S. Department of State, 'Ethiopia Human Rights Practices, 1993' (US State

in fact seems that it was the EPRDF, the rebel force that controlled the country in May 1991, which solely reached the decision to prosecute.[148]

The SPO Proclamation emphasized the mission and achievements of the EPRDF, which it appears to be linking to the decision to prosecute. The most relevant paragraph of the Proclamation in announcing the decision to prosecute reads,

> [i]n view of the fact that the historical mission of the *Ethiopian People's Revolutionary Democratic Front (EPRDF)* has been accomplished, it is essential that higher officials of the WPE (Workers Party of Ethiopia) and members of the security and armed forces who have been detained at the time the *EPRDF* assumed control of the country and thereafter…must be brought to trial.[149]

This paragraph purports two problematic assertions. Firstly, by mentioning only the EPRDF and its historical missions, it concealed the possible role played by other military and non-military groups that had been fighting to end human rights violations under the *Dergue* regime. In portraying the EPRDF as the only force that unseated the *Dergue* and as the only force that had a mission, it removed others from the political scene. It associated the EPRDF to the decision to prosecute and thus to any political benefit that doing so could enlist.

Secondly, what the Proclamation did not explain was why it was essential or necessary that the perpetrators be brought to trial. As pointed out earlier, neither national nor international legislation made prosecution mandatory for the crimes identified by the SPO as having been perpetrated by the *Dergue* officials. Again, even if we accepted that the EPRDF had the genuine and sincere impression that it was under a national or international obligation to prosecute the atrocities of the past, it would still be difficult to logically argue that such a belief led the EPRDF to decide on spending the scarce resources at its disposal, and to even go further to the extent of begging international donors for material and expert assistances. Such utopic form of commitment towards

---

Department, 31 January 1994), available at: <https://www.refworld.org/docid/3ae6aa4d10.html> accessed 25 March 2019.

148   In fact, and as also noted earlier, the EPRDF was the PGE, the TGE, and had been the FDRE. For a detailed analysis, see T.M. Vestal, *Ethiopia: A Post-Cold War African State* (Westport: Greenwood Publishing Group, 1999) 45–52.

149   SPO Proclamation, Preamble, para. 4. Emphasis added.

prosecution and political reform requires a truly democratic party, which the EPRDF, as circumstances of the time dictated, was not.[150]

In a politically ambiguous culture like that of Ethiopia in the early 1990s, a search for a 'why', a 'who', or a 'how' in relation to the decision to prosecute, or any other decision for that matter, is obviously not an easy task. Even clear and open governmental statements may not be exactly what they claim to be. For instance, as previously mentioned, it was reported, at one point, that the prime minister was open to the option of introducing amnesty,[151] which contradicts another one of his statements that the decision to prosecute was made by the TPLF earlier during the armed struggle, before the EPRDF was formed and thus before the London Conference was convened.[152] The question of who of the TPLF or the EPRDF made the decision may however not be that significant since the two groups are practically one and the same: the later was founded and also substantially controlled by the former, in particular during the period of transition.[153]

Irrespective of who took the decision, it is possible that it was taken for the EPRDF to acquire political legitimacy. At the time, there were clear indicators regarding the EPRDF's credibility deficit both internationally and internally

---

150   Nevertheless, Ethiopia has never been a democratic state. In 1991, by the time the *Dergue* regime had broken down, the only sign of 'democracy' that the incoming power carried with it was the phrase 'Democratic' within its party-nomenclature: Ethiopian People Democratic Revolutionary Front [EPRDF]. In this regard, the previous totalitarian regime, which succeeded in the 1974 revolution, had a similar disguising indicant as it had inserted the word 'democratic' in its 'Programme of the national democratic revolution of Ethiopia'. Yet, the Ethiopian revolution of 1991 was not accompanied by a genuine intention of transforming the country into a democratic regime. This was demonstrated by measures taken by the EPRDF both before and after the London peace talks of May 1991. The EPRDF's measures included mainly the building up of a single party system in the country. For details, see D.N. Sarbo, *Contested Legitimacy: Coercion and the State in Ethiopia* (PhD dissertation, University of Tennessee, 2009) 151–156; J. Harbeson, 'A Bureaucratic Authoritarian Regime: Is Ethiopia Democratic?' (1998) 9(4) *Journal of Democracy* 62–69; M. Gudina, 'Elections and democratization in Ethiopia,1991–2010' (2011) 5(4) *Journal of Eastern African Studies* 664–680; S. Pausewang *et al.* (eds.), *Ethiopia Since the Derg: A Decade of Democratic Pretension and Performance* (London: Zed Books Ltd, 2002) 1–44.

151   See Harden, 'Rebel leaders Pledges Coalition Government, then Free Elections', *supra* note 91, 1.

152   K. Tronvoll *et al.,* 'The 'Red-Terror' Trials: The Context of Transitional Justice in Ethiopia' in K. Tronvoll *et al.* (eds.), *The Ethiopian Red Terror Trials: Transitional Justice Challenged* (Martlesham: James Currey, 2009) 1–16, 6.

153   See A. Berhe, *A Political History of the Tigray People's Liberation Front (1975–1991): Revolt, Ideology and Mobilisation in Ethiopia* (PhD Dissertation, Vrijie Universiteit Amsterdam, 2009), 230.

and the decision to hold the *Dergue* officials accountable for the crimes of the old regime might have been adopted to ease the legitimacy challenges of the new government.

Internationally, the EPRDF had a perceived legitimacy crisis, probably caused by the manner in which it came to power and the political ideology it had allegedly carried along with itself, which was at odds with the international political order emerging at the time. 1991 was the year that marked the end of the cold war and the fall of socialist regimes in many places, including Ethiopia. Clearly, the Western World had a vested interest in ensuring that societies emerging out of a communist style governance be transformed into new and democratic political orders as there was no interest in replacing or approving the replacement of one communist regime by another. Both Europe and the US, the main powers in the cold war, perceived the EPRDF as an advocate of communist ideologies.[154] Being perceived as pro-Soviet was therefore among the factors that could, at that time, entail a legitimacy crisis with serious repercussions on the international recognition of governments.

According to Herman Cohen, who claims to have discussed the matter openly with the EPRDF during the London talks, the EPRDF had informed the US that it had already dropped fancying an Albanian-style socialist ideology.[155] Evidently, this was not regarded as sufficient to secure political legitimacy and therefore bilateral cooperation. At the end of the London talks, the US expressly communicated to the EPRDF that there would be no bilateral relationship provided that the formation and operation of the would-be TGE fell short of democratic standards, a position commonly known as 'no

---

154 It was reported that Herman Cohen (the US representative at the 1991 London Peace Talks) stated: 'We have argued with them about Ideology ... and has been assured that the Tigrayans as well as the powerful and previously Marxist Eritrean rebel group will welcome all points of view ... and that Marxism probably does not dominate either organizations as an ideology'. See Harden, 'Rebel leaders Pledges Coalition Government, then Free Elections', *supra* note 91, 1.

   It was not only the US that viewed the TPLF as having connections to a pro-Marxist ideology. The UK's Thatcher government had already discussed and dropped the option of assisting the rebel forces (TPLF and EPLF) in their struggle against the *Dergue*. According to an information recently released for public access, the rebel forces were regarded by the British Foreign Office to be as extreme in their broadly Marxist political attitudes as the *Dergue*. See The Foreign Secretary, Letter to the Foreign and Common Wealth Office (London SW1A 2AH), 10 January 1986, 2 available at: <https://discovery.nationalarchives.gov.uk/details/r/C14568616#imageViewerLink> accessed 28 September 2019.

155 J. Cohen, *Intervening in Africa: Superpower Peacemaking in a Troubled Continent* (New York: St. Martin's Press LL.C., 2000), 51.

democracy – no cooperation'.[156] It was thus the EPRDF's own task to prove that it was no more harboring a pro-socialist dogma, which could be done by advertising a gesture of respect for the rule of law and democracy. In addition to, and probably as part of, the no democracy – no cooperation condition, the US expressly recommended to the EPRDF that those responsible for atrocities committed during the *Dergue* regime be brought to trial.[157] Not complying with this recommendation could have been considered by the EPRDF as a course of action that would only exacerbate its credibility deficit.

The questionable nature of the manner in which the EPRDF ascended to power and took full control of the country was also a cause of concern for the European Union. The European Parliament released a resolution with a particular emphasis on the completion of the London talks,[158] in which it stated that it

> deplores the fact that, at the first negotiation held in London on 27 and 28 May 1991 under the auspices of the United States, only three opposition groups were invited...believes that a peaceful and democratic solution to the problem tearing the country apart must be found first and foremost by the Ethiopians themselves, without outside interference and in the presence of all the organisations and movements representing the Ethiopian civilian population.[159]

Around the time the TGE was established, it was clear that displaying a commitment towards the rule of law and human rights was being considered, in particular by the European Union, as a prerequisite for recognizing new states and governments such as those that were emerging from the former Yugoslavia.[160] That, coupled with the fact that the European Parliament had

---

156 T. Lyons, 'Great Powers and Conflict Reduction in the Horn of Africa' in I.W. Zaartman and V.A. Kremenyuk (eds.), *Cooperative Security: Reducing Third World Wars* (Syracuse: Syracuse University Press, 1995) 241–266, 255. See also B.K. Holcomb, 'Contending Democracies: US-Sponsored Democracy Encounters Indigenous Oromo Democratic Forms' in A. Jalata (ed.), *State Crisis, Globalisation, and National Movements in North-East Africa* (London: Routledge, 2004)122–164, 136.
157 See Haile-Selassie, *The Ethiopian Revolution, supra* note 92, 326.
158 Ibid.
159 Ibid., 327.
160 In 1991, the European Union developed a set of guidelines in relation to state recognition, some of which could possibly be considered as applicable to the issue of recognizing governments. See European Community, Declaration on Yugoslavia and On the Guidelines of the Recognition of New States, 16 December 1991, 31 I.l.m.1485 (1992). Among the requirements, respect for the rule of law, democracy and human rights was cited. Even if the guidelines were developed in relation to Eastern Europe and the Soviet Union, they

already deplored the manner in which the new government had been formed in Ethiopia,[161] might have forced the EPRDF, from a political point of view, to leave no stone unturned to convince European States into recognizing the TGE's status as government. Perhaps the decision to prosecute was reached to portray the TGE as a government with a manifest willingness to respect and implement international norms so that other countries would recognize it as legitimate and start bilateral or multilateral cooperations.[162]

Internally too, the eprdf was hardly considered as a legitimate government, and the tge lacked a peaceful start. As evidenced by numerous moderate protests as well as strong disapprovals against the transitional process, the legitimacy crisis was too vivid for the eprdf not to see it. Protests against the eprdf started as early as May 1991 when a group of independent Ethiopian experts deplored the eprdf's ascendency to power at the London Conference.[163] The eprdf was met with several other protests, mainly in Addis Ababa, to which it responded with violence. The transitional period was by and large full of political unrest and the EPRDF's legitimacy crisis was further reflected in the actions it took to control public dissent. For example, in an outright violation of Article 1 of the Transitional Period Charter, the eprdf banned the right to hold public demonstrations and public political meetings in June 1991, and restored it two months later pursuant to Proclamation No. 3/1991.[164] The strongest case of the eprdf's legitimacy crisis however relates to its disagreement with the olf, the second major group in the tge. The disagreement had

---

might have indicated the overall stand the EU held at the time in relation to state recognition, and might have been considered applicable to Ethiopia as the country was, just like Eastern European States, also emerging out of socialism and conflict.

161 See above for the statement of the European Parliament *cited in* Haile-Selassie, *The Ethiopian Revolution, supra* note 92, 327.

162 Recognition is, in general, a highly politicized matter. For a general perspective on governments' ability and willingness to fulfil international obligations as a requirement for recognition, see M.J. Peterson, *Recognition of Governments: Legal Doctrine and State Practice, 1815–1995* (London: Palgrave Macmillan UK, 1997) 68–72. See also J. Klabbers, *International Law* (Cambridge: Cambridge University Press, 2013) 76. In relation to Ethiopia, the issue of recognition is used here strictly with reference to the government not the State. Eritrea's secession did not have a bearing on Ethiopia's status as a State since the latter continued as an old parent State with the same legal identity, as is usually the case under international law. See M.N. Shaw, *International Law* (6th ed., Cambridge: Cambridge University Press, 2008) 960–963.

163 See Haile-Selassie, *The Ethiopian Revolution, supra* note 92, 328.

164 See Proclamation to Define a Procedure for Peaceful Demonstration and Public Political Meeting, Proclamation No. 3/1991, entered into force, 12 August 1991.

culminated in the olf's withdrawal from the tge on 23 June 1992, a situation that was accompanied by a brief period of armed conflict between the two factions.[165]

The tplf had already noted that, due to its narrow support base, it would not be regarded as a representative movement or as a legitimate government, whether it would pledge democracy or not.[166] That was apparently why it allegedly established Peoples' Democratic Organizations (pdos) and formed the eprdf in 1991: to appear representative and thus legitimate.[167] The decision to prosecute might have been made to reinforce a similar agenda. It could be one of the forward-looking approaches to deceitfully attempt to legitimize the illegitimate by conferring an appearance of democracy to the new government.

3.6 Post-TGE Decisions to Prosecute Core Crimes: The Persistence of Political Considerations

As examined in the foregoing, several factors might have contributed to the TGE's decision to bring the *Dergue* to justice. Significantly, such a decision might have been the result of political reasons that were considered relevant during the transitional period. This section explores the possible motivations behind the decision to prosecute core crimes committed later on after a new political order and government replaced the TGE in 1995. In particular, the following development discusses whether Ethiopia was under an obligation to prosecute the core crimes it tried in the *Anuak-Nuwer, the CUD* and *Oromo-Gumuz* cases. It is also assessed below whether the prosecution of core crimes in Ethiopia were overall driven by the country's willingness to uphold a duty to prosecute or whether political motivations still played a significant role in such decisions.

---

165 For a full account of the political unrest during the TGE, see Vestal, *Ethiopia: A Post-Cold War African State, supra* note 148, 1–57.

166 The TPLF's narrow support base was/is a result of its ethnic based nature and the small size of the ethnic group it represented coupled with the geographic remoteness of its support-base from the capital. For the history and nature of the TPLF and its movement, see J. Young, *Peasant Revolution in Ethiopia: The Tigray People's Liberation Front, 1975–1991* (Cambridge: Cambridge University Press, 1997) 172–197; Berhe, *A Political History of the Tigray People's Liberation Front, supra* note 153, 230.

167 See Gudina, 'Elections and democratization in Ethiopia,1991–2010' ,*supra* note 150, 664–680.

3.6.1 *The* Anuak-Nuwer, *the* CUD, *and the* Oromo-Gumuz *Trials: The Application of the Obligation to Prosecute Genocide*

Pentering into force in 1995 of a new constitution that established the FDRE,[168] is believed to have been founded upon a promise of non-repetition of core crimes. Such a promise was envisaged mainly in the TGE's decision to prosecute members and affiliates of the *Dergue*. The fact that the new constitution incorporated human rights provisions like never before was also largely viewed as a guarantee that the era of violence had departed for good.[169] In fact, the promise of non-repetition of violence is echoed in several paragraphs of the preamble of the Constitution such as those vowing to rectify 'historically unjust relationships', to ensure lasting peace and to consolidate prospects of democracy that 'our struggles and sacrifices have brought about'.[170]

Alas, the FDRE begun witnessing a trilogy of core crimes, even before the *Dergue* trials came to a conclusion. Large-scale violence that claimed the lives of many people occurred in various parts of the country on several occasions.[171] Prosecutions were held in relation to crimes committed in three instances. These are: the *Anuak-Nuwer* trials in connection with the genocide that took place in Gambella in 2002; the CUD trials involving attempted genocide during the post-election violence in Addis Ababa and some other cities in 2005; and the *Oromo-Gumuz* trials in relation to acts of genocide committed in districts of Benishangul-Gumuz and Oromia in 2008.[172]

Although no amnesty decree was issued in relation to these instances, the manner in which the different decisions to prosecute were reached is unknown. The investigations and the prosecutions were held discreetly, thus suggesting that no independent and impartial commission of inquiry was set up, either prior to or after the commencement of the trials. There hardly was a public announcement regarding the opening or the closing of the trials. Unlike the manner in which the government had reached a decision to prosecute the *Dergue* era crimes, no legislation was issued and no special prosecutorial mechanism was established in relation to any of these conflicts.

---

168 FDRE Constitution, Article 1.
169 Ibid., Chapter 3, Articles 13–43.
170 Ibid., Preamble, paras 1, 4, 6.
171 For notable allegations, see below section 3.6.2.
172 See FHC, *Federal Prosecutor v. Gure Uchala Ugira et al.*, (Indictment) 4 January 2004, 586/96, 3; FHC, *Federal Prosecutor v. Tadesse Jewanie Mengesha et al.*, (Indictment), 22 August 2008, File No. 70996/2000, 5; FHC, *Federal Prosecutor v. Engineer Hailu Shawul et al.*, (Indictment), 15 December 2006, File No. 43246/97, 14.

THE DECISIONS TO PROSECUTE: POSSIBLE MOTIVATIONS   131

One thing however is clear: all of the three trials were genocide trials, given that genocide (including attempt to commit genocide) is the only core crime prosecuted in these trials. Despite the absence of official explanations, these prosecutions might have resulted from the application of the obligation to prosecute genocide. In fact, in contrast to the situation surrounding the *Dergue* trials, Ethiopia was here under an explicit twofold (international and national) obligation to prosecute acts of genocide committed in the context of the Anuak-Nuwer, the CUD, and the Oromo-Gumuz conflicts.

The international obligation stems directly from the Genocide Convection, to which Ethiopia is a party since 1949. Acts of genocide committed in the Anuak-Nuwer, the CUD, and the Oromo-Gumuz situations fall within the scope of the conventional definition of genocide: in all of these cases, genocidal acts (murder and attempted murder) were alleged to have been committed with the intent to destroy in whole or in part members of ethnic groups, one of the four protected groups enumerated in Article II of the Convention.[173] Besides, the fact that the crime was committed on Ethiopian territory implies the absence of an exception that may limit the application on Ethiopia of the Convention's duty to prosecute.[174]

As for a national obligation to prosecute acts of genocide, as discussed earlier, if Ethiopian laws had allowed for the possibility to grant amnesty for all kinds of crimes,[175] this only holds true for the period until 1995, when the FDRE Constitution came into force with a provision imposing a duty to prosecute crimes it referred to as 'crimes against humanity'. Article 28 of the FDRE Constitution reads:

> Criminal liability of persons who commit crimes against humanity, so defined by international agreements ratified by Ethiopia and by other laws of Ethiopia, such as *genocide*, summary executions, forcible disappearances or torture shall not be barred by statute of limitations. Such offences *may not be commuted by amnesty* or pardon of the legislature or any other state organ.[176]

This provision has given birth to a new era of a 'national constitutional obligation', in which Ethiopia self-imposed an obligation to prosecute genocide

---

173   Only in the CUD cases were the victims regarded as having dual membership status, i.e. they were both Tigre (an ethnic group) and EPRDF (a political group).
174   See above, section 3.2.1.1.
175   See above, section 3.2.1.2.
176   The Constitution of FDRE, Article 28(1). Emphasis added.

and other crimes. It is noteworthy that the significance of this provision is not limited to imposing an obligation to prosecute genocide. Firstly, the provision's list of crimes is non-exhaustive, and deals not only with core crimes but also with domestic crimes such as summary executions.[177] Secondly, the provision outlaws amnesty irrespective of whether an obligation of a similar nature exists in international law. This means that, with respect to core crimes, Article 28 also imposes an obligation to prosecute war crimes committed in non-international armed conflicts and crimes against humanity, in relation to which the existence in international law of a duty to prosecute is less explicit.

It should be pointed out that the FDRE Constitution is not unique in providing a constitutional duty to prosecute various kinds of crimes. For instance, the 1988 Constitution of Brazil provides that amnesty shall not be granted for 'heinous crimes such as illicit trafficking in narcotics and similar drugs, terrorism, and torture'.[178] More recently, some states have undertaken legal reforms in which they incorporated in their respective constitutions a specific duty to prosecute core crimes; a development which appears to have resulted from the domestic implementation of the Rome Statute of the ICC. Examples include the Constitutions of Angola,[179] Colombia,[180] Ecuador,[181] Paraguay,[182] and Venezuela.[183]

For Ethiopia, the reason that led to the incorporation of a no-amnesty provision in the Constitution was connected to the atrocities that the country had experienced during the *Dergue* era. From the discussions held during the drafting of the Constitution, it was evident that Ethiopia wanted to close all

---

177 On the non-exhaustive nature of Article 28 as regards the crimes it covered, see Explanatory Notes to the FDRE Constitution 1995, 63.
178 Constituição Da República Federativa Do Brasil De 1988 Incluindo Reformas De 1992, 1993, 1994, 1995, 1996, Articles 5, XLIII.
179 See the Constitution of the Republic of Angola 2010, Article 61, available at: <https://www.constituteproject.org/search?lang=en&q=angola> accessed 28 September 2019.
180 Colombia's Constitution of 1991 with Amendments through 2005, Article 30, available at: <https://www.constituteproject.org/constitution/Colombia_2005.pdf> accessed 28 September 2019.
181 The Constitution of the Republic of Ecuador 2008 (Rev.2011), Article 80, available at: <https://www.constituteproject.org/search?lang=en&q=Ecuador> accessed 28 September 2019.
182 See The Constitution of Paraguay 1992 (rev. 2011) Article 5, available at: <https://www.constituteproject.org/search?lang=en&q=Paraguay> accessed 20 March 2019. Note, however, that the Constitution does not make a precise reference to crimes against humanity.
183 The Constitution of Venezuela (Bolivarian Republic of) 1999 (rev. 2009), Article 29, available at: <https://www.constituteproject.org/search?lang=en&q=venezuela> accessed 28 September 2019.

windows that could lead to a recurrence of crimes and to impunity for offences similar to those previously prosecuted by the SPO.[184] Ethiopia's desire to disassociate itself from the experiences of some countries in Africa and Latin America, where a culture of impunity was, at that time, seen as growing, was also invoked to explain why the country decided to abolish amnesty for certain crimes. This was pointed out in the *travaux préparatoires* of the Constitution in the following terms:

> [I]n some countries in Africa and Latin America a culture of impunity has developed in which dictator governments remain unaccountable for the atrocities they perpetrated against their own people, which encourages a recurrence of similar atrocities. It was also stated during the transitional period that amnesty should not be granted in relation to offences involving violations of human rights.[185]

3.6.2 *Beyond the* Anuak-Nuwer, *the* CUD, *and the* Oromo-Gumuz *Trials: Mapping Ethiopia's Trend in Prosecuting Core Crimes*

It could be possible to look at the *Anuak-Nuwer*, the *CUD* and the *Oromo-Gumuz* trials as indicative of Ethiopia's commitment to end impunity for core crimes by prosecuting perpetrators before its own courts. In line with these positive developments, Ethiopia now has a clear policy direction according to which, as stated in its Criminal Justice Policy (2011), amnesty should be granted only after the conduct of an inquiry to ascertain that doing so would not affect the possibility of prosecuting crimes under Article 28 of the Constitution.[186] In a similar vein, one could also mention the fact that a Parliamentary Commission of Inquiry (PCI) was set up in 2003 to investigate whether genocide was committed in a conflict that took place in the Gambella Regional State on 13 December

---

184 See 'The Minutes of the 43rd Meeting of the Constitutional Committee, (20 September 1993)' in The Constitutional Commission, *Minutes, Vol. I: Ordinary Sessions No 1- No 50 held from 25 February 1993 to 25 October 1993* (Addis Ababa: FDRE House of Federations, Unpublished) 201.

185 The discussion did not mention the specific countries to which it was referring. See 'The Minutes of the 84th Ordinary Session of the Constitutional Committee (24 February 1994)' in The Constitutional Commission, 'Minutes, Vol. II: Ordinary Sessions No 51- No 88 held from 2 November 1993 to 3 April 1994' (Addis Ababa: FDRE House of Federations, Unpublished) 199. Translation by the author. The original (Amharic) version reads:
የሚለው በኢትዮጵያ ሁኔታ እንዲሁም በ አፍሪካ በላቲን አሜሪካ ሀገሮች አምባገነን ግርዖች በህዝብ ላይ ግፍ ከፈጸሙ በኋላ በሰሩት ወንጀል ተጠያቂ ሳይሆኑ የሚቀሩበት ሁኔታ እየተለመደና ለተመሳሳይ ድርጊት የሚጋብዝ መሆኑን በሽግግሩ ወቅትም ሰብ አዊ መብትን ከተመለከተ ለተሰሩ ወንጀሎች ምህረት የማይሰጥ መሆኑ ተገልጿል።

186 FDRE Criminal Justice Policy, adopted 3 April 2011, 16.

2003.[187] Such a practice may be regarded as a progressive step towards developing a more robust system that fights impunity for core crimes, although the impartiality of this particular PCI could be contested insofar as its conclusion that genocide was not committed in Gambella during the said instance lacked sufficient explanation.[188]

However, a further assessment of Ethiopian practice reveals the existence of significant deviations from the promises of the law. Firstly, there have been several allegations that core crimes other than those already prosecuted have been perpetrated in various regions of Ethiopia.[189] The allegations were often dismissed by the government as political propagandas of the opposition political parties or as enemy campaigns aimed at intruding and disintegrating

---

187   A Proclamation to Provide for the Establishment of an Inquiry Commission to investigate the conflict occurred in Gambella Regional State on 13 December 2003, Proclamation No 398/2004. By only referring to 13 December 2003, it appears that the proclamation treated the situation as just a one day conflict. Nevertheless, the report of the Inquiry Commission found that crimes were committed between 13 to 15 December 2003. See Resolution on the Report of the Gambella Inquiry Commission adopted by the House of Peoples' Representatives of the Federal Democratic Republic of Ethiopia on 8 July 2004, para. 8.

188   In its investigation report, the PCI refuted the allegation that genocide was perpetrated in Gambella in December 2003, although it found that '65 persons died while close to 75 were wounded and thousands were displaced and fled across the border [while] 482 houses were burnt down'. See Resolution on the Report of the Gambella Inquiry Commission adopted by the House of Peoples' Representatives of the Federal Democratic Republic of Ethiopia on 8 July 2004, para. 8. Nonetheless, the PCI did not explain why and how these acts did not constitute genocide, when it pointed out that the targeted victims belonged to the *Anuak* ethnic group. See ibid., paras 4 and 10.

189   Notable allegations include: 1) the Anuak Situation which represents the continued commission of international crimes against the Anuak communities in South West Ethiopia allegedly by Ethiopian National Defence Force (ENDF) since 2003; see Human Rights Watch, 'Targeting the Anuak', available at <http://www.hrw.org /reports /2005/ 03/23/targeting-anuak> accessed 24 September 2019; 2) the Ogaden conflict in which alleged commissions of war crimes and crimes against humanity by the ENDF have been reported; see Human Rights Watch, 'Collective Punishment: War Crimes and Crimes against Humanity in the Ogaden area of Ethiopia's Somali Region', 13 June 2008, available at <http://www.hrw.org/node/62176> accessed 24 September 2019; 3) The eviction and deportation of members of the Amhara ethnic group from the Benishangul-Gumuz regional states have been widely portrayed as acts of ethnic-cleansing; see <http://www.ethiomedia.com/addis/5775.html> accessed 24 September 2019; 4) A widespread and systematic attack against the members of ethnic Oromos as reported by different organizations such as Amnesty International; see e.g.Amnesty International, 'Because I am Oromo: Sweeping repression in the Oromia region of Ethiopia' (Amnesty International Report, 27 October 2014), available at <https://www.amnesty.org/en/documents/afr25/ 006/2014/en/> accessed 24 September 2019.

the country. It was only in 2018 that, for the first time in Ethiopian history, an incumbent government publicly admitted that widespread and systematic acts of torture and terror had been perpetrated against the Ethiopian people by its own police and security forces.[190] Nevertheless, this acknowledgement of state criminality, although expressed while the country was undergoing its biggest political change since 1991,[191] did not indicate a political willingness to prosecute the alleged crimes, as discussed further below.

Secondly, even where an inquiry commission was established to look into allegations of gross human rights violations and core crimes, it seems to have been set up precisely to discount the scope and nature of such violations and crimes, notably when the government was implicated in their commission. A typical example is the parliamentary investigation conducted in the aftermath of the 2005 post-election conflict, which is discussed in detail in the next chapter due to its relevance to the manner in which the federal prosecutor selected who to prosecute in the CUD trials. In this particular investigation, the government went from blocking the release of the report of the investigation commission to releasing its own version of such a report.[192]

Thirdly, the current practice of amnesty could also be invoked as evidence of the lack of genuine commitment in Ethiopia to bring perpetrators of core crimes to justice. Although it is clear from Article 28 of the Constitution that certain crimes shall not be subjected to amnesty, it is also the case that no mechanism is available to ensure that the government does not infringe such a proscription in practice. In that respect, one could question the legality of the amnesty granted in October 2015 to members of the Tigray People's Democratic Movement (TPDM), an armed group, that, when defecting to Eretria, allegedly used to engage in some 'anti-peace activities' against the government of

---

190   See Prime Minister Abiy Ahmed Speech to the Parliament, 1 July 2018, available at <https://www.youtube.com/watch?v=wJnC2aX4jP8&t=8079s> accessed 22 September 2019.

191   On 11 April 2018, Ethiopia's ruling party, the EPRDF, appointed a new Prime Minister in order to accommodate demands aired by the public during a series of protests held across the country for over three years. Despite the absence of a transitional government and a formal declaration of regime change, Ethiopia seems to be in a state of transition from the Old EPRDF to the New EPRDF, which appears to be striving to forge a new (hopefully democratic) political order. It has released from prison thousands of individuals detained by the Old EPRDF on political grounds and removed opposition political groups from its lists of terrorist organizations in order to establish a more inclusive democratic process. It has also restored peaceful relations with Eritrea by ending an almost two decades long military stalemate between the two states. See further, Human Rights Watch, 'Ethiopia: Events of 2018' available at<https://www.hrw.org/world-report/2019/country-chapters/ethiopia> accessed 22 September 2019.

192   See Chapter 4, section 4.2.1.

Ethiopia.¹⁹³ According to the announcement made by the Ethiopian government, 'the amnesty was given as TPDM had not participated in any of the acts stated under Article 28 (1) of the Constitution'.¹⁹⁴ However, as the announcement did not specify the crimes for which amnesty was granted, it is not clear whether such 'anti-peace activities' involved the commission of crimes for which amnesty cannot be granted.

Furthermore, a recent practice seems to have allowed for the adoption of self-proclaimed *de facto* amnesty. This was the case with the above-mentioned admission of state criminality by the government, which was not accompanied by a declaration of any governmental plan to bring perpetrators to justice. Rather, Prime Minister Abiy Ahmed, winner of the Nobel Peace Prize for 2019,¹⁹⁵ claimed that the public had accepted his apology and forgiven the EPRDF, the ruling party since the 1991 transition.¹⁹⁶ This is however hardly defensible: there is no evidence supporting the Prime Minister's assertions that 'this honest and kind-hearted public has spoken and acted in favor of giving amnesty to the government'.¹⁹⁷

The fact that a popular opinion supporting the alleged amnesty never existed in reality may also be inferred from the Prime Minister's vague and unsubstantiated attempts to explain why amnesty, as compared to prosecution, is a better option for Ethiopia. In that sense, he claimed that, although the killings, corruptions, and tortures are more than enough reasons to detain government officials and affiliates,¹⁹⁸ the public understood that 'our going to prison has no use for Ethiopia'.¹⁹⁹ In what seemed an attempt to support his point about the futility of detention/prosecution, the Prime Minister highlighted that historical efforts to detain officials of the ousted regime had in

---

193   See 'President Mulatu Grants Amnesty to TPDM members' (Ethiopian Brodacatsting Service, 26 October 2015), available at <http://www.ebc.et/web/ennews/-/president-mulatu-grants-amnesty-to-tpdm-members> accessed 28 October 2015.
194   Ibid.
195   As announced by the Nobel Committee, Prime Minister Abiy Ahmed was awarded the2019 Nobel Peace Prize 'for his efforts to achieve peace and international cooperation, and in particular for his decisive initiative to resolve the border conflict with neighbouring Eritrea'. See <https://www.nobelprize.org/prizes/peace/2019/press-release/> accessed 05 November 2019.
196   See Prime Minister Abiy Ahmed Speech to the Parliament, *supra* note 190.
197   See ibid. Translation by the author. The original (Amharic) statement reads: 'ህዝቡ በንግግር ብቻ ሳይሆን በተግባር ይቅርታ አሳይቶናል'.
198   Ibid. Translation by the author. The original (Amharic) statement reads: 'ስብስቦ እኛን እስር ቤት ቢያስገባ ምክንያት ስላጣ አይደለም። ሌብነቱ፤ መግራፉ፤ መግደሉ፤ ብዙ ሰበብ አለ እኛን ላማሰር'.
199   Ibid. Translation by the author. The original (Amharic) statement reads: 'እኛ እስር ቤት ብንገባ ግን ለኢትዮጵያ ለውጥ የለውም'.

the past failed to solve the country's problems. Ironically, the Prime Minister's remarks omitted all reference to the TGE's decision to prosecute the *Dergue*, on the basis of which the obligation to prosecute core crimes was incorporated into the Constitution, as noted above. Instead, the historical instances invoked by the Prime Minster to justify amnesty over prosecution were the transition from Lij Iyasu to Emperor Haileselassie I in 1916 and the regime change from the Emperor to the *Dergue* in 1974.[200] Yet, in these instances, no attempt was made to bring the alleged perpetrators to justice; on the contrary, in all these instances, former government officials were indefinitely detained or summarily executed.

Be that as it may, it is clear that the Prime Minister's remarks could be characterized as self-proclaimed amnesty, for which he attempted to provide an *ex post facto* justification. As this was not introduced by any formal act of Parliament, this situation amounts to *de facto* amnesty. Such an amnesty, whether backed by popular support or not, remains unconstitutional as it constitutes a clear violation of Article 28 of the Constitution. This was further evidenced by the fact that some recent prosecutions instituted in Ethiopia against middle and low level security forces and the police have treated cases of widespread and systematic torture as corruption and abuse of power rather than as crimes against humanity.[201] In fact, Ethiopia still lacks a provision criminalizing torture and crimes against humanity as such, which is symptomatic of the country's lack of genuine commitment to prosecute core crimes at all times.

3.7 Conclusion

This chapter has examined the possible motives why Ethiopia prosecuted core crimes in the *Dergue*, the *Anuak-Nuwer*, the CUD, and the *Oromo-Gumuz* trials. Although several motivations might have played a role, the initial decision to prosecute the *Dergue* trials was predominantly a result of a political ambition to use the trials for political legitimacy. The fact that the *Dergue* was completely defeated and lacked all bargaining power might have helped the TGE to reach the decision to prosecute without making compromises. The overall development behind the decision to prosecute seemed to have been tailored by the TGE for its own political interests. In that sense, the decision-making process was not accessible by either the victims or the perpetrators.

---

200   Ibid.
201   See for instance, FHC, *Federal Prosecutor v. Getachew Aseffa et al.*, (Indictment), 7 May 2019, File No. 238040.

Political interests have remained to be the driving forces behind the other decisions to prosecute core crimes. Although Ethiopia was under both national and international obligations to prosecute the genocides that occurred in the *Anuak-Nuwer,* the CUD, and the *Oromo-Gumuz* situations, it is doubtful that these trials resulted from a genuine commitment to prosecute core crimes. In fact, the hidden nature of these trials could be a result of their political irrelevance to the government. As was also shown in the last part of the chapter, Ethiopia does not appear to be ready to prosecute core crimes at all times. As is discussed in detail in the next chapter, the question of who should be prosecuted for core crimes is indeed another aspect that indicates the significant weight of political considerations in shaping the nature and scope of Ethiopian core crimes trials.

CHAPTER 4

The Decisions to Prosecute

Who Should Be Brought to Justice?

4.1   Introduction

This chapter is a continuation of the analysis started in Chapters 2 and 3 regarding how the four instances of prosecution of core crimes in Ethiopia were set in motion. The previous chapters discussed the contexts in which Ethiopia decided to prosecute core crimes, the alleged motives behind the decisions, and, in the process, made a preliminary identification of the legal qualification of crimes investigated and prosecuted in the *Dergue,* the *Anuak-Nuwer,* the CUD, and the *Oromo-Gumuz* trials. This chapter aims to take the scope of the discussion one-step further. Although the decisions to prosecute are still the subject of the chapter, the focus is now on the aims and scope of these decisions to prosecute, and more particularly on who to prosecute. In other words, here, unlike in the two previous chapters, the discussion focuses not on *how* Ethiopia's decisions to prosecute core crimes came about but on *who* was and was not prosecuted in relation to these crimes.

As pointed out in section 1.7 of Chapter 1, the process of national prosecution of core crimes should be carried out in a manner that removes legal and institutional impediments that could hinder actual prosecutions from emerging or render them ineffective. As discussed in Chapter 2, apart from the application of amnesty laws,[1] legal impediments to the prosecution of core crimes could include statutes of limitations and laws on immunities.[2] As will be discussed in this chapter, legal provisions on jurisdiction or on prosecutorial scope may also contain stipulations that are aimed at shielding perpetrators from accountability through an unjustified selectivity of crimes and/or suspects.[3]

Using the relevant standards of international criminal justice as a comparison yardstick, that is, those standards in force at the time of the respective Ethiopian trials, this chapter explores the issue of jurisdiction over persons responsible for committing core crimes. It begins by examining how the prosecutorial power was delineated with regards to personal jurisdiction over those

---

1   For the discussion on amnesty in relation to the Ethiopian trials, see Chapter 2, sections 2.2.
2   See Chapter 1, section 1.7.
3   See also ibid.

responsible for crimes identified under the previous chapter. It analyzes both specific circumstances and laws behind these trials as well as the relevant practices.

Section 4.2. of this chapter explores some allegedly striking aspects of the Ethiopian trials, and notably discusses whether the Ethiopian process has created its own political impediments such as selectively targeting a specific group of individuals for prosecution. In connection to this, it also assesses the manner in which crimes were qualified.

The final section (section 4.3.) examines issues related to bringing fugitive offenders to justice. In particular, it analyzes the legality of trials *in absentia* (by default) held in Ethiopia in relation to thousands of defendants, notably in the *Dergue* trials. In addition to assessing whether the practice conforms to standards of international human rights law, this section also aims at highlighting whether the trials have complied with an additional requirement under Ethiopian law, namely, the obligation to request the extradition of fugitives before resorting to trials in their absence.[4]

4.2 Delineating Prosecutorial Scope: The Notion of Unjustified Selectivity

It has been alleged that during two of the four episodes of core crimes trials in Ethiopia the procedures could be characterized as victor's justice; an accusation that both international and internationalized prosecutions of core crimes have seldom escaped.[5] The CUD and the *Dergue* trials were indeed said to have only prosecuted defendants belonging to one side of a conflict.[6]

There are no similar accusations with respect to the other two trials, the *Anuak-Nuwer* and the *Oromo-Gumuz*, perhaps because of the completely hidden nature of these trials. Nonetheless, based on the trial documents, it is possible to determine whether these trials were selective in their choice of defendants or not. The following paragraphs examine this issue in relation to

---

4 See below, sub-section 4.3.2.1.
5 With regards to the Nuremberg Charter and the Tokyo Charter, which have been referred to as victors' charters for implicating, respectively, the European Axis and Far-Eastern (Japanese) war criminals only, see e.g. R.H. Minear, *Victors' Justice: The Tokyo War Crimes Trial* (Princeton: Princeton University Press, 1971) 93–95. With regards to the ICC, see e.g. W.A. Schabas, 'Victor's Justice: Selecting Situations at the International Criminal Court' (2009–2010) 43(1) *John Marshall Law Review* 535–552, 549–552.
6 See below, sections 4.2.1. and 4.2.2.

the *Anuak-Nuwer* and the *Oromo-Gumuz* trials before turning to an in-depth discussion of the victor's justice accusations raised against the CUD and the *Dergue* trials.

The *Anuak-Nuwer* incident related to an attack perpetrated by members of the *Anuak* ethnic group against defenseless *Nuwer* refugees from South Sudan.[7] This premeditated attack took place while the *Nuwer* refugees were travelling by bus and in the absence of any conflict preceding the incident. In fact, the *Anuak-Nuwer* trial was a prosecution that resulted from a single incident, not a conflict. Unsurprisingly therefore, the trial documents do not contain any indication as to the existence of a conflict either before or after the incident. As such, the incident represents a one-sided attack, the prosecution of which cannot reasonably give rise to the above-mentioned criticism of victor's justice.

The *Oromo-Gumuz* trials were conducted in relation to a conflict that took place from 16 to 31 May 2008 between members of the ethnic *Oromo* and those of the ethnic *Gumuz* in western Ethiopia, across the border shared by the Regional States of *Benishangul-Gumuz* and *Oromia*. The analysis of the court cases indicates that members of the *Gumuz* opened an attack against members of the *Oromo* and that the *Oromos* responded by attacking members of the *Gumuz*, thereby turning the situation into a two-sided conflict. Apart from the court cases, there is no additional and independent study that explains the context of the *Oromo-Gumuz* conflict, although it can be noted that, in 2014, the FDRE House of Federation allegedly finalized conflict-mapping studies throughout Ethiopia including that of the *Oromo-Gumuz* disputes. Yet, the outcomes of these studies have been regarded as classified.

Interestingly, the *Oromo-Gumuz* trials targeted both sides to the conflict. Of the 286 defendants prosecuted in three separate trials, 160 defendants from the *Kemashie* District of the *Benishangul-Gumuz* Regional State were prosecuted, in the cases of Federal *Prosecutor v. Tadesse Jewannie Mengesha et al.*[8] and *Federal Prosecutor v. Tesfaye Nenno Loya et al.*,[9] for perpetrating genocide against ethnic *Oromos*. The remaining 126 defendants, residents of the *East Wellega District* of the Oromia Regional State, were prosecuted in the case of *Federal Prosecutor v. Aliyu Yusuf Ibrahim et al.* for perpetrating genocide

---

7   See FHC, *Federal Prosecutor v. Gure Uchala Ugira et al.*, (Trial Judgment), 25 March 2005, File No. 586/96.
8   FHC, *Federal Prosecutor v. Tadesse Jewanie Mengesha et al.*, (Trial Judgment) 24 August 2009, File No. 70996/2000.
9   FHC, *Federal Prosecutor v. Tesfaye Neno Loya et al.*, (Trial Judgment), 30 April 2009, File No. 74796/2000.

against members of the *Gumuz* ethnic group.[10] As such, these trials dealt with what can be described as *retaliatory genocide* in the sense that perpetrators of genocide became victims of a genocidal attack by the survivors, as will be discussed in chapter 6.

Compared to the above two trials, both the CUD and the *Dergue* trials were conducted following complex situations of violence over long periods of time and involving multiple groups. In both cases, the victim or perpetrator status of the groups that participated in the respective conflicts was not always clear. Consequently, the manner in which the resulting trials selected their defendants might be put into question. The following subsections provide an in-depth separate discussion on how these two groups of trials chose their defendants. In particular, by turning to both the relevant law and practice and the situational background, it examines whether these trials were of a one-sided nature or not.

4.2.1 The Dergue *Trials: The Victors v. The Vanquished*

The *Dergue* regime ruled the country for 17 years (1974–1991) and between 175,000 to possibly 2,000,000 people lost their lives due to various forms of violence. The decision to prosecute was taken by the TGE in 1992 and by the time the SPO became operational in 1993 – six months after its establishment – more than 2,000 suspects had already been arrested and detained.[11] The forces of the EPRDF proceeded to the arrests mainly in May and June 1991, thus before the decision to prosecute was reached by the TGE. As noted in the previous chapter, the arrests and detentions of such a large number of people were effectuated without prior inquiry into who was, and was not, allegedly responsible for acts later referred to as 'heinous and horrendous crimes'.[12] Measures taken in May and June 1991, in particular the arrests and detentions, were directed entirely against officials and members of the vanquished: the *Dergue*.

What about the investigations and the prosecutions that were initiated a year later? In response to this question, several commentators and journalists have stated that the *Dergue* trials were one-sided.[13] Nevertheless, their

---

10   See FHC, *Federal Prosecutor* v. *Aliyu Yusufe Ibrahim et al.*, (Trial Judgment), 6 September 2009, File No. 7100/2000.

11   SPO, 'Report of the Office of the Special Prosecutor 1994: The Special Prosecution Process of War Criminals and Human Rights Violation in Ethiopia' in N.J. Kritz (ed.), *Transitional Justice: How Emerging Democracies Reckon with Former Regimes; Laws, Rulings and Reports* (Washington DC: United States Institute of Peace Press, 1995) 561 [Hereinafter: SPO Report (1994)].

12   See Chapter 2, sub-section 2.3.1.

13   See in general E. Kissi, *Revolution and Genocide in Ethiopia and Cambodia* (Lanham: Lexington Books, 2006) 107–114.

response lacks a comprehensive examination of the relevant law and practice, as it draws solely upon the alleged political motivation behind the decision to prosecute, which this book has looked into in Chapter 3.[14] Some authors have raised the issue of victor's justice more directly, but their claim seems to rest only on the criticisms raised by the defendants.[15]

This serious accusation of victor's justice begs for a meticulous scrutiny of the scope of the SPO's personal jurisdiction as well as of the context in which the *Dergue* era crimes were perpetrated. The next section thus examines the SPO's personal jurisdiction to determine whether the SPO defendants only belonged to one of the groups to the conflict. Insofar as it will be demonstrated that such was the case, the subsequent section proceeds to elucidate whether persons outside the *Dergue* were also implicated in crimes perpetrated during the *Dergue* regime.

4.2.1.1 The SPO's Personal Jurisdiction: 'The Others Were Left Untouched'
The issue of who should be prosecuted by the SPO was dealt with in Article 6 of the SPO Proclamation, under the heading 'the power of the office'. It read:

> The [SPO] shall, in accordance with the law, have the power to conduct investigation and institute proceedings in respect of any person having committed or responsible for the commission of an offence by abusing his position in the party, the government or mass organizations under the *Dergue*-WPE [Workers Party of Ethiopia] regime.[16]

It follows from this provision that for the SPO to exercise its personal jurisdiction two conditions had to be fulfilled. The first proviso was the requirement of a position of 'authority' i.e. *selethan* (ሥልጣን), as precisely stated in the Amharic version of the SPO Proclamation. The SPO's power was to be exercised only with regards to those persons who had allegedly perpetrated crimes falling under the SPO's jurisdiction by abusing and taking advantage of their position of authority (ሥልጣን መከታ በማድረግ). As such, the provision excluded from

---

14 See Chapter 3, in particular, section 3.5.
15 See M.T. Tessema, *Prosecution of Politicide in Ethiopia: The Red-Terror Trials* (The Hague: Asser Printing Press, 2018), 241–243.
16 SPO Proclamation, Amharic version, Article 6. Translation by the author. Emphasis added The original (Amharic) reads:
ሕፈት ቤቱ በደርግ ኢሥፓ ሥርዓት በፓርቲ፣ በመንግስት ዉይም በሕዝባዊ ድርጅት የነበረዉን ሥልጣን መከታ በማድረግ ወንጀል ፈጽሟል ወይም በወንጀል ተጠያቂ ነዉ በሚል በማንኛዉም ሰዉ ላይ በሕግ መሠረት ምርመራ የማካሄድ ክስ የመመሥረት ሥልጣን ይኖራዋል።.

the SPO's personal jurisdiction private individuals and officials who might have participated in the commission of the SPO crimes in *their private capacity*. The provision referred to any person with a position of authority without distinction of rank, thus explicitly stating that the SPO's jurisdiction was not limited to the 'big fish'. As such, the SPO had, arguably, a broader *ratione personae* jurisdiction as compared to some of the post-conflict international tribunals such as the ICTR and the ICTY, although in practice prosecutions before these tribunals have included low-ranking individuals.

The second proviso, which further qualified the first proviso, defined the requirement of 'position of authority' in terms of the administration of the *Dergue*. Thus, for the SPO to actually exercise its investigative and prosecutorial power over a particular person suspected of having committed crimes falling under its jurisdiction, that person must have held a *position of authority* within the organizational hierarchy of the *Dergue*, as opposed to any other organization or entity.

Thus, Article 6 played both exculpatory and incriminatory roles. In its incriminatory angle, the provision accused a specific category of defendants, namely the *Dergue*. In its exculpatory aspect, the provision excluded members or officials of non-*Dergue* organizations from being subjected to investigation and prosecution by the SPO. As far as the law was concerned, there was no visible reason justifying such exculpation and inculpation. This apparent lack of objectivity becomes even less tenable insofar as neither the decision to prosecute or the drafting of the proclamation was accompanied by an inquiry into the question of who was, or was not, responsible for the crimes committed during the *Dergue* regime.[17]

Concerning the practice, a brief glance at the SPO's list of defendants reveals that not all of the 5119 defendants had a position of authority in the *Dergue*'s administration (the government, the party, or mass organizations).[18] Private individuals were also prosecuted. From the beginning, a prosecutorial strategy prepared by the SPO in 1993 targeted the prosecution of three categories of offenders: policy makers, field commanders, and 'individual perpetrators'.[19] Unlike the first two, the last category was meant to refer to both private individuals and officials who actually carried out the crimes.[20] Already fairly wide,

---

17   See Chapter 2, sub-section 2.3.2.
18   For details regarding the number of defendants prosecuted by the SPO, see Special Prosecution Office, 'Annual Report to the House of Peoples' Representatives of Ethiopia' (Addis Ababa, 4 February 2010) 10.
19   Ibid.
20   Ibid.

this last category was *de facto* expanded so as to include any person, instead of any person *with a position of authority*. As a result, the SPO prosecuted individuals who held no position of authority for their participation in crimes committed under the auspices of the *Dergue* administration. Whether doing so was contrary to the SPO Proclamation went largely unexamined.

The list of individual perpetrators that the SPO prosecuted thus included ordinary members of society to which the SPO referred to using such labels as 'drivers',[21] 'cooperating individuals',[22] 'progressive individuals'[23] and 'informants'.[24] The SPO's total disregard for the position of authority proviso can also be inferred from other cases where defendants were described using the phrase 'position of authority unknown'.[25] At times, the SPO referred to its defendants using only their names (sometimes even just a part of a name) without any description as to their private or official positions.[26]

A clear objection, however, was raised in the case of *SPO v. General Tedela Desta et al.*,[27] one of the cases adjudicated by the Oromia Supreme Court's western division in Jimma. According to the objection raised by Ewunetu Akoma, defendant number 55 in the case at hand, the SPO had exceeded its mandate by indicting him for crimes allegedly committed at a time where he had no position of authority in the government.[28] According to the SPO, however,

---

21   See Special Prosecutor's Office, *Dem Yazele Dossie: Begizeyawi Wotaderawi Dergue Weyem Mengist Abalat Benetsuhan Zegoch Laye Yetefetsem Wenjel Zegeba* (Addis Ababa: Far-East Trading P.L.C., 2010). [Hereinafter: *Dem Yazele Dossie*] 137. See also FHC, SPO v. *Teshome Ashenie*, (Indictment, 29 June 2000) File No. 1937/1992,1; FHC, SPO v. *Ademasu Amare et al.*, (Revised Indictment), 7 July 1998, File No. 654/1989, 3: see in particular defendant number 16.

22   See e.g. defendants number 28, 54, 117, 140, 141, and 142 in FHC, SPO v. *Gesegesse Gebremeskel Aterega et al.*, (Indictment), 23 December 1996, File No. 03099/1989, 4–5, 12, 14. Several defendants were prosecuted as cooperating individuals in SNNPRS SC, SPO v. *Mekonnen Gelan et al.*, (Revised Indictment), 22 May 2001), File No. 1338/97,1-20. See defendants number 132, 138, and 152 in OSC, SPO v. *Brigadier General Tedela Desta et al.*, (Revised Indictment), 10 October 1999, File No. OSC 1/1989, 13–14.

23   See defendants number 41 and 46 in *Gesegesse Gebremeskel Aterega et al.*, (Indictment) *supra* note 22, 5.

24   See for instance defendant number 36 in FHC, SPO v. *Asazenew Bayyisa et al.*, (Indictment), 23 December 1996, File No. 643/1989, 7.

25   See for instance defendant number 62, in FHC, SPO v. *Demissie Weldemariam et al.* (Initial Indictment), 23 December 1996, File No. 963/1989, 6; See also several defendants in *Mekonnen Gelan et al.*, (Revised Indictment), *supra* note 22, 1–20.

26   See e.g. defendants number 36, 50, 51, 52, 58, 59 in *Ademasu Amare et al.*, (Revised Indictment), *supra* note 21, 4–6.

27   *Brigadier General Tedela Desta et al.*, (Revised Indictment), *supra* note 22, 13–14.

28   OSC, SPO v. *Brigadier General Tedela Desta et al.*, (Defendant Ewunetu Akoma's Preliminary Objection to the Initial Indictment), 11 November 1998, File No. 1/1989, 1.

its personal jurisdiction was never limited to persons who held a position of authority in the *Dergue* administration; a response with which the court concurred.[29] In support of its position, the SPO invoked Article 6 and the Preamble of the Proclamation.

The SPO recalled the terms of Article 6, which referred to 'any person having committed or responsible for the commission of an offence by abusing his position', and argued that this phrase was to be read disjunctively by distinguishing two categories: 'any person having committed an offence' on the one hand and 'any person responsible for the commission of an offence by abusing his position' on the other.[30] Neither the Amharic version nor the English version of Article 6 supports this admittedly illogical deconstruction of phrases. As stated above, Article 6 contains clear provisos on the investigative and prosecutorial powers of the SPO and a textual reading unequivocally suggests that the target of the law is not *any person*, but *any person with a position of authority*.

The SPO also relied on the Amharic version of the second paragraph of the Preamble, which, according to the SPO's understanding, was apparently not similar to the official English version that had identified the alleged perpetrators to be 'officials of the *Dergue* WPE-regime, members and auxiliaries of the security and armed forces'.[31] In contrast, the SPO's interpretation of the Amharic version of the paragraph added a category of 'collaborating individuals' to the list of targeted persons. As such, the SPO understood the last part of the second paragraph as referring to 'officials of the *Dergue* WPE-regime, members of the security and armed forces, *and collaborating individuals*'.[32]

The SPO's reliance on the Preamble of the Proclamation to determine the scope of its mandate is as unsustainable. Firstly, paragraph 2 – that the SPO invoked – hardly supported its claim: it dealt with who allegedly committed the crimes, not with who should be investigated and prosecuted. Rather, it is the fourth paragraph of the Preamble that clearly addressed the issue of who 'must be brought to trial'.[33] This paragraph identified four

---

29 OSC, SPO v. *Brigadier General Tedela Desta et al.,* (Ruling on Preliminary Objections), 11 November 1998, File No. 1/1989, 1.
30 OSC, SPO v. *Brigadier General Tedela Desta et al.,* (SPO's Response to Defendant Ewunetu Akoma's Preliminary Objection to the Initial Indictment), 25 May 1999, File No. 1/1989, 51.
31 See SPO Proclamation, Preamble, para. 2.
32 *Brigadier General Tedela Desta et al.,* (SPO's Response to Defendant Ewunetu Akoma's Preliminary Objection to the Initial Indictment), *supra* note 30, 51. Emphasis added.
33 SPO Proclamation, Preamble, para. 4:
    In view of the fact that the historical mission of the Ethiopian People's Revolutionary Democratic Front (EPRDF) has been accomplished, it is essential that higher officials of the WPE and members of the security and armed forces who have been detained at the time the EPRDF assumed control of the country and thereafter and who are suspected of

categories of alleged offenders: *i*) higher-officials of the WPE,[34] and officials of the government;[35] *ii*) members and auxiliaries of the security[36] and armed

---

having committed offences, as well as representatives of urban dwellers associations and peasant associations, and other persons who have associated with the commission of said offences, must be brought to trial.

34   The WPE, the first political party in the history of Ethiopia, was established by the *Dergue* in 1984, a decade after the *Dergue* took power and after other leftist political organizations were eliminated through the notorious Red-Terror campaign. For a historical analysis of the WPE, see R. Warner, 'The Workers' Party of Ethiopia' (A Report Prepared by the Federal Research Division of the Library of Congress under an Interagency Agreement, Washington DC, 12 October 1984) 1–17, available at: <http://oai.dtic.mil/oai/oai?verb=getRecord&metadataPrefix=html&identifier=ADA303418> accessed 19 October 2016. In 1987, upon the establishment of the People's Democratic Republic of Ethiopia (PDRE), the WPE acquired the status of the ruling vanguard party. See The 1987 Constitution of the PDRE, Article 6.

35   Only the Amharic version of paragraph 4 of the Preamble refers to 'officials of the government' የመንግስት በለሥልጣኖች. Because the objective of the Proclamation was to prosecute crimes committed throughout the *Dergue* regime from 1974 to 1991 (See Preamble, para. 1), a reference to the WPE that would exclude the 'government' is incorrect. The intermittent mentioning of the WPE in various paragraphs of the Preamble and Article 6 is rather confusing. Broadly seen, the *Dergue* was a collective name not only for the pre-WPE administration but also for the restructured administration during the PDRE. The establishment of the WPE, which was meant to transfer power from the military to the people, did not bring a fundamentally new arrangement. The same officials that were in the *Dergue* (the remaining 73 of the original 106 members) became members of the WPE's politburo and heads of its departments. In general, though few handpicked civilians were also included in the new administration, what essentially happened after the establishment of the WPE was, as had also happened previously on several occasions, a case of the *Dergue* restructuring and redefining itself. See A. Tiruneh, *The Ethiopian Revolution 1974–1987: A Transformation from an Aristocratic to a Totalitarian Autocracy* (Cambridge: Cambridge University Press, 1993) 227–265. See also T. Haile-Selassie, *The Ethiopian Revolution 1974–1991: From a Monarchical Autocracy to a Military Oligarchy* (London: Kegan Paul International, 1997) 253–259.

36   As deconstructed by the SPO, the Proclamation's reference to members of the security forces was understood as including those appointed or employed at various security and intelligence departments that were greatly expanded throughout the nation. The intelligence and security departments were structurally placed either under the *Dergue* Central Committee (DSC) or the Ministry of National and Public Safety and Security (MNPSS). Those under the DSC were: the Revolutionary Campaign and Security Department, the Central Revolutionary Investigation Office, the *Dergue* Investigation Unit, and the Revolutionary Intelligence Centre, all of which were staffed largely with persons from the military. Under the MNPSS were the special investigation offices such as the Police Force Main Department, and the Police Force Special Investigation Unit, which had several provincial sub-divisions throughout the country. Besides those falling within the official security apparatus of the government, various 'off-the-record' security units were created over the course of the 17 years of the *Dergue*'s rule. See *Dem Yazele Dossie, supra* note 21,

forces;[37] *iii*) representatives of urban dwellers associations and peasant associations,[38] (which are referred to as mass organizations under Article 6)[39]; and *iv*) *other persons* who have associated themselves with the commission of 'said offences', i.e. offences referred to as heinous and horrendous crimes

---

81–88. The structure of the *Dergue*'s institution of violence are discussed in Chapter 6. See Chapter 6, sub-section 6.3.1.1.

37 The *Dergue* regime was a military regime where virtually all of its organs were controlled by members of the armed forces. It should be noted that some of the members of the armed forces were higher officials, and therefore fell within the first category of offenders i.e. officials of the government. Those who were not fell into the second category of offenders. The distinction between the two was however not based on a military-ranking of the members in the sense that senior military officials were not necessarily higher officials too. Official positions during the *Dergue* were not assumed or assigned based on military-ranking; several higher officials, including Mengistu Hailemariam, the chairman of the *Dergue*, the secretary general of the WPE, and the president of the PDRE, were all junior officers in the military. In fact, senior military officials were deliberately excluded from the *Dergue* from the start on the ground that they were deemed compromised by their close association with the Haileselassie regime. Thus, all members of the armed forces who had allegedly participated in the commission of heinous and horrendous crimes, from ordinary soldiers to those members who assumed the highest ranking in the military, were categorized under the same group of offenders.

38 Urban Dwellers' Associations (UDAs) and Peasant Associations (PAs), represented civilian offenders as opposed to military or security forces. It was through UDAs and PAs that civilians were more or less able to assume offices at provincial, *aweraja*, and *kebele* levels. UDAs and PAs were established following *Dergue*'s land and property ownership Proclamations of 1975. See Tiruneh, *The Ethiopian Revolution 1974–1987*, supra note 75, 115. The same year, there were about 300 UDAs in Addis Ababa alone, while by September of 1976 about 22,000 PAs were established in the entire nation. See Haile-Selassie, *The Ethiopian Revolution 1974–1991*, supra note 35, 178. By referring to members of the UDAs and PAs, it should be noted that the Proclamation did not aim at prosecuting ordinary members of the associations, but those in leadership positions. In that regard, it was clear from the wording of the Preamble that the law referred to the representatives of UDAs and PAs. Usually, each mass organization had three organs: the executive committee, the judicial committee and the public welfare committee, which respectively had three, three and two committee members. See Tiruneh, *The Ethiopian Revolution 1974–1987*, supra note 35, 115–117.

39 The reason for the Proclamation to put an emphasis on the representatives of the UDAs and PAs is to be found in the notorious role they played in the execution of the Red-Terror campaign. Following intensive politicization and mobilization activities carried out against the mass organizations by the Provisional Office for Mass Organization Affairs (POMOA), an intermediary organ established by the *Dergue* to control the mass organizations, the PDAs and PAs became institutions of violence and converted their Public Affairs Committees into, respectively, Revolutionary Defense Squads and Defense Squads. See Tiruneh, *The Ethiopian Revolution 1974–1987*, supra note 35, 117. As such, the mass organizations were empowered to have armed-wings through which they were able to take, *inter alia*, independent 'revolutionary measures'. See ibid.

under paragraph 2 of the Preamble. Without any explanation, Article 6 does not mention this fourth category of offenders.[40]

Secondly, the SPO's argument is legally fragile because there was no actual need to refer to, or rely on, the Preamble. Although it admittedly disregarded the objectives of the decision to prosecute set out in the Preamble, Article 6's delineation of the power of the SPO is no less unequivocal. In cases where the operative provision is clear, the interpretative relevance of the Preamble is limited. By relying on the Preamble, the SPO might have abused the rules of interpretation to expand its own personal jurisdiction.

This, however, does not mean that persons not affiliated to the *Dergue* were prosecuted. Only the *Dergue* and its supporters (irrespective of a position of authority) were brought to justice. This was clearly indicated in the SPO's final report in 2010, not least by the use of the Amharic statement: ሌሎቹ አልተነኩም, which literally means *the others were left untouched*.[41]

4.2.1.2 The Victor's Justice Accusation

The fact that only those officials, members, and affiliates of the *Dergue* (the vanquished) were implicated in the Proclamation and prosecuted by the SPO is not *per se* sufficient to regard the *Dergue* trials as an exercise of victor's justice. Such a conclusion should also be based on the determination of whether groups or peoples fighting the *Dergue* have also participated in the commission of crimes. If so, it should be assessed whether a separate response (other than the SPO) was given to bring the non-*Dergue* groups/individuals to justice.

4.2.1.2.1 The Question of Multiple Actors

The SPO Proclamation does not mention any group other than the *Dergue* in relation to the crimes committed against the Ethiopian people from 1974 to1991.[42] However, the SPO process was criticized as unjustifiably selective for two reasons. The first set of criticism relied on allegations related to the context in which the Red-Terror era crimes were perpetrated while the second set was based on allegations as to the crimes perpetrated within the context of

---

40 On a closer look, one can identify a difference between the English and Amharic versions of the Proclamation regarding the identity of the 'other persons'. Contrary to 'other persons' which literally translates to *leloch sewoch* in Amharic, the Amharic version of the Proclamation used the phrase *begelesebe dereja* which refers to both officials and 'private individuals' who participated in the commission of crimes in a 'private capacity' as opposed to those holding official positions and who might have used their 'official capacity' to commit crimes. See SPO Proclamation, Preamble, para. 4.

41 See *Dem Yazele Dossie, supra* note 21, 2.

42 See SPO Proclamation, Preamble, para. 1.

the armed conflict. This division is essential not only because it, in theory, distinguishes crimes committed in the context of an armed conflict from those committed outside of it, but also because it has, as will be discussed, practical implications on the identity of the groups involved. The following sub-sections discuss these allegations separately.

4.2.1.2.1.1 Allegations Related to the Red-Terror

Several studies conducted on the context in which violence was perpetrated during the Ethiopian Red-Terror era largely disagree on one important aspect of that period, namely, the start date of the Red-Terror.[43] Closely seen, however, the disagreement emanates from the absence of a single straightforward answer to the question: who fired the first bullet? In a way, this disagreement is thus very much connected to the question this section seeks to answer, that is, whether the Red-Terror era was a period of one-sided violence.

As Edward Kissi noted, 'any objective assessment of terror in Ethiopia in the 1970s should lead to a conclusion that the widespread killings and terror that took place in the country during that period were not one-sided'.[44] Although the state of scholarship on the context of Red-Terror is highly partisan,[45] there actually exists no denial of the fact that there were multiple actorsand this cannot be considered a period of one-sided violence.

Notwithstanding its extremely asymmetrical nature, the Red-Terror era has been commonly understood as a violent struggle among the ruling and the opposition groups, notably through its colloquial Amharic reference 'Tenenqe' (ተነንቀ). The Red-Terror was declared by the *Dergue* against the opposition groups, and the government used the entire state apparatus to inflict extreme and extensive violence against all dissenting groups. Nevertheless, in what was referred to as the White-Terror, the opposition too had declared and used violence against the *Dergue*.

Simply put, the White-Terror was a sporadic campaign of assassination that targeted members and allies of the *Dergue*. As known by its other labels, such as 'urban guerrilla warfare', the assassination and terrorization acts were

---

43 For details on this, see P. Toggia, 'The Revolutionary Endgame of Political Power: The Genealogy of 'Red Terror' in Ethiopia' (2012) 10 (3) *African Identities* 265–280, 270; M. Tegegn, 'Mengistu's Red Terror' (2012) 10(3) *African Identities* 249–263, 250.

44 E. Kissi, 'Remembering Ethiopia's 'Red Terror': History of a Private Effort to Preserve a Public Memory' in ERTDRC, *Documenting the Red Terror: Bearing Witness to Ethiopia's Lost Generations* (Ottawa: ERTDRC North America Inc, 2012) 9–23, 9.

45 See generally J. Wiebel, 'The State of Scholarship on the Ethiopian Red Terror' in ERTDRC, *Documenting the Red Terror: Bearing Witness to Ethiopia's Lost Generations* (Ottawa: ERTDRC North America Inc, 2012) 89–96.

carried out in the cities, mainly in the capital Addis Ababa.[46] In the literature, it is widely accepted that the EPRP was the main, if not only, group behind the White-Terror.

For the most part, the jurisprudence of Ethiopian courts substantiates the assertion that there were non-*Dergue* groups that took part in the array of violence during the Red-Terror era. In their joint submission to the FHC, defendants in *Mengistu et al.* produced numerous evidence in support of their claim that they had committed the alleged crimes in self-defense i.e., in defense of the State and the Revolution.[47] The evidence (documents, laws, decrees, experts and witnesses)[48] demonstrated the perpetration of widespread crimes against members and affiliates of the *Dergue* administration. The defendants produced the names of about eighty-three individuals allegedly assassinated by the EPRP during its White-Terror campaign.[49] Evidence was also submitted by the defendants to establish that the assassination attempt on the Chairman of the *Dergue*, Mengistu Hailemariam, was the EPRP's doing.[50] The FHC noted that the defendants had produced sufficient evidence to establish that the EPRP had waged violence against the *Dergue* administration.[51] Most importantly, in a statement that concluded that the Red-Terror era was indeed not a period of one-sided violence, the FHC stated,

> Save the question whether the EPRP or some other political group was responsible, it can safely be concluded from the evidence that acts of killing had been perpetrated against persons considered affiliated to the *Dergue* government. The same is true for government properties allegedly destroyed by explosives.[52]

---

46 As opposed to the armed struggle of the peasants that was simultaneously carried out in the rural parts of the country, the White-Terror was not an armed struggle and, as it is generally understood, had no connection to the armed conflicts and thus to conducts that could potentially constitute war crimes.
47 See FHC, SPO v. *Colonel Mengistu Hailemariam et al.*, (Trial Judgment), 12 December 2006, File No. 1/87, 9.
48 See ibid., 11–109.
49 See ibid., 114. Recently, an alleged partial list of about 271 victims of the White-Terror was published by Fekereselssie Wogederes who still (even after serving eighteen years in prison) describes the SPO process as a case of victor's justice. See F. Wogederes, *Egnana Abiyotu* (Los Angeles: Tsehai Publishers, 2014) 274–296.
50 See *Colonel Mengistu Hailemariam et al.*, (Trial Judgment), *supra* note 47, 115.
51 Ibid.
52 See ibid. Translation by the author. The original (Amharic) version reads:
ስለዚህ ኢህአፓ ወይም ሌላ የፖለቲካ ቡድን ወይም አባላቱ የገደሏቸው መሆን አለመሆን እንዳለ ሆኖ በዚህ ማስረጃዎች መሰረት የደርግ መንግስት ደጋፊዎች የተባሉ ሰዎች ሲገደሉ እንደነበረ ማረጋገጥ ይቻላል። በንብረት ላይ ተፈጻሚ የተባለትም የፈንጂ አደጋዎች እንዲሁ።

The Court however did not outline the genealogy of the Red-Terror. At one point, it considered proven that the unleashing of the Red–Terror campaign by the *Dergue* was triggered by the EPRP's assassination of Fikre Meride,[53] who at the time was 'a prominent member of the AESM and the chairperson of the POMOA'.[54] In most parts of its discussion, however, the Court refrained from making reference to the Red-Terror, even if it did highlight that the Red-Terror was not an act of self-defense.[55]

In other cases, defendants were not limited to raising the self-defense argument. Instead, they challenged the SPO more directly, arguing that it had engaged in a one-sided prosecution. For example, in the case of *SPO v. Asazenew Bayissa et al.*, defendant number 21, Abebe Ahamed Hassen, submitted a preliminary objection stating that it was against the principle of equality before the law that acts committed by other groups were not regarded as crimes.[56] The SPO referred to the objection as improper and iniquitous, and stated that the others were just powerless civilians, incapable of defending themselves against the acts of torture inflicted upon them by the militarized apparatus of the *Dergue* administration.[57] Without going into the arguments on factual issues, the FHC rejected the objection on the ground that the issue of 'equality before the law' did not qualify as a preliminary objection pursuant to Article 130 (2) of the 1961 Code of Criminal Procedure.[58]

A similar objection was raised in the SPO proceedings conducted before regional courts. Fekadu Tegegne, defendant number 12 in *SPO v. Demetse Geberemedehen* before the Amhara Supreme Court (ASC), raised the issue of

---

53   Ibid., 115.
54   See Haile-Selassie, *The Ethiopian Revolution 1974–1991, supra* note 35, 184; Tiruneh, *The Ethiopian Revolution 1974–1987, supra* note 35, 186; *Dem Yazele Dossie, supra* note 21, 110.
55   The FHC concluded that the evidence had failed to establish the defendants' argument that they had acted in self-defense. According to the Court, the EPRP was not the group that shot the first bullet. Rather, the EPRP's declaration of violent struggle against the *Dergue* was a response to the acts of killing directed by the latter against the former, as a result of which EPRP's members were already forced to live in a state of misery and dismay. The Court thus concluded that the *Dergue* did not act in self-defense, owing to the fact that it was not only the one who shot the first bullet but also the one who inflicted an extremely greater amount of violence as compared to what the other groups did (this will be discussed in Chapter 6). See *Colonel Mengistu Hailemariam et al.*, (Trial Judgment), *supra* note 47, 115.
56   FHC, *SPO v. Asazenew Bayyisa et al.*, (Abebe Mohammed Hassen's Preliminary Objection on the Indictment) 14 December 1997, File No. 643/1989, 3.
57   FHC, *SPO v. Asazenew Bayyisa et al.*, (SPO's Response to the Defendant's Preliminary Objection on the Indictment), 01 April 1998, File No. 643/1989, 12.
58   Federal High Court, *SPO v. Asazenew Bayyisa et al.*, (Ruling on Preliminary Objections), 22 May 1998, File No. 643/1989, 19.

victor's justice in an explicit way.[59] As a preliminary objection to the charge brought against him by the SPO, the defendant argued:

> If the aim of these proceedings is to resolve those complex problems that took place during the *Dergue* regime through a trial process, those persons who participated in the 'white-terror' as well as in other unlawful conducts, which at the time forced the *Dergue* to respond by taking measures that are now regarded as criminal offences, must be brought to trial. A process that excludes those categories of people and focuses only on certain group of citizens is not only unfair and unjust but also violates guarantees and principles enshrined under Article 4 of the Criminal Code and Article 25 of the FDRE Constitution.[60]

The defendant's objection was not accepted by the Court. In ruling against the defendant, the ASC noted that the question of equality before the law did not qualify as a preliminary objection.[61] The Court concluded that 'even if the allegations were true they could not have absolved the defendant from criminal responsibility or stopped the court from proceeding with the current case'.[62] This decision was in line with Article 130 of the Code of Criminal Procedure, which exhaustively enumerated the grounds for preliminary objection to the charge: equality before the law was not included therein.[63]

---

59 ASC, SPO v. *Demetse Gebremedehen et al.*, (Fekadu Tegenge's Preliminary Objection on the Indictment), 21 July 1999, File No. 25/90, 3.
60 Ibid. Translation by the author. The original (Amharic) version reads:
    በደርግ ዘመነ መንግስት ተከስተው የነበሩ ውስብስብ ችግሮች በፍርድ ሂደት እልባት ማግኘት አለባቸው የሚባል ከሆነ በዚዜው ከነጭ ሽብር ጀምሮ በህግ ውጥነት እንቅስቃሴዎች ዉስጥ ተሳትፈና አሁን ወንጀል ተብለው ለተፈረጁት ጉዳቶች መከሰት የሆነት እንዲሁም ተካፋዮች የነበሩ ሁሉ ከህግ ፊት መቅረብ ይኖርባቸዋል። እናሊሆን ወገኖች ወደ ጎን በመተው በተወሰኑ ዘጎች ላይ ብቻ ተፈጻሚ ማድረግ ሚዛናዊ ፍትሃዊ ካለመሆኑም በላይ በወ/መ/ሕ/ቁ. 4 ዲንጋጌና በኢ.ፊ.ዲ.ሪ ህገ መንግስት አንቀጽ 25 መርህ ዊጭ ነው።
61 ASC, SPO v. *Demetse Gebremedehen et al.*, (Ruling on Preliminary Objection), 11 October 2000, File No. 25/90, 117.
62 Ibid.
63 See Criminal Procedure Code of Ethiopia, Article 130. According to this provision, the accused may object to the charge if: (a) the case is pending before another court; or (b) he has previously been acquitted or convicted of the same charge: or (c) the charge against him has been barred by limitation or the offence with which he has been charged has been made the subject of pardon or amnesty; or (d) he will be embarrassed in his defense if he is not granted a separate trial, where he is tried with others; or (e) no permission to prosecute as required by law has been obtained; or (f) the decision in the criminal case against him cannot be given until other proceedings have been completed: or (g) he is not responsible for his acts. The exhaustive nature of the list provided by this provision was also highlighted by the FHC in *Mengistu et al.*, where it declined to look into preliminary objections based on grounds that are not enumerated in this article. See FHC, SPO

Interestingly, the ASC did not turn a blind eye to the victor's justice accusation. It implied that selective prosecution could constitute a violation of the principle of equality before the law, even though it did not constitute a defense in criminal law.[64] In a more straightforward statement, the ASC asserted that 'provided that the allegations are true, a one-sided prosecution in violation of the principle of equality before the law entails accountability on the organ of the government that chose to proceed in such a manner'.[65]

4.2.1.2.1.2   Allegations Related to Armed Conflicts

The entire 17 years of Ethiopia's history under the *Dergue* regime witnessed several protracted civil wars in the northern, eastern, and western parts of the country, as well as the international armed conflict with neighboring Somalia.[66] Before the *Dergue* came to power, in 1974, there had already been numerous ethnic-based groups that had raised arms with secessionist ambitions. The main groups included: the Eritrean People's Liberation Front (EPLF), the Oromo Liberation Front (OLF), and the Tigray People's Liberation Front (TPLF). Sometime after the establishment of the *Dergue* and its absolute control of state power, the EPRP joined the armed struggle as the Ethiopian People's Revolutionary Army (EPRA).[67] The rebel groups ultimately succeeded in overthrowing the *Dergue* by force in 1991. While the EPLF managed to secure Eritrea's independence in 1993, the TPLF and the OLF dropped their ideology of secession and worked in 1991 towards conceiving the current federal state structure in Ethiopia.[68]

Like in the cases of the Red and the White Terrors, crimes perpetrated during the armed conflicts were admittedly not one-sided. Several reports alleged that the rebel forces had perpetrated acts that could constitute violations of common Article 3 to the 1949 Geneva Conventions or of the war crimes provisions of the Penal Code of 1957 of Ethiopia.[69] According to Amnesty

---

v. *Colonel Mengistu Hailemariam et al.,* (Ruling on Preliminary Objections), 10 October 1995, File No. 1/87, 10.

64 *Demetse Gebremedehen et al.,* (Ruling on Preliminary Objection), *supra* note 103, 117.
65 Ibid.
66 See T.P. Ofcansky, 'National Security' in T.P. Ofcansky and L. Berry (eds.), *Ethiopia: A Country Study* (Washington, D.C.: Federal Research Division Library of Congress, 1991) 267–325, 311–313.
67 It is stated in the literature that the EPRA was established as the armed wing of the EPRP even before the *Dergue* took power. See Tiruneh, *The Ethiopian Revolution 1974–1987*, *supra* note 35, 140–141.
68 As stated in Chapter 2, the EPRP did not participate in the discussions held in 1991 to form the TGE. See Chapter 2, sub-section 2.2.2.
69 See the Penal Code of 1957, Articles 282, 283, 284, 288, and 292.

International,[70] Human Rights Watch,[71] and the US State Department,[72] a wide range of acts, with varying degrees of cruelty and intensity, were reported to have been committed by the EPLF, the OLF and the TPLF in various parts of the country. The acts included: killings of civilians, executions of prisoners, executions of officials of the *Dergue*–WPE administration, executions of supporters of the government, forced military conscriptions, forced disappearances of party and government officials, use of civilians as human shields, attacks on refugees and UN aid agencies, destruction of religious places, attacks against religious leaders (priests and monks of the Ethiopian Orthodox Church), and acts of sexual assault including rape.[73]

As noted earlier, the SPO was only authorized to investigate crimes committed by officials and members of the armed forces of the *Dergue*. Unsurprisingly therefore, other groups were not investigated. And even as regards the *Dergue*, the SPO exhibited a frustrating performance as to the investigation and prosecution of war crimes. Out of the hundreds of SPO cases,[74] only one, *SPO v. Legesse Asfaw et al.*, dealt with the prosecution of war crimes, namely, war crimes against the civilian population in violation of Article 282 of the Penal Code.[75] As discussed in detail in Chapter 7, the absence of additional war crimes cases could not be justified on lack of evidence alleged by the spo, as several spo cases have dealt with potential war crimes cases as ordinary crimes.[76] Apparently, it was because the government (EPRDF) did not want to be implicated in war crimes investigation that there were no trials in Ethiopia for potential war crimes committed in various parts of the country during the civil war.[77]

---

70   See Amnesty International, 'Ethiopia: End of an Era of Brutal Repression – A New Chance for Human Rights' (Amnesty International, 18 June 1991) 48, available at: <https://www.amnesty.org/en/documents/afr25/005/1991/en/> accessed 28 March 2019.
71   See Human Rights Watch, 'Evil Days: 30 Years of War and Famine in Ethiopia' (Report of African Watch, September 1991) 1, available at: <https://www.hrw.org/sites/default/files/reports/Ethiopia919.pdf> accessed 10 September 2015. [Hereinafter: 30 Years of Evil Days].
72   Department of State, 'Country Reports on Human Rights Practices for 1990', 116, 118, 119, available at: <https://archive.org/details/countryreportson1990unit> accessed 28 March 2019.
73   See Amnesty International, 'Ethiopia: End of an Era of Brutal Repression – A New Chance for Human Rights', *supra* note 112, 45.
74   The exact number of SPO cases has not been reported, although the SPO stated that it investigated a total of 364 cases. See *Dem Yazele Dossie*, *supra* note 21, Annex 2.
75   See FHC, *SPO v. Legesse Asfaw et al.*, (Trial Judgment), 4 March 2008, File No. 03116.
76   See Chapter 7, section 7.7.
77   For details, see ibid.

4.2.1.3 The SPO's Final Defense to the Victor's Justice Accusation

In its final report and assessment of its process, the SPO attempted to respond to the general body of scholars and journalists that had characterized it as an exercise of victor's justice. It did so in its book: *Dem Yazele Dossie*.[78] The SPO's justifications were however filled with numerous unclear, unsubstantiated, and conflicting assertions.

For instance, at one point, it expressly conceded to the allegation that members of the EPRP also committed crimes against officials and affiliates of the *Dergue*. Highlighting the complicated and entangled phenomena of terror between the EPRP and the *Dergue*, the SPO wrote, in a manner that attempted to justify acts of the former,

> the EPRP had no judiciary. The *Dergue* was a government and it had a judiciary. The EPRP had no governmental responsibility, but the *Dergue* had. The one with no governmental responsibility was inflicting terror. The government chose to respond to the terror, with terror.[79]

At another point, the SPO implied the existence of a symmetry between the violence inflicted by the EPRP and the *Dergue*'s response to it. It stated:

> [o]f the urban strife that the *Dergue* administration had faced, the one caused by the EPRP was the most violent. *Dergue*'s response to halt the strife was *equally* vindictive. By taking individual actions, the EPRP exposed itself to further attacks.[80]

For the SPO, however, recognizing the two-sided nature of the violence in question was entirely different from accepting the victor's justice portrayal of

---

78 However, the SPO did not deal with the victor's justice accusations in a direct and explicit way; its responses were mostly implicit and scattered in different sections of the book.

79 See *Dem Yazele Dossie*, supra note 21, 145. Translation by the author. The original (Amharic) version reads:
ኢህአፓ ፍርድ ቤት አልነበረዉም። ደርግ መንግስት ነበር ፍርድ ቤትም ነበረዉ። ኢህአፓ የመንግስት ኃላፊነት አልነበረበትም፤ ደርግ ግን ነበረበት። ኃላፊነት የሌለዉ ያሸብራል። መንግስት ሸበርን በሸበር ይመልሳል።

80 See *Dem Yazele Dossie*, supra note 21, 108. Emphasis added. Translation by the author. The original (Amharic) version reads: ደርጉን በከተሞች ገጥሞት ከነበረዉ ታቃዉሞ በኢህአፓ የተሰነዘረበት ካዱ ነበር። ይሁንን ተቃዉሞ ለመደምሰስ ደርጉ የወሰደዉ እርምጃም ያንኑ ያህል የከፋ ነበር። ኢህአፓ የተናጠል እርምጃዎችን በመዉሰድ እራሱን ለበለጠ ጥቃት አጋለጠ። Some of the SPO's assertions appear to conflict with how the literature commonly portrays the nature and scale of the *Dergue* era of violence. In particular, with respect to the Red-Terror, the literature agrees on the point that the violence perpetrated by the *Dergue* was unparalleled.

THE DECISIONS TO PROSECUTE: WHO SHOULD BE BROUGHT TO JUSTICE? 157

the trials. In its final report, the Office put the aggregate blame only on the *Dergue* and claimed that

> it is a known fact that the injustice that had befallen Ethiopia during the [*Dergue* regime] signify the monstrosity of *only* Colonel Mengistu Hailemariam and his government, but not of Ethiopia and its people.[81]

This assertion seems an over-statement: even the SPO Proclamation, despite aiming for the prosecution of the *Dergue* alone, never expressly purported the idea that the *Dergue* was *the only perpetrator*.

Overall, the SPO invoked two reasons why the *Dergue* trials should not been seen as selective. Firstly, the SPO stated that it prosecuted the *Dergue* not only for having committed crimes against members of opposition political groups but also for having murdered its own members. In support of this argument, the SPO's report mentioned two victims: Major Birhanu Kebede and Colonel Atenafu Abate.[82] The former was the Director of the *Dergue* Investigation Unit while the latter was responsible for organizing and arming the revolutionary defence squads of the ADAs, and mostly known for promising to kill a thousand counter-revolutionaries for every revolutionary killed by the White-Terror.[83] Thus, according to the SPO, the process was not an exercise of victor's justice, because justice was also rendered in cases where the *Dergue* was a victim. This argument is however hardly convincing. From a point of fact, the victims mentioned by the SPO as members of the *Dergue* were actually no longer members of the *Dergue* at the time of their execution. As stated in the indictment of the SPO in *Mengistu et al.*, the above-mentioned two individuals, although initially members of the *Dergue*, were executed due to their alleged membership or affiliation to the EDU.[84] This was also not the only instance where the *Dergue* killed persons who were initially its own members. The *Dergue* did not allow its members to sympathize with the opposition, let alone change sides. It executed several of its members after identifying them as supporters and affiliates of opposition groups such as the EPRP. The clearest example in this regard is

---

81 Ibid., 438. Emphasis added. Translation by the author. The original (Amharic) version reads:
    በዚያ ዘመን በዚጎች ላይ የተፈጸመው ግፍ የኢትዮጲያና የሕዝብዋን ዛይሆን የኮሎኔል መንግስቱ ኃይለማርያም መንግስት አረመኔያዊ ተግባር የሚያረጋግጥ ብቻ መሆኑ ይታወቃል።
82 Ibid.,135.
83 Ibid.
84 FHC, SPO v. *Colonel Mengistu Hailemariam et al.*, (Revised Indictment), 27 November 1995, File No. FHC 1/87, 14.

the summary execution of seven high-ranking *Dergue* officials on 3 February 1977 at the meeting of the Standing Committee of the *Dergue*.[85] The victims included Lieutenant General Teferi Benti, Captain Alemayehu, Captain Moges, and Lieutenant Colonel Asrat Desta.[86] There are also other examples of the *Dergue* killing members of its own militia and armed forces who had aligned with opposition political groups.[87]

From a point of logic, the SPO's reasoning fails to grasp the essence of the accusation of victor's justice. The victor's justice criticism has never been so much about the identity of the victims, but about the identity of those who stood trial. The issue has been about the fact that both in the law and in the practice of the SPO only members and affiliates of the *Dergue* were targeted for prosecution. A logical answer should have focused on the (un)availability of responses concerning members and affiliates of the *Dergue* killed by non-*Dergue* groups or individuals, and not on responses concerning the *Dergue*'s killing of its ex-members.

The second reason advanced by the SPO to explain why the *Dergue* trials should not been seen as selective was that 'members and affiliates of the Mengistu regime were brought to trial not because they lost power but because they committed crimes against their own citizens during the time they were in power'.[88] This argument shares a stark similarity with the earlier-quoted statement used by Airy Neave in connection to the Nuremberg trials that the Nazis were put on trial not for losing the war but for having committed mass murder.[89] This argument however misses the point of the victor's justice accusation as it misconstrues it as a claim about the *Dergue*'s innocence. As it was established in the courts, there is strictly no doubt that the *Dergue* committed atrocities against the Ethiopian people. The point however is that members

---

85 Ibid., 23.
86 Ibid.
87 See ibid., 44, 46, 59.
88 *Dem Yazele Dossie, supra* note 21, 135. Translation by the author. The original (Amharic) version reads:

የግዚያዊ ወታደራዊ አስተዳደር ደርግ ወይም መንግስት አባላትና ተከታዮቻቸው ለፍርድ የቀረቡት መንግስታቸው ስለተሸነፈ አልነበረም። በልጣን ዘመናቸው ሕግን በመጣስ እያዳንዳቸው በንፁሃን ዜጎች ላይ በፈፀሙት ወንጀል ነው።.

89 Air Neave, member of the British War Crimes Executive during the Nuremberg trials, reported that he was faced by a British Major-General who said: 'Thank God, we won the war, Neave. Seems a shame to try men like Keitel and Jodl, both Generals, for losing it'. Neave replied: 'we're not trying them for losing it. We're trying them for mass murder, sir'. See A. Neave, *On Trial at Nuremberg* (Boston: Little, Brown and Company, 1978) 199.

of the *Dergue* were allegedly not the only ones to have committed atrocities during the period the *Dergue* ruled.

In sum, in trying to address the victor's justice accusations it seems that the SPO wanted to leave behind a positive legacy of its trials. In fact, the SPO was too pleased for discharging its responsibility 'successfully', in particular for doing so without significant international support. Celebrating its accomplishment in prosecuting the *Dergue* based solely on provisions of the Penal Code, the SPO referred sentimentally as 'our national effort' and 'our own laws'.[90]

There is no doubt that the SPO undertook the very complex and cumbersome task of prosecuting thousands of peoples who committed several atrocities over a period of 17 years. Yet, the SPO's high regard for its own accomplishments might have played a role in presenting solely the success story and in defending the *Dergue* trials against any stigma that could be inflicted by the victor's justice characterization.

4.2.1.4   The Issue of a Separate Response: The RPPO and the Others

In general, the foregoing revealed that the SPO process focused exclusively on the prosecution of the *Dergue*. Nevertheless, caution is required: it is neither unorthodox nor *per se* unfair to establish a specialized prosecution office with a focused mandate to investigate and prosecute specific categories of crimes perpetrated by specific categories of individuals. As is often the case, prosecutions of international crimes are by definition selective due to the large number of perpetrators. Starting with the Nuremberg and the Tokyo trials, post-conflict prosecution initiatives have been designed to be implemented through the establishment of specialized schemes aimed at selective prosecution. Such mechanisms were adopted due to political and practical reasons. What defines the existence of victor's justice is not the fact that one group is prosecuted by a specialized tribunal, but that the other group is granted amnesty or enjoys *de facto* impunity for the crimes it committed.

Even in the Ethiopian context, the SPO was not the first special mechanism established to prosecute certain categories of crimes and offenders. The country had already experienced special mechanisms (courts) in three instances before the establishment of the SPO. The first one was the 1922 Special Court, established pursuant to the 1908 Franco-Ethiopian treaty to try cases arising between Ethiopians and foreigners.[91] The second one was the 1974 Special

---

90   *Dem Yazele Dossie, supra* note 21, 438–439.
91   H. Scholler, *The Special Court of Ethiopia:1922–1935* (Stuttgart: F. Steiner Verlag Wiesbaden, 1985).

Courts-Martial,[92] established and operated as an organ distinct from both ordinary courts of law and courts-martial, to adjudicate offences proscribed by the Special Penal Code of 1974.[93] The third one was the 1981 Special Court, which was established as a successor to the 1974 Special Courts-Martial with jurisdiction to try offences under the Revised Special Penal Code of 1981.[94]

From a practical point of view, the establishment of the SPO with a special and specific mandate could be a defendable strategy. Firstly, unlike crimes allegedly committed by non-*Dergue* groups or individuals, crimes committed by the *Dergue* may have justified the establishment of a special prosecution office. Compared to crimes allegedly committed by non-*Dergue* groups, those allegedly committed by the *Dergue* represents a case of extensive and continued perpetration of atrocities for the purpose of which the government employed an entire State apparatus. The gravity and complexity of these crimes may have justified the need to address them using a specialized mechanism. Secondly, financial and infrastructural impediments that were apparent during the transitional period might have justified the need to establish the SPO and limit its mandate to crimes committed by the *Dergue*. A broader mandate might have simply been regarded as unattainable.

Turning to the Ethiopian criminal justice system during the transitional period, it should be pointed out that, in principle, the SPO was not the only organ with jurisdiction over crimes committed during the *Dergue* regime. As stated in Article 9 of the SPO Proclamation,

> [w]here, in the process of investigation, the Office [the SPO] discovers cases which are outside its jurisdiction, it shall transfer such cases to the regular public prosecutor's office [RPPO].

It could be inferred from this provision that the SPO's establishment did not create *de jure* impunity for non-*Dergue* offenders, for they could be prosecuted by the RPPO. This is indicative of the availability of a jurisdictional arrangement in which the SPO could simply be viewed as a special segment within a broader scheme. Article 9 of the SPO Proclamation may thus, at least theoretically, be regarded as the expression of the TGE's willingness to prosecute non-*Dergue* members for crimes they had allegedly committed during that regime.

---

92 See the Special Courts-Martial Establishment Proclamation, Proclamation No. 7/1974, *entered into force* 19 October 1974.

93 See ibid., Article 1(c).

94 The Special Court Establishment Proclamation, Proclamation No 251/1981, *entered into force* 8 September 1981.

THE DECISIONS TO PROSECUTE: WHO SHOULD BE BROUGHT TO JUSTICE?   161

In practice, however, the SPO never transferred cases to the RPPO.[95] There exists no evidence of a prosecution conducted by the RPPO for crimes committed by non-*Dergue* groups in the context of the Red-Terror or the armed conflict. In addition, there is no legal provision indicating the existence of governmental willingness to prosecute crimes committed by groups other than the *Dergue*. In the absence of any official statement indicating a plan or an intention to bring to justice the non-*Dergue* groups, the mere existence of the RPPO is not sufficient to, by and of itself, dismiss the claims of victor's justice. Ultimately, non-*Dergue* groups enjoyed impunity and the establishment of the SPO may indeed be seen as an exercise of victor's justice.

4.2.2   *The CUD Trials: The Perpetrators v. the Victims*

The CUD trials refer to prosecutions conducted in relation to crimes committed in the context of the violence that took place in connection with federal and regional parliamentary elections held on 15 May 2005. The elections, although reportedly marred by irregularities, were considered relatively peaceful and, arguably, the closest to genuine elections that Ethiopia has ever experienced.[96]

The post-election crisis was triggered in early June 2005 when the CUD, the second largest opposition coalition at that time,[97] refused to accept the results that declared a narrow victory for the ruling party, the EPRDF, alleging electoral manipulation. In turn, the EPRDF accused the CUD of conspiring to overthrow the government by force and rejected reports of international observers which largely confirmed the CUD's claims. Violence ensued and both sides contributed, in varying degrees, to the loss of lives and property that occurred from the beginning of June until the end of November 2005.

In December 2005, the government initiated a prosecution process, commonly known as the CUD trials, that targeted only one side to the conflict. 131

---

95 Interview with Mr. Yosef Kiros, Deputy Special Prosecutor of the SPO, 30 December 2017. Notes with the author.

96 See for example, A. Wijkman, 'European Parliament Delegation to Observe Federal and Regional Parliamentary Elections in Ethiopia: A Report, 12–17 May 2005' (June 2005), Annex C, 1. available at: <http://www.europarl.europa.eu/intcoop/election_observation/missions/2004–2009/20051505_ethiopia.pdf> accessed 28 March 2019. [Hereinafter: European Parliament Report on 2005 Elections in Ethiopia]. See also Human Rights Watch, 'World Report 2006: Ethiopia, Events of 2005' 1, available at: <https://www.hrw.org/world-report/2006/country-chapters/ethiopia> accessed 29 September 2019.

97 The CUD (ቅንጅት (Kinjit) in Amharic) was a coalition of four parties: The All Ethiopia Unity Party (AEUP), the Ethiopian Democratic League (EDL), the United Ethiopian Democratic Party-Medhin (UEDP-Medhin), and the Rainbow Party (Movement for Democracy and Social Justice).

defendants, including ten legal persons, were indicted in the main CUD trial, *Federal Prosecutor* v. *Engineer Hailu Shawul et al.*[98] In this case, in addition to official members and leaders of the CUD, individuals, human rights activists, and journalists deemed to have aligned with the CUD[99] were brought to justice for participation in the perpetration of both domestic crimes (mostly treason and related offences) and core international crimes. With respect to core crimes, 94 defendants, including ten legal persons,[100] were charged with attempt to commit genocide against the ruling political party, the EPRDF, and against members of the Tigray ethnic group.[101]

In a separate trial targeting only supporters of the CUD, *Federal Prosecutor* v. *Berehene Kehassaye Woldeselassie et al.,* five individuals were accused of targeting a victim they had identified as a member of both the EPRDF and the Tigray ethnic group, which according to the prosecutor constituted an act of genocide.[102] In another case dealing with low ranking members and supporters of the CUD, *Federal Prosecutor* v. *Kifle Tigneh et al.,* it was alleged by the prosecutor that 17 individuals had attempted to follow up on the call to destroy ethnic and political groups announced by the higher officials of the CUD.[103] Notwithstanding, the FHC ruled in all of the three above-mentioned

---

98   See FHC, *Federal Prosecutor* v. *Engineer Hailu Shawul et al.,* (Indictment), 15 December 2006, File No. 43246/97.

99   See ibid.

100   The prosecution of legal persons in the CUD trials for genocide had no legal basis in Ethiopia. Although the law recognizes corporate criminal responsibility, legal persons could only be prosecuted with respect to crimes for which such form of accountability had been expressly mentioned. See FDRE Criminal Code, Article 34. As there was no corporate criminal liability for war crimes and genocide in Ethiopia, the courts in the CUD trials rightly dismissed the proceedings against the legal persons in the genocide cases. See FHC, *Federal Prosecutor* v. *Kifle Tigeneh et al.,* (Trial Ruling), 16 April 2007, File No. 44562/99, 26.

101   See ibid., count 7. Defendants accused of committing genocide were those listed in the indictment from number 1 to number 39, number 70 to number 90, and number 96 to number 131. The juridical persons accused of participating in the commission of genocide were mentioned at numbers 70, 73, 76, 83, 86, 88, and number 128 to number 131. The indictment was amended in 2006, before the trial started, and the prosecutor dropped the genocide charge in favor of 11 of the 94 defendants, although no explanation was provided as to why the amendment was necessary. See FHC, *Federal Prosecutor* v. *Engineer Hailu Shawul et al.,* (Trial Ruling), 3 May 2007, File No. 43246/97, 5. Furthermore, as regards the remaining 83 defendants, the prosecutor amended the genocide charge to *attempt to commit genocide*, a violation of Article 27 and Article 269 of the FDRE Criminal Code. See ibid.

102   See FHC, *Federal Prosecutor* v. *Berehene Kehassaye Woldeselassie et al.,* (Indictment),15 December 2006, File No. FHC 45671/98. The details of the crime will be discussed further in Chapter 6.

103   FHC, *Federal Prosecutor* v. *Kifle Tigeneh et al.,* (Indictment), 30 June 2006, File No. 44562.

cases that the crimes committed by the defendants did not constitute genocide.[104] Instead, the court found the defendants guilty of outrages against the Constitution or the constitutional order; a crime under Article 238 of the FDRE Criminal Code.[105]

The CUD trials were conducted without adequate preparation. By the time the government announced its plan to bring the CUD to trial, no independent investigation into the violence had been conducted.[106] Likewise, by the time charges were pressed against the CUD, there still had not been an independent inquiry into the violence, in spite of the fact that international organizations, notably the European Parliament, had already called on the Ethiopian government to facilitate the establishment of a UN affiliated international commission of inquiry.[107]

Furthermore, unlike what is generally believed to be the period of electoral violence, that is the period from June to November 2005, the prosecution broadened the temporal scope of the violence to cover the pre-election campaign period. This meant that the CUD stood trial for crimes committed between 4 November 2004 and 14 November 2005. As will be analyzed in Chapter 6 of this book, the prosecutor referred to the pre-election campaign period to establish the existence of a conspiracy and a plan to commit the alleged crimes. The ways in which the members and officials of the CUD who were brought to justice and in which the crimes/time period for which they were prosecuted was determined thus appear questionable. Yet, the manner in which the government forces and officials were excluded from prosecution seems even more questionable.

The government itself did not deny its contribution to the violence. It acknowledged that the security forces perpetrated acts of killings but asserted that the death toll reported by international organizations and media outlets

---

104 See *Engineer Hailu Shawul et al.,* (Trial Ruling), *supra* note 101, 196; FHC, *Federal Prosecutor v. Berehene Kehassaye Woldeselassie et al.,* (Trial Judgment), 19 April 2007, File No. 45671/98, 7; *Kifle Tigneh et al.,* (Trial Ruling), *supra* note 100, 23.

105 See ibid. The nature of the crime and the judgment (of acquittal) will be discussed in detail in Chapter 6.

106 The government announced on 9 November 2005 that the CUD and its supports would be charged with treason and genocide. See The Carter Center, 'Observing the 2005 Ethiopian National Elections: Carter Center Final Report' December 2009, 37. Available at: <https://www.cartercenter.org/resources/pdfs/news/peace_publications/election_reports/ethiopia-2005-finalrpt.pdf> accessed 28 September 2019.

107 See European Parliament Resolution on the Situation in Ethiopia and the New Border Conflict (P6_TA(2005)0535), *adopted* 15 December 2005, para. 5, available at: <http://www.europarl.europa.eu/sides/getDoc.do?type=TA&reference=P6-TA-2005-0535&language=EN> accessed 28 September 2019.

were exaggerated.[108] Perhaps as a response to international pressures, the FDRE House of Peoples' Representatives (HoPR) issued on 21 December 2005 a Proclamation establishing an independent commission of inquiry to investigate what it referred to as 'the *disorder* that occurred in Addis Ababa and some parts of the country'.[109] However, this Proclamation, in itself, appeared to be yet another manifestation of the government's attempt to shield itself from criminal accountability through an inquiry aimed at discounting the scope and nature of the violence. One can point out three clear indicators which seem to confirm this.

Firstly, with respect to persons or groups involved in the violence, the Proclamation did not grant the Inquiry Commission a mandate to investigate crimes committed by all sides involved in the violence. The Inquiry Commission's mandate was limited to investigating actions taken by the security forces of the government.[110] Furthermore, the Proclamation referred to the violence as 'disorder', and required the Inquiry Commission to investigate whether the disorder had resulted in human rights violations.[111] Thus, the mandate of the Inquiry Commission was limited to investigating the consequences, not the causes, of the violence.[112] Such a mandate had the potential to avoid an inquiry into the background of the violence, in particular into whether public officials had helped design, co-ordinate and implement the violence inflicted by the security forces.

Secondly, in terms of the time and places of violence, the Proclamation further restricted the mandate of the inquiry commission to the well-known incidents. These are, according to the Proclamation, disorders which occurred: *i*) on 8 June 2005 in Addis Ababa; *ii*) from 1 to 10 November 2005 in Addis Ababa and some other parts of the country; and *iii*) from 14 to 16 November 2005 in Addis Ababa and some other parts of the country.[113]

---

108   For instance, the 'Federal police acknowledged the death of 26 persons on [8 June 2005] following an unlawful demonstration'. See U.S. Department of State, '2005 Country Reports on Human Rights Practices: Ethiopia' (Bureau of Democracy, Human Rights, and Labor, 8 March 2006), Section 1(a), available at: <https://www.state.gov/j/drl/rls/hrrpt/2005/61569.htm> accessed 28 September 2019.
109   An Inquiry Commission to Investigate the disorder that occurred in Addis Ababa and in Some Parts of the Country Establishment Proclamation, Proclamation No. 478/2005, *entered into force* 21 December 2005 [Hereinafter: 2005 Inquiry Commission Proclamation].
110   Ibid., Article 2.
111   2005 Inquiry Commission Proclamation, *supra* note 109, Article 5(a) and (b).
112   See ibid., Articles 2 and 5.
113   Ibid., Article 2.

The June and November incidents represented instances of direct confrontation between the security forces and demonstrators that resulted in most of the killings recorded during the 2005 post-election violence. Nonetheless, various international reports indicated that violence had never ceased between June and November 2005.[114] Therefore, by restricting the mandate of the Inquiry Commission to the specified dates and incidents, the Proclamation played a role in minimizing the overall context and nature of the offences committed during the post-election violence.

Thirdly, within the Proclamation there is no explicit indication of the government's willingness to prosecute crimes committed by its security forces. Instead, the Proclamation appears to have set up the Inquiry Commission to find out what the possible justifications for the violence were. In connection with the killings, it can be inferred from Article 5 of the Proclamation that the mandate of the Inquiry Commission was to investigate the number of lives lost[115] and to determine whether the security forces had used excessive force.[116]

Even more egregious was the mandate under Article 5 (b) which required the Inquiry Commission to assess whether the 'handling of human right in matters related to the problem was conducted in accordance with the Constitution and the rule of law'.[117] The phrase 'handling of human rights' was meant to refer to acts of violence including the alleged killings, as can be inferred from Article 5(c) of the Proclamation. Such a mandate, which implied the existence under Ethiopian law of a *constitutionally justifiable killing* was inherently problematic. The FDRE Constitution guarantees the inviolability and inalienability of the right to life, which suffers no exception apart from the case of a punishment pronounced by a court of law with respect to serious criminal offences determined by law.[118] In fact, the Constitution does not even expressly recognize the taking of life in self-defense. It may thus seem incorrect that the

---

114 For details of acts of killings perpetrated during the post-election violence, in particular in the months following June 2005, see U.S. Department of State, '2006 Country Reports on Human Rights Practices: Ethiopia' (Bureau of Democracy, Human Rights, and Labor, 6 March 2007), available at: <https://www.state.gov/j/drl/rls/hrrpt/2006/78734.htm> accessed 28 September 2019.
115 2005 Inquiry Commission Proclamation, *supra* note 109, Article 5(1)(c).
116 Ibid., Article 5(1)(a).
117 Ibid., Article 5(1)(b).
118 See FDRE Constitution: Article 14: Rights to life, Security of Person and Liberty: 'Every person has the inviolable and inalienable right to life the security of person and liberty'. See also ibid., Article 15: Right to Life: 'Every person has the right to life. No person may be deprived of his life except as a punishment for a serious criminal offence determined by law'.

Proclamation failed to out-right recognize as unconstitutional acts of killings committed by the government's security forces.

Arguably, pursuant to its Article 13(2), the Constitution's right to life may be interpreted in conformity with the scope of the right to life under international human rights treaties to which Ethiopia is a party, which recognizes that a life could be taken by law enforcement officials under exceptionally justified circumstances.[119] In that respect, the Constitution's lack of an 'emergency clause' might even be criticized as an untenable protection of the right to life. As stated by the African Commission in *Noah Kazingachire et al.* v. *Zimbabwe*, 'a system that is seen as too protective of the rights of suspects is unlikely to be effective in practice. The challenge clearly is to find the right balance between overly permissive and overly restrictive'.[120]

Be that as it may, the establishment of the Inquiry Commission was not intended to lead the government into bringing those responsible to justice. Rather, the Inquiry Commission was rather used later to politically and collectively justify the killings, as also became evident from how the investigation ended. Yet, the manner in which the killings were justified created much controversy. In particular, not all members of the Inquiry Commission were willing to produce a conclusion desired by the government, although all of them were hand-picked by the government.

The already unpleasant relationship between the government and the Inquiry Commission[121] deteriorated in early July 2006 when the latter was about to release its findings that excessive force had been used by the security forces of the government.[122] The disagreement was so strong that it interrupted the release of the report and two of the members of the Inquiry Commission,

---

119 For details, see R. Murray, *The African Charter on Human and People's Rights: A Commentary* (Oxford: Oxford University Press, 2019) 123–124. See also, B. Rainey et al., *The European Convention on Human Rights* (6th edn., Oxford: Oxford University Press, 2014) 143–149.

120 African Commission, *Noah Kazingachire, John Chitsenga, Elias Chemvura and Batanai Hadzisi (represented by Zimbabwe Human Rights NGO Forum)* v. *Zimbabwe*, (Decision), 2 May 2012, Communication 295/04, para. 109.

121 For details, see The Observatory, 'Ethiopia: The Situation of Human Rights from Bad to Worse' (FIDH-OMCT Report of International Mission of Judicial Observation, No.463, 2 December 2006), 12–15, available at: <http://www.omct.org/files/2006/12/3823/ethiopia_obs4632_1106_eng.pdf> accessed 28 September 2019. See also Amnesty International, 'Justice Under Fire: Trials of Opposition Leaders, Journalists and Human Rights Defenders in Ethiopia' (Amnesty International Report, 29 July 2011) 67–70, available at: <https://www.amnesty.org/en/documents/AFR25/002/2011/en/> accessed 28 September 2019.

122 See ibid. See also, U.S. Department of State, '2006 Country Reports on Human Rights Practices: Ethiopia', *supra* note 114, Section 1(a).

its chairperson and its vice-chairperson, fled the country because they were allegedly intimidated by the government.[123] Eventually, the process of inquiry ended with the partial release of two different reports: the official report and another unofficial one which was leaked.

The leaked report – a draft report of the original Inquiry Commission, the release of which was stopped by the government in July 2006 – was obtained by the Associated Press on 18 October 2006 and published the next day in *The New York Times*.[124] Among other things, the report revealed that government security forces killed 193 people while six police officers were killed by CUD-affiliated anti-government demonstrators.[125] The official report, presented by the members of the Inquiry Commission, except its Chair and vice-Chair who had fled the country, and allegedly published on the website of the HoPR two days after the release of the leaked report, acknowledged the same death toll.[126] The report also indicated that the violence resulted in causing serious and minor injuries to 763 civilians and 71 members of the security forces.[127]

The official report nonetheless denied the excessiveness of the force used by the security agents, thereby collectively exonerating those responsible for the killings and effectively blocking the possibility to eventually bring them to justice. The relevant part of the report reads:

> the Commission believes that according to the responsibility accorded to it by the proclamation, the actions taken by the security forces to control the violence was a legal and necessary step to protect the nascent system of government and to stop the country from descending in to a worse crisis and possibly never-ending violence upheaval. The issue of proportionality cannot be seen outside these realities.[128]

---

123   Ibid.
124   See The Associated Press, 'Inquiry Says Ethiopian Troops Killed 193 in Ballot Protests in '05', *The New York Times*, 19 October 2006, available at: <http://www.nytimes.com/2006/10/19/world/africa/19ethiopia.html> accessed 28 March 2019.
125   Ibid.
126   See The Observatory, 'Ethiopia: The Situation of Human Rights from Bad to Worse', *supra* note 121, 12–13. At least 17 arrested protestors died in detention. See U.S. Department of State, '2006 Country Reports on Human Rights Practices: Ethiopia', *supra* note 114, Section 1(c).
127   See ibid., Section 1(a).
128   See The Observatory, 'Ethiopia: The Situation of Human Rights from Bad to Worse', *supra* note 33, 13. See also, Amnesty International, 'Justice Under Fire' *supra* note 121, 68.

As noted earlier, the mandate of the Inquiry Commission was restricted to the events of June and November 2005 and the published reports reveal that the investigation indeed focused on the killings that took place on the designated dates. Insofar as the complete findings of the investigation were never published in full, it is possible that what was ultimately published concealed the context and scale of the post-election violence as well as the identity and official status of those who participated in orchestrating the violence.

There are reasons to believe that the 2005 post-election violence in Ethiopia represents more than just a case of sporadic chaos and riot resulting in the perpetration of domestic crimes. As can be deduced from numerous statements made and reports compiled by the U.S. Department of State,[129] Amnesty International,[130] Human Rights Watch,[131] the European Parliament,[132] and international observers to the elections,[133] uninterrupted and widespread violations of human rights took place from June to November 2005. In various locations in Ethiopia, the police, the militia, and the *Kebele* (local administrations) authorities participated in the numerous killings directed not only against CUD supporters but also against members and supporters of the United Ethiopian Democratic Forces (UEDF), the largest opposition coalition during the 2005 election.[134] In addition to the 193 killings, about 30,000 to

---

129 See U.S. Department of State, '2006 Country Reports on Human Rights Practices: Ethiopia', *supra* note 114, Sections 1(a), 1(c).
130 Amnesty International, 'Amnesty International Report 2006: Ethiopia', 23 May 2006, available at: <https://www.refworld.org/docid/447ff7a62f.html> accessed 28 September 2019. See also Amnesty International, 'Justice Under Fire', *supra* note 121 59–61.
131 See in general, Human Rights Watch, 'World Report 2006: Ethiopia, Events of 2005', *supra* note 96, 1.
132 Wijkman, European Parliament Delegation to Observe Federal and Regional Parliamentary Elections in Ethiopia: *supra* note 96. See also European Parliament Resolution on Ethiopia (P6-TA(2006)0501) adopted 16 November 2006, para. B, available at: <http://www.europarl.europa.eu/sides/getDoc.do?pubRef=-//EP//TEXT+TA+P6-TA-2006-0501+0+DOC+XML+V0//EN> accessed 28 March 2019; European Parliament Resolution on the Situation in Ethiopia (P6_TA(2005)0383), adopted 13 October 2005, para. N, available at: <http://www.europarl.europa.eu/sides/getDoc.do?type=TA&reference=P6-TA-2005-0383&language=BG&ring=B6-2005-0541> accessed 28 September 2019.
133 The Carter Centre, 'Observing the 2005 Ethiopian National Elections' *supra* note 106, 25–26. See also The Observatory, 'Ethiopia: The Situation of Human Rights from Bad to Worse', *supra* note 121, 10–12.
134 See U.S. Department of State, '2006 Country Reports on Human Rights Practices: Ethiopia', *supra* note 114, Section 1(a), indicating, among others, that about 24 members of the *Oromo* National Congress (ONC), one of the 12 opposition political parties in UEDF, were attacked during the violence. See ibid., Section 1(c).

50,000 civilians were arbitrarily arrested and detained for months *incommunicado*, some in undisclosed locations, and were allegedly subjected to torture and inhuman and degrading treatments.[135]

Even with regards to the June and November killings, the leaked report stated that the majority of the demonstrators, who were unarmed, died from shots to the head.[136] Besides, numerous arbitrary killings were perpetrated against old men while in their homes, and children while playing in their garden.[137] Although it is beyond the scope of this book to investigate fully each and every element of the crimes committed during the post-election violence, the alleged widespread attack against the civilian population, which could not have happened without the direct or indirect involvement of the officials of the State, appears to be satisfying the definition of crimes against humanity.[138]

From the foregoing, it can therefore be submitted that the judicial response to the 2005 post-election violence represents, in particular in relation to international crimes, an instance in which *victims* were prosecuted while *perpetrators* were granted impunity. In other words, the security forces of the government, those responsible for the alleged core crimes (crimes against humanity), were left unprosecuted, while the CUD, the group protesters accused of attempting to perpetrate another core crime (genocide), was brought to justice. In this regard, it is worth pointing out here that, whether characterized as crimes against humanity under ICL or not, an attack against civilian protestors constitutes one of the crimes that cannot be subjected to amnesty under Article 28 of the FDRE Constitution, as explained by the 1994 Constitutional Commission.[139]

---

135 Ibid., Sections 1(a) and 1(b). For alleged acts of torture and ill treatment, see Human Rights Watch, 'Ethiopia: Crackdown Spreads Beyond Capital, as Arbitrary Arrests Continue, Detainees Face Torture and Ill-Treatment' 15 June 2005, available at: <https://www.hrw.org/news/2005/06/15/ethiopia-crackdown-spreads-beyond-capital> accessed 28 March 2019. See also Human Rights Watch's Submission to the Committee against Torture on Ethiopia September 2010', 4, available at: <http://tbinternet.ohchr.org/Treaties/CAT/Shared%20Documents/ETH/INT_CAT_NGO_ETH_45_8752_E.pdf> accessed 28 September 20190; Amnesty International, 'Justice Under Fire' *supra* note 121, 59–61.
136 See The Associated Press, 'Inquiry Says Ethiopian Troops Killed 193 in Ballot Protests in '05', *quoting* the vice chairperson of the original Inquiry Commission, *supra* note 124.
137 See ibid., *quoting* the vice chairperson of the original Inquiry Commission.
138 Reference is here being made to the definition of crimes against humanity provided under Article 7 of the ICC Statute.
139 See the 1994 Constitutional Commission, *The FDRE Constitution: Explanatory Note* (Unpublished, available at the Library of FDRE House of People's Representatives), 63.

4.3   The Issue of Fugitive Offenders: Trial *in Absentia* / Trial by Default

The Ethiopian cases, with the exception of the *Anuak-Nuwer* trials, have tried a number of accused persons in their absence. Two out of 286 defendants were tried in their absence in the *Oromo-Gumuz* trials.[140] In the CUD trials, two of the 88 physical persons accused of attempt to commit genocide were not present at their trial.[141] The *Dergue* trials, however, showed a huge number of *in absentia* trials, perhaps like no other trial of international crimes in history. A shockingly high number of defendants – 2,188 out of 5,119 – were tried in their absence.[142] Out of the 73 high-ranking *Dergue* officials prosecuted in *Mengistu et al.*, 20 were prosecuted *in absentia*, including Mengistu Hailemariam, who fled to Zimbabwe a week before the total downfall of his regime.[143]

The fact that the Ethiopian trials have culminated in prosecuting a large number of defendants in their absence might give the impression that such proceedings are widely accepted as normal in the Ethiopian legal system. This should however be nuanced: although none of the four Ethiopian Constitutions (1931, 1955, 1987, and 1995) have expressly and directly recognized the right to be present at one's trial as a constitutional right,[144] as is the case with several other constitutions,[145] Ethiopian law does recognize this right. Recently, the Federal Supreme Court's Cassation Bench (FSC CB), the only court empowered

---

140   *Tadesse Jewanie Mengesha et al.*, (Trial Judgment), *supra* note 8, defendants number 74 and number 125.

141   These are defendants number 79 (Zelalem Gebre, Editor-in-Chief of *Minilik* newspaper) and number 85 (Abiy Gizaw, Editor-in-Chief of *Netsanet* newspaper). See *Engineer Hailu Shawul et al.*, *supra* note 18, 3- 4. However, the treason related charges in the CUD trials had 25 defendants *in absentia*.

142   See *Dem Yazele Dossie*, *supra* note 21, 444.

143   *Colonel Mengistu Hailemariam et al.*, (Trial Judgment), *supra* note 47, 77.

144   The 1931 Constitution failed to recognize this right even implicitly. The right had an implicit existence in the 1955 Revised Constitution and in the 1987 PDRE Constitution. See Articles 43 and 52 of the 1955 Revised Constitution, which respectively guaranteed the right of the accused to due process of law and to obtain attendance of and to examine witnesses testifying against or on behalf of him/her. See also Article 45(3) of the 1987 PDRE Constitution, which provided that the accused person has the right to defend himself/herself.

145   A survey of national constitutions conducted by Professor Bassiouni indicated that, by 1993, only about 25 countries incorporated in their constitution the right to be tried in one's own presence. See M.C. Bassiouni, 'Human Rights in the Context of Criminal Justice: Identifying International Procedural Protections and Equivalent Protections in National Constitutions' (1993) (3)1 *Duke Journal of Comparative & International Law* 235–298, 279.

to deliver binding interpretation of laws,[146] has highlighted that the right to be present at one's own trial has a constitutional status as it is firmly enshrined in the FDRE Constitution.[147] According to the FSC CB, the right to attend one's own trial is rooted in the Constitution's Article 20 (1), which guarantees the right to a public trial, and Article 20(4), which protects the right to challenge and produce evidence.[148] This conclusion was reached after the Cassation Bench interpreted these provisions in line with international human rights instruments to which Ethiopia is a party.[149] In support of its conclusion, the FSC CB referred to Article 14 (3) (b) and 14 (3) (d) of the ICCPR.[150] If relying on paragraph (d), which explicitly mentions the right of the accused '[t]o be tried in his presence', seems well-grounded, relying on paragraph (b) might seem more remote,[151] although it is possible that the FSC CB read in the right 'to communicate with counsel of his own choosing' the implication that the accused was indeed present.

From a terminology viewpoint, it should be noted that what is elsewhere referred to as trial *in absentia* is known as trial by *default* in Ethiopian law. Nowhere in the Code of Criminal Procedure is the expression '*in absentia*' used to designate the absence at trial of the accused. Instead, the law uses expressions such as 'cases of default' and 'judgments given in default' to refer to trials conducted in the absence of the accused.[152] Some commentators have already pointed out the existence of a distinction between 'trial *in absentia*' and 'trial by default'.[153] Although in both cases the accused is not present at his or her

---

146 See Federal Courts Proclamation Re-amendment Proclamation, Proclamation No.454/2005, *entered into force* 14 June 2005, Article 5(1).

147 See FSC CB, *Zewedu Tesfaye Semegne v. Tigray State Bureau of Justice*, (Decision), 1 December 2014, File No. 93577.

148 Ibid., 2.

149 This method of constitutional interpretation is required by Article 13 (2) of the FDRE Constitution itself, which reads: 'The fundamental rights and freedoms specified in this Chapter shall be interpreted in a manner conforming to the principles of the Universal Declaration of Human Rights, International Covenants on Human Rights and international instruments adopted by Ethiopia'.

150 *Zewedu Tesfaye Semegne v. Tigray State Bureau of Justice*, (Decision), *supra* note 147, 2–3.

151 See International Covenant on Civil and Political Rights, G.A. res. 2200A (XXI), 21 U.N. GAOR Supp. (No. 16) at 52, U.N. Doc. A/6316 (1966), 999 U.N.T.S. 171, *entered into force* 23 March 1976, Article 14 (3) (b), which guarantees the right of the accused '[t]o have adequate time and facilities for the preparation of his defense and to communicate with counsel of his own choosing'.

152 See Criminal Procedure Code of Ethiopia, Title II, Articles 160–166.

153 See P. Gaeta, 'Trial In Absentia Before the Special Tribunal for Lebanon' in A. Alamuddin *et al.* (eds.), *The Special Tribunal for Lebanon: Law and Practice* (Oxford: Oxford University Press, 2014) 229–250, 230–231; S. Starygin and J. Selth, 'Cambodia and the Right to be

trial, the former refers to being absent by choice, after summon is effectively served or even following an initial court appearance, while the latter stands for absence owing to the fact that the accused has not been informed *unequivocally* of the charges instituted against him or her.¹⁵⁴ In Amharic, trial *in absentia* may loosely translate into ስላልቀረበ/ች ተከሳሽ ችሎት while trial by default stands for ስለሌለ/ች ተከሳሽ ችሎት.

Based on this distinction, international criminal justice has seen rarer instances of trials by default as compared to trials *in absentia*. The SCSL, the ICTY, and the ICTR have in one way or the other practiced trials *in absentia*.¹⁵⁵ The ICC also has the option of conducting a trial *in absentia* by removing from the court an accused who continuously disrupts the trial. As for trial by default, the Rome Statute explicitly and outrightly rejects the option of going forward with trials without the accused being present at all.¹⁵⁶ If this now seems to be the usual standard in international criminal justice, such has not always been the case, as illustrated by the commonly cited trial by default of Martin Bormann at Nuremberg who was sentenced to death in his absence.¹⁵⁷ As for contemporary international criminal justice, the practice of the STL stands as an exception since it undertook several trials in which not one single accused ever appeared before the tribunal.¹⁵⁸

Ethiopian law advocates the existence of an inextricable link between the conduct of a trial and the presence of the accused. In particular, the accused person does not have a right not to appear at his or her trial, unlike the practice in other countries such as the U.S.¹⁵⁹ In principle, the Code of Criminal Procedure makes appearance before the court mandatory and, in order to compel attendance of an accused who fails to appear after having received

---

Present: Trials in absentia in the Draft Criminal Procedure Code' (2005) 1(1) *Singapore Journal of Legal Studies* 170–188, 171.

154   See Gaeta, 'Trial In Absentia Before the Special Tribunal for Lebanon', *supra* note 153, 230–231.
155   Ibid., 232 ff.
156   ICC Statute, Article 60(1).
157   See W.A. Schabas, 'In Absentia Proceedings before International Criminal Courts' in G. Sluiter and S. Vasiliev (eds.), *International Criminal Procedure: Towards a Coherent Body of Law* (London: Cameron May, 2009) 336- 342. It was later discovered that Martin Bormann had already died. The International Military Tribunal decided to try him *in absentia* because his death had not been established at the time of the trial. See also, Trial International. 'Martin Bormann' available at <'https://trialinternational.org/latest-post/martin-bormann/> accessed 28 September 2019.
158   For a detailed discussion see Gaeta, 'Trial In Absentia Before the Special Tribunal for Lebanon', *supra* note 153.
159   For the practice in the U.S., see ibid., 231.

summons, the trial court is required to issue a 'bench warrant' to effect the arrest of the accused, unless a representative appears to satisfactorily explain the absence of the accused.[160] Further, failure to re-appear before the court after initial appearance may cause a revocation of bail and entail the accused to be arrested and remain in police custody until the end of the trial.[161]

With regards to what is referred to above as trial *in absentia*, Ethiopian courts have no clear judicial mechanism at their disposal on how to respond to a defendant who continuously disrupts a trial.[162] The only leeway that is provided by the Code of Criminal Procedure is for the court to order the accused to appear chained and adequately guarded, which may be a solution, but only to avoid physical violence.[163] As for trials by default, the Code of Criminal Procedure contains special procedures, thereby allowing them in connection to some categories of crimes, as discussed below.[164]

It is also important to note that some Ethiopian courts have considered the right to be present at one's own trial as absolute. In the *Dergue* trials, the SPO's request to go forward with the case in the absence of the accused was initially rejected on the basis that doing so lacked legal basis.[165] This was later on reversed by the FSC, which ordered lower courts to conduct trials even though the accused was not present[166] and relied on the above-mentioned provisions of the Code of Criminal Procedure, which regulates trials by default.[167]

Although, as explained earlier, Ethiopian law does recognize trials by default, the question of the legality of such trials, in particular with respect to the *Dergue*, merits further attention.

---

160   Criminal Procedure Code of Ethiopia, Article 125, 160.
161   See Gaeta, 'Trial In Absentia Before the Special Tribunal for Lebanon', *supra* note 153, 237ff.
162   Ibid., 236 *citing* C. Whitebread and C. Slobogin, *Criminal Procedure: An Analysis of Cases and Concept*, (3rd edn, New York: The Foundation Press, 1993) 718–28.
163   Criminal Procedure Code of Ethiopia, Article 127. According to Article 443 of the Penal Code of 1957 and Article 449 of the FDRE Criminal Code, the court could found a violent accused guilty of contempt of court, and impose a fine or imprisonment. These measures might however prove ineffective and the trial court may find it difficult to conduct an orderly trial, not least in instances where the accused continues with a disruptive behavior labelling both the court and the trial as illegitimate and political – a problem witnessed in some recent trials involving opposition political groups, journalists, and bloggers.
164   Ibid., Article 160.
165   See FHC, SPO v. *Elias Tsegaye et al*, (Trial Ruling), 25 November 2000, File No. 632/89, 283.
166   Ibid.
167   Criminal Procedure Code of Ethiopia, Article 160.

4.3.1   Eligible Offenses

Not all offenses are eligible for trial by default. Before considering whether to conduct a trial by default, the law requires courts to first ascertain whether the alleged crime satisfies the requirement of the law. Indeed, an accused may only be tried in his absence in connection with two categories of crimes. The first category refers to crimes *punishable with rigorous imprisonment of no less than 12 years*.[168] The second category regroups the special of *offenses against the fiscal and economic interests of the State*[169] and a court can conduct a trial by default provided that offenses be 'punishable with rigorous imprisonment or fine not exceeding five thousand [Ethiopian Birr]'.[170]

The determination of the offenses of the first category calls for more remarks. To begin with, there is no available explanation as to why the '12 years of rigorous imprisonment' was set as a marker to distinguish between offenses that may or may not be prosecuted in the accused's absence. The draft Code of Criminal Procedure referred to 20 years and it is unclear why Parliament substituted it with 12 years.[171] One plausible explanation is that Parliament picked this benchmark because it roughly represents half of the maximum prison term prescribed under Ethiopian criminal law, which is 25 years of rigorous imprisonment, except for cases involving imprisonment for life. Still, this benchmark remains problematic since no crime in Ethiopian law is actually specifically punishable with 12 years of rigorous imprisonment. In other words, this marker is not in line with the penalty scheme under Ethiopian criminal law.

Ethiopian law prescribes prison sentences for each and every offense in terms of *range* of years, each having *minimum and maximum limits*. Using '12 years of rigorous imprisonment' as a penalty yardstick, one can divide criminal offenses into four categories. These are offenses entailing: *i*) a minimum penalty of less than 12 years of rigorous imprisonment; *ii*) a minimum penalty of 12 years of rigorous imprisonment and above, which would fall within the scope of offences eligible for trial by default; *iii*) a maximum penalty of 12 years of rigorous imprisonment or above; and *iv*) a maximum penalty of less than

---

168   Ibid. For the notion of rigorous imprisonment, see Chapter 8, section 8.2.1.2.1.
169   Ibid., Article 160 (2). See also the Penal Code of 1957, Articles 354 to 365; FDRE Criminal Code, Articles 343 to 354.
170   Criminal Procedure Code of Ethiopia, Article 160 (2).
171   For the parliamentary changes in the Code of Criminal Procedure prior to its enactment, see S.Z. Fisher, *Ethiopian Criminal Procedure: A Source Book* (Addis Ababa: Faculty of Law of Haile Selassie I University, 1969), Appendix E, 477.

12 years of rigorous imprisonment, which would *de facto* fall outside of the scope of offenses eligible for trial by default.

If the eligibility and non-eligibility for trial by default of categories ii and iv respectively is without contention, the fate of offenses falling into categories i and iii has been the object of disagreement among commentators and courts in Ethiopia. Commentators have suggested that courts should look at the minimum penalty prescribed for a crime. According to Fisher and Kiros, the law is clear: for the purpose of conducting a trial by default it is the minimum penalty prescribed for a particular offense that should be taken into account. According to them, a trial by default is only lawful if the minimum penalty prescribed does not allow the imposition of rigorous imprisonment of less than 12 years.[172] For Kiros, referring to the maximum penalty attached to the offense where the minimum penalty is less than 12 years of rigorous imprisonment amounts to convicting and punishing the accused before his or her trial.[173] Yet, it could also be argued that looking only at the minimum penalty, even where the maximum penalty is above 12 years of rigorous imprisonment, may also amount to passing a judgment of sentence before trial.

This could explain why the practice largely deviates from these theoretical assertions by relying on the maximum penalty prescribed for the crime that a fugitive or an absconder is suspected of having committed. As evidenced by the *Dergue* trials, the CUD trials, and the *Oromo-Gumuz* trials, both ordinary crimes and core crimes were prosecuted in the absence of the accused, as long as they carried the *maximum penalty of at least 12 years of rigorous imprisonment*, irrespective of the minimum penalty prescribed. This has however not always been the case, as could be inferred from the case of *Federal Anti-Corruption and Ethics Commission* v. *Asmare Abate et al.*, involving a crime of abuse of power, which was punishable under the Special Penal Code of 1974 with a minimum penalty of three years and a maximum penalty of 15 years of imprisonment.[174] In this case, the FHC refused to hold a trial by default, stating that the minimum penalty attached to the offense fell short of the requirement of 'no less than 12 years of rigorous imprisonment'.[175]

The FHC's ruling was however quashed on appeal by the FSC, which stated that thelegal requirement for trial by default refers to the maximum penalty

---

[172] See ibid., 374; S Kiros, *Criminal Procedure Law: Principles, Rules and Practices* (Bloomington: Xlbris, 2010) 413.

[173] Kiros, *Criminal Procedure Law, supra* note 172, 414.

[174] FHC, *Federal Anti-Corruption and Ethics Commission* v. *Asmare Abate et al.*, (Ruling on Prosecutor's Request for by Defualt Proceeding), 20 December 2004, File No. 35044.

[175] Ibid., 2.

attached to the offense, not to the minimum.[176] In criticizing the FHC's argument, the FSC stated,

> Because the punishment is not limited to less than 12 years, the decision not to try the accused in their abscence is not justified pursuant to article 161(2) Criminal Procedure Code. The court must consider not only the minimum limit but also the maximum limit of a given punishment. The FHC cannot limit the penalty to less than 12 years and decide beforehand that the maximum punishment would not be imposed on the accused, if found guilty.[177]

From a practical point of view, the FSC's decision seems more grounded since, by taking into account the maximum sentence prescribed by law for any particular crime under consideration, courts may avoid certain absurd consequences that would follow from taking the opposite view. Indeed, if the minimum limit of a prescribed sentence was taken into account, it would allow a trial by default of some ordinary crimes, but not of core crimes since all of the core crimes proscribed under Ethiopian criminal law carry a minimum penalty of less than 12 years of rigorous imprisonment,[178] while several ordinary crimes are punishable by a minimum of 15 years of rigorous imprisonment.[179] In fact, aggravated homicide is punishable with a minimum of life sentence.[180] Consequently, if the minimum penalty interpretation was to be followed, a person could be prosecuted in his absence for aggravated homicide but not for genocide, although the former is an underlying offense to the latter. Moreover, any interpretation that would exclude the core crimes from the reach of trials by default would be unwarranted, given the overwhelming assumption that trials in the absence of the accused are exceptionally justified based on the gravity of the alleged crime; a requirement that core crimes definitely fulfil as discussed earlier in Chapter 2.[181]

---

176 FSC, *Federal Anti-Corruption and Ethics Commission* v. *Asmare Abate* and *Kebede Kiros*, (Appeals Judgment), 24 May 2006, File No. 18127.
177 Ibid.,12. Translation by the author. The original (Amharic) version reads:
ቅጣቱ ከ 12 አመት በታች ተብሎ የተገደበ ሰላልሆነ በ/መ/ሕ/ስ/ስ/ቁ 161/2/ መሰረት በሌሉበት በሚል ጉዳዩ ሊታይ አይችልም የሚለው ተቀባይነት የለውም። የቅጣት መነሻ ብቻ ሳይሆን ጣሪያውም መታየት አለበት። ክፍተኛው ፍርድ ቤትም ከወዲሁ ጣሪያው ድረስ ሊቀጡ አይችሉም ብሎ የቅጣቱን መጠን ከ አስራ ሁለት አመት በታች በመገደብ ሊወስን አይችልም። .
178 See FDRE Criminal Code, Articles 269–280.
179 See ibid., Articles 507–511, 631.
180 Ibid, Article 539.
181 See Chapter 2, section 2.3.

THE DECISIONS TO PROSECUTE: WHO SHOULD BE BROUGHT TO JUSTICE? 177

4.3.2 *A Last Resort Proceeding: To Bring or To Notify*

Even if allowed under Ethiopian criminal law, trials by default are a last resort proceeding. This is implied in the Code of Criminal Procedure which refers to such trials as 'special procedures'.[182] Following the determination as to the eligibility of an alleged crime for a conduct of a trial by default, courts are expected to ascertain whether reasonable steps have been taken to ensure the accused person's presence at his or her trial.[183] In this regard, Ethiopian law requires that attempts be made to search for, and communicate with, the accused before allowing the conduct of a trial by default. The sections below discuss separately the distinct requirements of searching for and notifying the accused against whom an indictment has been filed.

4.3.2.1 The Obligation to Search for the Accused: Requesting Extradition

A mere non-appearance of the accused in court is not sufficient to hold a trial by default. According to the Code of Criminal Procedure, 'where the accused does not appear on the date fixed for the trial or no representative appears satisfactorily to explain his absence, the court shall issue a warrant for his arrest'.[184] The court may only begin to consider a trial by default as a possibility after having been officially informed by the relevant authorities that the warrant cannot be executed.[185] In Ethiopian criminal procedure, it is standard practice for a court to order the police to search for the absent accused before responding to the prosecutor's request for trial by default.

In relation to an accused known to have taken refuge in a foreign country, the court may hear the case in the absence of the accused provided that Ethiopia's request for extradition has become unsuccessful. This requirement is stipulated in Ethiopian criminal law in mandatory terms: 'if the criminal has taken refuge in a foreign country, his extradition *shall be* requested so that he may be tried under Ethiopian law'.[186] This obligation to request extradition exists irrespective of the nationality of the accused, as long as the crimes have been perpetrated on Ethiopian territory.[187] The Code of Criminal Procedure and the Penal Code both contain further requirements regarding the prosecution of foreign nationals who took refuge in a foreign country. Article 161(2)(c),

---

182 Criminal Procedure Code of Ethiopia, Title II.
183 Ibid.
184 Ibid., Article 160 (2).
185 Ibid., Article 160 (3).
186 See the Penal Code of 1957, Article 11(3); FDRE Criminal Code, Article 11(3). Emphasis added.
187 The Penal Code of 1957, Article 12; FDRE Criminal Code, Article 12.

which appears only in the Amharic version of the Code,[188] and Article 12 of the Penal Code both provide that the Ethiopian authorities shall request the State of refuge to bring the fugitive to trial in particular where the offence cannot be heard in the absence of the accused.

The practice has however largely failed to comply with the obligation to request extradition. From the beginning, the *Dergue* trials seem to have been framed in a manner that disregarded this requirement. For instance, one may recall a statement allegedly made by the president of the TGE in 1991 'that the extradition of Mengistu is not a priority'.[189] In fact, the numerous reports accusing Zimbabwe of refusing Mengistu's extradition to Ethiopia might have been too hasty as it is not clear whether Ethiopia had formally requested his extradition. As far as the SPO is concerned, it did not attempt to ensure Mengistu's extradition to Ethiopia.[190] This appears to be inconsistent with the requirement of the law. Provided that there is an intention to prosecute crimes committed on Ethiopian territory by an Ethiopian fugitive, the law gives no discretion to the authorities to not request the fugitive's extradition, as long as the crime in question is extraditable.

In practice, Ethiopian courts do not consider that the law requires them to check whether extradition has already been requested in relation to the absent accused before they decide to conduct a trial by default. In *Mengistu et al.*, following the FHC's decision to try Mengistu in his absence, the counsel for defendants requested the court to 'issue an order requesting the extradition of Mengistu from Zimbabwe'.[191] The FHC dismissed the request stating that the 'defense counsel should have understood that this is not a type of a question that could be brought to the court'.[192]

188　The original (Amharic) version of the provision, ፪፻፷፭ (፪)(ሐ), reads:
የተከሠሠው ሰው የውጭ አገር መንግስት ጥገኛ በመሆኑና ጥገኛ ያደረገው አገር አሳልፎ ያልሰጠው እንደ ሆነ ውይንም በሌለበት ነገሩ ሊሰማ የማይችል ቢሆን ጊዜ በወንጀላኛ መቅጫ ሕግ በቁ ፩፪ በተመለከትው መሰረት ተፈጻሚ ይሆናል።
This translates into: 'where the accused has taken refuge in a foreign country and the latter has refused to extradite the accused to Ethiopia, or when the case cannot be heard in the absence of the accused, the provisions of Article 12 of the Penal Code of 1957 [Article 13 of the FDRE Criminal Code] shall be complied with'. Translation by the author.
189　See Chapter 2, section 2.2.
190　Interview with Yosef Kiros, Deputy-Chief SPO, Addis Ababa, 31 December 2017. Notes with the author.
191　*Colonel Mengistu Hailemariam et al.*, (Ruling on Preliminary Objections), *supra* note 63, 21.
192　Ibid., 27.

THE DECISIONS TO PROSECUTE: WHO SHOULD BE BROUGHT TO JUSTICE?   179

In the *Dergue* trials, only two fugitives were returned to Ethiopia to stand trial in person[193] and only one, Melaku Teferra, was ultimately returned from Djibouti through a formal extradition process, pursuant to an extradition treaty signed between the two countries in 1994.[194] This extradition represents the only instance in which a high-ranking *Dergue* official was prosecuted by Ethiopia after exile.[195] The symbolic significance of Melaku Teferra's extradition is probably reinforced by the fact that the accused was arguably the most monstrous and feared provincial governors of the *Dergue* regime.[196]

The second fugitive, Kalbessa Negewo, was repatriated to Ethiopia from the U.S. He was a low-ranking *Dergue* official, who, from 1975 to 1979, had chaired the Higher District 9 and its revolutionary coordinating committee in Addis Ababa.[197] Kalbessa's deportation from the U.S. was a process that started in 1993, when, in its landmark decision that established a private right of action under the Alien Tort Claims Act (ATCA), the District Court for the Northern District of Georgia found the deportee liable for the torture and cruel, inhuman, and degrading treatment of three Ethiopian women in Higher District

---

193   Apparently, the Ethiopian government treats extradition correspondence as classified documents. Efforts made by this author to access a complete information on extradition requests to and from Ethiopia has been unsuccessful.

194   See Extradition Treaty between the Transitional Government of Ethiopia and the Republic of Djibouti, signed in Djibouti on 28 April 1994. The treaty was ratified by Ethiopia on 28 September 1994. See Proclamation No. 104/1994. Another defendant in *Mengistu et al.*, Tessema Belay, alleged that he was unlawfully taken from the compound of the Consular Office of the Republic of Djibouti in Dire Dawa. The FHC however stated that such a circumstance could not constitute a valid objection to a charge brought by the SPO against the person arrested, even if unlawfully. See *Colonel Mengistu Hailemariam et al.*, (Ruling on Preliminary Objections), *supra* note 63, 37.

195   Melaku Teferra was prosecuted as one of the high-ranking co-defendants in *Mengistu et al.* In this case, the defendant unsuccessfully attempted to challenge his extradition from Djibouti. See *Colonel Mengistu Hailemariam et al.*, (Ruling on Preliminary Objections), *supra* note 63, 41. He was also prosecuted as sole defendant in a separate case focusing on crimes perpetrated in Gonder province. See FHC, SPO v. *Melaku Teferra*, (Judgment), 11 November 2005, File No. 17/85.

196   In a poignant depiction of the scale of his mercilessness in detaining, killing, and forcefully conscripting their sons into the army, mothers in the Gonder province of northern Ethiopia had poetized him as: 'Melaku Teferra, God's younger brother; pardon my son, I would not bear another'. Translation by the author. The original (Amharic) lyrics read:
       መላኩ ተፈራ የግዚር ታናሽ ወንድም
       ያዛሬን ማርልኝ የነገን አልወልድም

197   See FHC, SPO v. *Kalbessa Negewo*, (Indictment), 13 January 2008, File No. 69/85,1. Kalbessa is apparently the first person to have stood trial in connection with acts of torture committed during the *Dergue* regime. His trial in the U.S. started in 1990, i.e. when the *Dergue* was still in power in Ethiopia.

9 prison in Addis Ababa.[198] Consequently, the Board of Immigration Appeals, following the revocation of his naturalized citizenship, deported Kalbessa to Ethiopia on 19 October 2006 pursuant to a final order of removal.[199]

Aside from these two cases, the whereabouts of most of those the SPO accused in their absence were unknown. Not all of the 2188 defendants tried in their absence were fugitives: some had already died before their trial[200] while others were still in Ethiopia and unaware of proceedings being instituted against them.[201] According to a report published in 1994, the SPO indicated that about 300 military officers and civil leaders of the *Dergue* regime were identified as having fled the country, and the office could only locate about 60 of them.[202] In addition to Zimbabwe, Djibouti, Kenya, the Netherlands, the U.S., and the Italian Embassy in Addis Ababa have given refuge to several members and affiliates of the *Dergue*. Kenya and the U.S. were found to have the highest number of Ethiopian fugitives.[203]

In the CUD trials, the absent defendants were not present in Ethiopia from the very beginning: they resided outside the country both during and after the commission of the crimes they were alleged to have orchestrated.[204] None of them were extradited back to Ethiopia. In 2014, Andargachew Tsige, a U.K. citizen of Ethiopian origins and one of the CUD defendants sentenced to death in his absence, was arrested at Yemeni's Sana'a International Airport from which

---

198   United States District Court, *Abebe-Jiri* v. *Negewo*, Case No. 1:90-CV-2010-GET, N.D. Georgia, Atlanta Division, 20 August 1993 (1993 WL 814304) paras 5–7. The United States Court of Appeal, Eleventh Circuit, later confirmed this decision. See United States Court of Appeal, (Eleventh Circuit, Judgment, 10 January 1996), Case No. 93–9133, *Abebe-Jiri* v. *Negewo*. The United States Federal Supreme Court denied Kalbessa's petition for writ of certiorari. See *Abebe-Jiri* v. *Negewo*, 519 U.S. 830, 117 S.Ct. 96 (Mem), 136 L.Ed.2d 51, 65 USLW 3258.

199   See United States District Court, *Negewo* v. *Chertoff*, (S.D. Alabama, Northern Division, 5 January 2007) Civil Action No. 06-00631-WS-C (2007 WL 38336) paras 1- 5.

200   For instance, six defendants in the case of *Elias Tsegaye et al.* were identified as dead at the later phase of the trial but the proceedings had progressed in their absence. See *Elias Tsegaye et al.*, *supra* note 165, 22.

201   See below section 4.3.3.

202   SPO Report (1994) *supra* note 11, 670.

203   Ibid.

204   Most of these were exiles residing in the U.S. where they have worked as academics, publishers, editors of private websites on Ethiopia, and journalists at the U.S.-based Voice of America (VOA) radio station. See Amnesty International, 'Justice under Fire' *supra* note 121, 13–14. Others reside in the U.K. and Denmark. See ibid. As discussed in detail in Chapter 6, the CUD leaders were not convicted of genocide, but of treason.

he was then deported to Ethiopia,[205] where he was detained until his release on pardon on 26 May 2018 as part of a governmental decision to release hundreds of political prisoners.[206]

4.3.2.2 The Obligation to Notify the Accused

The right to be present in one's own trial is not absolute, and an accused person could be tried in his or her absence under exceptional circumstances, generally in the interests of the proper administration of justice. As specified in the Model Treaty on Extradition (MTE),[207] as well as in decisions of the UNHRC[208] and of the ECtHR,[209] the legality of trials in the absence of the accused is predominantly based on the requirements of notice. Thus, the mere fact that the accused is a fugitive or that the crime is grave does not alone justify resort to such trials.[210] In this respect, Ethiopian law and practice appear to have been evolving towards the standard of notification as required under international human rights treaties.

Interestingly, the Code of Criminal Procedure stipulates the requirement of notice (*publication of summons*) irrespective of whether the accused is an absconder who has already received summons or a fugitive who has no knowledge of proceedings being instituted against him or her.[211] Content-wise, the notification is required to show the date fixed for the trial and a stipulation that the accused will be tried in his or her absence in case of non-appearance.[212] There is no requirement in the law that the notification should state the details of the charges brought against the accused. Nor does the law specify when, i.e. how long before the start date of the trial, the notification should be published.

---

205 See Amnesty International, 'Ethiopian Activist at Risk of Torture: Andargachew Tsige', 4 July 2014, Index number: AFR 25/003/2014, available at: <https://www.amnesty.org/en/documents/afr25/003/2014/en/> accessed 28 September 2019. Regarding the continued detention of Andargachew Tsige, see Human Rights Watch, 'World Report 2016: Ethiopia, Events of 2015' available at: <https://www.hrw.org/world-report/2016/country-chapters/ethiopia> accessed 28 September 2019.

206 See *Aljazeera News*, 'Andargachew Tsige Pardoned by Ethiopia' available at: <https://www.aljazeera.com/news/2018/05/andargachew-tsige-pardoned-ethiopia-180526163642586.html> accessed 28 September 2019.

207 Model Treaty on Extradition, Adopted by General Assembly resolution 45/116, subsequently amended by General Assembly resolution 52/88, A/RES/45/116, 68th plenary meeting, 14 December 1990, Article 3(g).

208 Human Rights Committee, General Comment 31, Nature of the General Legal Obligation on States Parties to the Covenant, U.N. Doc. CCPR/C/21/Rev.1/Add.13 (2004) para. 11.

209 ECtHR, *Sejdovic v. Italy*, (Judgment), 1 March 2006, Application No. 56581/00, para. 58.

210 See in this regard, ECtHR, *Colozza v. Italy*, (Judgment), 12 February 1985, Application, No. 9024/80,, para. 28.

211 Criminal Procedure Code of Ethiopia, Article 162.

212 Ibid.

Regarding the means of notification, Article 162 of the Amharic version of the Code of Criminal Procedure states that where the accused is absent, notice of the date of the hearing must be published in a national newspaper.[213] In practice, the *Addis Zemen*, a national Amharic newspaper, is the default means of notifying the absent accused. Yet, the Code of Criminal Procedure also states that the notification can be transmitted to the accused through *other means* that the court considers more fitting to serve the aim of notification.[214] The means of notification appears to be a contentious issue in practice. As shall be seen below, Ethiopian courts have treated this issue on a case-by-case basis, with the aim of giving due respect to the right to be present at one's own trial. The cases of *Zewedu Tesfaye Semegne* v. *Tigray State Bureau of Justice*[215] and of SPO v. *Selashi Tessema et al.* are the most relevant to explain the development.

In *Zewedu Tesfaye Semegne,* the FSC CB pointed out that the right to be present at one's own trial is one of the fundamental guarantees of a fair trial.[216] It then underscored that 'the right to a fair trial guaranteed by the FDRE Constitution and international human rights treaties adopted by Ethiopia must be enforced by the judiciary *with no reduction whatsoever*'.[217] Continuing on to the specific issue of notification, the FSC CB asserted that 'in order to conduct a trial in the absence of the accused in a manner that does not [further] restrict the accused's constitutional right to defend oneself, *the process of notification* must strictly adhere *to the provisions of the law*'.[218] The FSC CB

---

213   Ibid., Article 162(1).
214   Ibid., Article 162 (2).
215   See *Zewedu Tesfaye Semegne* v. *Tigray State Bureau of Justice,* (Decision), *supra* note 147, 1. In this case, the High Court of Southern Zone of Tigray Regional State convicted the accused of aggravated homicide in his absence, following his non-appearance in spite of a notification communicated prior to the start of the trial. The notification was affixed on a notice board at the *kebele* (local administration office) nearest to the accused's last known address. See ibid. Upon his arrest, the convicted objected to the conduct of trial in his absence, stating that he was not aware of any proceeding instituted against him and that the court had improperly deviated from using the means of communication designated by the law for such purpose.
216   Ibid., 3. On appeal brought to the FSC CB, the convicted argued that serving a notification to the nearest town hall of his last known address was not a proper means of communication, because pursuant to the tradition of the area in which he lived at the time of the alleged crime, a person who was suspected of having perpetrated murder had to change residence.
217   Ibid. Translation by the author. Emphasis Added. The original (Amharic) version reads: በሕገ መንግስቱና ኢትዮጲያ የጸደቀቻቸው የስብዓዊ መብት ድንጋጌዎች የተረጋገጠው ፍትሐዊ የዳኝነት መብት በየትኛውም መልኩ ሳይሸራረፍ በፍርድ ቤቶች ተግባራዊ ሊሆን ይገባል።
218   Ibid. Translation by the author. Emphasis Added. The original (Amharic) version reads: ...ተከሳሽ በሌለበት የሚደረገው ክርክር የተከሳሽ የመከላከል ሕገ መንግስታዊ መብት የሚያብብ አንዳይሆን የመጥሪያ አደራረስ ሥርዓት ሕጉ የዘረጋውን ድንጋጌ በጥብቅ በመተግበር ነው።

thus reiterated the mandatory nature of the publication in a newspaper rule, and stated that it implied the obligation for the courts to employ the means that could generally be regarded as widespread and accessible to notify the accused.[219] For the FSC CB, any deviation from this rule could thus only be justified by the existence of a means that could guarantee a receipt of notification by the accused.[220] As also discussed in the case of *The Federal Anti-Corruption Commission* v. *Alemetsehaye Wondemu,* courts shall not refuse a publication of notification in a newspaper unless there is a better means of communication.[221] Interestingly, publication in the *Addis Zemen* is not *per se* a guarantee that the accused will actually receive a notification as to a case being instituted against him or her in his or her absence.

In SPO v. *Selashi Tessema et al.,* defendant Kuma Ayyana argued before the Federal Supreme Court that his conviction by the Oromia Supreme Court (Jimma Bench) was in violation of his right to be present at his trial.[222] The appellant did not question the alleged fact that a notification was announced in a newspaper, but rather the *validity of the publication in a newspaper.* In support of his argument, the appellant raised: *i*) that he did not understand Amharic, the language of the *Addis Zemen*, and *ii*) that he was a farmer living in a countryside where the newspaper did not circulate.[223] In its majority decision, the FSC ruled that although the OSC had followed the publication in a newspaper rule, the inaccessibility of the newspaper in the appellant's place of residence meant that it could not be deemed that the appellant had been aware of a case being instituted against him. A judge dissented on the ground that the *Addis Zemen* maintains circulation in *Nekemte,* the nearest town to the appellant's place of residence.[224] Neither the dissenting nor the majority opinion discussed the issue of the language used in publishing the notification and its implication regarding the accessibility of the notification to the accused. Nonetheless, it stands to reason that a notification published in a language that the accused does not understand is no different from a notification that is never published, given that, for the purpose of trial by default, the court is required not just to publish but to notify the accused. It is noteworthy that in *Selashi Tessema et al.* the FSC deliberated on a broader aspect of the practice of

---

219   Ibid., 3.
220   Ibid.
221   FSC, *The Federal Anti-Corruption Commission* v. *Alemetsehaye Wondemu,* (Appeals Judgment), 16 June 2006, File No. 2093, 3.
222   FSC, SPO v. *Selashi Tessema et al.,* (Appeals Judgment), 7 June 2002, File No. 6/89, 3.
223   Ibid., 4.
224   Ibid., 5.

notification through a newspaper. Going beyond the issue raised in the particular case, the Court commented on the existence and implications of insufficient circulation of public media in the country. In particular, the Court stated that 'let alone in the rural areas, there is no sufficient reason to conclude that an individual could read notifications published in newspapers, even in the main cities'.[225]

4.3.3   The Availability of a Remedy: Retrial

International human rights law purports that a violation of the right to be present at one's own trial can be remedied by a retrial.[226] It is essential that the law that permits trials by default guarantees a retrial, because the accused might remain uninformed, despite the existence of sufficient efforts to notify him or her that there is a plan to prosecute him or her in his or her absence. On the international scene, it is noteworthy that, in the case of the STL, a retrial is regarded not as a remedy but as a *right*, irrespective of whether the right to be present at one's own trial is regarded as violated or not.[227]

Under Ethiopian law, retrial is guaranteed mainly for a person tried in his or her absence and who is unaware of the case instituted against him or her. As an exception, the accused who was prevented by *force majeure* from appearing in person or through a counsel during the first trial may be granted a retrial.[228] What constitutes *force majeure* in this case is not clarified either by the law or by the practice.

The only apparent limitation that may hinder an individual from benefiting from the remedy of retrial is the *time limit* for submitting an application to set aside a judgment rendered in default, which is 30 days from the date on which the applicant became aware of the judgment given in his or her absence.[229] In *Selashi Tessema et al.,* the Court applied the time requirement strictly: it denied the application for a retrial submitted by Seleshi Tessema, Tegenge Tolera, and Abiyu Bante (who were arrested after having already been tried and convicted in their absence), on the ground that the application had been submitted after the expiry of the 30 days.[230] The applicants however argued that they had submitted the application within 30 days after the date of their arrest by the police,

---

225   Ibid., 4.
226   See *Sejdovic* v. *Italy*, (Judgment), *supra* note 209, para. 82.
227   See STL Statute, Article 22(3); STL, *Prosecutor* v. *Ayyash et al*, Appeals Chamber, (Judgment), 1 November 2012, STL-11-01/PT/AC/AR126.1, para. 14.
228   Criminal Procedure Code of Ethiopia, Articles 197 and 199.
229   Ibid., Articles 197 and 198.
230   *Selashi Tessema et al.,* (Appeals Judgment), *supra* note 222, 4.

alleging that to be the date on which they had become aware of the judgment. This claim was dismissed by the Court who noted that *circumstances* showed that the applicants had been aware of the judgment rendered against them in their absence prior to their arrest by the police.[231]

A retrial is regarded as a fresh trial, where the prosecutor is not bound to limit its accusation to the facts included in the first hearing. In the case of *SPO v. Kalbessa Negawo*, a retrial conducted after the accused was deported to Ethiopia from the U.S., the defense counsel argued that the prosecutor should not amend the content of the indictment used during the first trial.[232] The Court ruled against this objection, precisely on the ground that a retrial involves a fresh consideration of accusations and evidence.[233]

A retrial should also be a fair trial. In this regard, the Code of Criminal Procedure has put in place a safeguard by providing that the same judge, court, or criminal bench that has adjudicated the first trial shall not conduct the retrial.[234] This is seen as appropriate in order to conduct an impartial retrial. Yet, a search of a new venue and judge for a retrial is apparently not easy in the Ethiopian context, owing to the fact that some towns have only one criminal bench with no additional judge other than the one who has already heard the case during the first trial. As a result, some cases of retrial have to be moved to another high court in a nearby town, as was the case in *Zewede Tesfaye Simegne* where a retrial was ordered by the FSC to be conducted by the high court in Mekele, a regional city, instead of the court of first trial in the town of Maychew.[235]

4.4 Conclusion

This chapter has examined whether Ethiopian trials were designed or conducted in a manner that brought to justice persons responsible for the commission of core crimes, irrespective of on whose side the perpetrators were while committing these crimes. The only group of trials in which perpetrators from both sides to the conflict were brought to justice was the *Oromo-Gumuz* trials. Apparently, the relevant conflict behind the *Oromo-Gumuz* cases did not involve participation of government forces, and in particular of the federal

---

231   Ibid.
232   FHC, *SPO v. Kalbessa Negawo*, (Trial Ruling), 14 January 2009, File No. 62185, 3.
233   Ibid.
234   Criminal Procedure Code of Ethiopia, (Amharic version), Article 202.
235   See *Zewedu Tesfaye Semegne v. Tigray State Bureau of Justice*, *supra* note 147, 4.

government's forces; an element which might explain why both sides to the conflict faced justice.

In situations where officials or agents of the government were suspected of having participated in the perpetration of violence, Ethiopian core crimes trials represented a typical case of victors' justice. The selection of defendants in the *Dergue* trials was carefully done in a manner that avoided bringing the victors to justice. Such an effort not only affected the selection of perpetrators but also that of the crimes, as evidenced by the absence of more trials for potential war crimes cases. In the CUD trials, the manner in which the government excluded criminal responsibility constitutes further evidence of how Ethiopia does not prosecute those in power, even when they might bear the greatest responsibilities.

The chapter further discussed the question of who should be brought to justice from the perspective of suspects that had fled the country. It is established from the discussion under section 4.3. that Ethiopia has so far failed to pay sufficient attention to the process of securing extradition for perpetrators of core crimes. It does not have extradition treaties with several of the countries in which Ethiopian fugitives have resided and the investigation process does not seem to have attempted to locate the whereabouts of fugitives. Instead, the criminal justice system has conducted more *in absentia* trials for the prosecution of core crimes than any other domestic system. In effect, the practice has treated trials *in absentia* as regular proceedings, although the law requires them to be considered as exceptional proceedings that should be adopted as a last resort.

PART 2

*Ethiopian Core Crimes Trials: Applicable
Laws, Crimes, and Punishment*

∴

CHAPTER 5

The Crime of Genocide in Ethiopian Law

5.1 Introduction

As noted earlier in this book, Ethiopia was the first country to have ratified the Genocide Convention, which was the first international instrument criminalizing genocide. It was also among the very few countries that incorporated the Convention's crime of genocide in its national law and it did so as early as the 1950s.[1] Besides this largely public information, no in depth explanation is available as to why and how the country took such a pioneering role. Nor is there a comprehensive analysis of the extent to which the elements of the crime of genocide were fully and correctly incorporated into Ethiopian law or of the status of the Convention within Ethiopian law. This chapter explores these issues methodically.

Section 5.2 provides for the historical background of the incorporation of the law of genocide into the Ethiopian legal system. It addresses such issues as the ratification of the Convention and Ethiopia's involvement in its drafting and the negotiations surrounding it. Section 5.3 thoroughly examines the municipal legislation proscribing genocide, using as a comparative benchmark the Convention's definition of the offense. It aims at pointing out and exploring the differences and similarities between the domestic and the international versions of the elements of the crime of genocide. Section 5.4. discusses the manner in which the domestic provision on genocide has evolved over time. It examines whether Ethiopian legislation has widened or narrowed potential discrepancies between its provisions and the Convention. Section 5.5 considers the status of the Convention in the Ethiopian legal system, giving due regard to a possible hierarchy of norms. Lastly, section 5.6 concludes the chapter by highlighting the dualism of the law of genocide in Ethiopia and how this was reflected in the choice of the applicable law in the Ethiopian genocide trials.

This chapter predominantly focuses on the analysis of the Ethiopian law on genocide and briefly engages with the court cases, which will be discussed in full in the next chapter. As another methodological point, it should be reiterated that the analysis in this and all other chapters of this book are primarily based on the Amharic versions of the domestic legislation, as was also noted

---

1 See below section 5.3.

in Chapter 1, section 1.5. Amharic, the official language of Ethiopia in the 1950s and the working language of its federal government since 1991, was the language used to incorporate the crime of genocide into the Ethiopian legal system. Disregarding the Amharic versions of the laws could thus result in reaching hasty and fragile conclusions, as is arguably the case in studies conducted by Asgedome and Tessema in relation to, for example, genocidal *mens rea* under the Ethiopian Penal Code of 1957.[2] In fact, in cases of linguistic inconsistency or difference, there is an obligation in Ethiopian law to favor the Amharic version of a piece of legislation over the English one.[3] From a practical point of view, the analysis of Ethiopian trials should also be based on the Amharic, not the English, version of the applicable laws, simply because the former has always been the language of core crimes trials in Ethiopia, as pointed out in Chapter 1[4] and as will appear from the overall discussion in Chapter 6. Amharic has been expressly regarded as the authoritative version of the Penal Code in the *Dergue* trials.[5]

---

2   See M.T. Tessema, *Prosecution of Politicide in Ethiopia: the Red Terror Trials* (The Hague: T.M.C Asser Press, 2018), 100–103. M. Asgedom, 'The Place of Crimes against Humanity under the Ethiopian Legal System: A Reflection' (2013) 3(2) *Bahir Dar University Journal of Law* 401–415.
3   Despite his analysis's self-defeating reliance on the English version of the Penal Code of 1957, Tessema noted that the Amharic version of the law is the authoritative one in case of discrepancy. See Tessema, *Prosecution of Politicide in Ethiopia, supra* note 2, 77.

In 1942, Ethiopia promulgated the obligation for all laws to be published in the official gazette in both the Amharic and English languages. See Administration of Justice Proclamation, Proclamation 1/1942, Article 22. Nonetheless, it is only in 1995 that a provision was enacted to specify that the Amharic version should be treated as authoritative. See Federal Negarit Gazeta Establishment Proclamation, Proclamation No. 3/1995, Article 2(4), which reads, 'the Federal Negarit Gazeta shall be published in both the Amharic and English Languages; in case of discrepancy between the two versions the Amharic shall prevail'.

Regarding the laws that predate 1995, the absence of a clear provision determining an authoritative version of legislation is perplexing, even more so when one recalls that it was a discrepancy between the Amharic and foreign (Italian) versions of a law that triggered a dispute between Italy and Ethiopia, which culminated in the battle of Adwa in 1896. See 'Treaty of Wuchale: Italy-Ethiopia [1889]' available at: <https://www.britannica.com/event/Treaty-of-Wichale> accessed 28 September 2019.

Nonetheless, and as stressed earlier, one could argue that there was a sort of unwritten law in Ethiopia that the Amharic version was indeed the authoritative version of the law, even prior to 1995. Amharic served as the official language of the country and English was never regarded as the second official language. Drafts of the laws promulgated by the Emperor as well as those passed by Parliament (both during the Emperor and the *Dergue*) were examined in their Amharic versions.

4   See Chapter 1, section 1.2.
5   See for instance FHC, SPO v. *Colonel Mengistu Hailemariam et al.*, (Ruling on Preliminary Objections), 10 October 1995, File No. 1/87, 119.

5.2 The Early Ethiopian Ratification of the Genocide Convention

Ethiopia's involvement in the international effort to prevent and punish genocide is virtually as old as the international effort itself. Its role began with its declaration, as the only African State, of adherence to the London Agreement of 1945 for the Prosecution and Punishment of the Major War Criminals of the European Axis.[6] This agreement culminated in bringing to justice those responsible for waging the aggressive war which blood-stained Europe. Even if not the actual focus at Nuremberg, the Holocaust was nonetheless prosecuted under persecution as a crime against humanity.[7] It wasn't qualified as genocide as the word, which was coined for the first time in 1944 by Raphael Lemkin,[8] had not yet been generally accepted by the international community.

In 1946, when discussions were held by the United Nations General Assembly (UNGA) to adopt a resolution on the crime of genocide, Ethiopia was one of the four African countries that had representatives in the UNGA's Sixth Committee.[9] As a result, it directly contributed to the approval of a resolution drafted by Sub-Committee 3 – later adopted by the UNGA as resolution number 96(1).[10] Subsequently, by maintaining its representation in the Sixth Committee, Ethiopia became one of the 60 States that participated in the process of drafting the Genocide Convention, from 1946 to1948.[11] However, as can be inferred from the *travaux préparatoires* of the Convention, Ethiopia's role was limited to casting votes or abstentions and as such did not have a direct impact on the actual drafting of the substantive provisions of the Convention.

---

6   United Nations, Agreement for the Prosecution and Punishment of the Major War Criminals of the European Axis (London Agreement), 82 U.N.T.C. 280, *entered into force* 8 August 1945.

7   See C. Fournet and C. Pégorier 'Only One Step Away from Genocide: The Crime of Persecution in International Criminal Law' 2010 (10)5 *International Criminal Law Review* 713, 720–722. See also G. Mettraux, *International Crimes and The Ad Hoc Tribunals* (Oxford: Oxford University Press, 2005) 193–199.

8   R. Lemkin, *Axis Rule in Occupied Europe: Laws of Occupation, Analysis of Government, Proposals for Redress* (Washington: Carnegie Endowment for World Peace, 1944) 79.

9   Ethiopia's representatives were Ato Zelleke Gashaou, Ato Kifle Egzi Gabremaskal, and Mr. H. Spencer. See H. Abtahi and P. Webb, *The Genocide Convention: the Travaux Préparatoires – Vol.II* (Leiden: Martinus Nijhoff Publishers, 2008) 1276. For a discussion on the list of state that attended the drafting process of the Convention, see H. Abtahi and P. Webb, 'Secrets and Surprises in the *Travaux Préparatoires* of the Genocide Convention' in M.M. deGuzman and D.M. Amann (eds.), *Arcs of Global Justice: Essays in Honour of William A. Schabas* (Oxford: Oxford University Press, 2018) 299- 319, 300.

10 G.A. Res. 96 (1), UN Doc. N231, (11 December 1946).

11 See Abtahi and Webb, 'Secrets and Surprises in the Travaux Préparatoires of the Genocide Convention' *supra* note 9, 300, *fn.* 1.

After signing the Convention on the date of its adoption, i.e. on 11 December 1948, Ethiopia only took a few months to make it binding upon itself and its citizens through ratification. According to Kissi, this immediate ratification of the Convention, on 1 July 1949, might be the result of the particular sensitivity triggered by the fact that the country had been a victim of atrocities perpetrated by Italian forces during the Second Italo-Ethiopian War, from 1935 to 1936.[12] Tessema appears to be sharing this view. For him, however, the relevant trigger, which explains not only the swift ratification of the Convention but also its incorporation in national law, was the Addis Ababa massacre of 19 February 1937 in which about 19,000 civilians were killed.[13]

The above arguments appear to be more relevant to explain why Ethiopia supported the London Agreement of 1945 rather than why it became the first country to ratify the Genocide Convention. As for the former, Ethiopia had hoped that the planned prosecution of the Axis Powers would include bringing Italy to justice for atrocities committed in Ethiopia.[14] Regrettably, that never happened, notably because the Second Italo-Ethiopian war was considered 'another war', not part of the Second World War.[15] This same reason was invoked to justify the exclusion of Ethiopia from membership to the UN War Crimes Commission, as discussed in Chapter 7.[16]

---

12   E. Kissi, *Revolution and Genocide in Ethiopia and Cambodia*, (Lanham: Lexington Books, 2006) 98. For a detailed historical context, see R. Pankhurst, 'Italian Fascist War Crimes in Ethiopia: A history of Their Discussion, from the League of Nations to the United Nations (1936–1949)' (1999) 6(1–2) *Northeast African Studies* 83–140, 83. For details on the second Italo-Ethiopian war, see C. Paoletti, *A Military History of Italy* (Westport: Praeger Security International, 2008) 151–161.

13   See Tessema, *Prosecution of Politicide in Ethiopia*, supra note 2, 68 *fn*. 13. It is not clear why Tessema emphasized the Addis Ababa massacre while several other atrocities were committed by Italian forces during the invasion and military occupation of Ethiopia. For details of the massacre of about 19,000 civilians in Addis Ababa by Italian forces upon the order of Benito Mussolini on 19 February 1937 and the following days, see I. Campbell, *The Addis Ababa Massacre: Italy's National Shame* (Oxford: Oxford University Press, 2017) 279–331.

14   See Chapter 7, section 7.2.

15   See Pankhurst, 'Italian Fascist War Crimes in Ethiopia' *supra* note 12, 96–97. Although it is true that the 1935–36 Italo-Ethiopian war was a pre-Second World War conflict, Ethiopia also had a belligerent status during the Second World War. In 1942, soon after the Italian occupation of Ethiopia came to an end with the latter regaining its independence, Ethiopia declared that, in support of what it called 'the fight for the liberation of the world', a state of war existed between itself and the Axis powers. See The Declaration of War Proclamation, Proclamation No. 33/1942.

16   See Chapter 7, section 7.2.

It is plausible that the atrocious invasion and occupation of Ethiopia by Italian forces, which could constitute a typical example of the crime of aggression[17] as well as certain types of war crimes[18] alerted the country to partake in international efforts aimed at the prevention and repression of similar forms of atrocities. Such vigilance might have contributed to the ratification of the Convention. Nonetheless, the immediate ratification might partly find an explanation in the fact that back then, and unlike now,[19] the Emperor could ratify a treaty in a non-time-consuming and straightforward procedure, without having to go through lengthy parliamentary debates. The 1931 Constitution of the Empire of Ethiopia indeed allowed for treaty ratification by exclusive decision of the Emperor.[20] Several elements support this suggestion. First, there is no evidence that the Ethiopian Parliament discussed the Convention before its ratification. This is also apparent from the absence of an Amharic translation of the instrument, which could have happened had Parliament discussed its ratification. Second, the fact that the Emperor was himself a victim forced into exile by the Italian forces might have encouraged him to use his prerogatives to swiftly ratify the Convention.[21]

---

17 Q. Wright, 'The Test of Aggression in the Italo-Ethiopian War' (1936) 30(1) *The American Journal of International Law*, 50–55.
18 See Chapter 7, section 7.2.
19 Under the current system of government in Ethiopia, the Federal House of Peoples Representatives has the power to 'ratify international agreements concluded by the executive'. See the FDRE Constitutions, Article 55(12) and 71(2).
20 See The 1931 Constitution of the Empire of Ethiopia, Article14. This provision stated that only the Emperor had the right to negotiate and sign all kinds of treaties. Although there was no provision specifically dealing with treaty ratification as different from negotiating and signing a treaty, it appears that the ratification power was always regarded as a prerogative of the Emperor. See A. Jembere, 'Treaty Making Power and Supremacy of Treaty in Ethiopia' (1970) 7(2) *Journal of Ethiopian Law* 409–434, 409–410.
21 This prerogative of the king remained intact until the coming into force of the 1955 Revised Constitution, which for some treaties required a parliamentary discussion and approval before ratification by the Emperor. See The 1955 Revised Constitution of Ethiopia, Article 30, which read:
    ... However, all treaties of peace and all treaties and international agreements involving a modification of the territory of the Empire or sovereignty or jurisdiction over any part of such territory, or laying a burden on Ethiopia subjects personally, or modifying legislation in existence , or requiring expenditures of State funds, or involving loans or monopolies shall, before becoming binding upon the Empire, and the inhabitants thereof, be laid before Parliament and if both Houses of Parliament shall approve the same in accordance with the provisions of Article 88–90 inclusive of the present Constitution, shall then be submitted to the Emperor for ratification.

5.3 Incorporating the Crime of Genocide into Ethiopian Law

Article V of the Genocide Convention imposes an obligation on the States Parties to provide for domestic legislation criminalizing and punishing genocide.[22] It took Ethiopia about eight years after ratification to comply with this obligation. Genocide became a punishable offense under Ethiopian law on 5 May 1957; date on which the Penal Code of 1957 came into force. There is thus little doubt that the Ethiopian reaction is is to be considered prompt domestic criminalization. Yet, the actual incorporation of the crime of genocide into Ethiopian law seems to have been carried out at a slower pace, notably in view of the speed with which the Convention was ratified. While Ethiopia, contrary to a significant number of State Parties which have yet to incorporate the provisions of the Convention in their legal system,[23] should be praised for having incorporated the provisions of the Convention, it is true that – given its immediate ratification of the Convention – one could have expected a swift incorporation of the crime of genocide, perhaps through the adoption of a separate act, as had been done in States such as Australia (1949),[24] Israel (1950),[25] and Brazil (1956).[26] Furthermore, the delay in proscribing genocide as a criminal offence in Ethiopia could have been avoided, for instance through the inclusion of relevant provisions in the Federal Crimes Act of 1953,[27] enacted precisely to proscribe and punish at

---

22 See Genocide Convention, Article V, which reads, 'the Contracting Parties undertake to enact, in accordance with their respective Constitutions, the necessary legislation to give effect to the provisions of the present Convention and, in particular, to provide effective penalties for persons guilty of genocide or of any of the other acts enumerated in article III. For details on this, see C.J. Tams *et al., Convention on the Prevention and Punishment of the Crime of Genocide: A Commentary* (München: Verlag C.H. Beck oHG, 2014) 217. See also P. Gaeta, 'Grave Breaches of the Geneva Conventions' in A. Clapham *et al.* (eds), *The 1949 Geneva Conventions: A Commentary* (Oxford: Oxford University Press, 2014), 615–646, 623 *fn.* 38.

23 For the domestic implementation of the Genocide Convention, see W.A. Schabas, *Genocide in International Law: the Crime of Crimes* (2nd edn., Cambridge: Cambridge University Press, 2009) 406–408.

24 Australia's Genocide Convention Act No. 27, 1949. However, the High Court of Australia ruled in 1997 in the case of *Kruger* v. *The Commonwealth* that the Convention had not been implemented by legislation in Australia and therefore did not form part of Australian law. See *Kruger* v. *The Commonwealth* (1997) 190 CLR 1, paras 70–71, 87-88,159.

25 Israeli Law No. 5710-1950 on the Prevention and Punishment of Genocide.

26 Brasil – Lei N°2.889, De 1° de Outubro de1956 – Genocidio.

27 Federal Crimes Proclamation, Proclamation No. 138 of 1953, *entered into force* 25 September 1953.

the federal level various offenses that were missing from the 1930 Penal Code of the Empire of Ethiopia.[28]

5.3.1 Naming Genocide in Amharic: ዘርን ማጥፋት

Genocide is a term coined in 1944 by Lemkin to name certain atrocities committed during the Second World War, some of which Winston Churchill referred to as 'a crime without a name'.[29] In Ethiopia, genocide did not have a name until 1957, when it was introduced into the legal system using the Amharic phrase ዘርን ማጥፋት, which may be pronounced in English as 'zerenmathefat'[30] and literally translated as 'destroying (*'mathefat'*) the race (*'zeren'*). Some authors have taken issue with this terminology, suggesting that the word *'zere'* (race)[31] misrepresents its English counterpart, i.e. *'genos'* (group) in genocide, and that it fails to include groups other than 'racial' ones.[32] Apparently, the issue was first raised by the defendants in the *Dergue* trials in which, as a preliminary objection to the charge of genocide against political groups, they stated that: 'since 'zere' does not refer to groups other than racial groups the legislator did not intend to include political groups into the protected groups'.[33]

According to Tessema, who considered *zeremathefat* as a misnomer, the English word genocide (ጄኖሳይድ, as written in Amharic) should have been used in the Amharic version *as is* or the legislator could have chosen the phrase ክልከላ የተደረገለትን ቡድን ማጥቃት ወይም ማጥፋት, which translates into the crime of 'attacking or destroying a protected group', instead of *zeremathefat*.[34] The first suggestion is absurd. To use the English word 'genocide' as the Amharic name of the crime is, to begin with, not something that the Ethiopian legislator would have allowed. It defeats the whole purpose and benefit of understanding the name of the crime in one's own language. For that matter, no foreign

---

28   Although the 1953 Federal Crimes Proclamation was focused on redefining the jurisdiction of Federal Courts that came into existence after the reunification of Eritrea with Ethiopia following the end of the Second World War, it also proscribed various crimes that did not exist in the 1930 penal code.

29   See C. Fournet, *The Crime of Destruction and the Law of Genocide: Their Impact on Collective Memory* (Aldershot: Ashget Publishing Limited, 2007), 3–12; Schabas, *Genocide in International Law, supra* note 23, 17.

30   See The Penal Code of 1957, Amharic Version, Article 281.

31   The dictionary meaning of the Amharic 'ዘር' includes: 'seed, descent (origin), offspring, line (descent), lineage, issue (offspring), species, race (human), root, pedigree, blood'. See T.L. Kane, *Amharic-English Dictionary: Volume II* (Wiesbaden: Otto Harrassowitz, 1990), 1623.

32   See Tessema, *Prosecution of Politicide in Ethiopia, supra* note 2, 77–78.

33   *Colonel Mengistu Hailemariam et al.*, (Ruling on Preliminary Objections), *supra* note 5, 85.

34   Tessema, *Prosecution of Politicide in Ethiopia, supra* note 2, 260.

word is used to name a crime in the Amharic version of the Penal Code of 1957, even though the Code was drafted in French. The same is true for the FDRE Criminal Code. Furthermore, one could hardly provide a logical reason to consider that the English 'genocide' provides a better meaning than the Amharic *zerenmathefat* to an Amharic speaking Ethiopian, not least in the 1950s, when Amharic was the official language of the country.

Tessema's second suggestion might make sense, only if it is necessary to capture the elements of the crime in its name. Even then, the suggestion is partly inaccurate because to 'attack' (ማጥቃት) a protected group is not necessarily to commit genocide. Such a name might result in confusing genocidal *mens rea* with that of crimes against humanity of persecution.[35] Nonetheless, if *zerenmathefat* has to be replaced by a terminology that more accurately mirrors the international definition of genocide, the phrase ከልካ የተደረገለትን ቡድን ማጥፋት (destroying a protected group) or, simply, ቡድንን ማጥፋት (destroying the group) could be used.

In general, the emphasis on the name of the crime seems to be overly confusing. It also overlooks the fact that finding a precise terminology to denote the crime of genocide is an inherently difficult, if not impossible, task.[36] As noted above, it was pointed out that the Amharic *zerenmathefat* only covered racial groups. This should however be expressly mitigated since overall, what matters is not the scope of the literal meaning of the terms, but rather the elements of the crime as defined in the operative paragraphs of the provision that criminalizes genocide. As the analysis of the relevant disposition will overwhelmingly demonstrate[37] the operative meaning of *zerenmathefat* as defined in Ethiopian criminal law is not limited to racial groups.

Most importantly, the question regarding the *zerenmathefat* nomenclature should be seen within the context it was originally raised, i.e. the *Dergue* trials. There, the main debate revolved around the issue whether genocide could be committed against political groups, and challenging the meaning of *zerenmathefat* was, apparently, one of the arguments raised by the defendants to challenge the SPO indictment.[38] It was however dismissed by the FHC, which unequivocally found that the notion of *zerenmathefat* as defined in the law was not limited to 'racial' groups.[39]

---

35 This is discussed further in Chapter 6, section 6.4.
36 See Fournet, *The Crime of Destruction and the Law of Genocide*, supra note 29, 5.
37 See Chapter 6, section 6.2.
38 Other objections raised by the defendants in the *Dergue* trials are discussed in several parts of this book as appropriate.
39 *Colonel Mengistu Hailemariam et al.*, (Ruling on Preliminary Objections), *supra* note 5, 92.

The Amharic version of Article 269 of the FDRE Criminal Code retained its predecessor's expression *zerenmathefat*, despite its enactment after the above discussions took place in the *Dergue* trials.[40] In the other Ethiopian languages of the Criminal Code, the translations of genocide mirror the Amharic version and literally mean 'destruction of a race'. In Afan Oromo, it reads 'Sanyii Balleessuu'.[41] In Eritrea, the version in Tigrigna of the Penal Code of 2015 refers to genocide as 'ማጥፊኢ ዘሪኢ ሰብ', which literally means *zerenmathefat* in Amharic.[42]

5.3.2 Genocide as 'Crimes against Humanity'

The title of Article 281 of the Penal Code of 1957 referred to both the word 'genocide' and the phrase 'crimes against humanity' which it separated by the use of a semi-colon. The implication of the caption had not been discussed in Ethiopia until after the decision was reached in 1992 to prosecute the *Dergue* for crimes committed between 1974 and 1991. Some of the reports released in the early 1990s, that is at the time the SPO was investigating the *Dergue* crimes and preparing the indictments, only made references to the phrase 'crimes against humanity'. For example, in 1994, a few months before it filed indictments against the top *Dergue* officials, the SPO reported that,

> our research shows that crimes such as summary executions, forced disappearances, and torture carried out systematically on a wide scale as a matter of state policy constituted flagrant violations of international law, and specially *crimes against humanity*. These types of violations were clearly established as crimes and in force during the previous regime.[43]

---

40 See also the Penal Code of 1957 Amharic Version (የ ፩፱፻፶ የኢ.ትዮጵያ ፌዴራላዊ ዲሞክራሳዊ ሪፐብሊክ የወንጀል ሕግ፣ አንቀጽ ፪፻፹), Article 281.
41 See Seera Yakkaa Rippaabiliika Dimokiraatawaa Federaalawaa Itoophiyaa 1997, Keewwata 269, available at: <http://ethcriminalawnetwork.com/system/files/FDRE%20 Criminal%20Code%20-%20Afan%20Oromo.pdf> accessed 29 September 2019.
42 See The Penal Code of the State of Eritrea of 2015, Article 105.
43 SPO, 'Report of the Office of the Special Prosecutor 1994: The Special Prosecution Process of War Criminals and Human Rights Violation in Ethiopia' in N.J. Kritz (ed.), *Transitional Justice: How emerging democracies reckon with former regimes; Laws, Rulings and Reports* (Washington DC: United States Institute of Peace Press, 1995) 559-575, 562. Emphasis added. Trials were planned to begin in May 1994, that is, three months after the time of this report. See ibid., 563. The first indictment in *Mengistu et al.*, was filed in October that year. See FHC, SPO v. *Colonel Mengistu Hailemariam et al.*, (Indictment), 25 October 1994, File No. 1/87.

In 1994, a few months before the *Dergue* trials were planned to commence, the TGE disseminated a Circular to the UN Human Rights Commission, which stated, with particular reference to paragraphs 60, 62, and 90 of the 1993 Vienna Declaration and Program of Action,[44] that,

> according to these principles, it is the duty of the Transitional Government of Ethiopia to bring to justice those persons with respect to whom there are serious reasons for considering that they are responsible for serious violations both of international law and domestic law that can be assimilated in some cases to crimes against humanity.[45]

The phrase 'crimes against humanity' also appeared, together with the term 'genocide', in all of the SPO indictments referring to the alleged violation of Article 281 of the Penal Code. Accordingly, the SPO accused the *Dergue* defendants of committing a crime phrased as: 'genocide; crimes against humanity', against which the defendants raised a preliminary objection requesting the court to dismiss the charge from the indictment on the ground of opacity. In stating that the SPO did not specify the crime for which they were made to stand trial, the defendants mentioned that it was not clear from the SPO indictment whether they were accused of having committed genocide or crimes against humanity.[46] This objection opened a discussion as to the implication of the title of Article 281 of the Penal Code of 1957.

In countering the objection as groundless, the SPO offered various explanations that are mostly focused on describing genocide as crimes against humanity. In *Mengistu et al.*, where the SPO highlighted that the indictment refers to a crime of genocide, it also stated that 'in principle we do not disagree that Article 281 consisted of two different crimes'.[47] Nonetheless, in what appeared to conflict with this statement, it defended its indictment based on the irrelevance of distinguishing genocide from crimes against humanity in a formula worth reproducing here: 'of all the crimes that could be committed against humanity, genocide is the most appalling and shocking. As committing

---

44 Vienna Declaration and Program of Action, Adopted by the World Conference on Human Rights in Vienna on 25 June 1993. Available at: <http://www.ohchr.org/EN/ProfessionalInterest/Pages/Vienna.aspx> accessed 12 May 2019.
45 See TGE's Letter to the UN, E/CN.4/1994/103, 4.
46 *Colonel Mengistu Hailemariam et al.*, (Ruling on Preliminary Objections), *supra* note 5, 104–105.
47 Ibid.

genocide is committing crimes against humanity, the indictment, therefore, refers to genocide'.[48]

In treating genocide as crimes against humanity, the SPO further argued that genocide has as its legal source Article 6(c) of the Charter of the IMT.[49] This provision, which is known to have defined crimes against humanity for the first time in international law, reads,

> murder, extermination, enslavement, deportation, and other inhumane acts committed against any civilian population, before or during the war, or persecutions on political, racial or religious grounds in execution of or in connection with any crime within the jurisdiction of the Tribunal, whether or not in violation of the domestic law of the country where perpetrated.[50]

The SPO statement might have some merits in the sense that the definition of crimes against humanity in the Nuremberg Charter had a significant relation to 'genocide',[51] which was already used by the IMT prosecutors to colloquially describe acts committed by Nazi troops.[52] Nonetheless, these statements, coupled with references to crimes against humanity previously made in the above-mentioned reports of the SPO and the TGE, might have created a scholarly misunderstanding that the *Dergue* stood trial for crimes against humanity.[53] Indeed, it is one thing to argue that crimes committed by the *Dergue* could

---

48   Ibid., 104. Translation by the author. The original (Amharic) version reads,

በመሰረቱ አንቀጽ 281 ሁለት የተለያዩ ወንጀሎች ይዟል የሚለውን ሀሳብ አንቀውምም። በእኛ በኩል ያቀረብነው ክስ ዘርን የማጥፋት ወንጀል ነው። ዘርን የማጥፋት ወንጀል በሰበዓዊ ፍረት ላይ ከሚፈጸሙ ወንጀሎች ሁሉ አስከፊዉና አስቀያሚው ነው። በመሆኑም ዝርን ማጥፋት በሰበዓዊ ፍጡረት ላይ ወንጀል መፈጸም በመሆኑ ክሱ የቀረበው ዘርን በማጥፋት።

49   Ibid.

50   See also Nuremberg Rules, in Agreement for the Prosecution and Punishment of the Major War Criminals of the European Axis, 82 U.N.T.S. 279, *entered into force* 8 August 1945.

51   See Note by the Secretariat, E/AC.25/3, which stated that genocide as constituting an act of extermination was 'covered by the terms of Article 6, paragraph (c) of the Charter of the International Military Tribunal'.

52   See J.B. Quigley, T*he Genocide Convention: An International Law Analysis* (Aldershot: Ashgate Publishing Limited, 2006), 6.

53   It has been frequently argued that: *i*) the SPO prosecuted crimes against humanity; and *ii*) the duty to prosecute crimes against humanity perpetrated in Ethiopia emanated from various international human rights treaties, as well as from customary international law. For instance Professor Bassiouni wrote, 'in Africa, Ethiopia undertook the national prosecution for CAH and other international crimes committed during the Mengistu regime, which controlled the country in the aftermath of the 1974 Revolution'. See M.C. Bassiouni, '*Crimes Against Humanity* (Cambridge: Cambridge University Press, 2011) 660.

be best described as 'crimes against humanity', it is another to state that those conducts were clearly proscribed as crimes against humanity in a law that was in force throughout the *Dergue* regime. The only instance in which the phrase 'crimes against humanity' was mentioned in Ethiopian criminal law in force during the *Dergue* was in the title of Article 281 of the Penal Code of 1957. In the Ethiopian trials, Article 281 was never invoked in a manner that refers either to the definition of crimes against humanity under Article 6(c) of the IMT Charter or to its customary international law understanding of a widespread or systematic attack against a civilian population. Simply put, crimes against humanity were never regarded in Ethiopian law as an independent crime, and, as detailed below, the phrase 'crimes against humanity' in Article 281 was a redundant addendum to the word 'genocide'.

First of all, no significant meaning should be attached to the caption of Article 281 of the Penal Code for referring to the phrase 'crimes against humanity' in addition to genocide. The Ethiopian Penal Code was not the first one to refer to genocide as crimes against humanity, as such an understanding can be traced back to the discussions made during the drafting of the Convention. In fact, some States were opposed to the separate criminalization of genocide in international law on the ground that it is 'closely analogous to'[54] or 'an aspect of'[55] crimes against humanity. Other states such as Saudi Arabia[56] and the Dominican Republic[57] had proposed for an express denunciation of genocide as an 'international crime against humanity' instead of formulating it as 'a crime in international law'.[58] Such considerations were put to an end with the General Assembly's decision, pursuant to resolutions 96(I) of 11 December 1946 and 180(II) of 21 November 1947, that genocide cannot be regarded as just one of the crimes against humanity mentioned in the Charter of the IMT.[59]

---

54   In this regard, the U.K. suggested that 'genocide is so closely analogous to the crimes against humanity covered by the Nürnberg judgment that the best thing to do would be to send it to the International Law Commission'. See A/PV.123.

55   France for example, criticized the General Assembly resolution for not using crimes against humanity instead of genocide which it referred to as a 'neologism'. It also stated that it 'regretted that the question of genocide was not considered in correlation with the principles affirmed in the Statute and sentences of the Nürnberg Tribunal, and as a parallel to the conception of crime against humanity, of which genocide was merely one of the aspects'. See Communication Received from France A/401.

56   See UN Doc. E/621.

57   The representative of the Dominican Republic stated that 'humanity is looking to us for the expression of this idea in a solemn form and for the denunciation of that crime as a crime against humanity'. See UN Doc. E/621.

58   See G.A. Res. 96 (I), *supra* note 10.

59   See Note by the Secretariat, E/AC.25/3.

Consequently, genocide has evolved as an independent crime with its own unique elements, most notably as regards the *mens rea*.[60]

Second of all, despite the title's indication of the phrase 'crimes against humanity', Article 281 of the Penal Code referred to the crime of genocide as defined under Article II of the Genocide Convention. As will be discussed in detail in the next chapter, both the *chapeau* and the remaining parts of Article 281 were meant to reproduce the elements of the crime of genocide in international law. Ethiopian courts have repeatedly stated that Article 281 of the Penal Code was a provision that domesticated Article II of the Convention. In particular, as underlined by the FSC in reference to the provision in question, 'the Convention is the source of the Ethiopian law on genocide'.[61] In *Mengistu et al.,* the FHC specified that the expression 'crimes against humanity' was an addendum meant to explain that genocide is a crime against humanity.[62] It also stated that Article 281 dealt exclusively with genocide when it further stated, 'should there be a need to describe the term 'genocide' separately; it is the commission *against human beings* of conducts listed under Article 281 (a), (b), (c) of the Penal Code'.[63]

Regardless, the reference to genocide as crimes against humanity in the Ethiopian legal system continued beyond the *Dergue* trials and the Penal Code. It reappeared in 1994 in the Constitution and again in 2005 in the Criminal Code. The Constitution, as discussed in Chapter 2, comprises a self-imposed obligation to prosecute 'persons who commit *crimes against humanity,* so defined by international agreements ratified by Ethiopia and by other laws of Ethiopia such as *genocide,* summary executions, forcible disappearances or torture'.[64] On its part, the Criminal Code removed the expression 'crimes against humanity' from the title of its provision on genocide, although it uses the same phrase elsewhere to refer to both genocide and war crimes.[65] In this regard, the *Explanatory Notes* stated,

---

60 See A. Cassese *et al., Cassese's International Criminal Law* (3rd ed., Oxford: Oxford University Press, 2013) 127–128.
61 FSC, SPO v. *Colonel Mengistu Hailemariam et al.,* (Appeals Judgment), 26 May 2008, File No. 30181, 68.
62 *Colonel Mengistu Hailemariam et al.,* (Ruling on Preliminary Objections), *supra* note 5, 105.
63 Ibid. Emphasis Added. Translation by the author. The original (Amharic) version reads, 'የዘር ማጥፋት ወንጀል ያሚለዉን ሀረግ ብቻዉን እንዲተነተን ከተፈለገ በሰው ልጆች ላይ በወንጀለኛ መቅጫ ሕግ ቁጥር ፪፻፹፩ በፊደል 'ሀ' 'ለ' 'ሐ' የተዘረዘሩትን የወንጀል አድራጎቶች መፈጸም ማለት ነው።'.
64 FDRE Constitution, Article 28. Emphasis added.
65 FDRE Criminal Code, Article 44.

concerning the naming of the provision, which was previously referred to as 'genocide; crimes against humanity', the phrase 'crimes against humanity' is now deleted. The reason is that 'genocide' is one of the crimes against humanity and that Article 270 and the following Articles are also concerned with crimes that are crimes against humanity.[66]

By referring to crimes against humanity as including crimes from Article 269 to Article 280,[67] the Explanatory Notes to the Criminal Code were apparently using the phrase crimes against humanity as synonym to the phrase 'fundamental crimes against international law' – employed by the Code as the title of Chapter II of its Book III to designate genocide and war crimes. This superfluous usage might find some support in the *travaux préparatoires* of the Constitution as well as in its *Explanatory Notes*.

Indeed, during the discussions of the 1994 Constitutional Commission, comments were made as to the meaning and scope of the phrase crimes against humanity. Some members of the Commission disputed the Amharic translation of the phrase as በስብዕና ላይ የሚፈጸሙ ወንጀሎች (which translates into crimes against the quality of being a human).[68] At times, the phrase was translated into በሰው ልጅ ላይ የተሰራ ወንጀል, which literally means 'crime committed against a human being/kind'.[69] There is no record in the *travaux* as to the specific international definition of crimes against humanity referred to by the comments. At the time this was discussed, crimes against humanity were already defined in the Statutes of the international criminal tribunals. Accordingly, several crimes (not including genocide) could constitute crimes against humanity 'when directed against any civilian population', according to Article 5 of the

---

66 See FDRE Criminal Code, *Explanatory Notes*, Article 269. Translation by the author. The original (Amharic) version reads,
ስያሜውን በተመለከተ ቀደምሲል ዘርን ስለማጥፋት ፤ በሰዉአዊነት ላይ ስለሚፈጸሙ ወንጀሎች (crimes against humanity) ይል የነበረ ሲሆንበሰብአዊነት ላይ ስለሚፈጸሙ ወንጀሎች የሚለው ሐረግ እንዲሰረዝ ተደርጓል። ምክንያቱም ዘር ማጥፋት በሰብአዊነት ላይ ከሚፈጸሙት ወንጀሎች አንዱ በመሆኑና ከአንቀጽ ፪፻፸ ጀምሮ ያሉት ተከታታይ አንቀጾች በሰብአዊነት ላይ ስለሚፈጸሙ ወንጀሎች ስለሆኑ ነው። .

67 Unlike Article 44 of the Criminal Code which by 'crimes against humanity' refers to genocide under Article 269 and to some of the war crimes listed in Articles 270 to 274, the *Explanatory Notes* appear to be referring to genocide and all war crimes contained in Articles 269 to 283.

68 See 'The Minutes of the 88th Ordinary Session of the Constitutional Committee (7 April 1994)' in The Constitutional Commission, 'Minutes, Vol. II: Ordinary Sessions No 51- No 88 held from 2 November 1993 to 3 April 1994' (Addis Ababa: FDRE House of Federations, Unpublished), 2.

69 See 'The Minutes of the 84th Ordinary Session of the Constitutional Committee (24 February 1994)' in The Constitutional Commission, 'Minutes, Vol. II', *supra* note 68, 5.

ICTY Statute[70] or 'when committed as part of a widespread or systematic attack against any civilian population on national, political, ethnic, racial or religious grounds', according to Article 3 of the ICTR Statute.[71]

The Constitutional Commission did not delve into establishing an accurate definition of crimes against humanity by consulting international law. When the need to do so was mentioned by a member of the Commission, it ignored it on the ground that 'doing so would require enormous amount of time and study'.[72] From a closer reading of the *travaux*, it appears that defining 'crimes against humanity' was in fact not regarded as the Commission's task. Its primary aim was to use this expression as a guarantee-clause in the Constitution to ensure that crimes such as those committed during the *Dergue* regime would not be subjected to amnesty or statute of limitations.[73]

In line with this purpose of 'crimes against humanity' as a guarantee of non-repetition of atrocities, it was also suggested that the use of the phrase should be construed as indicating any kind of 'inhumane crimes against Ethiopians'.[74] Apart from that, no specific definition was attached to this phrase in the *travaux* of the Constitution. Nonetheless, one may argue that whenever the 'expression crimes against humanity' was considered as referring to crimes under international law, it was the Nuremberg Charter that was on the mind of the Constitutional Commission. The Commission indeed stated at one point that the phrase crimes against humanity referred to the kind of atrocities committed against the Jews by Nazi Germany from 1941 to 1945.[75]

To one's dismay, the *Explanatory Notes* to the Constitution, prepared in 1994 by the Constitutional Commission, turned out to be a counterproductive attempt as far as clarifying the nature and scope of 'crimes against humanity' is concerned. It listed, non-exhaustively, eight offences that it considered as crimes envisioned by Article 28, which it referred to as በሰው ልጆች መብት ላይ የሚፈጸሙ ወንጀሎች (crimes against the rights of persons).[76] Four of the offences are similar to the crime of genocide and its underlying acts as provided under

---

70 The underlying offenses include crimes such as murder, extermination, enslavement, deportation, imprisonment, torture, rape; persecutions on political, racial and religious grounds, and other inhumane acts. See ICTY Statute, Article 5.
71 ICTR Statute, Article 3.
72 See 'The Minutes of the 84th Ordinary Session of the Constitutional Committee (24 February 1994)' *supra* note 69, 5.
73 Ibid.
74 Ibid.
75 See 'The Minutes of the 87th Ordinary Session of the Constitutional Committee (6 April 1994)' in The Constitutional Commission, 'Minutes, Vol. II', *supra* note 68,12.
76 See FDRE Constitution, *Explanatory Notes*, 64.

Article 281 of the Penal Code of 1957.[77] The remaining four offences, based on a literal translation, are: *i*) intentional act of causing a suffering to people;[78] ii) denationalization or forcible religious conversion;[79] iii) appropriation of civilian property and destruction of wealth;[80] and iv) inflicting an act of killing, torture, inhumane or degrading treatment, forced labor or grave willful injury against the prisoners of war or those peacefully protesting against the policy of the government.[81]

That being said, it should also be pointed out that the reference to 'crimes against humanity' in the Penal Code of 1957, the Constitution, and the Criminal Code of 2005 may not be dismissed as a mere case of misnomer devoid of implication on the definition of genocide in Ethiopian law. One could point out two aspects of the crime of genocide in Ethiopia that might have stemmed from the above discussed view that this crime is a subset of crimes against humanity. The first one is the protected groups' aspect of genocide, which now appears to be covering twice the number of groups protected under Article II of the Genocide Convention.[82] The second one is the treatment of genocide under the Penal Code of 1957 as a crime of plan (ዕቅድ) instead of as a crime of intent, as discussed below and, further, in Chapter 6.[83]

5.3.3 *Genocide as a Crime of ዕቅድ (Dessein)*

Ethiopian law has not determined genocidal *mens rea* in a self-evident manner. Article 281 of the Penal Code of 1957 contained a discrepancy in relation to how genocidal *mens rea* was defined in its Amharic and English versions. The Amharic version used the word በማቀድ (a verb form of the noun ዕቅድ) which literally meant 'with a plan' in English,[84] instead of the English version's 'with

---

77 These are crimes listed under the *Explanatory Notes*' Article 28 a, b, c, and e. See ibid., 63.
78 Ibid. Translation by the author. The original (Amharic) version reads : ሆን ብሎ ህዝብን ችግር እንዲደርስብት ማድረግ.
79 Ibid. Translation by the author. The original (Amharic) version reads :
በዘዴት ከትውልድ ገና ዜግነት ወደ በዓድ ገር ጥገኝነት እንዲዛወር ማረግ ወይንም ሃይማኖት እንዲክድ ማድረግ.
80 Ibid. Translation by the author. The original (Amharic) version reads : የህዝብን ንብረት መዉረስና ሃብት ማፍረስ.
81 Ibid. Translation by the author. The original (Amharic) version reads:
በጦር ምርክኝነት የታስሩ ወይንም የመንግስትን ፖሊሲ መሰርያ ሳያነሱ በሰላማዊ መንገድ የተቃወሙትን ሰዎች መግድል ማሰቃየት ከሰበአዊ ፍጥረት ውጭ የሆነ ይስቃይ ስራ እንዲፈጸምባቸው ከባድ የሆነ ስቃይና ጉዳት እንዲደርስባቸው ማድረግ.
82 For details, see Chapter 6, section 6.2.2.
83 For the practice of interpreting see ibid., section 6.4.1.
84 See Kane, *Amharic-English Dictionary: Volume II*, supra note 31, 1187; W. Leslau, *English-Amharic Context Dictionary* (Wiesbaden: Otto Harrassowitz, 1973) 936.

intent' which translated into the Amharic's በማሰብ (a verb form of the noun አሳብ).⁸⁵

This discrepancy could be examined by referring to the language of the original drafts from which the Amharic and the English versions were translated, i.e. French. Although the *avant-projets* (initial drafts) were not published, the definitive French version of the Penal Code is accessible. In referring to genocidal *mens rea*, Article 281 of the French version of the Penal Code used the phrase '*dans le dessein de détruire*'.⁸⁶ In the *Dictionnaire Français Amharique* the noun *dessiene* is defined as ዕቅድ (plan) or ግላማ (goal) in Amharic.⁸⁷ If one may thus conclude that the Amharic version of Article 281 of the Penal Code did not mirror the genocidal *mens rea* required by the Convention, there is however no explanation as to why the law chose 'plan' over 'intent'. The *travaux préparatoires* are either missing or were not recorded from the outset.⁸⁸ In this context, it might be useful to consult how the relevant terms are used in French language laws.

As was already used in the French versions of the Genocide Convention and later in the Statutes of the ICTY, the ICTR, and the ICC, it is the phrase '*dans l'intention de détruire*' that matches the English phrase 'with intent to destroy'.⁸⁹ One could thus notice that the Ethiopian Penal Code was the first, but not the only, French language legislation to refer to genocidal *mens rea* using the phrase '*dans le dessein de détruire*'.⁹⁰ Similar formulations exist in Penal Codes

---

85   Kane, *Amharic-English Dictionary: Volume II*, supra note 31,1169; Leslau, *English-Amharic Context Dictionary*, supra note 84, 654. In the legal usage too, the word '*plan*' is always defined as ዕቅድ in Amharic. See the Penal Code of 1957, Articles 269, 286, 344, 473; the FDRE Criminal Code, Articles 248, 257, 274, 308, 335, 338, 479.
86   See The Penal Code of 1957, French Version (Code Pénal De L'Empire D'Ethiopie), Article 281.
87   B. Abebe et É. Ficquet, *Dictionnaire Français Amharique* (Addis Abeba: Shama Books, 2003) 131.
88   In 1963, six years after the Penal Code came into force, Berhanu wrote that '[d]rafts and preliminary works in connection with the Ethiopian Codes have not yet been published'. See M.N. Berhanu, *Penal Code Index* (Asmara 1963) *cited in* J. Vanderlinden, 'An Introduction to the Sources of Ethiopian Law from the 13th to the 20th Century' (1966) 3 *Journal of Ethiopian Law* 227–302, *fn.* 229–230.
89   See Convention Pour La Prévention Et La Répression Du Crime De Génocide, Article II.
90   There was no French language domestic law defining genocide before the Penal Code of 1957 of Ethiopia. For States such as France, however, it could be argued that the Genocide Convention had a direct application upon ratification (1950) due to France's monist system. For details, see C. Fournet, 'Reflection on the Separation of Powers: The Law of Genocide and the Symptomatic French Paradox' in R. Henham and P. Behrens (eds.), *The Criminal Law of Genocide: International, Comparative and Contextual Aspects* (Farnham: Ashgate, 2007) 212–213.

such as that of Côte d'Ivoire[91] and Switzerland.[92] In unofficial English translations of these laws, 'with the intent to destroy' is used to denote *'dans le dessein de détruire'*.[93] However, in the laws of Belgium,[94] Canada,[95] Luxemburg[96] and Mali,[97] it is the French phrase *'dans l'intention de détruire'* that is applied to refer to the genocidal intent to destroy.

Perhaps, the terms *'dessein'* and *'intention'* could refer to the same thing in everyday French, although the latter might be considered the preferred legal parlance when it comes to *mens rea*, as endorsed by the relevant international instruments. The French word *'dessein'* may also mean 'design' in English and could refer to 'a plan conceived in the mind'.[98] This is however not to say that *'dessein'* is the word that French legal texts prefer while referring to the English word 'plan'. In French language laws defining genocide, it is the French word *'plan'* (not *dessein*) that refers to the English word 'plan', as can be inferred from the criminal laws of countries such as Andorra,[99] Burkina Faso,[100] and France,[101] where 'concerted plan to destroy' (not intent to destroy) is the required genocidal *mens rea*.

The question at this juncture could be whether Swiss drafter Jean Graven was referring to plan or to intent when using the French word *'dessein'*. This is a very difficult question to answer for the obvious lack of authoritative sources. However, it could be argued that the choice must have been a deliberate one. Because Professor Graven was familiar with the Convention's definition of genocide,[102] it is unlikely that the Code's use of *'dessein'* instead of *'intention'* was not intentional, given also that the Code was prepared after the Genocide Convention had been ratified by Ethiopia. In this respect, it may also be advanced that such *'dessein'* included a state plan or policy requirement.

---

91   Loi n° 1981-640 du 31 juillet 1981, instituant le Code pénal (modifiée par la loi n° 1995-522 du 6 juillet 1995), Article 137.
92   Code pénal suisse du 21 décembre 1937 (Etat au 1er septembre 2017), Article 264.
93   Swiss Criminal Code of 21 December 1937 (Status as of 1 January 2017) English version, Article 264.
94   Criminal Code of the Republic of Belgium (1867, as of 2016) French Version, Article 136bis.
95   Code Criminel. S.R., ch. C-34, Article 318(2).
96   Code pénal, En vigueur Dans Le Grand-Duché De Luxembourg (Législation: Jusqu'au 10 Juillet 2016), Article 136bis.
97   Loi N° 01-079 Du 20 Août 2001 Portant Code Pénal, Article. 30.
98   See M.H. Corréard and V. Grundy (eds.), *The Oxford-Hachette French Dictionary* (2nd edn., Oxford: Oxford University Press, 1997), 247.
99   Nouveau Code Pénal Andorre, Article, 456.
100 Loi n° 25–2018/AN, Article 313.
101 Code Pénal France (1994), Article 211-1.
102 See section 5.4.1. below.

THE CRIME OF GENOCIDE IN ETHIOPIAN LAW   207

As Schabas noted, Professor Bassiouni, who considered that genocide requires state plan or policy,[103] was at the time interning with Jean Graven and was thus involved in the drafting of the Code's provision on genocide.[104]

In sum, the Amharic meaning of '*dessein*', is far from clear. In fact, the Amharic version of the law translated '*dessein*' into ዕቅድ (plan) rather than ኣሳብ (intention).[105] Nonetheless, several provisions in the Amharic version used the same word, ዕቅድ(plan), to refer to their French counterparts' use of 'intention' ('*intentionnellement*'). Several other provisions had translated this same French word, 'intention', into ኣሳብ (intention)[106] Accordingly, the Amharic word ዕቅድ stood for both '*dessein*' and '*intention*'. As a result of this ambiguity, it is hard to say from its wording whether the genocidal *mens rea* defined under Article 281 of the Penal Code was in line with the Genocide Convention's *intent* to destroy.

It also seems important to note that not all discrepancies between the French and Amharic versions of the Penal Code of 1957 can be solved through etymological and lexical comparisons, notably because some of the Code's provisions – as drafted in French or as translated into Amharic – have not been approved as such. The codification process, as noted by Jembere, was rigorous – in addition to the foreign experts tasked with preparing the *avant projets* (*initial preparatory drafts*), the Codification Commission, the Council of Ministers, the two Chambers of Parliament, and finally the Emperor took part in the promulgation of the Penal Code.[107] After the *avant projets* were translated into Amharic, detailed discussions and debates were undertaken among Ethiopian members of the Codification Commission, following which amendments proposed by Ethiopian members were considered to insert, replace, or omit words, phrases, or ideas.[108] As Jembere observed, the drafts of the Civil Code and Penal Code were, in particular, subjected to heated debates and arguments that took much time and energy.[109] Even after the drafts were approved by the Codification Commission, 'every article was read, discussed, and some

---

103   See Bassiouni, *Crimes Against Humanity, supra* note 53, 117.
104   See Schabas, *Genocide in International Law, supra* note 23, 161, *fn*. 292.
105   Only once out of 27 times did the Code translated '*dessein*' into ኣሳብ (intention). See The Penal Code of 1957, Article 301.
106   In fact, Chapter II of the Penal Code that dealt with the concept of criminal culpability (*la culpabilité pénale*) employed the French word '*intention*', not '*dessein*', to refer to the English word 'intention'. Here, its Amharic counterpart refers to ኣሳብ (intention), not ዕቅድ(plan).
107   See A. Jembere, *An Introduction to the Legal History of Ethiopia: 1434–1974* (Lit Verslag: Münster, 2000),199–201.
108   Ibid.
109   Ibid.

alterations were inserted' by the two Chambers of Parliament.[110] By using ዕቅድ (plan/intent) in the Amharic version of Article 281, the Ethiopian members of the Codification Commission and/or members of Parliament might have considered that the commission of genocide requires the existence of a plan to destroy. In ordinary Amharic, with which members of Parliament were, presumably, more familiar, intention is not plan/intent ዕቅድ.

Be that as it may, it is noteworthy that the Criminal Code of 2005 did the exact opposite, i.e its Article 269 replaced the ዕቅድ (plan/intent) under Article 281 of the Penal Code of 1957 with አሳብ (intention).[111] Although the *Explanatory Notes* do not offer any explanation for this particular change, a relevant explanation may be found in Article 57 of the Criminal Code, which states that 'the preferred translation for the English 'intentionally' is the Amharic አስቦ'.[112] As a result of this change, the *mens rea* required for the crime of genocide under Ethiopian law depends on whether the applicable law is the Penal Code of 1957 or the Criminal Code of 2005, to which the book will revert in Chapter 6 with respect to the Ethiopian courts' jurisprudence.

5.4 Evolution of the Ethiopian Law on Genocide

Besides the Penal Code of 1957, there have been two laws with significant implications on the prevention and repression of genocide in the Ethiopian legal system. These are the 1989 Draft Criminal Code of the People's Democratic Republic of Ethiopia (PDRE)[113] and the Criminal Code of 2005. The following development discusses these three codes separately to show the evolution of the text of the crime of genocide in Ethiopia.

5.4.1 *The Penal Code of 1957*
The Penal Code recognized genocide (Article 281), together with several categories of war crimes (Articles 282–292), as crimes against international law. In the Code's expression, these crimes were 'fundamental offenses' in the

---

110   Jembere noted that it was only the Civil Procedure Code that did not pass through this process. See ibid.
111   See the FDRE Criminal Code, Article 269, which substituted its predecessor's 'በማቀድ' with 'በማሰብ'.
112   See FDRE Criminal Code, *Explanatory Notes*, Article 57. Translation by the author. The original (Amharic) version reads: ' "Intentionally" ለሚለው ቃል የተሻለው ትርጉም "አስቦ" የሚለው በመሆኑ ነው።' Emphasis in the original.
113   Draft Criminal Code of the PDRE, *submitted to the National Assembly in* Megabit 1981 Ethiopian Calender (March/April 1989).

category of 'offenses against the law of nations' as laid down under the second title of its Book III.[114] Under its Article 281, the Penal Code criminalized genocide irrespective of its commission in time of peace or war, as required by Article I of the Genocide Convention.

Insofar as the Penal Code also listed all the other acts prohibited by Article III of the Convention, it provided for a complete implementation of the Convention, as required under its Article V. Generally, crimes such as attempt and complicity in genocide are punishable by virtue of the Penal Code's general rules of participation.[115] Furthermore, the Penal Code comprised a separate provision on conspiracy to commit genocide.[116] Even further, the Penal Code stood in stark contrast to other domestic laws[117] by making direct and public incitement to commit genocide punishable as an inchoate offence (not as a mode of liability) under its Article 286 (a).[118]

Contrary to Tessema's suggestion, there is no evidence that the incorporation of genocide into the Penal Code resulted from Ethiopia's experience with atrocities perpetrated by Italian forces in Addis Ababa.[119] Rather, the domestication of the crime of genocide into the Ethiopian legal system appears to have resulted from the fact that the drafting of the Penal Code was entrusted to Professor Jean Graven, expert in international criminal law and, among others, a representative of Switzerland during the Nuremberg trials, as well as one of the early advocates for the establishment of a permanent international criminal court.[120] It was also pointed out later by the drafter that the incorporation of offenses against international law into the national law was a

---

114   The Penal Code's expression, 'crimes against the law of nations', was considered as synonymous to 'crimes against international law'. See J. Graven, 'The Penal Code of The Empire of Ethiopia' (1964) 1(2) *Journal of Ethiopian Law* 267–298, 295.
115   With regard to attempt to commit genocide, see the Penal Code of 1957, Articles 27 and 281. For complicity in genocide, see ibid., Articles 36 and 281.
116   The Penal Code of 1957, Article 286(b). In this regard, the Ethiopian law may appear to be unique.
117   For details, see Schabas, *Genocide in International Law*, supra note 23, 407: 'virtually [no state has] provisions for direct and public incitement [to commit genocide]'.
118   See the Penal Code of 1957, Article 286(a). This provision, captioned 'provocation and preparation', reads, 'whosoever, with the object of committing, permitting or supporting any of the acts provided for in the preceding articles[genocide and war crimes]: (a) publicly encourages them, by word of mouth, images or writings'. Although Ethiopian courts have not discussed it, which is why this book is not examining this inchoate offence, the SPO's first count in *Mengistu et al* accused the *Dergue* of 'provocation and preparation' to commit genocide. See Chapter 1, section 1.6.
119   See Tessema, *Prosecution of Politicide in Ethiopia*, supra note 2, 68 fn. 13.
120   At the time of the drafting, Jean Graven was the Dean of the Faculty of Law and President of the Court of Cassation in Geneva, Switzerland.

bold innovation, 'in order to guarantee the effectiveness of [the Penal Code's] provisions'.[121]

There is no doubt that Jean Graven made the Ethiopian Penal Code stood out as one of the most comprehensive and modern penal codes of its time and as one of the few that had incorporated provisions on core international crimes.[122] Yet, Article 281 of the Penal Code arguably had two major deficiencies. Firstly, the Convention's definition of genocide was not incorporated *verbatim* into the Penal Code. Secondly, the *avant-projets* of the Penal Code were prepared in French, the language of the drafter, before being translated into Amharic and English, the two languages used in the final version of the Code, with – as has been exposed earlier – the former having precedence over the latter in case of conflict. It is thus highly likely that most of the discrepancies in the mostly prolix final versions of the Code stem from the inherent difficulties of legal translation.[123] The often-cited English version of Article 281 of the Penal Code, whose title blended genocide with crimes against humanity, reads:

> Genocide; Crimes against Humanity
>
> Whosoever, with intent to destroy, in whole or in part, a *national, ethnic*, racial, religious or political group, organizes, orders or engages in, be it in time of war or in time of peace:
> (a) killings, bodily harm or serious injury to the physical *or* mental health of *members* of the group, in any way whatsoever; or
> (b) measures to prevent the propagation or continued survival of its members or their progeny; or
> (c) the compulsory movement or dispersion of peoples or children, or their placing under living conditions calculated to result in their death or disappearance, is punishable with rigorous imprisonment from five years to life, or, in cases of exceptional gravity, with death.[124]

By contrast, Article 281 of the Amharic version of the Penal Code translates into:

> Genocide; Crimes against Humanity

---

121 Graven, 'The Penal Code of the Empire of Ethiopia' *supra* note 114, 295.
122 Ibid. See also Jembere, *An Introduction to the Legal History of Ethiopia, supra* note 107, 202.
123 For details on this, see Jembere, *An Introduction to the Legal History of Ethiopia, supra* note 107, 198. See also R. Briottet, 'French, English, Amharic: the law in Ethiopia' (2009) 9(2) *Journal of Romance Studies* 1–9.
124 The Penal Code of 1957, Article 281. Emphasis added.

Whosoever, in time of war or in time of peace, *by planning to destroy*, in whole or in part, *a social unit of a multinational population unified in language and culture* organized on the basis of race, religion, or political affiliation, organizes an act of destruction, orders, or engages in:

(a) killing, causing bodily injury, or causing serious harm to the external *and* internal health of *one of the members* of the unit, in any way whatsoever

(b) the placing of measures necessary to prevent the propagation or continued survival of its members or their progeny; or

(c) forcibly moving peoples or children from place to place, or causing their dispersion, or placing them under living conditions calculated to result in their death or disappearance, is punishable with rigorous imprisonment from five years to twenty-five years, or, in more serious cases, with life imprisonment or death.[125]

There are five apparent conflicts between the two versions of the Penal Code. Firstly, the phrase 'intent to destroy' does not appear in the Amharic version, which instead uses the phrase 'ዕቅድ to destroy', as discussed above. Secondly, the Amharic version employs a lengthy phrase, 'a social unit of a multinational population unified in language and culture', which stands for the word 'group' in the English version. Thirdly, and concerning the protected groups, the English version of the provision recognizes five groups, namely national, ethnic, racial, religious, and political groups. The Amharic version is different in that it did not expressly recognize *national* and *ethnic* groups. Fourthly, as to prohibited acts, the English version of Article 281(a) uses the disjunctive 'or' to refer to 'serious injury to the physical *or* mental health' of members of the group. However, the corresponding Amharic version uses the conjunctive 'and',

---

125 Translation by the author. Emphasis added. The original (Amharic) version reads:
ቁ፤ ፪፻፹፩፡፡ ዘርን፡ ሰለ ማጥፋት በሰብአዊ ፍጥረት ላይ ስለሚደረግ ወንጀል

ማንም ሰው በሰላምም ጊዜም ሆነ በጦርነት ጊዜ በቋንቋና በልማድ አንድ የሆነውን በዘር በያይማኖት ወይም በፖለቲካ ተሳስሮ የተቋቋመውን የኀብረ ብሔርን ማሕበራዊ የሆነ አንድ ክፍል ሕዝብ በመላው ዉይም በከፊል ለማጥፋት በማቀድ የጥፋቱን ሥራ በማቋቋም ትእዛዝ በመስጠት ወይም ይህን አድራጎት በሥራ ላይ በማዋል ፤

(ሀ) ነፍስ የገደለ ፣ አካል ያቆሰለ፣ ወይም ከዚሁ ክፍል አባሎች በአንደኛው አፍአዊና ውስጣዊ ጤንነት ላይ በማናቸውም ሁኔታ ጉዳት ያደረሰ እንደ ሆነ

(ለ) እነዚሁ አባሎች በዘር እንዳይራቡ ወይም በአይዎታ እንዳይኖሩ ላማገድ አስፈላጊዉን ዘዴ ያደረገ እንደ ሆነ

(ሐ) ሕዝብን ወይም ሕፃናትን በኃይል ከስፍራ ወደ ስፍራ በማዛወር ወይም በመበተን ወይም ዝርያቸዉ እንዳይተን ወይም ጨርሶ እንዲጠፋ የሞት አደጋ ባሚያደርስባቸው ሁኔታ ባንድ ስፍራ በግዞት በማስቀመጥ ማንበራዊ ጉዳት እንዲደርስ ያደረገ እንደ ሆነ ካምስት ዓመት እስከ ዕድሜ ልክ ሊደርስ በሚችል ጽኑ እስራት ወይም ሁኔታዉ እጅግ ከባድ ሆኖ ጊዜ በሞት ፍርድ ይቀጣል.

as in 'serious harm to the external *and* internal health of one of the members of the unit'. It is in fact not self-evident whether the Amharic version of the Penal Code actually recognizes mental harm.[126] Fifthly, regarding the number of victims, the Amharic version of Article 281(a) mentions that causing serious harm to the external and internal health of one member is sufficient, while the English version uses the plural marker, 'members', in such cases.

The Amharic version of the Penal Code is also not similar to the final version of the French draft of the Penal Code. The latter, which is more or less identical to the English version of the Code, reads:

> ART. 281. – Génocide, crimes contre l'humanité.
> Celui qui, dans le dessein do détruire totalement ou partiellement un groupe national, ethnique, racial, confessionnel ou politique, aura organisé, ordonné ou pratiqué, que ce soit en temps de paix ou de guerre:
> a) des homicides, des lésions corporelles ou des atteintes graves à la santé physique ou mentale de membres du groupe, sous quelque forme que ce soit;
> b) des mesures en vue d'empêcher la procréation ou la survie de la descendance de ses membres;
> c) le déplacement ou la dispersion forcés de populations ou d'enfants ou leur placement dans des conditions de vie telles qu'elles doivent aboutir à leur mort ou leur disparition, encourt la réclusion, de cinq ans à perpétuité, ou, dans les cas les plus graves, la peine de mort.[127]

It is not clear why the Amharic translation reads so differently from both the French and English versions. Due to the inaccessibility of the *legislative minutes* of the Code, it is difficult to conclude whether these differences are the result of poor translation or a deliberate choice of words and phrases by the Ethiopian Parliament.[128] Some have opined that the discrepancies between the French and Amharic versions of the Penal Code resulted from the fact that 'Amharic as a language lacks a settled and precise body of legal terminology

---

126 This is discussed further in Chapter 6, section 6.3.2.
127 See Le code pénal de l'Empire d' Éthiopie du 23 juillet 1957, Article 28, available at: <http://ethcriminalawnetwork.com/system/files/The%20Ethiopian%20Penal%20Code%20of%201957%20-%20French%20Version.pdf> accessed 29 September 2019.
128 As noted earlier, the Parliament had read and discussed every article and inserted some alterations to the final draft. See Jembere, *An Introduction to the Legal History of Ethiopia*, *supra* note 107, 201. See also section 5.3.3 above.

...[and] translators may have to use vague terminology, or long descriptive phrases which lose the exact meaning of the original text'.[129]

In fact, the significance of the final French version of the Penal Code of 1957 is not known, as it was never recognized as an official version of the law. Although the Code's initial draft were prepared in French, the FHC only referred to it in one instance, to interpret a prolix phrase in the Amharic version of the Code. In that one instance, the FHC stated that Article 275 of the French draft of the Penal Code contained 'political groups', and concluded that the same groups were referred to in the phrase 'a social unit of a multinational population unified in language and culture organized on the basis of...political affiliation' in the Amharic version of the Code.[130]

Although ambiguous legal texts can be interpreted based on *travaux préparatoires* or legislative minutes, which are deemed to be reflecting the intention of the legislator, the FHC's reference to the *avant projet* was problematic. Firstly, the Court did not refer to the actual *avant projet*. Instead, it based its conclusion on an information included in a secondary source, i.e. a journal article referring to the inclusion of political groups under the French drafts.[131] Secondly, the *avant projets* was not discussed by the Ethiopian Parliament or the Codification Commission until after it was translated into Amharic. It was thus not by and of itself reflective of the intent of the legislator, but only of the drafter. As pointed out earlier, the Parliament had discussed the Amharic translation of the *avant projet* article by article to which it inserted several changes. Therefore, the Amharic translation of the *avant projet* and the parliamentary discussions thereof were the relevant documents that should have been regarded, for all intents and purposes, as the *travaux préparatoires* of the Penal Code of 1957. In relying on the *avant projet* to clarify ambiguity in the final Amharic version of the Code, the FHC might have substituted the intention of the legislator with that of the drafter.

It may be pointed out here that the existence of an official version in English has no practical significance in terms of legal interpretation, and its relevance may not go beyond its application in the academic sphere where the medium of instruction of Ethiopian law schools is English.[132] Be this as it may, the

---

129 P.L. Strauss 'On Interpreting the Ethiopian Penal Code' 1968 5(2) *Journal of Ethiopian Law* 375–377.
130 see *Colonel Mengistu Hailemariam et al.*, (Ruling on Preliminary Objections), *supra* note 5, 97.
131 Ibid.
132 In fact, English is limited to university level teachings, as Amharic takes over as a medium of training in post-university judicial trainings at the Federal level. Other regional languages are used for similar trainings at regional levels.

Amharic version remains the authoritative one in case of conflict and is the one applied by Ethiopian courts in the relevant core crimes trials, as noted above.[133]

At this juncture, it is imperative to highlight the – numerous – differences between the Amharic version of Article 281 of the Penal Code of 1957 and Article II of the 1948 Genocide Convention. The differences between the two texts relate to virtually all the elements of the crime of genocide. In specifying genocidal *mens rea*, Ethiopian law refers to 'ዐቅድ to destroy' instead of 'intent to destroy'.[134] While there is no qualifier to elucidate the word 'group' in the Genocide Convention, a group is understood in the Ethiopian Penal Code as 'a social unit of a multinational population unified in language and culture'. With reference to protected groups, the widely pointed out discrepancy between Article 281 of the Penal Code and Article II of the Genocide Convention is the fact that the former extends its protection to members of *political groups*. Nonetheless, the Penal Code did not recognize *national* and *ethnic groups*[135] and failed to recognize the phrase 'as such'.[136]

With respect to the prohibited acts, one can easily see that the Penal Code had substantially rephrased the corresponding formulations of the Convention. Three discrepancies can be pointed out. Firstly, unlike Article II(b) Convention, which contains an alternative prohibition, namely causing serious bodily or mental harm to the members of the group, Article 281(a) provided for a conjunctive prohibition of causing serious harm to the internal and external health of one of the members of the unit. The use of the conjunctive is confusing and, as noted above, it is not clear whether mental harm was proscribed by and of itself.[137] Secondly, if Article 281(c) of the Penal Code added a prohibited act – that of the compulsory movement of people –[138] it however failed to explicitly proscribe the act of 'forcibly transferring children of the group to another group' as prohibited under Article II(e) of the Convention.[139] It only prohibited the forced movement of people, including, children from *place to place*. Thirdly and relatedly, the Penal Code also prohibited the act of causing the compulsory movement or dispersion of peoples or children; an act which is absent from the conventional list.[140]

---

133 See section 5.1. above.
134 See section 5.3.3. above.
135 For a summary of the differences, See Table 2 below.
136 This is discussed further in Chapter 6, section 6.4.5.
137 See also Chapter 6, section 6.3.2.
138 See ibid., section 6.3.4.
139 See ibid.
140 See ibid.

5.4.2 The PDRE Draft Criminal Code: An Abortive Attempt to Rectify Discrepancies

Between March and April 1989 (Megabit 1981 Ethiopian Calender), the People's Democratic Republic of Ethiopia (PDRE)[141] submitted to the National Assembly (Parliament) a final draft of a criminal code. The Draft Criminal Code aimed at repealing and replacing both the Penal Code of 1957 and the Revised Special Penal Code of 1981, which were not considered as reflecting the socialist ideals seen as the cornerstones for the formation of the PDRE.[142] Although the Draft Criminal Code never entered into force as the regime fell about a year and a half later, it proposed notable changes to the criminal law of genocide in force at the time, i.e. Article 281 of the Penal Code of 1957.

The Draft Criminal Code's provision on genocide (Article 281) was, compared to Article 281 of the Penal Code, formulated in a manner that better mirrored the Convention's definition of genocide, although it did retain the caption that amalgamated genocide with crimes against humanity. It read:

> Article 281: Genocide; Crimes against Humanity
> Whoever, in time of peace or in time of war, with intent to destroy, in whole or in part, national, ethnical, racial, or, religious groups, organizes, orders, or engages in:
> (a) Killing or causing bodily injury by harming the bodily or mental health of members of the group, in any way whatsoever
> (b) Putting in place measures necessary to prevent the propagation or continued survival of its members; or
> (c) Compulsory movement or dispersion of members of the group or their children; placing them under conditions of life calculated to bring about their death in order to bring their total destruction is punishable with rigorous imprisonment from ten years to life or, in more serious cases, with death. [143]

---

141 The PDRE was the *Dergue* government that replaced in 1987 what was used to be known as the Provisional Military Government (PMG). See The Declaration of the Establishmnet of the People's Democratic Republic of Ethiopia, Proclamation No. 2/1987, Articles 2 and 3.
142 See Draft Criminal Code of the PDRE, Article 1.
143 Translation by the author. The original (Amharic) version reads:
አንቀጽ 281 ዘርን ስለማጥፋት በሰባዊ ፍጥረት ላይ ስለሚፈጸሙ ወንጀሎች
ማንም ሰው በሰላልምም ሆነ በጦርነት በብሔረሰብ፤ በጎሳ፤ በዘር፤ ውይም በሃይማኖት አንድ የሆነዉን ማኅበረሰብ በመላ ወይም በከፊል ለማጥፋት በማሰብ፤
ሀ/ በማናቸውም ሁኔታ የማኅበረሰቡን አባሎች ሕሊና ወይም አካላዊ ጤንነት በመጉዳት የገደያ ወይም የአካል ጉዳት በማድረስ፤ ውይም

The Draft Criminal Code attempted to rectify many of the discrepancies between Article II of the Genocide Convention and the Penal Code of 1957. With respect to *mens rea*, the Draft Criminal Code replaced the Penal Code's 'plan to destroy' (ለማጥፋት በማቀድ) with the Convention's expression 'intent to destroy' (ለማጥፋት በማሰብ). It avoided the above-mentioned complex expression the Penal Code used to refer to 'groups' and instead employed the Amharic ማኅበረሰብ, which translates into 'society'. It also proposed to limit the list of protected groups to those exhaustively covered by the Convention. As such, it excluded political groups and included national and ethnic groups.

Concerning prohibited acts, however, the Draft Criminal Code's proposed provision on genocide failed to mirror the Convention in full. Firstly, unlike both the Penal Code and the Genocide Convention, it did not treat acts of killing and bodily injury as independent of acts of harming the bodily or mental health of members of the protected groups. Instead, it used the latter as a means to cause the former, i.e. harming the bodily or mental health of the members of the group to kill them or cause them a bodily injury. Secondly, unlike the Genocide Convention, it did not expressly prohibit the act of 'forcibly transferring children of the group to another group'. In that respect, its prohibition is, similar to the Penal Code, limited to the forced movement of children from place to place. Thirdly, regarding acts that are not recognized under Article II of the Convention, the Draft Criminal Code reiterated the Penal Code's proscription of compulsory movement or dispersion of members of the group or their children as an underlying offense to genocide.

It is also noteworthy that the Draft Criminal Code regarded as too lenient the five years of rigorous imprisonment the Penal Code prescribed as the minimum penalty for genocide. It instead proposed that genocide be punishable by at least ten years of rigorous imprisonment, which has a significant implication on the perceived gravity of core crimes under Ethiopian law, as discussed under Chapter 7. Notwithstanding these developments, the Draft Criminal Code never came into force because the National Assembly did not manage to discuss and approve it due to the heightened state of conflict that brought about an unconstitutional change of government in 1991. As a result,

---

ለ/ የሙኅበረሰብ አባሎች በዘር አንዳይራቡ ውይም በሕይወት እንዳይኖሩ ለማድረግ አስፈላጊዉን ዘዴ እሥራ ላይ በማዋል፤ ወይም

ሐ/ የሙኅበረሰብን አባላት ውይም ልጆቻቸዉን በኃይል ከሥፍራ ወደ ሥፍራ በማዘዋወር፣ በመበተን ወይም ጨርሰው እንዲጠፉ የሞት አደጋ በሚያደርስባቸው ሁኔታ እንዲኖሩ በማደረግ፤

ያደራጀ፣ ያዘዘ ወይም በዚሁ ድርጊት የተሳተፉ እንደሆነ፤ ከአሥር ዓመት እስከ እድሜ ልክ ለመድረስ በሚችል ጽኑ እሥራት ወይም ነገሩ በጣም ከባድ ሆኖ ጊዜ በሞት ይቀጣል።

the Penal Code of 1957 remained in force until the promulgation in 2005 of the new Criminal Code.

5.4.3 *The FDRE Criminal Code: Broadening the Discrepancies?*

The FDRE Criminal Code came into force in 2005 by repealing and replacing a virtually half a century old Penal Code in its entirety. The need to fix the discrepancies between the Penal Code and the Genocide Convention was not among the several reasons mentioned to justify the need to repeal and replace the Penal Code.[144] Still, at the time of the drafting of the Criminal Code, the *Dergue* trials had already generated in-court debates on several inconsistencies between Ethiopian law and the Genocide Convention.[145] Further, the Criminal Code did not leave the Penal Code's genocide provision intact. To the contrary, it made significant alterations, and the current provision on genocide reads:

> Article 269- Genocide.
> Whoever, in time of war or in time of peace, with intent to destroy, in whole or in part, a nation, nationality, ethnical, racial, national, colour, religious or political group, organizes, orders or engages in:
> (a) Killing, bodily harm or serious injury to the physical or mental health of members of the group, in any way whatsoever or causing them to disappear; or
> (b) measures to prevent the propagation or continued survival of its members or their progeny; or
> (c) the compulsory movement or dispersion of peoples or children or their placing under living conditions calculated to result in their death or disappearance, is punishable with rigorous imprisonment from five years to twenty-five years, or, in more serious cases, with life imprisonment or death.

There is no apparent discrepancy between the Amharic and English versions of Article 269 of the Criminal Code. Interestingly, this provision resolved the differences that existed between the Penal Code of 1957 and the Convention with respect to genocidal *mens rea* insofar as it replaced the Penal Code's 'plan to destroy' with the Convention's 'intent to destroy'. Furthermore, here also bringing the domestic definition in line with the international one, in place of the Penal Code's 'social unit of a multinational population unified in language

---

144 For a summary of the reasons behind the repeal of the Penal Code, see FDRE Criminal Code, Preface, 1–5.
145 See for instance, section 5.5 below.

TABLE 2 Summary of Ethiopian laws on major omissions and additions to the Convention's definition of genocide

Elements	Protected groups	Mens rea	Actus reus	Criminal Codes
Omissions	National Ethnic	Intent to destroy 'as such'	Transfer of children from one group to the other	1957
	-	'as such'	Transfer of children from one group to the other	2005
Additions or Substitutions	Political	Plan to destroy	Bodily and mental harm Compulsory dispersion of children	1957
	Political Color Nationality Nation	-	Bodily and mental harm Compulsory dispersion of children Enforced disappearance	2005

and culture', the Criminal Code employs the Amharic word 'ቡድን', which can be straightforwardly translated into the English word 'group'. Finally, it also recognizes all of the four protected groups listed under Article II of the Genocide Convention, namely racial, ethnic, national and religious groups.[146]

Notwithstanding these admittedly positive changes, Article 269 has not rectified the rest of the discrepancies discussed above. Although some judges have regarded the Criminal Code's genocide provision as not significantly different

---

146 The Criminal Code of 2005's inclusion of all of the four groups protected by the Convention could be seen as a move aimed at ensuring that municipal law mirrors its international counterpart. As noted by the courts, the domestic provision on genocide is expected not to contradict the Convention, which could occur if some of the protected groups are excluded. See section 5.5 below. By including groups that the Penal Code of 1957 had excluded, namely, ethnic and national groups, one could therefore argue that the Criminal Code of 2005 is just avoiding inconsistency with the Convention. Nonetheless, these additions were not noted in the *Explanatory Notes* to the Criminal Code. Even further, the fact that the two groups (ethnic and national) were omitted in the Amharic version of the Penal Code was never pointed out during the trials, including in the *Anuak-Nuwer* trials where defendants were prosecuted for ethnic genocide on the basis of the Penal Code of 1957. See section 5.6 below.

from the international definition of the offense,[147] it should be noted that, in some respects, the former has actually broadened the disparity between Ethiopian law and the Convention. By extending its protection to political, nation, nationality, and colour groups, it covers twice the number of groups protected by the Convention. Unlike its predecessor or the Convention, it also recognizes as a prohibited act 'causing members of a group to disappear'.[148]

5.5   The Status of the Genocide Convention in the Ethiopian Legal System

Neither Article 281 of the Penal Code of 1957 nor Article 269 of the 2005 Criminal Code made specific reference to the Genocide Convention, contrary to the war crimes provisions which expressly revert to the applicability of international humanitarian law conventions.[149] This is all the more problematic insofar as there is no particular legislation devoted to laying down the status of international treaties within the Ethiopian legal system. One may find some treaty-related provisions in the ephemeral constitutions of the country. With the exception of the FDRE Constitution of 1995, however, neither the monarchical constitutions of 1931 and 1955 nor the PDRE Constitution of 1987 dealt with treaty-related issues other than determining the ratification procedure of treaties. Although the 1995 Constitution attempts to define the positional hierarchy of treaties in the current legal system, the relevant provisions have been deemed by several commentators to be lacking sufficient clarity.[150]

Under its supremacy clause, the 1995 Constitution states that 'all international agreements ratified by Ethiopia are an integral part of the law of the land'.[151] Two essential rules can be deciphered from this provision. First, the Constitution contains no procedural proviso: ratification thus results in the

---

147   See FHC, *Federal Prosecutor* v. *Tesfaye Neno Loya et al.*, (Judgment: Dissenting Opinion of Judge Aseffa Abreha), 30 April 2008, File No. 74796, 45.
148   This is further discussed in Chapter 6, section 6.4.6.
149   See Chapter 7, section 7.3.
150   See A.K. Abebe, 'Human Rights under the Ethiopian Constitution: A Descriptive Overview' (2011) 5(1) *Mizan Law Review* 41–71, 47; I. Idris, 'The Place of International human rights conventions in the 1994 Federal Democratic Republic of Ethiopia (FDRE) Constitution' (2000) 20(1) *Journal of Ethiopian Law* 113–138, 114; G.A. Woldemariam, 'The Place of International Law in the Ethiopian Legal System' (2016) 1(1) *Ethiopian Yearbook of International Law* 61–93, 63; T.S. Bulto, 'The Monist-Dualist Divide and the Supremacy Clause: Revisiting the Status of Human Rights treaties in Ethiopia' (2009) 23(1) *Journal of Ethiopian Law* 132–160, 133.
151   FDRE Constitution, Article 9(4).

automatic integration of a treaty into the Ethiopian legal system. In that sense, the publication of a newly ratified treaty in the official *Gazette* is not required for the treaty to be regarded as part of the law of the land. From a practical point of view, this provision could have more significance with respect to self-executing treaties. Since the Genocide Convention is a non-self-executing treaty, it always requires a domesticating law that defines the offense and attaches to it an adequate penalty, as envisaged by Article V of the Convention. Second, in terms of hierarchy, an international treaty is below the Constitution and is equivalent to a proclamation. This hierarchical position, as highlighted in the *Explanatory Notes* of the Constitution, implies that the Constitution has precedence over an international treaty where there is a contradiction between the two.[152] In case the conflict is between a treaty and other domestic laws, courts may solve the problem by applying traditional doctrines of interpretations such as *lex specialis derogat legi generali* or *lex posterior derogat (legi) priori*.[153]

Notwithstanding the provision of Article 9(4), Article 13(2) of the Constitution provides for the special status of human rights treaties. This provision states that the fundamental rights and freedoms guaranteed in the Constitution 'shall be interpreted in a manner conforming to the principles of the Universal Declaration of Human Rights, International Covenants on Human Rights and international instruments adopted by Ethiopia'. It is the consideration that international instruments served as sources of the Constitution's fundamental rights and freedoms that justified such special treatment.[154] By virtue of Article 13(2), the Constitution therefore places itself hierarchically below international treaties as far as human rights are concerned.[155] Admittedly a human rights treaty, the Genocide Convention may fall within the ambit of Article 13(2) of the Constitution. As a result, one may argue that the Convention is as supreme as the Constitution is, if not hierarchically above.

So far, in practice, there has not been a significant controversy between the Constitution and international treaties. In case a significant dispute requiring

---

152　FDRE Constitution, *Explanatory Notes*, Article 9.
153　Ibid.
154　Ibid., Article 13.
155　This could be the case even when the relevant treaties are not ratified by Ethiopia. Unlike Article 9 of the Constitution, Article 13(2) does not specifically require that treaties be ratified by Ethiopia, but 'adopted'. Some commentators have however argued that 'all kinds of treaties or international agreements Ethiopia enters into can only be brought to domestic effect upon ratification by [the House of Peoples' Representatives]'. See Woldemariam, 'The Place of International Law in the Ethiopian Legal System' *supra* note 150, 72.

THE CRIME OF GENOCIDE IN ETHIOPIAN LAW   221

constitutional interpretation emerges, it would have to be resolved by the House of Federations (HoF), a non-legislative assembly of nations, nationalities, and peoples.[156] Interestingly, during core crimes trials, the Genocide Convention was discussed on several occasions and, in the process, Ethiopian courts touched upon issues related to its status in the Ethiopian legal system. The courts' jurisprudence shows that expansive domestic laws are acceptable while restrictive laws that are considered contrary to the Genocide Convention are to be disregarded as inapplicable.

5.5.1   *The Permissibility of Expansive National Laws*

As discussed earlier, Ethiopian law contains an expansive definition of genocide – it notably added elements that are not mentioned in the conventional definition. More groups are protected and acts that are not prohibited by the Convention are criminalized as genocide in Ethiopia, as summarized in Table 2. Some of these additions were discussed during the trials.

As for the protected groups, it was held in the *Dergue* trials, in relation to political groups, that the Convention does not prohibit broader protection under national law.[157] As noted in Chapter 2, it is generally held by Ethiopian courts that an expansive or idiosyncratic definition of genocide in the municipal system is not *per se* problematic, at least as long as there is no direct conflict between the domestic and the conventional definitions of the offense.[158] In *Geremew Debele*, where the Penal Code of 1957 was hailed as the most advanced law as compared to the Convention, the FHC stated:

> Perhaps, the inclusion of political groups in the Penal Code indicates that this law is very civilized. Moreover, it should rather be acclaimed than criticized for offering broader legal protection to human rights [in general] and to the right to life [in particular]. It does not contradict the international convention on genocide.[159]

---

156   The HoF has no judicial power except the power to interpret the Constitution. See FDRE Constitution of 1995, Articles 61 and 83. It is the supremacy of the nations, nationalities and peoples of Ethiopia and the consideration of the Constitution as an agreement among them that made the HoF constitutional adjudicator. See FDRE Constitution, *Explanatory Notes*, Article 83.
157   See Chapter 2, Section 2.4.2.2.
158   See Ibid.
159   See FHC, SPO v. *Geremew Debele*, (Ruling on Preliminary Objections), 13 April 1998, File No. 952/89, 17. Translation by the author. The original (Amharic) version reads:
የዚህ የፖለቲካ ቡድን ክፍል በኢትዮጵያ ወንጀለኛ መቅጫ ሕግ ላይ መጨመሩ ምናልባትም ሕጉ እጅግ ዘመናዊ ፤ ይበልጡን የሰው ልጅ ሰብዓዊ መብት፤ የመኖር መብቱ ሰፋ ተደርጎ የሕግ ጥበቃ ተደርጎለታል ተብሎ ሊመሰገን የሚገባ እንጂ የሚነቀፍ፣ ከአለም አቀፍ ጀኖሳይድ ኮንቬንሽንም ጋር የሚጋጭ አይደለም።

Several other courts have taken a similar view, although only the FHC in *Mengistu et al.* attempted to find evidence that could support its conclusion that the Genocide Convention does not prohibit the existence of expansive domestic provisions.[160] In that respect the Court invoked the savings clause in Article 1 (2) of the Convention against Torture (CAT), which reads, 'this article is without prejudice to any international instrument or *national legislation* which does or may contain provisions of wider application'.[161] Although the Court did not add further comment to this reference, it appears that it wanted to use the CAT to make a general inference that international human rights treaties including the Genocide Convention 'only provide minimum standards which, of course, may be exceeded by domestic law'.[162]

When the issue was taken on appeal, the FSC upheld the lower court's argument and underlined that Article 281 of the Penal Code of 1957 did not contradict the Convention.[163] The Court stated, 'for its bold move to protect political groups against genocide in its domestic law, an issue that other countries had hesitated to address [in the Convention], the Ethiopian government deserves a praise, not a criticism'.[164] The FSC added that by protecting political groups, 'Ethiopian criminal law does not contradict the Genocide Convention, but complements it further'.[165]

At this juncture, the question should go beyond asking whether states are allowed to protect groups other than those recognized under the Convention, which as shown in the foregoing the FHC, the FSC, have all answered in the positive. The ECtHR seems to have adopted a similar approach, as illustrated by its judgment in *Vasiliauskas* v. *Lithuania*.[166] More interesting is the question *why* Ethiopian law included protected groups that were not mentioned in the Convention and the analysis of the Ethiopian law of genocide does provide

---

160 *Colonel Mengistu Hailemariam et al.*, (Ruling on Preliminary Objections), *supra* note 5, 86.
161 Convention against Torture and Other Cruel, Inhuman or Degrading Treatment or Punishment, G.A. res. 39/46, [annex, 39 U.N. GAOR Supp. (No. 51) at 197, U.N. Doc. A/39/51 (1984)], *entered into force* 26 June 1987, Article 1(2). Emphasis added.
162 For such an interpretation, see M. Nowak and E. McArthur, *The United Nations Convention against Torture: A Commentary* (Oxford: Oxford University Press, 2008) 85.
163 *Colonel Mengistu Hailemariam et al.*, (Appeals Judgment), *supra* note 62, 70.
164 Ibid. Translation by the author. The original (Amharic) version reads:
    የኢትዮጵያ መንግስት የጀኖሳይድ ኮንቬንሽን ከተቀበለ በኃላ በአገር ውስጥ የራሱን የወንጀል ህግ ሲያወጣ ሌሎች አገሮች ያንገራገሩበትን ጉዳይ ደፍሮ በመቀበል ዘር ማጥፋት የሚለው በፖለቲካ ቡድን አባላት ላይ የሚፈፀሙትን ድርጊቶችም እንዲያካፍ በማድረግ በወንጀለኛ መቅጫ ሕግ ቁጥር ፪፻፹፩ ላይ መደንገጉ የነበረውን የላቀ አስተሳሰብ የሚያሳይ እንጂ የሚያስተችው አይደለም።
165 Ibid. Translation by the author. The original (Amharic) version reads: 'የኢትዮጵያ የወንጀል ሕግ የጀኖሳይድ ኮንቬንሽንን በበለጠ የሚያዳብር እንጂ የሚቃረንም አይደለም።'.
166 See Chapter 3, Section 3.2.2.

certain guidance as to plausible answers. As detailed below, the scope and evolution of protected groups under Ethiopian law could be explained in three somewhat interrelated ways.

Firstly, the Penal Code of 1957's extension of the protected status to political groups could be due to the drafter's understanding that such groups should not have been excluded from the international definition in the first place. Although the issue was discussed in the *Dergue* trials, the courts did not explore directly why and how political groups were included in the Penal Code, as the focus was on whether the State had a *right* to protect them. The FHC however remarked in *Mengistu et al.* that the exclusion of political groups from the Convention's definition was in itself political, lacking any philosophical and legal justifications.[167] In that sense, Ethiopian courts rejected the 'stable and permanent groups' argument long before it was raised in international trials.

Secondly, the fact that Ethiopian law has considered genocide as 'crimes against humanity' could be the reason for the inclusion in the Criminal Code of other groups than those conventionally protected, namely, political color, nationality, and nation.[168] The legislator, prosecutors, and judges believed, albeit erroneously, that genocide was still a sub-category of 'crimes against humanity' rather than a self-standing independent crime.[169] 'Crimes against humanity' have been considered as an umbrella category encompassing both genocide and war crimes.[170] As noted in the *Explanatory Notes* to the 2005 Criminal Code, the addition of new groups within the list of protected groups was justified by the fact that they embodied qualities connected to the interests protected by 'crimes against humanity' such as humanity (ሰብአዊነት) and humanness (ስብዕና).[171] The *Explanatory Notes* further considered that all of the groups protected by the law of genocide are fundamentally linked to the concept of humanity and humanness.[172] The problem with this assertion is that there is no precise definitional scope attached to the notions of 'humanity' and 'humanness' in the *Explanatory Notes*.

---

167 FHC, SPO v. *Colonel Mengistu Hailemariam et al.*, (Trial Judgment), 12 December 2006, File No. 1/87, 115.
168 This does not mean that 'crimes against humanity' in Ethiopia is similar to what is defined as such in international law, as will be discussed below under section 5.3.2.
169 *Colonel Mengistu Hailemariam et al.*, (Ruling on Preliminary Objections), *supra* note 5, 104–105. See also Chapter 5, section 5.3.2.
170 See FDRE Constitution, Article 28; FDRE Criminal Code, Article 44 FDRE Criminal Code, *Explanatory Notes*, Article 269.
171 FDRE Criminal Code, *Explanatory Notes*, Article 269.
172 Ibid.

Thirdly, some of the decisions in the *Dergue* trials might have induced the expansion of protected groups in the Criminal Code. As already noted, the question of the scope of protected groups in Ethiopian law was central to the preliminary objections raised in most of the cases in the *Dergue* trials. In the above-mentioned Ruling on Preliminary Objections, the FHC averred that the State had a sovereign right to recognize groups that were not already protected by the international law of genocide.[173] By failing to restrain its ruling specifically to political groups, the decision appears to have opened a Pandora's box of protected groups as it implied that the protection could be extended to any groups that the State wishes to protect 'depending on prevailing circumstances of the time'.[174]

5.5.2   The Impermissibility of Conflicting National Laws

In the *Dergue* trials, the defendants raised a preliminary objection to the indictment claiming that Article 281 of the Penal Code of 1957 had been repealed by proclamations issued between 1974 and 1977 by the *Dergue* itself.[175] In support of their objection, the defendants invoked eight proclamations: No.1/74,[176] No. 2/74,[177] No.12/74,[178] No. 26/75,[179] No. 31/75,[180] No. 91/76,[181] No. 110/77,[182] and No.129/77.[183] All of these proclamations had, according to the defendants, allowed in one way or another the taking of counter-revolutionary measures (killing, torture, unlawful arrest, and detention) against members of political

---

173   *Colonel Mengistu Hailemariam et al.*, (Ruling on Preliminary Objections), *supra* note 5, 86–87.
174   Ibid., 86.
175   *Colonel Mengistu Hailemariam et al.*, (Ruling on Preliminary Objections), *supra* note 5, 113.
176   Provisional Military Government Establishment Proclamation, Proclamation No.1 of 1974, *entered into force*, 12 September 1974.
177   Definition of Powers of the Provisional Military Administration Council and its Chairman Proclamation, Proclamation No.2 of 1974, *entered into force*, 15 September 1974.
178   Provisional National Advisory Commission Establishment Proclamation, Proclamation No.12 of 1974, *entered into force*, 16 December 1974.
179   Government Ownership and Control of the Means of Production Proclamation, Proclamation No.26 of 1974, *entered into force*, 7 February 1975.
180   Public Ownership of Rural Lands Proclamation, Proclamation No.31 of 1975, *entered into force*, 4 March 1975.
181   Peoples Organizing Provisional Office Establishment Proclamation, Proclamation No.91 of 1976, *entered into force*, 21 April 1976.
182   Redefinition of Powers and Responsibilities of the Provisional Military Administration Council and the Council of Ministers Proclamation, proclamation No. 110 of 1977, *entered into force*, 11 February 1977.
183   National Revolutionary Operation Command Proclamation, Proclamation No. 129 of 1977, *entered into force*, 27 August 1977.

parties who, at the time, were labeled as *anti-revolutionary* and *anti-unity* elements. As such, the defendants argued that the proclamations justified the perpetration of acts prohibited under Article 281 of the Penal Code of 1957, the alleged violation of which brought them to trial.[184]

It is noteworthy that for about 13 years after the coming to power of the *Dergue* (1974–1987), Ethiopia was ruled without a constitution. The 1995 Revised Constitution was suspended by Proclamation No.1/74 on 12 September 1974, the date on which the *Dergue* officially established the Provisional Military Government (PMG). The next constitution materialized only in 1987, although a process to draft one was already in place as early as March 1974.[185] As a result, between 1974 and 1978, the country was ruled by a series of decrees issued by the *Dergue* such as those invoked by the defendants.

In the absence of a constitution, the *Dergue*'s proclamations acquired precedence over any legislation enacted by the *ancien régime*. In particular, Proclamation No. 1/74 declared that 'all existing laws that do not conflict with the provisions of this proclamation and with all future laws orders and regulations shall continue in force'.[186] It was therefore against this background that the defendants questioned the applicability of Article 281 of the Penal Code of 1957 in relation to the alleged acts of politicide committed during the *Dergue* regime.

The objection was, nonetheless, swiftly rejected by the FHC in its ruling of 10 October 1995 at the time of the opening of the trials as well as later during the trial phase when the issue resurfaced as a substantive defense. In the majority judgment, in *Mengistu et al.*, the FHC put forward three reasons for rejecting the defense and concluded that Article 281 was never repealed and that, as a result, genocide, as defined by this article, had constantly been a crime in Ethiopia since 5 May 1958.[187]

The FHC began by stating that the proclamations mentioned by the defendants were not meant to repeal the Penal Code of 1957 because none of them, except Proclamation No. 129/77, had a repealing clause.[188] This was however incorrect, both in fact and in law. It was factually inaccurate since Proclamation

---

184 Ibid.
185 The process started during the final days of the Haileselassie regime and months before the *Dergue* officially took over power. See T. Haile-Selassie, *The Ethiopian Revolution 1974–1991: From a Monarchical Autocracy to a Military Oligarchy* (London: Kegan Paul International, 1997) 106–108.
186 Proclamation No.1/74, Article 10.
187 *Colonel Mengistu Hailemariam et al.*, (Trial Judgment), *supra* note 166, 116.
188 Ibid.

No.129/77 was not the only one with a repealing clause.[189] It was also legally erroneous since it effectively set aside the application of *repeal by implication* where the earlier law is considered repealed pursuant to the doctrine of *lex posterior derogat (legi) priori* because it contradicts the recently promulgated one. In other words, the enforcement of the new law renders the older one inapplicable and there is no way that the two can stand together.

The second reason put forward by the Court was rather ambiguous and self-contradictory. At one point, the majority stated that Proclamation No. 129/77 did not allow the killing of members of political opposition groups.[190] At another point, they mentioned that this Proclamation allowed for acts of killing but only in time of war.[191] In a manner that added more confusion to the issue, the majority wrote, 'these laws were promulgated to announce the definition of powers and a chain of command established by the *Dergue* to carry out its preconceived policy of destroying political opposition parties and members thereof, but not to repeal the law they stood trial for violating'.[192] The problem with this statement is that it did not explain further how or why the laws that allowed for the establishment of a system to destroy political groups were not considered in contravention of Article 281 of the Penal Code, which prohibited the destruction of those same groups.

The FHC's third reason for rejecting the defendants' argument was the most significant in the sense that it drew mainly on the relationship between domestic and international laws. According to the Court, even if acts of killings were permitted by the alleged proclamations, that could not have repealed Article

---

189   Three more proclamations, No. 1/74, No. 31/75 and No. 110/77, had repealing clauses. As far as the criterion for selecting the proclamations to be analyzed by the Court in order to settle the issue at hand was whether a particular proclamation contained a repealing clause, the Court should have looked into these proclamations to assess whether the defendants' allegations were grounded.

190   The majority argued, 'the Proclamation did not allow for an action that involved killings or assaulting individuals suspected of having carried out *anti-revolutionary* activities but stated that these individuals be detained and brought before a court of law. In this regards too, the Proclamation did not contradict the content of the law mentioned in the indictment'. See *Colonel Mengistu Hailemariam et al.*, (Trial Judgment), *supra* note 166,, 116. Emphasis added. Translation by the author. The original (Amhari) version reads,

በሌላ በኩልም አዋጁ ብዕረአብዮት ተግባር የተጠረጠረ ሰው እንዲታሰር ውይም ለፍርድ ቤት እንዲቀርብ ይላል እንጇ ተከሳሾቹ የተከሰሱበትን የመደብደብ እና የመግደል ተግባር እንዲፈጸም እይፈቅድም። በዚህም ረገድ አዋጁ ተከሳሾቹ በተከሰሱበት ህግ ዉስጥ ካለው ሃሳብ ጋር አይቃረንም።

191   Ibid.

192   Ibid., 116–117. Translation by the author. The original (Amharic) version reads as follows:

... ደርግ አስቀድሞ የነበረውን ተቃዋሚ የፖለቲክ ቡድኖችንና አባላቱን የማጥፋት ሃሳቡን ለማስፈፀም የስልጣን ክፍፍልን እና ትዕዛዝ መስጠት ለመግለጽ የወጡ እንጇ ክስ የተረበበትን ህግ ለመሻር የወጡ ስላልሆኑ ህጉ ተሽሯል ማለት አይቻልም።

281. For the Court, 'because genocide is prohibited both under Ethiopian and international law, any law that is promulgated to allow for the perpetration of acts of genocide shall be regarded null and void for it violates international law'.[193] This last reasoning is nonetheless faulty, not least because it turned to the Genocide Convention as the relevant international law to address the status of Article 281 of the Penal Code of 1957. The defendants argued that the proclamations called for, and imposed a duty on them to participate in, the 'liquidation' of political opposition groups. They thus claimed that any provision of the Penal Code of 1957 that contradicted these proclamations was therefore considered repealed.[194] As such, central to the preliminary objection was the question of political genocide. The FHC's reliance on the Genocide Convention to reject this preliminary objection is therefore very fragile for the obvious reason that the Convention does not protect political groups.

Judge Nuru Seid's dissenting opinion contains sufficient explanation as to how and why the majority argument is unconvincing, although some of his arguments are based on weak legal basis, as pointed out below. He first addressed the question whether killing or harming political opposition groups was allowed in the proclamations mentioned by the defendants. In arguing in favor of the defendants, the dissenting opinion relied on Proclamations No.10/1977 and No. 129/77.[195] It discussed the latter with more details; and explained that:

> Proclamation No.129/77 established a national revolutionary operations command, consisting of multi-level organs headed by the chairman of the *Dergue*. The organs of the national revolutionary operations command were, pursuant to Article 8(3) of Proclamation No.129/1977 and in line with the chain of command, vested with the responsibility of coordinating the regular army, the police and the militia to liquidate anti-unity and anti-revolution forces. Their powers included the taking of *necessary measures* against anti-unity and anti-revolution forces (Articles 14(7), 16(6)), and the agitation and coordination of the people to participate in the search campaigns to liquidate anti-unity and anti-revolution forces

---

193 *Colonel Mengistu Hailemariam et al.*, (Ruling on Preliminary Objections), *supra* note 5, 116. Translation by the author. The original (Amharic) text reads as follows:
...የዚህን ህግ ክልከላ በመጣስ የዘር መማጥፈት ተግባር ለመፈፀም ህግ ቢታወጅ ዓለም ዓቀፍ ህግን ስለሚጥስ አዋጁ ፍርስ መሆን አለበት መክንያቱም ዘር ማጥፋት በዓለም ዓቀፍ ደረጃም ሆነ በኢትዮጵያ ወንጀል ስለሆነ ነው ... ።

194 Ibid., 114.

195 *Colonel Mengistu Hailemariam et al.*, (Trial Judgment), *supra* note 166, Dissenting Opinion of Judge Nuru Seid, 462–463.

(Articles 18(7), 16(5), 14(8) etc.). Therefore, the destruction of various political groups, namely those considered to be anti-revolutionary, was allowed by these proclamations.[196]

This conclusion is well founded. To begin with the *Dergue's* alleged crimes, there is no doubt that they were perpetrated against those labeled by the regime as *anti-people* and *anti-revolutionary* and under the guise of safeguarding the peace and order of the people and the unity of the country, as also established by prosecution evidence.[197] The call for elimination of political opposition groups was officially announced using various means, including through the promulgation of proclamations that conferred on the *Dergue* and its affiliates the power to take '*necessary* measures against *anti-people* and *anti-revolutionary*'.[198] The taking of *necessary measures,* as was already noted by the FHC in the case in question and several other courts as well as by Judge Nuru Seide in his dissenting opinion,[199] denoted acts of killing.[200]

The next question addressed in the dissenting opinion was whether the said proclamations had repealed the crime of politicide under Article 281 of the Penal Code o 1957. In that respect, Judge Nuru asserted, 'the proclamations contravened Article 281 of the Penal Code, particularly with the part of the Article that prohibited the destruction of, or causing harm to, members of a group established based on political affiliation, which is why that part of the Article could no longer be in force'.[201] Invoking *lex posterior derogat (legi)*

---

196 Ibid. Emphasis added. Translation by the author. The original (Amharic) version reads,

በደርጉ ሊቀመንበር የሚመራ በተዋረድ በሀገር አቀፍ ደረጃ የተለያዩ አካላት ያሉት የመጮ መምሪያ ተቋቁሟል (አዋጅ ቁ 129/69 ። እነዚህ የመጮ መምሪያ አካላት እንደተዋረዳቸው የመደበኛ ጦር፣ ፖሊስ ሠራዊት እና ሕዝባዊ ሠራዊትን በማስተባበር ፀረ አንድነትና ፀረ አብዮት ኃይሎችን የመደምሰስ (አዋጅ ቁ 129/69 ቁ 8(3))ፀረ አንድነትና ፀረ እና አብዮት ተግባሮች ላይ አስፈላጊዎቹ እርምጃዎች እንዲወሰዱ የማደረግ (አዋጅ ቁ 129/69 ቁ 14(7) ፤16(6)) ፀረ አንድነትና እና ፀረ አብዮት ኃይሎችን ለመደምሰስ በሚደረገው አሰሳ ሕዝብ ተካፋይ እንዲሆን የመከሰቅስ፣ ማስተባበር፣ ማሰማራት (አዋጅ ቁ 18(7) ፤16(5) ፤14(8) ፤) ወዘተ ሥልጣን ተሰጥቷቸዋል። ስለዚህ በእነዚህ አዋጆች መሠረት ፀረ አብዮት የተባሉትን የተለያየ የፖለቲካ ቡድኖችን መደምሰስ ተፈቅዷል ማለት ነው።

197 See FHC, SPO v. *Colonel Mengistu Hailemariam et al.,* (Trial Ruling), 23 January 2003, File No. 1/87.

198 For details, see Chapter 6, section 6.4.1.1.

199 FSC, SPO v. *Colonel Mengistu Hailemariam et al.,* (Appeals Judgment), 26 May 2008, File No. 30181, 42.

200 *Colonel Mengistu Hailemariam et al.,* (Trial Judgment), *supra* note 166, Dissenting Opinion of Judge Nuru Seid, 463.

201 Ibid. Translation by the author. The original version reads,

አዋጅ ቁ 110/69 [...] ሲታወጅ ይዘዋቸው የውጡ ድንጋጌዎች ይሚፍቅዱት ነገር በ/መ/ሕ/ቁ 281 ከተከለከሉት ውስጥ የፖለቲካ ትስስርን መሠረት አድርጎ የተሳሰሩ አባላትን ማጥፋት ወይም ጉዳት እንደደርስባቸው ማድረግን ከሚከለክለው ክፍል ጋር ስለሚቃረን ብጊዜው ብሥራ ላይ የነበረው በ/መ/ሕ/ቁ 281 የተወሰነ ክፍል አይፀናም ማለት ነው።

priori, he added that it is a well-established practice in the Ethiopian legal system that an old law (specific provision or a proclamation) shall be regarded as repealed if it contradicts a newly enacted law.

In explaining his arguments further, Judge Nuru highlighted the Court's unanimous ruling that states are not prohibited from expanding the protection provided by the Genocide Convention to political groups.[202] Unlike genocide against racial, religious, ethnic, and national groups, the criminalization of politicide was from the outset, according to the dissenting opinion, the result of a purely domestic choice.[203] According to the dissenting opinion, the fact that some other states, in addition to Ethiopia, also grant such a protection to political groups does not mean that this holds true under international law.[204] In highlighting that Ethiopia was and is not under an obligation to protect political groups, the dissenting opinion concluded that it was because politicide was criminalized by the decision of the Ethiopian legislator that it could be repealed by the decision of the same body.[205] As a last resort, Judge Nuru stated that the defendants could be found guilty of committing offenses such as *aggravated homicide and grave bodily injury instead of politicide*, because these offenses were never repealed.[206]

Strongly disagreeing with the dissenting opinion, Tessema criticized Judge Nuru's argument as illogical and self-contradictory, and stated: 'if killing a member of a political group remained a crime (as aggravated homicide) despite the *Dergue* laws, there is no reason why the same killing did not amount to politicide'.[207] Tessema goes further in his criticism of Judge Nuru's dissenting opinion and, for him, to state that part of Article 281 'was repealed is [to connote] that the acts of killing members of political groups were legal'.[208] He added that there was no logic in the reasoning of Judge Nuru that killings carried out during the *Dergue* could amount to aggravated homicide.[209]

Nonetheless, a closer look at Tessema's criticism reveals that he actually did not argue that Article 281's proscription of politicide was not or could not have been repealed at all. Instead, he stressed that if it were repealed the same could have been true for Article 522 of the Penal Code (aggravated homicide).

---

202 Ibid., 464.
203 Ibid.
204 Ibid.
205 *Colonel Mengistu Hailemariam et al.*, (Trial Judgment), *supra* note 166, Dissenting Opinion of Judge Nuru Seid, 464.
206 Ibid., 465.
207 Tessema, *Prosecution of Politicide in Ethiopia*, *supra* note 2, 210–212.
208 Ibid., 212.
209 Ibid.

That might not be correct. If politicide under Article 281 were repealed, it could have simply meant that the killing of members of political groups was no longer criminalized as such. The repeal or absence of politicide as a crime under the law cannot negate the possibility to prosecute defendants for aggravated homicide. In fact, it could have meant that in prosecuting the *Dergue* for the killings, the prosecution was not required to establish the identity of the group to which the victims allegedly belonged at the time of the commission of the crime.

As for aggravated homicide, Judge Nuru's dissenting opinion was composed of the 'was not' and 'could not have been' arguments. The former was mainly an argument of fact, i.e. aggravated homicide was not repealed by the *Dergue*. In support of this, Judge Nuru stated that aggravated homicide has been treated as a criminal offense in Ethiopia since its incorporation in the Penal Code in 1957.[210] He also emphasized that the offense had always been a crime that had always been punished by Ethiopian courts during the *Dergue* regime.[211] If one may challenge this assertion on the ground that the fact that courts apply a particular law does not *per se* indicate that it was not repealed, it nonetheless remains that the factual assertion was true: courts during the *Dergue* did punish perpetrators for committing aggravated homicide, including individuals later on brought to trial for genocide by the SPO.[212]

It is the 'could not have been repealed' part of the dissenting opinion that is interesting in the sense that it involved an argument of law, although it lacked a firm legal ground. In that respect, Judge Nuru stated that the *Dergue* could not have repealed Article 522 of the Penal Code even if it had wanted to, because doing so could violate principles that should be respected at all times.[213] In referring to these principles, he only stated that aggravated homicide had already been treated as an offense in the laws of all civilized nations before it was listed in the Nuremberg Charter.[214] This argument is unconvincing and unsubstantiated. In particular, it is not clear how and why the prohibition of aggravated homicide in municipal laws of countries all over the world could be

---

210 *Colonel Mengistu Hailemariam et al.*, (Trial Judgment), *supra* note 166, Dissenting Opinion of Judge Nuru Seid, 465.
211 Ibid.
212 For instance, Elias Nuru Mohammod, one of the defendants in *Tsegaye Mamo et al.*, had served prison terms for committing aggravated murder during the time the *Dergue* was still in power. See FHC, SPO v. *Tsegaye Mamo et al.*, (Sentencing Judgment), 3 August 2003, File No. 631/89, 6.
213 *Colonel Mengistu Hailemariam et al.*, (Trial Judgment), *supra* note 166, Dissenting Opinion of Judge Nuru Seid, 465.
214 Ibid.

invoked as capable of limiting the powers of any national legislator to repeal the relevant domestic provision.

Be that as it may, the gist of the debate regarding whether politicide was repealed or not was linked to whether a state could repeal a law prohibiting a conduct that is also a crime under international law. Both the majority judgment and the dissenting view concurred on this point, answering the question by the negative. They both treated international law as above domestic law, and, thereby, highlighted that a dictatorial regime could not be allowed to perpetrate crimes by making its law superior to other laws.[215] Such a view had already gained support in other jurisdictions as well. For instance, in the *German Border Guard* case, it was held by the *Bundesgerichtshof* that international human rights law renders inapplicable provisions of domestic law allowing for the arbitrary deprivation of one's life.[216] However, unlike the *Bundesgerichtshof*, the FHC failed to sufficiently and correctly spell out its legal reasoning for reaching such a conclusion – as nowhere in its decision did it explain and analyze the relevant international law and how it supports the conclusion reached. The same could be said with respect to Judge Nuru's dissenting opinion as regards his claim for aggravated homicide. In sum, it could generally be inferred from the above discussion that Ethiopian courts hold the opinion that international treaties such as the Genocide Convention impose an obligation on a State not to decriminalize acts considered as criminal under international law.

5.6 Conclusion: The Duality of Laws Applicable to the Crime of Genocide in Ethiopia

As discussed in this chapter, genocide has been regarded as a crime in the Ethiopian legal system since 1957. In fact, it is clear from the foregoing that the proscription of the crime of genocide in Ethiopia is subject to the application of dual legal regimes. Firstly, the crime was proscribed under Article 281 of the Penal Code of 1957, which was replaced by Article 269 of the Criminal Code of 2005, the law currently in force. Secondly, the Genocide Convention holds a

---

215   For a similar reasoning, see SPO Investigation File No.401/1993, 'a reply submitted by the Special Prosecutor pursuant to Art. 131(1) of the Criminal Procedure Code in response to the objection filed by counsels for defendants on March 07, 1995', 23 May 1995, 9.

216   For an elaborated discussion of the complex reasoning of the *Bundesgerichtshof*, see R. Geiger, 'the German Border Guard Cases and International Human Rights' (2009) 9(1) *European Journal of International Law* 540–549.

significant place in determining the scope of the law of genocide in Ethiopia as it was considered to be the legal source for the relevant domestic provisions. Because the definition of genocide in the Convention is placed hierarchically above the definition of the crime in the domestic provisions, the latter cannot contravene the former. Nonetheless, the domestic law could broaden the protection envisaged by the Convention.

None of the genocide trials in Ethiopia were based on international criminal law, be it the Genocide Convention or the relevant customary international law. The issue of the applicability of international law in Ethiopia was discussed only briefly in 1994 when the SPO was finalizing its preparation to file its first indictments against the *Dergue* officials.[217] At that time, the SPO reached the conclusion that it would use as the applicable law the Genocide Convention and rules of international humanitarian law that have attained the status of customary international law.[218] In reaching this conclusion, the SPO considered that, in relation to the domestic application of international law, the principle of legality only allowed for the use of those laws that have reached the status of customary international law.[219]

Ultimately, the SPO however chose to rely solely on the more familiar law, i.e. the Penal Code of 1957, on the ground that this legislation was not only clear and precise but also already consistent with the basic principles of criminal law and international legal norms.[220] Most importantly, the reliance on the extant domestic provisions was justified in relation to the need to respect the principle of legality.[221] Accordingly, the SPO considered that the genocide provisions in the Penal Code had been in force for nearly half a century (1958–2005) and were, therefore, applicable to the *Dergue* era genocide (1974–1991).

It is noteworthy that the SPO's choice of applicable law had gained support from, if not was influenced by, the late Professor Cherif Bassiouni, who had opined, in relation to what he referred to as 'the prosecution of war crimes and crimes against humanity in Ethiopia', that,

---

217 See T.S. Engelschiøn, 'Ethiopia: War Crimes and Violations of Human Rights' (1995) 34(9) *Military Law and Law of War Review* 9–32, 14–15.

218 In addition to the Genocide Convention, the Geneva Conventions of 1949, The Hague Convention IV, and the Charter of the International Military Tribunal of 8 August 1945 were seen as directly applicable. See ibid.

219 Ibid.

220 Special Prosecutor's Office, *Dem Yazele Dossie: Begizeyawi Wetaderawi Dergue Weyem Mengist Abalat Benetsuhan Zegoch Laye Yetefetseme Wenjel Zegeba* (Addis Ababa: Far-East Trading P.L.C., 2010) 131.

221 Ibid.

the decision to prosecute under Ethiopian Penal Code of 1957 is well advised; it is likely to be perceived as the fairest approach and is the one with which the courts, prosecutors and defense council are most familiar. This decision also seems to have largely obviated concerns relating to bringing charges that might be incompatible with the well-established prohibition of ex-post facto punishment. Consistent with the principle of legality and *international legal norms* and the relevant provisions of the code satisfy the notions of fairness and justice inherent in the rule of law.[222]

The SPO's decision to apply the Penal Code to prosecute the *Dergue* should not be taken as implying a total exclusion of international law from the Ethiopian trials. Although its indictments did not refer to international instruments such as the Genocide Convention, the SPO, on several occasions, made a general reference to international treaties on human rights and humanitarian law as well as to the practice of international criminal tribunals, notably while responding to preliminary objections raised by the defendants.[223]

Subsequently, it appears that the genocide trials in Ethiopia followed the trend set by the SPO's decision to prosecute the *Dergue* era international crimes on the basis of the relevant domestic law and out of respect for the principle of legality. Accordingly, it was again the Penal Code of 1957 that was applied in the prosecution of the *Anuak-Nuwer* genocide in 2004. In May 2005, the FDRE Criminal Code came into force by entirely repealing and replacing the Penal Code.[224] The CUD and the *Oromo-Gumuz* trials, in response to genocidal acts committed in 2005 and 2008 respectively, were thus conducted on the basis of the Criminal Code of 2005, and in particular of its Article 269. Exceptionally, this law was also invoked at the sentencing stage in the *Dergue* and *Anuak-Nuwer* trials, not least to give effect to the principle of *lex-mitior*, as will be discussed in Chapter 8.

---

[222] See Memorandum on the Applicable law for the prosecution of persons charged with war crimes and crimes against humanity in Ethiopia: an interpretive and analytical study of the Ethiopian penal code of 1957 and international humanitarian law (submitted to the office of the special prosecutor for the transitional government of Ethiopia), 28, 36 cited in *Dem Yazele Dossie, supra* note 220, 132 [emphasis added].

[223] See *Colonel Mengistu Hailemariam et al.*, (Ruling on Preliminary Objections), *supra* note 5, 14, 28,35. In fact the judgments in the *Dergue* trials were not devoid of references to international law when deemed relevant, as also pointed in Chapter 3, section 3.3.2.

[224] Two special penal laws (the 1974 Special Penal Code and the 1981 Revised Special Penal Code) were also repealed by the FDRE Criminal Code. See FDRE Criminal Code, Preface, No. 2.

Due concern for the principle of legality seems however to have been overlooked in the *Anuak-Nuwer* trials, in which the Penal Code of 1957 was applied.[225] At the time the crime of genocide was committed against the *Nuwer* ethnic group, no legislation in Ethiopia prohibited the genocidal destruction of ethnic groups.[226] Perplexingly, the trial did not discuss the issue of protected groups, and therefore the potential question involving the principle of legality appears to have slipped away. Had it been discussed, the courts could have reached two opposing conclusions depending on the applicable law. From the viewpoint of domestic law, the courts could have found the *Anuak-Nuwer* trials to be in violation of the principle of legality for lack of an applicable law. They could even have considered the prosecutions unconstitutional under Article 22(1) of the FDRE Constitution, which reads,

> No one shall be held guilty of any criminal offense on account of any act or omission which did not constitute a criminal offense at the time when it was committed. Nor shall a heavier penalty be imposed on any person than the one that was applicable at the time when the criminal offense was committed.

Had Ethiopian courts had turned to international law as the applicable law however, the *Anuak-Nuwer* trials would have been deemed lawful. Since genocide against ethnic groups was already a crime under international law, domestic prosecutions could be regarded as lawful even in the absence of a domestic legislation incorporating the international prohibition. Article 15(2) of the ICCPR, to which Ethiopia is a party, expressly allows for the national prosecutions of crimes already defined in international law, despite the unavailability of corresponding domestic laws.[227] Furthermore, a cumulative reading of

---

225 The Penal Code of 1957, Article 2(1) defined the principle of legality as follows: 'Criminal law specifies the various offenses which are liable to punishment and the penalties and measures applicable to offenders. The court may not treat as a breach of the law and punish any act or omission which is not prohibited by law. It may not impose penalties or measures other than those prescribed by law. The court may not create offenses by analogy'.

226 See section 5.4.1. above.

227 See International Covenant on Civil and Political Rights, G.A. res. 2200A (XXI), 21 U.N. GAOR Supp. (No. 16) at 52, UN Doc. A/6316 (1966), 999 U.N.T.S. 171, *entered into force* 23 March 1976, Article 15(2). The provision reads: 'nothing in this article shall prejudice the trial and punishment of any person for any act or omission which, at the time when it was committed, was criminal according to the general principles of law recognized by the community of nations'.

Articles 22(1) of the FDRE Constitution and Article 15(2) of the ICCPR would have kept the *Anuak-Nuwer* trials within the scope of constitutionality. This is possible in Ethiopian law pursuant to Article 13(1) of the FDRE Constitution, according to which,

> the fundamental rights and freedoms specified [under Articles 13 to 44 of the Constitution] shall be interpreted in a manner conforming to the principles of the Universal Declaration of Human Rights, International Covenants on Human Rights and international instruments adopted by Ethiopia.

That being said, this exception to the principle of non-retroactivity does not imply that an Ethiopian prosecutor could prosecute a suspect for a crime under international law without further procedural requirement. As will be noted in Chapter 7, prosecutions based on crimes that are only defined in international law require the existence of a domestic statute prescribing penalties for such crimes.[228]

---

228 See Chapter 7, sub-section 7.5.2.

CHAPTER 6

The Crime of Genocide in Ethiopian Trials
Elements of the Crime

6.1 Introduction

This chapter discusses the elements of the crime of genocide by focusing mainly on how Ethiopian courts have interpreted and applied them in practice. The four instances of prosecution of core crimes pointed out in the general introduction,[1] were mainly trials for genocide[2] which – taken as a whole – resulted in the prosecution of *all* of the acts prohibited under Article III of the Genocide Convention. As abridged in the table below, all of the four trials dealt with genocide and conspiracy to commit genocide. Attempt to commit genocide was only tried in the CUD trials while all the trials, except the CUD trials, dealt with complicity to commit genocide. Prosecution for incitement to commit genocide occurred in the *Dergue* and the *Oromo-Gumuz* cases.

TABLE 3   Genocide trials in Ethiopia

Trials	Genocide	Inchoate Offences			
		Attempt	Complicity	Conspiracy	Incitement
Dergue	Political	N/A	√	√	√
Anuak-Nuwer	Ethnic	N/A	√	√	N/A
CUD	Political & Ethnic	√	N/A	√	N/A
Oromo-Gumuz	Ethnic	N/A	√	√	√

N/A: Not Applicable √: Applicable

---

1 See Chapter 1, section 1.2.
2 This is not without noting that a single prosecution of war crimes against the civilian population took place in the *Dergue* trials, which is discussed in Chapter 7.

Nonetheless, as pointed out in Chapter 1, Ethiopian courts have not discussed these inchoate forms of genocide.

Discussing elements of a crime is, in general, a daunting task, and even more so when it comes to the crime of genocide. This could be even more complicated when it involves the case of Ethiopian law and practice. The prolixity of the Ethiopian provisions coupled with the fact that the vocabulary of the law has yet to develop into a more precise language could be mentioned as one of the factors that make the analysis of the elements of the crime frustrating, if not incomplete. The other is that Ethiopian courts rarely pay attention to each and every element of an offense, even when referring to the appalling crimes defined in international treaties. In that respect, the Ethiopian practice stands in stark contrast to the well-established principle of treaty interpretation, which is that, as stated by the ICJ in the *Anglo-Iranian Oil Co.* case, the text of a treaty 'should be interpreted in such a way that a reason and a meaning can be attributed to every word in the text'.[3]

The text of the Genocide Convention, although passed through a painstaking drafting process,[4] is mostly not self-explanatory,[5] as is commonly the case in legal drafting. For over four decades, the Convention has remained largely unexposed to judicial scrutiny until the establishment of the ICTY and ICTR in the early 1990s. The two international criminal tribunals have significantly contributed to elaborating on the meaning and concept of the crime of genocide.[6] Coincidentally, the Ethiopian genocide trials were carried out at around the same time.

International tribunals and Ethiopian courts conducted parallel trials in their own parochial ways without one referring to, and even noticing, the other. For example, in entering the country's first genocide conviction at the beginning of 1999 in *Geremew Debele*,[7] the FHC did not make a single mention of the landmark genocide judgment delivered sixth months before by the ICTR in the

---

3   ICJ, *United Kingdom v. Iran, Anglo-Iranian Oil Co.*, Judgment of 22 July 1952, para. 105, available at: <https://www.icj-cij.org/files/case-related/16/016-19520722-JUD-01-00-EN.pdf> accessed 4 May 2019.
4   For a brief introduction to the drafting process of the Genocide Convention, see C.J. Tams et al., *Convention on the Prevention and Punishment of the Crime of Genocide: A Commentary* (München: C.H.Beck. Hart.Nomos, 2014) 5–12. For a more elaborated account, see W.A. Schabas, *Genocide in International Law: The Crime of Crimes* (2nd ed., Cambridge: Cambridge University Press, 2010) 59–116.
5   See Y. Shany, 'The Road to the Genocide Convention and Beyond' in P. Gaeta (ed.), *The UN Genocide Convention: A Commentary* (Oxford: Oxford University Press, 2009) 3–26, 4.
6   See G. Mettraux, *International Crimes and the Ad Hoc Tribunals* (Oxford: Oxford University Press, 2005) 199–202.
7   FHC, *SPO v. Geremew Debele*, (Trial Judgment), 8 February 1999, File No. 952/89.

case of *Akayesu*.[8] Besides, neither the 2003 ruling[9] nor the 2006 judgment[10] in *Mengistu et al.*, the main genocide case in the *Dergue* trials, contains references to the decisions and judgments of international courts and tribunals. Conversely, the same could be said for the international criminal tribunals.

This mutual exclusivity between international and Ethiopian trials could be seen as an interesting phenomenon to assess the interpretation of the crime of genocide and the application of the Genocide Convention. It may provide a fresh understanding of how the Convention was interpreted by different courts that did not exercise any influence (direct or indirect) on each other. Nonetheless, this comparison contains certain limits. First, international and Ethiopian courts can hardly be deemed of an equal standing. Unlike their international counterparts, Ethiopian genocide trials could be best characterized as isolated trials by judges and lawyers who lacked the requisite background in international criminal law. In the *Dergue* cases, the trials were conducted by prosecutors and judges most of whom were fresh graduates, because the senior ones had been excluded owing to their previous involvement with the ousted regime, the *Dergue*.[11] Second, comparing international courts and tribunals with Ethiopian courts in terms of available resources could be like comparing, as one commentator wrote, 'the weight of an elephant with that of a mouse'.[12]

That being said, as far as their function is concerned, there is an equivalence between international and domestic courts that tried persons responsible for genocide:[13] all are tasked with the interpretation of the elements of crimes enshrined in the Genocide Convention. International criminal courts and tribunals have applied the Convention through their Statutes, which reproduced the exact definition of genocide provided under Article II of the Convention. Ethiopian courts had a similar option, although the crime of genocide was incorporated into Ethiopian law in a manner that did not mirror the international definition. Yet, as noted in Chapter 5, the Convention was considered by Ethiopian courts as the source behind the Ethiopian law on genocide.

---

8   See ICTR, *Prosecutor v. Akayesu*, Trial Chamber, (Judgment), 2 September 1998, ICTR-96-4-T.
9   See FHC, SPO v. *Colonel Mengistu Hailemariam et al.*, (Trial Ruling), 23 January 2003, File No.1/87.
10 FHC, SPO v. *Colonel Mengistu Hailemariam et al.*, (Trial Judgment), 11 December 2007, File No. 1/87.
11 See M. Redae 'The Ethiopian Genocide Trial' (2002) 1(1) *Ethiopian Law Review* 1–26, 21.
12 Y. Hailemariam, 'The Quest for Justice and Reconciliation: The international Criminal Tribunal for Rwanda and the Ethiopian High Court' (1999) 22(1) *Hastings International and Comparative Law Review* 667–745, 722.
13 See the discussion in Chapter 1, section 1.5.

It is against this backdrop that this chapter aims at providing an in-depth analysis of whether genocide trials in Ethiopia were conducted in line with standards of ICL. To this end, the relevant ingredients of the offense are treated separately. It will be discussed how Ethiopian courts have pointed out and addressed similarities and differences between the Convention and Ethiopian criminal law as well as the manner in which they have interpreted the crime's material elements (Section 6.2), *actus reus* (Section 6.3), and *mens rea* (Section 6.4).

This chapter mainly deals with the analysis of the law and the trials. As a result, it does not engage in providing a historical or factual analysis of issues related to genocide, although doing so could be interesting from the perspective of other disciplines. At times, however, the discussion resorts to factual issues in order to provide a clearer explanation of a given legal issue. In those circumstances, as is notably the case in relation to genocidal *mens rea* (Section 6.4.1.1.), the discussion will be strictly limited to the factual issues discussed by the courts in the context of the trials.

6.2 Material Element: Protected Groups

6.2.1 *Group* / ቡድን

Genocide is a crime against a group – not against a member of a group *per se*.[14] As such, the law that criminalizes genocide aims at protecting the group and when it protects members of a group, it does so for the sake of protecting the group which the members make up. Although both the French and English versions of Article 281 of the Penal Code of 1957 contained the words *groupe* and group respectively,[15] their Amharic counterpart used a lengthy phrase instead of using just ቡድን, the direct Amharic translation of the term 'group'.

---

14 See ICTY, *Prosecutor v. Krstić*, Trial Chamber, (Judgment) 2 August 2001, IT-98-33, para. 580; ICTY, *Prosecutor v. Tolimir*, Trial Chamber, (Judgment), 12 December 2012, IT-05-88, para. 741; ICTR, *Prosecutor v. Seromba*, Trial Chamber, (Judgment), 13 December 2006, ICTR-2001-66-T, para. 319; ICJ, *Bosnia and Herzegovina v. Serbia and Montenegro*, (Judgment), 26 February 2007, ICJ Reports 20076, paras 190, 328; Report of the International Commission of Inquiry on Darfur to the Secretary General Pursuant to SC Res. 1564, 18 September 2004, Annex to Letter dated 31 January 2005 from the Secretary-General addressed to the President of the Security Council, S/2005/60, 1 February 2005, paras 515, 517–20; L. Berster, 'Article II' in C.J. Tams *et al., Convention on the Prevention and Punishment of the Crime of Genocide: A Commentary* (München: C.H.Beck.Hart.Nomos, 2014), 79–156, 81.

15 See Le Code Pénal de l'Empire d'Éthiopie du 23 juillet 1957, Article 281; The Penal Code of 1957, Article 281.

This lengthy phrase, employed in the Amharic version for no apparent reason, translates into: 'a social unit of a multinational population unified in language and culture'.[16] Before dismissing it for prolixity, it might be useful to consider whether this lengthy phrase contained any criteria based on which a group can be identified or defined, something the Genocide Convention failed to do.

By a 'social (ማኅበራዊ) unit', it can be safely asserted that the law was referring to human groups. The expression 'population' suggests that a group consists of individuals.[17] A commentary on the first draft of the Genocide Convention (The Secretariat Draft) considered that 'a human group is made up of certain part of the population whose members have common characteristics distinguishing them from other members of society'.[18] The Amharic phrase, however, contains several ambiguities. The use of *multinational* is not precise, as it seems to be requiring a group to be heterogeneous in composition, which may defeat the very idea that a group should have some kind of shared identity.

Although one group can be distinguished from other groups by specific characteristics common to its members, the requirement in Ethiopian law that a group be something unified based on *language and culture* creates a problem. No doubt, linguistic groups are unified based on language, although they were excluded from the Genocide Convention's list of protected groups on the basis of 'unnecessary reference'.[19] Of the four protected groups listed in the Convention, it appears that neither *racial* and *religious* groups may be defined based on a common language and culture. Racial groups are defined mainly based on common hereditary traits,[20] while religious groups are defined in connection to a mode of worship or a common belief.[21] The other two groups listed in the Convention, *ethnic* and *national*, may however be identified based on common language and culture. Yet, ethnic groups may also be distinguished

---

16 Translation by the author. The original (Amharic) version reads, 'በቋንቋና በልምድ አንድ ያሆኑውን ... የጎብረ ብሔርን ማኅበራዊ የሆነ አንድ ክፍል ሕዝብ'. See የ፩፱፱፱ ዓ. ም የወንጀላኛ መቅጫ ሕግ አዋጅ፣ አንቀጽ ፪፻፳፱.

17 For a similar understanding of a group in the Genocide Convention, see N. Robinson, *The Genocide Convention: A Commentary* (New York: Institute of Jewish Affairs, World Jewish Congress, 1960), 58; Schabas, *Genocide in International Law, supra* note 4, 121–122. See also, ICTY, *Prosecutor v. Stakić*, Appeals Chamber, (Judgment), 22 March 2006, IT-97-24-A, para. 20.

18 UN Doc. E/447, 21.

19 See Schabas, *Genocide in International Law, supra* note 4, 167–168.

20 *Akayesu*, Trial Chamber, (Judgment), *supra* note 8, para. 513. See also *Kayishema and Ruzindana*, Trial Chamber, (Judgment), *supra* note 20, para. 98.

21 See *Kayishema and Ruzindana*, Trial Chamber, (Judgment), *supra* note 20, para. 98; *Akayesu*, Trial Chamber, (Judgment), *supra* note 8, para. 514.

by common traditions and/or by historical or religious features.[22] National groups are viewed in scholarly circles as related to ethnic groups or minority communities,[23] although they are defined within the context of citizenship and State by the ICTR in *Akayesu*.[24]

A commonality of language and culture criterion is also not helpful in defining or identifying a political group, one of the protected groups listed under Article 281 of the Penal Code of 1957. In the *Dergue* trials, where political groups were the alleged victims, Ethiopian courts have defined political groups using features other than common language and culture. According to the FSC, the expression political groups 'referred to persons that came together around a single political view and thought',[25] although there was no discussion as to what could distinguish one political group from another.[26] Accordingly, the Penal Code's use of the expression 'unified in language and culture' may not be regarded as a helpful tool to define the protected groups. Be that as it may, the 2005 Criminal Code removed the Penal Code's phrase and replaced it with a simple word ቡድን (group).[27]

Regarding the size of a group, no specific threshold has been suggested as a marker. Looking at ethnic groups, the numeric size of a group in Ethiopia could consist of as few as 289 members, as per the latest National Census reported in 2007,[28] or as many as over 25 million people.[29] Determining the existence of a group can thus not reasonably rely on the number of its members. Unsurprisingly therefore, in the Ethiopian trials, the size of a group was never considered a subject of discussion, except in relation to the 'in whole' or 'in part' element of the intent to destroy.[30]

---

22 See Berster, 'Article II', *supra note* 14,109.
23 See Schabas, *Genocide in International Law*, *supra* note 4, 134–138.
24 *Akayesu*, Trial Chamber, (Judgment), *supra* note 8, para. 511, in which the Trial Chamber stated that a racial group refers to 'a collection of people who are perceived to share a legal bond based on common citizenship, coupled with reciprocity of rights and duties'.
25 FSC, SPO v. *Colonel Mengistu Hailemariam et al.*, (Appeals Judgment), 26 May 2008, File No. 30181, 68.
26 See section 6.2.3.1. below.
27 See የ ፲፱፻፺፯ የኢትዮጵያ ፌዴራላዊ ዴሞክራሳዊ ሪፓብሊክ የወንጀል ሕግ፣ አንቀጽ ፪፻፸፱.
28 In the 2007 National Census, the Qewama and the She were both referred to as ethnic groups and had 289 and 319 members respectively. See Central Statistical Agency, 'Census 2007 Report: National Statistical', 72–73, available at: <http://www.csa.gov.et/census-report/complete-report/census-2007> accessed 29 September 2019.
29 The 2007 National Census reported that the *Oromo*, referred to as an ethnic group in the census, had 25,363,756 members. See ibid., 73.
30 See section 6.4.4. below.

As a material element of the crime, the issue of the existence of a group is central to the *mens rea* elements of genocide, as the attack against members of the groups must be carried out with the intent to destroy the group as such.[31] Overall, to consider that genocide has been committed, victims' membership to a group is essential, as highlighted by the ICTR in *Akayesu*[32] and as understood by Ethiopian courts, which refrained from entering genocide convictions when victims were targeted for other reasons than their membership to political groups.[33] In *Mengistu et al.,* the FSC reversed the FHC's judgment and stated that the first mass-killing by the *Dergue,* i.e. the summary execution of 59 officials of the *ancien régime,* was not genocidal because the victims did not belong to any of the political groups identified for destruction by the perpetrators.[34]

6.2.2   *The Expansion of the List of Protected Groups*

The issue of groups protected by the criminalization of genocide is one of the most debated and noted topics in Ethiopian criminal law. Whenever there is a discussion on the law of genocide in Ethiopia, commentators mainly, if not exclusively, emphasize that Ethiopian law extends its protection to political groups, which were excluded from the Convention at a later stage of its drafting by the Sixth Committee.[35] This issue was also a subject of debate in almost every case in the *Dergue* trials and even a significant reason for the dissenting opinion in *Mengistu et al.*[36]

Such debates are perhaps due to the fact that the protected group element of genocide in Ethiopian law is highly complex, if not confusing. The only legislation that attempted to reproduce the conventional definition of genocide was the abandoned Draft Criminal Code of 1989.[37] Compared to the Genocide Convention, the Penal Code of 1957 added political groups and excluded national and ethnic groups[38] while the 2005 Criminal Code covers such groups as political, color, nationality and nation in addition to those already protected under the Convention (thereby rectifying its predecessor's deficiency by including national and ethnic groups).[39]

---

31   See section 6.4.5. below.
32   *Akayesu,* Trial Chamber, (Judgment), *supra* note 8, para. 710; Schabas, *Genocide in International Law, supra* note 4,179–180.
33   This is discussed further below.
34   *Colonel Mengistu Hailemariam et al.,* (Appeals Judgment), *supra* note 25, 71.
35   UN Doc. E/AC.25/SR.13, 2.
36   See Chapter 5, section 5.5.
37   See ibid., section 5.4.2.
38   See above, Table 3.
39   See Chapter 5, section 5.4.3.

In international criminal law, the Convention's list of protected groups has been regarded as exhaustive. The reason for the exclusion of other groups was laid out by the ICTR in *Akayesu* when it stated,

> on reading through the *travaux préparatoires* of the Genocide Convention it appears that the crime of genocide was allegedly perceived as targeting only "stable" groups, constituted in a permanent fashion and membership of which is determined by birth, with the exclusion of the more "mobile" groups which one joins through individual voluntary commitment, such as political and economic groups. Therefore, a common criterion in the four types of groups protected by the Genocide Convention is that membership in such groups would seem to be normally not challengeable by its members, who belong to it automatically, by birth, in a continuous and often irremediable manner.[40]

Regardless, many municipal criminal laws have expanded the Convention's list of protected groups. As noted in Chapter 5 in relation to the inclusion of political groups under Article 281 of the Penal Code of 1957, the Convention was never seen as prohibiting such an addition.[41] The ICTR's 'stable' groups' argument did not appear to have had much impact in the practice of States such as Ethiopia, given that the 2005 Criminal Code, enacted after the *Akayesu* judgment, now contains twice the number of groups protected by the Convention.

Overall, the expansive list of protected groups in the Ethiopian law of genocide, which allegedly began with the need to rectify the Convention's exclusion of political groups, lacks clear parameters as to which group should be excluded or included. Defining the protected groups based on the relationship between crimes against humanity and genocide is in itself confusing given that the former is nowhere defined in Ethiopian law. Adding more groups to the list of protected groups to protect abstract concepts such as humanity or humanness might result in absurd consequences. If the legislator pursues this line of argument, there could eventually be nothing that could prevent the treatment of all human groups as protected groups in the Ethiopian law of genocide.

6.2.3 *The Protected Groups in Practice*

Providing for a precise meaning of any of the protected groups under the Genocide Convention is another challenging task. Nowhere in Ethiopian law

---

40   *Akayesu*, Trial Chamber, (Judgment), *supra* note 8, para. 511. See however Schabas, *Genocide in International Law*, *supra* note 4, 152.

41   See Chapter 5, section 5.5.

is a definition supplied for any of the eight protected groups under Article 269 of the 2005 Criminal Code. As providing a definition for each of these groups in the absence of case law would hold the risk of leading to extrapolations and erroneous conclusions, this section discusses how Ethiopian courts have considered the meaning of the two protected groups in relation to which genocide trials were conducted, i.e. *political* and *ethnic* groups.

6.2.3.1 Political Groups

In the *Dergue* trials, the FHC found that a political group consists of individuals who share a common political belief but does not necessarily designate a political party. Ethiopian courts have noted that a registration as a political party is not a requirement for a given group to be recognized as political.[42] This finding had the benefit of removing procedural requirements from intervening with the protected status of a group and of effectively protecting groups that are not recognized as political parties because they have failed or were unable to register with the electoral commission. This is all the more important in the context of crimes committed during the *Dergue* regime, not the least because political parties were banned in connection to the regime's bid to forge a single-party system.[43] Accordingly, recognizing political groups as protected irrespective of their registration should be seen differently from the mandatory requirement of registration without which a party or an organization may not be recognized for purposes such as running for election.[44]

---

42 Ibid.
43 The major policies of the *Dergue*'s Ethiopian Socialism were:
    1) Government Structure: A decentralized government structure with a minimum interference from the center to be introduced; 2) Political Organizations: There would be one political national party that would have as its members all progressive elements. No room for opposition parties; 3) Economic Policy: All resources of the nation and means of production would be owned by the State. The private sector would have a role in areas where it is beneficial for the development of the nation: 4) Social Policy: The Ethiopian family is an essential element of the society. It would be protected against negative forces that would undermine its cohesiveness and viability. All Ethiopians have a right to free basic education; and access to health services would be expanded.; and 5) Foreign Policy: The foreign policy would be essentially the same except a change of emphasis in the light of recent developments. Non-interference in the internal affairs of other nation, non-alignment, peaceful coexistence and the principles enshrined in the charters of the United Nations and the Organizations of African Unity would form the foreign policy component.
    See T. Haile-Selassie, *The Ethiopian Revolution 1974–1991: From a Monarchical Autocracy to a Military Oligarchy* (London: Kegan Paul International, 1997) 113–114.
44 See The Revised Political Parties Registration Proclamation, No. 573/2008, Article 2(2).

Under normal circumstances, political groups may be required to pursue their aims in a lawful manner, the absence of which may result in, among others, getting banned from participating in elections.[45] Lawfulness, however, is not a requirement for the purpose of status as a protected group under the law of genocide. In the *Dergue* trials, this could be inferred from the fact that participation in the assassination campaigns used to be known as the White-Terror has not affected the EPRP from being considered as a protected group.[46] The reason behind such an understanding is probably to be found in the idea that genocide is never justified, even though this is not explicitly stated anywhere in the judgments. This finds an echo in the *Oromo-Gumuz* trials, where victims of genocide were found guilty of committing genocide against their perpetrators.

It is noteworthy that, as a common feature, none of the political groups targeted by the *Dergue* were registered political parties. This however did not create difficulties in ascertaining an individual victim's membership to those groups, largely because membership to a group was determined subjectively rather than objectively. The subjective test was based on the individual perpetrator's perception of the victim's membership at the time he or she committed the *actus reus*. The existence of such a subjective test may be inferred from the absence in the *Dergue* trials of any attempt by the Prosecution to establish whether the victim was actually a member of a particular political group. According to the membership test, it was required that at the time of the attack the perpetrator believed that the victim belonged to the group he or she planned/intended to destroy. In international jurisprudence, determination of membership to a group depends on both subjective and objective tests. Nonetheless, the objective test was viewed as complementary, dictated apparently by the 'permanent and stable' criterion attached by international

---

45 See ibid., which requires that political parties operate in 'a democratic way. For an express reference to the requirement of promoting political programs 'in a lawful manner', see The Amended Electoral Law of Ethiopia Proclamation, Proclamation No.532/2007, Article 12. A draft proclamation being discussed by the Parliament also defines 'a political organization or a political party' as 'a grouping which, having formulated a political program, pursues its aims in a lawful manner'. See National Electoral Board of Ethiopia Establishment Draft Proclamation, February 2019, Article 2(5).

46 This was raised by the defendants as a substantive defense in *Mengistu et al.*, which the courts dismissed stating that the *Dergue* was not only the one who shot the first bullet but also inflicted an extremely greater amount of violence as compared to what the other groups did. See *Colonel Mengistu Hailemariam et al.*, (Trial Judgment), *supra* note 10, 115. See also ASC, SPO v. *Demetse Gebremedehen et al.* (Ruling on Preliminary Objections), 11 October 2000, File No. 25/90, 117; FHC, SPO v. *Asazenew Bayyisa et al.*, (Ruling on Preliminary Objections), 22 May 1998, File No. 643/1989, 19.

courts and tribunals to the groups protected by the Convention, as stated by the ICTs and the ICJ.[47]

An exclusive assessment of membership to political groups based on a subjective test appears to be a reasonable approach, at least when it comes to the Ethiopian cases. On the one hand, since political groups do not fulfil the permanent and stable criterion, the objective test should be regarded as inapplicable.[48] On the other hand, given that the political opposition groups were operating in clandestine ways, membership to such groups was secretive, which should make the subjective test not only necessary but also lenient. In other words, due to the surreptitious nature of the activities of a targeted group, the perpetrator's mere belief that the victim belonged to that group could be sufficient to satisfy the subjective test. Imposing an additional requirement, such as whether the perpetrator had a reasonable ground to consider the victim as a member of a targeted group, could amount to establishing an objective test that the victim actually belonged to the said group. Such a requirement would defy the whole purpose of protecting political groups that are neither registered nor expected to act lawfully, but rather secretively, as a result of which fluidity of membership might be inevitable.

Adopting an exclusive subjective test did not mean that courts were not careful in ascertaining whether the victims were killed due to their membership to a group or because of other reasons. In that sense, killing for political reasons did not necessarily mean targeting political groups. In *Mengistu et al.*, the FSC highlighted that some people were killed for other reasons than their membership to political groups. As noted above, it was precisely on the ground that the victims did not belong to political groups that the *Dergue's* first mass-execution was not regarded genocidal.[49] Similarly, the ASC stated in *Degenet Ayalew et al.* that killings carried out against victims labeled 'anti-revolutionary' or 'anti-people' did not constitute genocide since the victims were not targeted based on membership to a particular group.[50] One could also add the killing of the Emperor to the list of non-genocidal crimes due to lack of membership to a

---

47 *Bosnia and Herzegovina* v. *Serbia and Montenegro*, (Judgment), *supra* note 14, para. 191; *Stakić*, Appeals Chamber, (Judgment), *supra* note 17, para. 25; ICTR, *Prosecutor* v. *Rutaganda,* Trial Chamber, (Judgment), 6 December 1999, ICTR-96-3-T, para. 56.

48 *Akayesu*, Trial Chamber, (Judgment), *supra* note 8, para. 511; *Rutaganda,* Trial Chamber, (Judgment), *supra* note 47, para. 57.

49 *Colonel Mengistu Hailemariam et al.,* (Appeals Judgment), *supra* note 25, 71. In line with this argument, one could also consider that membership to a group was deemed essential for the commission of genocide in the jurisprudence of international criminal tribunals. See *Akayesu,* Trial Chamber, (Judgment), *supra* note 8, para. 710.

50 ASC, SPO v. *Dagnenet Ayalew et al.,* (Trial Judgment), 26 January 2004, File No. 13/90, 38.

protected group. As the FSC highlighted, 'the Emperor was assassinated owing to the *Dergue's* phony belief that his continued existence might have left the innocent public with a hope that he might reign again'[51] and thus not because of his belonging to a particular group.

In sum, Ethiopian courts have defined the notion of political groups in a manner that has largely taken into account the circumstances of the time under which political groups had operated – and were targeted. As a result, the determination of membership to political groups has predominantly followed a subjective criterion. Because politicide is not a crime under international law, the exact similar discussion did not exist in international trials. Nevertheless, international jurisprudence has often defined protected groups using the subjective test, i.e. based on the perpetrator's (or even the victim's) perception of the targeted group.[52] The subjective criterion was employed by international courts more often than the objective test[53] or the combined objective-subjective test.[54] However, the predominantly subjective approach followed by Ethiopian courts in defining political groups and membership to such groups could be justified based in these groups lack of 'stable' and 'permanent' nature – terms used precisely by the *Akayesu* Trial Chamber and the Darfur Commission to typify the four groups protected under the Convention.[55]

Yet, the application of the subjective test was not consistent and, at times, Ethiopian courts have leaned towards an objective requirement. For instance, in assessing the killing of Brigadier General Teferi Benti, the first Chairman of the *Dergue*, the FHC stated that it constituted an act of genocide as the victim was killed because he was found holding the EPRP's leaflet.[56] This was reversed

---

51 *Colonel Mengistu Hailemariam et al.,* (Appeals Judgment), *supra* note 25, 71.
52 As stated in *Jelisić,* 'to attempt to define [the protected groups] using objective and scientifically irreproachable criterion would be a perilous exercise whose result would not necessarily correspond to the perception of the persons concerned by such categorization'. See ICTY, *Prosecutor* v. *Jelisić,* Trial Chamber, (Judgment), 14 December 1999, IT-95-10-T, para. 70. See also *Rutaganda,* Trial Chamber, (Judgment), *supra* note 47, para. 55.
53 See *Akayesu,* Trial Chamber, (Judgment), *supra* note 8, paras 512–515.
54 See for instance ICTR, *Prosecutor* v. *Brđanin,* Trial Chamber, (Judgment), 1 September 2004, para. 209; *Kayishema and Ruzindana,* Trial Chamber, (Judgment), *supra* note 20, para. 98.
55 See *Akayesu,* Trial Chamber, (Judgment), *supra* note 8, para. 515. Report of the International Commission of Inquiry on Darfur to the Secretary General. *Supra* note 14, para. 501. For a criticism on the use of the subjective test to define the racial, ethnic, national and religious groups, see Berster, 'Article 11' *supra* note 14, 102–105; C. Kreß, 'The Crime of Genocide Under International Law' (2006) 6(4) *International Criminal Law Review* 461–502, 477–478.
56 Ibid., 72.

on appeal, and the FSC stated that holding a leaflet advertising EPRP's slogans could not have made the victim an EPRP member.[57] The court did not explain why or what other criteria should have been taken into account to determine the victim's membership to a given covert political group.

6.2.3.2 Ethnic Groups

Ethnic groups were recognized as victims of genocide in the trials discussed in the book, save in the *Dergue* trials. Ethnic genocide appeared before Ethiopian courts for the first time in 2004 in the *Anuak-Nuwer* trials, where the victims were South Sudanese refugees of ethnic *Nuwer*.[58] It was mentioned again in the CUD trials, which dealt with the 2005 post-election violence and which saw members and affiliates of political opposition groups accused of attempting and committing genocide against the Tigre ethnic group.[59] Yet, ethnic groups were not discussed as such as the court ruled on the absence of intent to destroy before arriving at the point where it could have addressed the status of the protected groups.[60] Later, the crime of genocide discussed in the *Oromo-Gumuz* trials was committed as a result of an inter-ethnic conflict between the ethnic *Gumuz* and the ethnic *Oromos*. As mentioned in the indictments prepared in 2008, both were regarded victims of genocide.[61]

In the *Anuak-Nuwer* and *Oromo-Gumuz* trials, the perpetrators were found guilty of committing genocide against ethnic groups. Nevertheless, none of these trials actually examined whether the *Gumuz*, the *Nuwer*, or the *Oromos* were indeed ethnic groups. It is possible that the courts considered that the ethnic identity of the *Gumuz*, the *Nuwer*, and the *Oromos* was too obvious to be debated. For instance, unlike the Hutu and the Tutsi in Rwanda, they spoke distinctive languages and Ethiopian courts were thus not faced with the same identification challenge as the ICTR.[62] Furthermore, the ethnic identity of the

---

57 Ibid.
58 See FHC, *Federal Prosecutor* v. *Gure Uchala Ugira et al.*, (Indictment) 4 January 2004, File No. 586/96, 1–2.
59 See FHC, *Federal Prosecutor* v. *Engineer Hailu Shawul et al.*, (Indictment), 15 December 2006, File No. 43246/97, 22; FHC, *Federal Prosecutor* v. *Berehene Kehassaye Woldeselassie et al.*, (Indictment), 15 December 2006, File No. FHC 45671/98, 7; FHC, *Federal Prosecutor* v. *Kifle Tigeneh et al.*, (Indictment), 30 June 2006, File No. 44562, 1.
60 See section 5.5.2 below.
61 See FHC, *Federal Prosecutor* v. *Aliyu Yusufe Ibrahim et al.*, (Indictment), 3 September 2008, File No. 71000, 1–8; FHC, *Federal Prosecutor* v. *Tadesse Jewannie Mengesha et al.* (Indictment), 22 August 2008, 1–9; FHC, *Federal Prosecutor* v. *Tesfaye Neno Loya et al.*, (Indictment), 20 September 2008, File No. 74796, 1–4.
62 In *Akayesu*, where ethnic group was regarded as the one that shares common language and culture, the fact that the Hutu and the Tutsi shared a common language was seen as

groups identified in the Ethiopian trials could, arguably, find support in the fact that these groups are recognized as ethnic groups by institutions such as the Central Statistical Agency and the House of Federations.[63] The problem, however, is that, in referring to ethnic identity, these institutions rarely distinguish between ethnicity, nation, nationality, or tribal origin. For instance, the Central Statistical Agency (CSA) has used the national or tribal origin of a person to identify her/him in a given ethnic group.[64]

It is also common to see different bodies referring to the same group as either ethnic or national/nationality. For instance, the *Anuak*, a group in the Gambella Regional State, is referred to as an ethnic group by the CSA.[65] The same group is mentioned as a 'nationality' group by the Parliamentary Commission of Inquiry that investigated the December 2003 conflict in Gambella.[66] Yet, in the *Anuak-Nuwer* trials, both the indictment and the judgment have referred to the *Anuak* as an ethnic group.[67]

In Ethiopia, 'ethnicity' is a term that is too familiar, if not overused, in the sense that its usage is inextricably linked to discourses involving the country's current federal structure of governance, commonly referred to as 'ethnic federalism'. In establishing a federal state structure in 1994, the FDRE Constitution restructured the country into nine Regional States[68] composed of 'nations, nationalities, and peoples'.[69] Supposedly, these terms are the ones implied in the expression 'ethnic federalism', as there is no single mention of the word 'ethnicity' in the Constitution. The grouping of 'nations, nationalities and peoples' into the nine Regional States was, according to the Constitution, based on factors such as 'settlement patterns, language, identity and consent of the peoples concerned'.[70] What these parameters imply in practice is far from

---

a problem to characterize the Tutsi as an ethnic group. Instead, the Trial Chamber relied on the official classification of the Tutsi as an ethnic group. See *Akayesu*, Trial Chamber, (Judgment), *supra* note 8, para. 702.

63   Official Census of 2007, *supra* note, 71.
64   Ibid.
65   Ibid.
66   Resolution on the Report of the Gambella Inquiry Commission adopted by the House of Peoples' Representatives of the Federal Democratic Republic of Ethiopia, adopted on 8 July 2004, para. 4.
67   See *Gure Uchala Ugira et al.*, (Indictment) *supra* note 58, 1. See also FHC, *Federal Prosecutor v. Gure Uchala Ugira et al.*, (Trial Judgment), 25 March 2005, File No. 586/96, 4.
68   See the FDRE Constitution, Article 47. The nine Member States as named in the Constitution are: Tigray, Afar, Amhara, Oromia, Somalia, Benshangul Gumuz, the Southern Nations, Nationalities and Peoples, the Gambela Peoples, and the Harari People. See ibid., Article 47(1).
69   See ibid., Article 46.
70   Ibid., Article 46(2).

clear. Some of the Regional States are composed of over 40 different linguistic groups, while some others Regions, such as the Ethiopian Somali and Oromia, are made up of people admittedly speaking a common language.

Some writers have noted the confusing and overly politicized usage of the term 'ethnicity' in Ethiopia, notably in the post-1991 political development. According to Gebrehiwot and Haftesion, who argue that the government structure in Ethiopia could be better described as a *multinational* federation, ethnicity 'requires common descent'.[71] While this definition might add complexity to the matter, it is however striking that it seems to overlap with the definition of racial groups rendered by the ICTR.[72]

In the only instance where remarks were made regarding the identity of the targeted group, the FHC noted in the *Oromo-Gumuz* trials that the members of the *Gumuz* ethnic group identified their victims based on skin color. In *Aliyu Yusufe et al.*, it was stated that in referring to the *Oromos*, the orchestrators of the attack had instructed their co-perpetrators to attack those who were light complexioned.[73] Although this was used to emphasize the finding that the attack was directed against the *Oromos*,[74] the Court did not explain how being light skinned was the distinctive marker of the targeted group, nor did it comment in general on whether skin color could be used to distinguish one ethnic group from the other. Such a subjective description of the victims by the perpetrators should have been explained by the court, given that, as compared to the *Gumuz*, several other groups in Ethiopia could be described as light skinned.

Simply put, unlike the practice in international trials,[75] the question of the ethnic identity of the targeted group was not scrutinized in the Ethiopian trials. As reflected in the definition of Ethiopian writers and the practice of the country's Central Statistical Authority, the definition of ethnicity overlaps with that of racial and national groups. Similar difficulties have been pointed out in international doctrine and jurisprudence that attempted to define ethnical groups.[76]

---

71 M. Gebrehiwot and F. Haftetsion, 'The Politics in Naming the Ethiopian Federation' (2015) 48 *Journal of Ethiopian Studies* 89–117, 97.
72 See *Akayesu*, Trial Chamber, (Judgment), *supra* note 8, para. 513. See also *Kayishema and Ruzindana*, Trial Chamber, (Judgment), *supra* note 20, para. 98.
73 See FHC, *Federal Prosecutor v. Aliyu Yusufe Ibrahim et al.*, (Trial Judgment), 6 September 2009, File No. 7100/2000, 23.
74 Ibid.
75 See *Akayesu*, Trial Chamber, (Judgment), *supra* note 8, para. 513; *Kayishema and Ruzindana*, Trial Chamber, (Judgment), *supra* note 20, para. 98.
76 See Schabas, *Genocide in International Law*, *supra* note 4, 143–147.

6.3 *Actus Reus* of Genocide: Underlying Offenses

By their order of appearance when first introduced into Ethiopian law, the *actus reus* elements of genocide are:
1) Killing members of a group,
2) Bodily injury or causing harm in any way whatsoever to the external and internal health of a member of the group,
3) Imposing measures to prevent propagation or continued survival of members of the group or their progeny,
4) Compulsory movement or dispersion of peoples or children,
5) Placing members of the group under living conditions calculated to result in their death, and
6) Enforced disappearance[77]

Although for the purpose of genocide these individual acts represent only the *actus reus* element of the crime, it should be noted that each of them constitutes a separate offense by and of themselves and are usually punishable as ordinary crimes in municipal laws. As a result, each of them comprises, as any other offense in criminal law, its own *actus reus* and *mens rea*. The *mens rea* required for these 'underlying offenses'[78] is not to be confused with the *mens rea* required for genocide, i.e. the specific intent to destroy, as discussed in section 6.4 below.

It can be safely submitted here that under Ethiopian law intent is the requisite *mens rea* for each of these underlying offenses. Ethiopian criminal law (both the Penal Code of 1957 and the 2005 Criminal Code) operates based on the principle that all crimes are intentional, except those offenses for which the law considers negligence to be a sufficient mental element. The requirement of intent, unlike the case of negligence, does not have to be expressly stated.[79] Criminal intent under Ethiopian law takes two forms: direct[80] and indirect.[81] In principle, the prosecutor has the duty to establish that the defendant acted

---

77 See The Penal Code of 1957, Article 281; The FDRE Criminal Code, Article 269.
78 For the significance of using the reference 'underlying offenses', see Mettraux, *International Crimes and the Ad Hoc Tribunals*, supra note 6, 235.
79 See The Penal Code of 1957, Articles 23 and 59; The FDRE Criminal Code, Articles 23 and 59.
80 This is the case when a person commits the *actus reus* 'with full knowledge and intent in order to achieve a given result'. See The Penal Code of 1957, Article 58(1)(a); The FDRE Criminal Code, Article 58(1)(a).
81 This form of intention materializes when a person commits the *actus reus* 'with the awareness that his act may cause illegal and punishable consequences', and regardless of the fact that such consequences may follow. See The Penal Code of 1957, Article 58(1)(b); The FDRE Criminal Code, Article 58(1)(b).

with the required type of intent to commit a crime. Exceptionally, the law adopts a *presumptive mens rea*, for which the prosecutor is absolved from having to prove the existence of intent because the law presumes that the commission of the *actus reus* implies the requisite intent, in whole or in part.[82] This however does not apply here as none of the underlying offenses listed above fall in the category of crimes with presumptive *mens rea*.

For the purpose of genocide, the commission of the underlying offenses needs to be carried out against a member or members of a protected group. This necessitates the application of a general *mens rea,* the proof of which requires showing that the perpetrator intentionally committed the *actus reus* with the knowledge that the victim belonged to a protected group.[83] The *general mens rea* required to accompany the underlying offenses should be distinguished from the specific intent to destroy required for the commission of genocide.[84] The former requires a proof of the perpetrator's knowledge as to the victim's membership to a targeted group while the latter requires proof of the perpetrator's intent to destroy the targeted group.

In Ethiopian law, the existence of such a requirement can be deduced more directly from the fact that the prohibited acts were formulated in reference to members of a group.[85] In practice, it seems that Ethiopian courts did not see the need to discuss and underline the details of *mens rea* required for the underlying offenses. Nonetheless, the overall practice shows that the perpetrator's knowledge of the victim's membership to the group was considered decisive for the commission of the genocidal *actus reus*.[86] The problem is that the courts have regarded the proof of the *general mens rea* as sufficient to establish the commission of genocide, which, as will be shown under section 6.4.3.

---

82   See for example, The FDRE Criminal Code, Articles 306 and 403.
83   See *Rutaganda,* Trial Chamber, (Judgment), *supra* note 47, para. 59; *Prosecutor* v. *Musema*, Trial Chamber, (Judgment), 27 January 2000, ICTR-96-13-T, para. 165; ICTR, *Prosecutor* v. *Bagilishema*, (Trial Judgment of 7 June 2001), ICTR-95-1A-T, para. 61; ICTR, *Prosecutor* v. *Semanza*, Trial Chamber, (Judgment), 15 May 2003, ICTR-97-20-T, para. 427; *Jelisić,* Trial Chamber, (Judgment), *supra* note 52, para. 66.
84   For the discussion of the specific genocidal *mens rea*, see below, section 6.4.
85   For example, an act of 'killing members of a group' under the genocide provision of the law is different from an act of killing provided as a separate and ordinary crime under the provisions of the law dealing with homicide. The former requires, in addition to intent, the knowledge that the victims were a member of a targeted group, which the latter does not. Simply put, killing under Article 281 of the Penal Code of 1957 required that it was inflicted upon a member of a group while killing under Article 522 of the same Code required the victim to be just any person. See also Articles 269 and 539 of the 2005 Criminal Code, respectively.
86   This is discussed above under section 5.3.3.

below, is symptomatic of the fact that Ethiopian courts have confused the general *mens rea* with the specific intent to destroy.

6.3.1   *Killing Members of the Group*

Killing members of a group, as listed under Article 281(a) of the Penal Code and Article 269(a) of the Criminal Code, represents the most common genocidal act committed in Ethiopia. In the *Dergue* trials, the SPO established that the *Dergue* took the life of 9,546 people in pursuance of its genocidal plan.[87] In the *Anuak-Nuwer* trials, six individuals were killed while the number of victims killed in the *Oromo-Gumuz* cases was 198.[88] In all of these cases, the accused were indicted for aggravated homicide as an alternative to the principal charge of genocide that was based on killing members of a group. In the *Dergue* and the *Oromo-Gumuz* trials, perpetrators were ultimately found guilty of aggravated homicide instead of genocide for lack of evidence showing genocidal *mens rea*.

Homicide in Ethiopian law refers not only to an act of killing but also to an act of 'causing death',[89] as is also the case with the concept of killing in international criminal law.[90] Intentional homicide takes three forms: aggravated,[91] ordinary,[92] and extenuated.[93] Ordinary homicide represents a simple case of causing death intentionally with no additional circumstances indicating the perpetrator's degree of cruelty or dangerousness.[94] In that sense, intentional homicide could be seen as aggravated homicide provided that circumstances such as, *inter alia*, premeditation, motive, use of weapons, membership to a homicidal gang or group, or intent to conceal or further another crime are present.[95] Extenuating homicide refers to cases of intentional homicide where

---

87   *Dem Yazele Dossie*, Annex, Table II.
88   See FHC, *Prosecutor v. Tadesse Jewanie Mengesha et al.*, (Trial Judgment), 24 August 2009, File No. 70996, 4; FHC, *Prosecutor v. Tesfaye Neno Loya et al.*, (Trial Judgment), 30 April 2009, File No. 74796; *Aliyu Yusufe Ibrahim et al.*, (Trial Judgment), *supra* note 73, 5.
89   See the Penal Code of 1957, Article 521; The Criminal Code of 2005, Article 538.
90   See ICC Elements of Crimes, Article 6(a), n. 2. See also *Akayesu*, Trial Chamber, (Judgment), *supra* note 8, para. 500; *Rutaganda*, Trial Chamber, (Judgment), *supra* note 47, para. 49; *Musema*, Trial Chamber, (Judgment), *supra* note 83, para. 155; ICTR, *Prosecutor v. Muvunyi*, Trial Chamber, (Judgment), 15 September 2006, ICTR-2000-55A-T, para. 486.
91   FDRE Criminal Code, Article 539. This was referred to as 'homicide in the first degree' under Article 522 of the Penal Code.
92   Ibid., Article 540. This was referred to as 'homicide in the second degree' under Article 523 of the Penal Code.
93   Ibid., Article 541. See also the Penal Code of 1957, Article 524.
94   See FDRE Criminal Code, Article 538.
95   Ibid., Article 539.

the perpetrator acted in the presence of extenuating factors that fall short of exculpating him or her from criminal responsibility.[96]

The jurisprudence of Ethiopian courts does not offer a meaningful discussion as to which form of intentional homicide could be considered sufficient as an underlying offense to genocide. Whenever there was a charge of genocide by killing, judges seemed to have been solely interested in the fact that the perpetrator caused the death of the victim. In that sense, the existence of premeditation or motive was not regarded necessary to establish intentional homicide, although most of the killings took place in the context of a plan to destroy (in the *Dergue* trials) or with a motive of gain (in the *Oromo-Gumuz* trials), as discussed below.[97]

Although it could be said that, akin to international jurisprudence,[98] Ethiopian courts did not require premeditation as an element of genocidal killing, such a conclusion might not tell the whole story. This is because one should also take into account the numerous cases where perpetrators were found guilty of aggravated homicide instead of genocide for lack of evidence showing genocidal *mens rea*. In such instances, Ethiopian courts failed to explain why the act of killing did not constitute ordinary homicide instead of aggravated homicide. They commonly put forward a rather simplistic argument based on the following reasoning: the acts of killing did not constitute genocide (because, for instance, the victims were not a member of a protected group); therefore, the perpetrator is found guilty of committing an aggravated homicide mentioned in the alternative charge.[99] It is not possible to tell whether such conclusions were reached just because the judges did not have the time to explain their arguments due to the overload of cases they had to deal with[100] or because they were of the view that killing as an underlying offense to genocide constitutes an aggravated homicide.

---

96 Ibid., Article 541.
97 See the discussion below under intent/plan to destroy.
98 See *Kayishema and Ruzindana*, Trial Chamber, (Judgment), *supra* note 20, paras 101–104. See also *Akayesu*, Trial Chamber, (Judgment), *supra* note 8, paras 500–501; *Rutaganda*, Trial Chamber, (Judgment), *supra* note 47, para. 50; *Musema*, Trial Chamber, (Judgment), *supra* note 83, para. 155; *Bagilishema*, Trial Chamber, (Judgment), *supra* note 83, para. 57; *Semanza*, Trial Chamber, (Judgment), *supra* note 83, para. 319; ICTR, *Prosecutor v. Kajelijeli*, Trial Chamber, (Judgment), 1 December 2003, ICTR-98-44A-T, para. 813; ICTR, *Prosecutor v. Kamuhanda*, Trial Chamber, (Judgment), 22 January 2004, ICTR-95-54A-T, para. 632.
99 *Colonel Mengistu Hailemariam et al.*, (Appeals Judgment), *supra* note 25, 71–73.
100 In the *Dergue* trials, judges were overly burdened with the number of cases they had to deal with. There were generally not many experienced judges left to deal with the cases as most of them had been disqualified on the basis of prior involvement with the *Dergue* regime. This was further exacerbated by the inaccessibility and insufficiency of reference

In addition to *mens rea,* homicide requires the proof of the *actus reus,* namely, that the perpetrator caused the death of the victim or that the victim actually died as a result of the perpetrator's acts.[101] If this requirement of death distinguishes killing from enforced disappearance, for which the fact that the victim is alive or dead cannot, by definition, be established,[102] Ethiopian courts seem to have, at times, confused the two. For instance, the Southern Nations Nationalities and Peoples' Regional State Supreme Court (SNNPRS SC) stated in *Mezemer Abebe et al.* that the fact that the victims were never returned showed that they were murdered, although there was no evidence that the victims were killed or even that they were released for execution.[103] There are in fact several other cases in the *Dergue* trials where the commission of homicide was established in relation to deceased persons whose bodies were never found, a phenomenon that could be referred to as the case of 'disappeared deceased'.[104] At other times however, Ethiopian courts distinguished the two crimes in such a strict way that they acquitted defendants because no bodies had been found.[105]

This does not mean however that the Ethiopian law of homicide necessarily requires the recovery of the victim's body or eyewitness testimony. Other forms of direct or circumstantial evidence are sufficient to establish the commission of homicide, as is also the case in international criminal trials.[106] Yet, the Cassation Bench of the FSC, while cautioning the need to evaluate circumstantial evidence with extreme care, stated that such form of evidence could

materials (such as legislation and scholarly works), the lack of research assistants and even of court clerks. See G.A. Aneme, 'Apology and s: The Case of the Red-Terror Trials in Ethiopia' (2006) 6(1) *African Human Rights Law Journal* 64–84, 78; Redae 'The Ethiopian Genocide Trial' *supra* note 11, 7.

101   See *Akayesu,* Trial Chamber, (Judgment), *supra* note 8, para. 588.
102   See below, section 5.4.6.
103   SNNPRS SC, SPO v. *Mezemer Abebe et al.,* (Trial Ruling), 16 November 2003, File No. 0457, 70–71.
104   The *Dergue* had engaged in a concerted plan of disappearing the deceased by concealing the bodies in mass graves, dumping them in rivers and abysses, feeding them to the beasts. See T.S. Metekia, 'Violence Against and Using the Dead: Ethiopian Dergue Cases' (2018) 4(1) *Human Remains and Violence* 76–92, 86. To a negligible extent, acts aimed at disappearing deceased individuals were also witnessed in the *Oromo-Gumuz* cases, where it was established that victims were thrown into a running river. See *Tesfaye Neno Loya et al.,* (Trial Judgment), *supra* note 88, 6.
105   See HSC, SPO v. *Amanshoa Gebrewolde et al.,* (Trial Ruling), 5 August 2003, File No. 4/90/1/ (00021), 362–363.
106   See Schabas, *Genocide in International Law, supra* note 4, 180.

be considered acceptable only if it clearly shows each of the elements of a crime without causing the inference of something that is not there.[107]

6.3.2 Bodily Injury or Causing Harm in Any Way Whatsoever to the External and Internal Health of a Member of the Group

In addition to killing members of a group, Article 281 (a) of the Penal Code contained a lengthy phrase that read: 'bodily injury or causing harm in any way whatsoever to the external and internal health of a member of the group'.[108] This phrase, as it appeared in the Amharic version of the law, was constructed from Amharic and Geez (a semantic language) words.[109] The English version read somehow differently: 'bodily harm or serious injury to the physical or mental health of members of the group, in any way whatsoever'.[110] This phrase, in its Amharic version, was discussed in the course of the *Dergue* trials and it appeared that it was meant to reproduce the physical element of genocide under Article II (b) of the Convention, namely, 'causing serious bodily or mental harm to members of the group'. Although Article 269 (a) of the 2005 Criminal Code replaced its predecessor's formulation with 'causing bodily injury; or harming bodily or mental health of members of the group, in any way whatsoever',[111] it might still be put forward that the intention of the drafters was to, here again, integrate the conventional act of 'causing serious bodily or mental harm to members of the group'.

Be that as it may, several differences with the conventional text can be pointed out. Firstly, unlike the Convention, Ethiopian law uses the word 'health' in referring to bodily or mental harm. Perhaps more problematically, it is not clear whether there is a specific meaning attached to the word 'health' and the case law shows no consistency in the references to 'health', which was either omitted or replaced by the word 'body', as in 'external and internal body'.[112]

---

107 See FSC CB, *Prosecutor* v. *Semachew Lengereh Alemu* (Decision), 15 November 2011, File No. 75980, 3; FSC CB, *Prosecutor* v. *Woldu Gebrezgi et al.*, (Decision), 29 August 2014, File No.94070, 5; FSC CB, *Prosecutor* v. *Ennat Hanacho et al.*, (Decision), 15 November 2011, File No. 75980, 3.

108 Translation by the Author. The original (Amharic) version reads: 'አካል ያቆሰለ ወይም ከዚሁ ክፍል አባሎች በአንደኛው አፍአዊና ውስጣዊ ጤንነት ላይ በማናቸውም ሁኔታ ጉዳት ያደረሰ'.

109 The word አፍአዊ in this provision is a geez word which refers to external in English and ውጫዊ in Amharic.

110 See the Criminal Code of 2005, Article 269(a); the Penal Code of 1957, Article 281(a).

111 Translation by the author. The original (Amharic) version reads: 'በማናቸውም ሁኔታ ያማገበረሰበን አባሎች ... አካላዊ ወይንም ኅሊናዊ ጤንነት የጎዳ፤ ወይንም የአካል ጉዳት ያደረሰ'.

112 FSC, *SPO* v. *Colonel Mengistu Hailemariam et al.*, (Revised Indictment), 28 November 1995, File No. 1/87, 92.

In fact, bodily injury and external injury could be used interchangeably, and an internal injury could also mean an injury to the internal organs, as can be inferred from the ICTR case law.[113] All of these three words (bodily, external, and internal) are covered under the expression of *bodily* harm.[114] Secondly, unlike the Genocide Convention, Ethiopian law makes no reference to 'seriousness' of mental or bodily harm, as discussed in the following sections.

6.3.2.1 Mental Harm

At least until the entry into force of the 2005 Criminal Code, Ethiopian law did not recognize causing injury to the mental health of members of the group as an *actus reus* element of genocide. This had serious consequences in practice. For instance, in *Mengistu et al.*, the indictments did not refer to mental harm of members of the group,[115] in spite of the fact that the crimes perpetrated most certainly caused such harm. Likewise, in the most notable torture cases such as *Teshoma Bayyu et al.*,[116] *Debela Dinsa Wege et al.*,[117] and *Abera Ayalew et al.*,[118] no charges were brought against the defendants for having caused mental harm to members of the group, thereby overlooking one crucial aspect of the crime of torture, namely, its psychological consequences.

Although the *Dergue* employed methods of mental torture such as threats of execution, no case dealt directly with acts of causing mental harm.[119] If judges in the *Dergue* trials made remarks that some of the torture techniques

---

113 See *Kayishema and Ruzindana*, Trial Chamber, (Judgment), *supra* note 20, para. 109. See also *Semanza*, Trial Chamber, (Judgment), *supra* note 83, para. 320; *Seromba*, Trial Chamber, (Judgment), *supra* note 14, para. 317.

114 As stated by the ICTR in *Kayishema* and *Ruzindana*, bodily harm refers to injury caused to 'the external, internal organs or senses'. *Kayishema and Ruzindana*, Trial Chamber, (Judgment), *supra* note 20, para. 109.

115 See *Colonel Mengistu Hailemariam et al.*, (Revised Indictment), *supra* note 112, 87–90. However, references to the English version of the law might have created the impression that the *Dergue* trials involved the prosecution of 'causing serious bodily and mental injuries'. See M.T. Tessema, *Prosecution of Politicide in Ethiopia: The Red Terror Trials* (The Hague: T.M.C Asser Press, 2018) 182.

116 FHC, SPO v. *Teshome Bayyu et al.*, (Indictment). 15 May 2001, File No. 07415.

117 FHC, SPO v. *Debela Dinsa Wege et al.*, (Indictment), 8 November 2000, File No.912/89.

118 ASC, SPO v. *Abera Ayalew et al.*, (Indictment), 24 September 1999, File No.22/90.

119 See FHC, SPO v. *Melaku Teferra*, (Trial Judgment), 11 November 2006, File No. 03112, 37–38. See also *Dem Yazele Dossie*, 278–279. Victims suffered severe mental pain because they were, for instance, forced to watch the killing or torturing of others, frightened by unmuzzled dogs, subjected to rape after *wefalala*, and taken for false execution.

have also caused mental or 'psychological' harm,[120] these were made in passing in the judgments or mentioned as aggravating factors in sentencing.[121] As a consequence of the lacunae in the applicable law, none of the genocide trials conducted in Ethiopia based on the Penal Code of 1957 actually dealt with the act of causing serious mental harm, thereby contrasting with the law and practice at the international level.[122]

Genocide trials based on the 2005 Criminal Code have however brought a whole different scenario into the picture, i.e. the possibility that genocide could be committed by causing mental harm alone. In *Berhene Kahassaye Woldeselassie et al.* of the CUD trials, the Federal Prosecutor indicted five defendants for having committed genocide by causing mental harm in violation of Article 269(a) of the 2005 Criminal Code. No other underlying offense was mentioned to have been committed.

The case of *Berhene Kahassaye Woldeselassie et al.* could also be interesting from the perspective of the 'seriousness' of mental harm, which does not appear as a requirement in Ethiopian law.[123] In the case at hand, the prosecutor claimed that the victim had sustained a mental injury as a result of perpetrators' acts that involved shouting at him, insulting him, and burning down his house.[124] The Court did not reject the acts on the ground of seriousness nor did it accept them as underlying offenses of genocide. Rather, it dismissed the genocide charge on the ground that the acts were not committed with a plan/intent to destroy a protected group.[125] A dissenting judge, who argued that the perpetrators had a plan/intent to destroy ethnic and political groups, however stated that such acts constituted harm to the mental health of the victim.[126] It is nonetheless arguable that considering such acts as constituting an injury to the mental health of the group is too far-fetched and hardly fits

---

120 See for instance HSC, *SPO* v. *Bekele Kassa et al.*, (Trial Judgment), 26 April 2004, File No. 4/95(00254), 10; FHC, *SPO* v. *Debela Dinsa Wege et al.*, (Sentencing Judgment), 10 August 2007, File No.912/89, 5–7.
121 This will be discussed further in Chapter 7.
122 See Berster, 'Article 11', *supra* note 14, 118–121; F. Jessberger, 'The Definition of and the Elements of the Crime of Genocide' in P. Gaeta (ed.), *The UN Genocide Convention: A Commentary* (Oxford: Oxford University Press, 2009) 87–111, 98.
      See *Kayishema and Ruzindana*, Trial Chamber, (Judgment), *supra* note 20, para. 110.
123 'Seriousness' is also not an element of bodily injury as discussed in section 6.2.3.2. below.
124 *Berehene Kehassaye Woldeselassie et al.*, (Indictment), *supra* note 59, 2.
125 FHC, *Federal Prosecutor* v. *Berehene Kehassaye Woldeselassie et al.*, (Trial Judgment),19 April 2007, File No. 45671/98, 7.
126 FHC, *Federal Prosecutor* v. *Berehene Kehassaye Woldeselassie et al.*, (Trial Judgment: Dissenting Opinion of Judge Aseffa Abereha),19 April 2007, File No. 45671/98, 8.

into the definitional scope of genocide. Even if 'seriousness' of the injury is not expressly mentioned in relation to the underlying offense, its existence should be deduced from the seriousness of genocide itself.[127]

In international criminal law, mental harm was initially aimed to cover cases similar to the production and use of narcotics against the Chinese victims by Japanese perpetrators during the Second World War.[128] In the practice of international courts and tribunals, this has been broadened to include other acts that may constitute 'some type of impairment of mental faculties, or harm that causes serious injury to the mental state of the victim'.[129] Indeed, any act that carries an effect that is not limited to causing 'temporary unhappiness, embarrassment or humiliation' may suffice as mental harm, according to international jurisprudence.[130]

According to Fournet, what prevented such a broad interpretation from amounting to the trivialization of the acts proscribed under Article II(b) of the Genocide Convention is the international criminal tribunals' consistency in examining whether such acts were carried out with the intent to destroy the group;[131] an examination that is often missing in Ethiopian trials. In that sense, one may consider that Ethiopian trials have indeed trivialized the specificity of the crime of genocide. This is also the case with 'bodily harm', as will be discussed below.

6.3.2.2   Bodily Harm

Under Ethiopian law, the material acts that could constitute the crime of causing bodily injury (harm) may range from a simple form of beating to the most severe cases of torture. The shocking acts of torture committed during the

---

127   Nonetheless, in relation to the targeted group, the harm does not need to be so serious as to threaten the physical and biological survival of a group. See Jessberger, 'The Definition of and the Elements of the Crime of Genocide', *supra* note 122, 99.
128   For relevant details on the discussion on mental harm during the drafting of the Genocide Convention, see S. Gorove, 'The Problem of Mental Harm in the Genocide Convention' (1951) 2(2) *Washington University Law Review* 174–187.
129   ICTR, *Prosecutor v. Gacumbitsi,* Trial Chamber, (Judgment), 17 June 2004, ICTR-2001-64-T, paras 291–293.
130   *Akayesu*, Trial Chamber, (Judgment), *supra* note 8, paras 502–504; *Krstić*, Trial Chamber, (Judgment), *supra* note 14, para. 513.
131   Fournet writes, 'while it is perfectly true that [international criminal tribunals] have read the act of 'causing serious bodily or mental harm' in an extensive fashion, they have, however, not unduly stretched and trivialized its definitional scope'. See C.I. Fournet, 'The Actus Reus of Genocide' in P. Behrens and R. Henham (eds.), *Elements of Genocide* (Abingdon: Routledge, 2012) 53–69, 63.

Dergue regime such as the *wofelala*¹³² were prosecuted as genocide under this provision.¹³³ In a similar vein, under international criminal law, the offense of causing serious bodily or mental harm to members of a group appears to be a catch-all offense that comprises several acts including torture, interrogations combined with beatings, inhuman and degrading treatment, persecution, rape and other crimes of sexual violence, and deportation.¹³⁴ The list seems to be non-exhaustive.¹³⁵ For a certain act to fall under this category the test

---

132   Torture techniques such as the *wofelala* were used to obtain confessions or as a form of extrajudicial punishment and caused the victims such severe suffering that the SPO referred to it as 'hell-on-earth'. See *Dem Yazele Dossie*, 63–71.

133   In relation to this, writings on Ethiopia's prosecution of the crimes of the *Dergue* era have assumed that the SPO brought to trial the *Dergue* officials for their involvement in committing horrific acts of torture. See for instance F.K. Tiba, 'The Trial of Mengistu and other Derg Members for Genocide, Torture and Summary Executions in Ethiopia' in C. Murungu and B. Japhet (eds.), *Prosecuting International Crimes in Africa* (Pretoria: Pretoria University Law Press, 2011) 306–324. The 2010 final report of the SPO to the House of People Representatives of Ethiopia was notable, among others, for Mr. Girma Wakjira's (Chief Special Prosecutor) intermittent use of the English word 'torture' throughout his speech. See Ethiopia Television, Documentary: findings of human rights abuse during Red Terror era – Part 1 (ETV Documentary part 1, 2010), available at: <http://www.ethiotube.net/video/8192/documentary-findings-of-human-rights-abuses-during-red-terror-era-part-1> accessed 22 September 2015. From the overall speech, it seemed that 'torture', compared to genocide or murder, was the main crime that was extensively perpetrated during the course of those 17 years. See also T.S. Engelschion, 'Ethiopia: War Crimes and Violations of Human Rights' (1995) 34(9) *Military Law and Law of War Review* 10–23. The SPO itself revealed that it was in possession of sufficient evidence implicating that torture was perpetrated by the *Dergue* officials. See *Dem Yazelew Dossie*, 63–71. Yet, not a single person was prosecuted by the SPO for perpetrating torture as such. The scholastic blur might have resulted from taking the crime of 'grave willful injury' under Article 538 of the Penal Code, which the SPO included in its alternative charges, for a crime of torture. Grave willful injury under Article 538 is however different from the crime of torture: it fulfils none of the elements of torture as understood under international law and as defined under Article 1 of the Convention Against Torture, which Ethiopia signed and ratified (only) in 1994. See Convention against Torture and Other Cruel, Inhuman or Degrading Treatment or Punishment, G.A. res. 39/46, [annex, 39 U.N. GAOR Supp. (No. 51) at 197, U.N. Doc. A/39/51 (1984)], *entered into force* 26 June 1987.

134   See *Akayesu*, Trial Chamber, (Judgment), *supra* note 8, paras 706–7; *Kayishema and Ruzindana*, Trial Chamber, (Judgment), *supra* note 20, para. 108; *Bagilishema*, Trial Chamber, (Judgment), *supra* note 83, para. 59; See *Krstić*, Trial Chamber, (Judgment), *supra* note 14, para. 513.

135   *Akayesu*, Trial Chamber, (Judgment), *supra* note 8, para. 502; *Kayishema and Ruzindana*, Trial Chamber, (Judgment), *supra* note 20, para. 110; *Rutaganda*, Trial Chamber, (Judgment), *supra* note 47, para. 51; *Musema*, Trial Chamber, (Judgment), *supra* note 83, para. 156; *Semanza*, Trial Chamber, (Judgment), *supra* note 83, paras 320–321; *Seromba*, Trial Chamber, (Judgment), *supra* note 14, para. 317.

is whether the act in question caused serious bodily or mental harm, which should be assessed on a case by case basis.[136] In this regard, it is interesting to note that Ethiopian law does not refer to any element of seriousness, as it simply refers to 'injury', as opposed to 'serious injury'. This might have been the result of a conscious choice, given that Ethiopian criminal law knows of different gravity levels of injuries and proscribes both 'grave willful injury'[137] (which might be equated with serious bodily injury) and 'common willful injury',[138] its mitigated form. The former refers to cases where a person:

> a) wounds [another] so as to endanger his life or permanently jeopardize his physical or mental health; or b) maims his body or one of his essential limbs or organs, or disable them, or gravely and conspicuously disfigures him; or c) in any other way inflicts upon another an injury or disease of a serious nature.[139]

Any intentional act of harming the physical health of an individual that falls short of the threshold set for grave willful injury remains a common willful injury. In that sense, the fact that Ethiopian law does not require *seriousness* of an injury as part of the genocidal *actus reus* could be seen as both useful and problematic at the same time. On the one hand, had Ethiopian law required the seriousness of an injury as an underlying offense to genocide, an Ethiopian judge could have understood it within the context of grave willful injury and thus as requiring permanent or irremediable harm; a finding which would have been in contradiction with the decisions of international criminal tribunals.[140] On the other hand, by omitting the requirement of 'seriousness', Ethiopian law might have trivialized the notion of genocide because it may entail that any injury could be regarded as satisfying the *actus reus* of genocide. There appears to be no criterion developed by Ethiopian courts as to what qualifies an act as constituting a bodily injury, which is also the case for mental injury, as noted above. The phrase 'in any way whatsoever' further suggests that such acts are open to judicial interpretation. Ethiopian courts often entered convictions for

---

136 See A. Cassese *et al.*, *Cassese's International Criminal Law* (3rd ed., Oxford: Oxford University Press, 2013) 116. See also *Kayishema and Ruzindana*, Trial Chamber, (Judgment), *supra* note 20, para. 108; *Kajelijeli*, Trial Chamber, (Judgment), *supra* note 98, para. 815.
137 The Penal Code of 1957, Article 358.
138 Ibid., Article 539.
139 Ibid., Article 358.
140 *Akayesu*, Trial Chamber, (Judgment), *supra* note 8, paras 502–504; *Krstić*, Trial Chamber, (Judgment), *supra* note 14, para. 513.

genocide against persons who had acted in a manner that caused injury of *any intensity* to a *single* member of the protected group without carefully considering whether he or she had acted with the intent to destroy the group in whole or in part.[141]

6.3.3 *Imposing Measures to Prevent Propagation or Continued Survival of Members of the Group or their Progeny*

The third genocidal conduct proscribed under Article 281(b) of the Penal Code of 1957 was the act of 'imposing measures to prevent the propagation or continued survival of members of the group or their progeny'; a phrase that contained no discrepancy between the Amharic and English versions of the Code. Its successor, the Criminal Code of 2005, removed the phrase 'or their progeny' from the offense,[142] perhaps because of the redundant aspect of this specification. Under international law, this *actus reus* of genocide is known as 'imposing measures intended to prevent births within the group'.[143] As understood in international criminal law, this offense aims at protecting a group from biological genocide that may result from acts damaging the group's capability to reproduce.[144] Sterilization appears to have pioneered the list of acts that prevent births[145] but other acts such as forced birth control, prohibitions of marriages and segregation of sexes would also fall under this category.[146]

In *Akayesu*, the ICTR held that rape may also fall within this *actus reus* when carried out to change the ethnic identity of the child, i.e. with the intention to pass on the perpetrator's own ethnicity.[147] According to Akhavan however, this finding may have unduly stretched the scope of this act as the ICTR here confused the notion of genocide with that of the crime against humanity of

---

141   See ASC, SPO v. *Abera Ayalew et al.*, (Trial Judgment), 4 December 2006, File No. 16170, 87.
142   See the FDRE Criminal Code, Article 269(b).
143   See Genocide Convention, Article II (d).
144   See Jessberger, 'The Definition of and the Elements of the Crime of Genocide', *supra* note 122, 101–102.
145   See Robinson, *The Genocide Convention*, *supra* note 17, 64. See also Schabas, *Genocide in International Law*, *supra* note 4, 198 *citing* the prosecution of sterilization as genocide as early as 1948 by the Supreme National Tribunal of Poland and the United States Military Tribunal.
146   *Akayesu*, Trial Chamber, (Judgment), *supra* note 8, para. 507. See also *Kayishema and Ruzindana*, Trial Chamber, (Judgment), *supra* note 20, para. 117; *Musema*, Trial Chamber, (Judgment), *supra* note 83, para. 158. Segregation of sexes may occur through the 'systematic allocation of works to men and women in different locations'. See UN Doc, E/477, 26.
147   *Akayesu*, Trial Chamber, (Judgment), *supra* note 8, para. 507.

forced pregnancy as defined under Article 7(2)(f) of the ICC Statute.[148] Yet, as long as rape is committed to change the ethnic identity of the child and as long as, in doing so, the perpetrator intended to destroy the group in whole or in part, there appears to be no reason why this should be characterized as crimes against humanity and not genocide.

Perhaps more unconvincingly, another rape-related significant statement that came out of the *Akayesu* judgment was that rape could be a measure intended to prevent births when the person raped refuses subsequently to procreate.[149] This could be loosely described as genocide through Rape Trauma Syndrome (RTS). Nonetheless, unlike in the case of rapes aimed at changing the ethnic composition of the group, RTS-genocide does not seem to automatically fall under the category of genocidal acts intended to prevent births. This is not because a victim of rape may not refuse to procreate but because the perpetrator may not have foreseen such a refusal, in which case it could be unconvincing to conclude that the perpetrator *intended* to impose on his victim a psychological trauma that could lead to a refusal of procreation. Furthermore, given that acts intended to prevent births should be seen within the context of genocidal *mens rea*, rape may only fall under this category if it is possible to prove that the person who committed the rape did so with the intent to destroy the group – here, by traumatizing its members into refusing to procreate.

At the international level, RTS-genocide that relies on the victim's refusal to procreate is, in fact, an *obiter dictum*, the significance of which is not yet known, given that no accused so far has been charged with genocide through that kind of rape. Nonetheless, RTS-genocide's emphasis on the perceived or real effects of a criminal act is troubling insofar as it relies entirely on the effects of the rape (the victim's refusal to procreate) before looking into the intent of the perpetrator. Such a construction defies the concept of intent in criminal law in general and finds no support in the case law of the international tribunals. As mentioned in *Kayishema and Ruzindana,* the formation of the specific intent must occur 'prior to the commission of the genocidal acts'.[150] If that intent was not formed at the time of the commission of the crime, attempting to establish it retrospectively out of the consequences of the prohibited act may amount to reducing genocidal *mens rea* to recklessness or *dolus eventualis*. Perhaps, what the *Akayesu* Trial Chamber attempted to formulate as RTS-genocide may best

---

148 See P. Akhavan, 'The Crime of Genocide in the ICTR Jurisprudence' (2005) 3(1) *Journal of International Criminal Justice* 989–1006, 1005.
149 *Akayesu*, Trial Chamber, (Judgment), *supra* note 8, para. 508.
150 See *Kayishema and Ruzindana*, Trial Chamber, (Judgment), *supra* note 20, para. 91.

fit into the notion of crimes against humanity if committed in the context of a widespread or systematic attack against a civilian population.

Turning to the Ethiopian situation, none of the Ethiopian trials have discussed rape as genocide for such an act was not identified as having occurred in Ethiopia. Nonetheless, it is essential to point out that the specific provision in Ethiopian law is not immune from the recurrent problem of omissions and additions when juxtaposed with the Genocide Convention. As for the omission, it has not included the word 'intended', which might indicate that, under Ethiopian law, this offense is one that requires a result, i.e. that the measures imposed have actually prevented births, a proof of which is not needed in international criminal law.[151]

Regarding the additions, Ethiopian law contains the phrase 'continued survival of members of the group', which does not appear in the Genocide Convention and which might indicate that the offense is not confined to preventing births, an act which the law also covers under the term 'propagation'. It is however unclear what other acts this phrase actually encompasses. Although erased from the 2005 Criminal Code, the Penal Code of 1957 also used the term 'progeny', the meaning of which is fairly opaque. A positive interpretation might have considered that the legislator wanted to give special attention to the children by explicitly ensuring that they should not be subjected to acts that are intended to destroy their future capability to reproduce through, for example, enforced or clandestine sterilization or irreversible birth control vaccination. As mentioned earlier, this addition was however considered unnecessary and redundant: in stating the reason for removing the word 'progeny', the *Explanatory Notes* to the Criminal Code stated that children of the group were already included in the expression 'members of the group'.[152] Indeed, there is nothing in Article II(c) of the Genocide Convention that suggests the age of the victim to be a decisive element for the purpose of considering measures intended to prevent births. Accordingly, it could be submitted here that the current Ethiopian law is in line with the Genocide Convention.

6.3.4 *Compulsory Movement or Dispersion of Peoples or Children*

'Compulsory movement or dispersion of peoples or children' represents the fourth *actus reus* of genocide and the only one to have been written into the law with no discrepancy between the English and Amharic versions of both the Penal Code of 1957 and the 2005 Criminal Code.[153] Since there was no

---

151 See Berster, 'Article II', *supra* note 14, 127–128; Schabas, *Genocide in International Law, supra* note 4, 198.
152 See FDRE Criminal Code, *Explanatory Notes*, Article 269.
153 The Penal Code of 1957, Article 281(c); FDRE Criminal Code, Article 269(c).

prosecution on the basis of this conduct and since the Genocide Convention does not use this terminology, what this act actually covers is open to interpretation. It appears to contain similarities with the act of 'forcibly transferring children of the group to another group', mentioned under Article II(e) of the Convention. There are however some clear differences.

Firstly, the Ethiopian law refers to 'people or children' instead of 'children of the group'. This could be seen as the fundamental difference between the two laws, as the whole purpose of Article II(e) of the Genocide Convention lies in protecting the group through protecting not the other members, but exclusively the children of the group. Through protecting the children from getting forcibly transferred to another group, the international law on genocide has proscribed the cultural destruction of the protected group.[154] By treating children and the rest of the members of the group alike, the Ethiopian law ignores the Convention's reasons for focusing on the children, namely, that cultural genocide may occur by subjecting persons to another culture and mentality at a time when they are of 'impressionable and receptive age'.[155]

Secondly, unlike the Convention, the Ethiopian law does not use 'transferring', but 'movement or dispersion'. Although the violation of Article II(e) of the Convention may involve preparatory acts such identifying the children and the group to which they would be transferred, it is essentially the actual act of 'transferring' that completes the offense in question. Transferring, as an 'essential element' of the offense, is a process that begins with an act of *separation* of the children from their group and ends with an act of *placing* them with another group.[156] Such a process is admittedly not fully captured in the expression 'movement or dispersion' as used in the Ethiopian law. That 'movement or dispersion' is not accompanied by another important word, i.e. 'group', further broadens the difference between the municipal and international laws. In short, even if one may argue that 'movement or dispersion' in this context may

---

154 Berster, 'Article II', *supra* note 14, 128–129.
155 Secretariat Draft Commentary (UN Doc. E/447), 27. This reason might have affected interpretations regarding the age of childhood. In particular, there are different opinions as to whether the near-adult children may fall under the protection of Article II(e) of the Convention. See Berster, 'Article II', *supra* note 14, 129; Schabas, *Genocide in International Law, supra* note 4, 203. See however the ICC Statute, Elements of Crimes, Article 6 (d), which states: 'The perpetrator knew, or should have known, that the person or persons were under the age of *18 years*'. Emphasis added.
156 See K. Mundorff, 'Other People's Children: A Textual Contextual Interpretation of the Genocide Convention, Article 2(e)', 2009 (50)1 *Harvard International Law Journal* 61–129, 91; G, Werle and F. Jessberger, *Principles of International Criminal Law* (3rd ed., Oxford: Oxford University Press, 2014) 203.

inevitably begin with an act of separation of children from their group, it does not imply their placement with another group. For the crime to be qualified as such under the law of the Genocide Convention however, the end part of the process is essential, although proof that the children have integrated within the other group is not required.[157]

Thirdly, rather than using the conventional term 'forcibly', the Ethiopian law prefers 'compulsory'. Although these two words could admittedly be used interchangeably, compulsorily – unlike forcibly – does not necessarily imply the use of physical force. In ordinary usage, one may consider that compulsory transfer occurs when, for example, a government issues a decree imposing an obligation to the parents to comply with a set of plans put in place to transfer children of one group to another. In a similar context, the concept of forcible transfer may come into play if the government uses force to enforce that same law against those who refuse or resist its application. Nonetheless, this difference may not have practical relevance, given that 'forcibly' has not been interpreted conservatively. The term received a broad meaning by the ICTR in *Akayesu*,[158] before it was given a wider definition under the ICC Elements of Crimes, which state that:

> the term "forcibly" is not restricted to physical force, but may include threat of force or coercion, such as that caused by fear of violence, duress, detention, psychological oppression or abuse of power, against such person or persons or another person, or by taking advantage of a coercive environment.[159]

In search of a proof that the crime of 'compulsory movement or dispersion of peoples or children' under Ethiopian law was an entirely new addition[160] to the Convention's list of genocidal acts, one may find some guidance in the Penal

---

157   See Berster, 'Article II', *supra* note 14, 130.
158   *Akayesu*, Trial Chamber, (Judgment), *supra* note 8, para. 509.
159   ICC Elements of Crime, Article 6, Element 1, *fn.* 5.
160   It is hard to say with certainty what the law has meant to address with the crime of 'compulsory movement or dispersion of peoples or children'. One may wonder if the offense envisaged cases of forced villagization or resettlement, where members of a community are moved and dispersed across the country against their will. Such instances have occurred in Ethiopia on several occasions for reasons related to droughts and famine. During the *Dergue* regime, where several poorly managed resettlements were carried out, critics have compared the situation to the Nazi concentration camps. See R. Pankhurst, *The History of Famine and Epidemics in Ethiopia prior to the Twentieth Century* (Addis Ababa: Relief and Rehabilitation Commission, 1985/1986). Nonetheless, there is no need to have an independent *actus reus* to proscribe such conducts for as long

Code of Eritrea,[161] where, until 2015, the 1957 Ethiopian Penal Code applied, owing to the country's history as part of Ethiopia until 1991. Article 107 of the Eritrean Penal Code of 2015 reproduced all of the underlying offenses of genocide contained in Article 281 of the Ethiopian Penal Code[162] with one notable exception: while Article 107(e) lists 'compulsory movement or dispersion of the group or their children', Article 107(f) also reproduces the conventional act of 'forcibly transferring children of the group to another group'.[163] These two distinct sub-articles seem to indicate that these two acts are different and that, by only integrating the former, Ethiopian law does depart from the Genocide Convention. In the absence of judicial interpretation, the extent of this differentiation however remains unclear.

6.3.5 *Placing Members of the Group under Living Conditions Calculated to Result in Their Death*

The fourth physical element of genocide under Ethiopian law is the offense of 'placing members of the group under living conditions calculated to result in their death', as enshrined in the English version of the Penal Code of 1957 and the English and Amharic versions of the 2015 Criminal Code. Its international counterpart employs a slightly different terminology, referring to the act of 'deliberately inflicting on the group conditions of life calculated to bring about its physical destruction in whole or in part'.[164]

In the Amharic version of the Penal Code, this offense fell under a prolix phrase which could loosely translate into 'causing social harm to bring the total destruction of members of a group by placing them under servitude in a certain place and under conditions that could result in their death'.[165] In practice, the SPO referred to this offense as 'harming members of a group to cause their total destruction by putting them in a certain place and under conditions that could result in their death'.[166] The case law reveals that this offense has four main elements: harm, place, condition, and death.

---

as they are carried out with genocidal *mens rea* they could be treated as genocidal conducts of 'deliberately inflicting on the group conditions of life calculated to bring about its physical destruction'.

161   See the Penal Code of the State of Eritrea, Article 107, unofficial translation available at: <http://www.ilo.org/dyn/natlex/docs/ELECTRONIC/101051/121587/F567697075/ERI101051%20Eng.pdf> accessed 29 September 2019.
162   Ibid.
163   Ibid.
164   The Genocide Convention, Article II(c).
165   The Penal Code of 1957, Article 281(c).
166   See *Colonel Mengistu Hailemariam et al.*, (Revised Indictment), *supra* note 112, 106. Translation by the Author. The Original Amharic version of the indictment

With respect to harm, the SPO merely referred to acts of causing external and internal injury, as discussed above under section 5.4.2. Accordingly, the SPO cases mostly focused on torture as constituting harm.[167] With respect to the place, the SPO's list included black-sites, dungeons, interrogation rooms and torture chambers, such as the CRID investigation centers, police force special investigation centers, *Meakalawi* (the central prison), and an old mansion in Addis Ababa used to be known by the *Dergue* interrogators as *Bermuda* or *Setan Bet* (Satan's House).[168] With respect to the conditions element, the SPO mentioned that victims were kept in rooms without sufficient food and air, in a manner that deprived them of proper sleep and with no access to medical care.[169] With respect to death, the SPO indictments mentioned that, after being tortured, victims were generally left to die in those places.

For Ethiopian courts, what was needed to enter a conviction was for the SPO to establish the above elements; a judicial practice which led to two series of problems. Firstly, it did not reflect the spirit of the domestic law in question, according to which this particular form of *actus reus* was not meant to include interrogation related acts of torture and inhumane treatments in prisons cells. As can be inferred from the use of the Amharic word ግዞት (servitude) used in the context of ባንድ ስፍራ በግዞት ማስቀመጥ (keeping them under servitude in one place), the domestic law was aimed at criminalizing situations in which members of a protected group could be kept under servitude in places with conditions that could bring their gradual death. A point of concern may however arise out of the Ethiopian law's expression of 'servitude' which includes a requirement of *place*, in the sense that the infliction of acts of servitude may only be carried out after putting the victims in one particular place. This additional requirement might have meant to refer *inter alia* to camps, parts of towns or regions, deserts or mining areas to which people could be expelled or detained. It thus risks leaving aside cases in which this requirement of place is not fulfilled.

Secondly, the manner in which the *Dergue* trials have understood and interpreted this conduct is different from how its counterpart is interpreted in international criminal law, where the act of deliberately inflicting on the group conditions of life calculated to bring about its physical destruction has been

---

reads: '[የ]ቡድን አባላት ጨርሰው እንዲጠፉ የሞት አደጋ በሚያደርስባቸው ሁኔታ ባንድ ሥፍራ ባማስቀመጥ ጉዳት እንዲደርስባቸው ማድረግ'.

167 See above, section 5.4.2.
168 See *Dem Yazele Dossie*, 69–71.
169 See *Colonel Mengistu Hailemariam et al.*, (Revised Indictment), *supra* note 112, 106–122.

largely understood as 'slow death genocide'.[170] According to judgments of the ICTY and ICTR, this underlying offense may include acts such as lack of proper housing, clothing, hygiene and medical care or excessive work or physical exertion including rape, the starving of a group of people, reducing required medical services below a minimum, and withholding sufficient living accommodation for a reasonable period.[171] This list is admittedly non-exhaustive and, as Robinson stated, 'it is impossible to enumerate in advance the 'conditions of life' that would come within the prohibition of Article II' of the Genocide Convention.[172]

By referring to 'placing members of the group under living conditions calculated to result in their death' in both its versions, the 2015 Criminal Code mirrors the Convention's formulation. Ethiopian courts could thus enter a conviction for genocide on the basis of various acts as long as they do not overlook the requirement that such acts need to be committed with intent to destroy. Furthermore, neither Ethiopian law nor the Genocide Convention require the materialization of the destruction. Yet, Ethiopian courts appear to have required proof of a result. The SPO cases, in particular, have emphasized that harm must have actually occurred against the victims, thus confusing this particular act with the acts of killing or of causing bodily or mental harm. On closer look, the SPO's interest in prosecuting the *Dergue* for this specific genocidal act seems to have been linked not to the death of the victims, but to their disappearance. This was indicated by phrases such as 'left to die inside those places' and 'their bodies were never found'.[173] It was also expressly claimed by the SPO in *Solomon Negussie et al.* that enforced disappearance could be covered under the genocidal act of placing members of the group under living conditions calculated to result in their death.[174] This however does not solve the uncertainty as to the harm requirement since the crime of enforced disappearance is expressly listed as a distinct genocidal act in Ethiopian law.

---

170 See Fournet, 'The Actus Reus of Genocide', *supra note* 131, 65. See also *Kayishema and Ruzindana*, Trial Chamber, (Judgment), *supra* note 20, para. 115.

171 See *Kayishema and Ruzindana*, Trial Chamber, (Judgment), *supra* note 20, para. 116; *Musema*, Trial Chamber, (Judgment), *supra* note 83, para. 157; ICTY, *Prosecutor v. Stakić*, Trial Chamber, (Judgment), 31 July 2003, IT-97-24-T, para 517; ICTY, *Prosecutor v. Sikirica et al.*, Trial Chamber, (Judgment on Defence Motions to Acquit), 3 September 2010 IT-95-8-T, para. 42.

172 Robinson, *The Genocide Convention*, *supra* note 17, 63–64.

173 In this regard, the English version of Article 281(c) of the Penal Code of 1957 proscribed the disappearance of members of the group as an alternative to causing their death. This is discussed further below.

174 See HSC, SPO v. *Solomon Negussie et al.*, (SPO Response to Preliminary Objections), 24 May 1999, File No. 4/91, 32.

6.3.6   *Enforced Disappearance*

Although it is well-established under international law that the Genocide Convention's list of the *actus reus* elements of genocide is exhaustive,[175] Ethiopian law nonetheless added the crime of enforced disappearance.[176] Under Article 281 of the Penal Code of 1957, enforced disappearance had a sort of shadowy existence. It was mentioned as an alternative to causing death under paragraph c of the provision, which proscribed 'forcibly moving peoples or children from place to place, or causing their dispersion, or placing them under living conditions calculated to result in their death *or disappearance*'.[177] In the *Dergue* trials, locating the whereabouts of several victims proved challenging, although the SPO had evidence showing that at a certain point they were arrested and tortured by the regime or that they were released from prison but never to return home. In spite of Article 281, some of the courts, in line with the case law of both the IACtHR and the ECtHR, assumed that the victims were taken out of the prisons for execution and thus considered such instances as acts of killing.[178]

More radically, the 2005 Criminal Code expressly lists enforced disappearance as an independent *actus reus* element of genocide. If it retains the Penal Code's criminalization of the act of 'placing people under living conditions calculated to result in their *disappearance*',[179] it also specifically lists, under its Article 269 (a), the act of 'causing the disappearance of members of a group in any way whatsoever'. As stated in the *Explanatory Notes* to the Criminal Code, the express listing of enforced disappearance as a genocidal act resulted from the need to recognize the challenges in the *Dergue* trials and deter similar atrocities in the future.[180]

Perhaps paradoxically, enforced disappearance is not a self-standing crime and is only punishable in Ethiopia when committed as an act of genocide. The exact elements of the crime are however left undefined and, although it was noted in the *Dergue* trials that the victims were made to disappear, there was no

---

175   For a detailed background of the exhaustive nature of the list of *actus reus* elements of genocide under the Genocide Convention, see Schabas, *Genocide in International Law*, supra note 4, 174–175.

176   It may be pointed out here that some other national laws have also expanded the *actus reus* elements of genocide. See B. Saul, 'The Implementation of the Genocide Convention at National Level' in P. Gaeta (ed.), *The UN Genocide Convention: A Commentary* (Oxford: Oxford University Press, 2009) 58–86, 65.

177   See FDRE Criminal Code, Article 269 (c). Emphasis added.

178   See above, section 5.4.1.

179   See the FDRE Criminal Code, Article 269(c).

180   See FDRE Criminal Code, *Explanatory Notes*, Article 269.

THE CRIME OF GENOCIDE IN ETHIOPIAN TRIALS: ELEMENTS OF THE CRIME   271

significant discussion as to these elements. Although Ethiopia is not a Party to the International Convention for the Protection of All Persons from Enforced Disappearance (CED),[181] Ethiopian courts could admittedly find guidance in the definition it provides:

> enforced disappearance is considered to be the arrest, detention, abduction or any other form of deprivation of liberty by agents of the State or by persons or groups of persons acting with the authorization, support or acquiescence of the State, followed by a refusal to acknowledge the deprivation of liberty or by concealment of the fate or whereabouts of the disappeared person, which place such a person outside the protection of the law.[182]

By not criminalizing enforced disappearance as a discrete offence, Ethiopia has also failed to comply with Articles 3 and 4 of the General Assembly Resolution 47/133.[183] As a result, acts that could constitute enforced disappearances may remain unpunishable in Ethiopia, as was the case in some of the *Dergue* trials where courts were unwilling to treat disappeared persons as murdered.[184] It is only when it can be proven that enforced disappearances are genocidal acts, that is, committed with the intent to destroy a group, that they can be prosecuted before Ethiopian courts: short of this intent, enforced disappearances will go unpunished since, as discussed in Chapter 5, Ethiopian law does not recognize crimes against humanity.

6.4   Mental Element of Genocide

Of all the elements of genocide, the mental element is admittedly the most challenging to analyze. Genocide in international law is a crime of specific

---

181   International Convention for the Protection of All Persons from Enforced Disappearance, G.A. res. 61/177, UN Doc. A/RES/61/177 (2006), adopted 20 December 2006. To date, Ethiopia has neither signed nor ratified the CED. It also does not accept individual complaint procedures and inquiry procedures under the Convention. See <https://tbinternet.ohchr.org/_layouts/TreatyBodyExternal/Treaty.aspx?CountryID=59&Lang=EN> accessed 29 September 2019.
182   Ibid., Article 2.
183   See A/RES/47/133, Declaration on the Protection of All Persons from Enforced Disappearance, 18 December 1992, Articles 3 and 4.
184   See *Amanshoa Gebrewolde et al.,* (Trial Ruling), *supra* note 105, 362–363; FSC, SPO v. *Hailu Burayu et al.,* (Trial Ruling),13 June 2003, File No. 428/92, 77, 79.

(special) intent. Mere negligence or recklessness does not entail genocidal culpability.[185] Besides, the existence of a 'plan' does not constitute an element of genocide in international law,[186] despite scholarly opinions purporting that genocide cannot be committed without a state plan or policy.[187] The specific intent required for genocide has specific ingredients: intent, to destroy, in whole or in part, and 'as such'. This section is structured so as to offer a separate discussion on each of these ingredients.

Regarding the 'intent' element of specific intent, Ethiopian law carries ambiguity as to whether the required genocidal *mens rea* is a 'plan' or an 'intent', as noted in Chapter 5.[188] Ethiopian law has, in fact, evolved from describing the mental element of genocide using ዓቅድ (plan/intent) in the Penal Code of 1957 to using አሳብ (intent) in the 2005 Criminal Code.[189] Nonetheless, two of the four trials (the *Dergue* and the *Anuak-Nuwer* trials) were conducted on the basis of the law of ዓቅድ (plan/intent) while the remaining two (the CUD and the *Oromo-Gumuz* trials) employed the law of አሳብ(intent).[190] This demands a separate examination of the two categories of trials in order to avoid any confusion that would arise from a combined treatment of the trials. As regards the remaining ingredients, (to destroy, in whole or in part, and 'as such') all of the trials are discussed together.

6.4.1   Intent/Plan: 'ዓቅድ' in the Dergue and the Anuak-Nuwer Trials

From a plain reading of the law, the word ዓቅድ (intent/plan) proved to be ambiguous.[191] The analysis of the practice may however offer some help. In the

---

185   For proposals made during the drafting of the Genocide Convention to include negligent genocide or genocide in the second degree, see Schabas, *Genocide in International Law*, supra note 4, 269.

186   *Prosecutor v. Jelisić*, Appeals Chamber, (Judgment), 5 July 2001, IT-95-10-A, para. 48; *Sikirica et al.*, Trial Chamber, (Judgment on Defence Motions to Acquit), supra note 171, para. 62; ICTR, *Prosecutor v. Semanza*, Appeals Chamber, (Judgment), 20 May 2005, ICTR-97-20-A, para. 260; ICTR, *Prosecutor v. Simba* Appeals Chamber, (Judgment), 27 November 2007, ICTR-01-76-A, para. 260; ICTR, *Prosecutor v. Kayishema and Ruzindana*, Appeals Chamber, (Judgment), 1 June 2001, ICTR-95-1-A, para. 172.

187   According to Schabas, the requirement of a plan as an element of genocide was widely debated upon in the Rome Conference of 1998. See on this Schabas, *Genocide in International Law*, supra note 4, 130–131. A draft element's text prepared by the U.S. at the Rome Conference contained plan to destroy instead of intent to destroy. See UN Doc. A/CONF.183/C.1/L.10, 1 *cited* in Schabas, *Genocide in International Law*, supra note 4, 110 fn. 337.

188   See in particular Chapter 4, section 4.3.3.

189   See ibid.

190   See above section 5.2.

191   See in particular Chapter 5, section 5.3.3.

Anuak-Nuwer trials, the Federal Prosecutor accused the defendants of having committed genocide by attacking 32 members of the *Nuwer* ethnic group while they were travelling by bus together with other (non-*Nuwer*) South Sudanese refugees.[192] The relevant part of the indictment meant to indicate *mens rea* was not more than a confusing assortment of several words such as intention, desire, willingness, and ዕቅድ (intent/plan). According to the prosecutor, the defendants acted 'with a great desire and complete willingness to intentionally cause harm against others and by planning to destroy the Nuwer ethnic group in whole...'[193] None of these elements were discussed by the court. Neither the ruling nor the judgment addressed genocidal *mens rea* in any meaningful way, although three of the defendants were found guilty of genocide against ethnic groups because they killed six of the 32 members of the *Nuwer* ethnic group.[194] Precisely, no mention of intent or plan to destroy could be found in the court's analysis. Apparently, the facts that the *actus reus* (killing) was fulfilled and that the victims were targeted on the basis of their ethnicity was regarded sufficient to convict the defendants of genocide. This is however not how genocide is understood in international law. As noted above, establishing the *general mens rea*, i.e. the fact that the attack was targeted against a member or members of a group with the knowledge that the victim belonged to the targeted groups, only proves the underlying offence of genocide,[195] not the genocide itself, that is, the specific intent to destroy the targeted group.[196]

In the *Dergue* trials, the whole accusation of political genocide relied upon the existence of a State ዕቅድ (intent/plan) to eliminate members of political opposition groups. The SPO's indictments alleged that the *Dergue* acted with ዕቅድ (intent/plan) to destroy political groups. From the context, the use of ዕቅድ (intent/plan) in the indictments refers to a plan. In the cases involving the so-called 'big fish', the SPO indictments alleged that the top officials had, in collaboration, planned (በገብረርነት በማቀድ) to destroy political opposition groups.[197] In its final report, the SPO mentioned that the genocide during the *Dergue* was committed pursuant to a state plan and policy in which crimes were planned

---

192   See *Gure Uchala Ugira et al.*, (Indictment) *supra* note 58, 1.
193   Ibid., Translation by the author. The original (Amharic) text reads: 'ተከሳሾቹ በወንጀል ስራ በሚሰጠው ውጤት ሙሉ ተካፋይ በመሆን በከፈተኛ ፍላጎት ሆን ብለው ሰዉን ለመጉዳት ፍጽም ፍቃደኛ በመሆን ...የኑዌር በሔረሰብ በመላው ለማጥፋት በማቀድ'.
194   *Gure Uchala Ugira et al.*, (Trial Judgment), *supra* note 67, 6.
195   See section 6.3. above.
196   This is further discussed below under 'to destroy'.
197   See *Colonel Mengistu Hailemariam et al.*, (Revised Indictment), *supra* note 112, 7; FHC, SPO v. *Melaku Teferra*, (Indictment), 23 November 1996, File No. 03112, 1; FHC, SPO v. *Getachew Tekeba*, (Indictment), 23 November 1996, File No. 914/89,1.

following overt official policies and executed through the involvement of a large number of people and state infrastructure.[198] In fact, for the SPO, the international crime of genocide required the existence of a state plan or policy, which it referred to by clearly stating that genocide is a crime the commission of which is state-sponsored in the sense that it requires the existence of state action or policy.[199]

From the language and the context in which it was used in the SPO indictments, there is further evidence that ዕቅድ (intent/plan) referred to 'a plan' rather than to intent. According to the indictments, it is the *Dergue's* establishment of institutions, commands, orders, campaigns, and the mobilization of state resources that indicated the existence of a plan. Furthermore, the use of the Amharic adjective, የተነደፈውን, (which means contrived or laid out), shows that the SPO used ዕቅድ (intent/plan) to mean 'plan', not intent.[200] This could be inferred further from phrases such as 'overarching plan to destroy contrived' by the top officials (ለማጥፋት የተነደፈውን አጠቃላይ ዕቅድ), which the middle and low level officials had allegedly accepted to execute.[201] Other indictments alleged the existence of a comprehensive plan to destroy[202] while others accused the *Dergue* of having 'laid out an unlawful plan to destroy'.[203]

Furthermore, the SPO's references to the existence of a plan to destroy opposition groups was not limited to cases involving top-ranking *Dergue* officials. The SPO's use of the word ዕቅድ to refer to a plan can be deduced from several cases involving middle and low level *Dergue* officials, who collaborated among themselves and planned the execution of the overarching plan.[204] In

198 *Dem Yazele Dossie*, 104–107.
199 *Solomon Negussie et al.*, (SPO Response to Preliminary Objections), *supra* note 174, 4.
200 On the specific use of the term የተነደፈውን with the word 'plan', See T.L. Kane, *Amharic-English Dictionary: Volume I* (Wiesbaden: Otto Harrassowitz, 1990) 1057.
201 These types of cases mainly dealt with crimes committed by officials in various provinces, as opposed to the highest ranking *Dergue* officials who were mainly based in the central government in Addis Ababa, the capital. See for instance OSC, SPO v. *Colonel Sahile Barie et al.*, (Indictment), 16 November 1999, File No. 7/92, 2; TSC, SPO v. *Colonel Ayenaw Mengistie et al.*, (Indictment), 23 November 1999, File No. 3/90, 6; ASC, SPO v. *Brigadier General Girma Neway et al.*, (Indictment), 23 December 1997, File No. 24/90, 2; HSC, SPO v. *Denbi Disassa et al.*, (Indictment), 3 October 2002, File No. 3/95. 2; FHC, SPO v. *Gesgese Geberemeskel Ateraga et al.*, (Indictment), 23 December 1997, File No. 03099, 15.
202 See FHC, SPO v. *Zenebe Ayele et al.*, (Indictment of 23 December 1997), File No 641/89, 3.
203 See OSC, SPO v. *Colonel Debeb Hurrissie et al.*, (Indictment. 16 November 1999) File No. 463/92, 5.
204 See *Colonel Sahile Barie et al.*, (Indictment), *supra* note 201, 2; *Colonel Ayenaw Mengistie et al.*, (Indictment), *supra* note 201, 6; *Brigadier General Girma Neway et al.*, (Indictment), *supra* note 201, 2; *Denbi Disassa et al.*, (Indictment), *supra* note 201, 2; *Gesgese Geberemeskel Ateraga et al.*, (Indictment), *supra* note 201, 15.

fact, planning in the *Dergue* cases does not necessarily require the participation of two or more persons, as is also the case in the case law of the UNICTs and the ICC.[205] In *Geremew Debele*, a single individual was accused of planning on his own to execute the overarching plan to destroy political groups.[206]

Nonetheless, Ethiopian courts have not discussed the issue of a plan to destroy in a consistent and vivid manner. In *Geremew Debele*, the first genocide judgment issued by an Ethiopian court, the court framed three main issues that were directly related to the plan to destroy: i) whether there was an overarching plan to destroy political groups; ii) whether the defendant, as the head of national slaughterhouses, had endorsed the overarching plan; and iii) whether the defendant has executed the overarching plan.[207] However, neither the ruling nor the judgment meaningfully discussed the existence of the overarching plan to destroy. The existence of such a plan was established based on one single document: the WPE membership application form submitted to the *Dergue* by the defendant in 1980.[208] According to the court, the defendant mentioned in the membership application form that 'he had already accepted the overarching plan and eliminated members of political groups in his organization'.[209]

The *Geremew Debele* case was not an isolated instance in this regard. Most of the *Dergue* cases did not discuss how and when the overarching plan to destroy was contrived. The apparent exception, if not the only, is the FHC's ruling in *Mengistu et al*, which started its examination of the SPO's accusation by framing it as: 'whether the defendants had ዐቅድ *(the intent/plan) to destroy* in whole or in part a section of population unified by political affiliation …'.[210] After examining numerous evidence, the Court concluded that the *Dergue* was established *from the outset* with ዐቅድ (intent/plan) to destroy opposition political groups which it carried with itself all along.[211]

---

205 See *Prosecutor v. Jean-Pierre Bemba Gombo et al.*, Trial Chamber, (Judgment), 19 October 2016, ICC-01/05-02/13, para. 29.
206 FHC, SPO v. *Geremew Debele*, (Indictment), 23 December 1997, File No. 952/89, 1.
207 FHC, SPO v. *Geremew Debele*, (Ruling on Preliminary Objections), 13 April 1998, File No. 952/89, 15.
208 FHC, SPO v. *Geremew Debele*, (Trial Ruling), 8 February 1999, File No. 952/89, 80; *Geremew Debele*, (Trial Judgment), *supra* note 7, 8–9.
209 *Geremew Debele*, (Trial Judgment), *supra* note 7, 8–9.
210 Emphasis added. See *Colonel Mengistu Hailemariam et al.*, (Trial Ruling), *supra* note 9, 5.
211 Ibid., 5–14. Emphasis added. Nonetheless, the defendants later on attempted to show that the *Dergue* was not established with a plan to destroy political groups, in support of which they stated that the *Dergue's* establishment had a popular basis. The FHC dismissed the defense by simply stating that such a fact 'could not have led to the conclusion that the *Dergue* could not have developed the intent to destroy opposition political groups after it was established'. See *Colonel Mengistu Hailemariam et al.*, (Trial Judgment), *supra* note

The following development provide the factual details on how the *Dergue's* ዐቅድ intent/plan to destroy was established,[212] following which an analysis will be made on whether and how the courts interpreted ዐቅድ in terms of plan and intent.

6.4.1.1   Establishing ዐቅድ in the *Dergue* Trials: Factual Issues

In its very hard-to-read ruling of 21 January 2003,[213] the FHC discussed numerous pieces of evidence that helped to reach the conclusion that the *Dergue* had ዐቅድ (intent/plan) to destroy political groups. In particular, the court's analysis relied on: *i)* official commands, pronouncements, and campaigns of violence; *ii)* establishment of institutions of violence; *iii)* restructuring institutions of violence; and *iv)* direct involvement of state officials in orchestrating and implementing the system of violence.[214]

6.4.1.1.1   *Orders, Announcements, and Campaigns of Violence*

Under this category, the Court evaluated evidence that included public statements, military commands, minutes of meetings, and campaign orders in connection with the removal of political opposition groups by the *Dergue*.[215] In this regard, it was established in evidence that the *Dergue* had given *combat and security commands* immediately following its ascension to power.[216] The minutes of 19 November 1976 from the *Dergue*'s National Assembly sessions revealed that a decision was reached by the *Dergue* to destroy groups that had opposing political views to the revolution.[217] Following this decision, a memo was dispatched to selected offices with orders to take every measure necessary

---

10, 111–112. This conclusion was not explained further, and it clearly contradicted the same Court's ruling that the *Dergue* was, from the beginning, established with the intent to destroy.

212   The factual details mentioned here are those discussed mainly by the FHC in *Mengistu et al*. As a result, the facts provided here may appear different from what is recorded in other studies that are based predominantly on other sources.

213   See *Colonel Mengistu Hailemariam et al.,* (Trial Ruling), *supra* note 9, 5–16. This ruling is difficult to read in the sense that not only was it not paragraphed but also because it was written without punctuation marks which makes the reader struggle to know where a sentence begins and ends.

214   Ibid., 5–16.

215   Ibid., 5–7.

216   Ibid. The commands were given between 7 July and 16 October 1974 to destroy unidentified individuals and groups that were engaged in countering activities that were being carried out by the *Dergue*.

217   Ibid. In the Assembly Sessions, a determination was made as to which government organ was responsible to carry out the decision.

THE CRIME OF GENOCIDE IN ETHIOPIAN TRIALS: ELEMENTS OF THE CRIME 277

to implement the *Dergue*'s future plan to destroy the enemies of the revolution and reactionaries (አድራጊያን).²¹⁸

In addition, there were two public announcements that the Court considered relevant to establish the existence of the *Dergue*'s ዓቅድ (intent/plan) to destroy members and affiliates of political groups. The first related to Colonel Mengistu Hailemariam's radio speech known as *Key Shiber Yefafame* ('let the Red-Terror intensify').²¹⁹ The second was Captain Legesse Asfaw's announcement in which he pledged on behalf of the *Dergue* to continue the *Netsa Ermija* (free measure),²²⁰ and promised that the *Kebeles* would not be held accountable for doing so.²²¹

The Court also found that the SPO had submitted sufficient evidence establishing that the *Dergue* had planned and carried out anti-revolutionary elimination campaigns on several occasions.²²² Following a study conducted by the Revolutionary Information Unit (RUI)²²³ on the identity of anti-revolutionary groups,²²⁴ a campaign dubbed 'Hit the Anti-Revolutionaries' and spearheaded

---

218   Following the decision, a memo written by the then Chairman of the *Dergue*, Brigadier General Tefer Benti, was dispatched to the provinces and the various offices, including the Special Supreme Court Martial, indicating the *Dergue*'s future plan. Ibid., 8.
219   The speech was made following the assassination of Colonel Atenafu Abate. In the speech aired on Ethiopian Radio, the *Dergue* called upon the public to blazon Red-Terror in the reactionary neighbourhoods, to consider the impeding and halting of anti-revolutionary intrigues its primary job, and to intensify the Red-Terror. The *Dergue* also promised that it would stand with the public in carrying out these activities. *Colonel Mengistu Hailemariam et al.*, (Trial Ruling), *supra* note 9, 8. It should be pointed out that this evidence was about the intensification of the Red-Terror As such, the exact date on which the Red-Terror was launched was not discussed by the Court.
220   *Netsa Ermija* was a codename denoting the permission given to the local actors (*Kebeles*) to take revolutionary measures (killing anti-revolutionaries) without seeking approval from higher level government officials.
221   *Colonel Mengistu Hailemariam et al.*, (Trial Ruling), *supra* note 9, 8. Based on evidence obtained from the Ethiopian Radio Organization, an announcement was made by Captain Legesse Asfaw on behalf of the *Dergue* at the Addis Ababa City Council on the municipal councillors' oath-taking ceremony. During the event, the Captain asserted that *Netsa Ermija* had been carried out with cooperation between the *Dergue and* the city administration and promised that the cooperation in this regard will continue. The evidence did not indicate when the *Dergue*'s *Netsa Ermija* began; it simply talked of the decision to continue them. According to Tola, however, the *Netsa Ermija* was launched in September 1977. See B. Tola, *To Kill the Generation: The Red Terror in Ethiopia* (2nd.ed., Washington, D.C.: Free Ethiopia Press, 1997) 146.
222   See also *Colonel Mengistu Hailemariam et al.*, (Trial Judgment), *supra* note 10, 4.
223   For the structure of the institutions, see below sections 6.4.1.1.2. and 6.4.1.1.3.
224   At this time, those considered enemies of the revolution included EPRP, EDU, Tesfa Le Zewede and its affiliates, members of the ELF, ECOP, youth associations. It was stated

by the *Dergue* Campaign and Security Department (DCSD) was launched in April 1977. This campaign, which involved the collaboration of civilian and military units, was designed to be carried out intensively day and night until anti-revolutionaries were fully destroyed.[225] Besides, a recurrent campaign called *Zemecha Mentir* (Identify and Eliminate) was carried out by the *Dergue* frequently at different levels to identify and eliminate members of opposition factions.[226]

6.4.1.1.2 *The Establishment of Institutions of Violence*
According to the FHC, the *Dergue* had organized itself with institutions of repressions, some of which were established for the sole purpose of destroying political groups while others were reorganized in order to intensify the execution of the ዐቅድ (intent/plan) to destroy. The first such institution was the *Dergue* Campaign and Security Department (DCSD), established at the beginning of July 1974 to prepare and coordinate the armed forces for combat activities.[227] The DCSD had a Hit-squad[228] and a Daily Situations Follow-up Unit (DCFU).[229] The Department was later reorganized under the *Dergue* Military Committee (DMC) in February 1975 in order to destroy individuals and groups with anti-revolutionary agendas.[230]

in the order document that the campaign was carried out by decision of the Provisional Military Government.

225 Colonel Mengistu Hailemariam gave an order to launch a 'hit the anti-revolutionaries' campaign, which was carried out through the collaboration of the armed forces, the police and other civilian bodies such as the *Kebele* revolutionary guards and workers' revolutionary guards. See *Colonel Mengistu Hailemariam et al.*, (Trial Ruling), supra note 9,10.

226 In October 1977, lieutenant colonel Debela Dinsa gave the order to the *Kebeles* in Addis Ababa. Similarly, on 1 July 1978, Colonel Tesfaye Gebrekidane prepared a procedural guideline based on which the armed forces would be able to identify and eliminate anti-revolutionary forces in the army. *Colonel Mengistu Hailemariam et al.*, (Trial Ruling), *supra* note 9, 10,14.

227 See ibid., 6. The department was composed of nine military members including lieutenant Colonel Fisseha Desta.

228 Ibid., 10. The Hit-squad was composed of soldiers handpicked from various divisions of the army by order of Colonel Mengistu Hailemariam. The Court also noted that the Hit-squad and the security unit of the DCSD were often sent on missions to attack anti-revolutionaries which they carried out in collaboration with the *Kebeles* and the police. Besides, there was no evidence that the Hit-squad was established on a short-term basis. In a document prepared in February 1978, it was stated that the Hit-squad had been carrying out such an assignment since the time of its establishment. See ibid.

229 Ibid.
230 Ibid.

In October 1974, the *Dergue* established the Central Prison (Maekalawi), the administration of which was carried out by high-ranking government officials in collaboration with the *Dergue* Investigation Team (DIT).[231] The latter was established initially with the aim to carry out investigations on the already arrested and suspected officials of the *ancien régime*.[232] Later on, the DIT's investigative power was extended to include members of the defense forces who did not accept the *Dergue*'s *Ethiopia Tikdem* ('let Ethiopia first') motto[233] as well as persons who engaged in activities disruptive to the *Dergue*'s policies.[234]

In August 1976, four organizations were added to the *Dergue*'s institutions of violence. These were: *i*) the Information Evaluation and Dissemination Unit (IEDU);[235] *ii*) the Public Security Protection Committee (PSPC);[236] *iii*) the Revolutionary Information Unit (RIU);[237] and *iv*) the Police Force Special Investigation Unit (PFSIU).[238] All of these institutions were structured to work together to carry out a coordinated attack against those identified by the *Dergue* as anti-revolution and anti-unity.[239] The establishment of these institutions of violence indicated that the *Dergue* had a whole system set up to destroy opposition political groups.

6.4.1.1.3 *Intensifying and Coordinating Institutions and Violence*
In the late 1970s, the *Dergue* started reorganizing the institutions of violence for the purpose of coordinating and intensifying the measures it had been taking against anti-revolutionaries. In May 1977, Higher Urban Dwellers

---

231 Ibid., 11.
232 Ibid., 10.
233 The motto Ethiopia Tikdem (ኢትዮጵያ ትቅደም) which means, literally, 'Ethiopia First' was first used in the earliest stages of the 1974 revolution as a slogan, according to Shifaw, against corruption and corrupted officials of the Haile-Selassie regime. Soon, the motto evolved to incorporate a notion of putting the country's interests above and beyond anything and anyone. It became a caption to a more elaborated manifesto of the *Dergue* issued on 1 November 1974. See D. Shifaw, *The Diary of Terror: Ethiopia 1974–1991* (Bloomington: Trafford Publishing, 2012) 16.
234 Ibid., 10.
235 The IEDU was established by order of Colonel Mengistu Hailemariam and had a mandate to track and report persons who could attempt to destabilize the *Dergue*'s position of control, its work programs, and its *Ethiopia Tikdem* ideology. Ibid., 11.
236 Ibid. The PSPC was established to work in collaboration with the DIT and the IEDU and to report the investigation results by including its suggestions to the *Dergue* or its chairman.
237 The RIU was empowered to render opinions regarding whether anti-revolutionaries were to be detained, released or subjected to revolutionary measures. Ibid.
238 The PFSIU was created within the police force with a power similar to that of the RIU. See ibid.
239 Ibid.

Associations (HUDAS) were established by decision of the Urban Development and Housing Minister.²⁴⁰ In order to undertake a coordinated attack against anti-revolutionaries and to ensure the involvement of public and professional organizations in the violence, the *Dergue* established a Revolution Protection Units Coordination Committee (RPUCC).²⁴¹ Efforts were also made to arm the *Kebeles* and coordinate ongoing measures against the anti-revolutionaries.²⁴² A school counter-anti-revolutionary force was established to remove the enemies of the revolution from schools.²⁴³ In January and May 1978, orders were issued to ensure that the *Kebeles* and HUDAS carry out interrogations jointly with the *Dergue* investigation units.²⁴⁴ Such a coordinated and supervised structure signified centralization of investigations and interrogations.

It was in August 1978 that the most advanced institution of violence was established, namely, the Central Revolutionary Investigation Department (CRID), formed out of a merger of the DIT and the PFSIU²⁴⁵ and equipped with modern communication systems, security clearance and a separate hit-squad to destroy anti-revolutionary groups.²⁴⁶ It established direct communication with *Kebeles* and HUDAS to carry out its investigations on anti-revolutionaries, thereby strengthening an already centralized system of investigation. Widening this system further, it operated both in Addis Ababa and in the provinces, notably by sending special investigators to the provinces and by having detainees transferred from the provinces to its Addis Ababa center.²⁴⁷

---

240   The reason for the establishment of the HUDAs was, according to the court, to push forward the revolution's offensive. Ibid.

241   Captain Legesse Asfaw worked in the committee and carried out activities such as submitting requests to the *Dergue* for the purpose of arming the coordinating committee. Ibid., 15.

242   The *Dergue* supplied weapons, gave trainings to the *Kebeles* and helped them organize themselves. According to the Court, this was done as part of an initial promise made by the *Dergue* to arm the *Kebeles* and HUDAs with weapons necessary to take revolutionary measures against the anti-revolutionaries. However, the Court did not mention when the promises were made and by whom. In the 1970s, it was discussed in several meetings held by the *Dergue* that *Kebeles* in Addis Ababa had begun killing detainees in local prisons and that dead bodies were seen left on different places and on the streets. The meetings also noted that there was a widespread practice of interrogations accompanied with flogging and beatings, as recorded in the diary of Colonel Tesfaye Woldeselessie (who served as the Chairman of the Information Evaluation and Dissemination Committee). See ibid., 12–15.

243   This was carried out under the leadership of Lieutenant Colonel Endale Tessema. Ibid., 14.

244   The order was given by Lieutenant Colonel Debela Dinsa. Ibid., 16.

245   Ibid., 11.

246   Ibid.

247   The CRID had investigation centers in Addis Ababa city administration, Addis Ababa Police Sprinter Division, Eritrea, and Tigray (Mekelle). Ibid., 12. For the SPO case dealing

As such, this well thought-through and centralized system of violence was meant to destroy opposition political groups throughout the country.

6.4.1.1.4 The Direct Involvement of Higher Officials in Perpetration of Violence

On top of giving orders, initiating and organizing campaigns, and making public announcements concerning the elimination of members and affiliates of political opposition groups, the *Dergue* higher officials were responsible for arming *Kebele* administrations,[248] supervising prisons,[249] and running the CRID.[250] Even more, they directly and regularly participated in deciding measures to be taken against anti-revolutionaries. In particular, officials at the National and Public Security Affairs (NSPA) /ሀገርና ሕዝብ ደህንነት ጉዳይ ሃላፊዎች/ were responsible for rendering the final decision on the fate of anti-revolutionaries.[251]

The usual procedure was well-oiled and followed clearly determined steps. After receiving investigation results from the Director of the DIT, the NPSA officials (such as Lieutenant Colonels Kassahun Tafesse and Teka Tulu) had the power to send their final decisions to the DIT or directly to the DCSD.[252] Their decisions often contained death sentences which were usually coded in phrases such as *take a revolutionary measure, move them to the district, take them across, join them with Jesus*, and *send them with any transport available*.[253]

An alternative procedure was also available: the NPSA officials could pass on their decisions to the general secretary of the *Dergue*, Captain Fikreselassie Wogederesse, or the deputy general Secretary, Lieutenant Colonel Fisseha Desta.[254] The two could either change or approve the decisions and send them back to the NPSA officials with instructions to notify the DCSD.[255] In 1971, when the CRID replaced the DIT and the PFSIU, both the usual and the alternative

---

with the CRID special investigators, see FHC, SPO v. *Teshome Bayyu et al.*, (Trial Judgment), 15 January 2009, File No. 07415, 4–5.

248 The list of officials included: Captain Fikreselassie Wegderess, Colonel Tesfaye Gebrekidane, Colonel Demessie Duressa, Letenal Colonel Fesseha Desta. Ibid., 13.
249 According to documentary evidence produced by the SPO in this regard, the prison administration committee included Major Kassaye Aragaw, *meto-aleqa* Petros Gebre, *mikitel meto-aleqa* Aragaw Yimer, Major Dejene Wolde Agegnehu, *miktel meto-aleqa* Fesseha Andeto and others. Ibid., 11.
250 The CRID used as its office an off-site location, Prince Asarat Kassa's villa, and was run by Lieutenant-Colonel Fisseha Desta. Ibid., 11.
251 Ibid., 12.
252 Ibid., 13.
253 Ibid.
254 Ibid.
255 Ibid.

procedures were maintained.[256] While these procedures were followed, arrestees were kept in the Central Prison (Maekalawi) and several other prisons.[257]

High-ranking officials were found to have participated not only in rendering the aforementioned decisions but also in their implementation. Executions usually happened in strictly official places in a manner that indicated the direct involvement and participation of higher officials. In particular, witnesses (ambulance chauffeurs, assistant chauffeurs, grave diggers, hospital personnel) have testified that, between 1976 and 1978, on a daily basis about 70 dead bodies were collected from *Arat-Kilo* Palace (Presidential Palace) and sent to Minilik II Hospital before they were dumped in mass graves.[258]

6.4.1.2   The Courts' Failure to Note and Clarify the Ambiguity of ዕቅድ

From the foregoing, it could be established that the *Dergue* had a plan contrived to destroy political opposition groups for the purpose of which decisions were made, institutions were established and reorganized, and actions were coordinated. The involvement of state officials and the putting in place of resources and mobilization of local actors suggest the existence of a methodical plan to destroy those identified as enemies of the *Dergue*. Notwithstanding, the FHC did not use the word ዕቅድ to specifically denote a plan. Rather, it used the term ambiguously, in a manner that could be interpreted as either plan or intent.

The FHC's ruling in *Mengistu et al.* was devoid of consistency. At times, judges used the word ፍላጎት(desire) to destroy[259] or አሳብ(intent) to destroy[260] instead of ዕቅድ (plan) to destroy. The usage by the Court suggests that these three words are interchangeable. Sometimes, ዕቅድ (plan) and አሳብ (intent) appeared jointly in a single statement and separated with an 'or' – thus implying the functional equivalence of the two terms without necessarily indicating that they mean the exact same thing. For example, in concluding that the *Dergue* had the requisite genocidal *mens rea*, the FHC stated that, 'therefore the court has established from the prosecution evidence that the *Dergue* had ዕቅድ (plan) or intent (አሳብ) to destroy a section of people unified on the basis of political affiliation ...'[261]

---

256 Ibid.
257 Ibid.,12.
258 Ibid., 13.
259 Ibid., 14.
260 Ibid., 12.
261 Ibid., 9. Translation by the author. The original (Amharic) text reads: 'ስለሆነም በፖለቲካ ተሳስሮ የሚገኘን የህዝብ ክፍል የማጥፋት ዕቅድ ወይንም አሳብ ደርግ የነበረው ...መሆኑን ፍርድ ቤቱ በዐ/ህግ ማስረጃ አረጋግጧል።'.

The meaning of **ዕቅድ** (plan) in the case at hand was to some extent clarified on appeal by the FSC, where its use was confined to the term 'plan'. According to the Court,

> since the appellants have not contested the killings, the relevant issue should not be whether people were killed, but who caused their death or *whether the killings were carried out in pursuance of a plan allegedly prepared by the defendants to destroy members of political groups*.[262]

In rejecting the defendants' appeal, the FSC, after reviewing the above mentioned factual issues that were already discussed by the FHC, concluded that 'it was established by sufficient evidence that the *Dergue* had prepared a comprehensive plan to destroy political groups, which it actually implemented'.[263] In that sense, the FSC had in fact heavily relied on the existence of plan to conclude whether genocide was committed by the *Dergue*. It criticized the FHC for indiscriminately characterizing most of the killings as genocidal while failing to examine how each of the killings fell within the scope of the plan laid out by the *Dergue*.[264] In finding the killing of the Emperor as not constitutive of genocide, the FSC mentioned that it was not carried out in pursuance of the *Dergue*'s plan to destroy political groups.[265] It also held: 'the reason behind the assassination of the Patriarch of the Ethiopian Orthodox Church was not mentioned anywhere, and therefore it was not clear if it had connection to *the plan*'.[266]

A closer look, however, reveals that in convicting the defendants for genocide on the basis of the existence of a comprehensive plan to destroy political groups, the FSC did not specifically found that establishing the existence of a plan was a legal requirement nor did it expressly state that it was not. In highlighting that the need to focus on the plan element of the case was merely

---

262 *Colonel Mengistu Hailemariam et al.*, (Appeals Judgment), *supra* note 25, 19. Emphasis added. Translation by the author. The original(Amharic) version reads: ተከሳሾች ሰዎቹ አልተገደሉም የሚል ክርክር የላቸውም፡፡ አከራካሪም ሆኖ የተገኘው የሰዎች መገደል አለመገደል ሳይሆን እንዚህ ሰዎች እንዲገደሉ ያደረገው ማን ነው የተገደሉት ተከሳሾች የፖለቲካ ትስስሩን አባላት ለማጥፋት አውጥተው ነበር በተባለው ዕቅድ መሠረት ነው አይደለም የሚለው ጉዳትይ ነው.

263 Ibid., 25. Translation by the author. The original (Amharic) version reads:
ደርግ የፖለቲካ ት ስ ስሩን አባላት ውይንም የ አንዲን የፖላቲካ ቡድን አባላት የማጥፋት ሰፊ ዕቅድ በማዉጣት እንዲፈጸም ያደረገ መሆኑ በበቂ ማስራጃ ሊራጋገጥ የቻለ ሲሆን...

264 See also the discussion above in section 5.5.1.1.
265 *Colonel Mengistu Hailemariam et al.*, (Appeals Judgment), *supra* note 25, 72.
266 Ibid.

because the SPO's accusations were based on the fact that the *Dergue* committed genocide by orchestrating a plan to destroy, the FCS further stated:

> given that the SPO fervently argues that the victims were killed on the basis of a plan prepared by the defendants to destroy members of political groups, it is essential to examine and determine whether there was a plan to destroy members of political groups and whether there were victims executed and harmed on the basis of the alleged plan prepared by the defendants.[267]

One could ask: if a plan is not the legal element of genocide, then what is? Alternatively, one could also ask: how is it even lawful to punish the defendants based on the existence of a plan, if this is not the legal element of the crime? The FSC did not contemplate these questions. Even more, neither the FHC nor the FSC mentioned whether genocidal intent could or should be derived from the existence of the above facts establishing a plan. Such a statement could have been written in Amharic as ዕቅዱ ተከሳሾች ዘርን የማጥፋት አሳብ እንደነበራቸው ይሳያል ('the existence of such a plan shows that the defendants had intent to commit genocide'), but it is nowhere to be found.

Ultimately, these unexplained and confusing judgments failed to clarify whether what is referred to as ዕቅድ in the genocide provision of the Penal Code of 1957 meant plan or intent, or both. As such, the practice in the *Dergue* trials neither contradicted nor conformed to the international jurisprudence in which the intent, not the plan, is the element of genocide, although the latter could help prove the existence of the former.[268] For similar reasons, it cannot

---

267 Ibid., 19–20 Translation by the author. The original (Amharic) version reads:
ዐቃቤ ሕግ የፖለቲካ ትስስሩን ውይንም የ አንድን የፖለቲካ ቡድን አባላት ላማጥፋት ባወጡት ዕቅድ መሠረት ነው በሚል አክክሮ ስለሚከራከር የፖለቲካ ት ስ ስ ሩን አባላት ላማጥፋት ዕቅድ መኖሩ አለመኖሩን፣ የፖለቲካ ቡድን አባላት ላማጥፋት ወጥቶ ነበር በተባለው ዕቅድ መሠረት የተገደሉና ጉዳት የደረሰባቸው ሰዎች መኖራቸዉን አለመኖራቸዉን በመመርመር መወሰን ይስፈልጋል።

268 See for instance *Kayishema and Ruzindana,* Appeals Chamber, (Judgment), *supra* note 186, para. 172, which reads,
> The Appeals Chamber is of the opinion that the existence of a plan or policy is not a legal ingredient of the crime. However, in the context of proving specific intent, the existence of a plan or policy may become an important factor in most cases. The evidence may be consistent with the existence of a plan or policy, or may even show such existence, and the existence of a plan or policy may facilitate proof of the crime.

See also *Jelisić,* Appeals Chamber, (Judgment), *supra* note 186, para. 48; *Bosnia and Herzegovina v. Serbia and Montenegro,* (Judgment), *supra* note 14, paras 373 and 376. See also Cassese who shares the view that a plan is not the element of genocide committed through killing member of a group or causing serious bodily or mental harm to members

be said whether the Ethiopian jurisprudence supports the position reflected in the ICC Elements of Crimes.[269]

6.4.2 Intent/Plan: 'አሳብ' in the CUD and the Oromo-Gumuz Trials

In the *Oromo-Gumuz* trials, the Federal Prosecutor accused the defendants of having committed genocide against ethnic groups in violation of Article 269 the FDRE Criminal Code. In these cases, the required *mens rea* mentioned in the indictments referred primarily to አሳብ (intent) to destroy. The courts however only gave a marginal treatment to the issue of genocidal *mens rea*. In all of the three cases in the *Oromo-Gumuz* trials, judges did not discuss genocidal *mens rea*, not even at the ruling stage.[270] Interestingly, in all of these cases, the same bench was rendering the judgment with judge Adem Ibrahim and judge Desta Letemo issuing the rulings and the judgments by majority, and judge Aseffa Abraha dissenting at both stages.

In *Ibrahim et al.*, the dissenting judge explained that genocide requires a separate and additional *mens rea* to the one required for the underlying offenses.[271] In his opinion, perhaps the longest in all of the genocide cases, Judge Aseffa Abraha stated that the difficult task, and the one that requires a careful analysis of the evidence, is not the *actus reus* but the genocidal *mens rea*, which could be established from orders given or expressions used at the time the defendants were committing the underlying offenses.[272] Nonetheless, by genocidal *mens rea*, the dissenting judge was referring to a 'plan' and not to 'intent', although article 269 of the FDRE Criminal Code unequivocally states that it is the latter that is required to establish the commission of genocide. According to the judge, as its fundamental element, the commission of genocide 'requires the existence of a *strategically coordinated plan*, which the defendants could not have come up with due to their low-level education'.[273]

---

of a group. A. Cassese, 'Is Genocidal Policy a Requirement for the Crime of Genocide?' in P. Gaeta (ed.), *The UN Genocide Convention: A Commentary* (Oxford: Oxford University Press, 2009) 128–136, 135.

269　ICC Statute, Elements of Crimes, Article 6, which specify: 'the conduct took place in the context of a manifest pattern of similar conduct directed against that group or was conduct that could itself effect such destruction'.

270　The ruling refers to the stage where the court, after hearing and analyzing prosecution evidence, makes a determination as to whether the case against the accused has been made out in a manner that warrants conviction, if unrebutted. This is not to be seen as different from the final judgment, in particular in *in absentia* trials. See Criminal Procedure Code of 1960, Articles 141 and 142.

271　See FHC, *Prosecutor v. Aliyu Yusufe Ibrahim et al.*, (Trial Ruling: Dissenting Opinion of Judge Aseffa Abreha) 21 May 2009, File No. 71000, 3.

272　Ibid.

273　Ibid., 5.

Judge Aseffa Abraha's comment regarding the significance of distinguishing genocidal *mens rea* from the commission of the *actus reus* was picked upon by the other two judges at the judgment stage in *Mengesha et al.* and *Loya et al.* In both cases, the two judges paused and explained whether the killings that were established by prosecution evidence constituted murder or genocide.[274] In concluding the latter, the majority judgments established the existence of genocidal intent (አሳብ) from the nature and scale of the killings (which they referred to as mass massacre), and statements used by the perpetrators (such as 'do not spare a single *Oromo*') while committing the killings.[275] For some reason, a similar explanation is not available in *Ibrahim et al.*, although the judges were the same. The defendants in *Ibrahim et al.* were thus convicted of genocide without any explanation other than that they were found guilty of committing the underlying offenses, as was the case in the *Anuak-Nuwer* trials and some of the cases in the *Dergue* trials.[276]

In the CUD trials, where attempt to commit genocide and genocide itself were discussed, the issue of intent to destroy political and ethnic groups was touched upon more directly. In *Shawul et al.*, the prosecutor accused 96 high-ranking officials and affiliates of the CUD of attempting to commit genocide against members of the ruling party (EPRDF) and ethnic *Tigrians* through attacking, defaming, and ordering acts of discrimination against them.[277] Defendants in *Tigneh et al.* were accused of attempted genocide for trying to carry out a 'call' to destroy the *Tigrians* and the EPRDF announced by the higher officials of the CUD.[278] Those in *Woldeselassie et al.* were accused of genocide through executing the alleged call.[279]

In *Woldeselassie et al.*, the FHC discussed whether there was a plan to destroy political groups as a legal element of the crime of genocide. After finding that all of the underlying offenses had been committed as alleged by the prosecutor,[280] the Court stated that the prosecutor did not provide evidence establishing the existence of a fundamental element of genocide, i.e. a 'plan (ዕቅድ) to destroy' political or ethnic groups.[281] The Court added, 'without the

---

274 See *Tadesse Jewanie Mengesha et al.*, (Trial Judgment), *supra* note 88, 45; *Tesfaye Neno Loya et al.*, (Trial Judgment), *supra* note 88, 41.
275 See *Tadesse Jewanie Mengesha et al.*, (Trial Judgment), *supra* note 88, 45; FHC, *Prosecutor v. Tadesse Jewanie Mengesha et al.*, (Trial Ruling), 22 May 2009, File No. 70996/2000, 41.
276 See *Aliyu Yusufe Ibrahim et al.*, (Trial Judgment), *supra* note 73, 12.
277 See *Engineer Hailu Shawul et al.*, (Indictment), *supra* note 59, 25.
278 *Kifle Tigeneh et al.*, (Indictment), *supra* note 59, 4.
279 *Berehene Kehassaye Woldeselassie et al.*, (Indictment), *supra* note 59, 2.
280 *Berehene Kehassaye Woldeselassie et al.*, (Trial Judgment), *supra* note 125, 6.
281 Ibid., 7.

THE CRIME OF GENOCIDE IN ETHIOPIAN TRIALS: ELEMENTS OF THE CRIME 287

existence of a plan to destroy, it cannot be said that the defendants have organized, ordered, and enforced the commission of genocide'.[282] A dissenting judge, who also read the requirement of a 'plan' to destroy into the law, stated that the evidence actually showed the existence of plan to destroy political and ethnic groups and that the defendants should thus have been found guilty of genocide.[283]

Apart from the largely confusing usage of 'plan' or/and 'intent' in Ethiopian genocide trials, some courts paid closer attention to the question of how genocidal intent could be established. As can be inferred from the above-mentioned cases in the *Oromo-Gumuz* trials, whether the defendants acted with specific intent to destroy can be established from the manner of their participation in the commission of the underlying offenses and, in particular, from verbal expressions and other communications accompanying the perpetration of the crimes. In the main CUD case, *Shawul et al.*, the FHC emphasized that the existence of intent shall not be limited to the spoken and written statements of the defendants, but can also be derived from the manner in which the underlying offenses were committed.[284] In this regard, international trials have followed a similar approach in identifying genocidal *mens rea*. Referring to it as 'a circular situation of inter-dependence', Fournet summarized,

> more than a mere dependence of the genocidal actus reus on the genocidal intent, there now arguably exists a circular situation of inter-dependence in which an act can only be characterized as genocidal if it is perpetrated with the specific intent to destroy, while the proof of this intent finds itself heavily dependent on the judicial assessment of the facts of the case and of the acts committed.[285]

6.4.3   *To Destroy /ለማጥፋት*

Genocide refers to the destruction of a group, namely, to its material destruction by either physical or biological means.[286] International tribunals and

---

282   Ibid.
283   Ibid., Dissenting Opinion of Judge Aseffa Abereha, 8. In the dissenting opinion the reference to 'plan' as the required *mens rea* is mentioned using the English word 'plan' in addition to the Amharic 'ዕቅድ'.
284   FHC, *Federal Prosecutor v. Engineer Hailu Shawul et al.,* (Trial Ruling), 3 May 2007, File No. 43246/97, 23, 25.
285   Fournet, 'The Actus Reus of Genocide', *supra* note 131, 68.
286   'Report of the Commission to the General Assembly on the Work of its Forty-First Session', UN Doc. A/CN.4/SER.A/1989/Add.1 (Part 2), 102, para. 4. See also ICTY, *Prosecutor*

courts have noted, with very few exceptions,[287] that genocidal intent should show that the perpetrator targeted the physical destruction of the protected group.[288] This implies that not all killings targeting the members of a protected group do constitute genocide. Such a judicial position only finds a limited echo in Ethiopian practice and, as it will now be shown, the jurisprudence of Ethiopian courts is not only divided on this issue but is also devoid of sufficient explanation.

As noted above, Ethiopian trials have on several occasions characterized as genocide an attack that targeted members of a protected group without further considering whether the attack was the result of discrimination or of an intent to annihilate the group.[289] This was the case in the *Anuak-Nuwer* trials, in several of the *Dergue* cases,[290] and in the case of *Ibrahim et al.* in the *Oromo-Gumuz* trials. In all those cases, courts have emphasized as the qualifying element of genocide the protected status of the group with which the victims were identified rather than – as they arguably should have – the intent to destroy.

The material destruction of a group is not in itself sufficient for the qualification of genocide if the intent of the perpetrators was to remove victims from a certain area, as discussed in the Darfur Report[291] and in the jurisprudence of international tribunals.[292] A similar issue was considered in the *Oromo-Gumuz* trials where the dissenting judge argued that the perpetrators did not commit genocide because they did not intend more than just removing the

---

v. *Mladić*, Trial Chamber I, (Judgment: Volume III of V), 22 November 2017, IT-09-92-T, para. 3435.

287 ICTY, *Prosecutor* v. *Blagojević*, (Trial Judgment of 17 January 2005), Case No. IT-02-60-T, paras 659–66. See also See Berster, 'Article II', *supra* note 14, 81. A broader interpretation which included social existence of a group was also rendered by the Federal Constitutional Court of Germany, the *Bundesverfassungsgericht*. See K. Ambos, *Treatise on International Criminal Law: Vol II, The Crimes and Sentencing* (Oxford, Oxford University Press, 2014) 36.

288 In *Krstić*, the ICTY Trial Chamber stated that the focus of genocide on the physical destruction of the protected group has a basis in customary international law. See *Krstić*, Trial Chamber, (Judgment), *supra* note 14, para. 580.

289 See above sections 5.3.3.1 and 5.5.1.

290 In several cases, the courts in the *Dergue* trials have limited their analysis to such issues as whether the defendants committed the underlying offenses, thereby leaving aside the central question, i.e. whether the defendants committed genocide. See for instance FHC, SPO v. *Feyyisa Seboka et al.*, (Trial Judgment of 20 November 2000) File No. 934/89, 10; FHC, SPO v. *Ali Musa et al.*, (Trial Judgment of 9 May 2001) File No. 925/89, 22–23.

291 Report of the International Commission of Inquiry on Darfur to the Secretary General, *supra* note 14, para. 518.

292 *Stakić*, Trial Chamber, (Judgment), *supra* note 171, para. 519.

Oromo farmers from an area of a land.²⁹³ The majority disagreed and argued in the conviction judgment that the perpetrators had intended to destroy the group, based on facts such as that the killings occurred after the perpetrators had made preparations to attack the victims,²⁹⁴ that the perpetrators had identified and targeted the *Oromos*, that at first they aimed at killing the male members of the *Oromo* community in the area, that during the attack the perpetrators were avowing not to spare any *Oromo*, and that the attack took the form of a massacre.²⁹⁵

Neither the dissenting opinion nor the majority judgment is convincing, mainly because they both fail to substantiate and explain their conclusions, as is often the case with most of the Ethiopian judgments. The dissenting judgment limited its discussion to the perpetrators' intent to expel the victims from a geographic area without clearly discussing whether a genocidal intent to destroy could co-exist with such an intent to expel. One could identify a similar deficiency in the CUD trials, with the exception of *Shawul et al.*²⁹⁶ where the unavailability of the intent to destroy was established from the fact that the defendants were found to possess an intent to remove the government by force without explaining how that intent did not also include the intent to destroy a political group (the EPRDF) and an ethnic group (*Tigre*).²⁹⁷

The majority judgments in the *Oromo-Gumuz* cases did not specify its findings further. It is noteworthy that in stark similarity to genocidal acts committed elsewhere,²⁹⁸ the perpetrators in the *Oromo-Gumuz* conflict spared the women and the children, which they soon forcefully expelled from the area.²⁹⁹

---

293   See *Aliyu Yusufe Ibrahim et al.*, (Trial Ruling: Dissenting Opinion of Judge Aseffa Abreha), *supra* note 271, 8.
294   Including mobilization of their supporters and supply of arms which were used in the attacks. See *Tadesse Jewanie Mengesha et al.*, (Trial Judgment), *supra* note 88, 45.
295   See ibid., 45; *Tesfaye Neno Loya et al.*, (Trial Judgment), *supra* note 88, 41.
296   See below.
297   See FHC, *Federal Prosecutor* v. *Kifle Tigeneh et al.*, (Trial Ruling), 16 April 2007, File No. 44562/99, 23. The Court failed to clarify the fact that genocide may be committed with a motive to remove a certain ethnic or political group, although motive is not a requsiete element of egnocide. It also did not discuss the fact that a certain violence may carry more than one intent. That is to say, it is possible for post-election violence to comprise both the intent to oust a government by force (which is an element of treason under Ethiopian law) and simultaneously the genocidal intent to destroy ethnic or political groups affiliated with the incumbent government.
298   For a discussion of the Srebrenica genocide, see *Krstić*, Trial Chamber, (Judgment), *supra* note 14, paras 568 and 720.
299   See *Tadesse Jewanie Mengesha et al.*, (Trial Judgment), *supra* note 88, 45; *Tesfaye Neno Loya et al.*, (Trial Judgment), *supra* note 88, 41.

Nonetheless, no discussion was provided as to whether the male members were killed to eliminate all possible resistance to the process of removing the *Oromos* from the area or because it was seen as essential to bring about the physical destruction of the group. Only the latter could justify the qualification of the acts as genocide. In cases involving Srebrenica, where the *génocidaires* decided not to kill the women and children, the ICTY Appeals Chamber in *Krstić* considered that such a decision did not negate the existence of a specific intent to destroy the group on the ground that it 'may be explained by the Bosnian Serbs' sensitivity to public opinion'.[300] In fact, the fact that a genocidal campaign may not have been implemented in the 'most direct and efficient way' does not have a bearing on the existence of the intent to destroy.[301]

The law preventing and punishing genocide plays a preventive role. 'To destroy' is, thus, an element of intent, not a requirement of a genocidal result. Put differently, the evidence does not need to establish whether the perpetrators succeeded in destroying the protected group. Ethiopian jurisprudence appears to have been muted on this point. However, it could be deduced from the Ethiopian genocide cases that killing a substantial number of members of the protected groups is not a requirement.[302] For instance, only six, 78, and 120 members of an ethnic group were identified as victims of genocide against, respectively, the *Nuwer*,[303] the *Oromos*,[304] and the *Gumuz*.[305]

In the *Dergue* trials, it was noted that the perpetrators had released several prisoners on various occasions on the ground that they had relinquished their anti-revolution sentiments and renounced their membership to political opposition groups. This fact has been used by some commentators to argue that the *Dergue* had, in general, lacked the intent to destroy political groups.[306] The release of anti-revolutionaries, once they had been forced to abandon their political views, may indeed cast doubt on the *Dergue's* intent to destroy, given that genocide in international law protects the physical destruction of the

---

300 See ICTY, *Prosecutor* v. *Krstić*, Appeals Chamber, (Judgment), 19 April 2004, Case No. IT-98-33-A, para. 31. According to the Appeals Chamber, the alleged sensitivity to public opinion might have resulted from the fact that killing women or children 'could not easily be kept secret, or disguised as a military operation, and so carried an increased international censure'. See ibid.
301 See ibid., para. 32.
302 See also the discussion in section 6.4.4. below.
303 *Gure Uchala Ugira et al.*, (Trial Judgment), *supra* note 67, 4.
304 See *Tadesse Jewanie Mengesha et al.*, (Trial Judgment), *supra* note 88, 4; *Tesfaye Neno Loya et al.*, (Trial Judgment), *supra* note 88, 4.
305 See *Aliyu Yusufe Ibrahim et al.*, (Trial Judgment), *supra* note 73, 5.
306 See Redae, 'The Ethiopian Genocide Trial' *supra* note 11, 21–22.

protected groups, not *per se* other qualities such as the identity of the group. This was the position adopted by the ICTY in the *Milošević* case,[307] while citing the 1996 International Law Commission's report that stated,

> as clearly shown by the preparatory work for the Convention, the destruction in question is the material destruction of a group either by physical or by biological means, not the destruction of the national, linguistic, religious, cultural or other identity of a particular group.[308]

Regardless, the analysis of the specific intent to destroy should make a distinction between the general (the *Dergue*, in this case) and the specific (individual perpetrators), on the one hand, and note the insignificance of 'random mercy', on the other. Such a distinction could be useful to distinguish a general determination of whether genocide has occurred from a specific determination of whether a given individual has participated in the commission of genocide. The *Dergue* had, as discussed above, an overarching plan to destroy political groups, which was largely unmitigated as the evidence did not evince that the plan had a mercy-clause whereby, as a general rule, those who repented and disavowed anti-revolutionary activities would be forgiven. In rejecting the defendants' argument based on the release of prisoners, the FHC explained:

> As prisoners were released only after having renounced their opposition and pledged to stand with the *Dergue*, it cannot be concluded that the *Dergue* had the willingness to release persons other than his supporters and, therefore, had no intent to destroy opposition [political] groups.[309]

When such was convincingly the case, Ethiopian courts have reached a different conclusion with regards to some members of the *Dergue* who might have released prisoners. For instance, the only acquittal from the genocide charge that was rendered in *Megistu et al.* in favor of Begashaw Gurmessa was notably based on the fact that he had released members of political opposition

---

307 See ICTY, *Prosecutor* v. *Milošević*, (Trial Decision on Motion for Judgment of Acquittal), 16 June 2004, IT-02-54-T, para. 124.
308 Draft Code of Crimes against the Peace and Security of Mankind with Commentaries 1996, 45–46, available at: <http://legal.un.org/ilc/texts/instruments/english/commentaries/7_4_1996.pdf> accessed 12 May 2019.
309 See *Colonel Mengistu Hailemariam et al.*, (Trial Judgement), *supra* note 10,112.

groups from prison instead of arranging or ordering their execution.[310] In stating the defendant's decision to release prisoners as the significant factor for his acquittal, the Court stated that, 'by releasing persons imprisoned pursuant to the *Dergue's* orders he has clearly demonstrated his objection [to the *Dergue's* plant to destroy political groups]'.[311]

Furthermore, even in relation to individual perpetrators, the fact that the perpetrator decided not to commit the *actus reus* elements against some of the members of the targeted group does not automatically establish the absence of his or her lack of specific intent to destroy. As stressed by the ICTY Appeals Chamber in *Jelisić*, the randomness of the killings or the showing of aberrational mercy cannot negate other evidence establishing the intent to destroy.[312] In some of the *Dergue* cases, SPO witnesses testified that they were once arrested due to an alleged membership to a political opposition group such as the EPRP, and released later upon paying a certain amount of fee.[313] However, such exceptions were not considered sufficient to grant the defendants an acquittal from the genocide charge.

It could also be inferred from the Ethiopian cases that, as part of establishing the 'to destroy' element of genocide, significant attention was given to killings aimed at bringing about the physical destruction of members of a group.[314] In *Teshome Bayyu et al.*, the CRID case, the FHC noted that the plan laid out by the *Dergue* to destroy political groups required the hunting down and destroying of members of the group.[315] In *Dagnet Ayalew et al.*, the ASC stated that the killings which resulted in the reduction of the number of members of political groups were aimed at erasing the existence of the group (ሕልውና).[316] As such, Ethiopian courts have considered that the law of genocide protects the groups' right to physical and biological existence. However, this does not in itself suggest that the courts did not consider the social existence of a group as the protected interest, given that such a debate was not raised in the trials.

By paying significant attention to the fact that perpetrators of genocide in the *Dergue* cases had planned/intended to bring about the physical destruction

---

310 The other factors mentioned by the court as establishing the defendant's lack of intent to destroy political groups were that the defendant was imprisoned by the *Dergue*, and that he was outside of the country at a certain point in time. See ibid., 412.
311 Ibid.
312 *Jelisić*, Appeals Chamber, (Judgment), *supra* note186, para. 71.
313 See for instance *Abera Ayalew et al.*, (Trial Judgment), *supra* note 141, 32; FSC, SPO v. *Tafa Gurmu*, (Appeals Judgment), 22 March 2001, File No.4896, 2–3.
314 See FHC, SPO v. *Zenebe Ayele et al.*, (Sentencing Judgment), 28 July 2003, File No. 641/89, 3.
315 *Teshome Bayyu et al.*, (Trial Judgment), *supra* note 247, 15.
316 See *Dagnenet Ayalew et al.*, (Trial Judgment), *supra* note 50, 41.

of the protected groups, it appears that Ethiopian courts have pointed to the true ambit of genocidal *mens rea*, i.e. that it is not only to attack or discriminate against, but 'to destroy a group, altogether'.[317] Indeed, it is in that sense that genocidal intent is different from discriminatory intent, which is required to establish the crime of persecution, although such an intent is just one step away from intent to destroy,[318] and genocide could be seen as an evolving process.[319] The Court in *Shawul et al.* seems to have explained this point more accurately. It first stated that the prosecution evidence had shown the existence of a plan to bring about the unconstitutional removal of the government through the taking of measures intended to coerce the government into relinquishing power. Diverse measures aimed at excluding members of the EPRDF and the *Tigrian* ethnic group from the public and social life were taken, ranging from avoiding them during coffee drinking routines, expelling and uninviting them to Ekubs[320] and Eders[321] to, in the more rural areas, avoid 'sharing a cooking fire' with them.[322] The Court noted that these measures were discriminatory in nature and that some of the speeches made by the defendants against the targeted groups could constitute hate speech.[323]

Whether these measures could have by and of themselves constitute valid evidence of an intent to destroy the political or ethnic groups remains an unsettled issue. And indeed, if the Court did find that no intent to destroy existed, this was because the time of the commission of the crimes overlapped with the time of post-election violence when the CUD acted in pursuance of a plan to forcibly and unconstitutionally remove the government from power.

---

317 *Krstić*, Trial Chamber, (Judgment), *supra* note 14, para. 684.
318 See ICTY, *Prosecutor v. Kupreškić*, Trial Chamber, (Judgment), 14 January 2000, IT-95-16, para. 751. For details, see C. Fournet and C. Pégorier, 'Only One Step Away From Genocide: the Crime of Persecution in International Criminal Law' (2010) 10(5) *International Criminal Law Review* 713–738.
319 See Mettraux, *International Crimes and the Ad Hoc Tribunals*, *supra* note 6, 216. Scholars have also identified that genocide is the final result of a continuum of destruction that passes through multiple steps. See for example, A. Smeulers and F. Grünfeld, *International Crimes and other Gross Human Rights Violations: A Multi- and Interdisciplinary Textbook* (Leiden: Martinus Nijhoff Publishers, 2011) 178-18; E. Staub, *The Roots of Evil: The Origins of Genocide and Other Group Violence* (Cambridge: Cambridge University Press, 1989) 51.
320 Ekub or Iqub is a rotating credit association in which each member contributes money periodically and the amount collected at each period is awarded to one of the members, often on a lottery system.
321 Eder or Ider is a traditional community organization in different parts of Ethiopia whose members assist each other during the mourning process.
322 See *Engineer Hailu Shawul et al.,* (Trial Ruling), *supra* note 284,196.
323 Ibid.

The Court thus found that the supporters of the EPRDF were targeted as part of this violence to evict the ruling coalition.[324] The Court however noted that the announcements and the calls could have instigated the commission of genocide, if they had been strengthened further.[325] It also added that it was because they ended prematurely that these measures did not constitute genocidal *mens rea*.[326] This is not without reminding the ICTY's *Krstić* judgment that found the existence of a genocidal intent to destroy only after 'the plan to ethnically cleanse the area of Srebrenica escalated to a far more insidious level that included killing all of the military-aged Bosnian Muslim men of Srebrenica'.[327]

The conclusion in *Shawul et al.* seems sound, although it could admittedly have been strengthened further had the Court thoroughly discussed some the relevant prosecution evidence. For instance, it was stated in the prosecution evidence that in a speech alleging and denouncing the accumulation of political power in the hands of the *Tigrians*, a CUD official stated that 'by the force of the people, the one on power will go back to where it has come from'.[328] This speech, submitted by the prosecutor to prove the existence of genocidal *mens rea*, could have been used by the Court to highlight that it actually proves the opposite, i.e. that the CUD had no intent to bring about the physical destruction of the targeted group, but only to unseat the EPRDF and to return its leaders to the Tigray region, where they allegedly came from.

6.4.4 *In Whole or in Part*

For a genocide to occur, a perpetrator does not need to intend to destroy a protected group in its entirety (in whole).[329] The intention to destroy a group 'in part' is sufficient for the act to be considered genocide. The problem however is that it is not clear how many members of a group constitute a group 'in part'. Since genocide protects the existence of a group, the 'in part' element of the intent to destroy a group needs to be determined in that perspective. The relevant international instruments and case law have provided two interpretations of what constitutes a group 'in part'.

The first interpretation, which appears to have the prevailing support in the doctrine and jurisprudence, is that 'in part' refers to a 'substantial part of the

---

324   Ibid.
325   Ibid.
326   Ibid.
327   *Krstić*, Trial Chamber, (Judgment), *supra* note 14, para. 619.
328   See *Engineer Hailu Shawul et al.,* (Trial Ruling), *supra* note 284,196.
329   ILC Draft 1996, Yearbook of International Law Commission 1996 II, Article 17, para. 8.

group'.³³⁰ This requirement appears to have resulted from the assumption that the Genocide Convention 'is intended to deal with action against large numbers'.³³¹ According to this interpretation, that a perpetrator intended to destroy a substantial part of a group can be inferred from the numeric size of the targeted group relative to the size of the group in whole,³³² from the targeted members' relevance to the existence of the group,³³³ and from other aspects related to the members of the targeted group the attack against which could result or amount to a genocidal attack against the group in whole.³³⁴

This interpretation was upheld most recently by the ICTY Trial Chamber in *Mladić*, which treated 'substantiality of part of the protected groups' as an element of the crime of genocide.³³⁵ On Count 1 – genocide, the Trial Chamber concluded that intent to destroy short of a certain number of victims is not genocide, although it did not specify what size is too small to constitute substantiality of part of a protected group. In summary, the Chamber explained:

> the Bosnian Muslims targeted in each individual municipality formed a relatively small part of the Bosnian-Muslim population in the Bosnian-Serb claimed territory or in Bosnia-Herzegovina as a whole. The trial Chamber received insufficient evidence indicating why the Bosnian Muslims in each of the above municipalities or the municipalities themselves had a special significance or were emblematic in relation to the protected group as a whole.³³⁶

The same 'substantiality' requirement was applied by the Tribunal in finding the commission of genocide, under Count 2 – Bosnian Muslims in Srebrenica. According to the Trial Chamber, the Bosnian Muslims in Srebrenica constituted a substantial part of Bosnian Muslims in Bosnia-Herzegovina, although they were found to have formed less than two percent of the latter.³³⁷ One could wonder as to why a 'relatively small' number could not satisfy the requirement of substantiality in Count 1 if 'less than two percent' did in Count 2.

---

330   See Schabas, *Genocide in International Law, supra* note 4, 277–282.
331   See A. Zahara and G. Sluiter, *International Criminal Law* (Oxford: Oxford University Press, 2008) 176. See also Cassese *et al.*, *Cassese's International Criminal Law, supra* note 136, 117.
332   See *Krstić*, Trial Chamber, (Judgment), *supra* note 14, para.12.
333   See *Tolimir*, Trial Chamber, (Judgment), *supra* note 14, para.782.
334   See in general Berster, 'Article 11', *supra note* 14, 149.
335   See *Mladić*, Trial Chamber, (Judgment), *supra* note 287, paras 3437, 3550.
336   Ibid., para. 3535.
337   Ibid., paras 3551–3555.

The second interpretation of the 'in part' element of the intent to destroy is to be found expressly mentioned in the text of ICL, under the ICC Elements of Crimes, where it is stated that 'one or more persons' can be the victim of genocide.[338] In that sense, the qualification of genocide under the Rome Statute does not need a substantial number of victims. If this has yet to be specified and confirmed by the ICC if and when it tries cases involving genocide, this approach might already find some support in the case law of the ICTR. In *Mpampara* the ICTR Trial Chamber stated that 'the commission of even a single instance of one of the prohibited acts is sufficient, provided that the accused genuinely intends by the act to destroy at least a substantial part of the group'.[339] In fact, it was already stated in *Akayesu* – thus before the coming into force of the Rome Statute – that:

> in concrete terms, for any of the acts charged under Article 2 (2) of the Statute to be a constitutive element of genocide, the act must have been committed against one or several individuals, because such individual or individuals were members of a specific group, and specifically because they belonged to this group. Thus, the victim is chosen not because of his individual identity, but rather on account of his membership of a national, ethnical, racial or religious group. The victim of the act is therefore a member of a group, chosen as such, which, hence, means that the victim of the crime of genocide is the group itself and not only the individual.[340]

Ethiopian law and case law seem to be in line with this approach. The Penal Code of 1957 used a singular marker in proscribing 'killing, causing bodily injury, or causing serious harm to the external and internal health of *one of the members* of the unit, in any way whatsoever'.[341] This has been amended by

---

338   ICC Elements of Crimes, Article 6 (a)-(e), Elements 1.
339   See ICTR, *Prosecutor* v. *Mpampara*, Trial Chamber, (Judgment), 11 September 2006, ICTR-01-65-T, para. 8.
340   See *Akayesu*, Trial Chamber, (Judgment), *supra* note 8, para. 521. According to Cassese however, such practices have not only broadened the text of the Convention by interpretation but have also ignored that the conduct under the Convention's Article II(C) 'by necessity must be carried out against a plurality of members of the group'. See Cassese et al., *Cassese's International Criminal Law*, *supra* note 136, 117.
341   See the Penal Code of 1957, Amharic Version, Article 281 (a). Translation by the author. The original (Amharic) version reads: 'ነፍስ የገደለ ፤ አካል ያቆሰለ፤ ወይም ከዚሁ ክፍል አባሎች በአንደኛው አፍኣዊና ውስጣዊ ጤንነት ላይ በማናቸውም ሁኔታ ጉዳት ያደረሰ እንድ ሆነ'. However, the singular marker did not appear with respect to other prohibited acts listed under sub-paragraphs b and c of Article 281.

the Criminal Code of 2005, which instead prohibited 'killing, bodily harm or serious injury to the physical or mental health of *members* of the group'.[342] It is not mentioned in the Code's *Explanatory Notes* why the plural marker is preferred. Nonetheless, even in the genocide cases where the Criminal Code was used as the applicable law, there exists no evidence that genocidal intent only materializes when the perpetrator kills or victimizes more than one person. To the contrary, several perpetrators were convicted of genocide and punished in the *Oromo-Gumuz* cases for killing just one person.[343]

Most importantly, the Criminal Code's pluralized reference to victims of genocide did not appear to have any impact on using the qualification of genocide even when there was just a single victim or a single instance of commission of prohibited acts. The only case that dealt with genocide in the CUD trials,[344] i.e. *Brehene Kahassaye Woldeselassie et al.,* involved a single victim and a single incident.[345] Although the defendants were acquitted of the genocide charge in a majority ruling, the number of victims was not the issue, but the perpetrators' lack of plan to destroy was.[346] Precisely, the lack of 'plan to destroy' was established from circumstantial evidence that indicated the perpetrators' intent to overthrow the government by force, and not their intent to commit genocide.[347] The fact that the number of victims and incidents did not matter in this case can be further inferred from the dissenting opinion which found that genocide was committed by the defendants.[348]

Nonetheless, it should be clarified that in the Ethiopian trials, it was common not to specify in the indictments whether the defendants had allegedly planned/intended to destroy a group in whole or in part. Besides, the courts largely avoided discussing the issue of 'in whole or in part', except for a brief mention in *Loya et al.*[349] Even in the *Dergue* trials, the SPO stated that the overarching plan laid out by the *Dergue*, as stated in the indictment, was to destroy political groups 'in whole or in part', without mentioning which of the two was

---

342 See FDRE Criminal Code, Article 269(a). Emphasis added.
343 In *Mengesha* et al., 27 defendants were sentenced to 20 years each because, according to the Court, 'they killed one person each'. See FHC, *Prosecutor v. Tadesse Jewanie Mengesha et al.,* (Sentencing Judgment), 4 September 2009, File No. 70996, 58–59.
344 The other two cases in the CUD trials (*Shawul et al.* and *Tigneh et al.*) were cases of attempted genocide. See section 6.4.3 above.
345 See *Berehene Kehassaye Woldeselassie et al.,* (Indictment), *supra* note 59.
346 See section 6.4.2. above.
347 Ibid.
348 See ibid.
349 See *Colonel Mengistu Hailemariam et al.,* (Trial Ruling), *supra* note 9, 5.

actually planned.³⁵⁰ Neither the FHC nor the FSC considered this element of the accusation relevant to address.

In fact, both the FHC and FSC have altogether avoided writing the phrase 'in whole or in part' in their respective judgments and merely stated that the *Dergue* had a plan to destroy *all* (ሁሉንም) political opposition groups.³⁵¹ Apparently, 'all' is used in the judgments to refer to each and every one of the numerous political opposition groups, in the sense that, contrary to popular belief, it was not just the EPRP that the *Dergue* targeted for destruction.³⁵² Nonetheless, there was no discussion as to whether the *Dergue's* plan to destroy opposition groups was to destroy each and every one of them in whole or in part.

The only brief and direct engagement with the issue of 'in whole' or 'in part' occurred in *Loya et al.* of the *Oromo-Gumuz* trials. There, the FHC attempted, by its own motion, to clarify the issue of whether the perpetrators, by targeting the *Oromo* families living across the borders between the Benishangul-Gumuz and Eastern-Wellega zones of the Oromia region, constituted a plan/intent to destroy the ethnic *Oromos* in whole or in part. It swiftly concluded that the perpetrators must have intended to destroy the *Oromos* in part since it could not have been possible for them to contemplate destroying the entire *Oromos* who cover several parts of the country.³⁵³

Although the FHC's conclusion lacked sufficient explanation, the view that the attack by the *Gumuz* against the *Oromos* could not have fulfilled the 'in whole' element of genocidal *mens rea* seems correct. It is indeed hardly plausible to imagine that the perpetrators intended to destroy the *Oromos* in whole: not only does the large size of the *Oromos* as an ethnic group would make such intent unrealistic, but also the motive behind the intent was to remove the *Oromo* farmers from a disputed land of a very small size.

Yet, the Court's conclusion regarding the 'in part' element may also be regarded as unconvincing, if the above-mentioned requirement of 'substantiality' is taken as assessment yardstick. Unlike what the Court held in its abrupt conclusion, the 'in part' requirement does not depend solely on the unattainability of the 'in whole' element. Rather, it should be assessed on its potential impact on the destruction of the group in whole. Furthermore, from a numerical point of view, members of the *Oromo* ethnic group targeted by the

---

350   *Tesfaye Neno Loya et al.*, (Trial Judgment), *supra* note 88, 41.
351   See *Colonel Mengistu Hailemariam et al.*, (Trial Ruling), *supra* note 9, 5; *Colonel Mengistu Hailemariam et al.*, (Appeals Judgment), *supra* note 25,70.
352   See on this *Dem Yazele Dossie*, 132.
353   *Tesfaye Neno Loya et al.*, (Trial Judgment) *supra* note 88, 41.

perpetrators in *Loya et al.* constituted less than 0.2 percent of the overall number of *Oromos* in the country.[354] This ratio might appear too small to constitute a substantial part of a group, although, as noted above, there is no percentage threshold to determine a numerical size of victims that could satisfy the requirement of substantiality of the part. Furthermore, evidence was also not available to assess whether the targeted victims were relevant to the existence of the *Oromo* ethnic group as a whole.

One could use the exact same line of argument with respect to the *Anuak-Nuwer* case and claim that it did not fulfil the 'in part' element of the intent to destroy. At about 0.02 percent of the whole group, the targeted members were numerically too small to satisfy the substantiality requirement.[355] Besides, the victims were refugees who were, apparently, possessing no special status; this makes it difficult to consider that their killings was meant to endanger the survival of the group to which they belonged.[356]

In sum, Ethiopian courts did not read the 'substantiality' of the number of victims as a requirement to the commission of genocide. As shown above, the change in the applicable criminal law did not affect the courts' interpretation that the determination of the crime of genocide is not dependent on the actual number of victims. As a result, the Ethiopian practice appears to support the idea that any attack conducted with intent to destroy could constitute genocide, although Ethiopian courts did not address this issue more directly and comprehensively.

6.4.5   *As Such /ን?*

As noted in Chapter 5, neither the Penal Code of 1957 nor the Criminal Code of 2005 included the words 'as such' (in their English versions) or its equivalent in their Amharic versions. These words appear in the *chapeau* of Article 11 of

---

354   Although the exact size of members of the targeted population in that *Kebele* was unknown, the 2007 Census showed that the targeted area (Hora Limu Woreda) had about 52,163 residents while the size of the *Oromo* group in whole was estimated at around 25 million.

355   In the *Anuak-Nuwer* trials, the prosecutor did not provide evidence as to what the abduction of 32 members of the *Nuwer* ethnic group as well as the killing of 6 of them could constitute in terms of the 'in whole or in part' requirement. Precisely, there was no evidence to show that the killings were aimed at destroying the *Nuwer* in part or not. From a numerical point of view, the number of *Nuwers* targeted by the attack constitutes around 0.02 percent of the whole group that lived in Ethiopia around the same time, based on the data from the 2007 Population Census.

356   For the case law interpreting the 'in part' element in line with the victims' significance to the group, see *Sikirica et al.*, Trial Chamber, (Judgment on Defence Motions to Acquit), *supra* note 171, para. 80.

the 1948 Genocide Convention as well as in the corresponding provisions of the Statutes of the ICTs and of the ICC. It was Venezuela's proposal that led to the insertion of 'as such' in the Convention's definition of genocide so that it could serve as a compromise clause to bring pro and anti-motive groups to an agreement.[357]

Commentators have attached differing meanings and significance to the words 'as such'. Some have considered it as indicating a motive requirement[358] while others have regarded it as precisely excluding it, since motive is considered as irrelevant in international criminal law.[359] It is also stated that 'as such' is an ambiguous and puzzling addition to the definition of genocide that does not specifically indicate whether the commission of genocide requires proof of motive or not.[360] It was also referred to as 'the vague addendum' to the definition of genocide[361] and some scholars have simply desisted from referring to it as an element of the crime.[362] In practice, courts have interpreted the words as denoting either *emphasis* or *motive*.

In describing them as emphasis markers, the ICJ stated that 'the words "as such" *emphasize* the intent to destroy the protected group'.[363] A similar understanding, that 'as such' signifies 'that the victim of crime of genocide is not merely the person but the group itself', is to be found in the judgments reached by the ICTR, ICTY, and, more recently, by the ECCC.[364] In view of this interpretation of 'as such', these words could have been represented by 'ን' (as such) in Amharic. In that sense, the Ethiopian law could have used 'በዳኙ' to refer to

---

[357] Schabas, *Genocide in International Criminal Law*, supra note 4, 298–299.
[358] See J.B. Quigley, *The Genocide Convention: an International Law Analysis* (Aldershot: Ashgate Publishing Limited, 2006) 120–126.
[359] See F. Jessberger, 'The Definition of the Elements of the Crime of Genocide', supra note 122, 110.
[360] See W.A. Schabas, 'Article 6: Genocide' in O. Triffterer and K. Ambos (eds), *The Rome Statute of the International Criminal Court: A Commentary* (3rd ed., München: C.H.Beck. Hart.Namos, 2016) 127–143, 136; See also W.A. Schabas, *An Introduction to the International Criminal Court* (5th ed., Cambridge: Cambridge University Press, 2017) 93. See also Robinson, *Genocide Convention*, supra note 17, 61.
[361] See Berster, 'Article 11', supra note 14, 152.
[362] See Ambos, *Treatise on International Criminal Law*, supra note 287, 37.
[363] See *Bosnia and Herzegovina v. Serbia and Montenegro*, (Judgment), supra note 14, para. 187. Emphasis added.
[364] ECCC, *Prosecutor v. Nuon Chea and Khieu Samphan*, Trial Chamber, (Judgment), 16 November 2018, Case File/Dossier No. 002/19-09-2007/ECCC/TC, para. 798; ICTR, *Niyitegeka v. Prosecutor*, Appeals Chamber, (Judgment), 9 July 2004, ICTR-96-14-A, para. 53; *Sikirica et al.*, Trial Chamber, (Judgment on Defence Motions to Acquit), supra note 171, para. 89.

a 'group as such' instead of using just 'ቡድን' which means 'group'. Had it been inserted in the definition of genocide, 'ን' (as such) could have emphasized that the primary target of genocide is the protected group as 'a separate and distinct entity',[365] not members of the group. Nonetheless, it is worth asking at this point whether the absence of 'as such'/'ን' in the Ethiopian definition of the crime of genocide has affected the judicial determination of genocide.

Some of the Ethiopian judgments stated that the main target of a genocidal campaign is the protected group not its members, save their general lack of meticulous examination of the genocidal *mens rea*. This may notably be inferred from judgments of the ASC which stated that the ultimate aim of the perpetrators was to destroy the group by annihilating its members.[366] The ASC also emphasized that to enter a conviction for genocide, it should be proved that the targeted group has a separate and distinctive existence, without which it cannot be said that there existed a plan/intent to destroy a protected group.[367] In a similar vein, the FSC also argued that the law of genocide focuses on the destruction of groups. It reversed the lower court's conviction owing to the insufficiency or unavailability of evidence placing the victims within the protected groups.[368] It also stated that political killings do not necessarily imply that the destruction of a political group was intended.[369] Admittedly, such decisions seem to have mirrored the international jurisprudence that genocide targets the destruction of a group as such, even in the absence of the words 'as such' in Ethiopian law.

However, Ethiopian courts have continuously handed out rulings and judgments that are inconsistent and self-contradictory. The fact that individuals were executed due to their real or perceived membership to a group was *in itself* regarded sufficient for the purpose of genocide.[370] Courts have often used interchangeably the expressions *plan to destroy* a group and *plan to destroy members of a group*, thus making it difficult to decipher whether it is the destruction of a group or that of its members that is a prerequisite to establish genocidal *mens rea*.[371]

---

365   See ILC Draft 1996, *Yearbook of International Law Commission 1996 II*, Article 17, para. 7.
366   In *Dagnenet Ayalew et al.*, the ASC stated that 'the *Dergue* planned to destroy the group by reducing the size of its members through killing'. See *Dagnenet Ayalew et al.,* (Trial Judgment), *supra* note 50, 4.
367   In not considering the executions of several individuals labelled *anti-revolutionaries* or *anti-people* as genocidal, the ASC stated that such expressions failed to denote the separate and distinctive existence of a group. See ibid.
368   *Colonel Mengistu Hailemariam et al.,* (Appeals Judgment), *supra* note 25, 71.
369   Ibid.
370   See above sections 5.5.1.1 and 5.5.3.
371   That was the case even with the FSC, which, by acquitting the *Dergue* leaders of genocide in relation to some of the counts, appeared to be more careful in its analysis, compared

Based on the foregoing, one may argue that Ethiopian courts would have been more careful in highlighting that genocide protects a group, had Ethiopian criminal law used the emphasis marker '፯' (as such) to identify a group. Nonetheless, this could be too simplistic an argument as it could amount to treating 'as such'(፯) as genocide's magical element, which it hardly is. To the contrary, it has been highlighted by commentators, as well as by some courts, that what is required by 'as such' is already required by the 'specific intent' element of genocide.[372]

As for the motive requirement, it is stated in the jurisprudence of international courts that the application of 'as such' requires establishing that it was the individual victim's membership to a protected group that drove the perpetrator to attack him or her, although such membership does not have to be the sole basis for the perpetrator's decision to attack.[373] Similar to what is said above, this interpretation was also regarded as already covered by the requirement of specific intent to destroy.[374] Indeed, in rejecting Ruzindana's appeal seeking acquittal based on the fact that his actions were accompanied by personal motives, the ICTR Appeals Chamber made no reference to the words 'as such', but only to intent to destroy:

> criminal intent (mens rea) must not be confused with motive and that, in respect of genocide, personal motive does not exclude criminal responsibility providing that the acts proscribed in Article 2(2)(a) through to (e) were committed 'with intent to destroy, in whole or in part a national, ethnical, racial or religious group'.[375]

---

to the lower courts. See *Colonel Mengistu Hailemariam et al.,* (Appeals Judgment), *supra* note 25, 70–73.

372 See Berster, 'Article II', *supra* note 14, 152: stressing that the protective purpose of the criminalization of genocide 'is already expressed by the specific intent-requirement with great clarity'; Werle and Jessberger, *Principles of International Criminal Law, supra* note 156, 315, referring to the 'as such' element as making the intent to destroy a group 'more precise'. See also ICTY Trial Chamber in *Zdravko Tolimir,* stating that 'the term "as such" reemphasizes the crime's prohibition of the destruction of the protected group itself'. *Tolimir,* Trial Chamber, (Judgment), *supra* note 14, para. 747. See however ICTR Appeals Chamber in *Niyitegeka* stating that 'the term "as such" clarifies the specific intent requirement', thus implying that the scope and meaning of specific intent is not clear enough without this addition. *Niyitegeka,* Appeals Chamber, (Judgment), *supra* note 364, para. 53.

373 See *Akayesu,* Trial Chamber, (Judgment), *supra* note 8, para. 521; ICTY, *Prosecutor v. Blagojević and Jokić,* Trial Chamber, (Judgment), 17 January 2005, IT-02-60-T, para. 669.

374 See Berster, 'Article II', *supra* note 14, 152–153.

375 *Kayishema and Ruzindana,* Appeals Chamber, (Judgment), *supra* note 186, para. 161.

As far as Ethiopian law is concerned it could simply be submitted here that it does not, at least theoretically, confuse intention with motive. Although at times it mentions a specific category of motive (often 'motive of gain') to distinguish an aggravated form of a crime from an extenuated version,[376] motive is not an element of a crime.[377] In relation to genocide, Ethiopian law does not indicate motive as a required element, nor did the practice. As an element of crime, prosecutors did not need to prove the existence of any kind of motive, although showing its nature and presence prior to or at the time of the commission of the crime may help prove the existence of the required intent. In the genocide trials, the existence of a particular motive was highlighted by the courts to be indicative of the absence or existence of intent to destroy a protected group.

As can be inferred from the CUD trials, a particular motive may indicate a particular intent insofar as a motive seen as indicating the intent required to establish treason was not regarded as sufficient to establish genocidal intent. From the discussion in this case, it was also clear that a motive may trigger a certain intent, but has no impact on the evolution of that intent in the sense that an intent to commit treason may evolve into intent to destroy an ethnic, racial or national group to which the most influential members of the ruling political party belong.[378].

In the *Oromo-Gumuz* trials, the FHC noted that the perpetrators were motivated to acquire a farming land occupied by *Oromo* farmers. On the face of it, a motive to acquire a land does not necessarily require destroying its inhabitants. It could be achieved by subjecting the inhabitants to various forms of attack, including killing and causing bodily injury aimed at expelling the inhabitants from the disputed land by force. The fact that the perpetrators

---

376 See Criminal Code of 2005, Articles 92, 373, 514, 525.
377 It may however have significance at the sentencing stage as it could serve to either aggravate or mitigate a sentence as the case maybe. Ibid., Articles 82(1), 84(1). Exceptionally, the law may consider motive as an element of a crime as it did in relation to crimes such as refusal to provide for medical assistance and aggravated homicide. Ibid., Articles 373 and 539. Even for these crimes, motive is just an alternative element, as opposed to a *sine qua non* element. Aggravated homicide, for example, could be considered committed if accompanied by any kind of motive or other factor or a manner of commission that could show the perpetrator's exceptional cruelty or dangerousness. Furthermore, aggravated homicide may be considered to have occurred if an act resulted from theperpetrator's membership to a criminal group or from his or her intention to further another crime. See ibid, Article 539.
378 See *Engineer Hailu Shawul et al.,* (Trial Ruling), *supra* note 284,196.

acted with such a motive does not have a direct effect on the formation of the intent to destroy. In *Mengesha et al.*, such motive did not not negate the existence of the required genocidal *mens rea*:[379] the motive was here considered as irrelevant, and the existence of the intent to destroy was established from relevant circumstantial evidence.[380]

In the *Dergue* trials, where it was stated that the *Dergue* was from the outset established with the intent/plan to destroy political groups, the defendants argued that there was no reason (motive) for the *Dergue* to have emerged with such an intent/plan. According to the defendants, the *Dergue* had popular support and good intentions aimed at ensuring the peace and unity of the country and therefore could not have had the urge to destroy political groups.[381] The FHC dismissed this argument by stating that having several well intentioned objectives does not exclude the fact that a crime may be committed just out of one ill-intentioned governmental objective.[382] In a similar vein, the Court highlighted that once the existence of an intent or plan to destroy political groups was established in evidence, it cannot be refuted by showing other unrelated intentions the perpetrators might have had.[383] As such, the existence or absence of a particular motive was not regarded as a decisive factor in determining genocidal *mens rea*, and even in establishing the existence of the intent to destroy among the highest ranking perpetrators or orchestrators of genocide.[384]

Be that as it may, one may wonder whether the absence of 'as such' may render the Ethiopian law on genocide incomplete. One possible argument is that the Criminal Code of 2005 should have rectified its predecessor's defect in this regard. At the time the Criminal Code was being drafted, Ethiopian courts had already highlighted that the legislator may not omit but only expand the elements of genocide as layed out in international

---

379 See *Tadesse Jewanie Mengesha et al.*, (Trial Judgment), *supra* note 88, 42–45. See also *Tesfaye Neno Loya et al.*, (Trial Judgment), *supra* note 88, 41–44.
380 The dissenting judge opined that the existence of the motive to acquire a piece of land showed the existence of no more than the intention to remove the farmers by force, and, therefore, the perpetrators lacked intent to destroy. See section 6.4.3 above.
381 See *Colonel Mengistu Hailemariam et al.*, (Trial Judgment), *supra* note 10, 110–111.
382 Ibid., 111.
383 Ibid.
384 Some commentators have however suggested that 'as such' could be reconsidered and interpreted in a manner that attaches to the definition of genocide a requirement of collective motive of a general nature (an overarching genocidal motive), although individual perpetrators should not be allowed to invoke personal motives as a defense for attacking individual members of a group. See Berster, 'Article II', *supra* note 14, 155; Schabas, *Genocide in International Law*, *supra* note 4, 254–256.

THE CRIME OF GENOCIDE IN ETHIOPIAN TRIALS: ELEMENTS OF THE CRIME   305

law.[385] However, the Ethiopian law on genocide has never been a *verbatim* copy of the Convention's definition. Furthermore, the fact that the phrase 'as such' has been viewed as redundant – either because its purpose could be served by the existence of *dolus specialis* or because motive is not a required element of genocidal *mens rea* – might also discourage any attempt to include it in domestic laws.

Had the Ethiopian legislator wanted to reproduce the exact terms of the international definition of genocide and incorporate the phrase 'as such' into the domestic law by using the Amharic language, it is unclear whether this would even have been possible. This is a tricky point because the answer depends on whether the domestic legislator can fairly determine the meaning of 'as such' in the context of the Convention. As noted in the foregoing discussion, both the doctrine and the international case law have shown that 'as such' is an ambiguous terminology and it could simply be nonsensical to try to find the right Amharic word that could describe it.

In this respect, one may point out that an attempt by the FHC to provide an Amharic translation of the definition of genocide under Article II of the Genocide Convention also omitted the words 'as such'. In *Mengistu et al.*, in a bid to explain the differences between the Convention and the Penal Code of 1957, the FHC produced its own Amharic translation of the Convention's definition of genocide[386] and omitted the phrase 'as such'. It is suggested here that either the terms were viewed as redundant additions by the Court or that their exact meaning was actually not obvious to the Court.

6.5   Conclusion: Undiscussed Genocides

This chapter has discussed the elements of the crime of genocide and their interpretation in Ethiopian trials. The following striking aspects of the Ethiopian case law on genocide could be pointed out. Firstly, unlike their international counterparts, Ethiopian courts have excessively relied on victims' membership to a protected group in a manner that equated any attack against a protected group with a genocidal attack. At times, it is not clear from the case

---

385   See Chapter 5, section 5.5.
386   See FHC, SPO v. *Colonel Mengistu Hailemariam et al.*, (Ruling on Preliminary Objections), 10 October 1995, File No. 1/87, 84. The Court's Amharic translation of Article II of the Genocide Convention reads, 'ማንም ሰው በቅንቅና ልማድ አንድ የሆነውን ዘር በሃይማኖት በጎሳ ወይም በብሔር ተሳስሮ የተቋቋመውን የጎብረ ብሔርን ማሕበራዊ የሆነ አንድ ክፍል ሕዝብ በመላው ዊይም በከፊል ለማጥፋት በማቀድ የጥፋቱን ሥራ በማቋቋም ትእዛዝ በመስጠት ወይም ይህን አድራጎት በሥራ ላይ በማዋል'.

law whether, in the courts' understanding, it is members of the group or the group itself that are protected by the law criminalizing genocide. Even then, Ethiopian courts did not attempt to determine and define whether a targeted group was indeed a protected group in the eyes of the law of genocide. This was notably the case in the genocide trials that dealt with genocide against ethnic groups, where no definitional parameter was provided to characterize such groups.

Secondly, Ethiopian courts have often failed to draw a clear connection between the *actus reus* elements of genocide and the genocide itself. Mostly, a proof of *actus reus* was considered *per se* sufficient to prove the commission of genocide. In the process, the Ethiopian case law overlooked the importance of linking the *actus reus* to the genocidal *mens rea*, as a result of which defendants were convicted just because they had committed the prohibited acts and their victims belonged to a protected group, as alleged by the prosecutor.

Thirdly, the practice has not clarified the requisite genocidal *mens rea*, which was, as discussed in Chapter 5, ambiguously defined in Ethiopian law. Courts remain divided on the question whether a plan or an intent is the required *mens rea* for genocide. This happened to be the case even after the Criminal Code of 2005 replaced its predecessor's 'plan to destroy' with 'intent to destroy'. Nonetheless, the courts have developed consensuses as regards some aspects of the genocidal *mens rea* such as the irrelevance of the substantiality of the number of victims, regarding which international practice stands divided.

That being said, it is worth recalling the statement made at the outset of the chapter: discussing the elements of genocide under Ethiopian law could prove a difficult task because of the prolixity of the law and of the judges' reluctance to examine each and every element of the crime. Indeed, it is pointed out in several parts of this chapter that Ethiopian judges have rendered unsubstantiated conclusions. They often reached their conclusion without thoroughly examining the complex elements of the crime of genocide. As such, any conclusion as to whether the Ethiopian genocide trials were in line with international standards needs to be accompanied with a disclaimer that Ethiopian courts did not discuss each of the elements expressly and directly, but briefly and in general terms. In that respect, the Ethiopian practice convicted defendants without fully and methodically discussing whether genocide had indeed been committed. These numerous instances could thus be best described as cases of undiscussed genocides.

In fact, this problem of convicting defendants for genocide without discussing the elements of the crimes was not limited to the practice of trial courts. Several appeals that were lodged against genocide convictions were often dismissed by the appellate court, the FSC, without explanation. This was notably the case in the *Oromo-Gumuz* trials where the FSC's majority decision dismissed all of the 99 appeals against the FHC's genocide conviction in *Mangesh et al.* by merely stating: 'after examining the issue in light of the indictment, the evidence, and the applicable law, we have dismissed the appeal pursuant to Article 195(1) of the Code of Criminal Procedure due to lack of sufficient ground for interference'.[387]

---

387   See for instance, FSC, *Jarmosa Ayansa Jamato* v. *Federal Prosecutor*, (Appeals Decision), 07 April 2010, File No. 53594, 2. Translation by the author. The original (Amharic) version reads: 'ይግባኝ ከክሱ ፡ ከቀረቡት ማስረጃዎችና ከሕጉ ጋር ባገገናዘብ እንደመረመርነው ወደ ጉዳዩ ለመግባት የሚያስችል በቂ ምክያት ባለመገኘቱ ይግባኙን በወ/መ/ሕ/ሥ/ሥ/ቁ 195/2/ መሠረት ባለመቀበል መዝገቡን ዘግተናል።'.

CHAPTER 7

War Crimes in Ethiopia
Law and Practice

7.1 Introduction

By definition, war crimes occur in the context of an armed conflict, a phenomenon that has commonly happened in Ethiopia. Like several other states, Ethiopia has a long history of fighting wars, be they internal or international in character. It went to war with all of its neighbors except for Djibouti and Kenya.[1] It also fought with countries with which it does not share any official boarder, such as Egypt,[2] the United Kingdom,[3] and Italy. Of all these wars, the ones that had the most significant sociopolitical and legal impact are the two wars with Italy: the battle of Adwa in 1896[4] and the Second Italo-Ethiopian war in 1935–1936.[5] The former is still seen as a symbol of victory and pride not only for Ethiopia but also for the whole African continent.[6] The Second

---

1   For details of the Mahdist war with Sudan, see B. Zewde, *A History of Modern Ethiopia:1855–1991* (2nd ed., Oxford: James Currey, 2001) 55–59. The Ogaden war was fought in the late 1970s between Ethiopia and Somalia. See G. Tareke, *The Ethiopian Revolution: War in the Horn of Africa* (New Haven: Yale University Press, 2009) 182–217. The recent war with Eritrea, referred to as the meaningless war, resulted in a two decades long military stalemate between the two countries until 2018. S. Kiley, 'A pointless, savage war is finally over' *CNN* (18 September 2018), available at: <https://edition.cnn.com/2018/09/18/opinions/ethiopia-eritrea-war-comes-to-an-end-kiley-opinion-intl/index.html> accessed 28 September 2019.
2   For the 1875 and 1876 war with Egypt, see C. Jesman, 'The Egyptian Invasion of Ethiopia' (1959) 58(230) *African Affairs* 75–81.
3   In 1867, the British expedition to Abyssinia (now Ethiopia) ended with a war at Magdala. See C.R. Markham, *A History of the Abyssinian Expedition* (London: Macmillan and Co., 1869) 314–354.
4   For a brief summary, see R. Overy, *A History of War in 100 Battles* (New York: William Collins, 2014) 268–274. For a comprehensive history, see J. Raymond, *The Battle of Adwa: African History in the Age of Empire* (Cambridge: Harvard University Press, 2011) 111–208.
5   See Zewde, *A History of Modern Ethiopia, supra* note 1, 150–178.
6   See T.M. Vestal, 'Reflections on the Battle of Adwa and its Significance for Today' in P. Milkias and G. Metaferia (eds.), *The Battle of Adwa: Reflections on Ethiopia's Historic Against European Colonialism* (New York: Algora Publishing, 2005) 21–36. The battle of Adwa is still remembered as a heroic achievement in Ethiopia's military history and the highest award that may be bestowed upon an Ethiopian individual in military spheres is known as the *Medal of the Victory of Adwa*. See Defense Forces (Amendment) Proclamation, Proclamation No. 123/1998, *entered into force* 30 June 1998, Article 38(1).

Italo-Ethiopian war portrays the exact opposite as it resulted in the country's occupation from 1937–1942; period during which atrocities were perpetrated.[7] It is precisely this war and the consequent occupation that triggered Ethiopia's involvement in the international effort to prevent and punish war crimes.[8]

Internally, it could prove difficult to point out a substantial period of time in Ethiopia free from a protracted armed conflict.[9] Civil wars occurred in the aftermath of every other international conflict, if not during the exact same period the State was fighting another sovereign. The pre-unification era, in particular the period between 1855 and 1896, also known as the era of princess, is often typified by countless armed conflicts fought between several war lords.[10] In the near past, from 1961 to 1991, a 30 years long armed conflict, 'the longest in post-colonial Africa', took place between the Ethiopian government and various armed groups, most of which referred to themselves as liberation fronts.[11] Of the liberation fronts, the Eritrean Peoples' Liberation Front (successor of the Eritrean Liberation Front (ELF)) was the first to embark on the longest journey of what could be characterized as a war of liberation, which ended in 1991 with the creation of the independent State of Eritrea. The *Tigray* Liberation Front (TPLF), which started an armed struggle in 1975 from the northern part of the country, was later on joined by other groups and formed the Ethiopian Peoples' Revolutionary Democratic Front (EPRDF) which succeeded at overthrowing the *Dergue* in May 1991.[12] In the East, the *Oromo* Liberation Front (OLF) had fought the *Dergue* until it was forced to reestablish itself in the western part of the country.[13] Other groups

---

7   See section 7.2. below.
8   Ibid.
9   Bulcha characterizes all of the internal wars fought in Ethiopia for the past 150 years as genocidal wars. See M. Bulcha, 'Genocidal Violence in the Making of Nation and State in Ethiopia' (2005) 9(2) *African Sociological Review* 1–54. Such a generalized characterization could be challenged from various aspects, including the absence in Bulcha's study of a separate treatment of the countless internal conflicts.
10 See P.B. Henze, *Layers of Time: A history of Ethiopia* (New York: Palgrave, 2000) 119–167.
11 See Tareke, *The Ethiopian Revolution*, supra note 1, 59.
12 See A. Berhe, *A Political History of the Tigray People's Liberation Front (1975–1991): Revolt, Ideology and Mobilisation in Ethiopia* (PhD Dissertation, Vrijie Universiteit Amsterdam, 2009), 313–345.
13 M. Plaut, 'Ethiopia's Oromo Liberation Front' (2006) 33(109) *Review of African Political Economy* 587–593; A. Tiruneh, *The Ethiopian Revolution 1974–1987: A Transformation*

such as the Ethiopian Democratic Union (EDU) and the Ethiopian Peoples' Revolutionary Army (EPRA), the armed wing of the Ethiopian Peoples' Revolutionary Party (EPRP), were also involved in relatively less significant armed conflicts in the 1970s.[14]

It was in 1991 that the lengthy civil war ended and a new political chapter began in Ethiopia, following which the country started reflecting on how to respond to the atrocities committed during the armed conflicts, as discussed in Part 1 of this book. The reckoning culminated in the establishment of the SPO, aimed at bringing to justice alleged perpetrators of war crimes and other international and domestic crimes (see Chapter 2). In 2010, by the time the SPO submitted a completion report to the Federal House of Peoples Representatives (the Parliament), it was stated that out of the hundreds of investigations it carried out, the SPO could only prosecute one single case involving war crimes.[15] This was the *SPO v. Legesse Asfaw et al.* case, which dealt with the prosecution of war crimes against the civilian population in violation of Article 282 of the Penal Code of 1957.[16] This case thus constitutes the focal point of this chapter, in addition to the discussion of the specific Ethiopian legal provisions on war crimes.

Legesse Asfaw et al. is however not the only case that dealt with war crimes committed in Ethiopia. The District Court of the Hague in the Netherlands took up a case in 2017, the case of *Eshetu Alemu* in which it exercised universal jurisdiction over war crimes committed in Ethiopia,[17] although the same facts had already been prosecuted as genocide against political groups by the FHC and the same accused had been convicted and sentenced to death *in absentia*.[18] This chapter thus also makes reference to this case whenever necessary to

---

from an Aristocratic to a Totalitarian Autocracy (Cambridge: Cambridge University Press, 1992) 366–367.

14   These groups were more active in what was referred to as the White-Terror than in the armed struggle. Their less intense armed struggle did not last long as both groups were defeated by the TPLF by the end of the 1970s. See Tareke, *The Ethiopian Revolution, supra* note 1, 86–88; Tiruneh, *The Ethiopian Revolution 1974–1987, supra* note13, 213–214.

15   See Special Prosecutor's Office, *Dem Yazele Dossie: Begizeyawi Wotaderawi Dergue Weyem Mengist Abalat Benetsuhan Zegoch Laye Yetefetsem Wenjel Zegeba* (Addis Ababa: Far-East Trading P.L.C., 2010), Annex 2.

16   See FHC, *SPO v. Legesse Asfaw et al.,* (Trial Judgment), 4 February 2008, File No. 03116.

17   District Court of The Hague, *Prosecutor v. Eshetu Alemu,* Judgment, 15 December 2017, (ECLI:NL:RBDHA:2017:14782).

18   FHC, *SPO v. Eshetu Alemu,* (Trial Judgment) 8 May 2000, File No. 921/89.

draw a comparison as to how the two courts have interpreted issues common to war crimes trials, such as the existence of an armed conflict and the nexus requirement.

The focus of this chapter is to examine the Ethiopian law on war crimes and the practice of Ethiopian courts in the light of the relevant standards developed in international criminal law through, in particular, the jurisprudence of the *ad hoc* international tribunals and the ICC. It is striking that, similarly to the Ethiopian genocide trials discussed in the previous chapter, the war crimes trial did not refer to the jurisprudence of international court and tribunals. Neither in its 2007 ruling[19] nor in its 2008 judgment[20] or sentencing[21] did the FHC make reference to any of the judgments issued at the international level. For some reason, the FHC did not notice – or deliberately ignored – the relevance of seminal decisions and judgments of the ICTY Appeals Chamber, such as the 1995 *Tadić* interlocutory decision on jurisdiction[22] or the 2002 *Kunarac* judgment (in relation to the nexus to an armed conflict),[23] and of the ICTR Appeals Chamber in the *Rutaganda* case.[24] This puts the trial of *Legesse Asfaw et al.* in stark contrast with the above-mentioned *Eshetu Alemu* case, in which the District Court of The Hague heavily relied on the jurisprudence of the ICTY, ICTR and ICC to determine many of the issues raised.[25]

It should however be pointed out here that *Legesse Asfaw et al.* possesses a unique position in the trials of core crimes in Ethiopia, not just because it is, so far, the only war crimes trials held in the country but also because it seems to be the only case that, perhaps paradoxically considering its disregard for international case law, extensively relied on the letter of international law. As will be shown, the FHC referred to rules of international humanitarian law (IHL) in the same way a municipal court would refer to its own domestic laws. This could be seen as the most interesting aspect of the comparison between the

---

19   See FHC, SPO v. *Legesse Asfaw et al.* (Trial Ruling), 10 January 2007, File No. 03116.
20   *Legesse Asfaw et al.*, (Trial Judgment), *supra* note 16.
21   FHC, SPO v. *Legesse Asfaw et al.*, (Sentencing Judgment), 4 February 2008, File No. 03116.
22   See ICTY, *Prosecutor v. Tadić*, Appeals Chamber, (Decision on the defense motion for interlocutory appeal on jurisdiction), 2 October 1995, IT-94-1-A.
23   ICTY, *Prosecutor v. Kunarac et al.*, Appeals Chamber, (Judgment), 12 July 2002, IT-96-23/1-A.
24   ICTR, *Prosecutor v. Rutaganda*, Appeals Chamber, (Judgment), 26 May 2003, ICTR-96-3-A.
25   *Prosecutor v. Eshetu Alemu*, *supra* note 18.

Ethiopian trial and international trials as it offers the opportunity to examine how Ethiopian and international courts have interpreted rules of IHL without referring to each other's prior decisions.

To conduct this examination, this chapter comprises eight sections, which firstly address the analysis of the law before examining the practice. Section 7.2 discusses the incorporation and evolution of war crimes law in Ethiopia. It also presents the early failed attempts to prosecute war crimes in Ethiopia. The subsequent four sections, sections 7.3–7.6, focus on the state of Ethiopian law on war crimes. Section 7.3 identifies war crimes provisions in Ethiopian criminal law by examining provisions that are usually referred to as war crimes in the light of the serious violations of IHL requirement advanced by the ICTY Appeals chamber in *Tadić*.[26] Section 7.4. appraises the fact that Ethiopian war crimes provisions are not subjected to the traditional classification of war crimes based on the type of armed conflict. Section 7.5 examines the manner and the extent to which rules of IHL could be considered as having a direct or an interpretative application in Ethiopian war crimes law; an examination which also involves an in-depth discussion on the principle of legality. Section 7.6 finalizes the chapter's discussion on the Ethiopian war crimes law by summarizing those individual acts of war crimes which are expressly and specifically listed in Ethiopian law and those which can be considered punishable in Ethiopia through the direct application of IHL. In so doing, it adopts a comparative approach by using Article 8(2) of the ICC Statute, which, to date, constitutes the most comprehensive list of war crimes and can admittedly be seen as the criminalization of IHL norms. The last two sections discuss the actual prosecution of war crimes in Ethiopia. Section 7.7. provides for a separate examination of the war crimes prosecuted in the *Legesse Asfaw et al.* case. It introduces the case, the counts, and explores the individual war crimes tried by the court and the manner in which the nexus to an armed conflict requirement was established by the FHC. Beyond examining the law and the trial in Ethiopia, this chapter critically discusses and questions, under section 7.8., the absence of more war crimes trials in Ethiopia.

---

26   *Tadić*, (Decision on the defense motion for interlocutory appeal on jurisdiction), *supra* note 22, para. 92.

7.2 Early Efforts to Punish War Crimes in Ethiopia: The UNWCC and the EWCC

Ethiopia does not have a separate legislation on war crimes. The rules on war crimes were incorporated into the Ethiopian legal system in 1957 – a decade before Ethiopia became a party to the Geneva Conventions of 1949.[27] It had, however, already acceded to several IHL treaties concluded at the end of the 19th and early 20th centuries, commonly referred to as the 'law of The Hague'.[28]

---

27 On 2 October 1969, Ethiopia ratified: Geneva Convention for the Amelioration of the Condition of the Wounded and Sick in Armed Forces in the Field, 75 U.N.T.S. 31, *entered into force* 21 October 1950 [Hereinafter: GC I]; Geneva Convention for the Amelioration of the Condition of Wounded, Sick and Shipwrecked Members of Armed Forces at Sea, 75 U.N.T.S. 85, *entered into force* 21 October 1950 [Hereinafter: GC II]; Geneva Convention relative to the Treatment of Prisoners of War, 75 U.N.T.S. 135, *entered into force* 21 October 1950 [Hereinafter: GC III]; Geneva Convention relative to the Protection of Civilian Persons in Time of War, 75 U.N.T.S. 287, *entered into force* 21 October 1950 [Hereinafter: GC IV].

28 In August 1935, Ethiopia acceded to The Hague laws on methods and means of warfare: Hague IV, Declaration II- Concerning the Prohibition of the Use of Projectiles Diffusing Asphyxiating Gases, 29 July 1899, 26 *Martens Nouveau Recueil* (ser. 2) 998, 187 Consol. T.S. 453, *entered into force* 4 September 1900; Hague IV, Declaration III- Concerning the Prohibition of the Use of Expanding Bullets, 29 July 1899, 26 *Martens Nouveau Recueil* (ser. 2) 1002, 187 Consol. T.S. 459, *entered into force* 4 September 1900; Hague Convention IV – Laws and Customs of War on Land: 18 October 1907, 36 Stat. 2277, 1 Bevans 631, 205 Consol. T.S. 277, 3 *Martens Nouveau Recueil* (ser. 3) 461, *entered into force* 26 January 1910 [Hereinafter: Hague Convention IV]; Hague Convention IX concerning Bombardment by Naval Forces in Time of War, 3 *Martens Nouveau Recueil* (ser. 3) 604, 205 Consol. T.S. 345, *entered into force* 26 January 1910; Declaration (XIV) Prohibiting the Discharge of Projectiles and Explosives from Balloons. The Hague, 18 October 1907, *entered into force* 27 November 1909.

At the same time, it acceded to: Hague Convention VI – Status of Enemy Merchant Ships at the Outbreak of Hostilities: 18 October 1907, 205 Consol. T.S. 305, 3 *Martens Nouveau Recueil* (ser. 3) 533, *entered into force* 26 January 1910; Hague Convention VII relating to the Conversion of Merchant Ships into War-Ships, 3 *Martens Nouveau Recueil* (ser. 3) 557, 205 Consol. T.S. 319, *entered into force* 26 January 1910; Hague Convention VIII relative to the Laying of Automatic Submarine Contact Mines, 3 *Martens Nouveau Recueil* (ser. 3) 580, 205 Consol. T.S. 331, *entered into force* 26 January 1910; Hague Convention IX concerning Bombardment by Naval Forces in Time of War, 3 *Martens Nouveau Recueil* (ser. 3) 604, 205 Consol. T.S. 345, *entered into force* 26 January 1910; Hague Convention XI – Restrictions With Regard to the Exercise of the Right of Capture in Naval War: 18 October 1907, 36 Stat. 2396, 1 Bevans 711, 205 Consol. T.S. 367, 3 *Martens Nouveau Recueil* (ser. 3) 663, *entered into force* 26 January 1910; Hague Convention XIII -Rights and Duties of Neutral Powers in Naval War: 18 October 1907, 36 Stat. 2415, 1 Bevans 723, 205 Consol. T.S. 395, 3 *Martens Nouveau Recueil* 713 (ser. 3), *entered into force* 26 January 1910.

It also acceded (still in 1935) to: Hague Convention III- Opening of Hostilities: 18 October 1907, 36 Stat. 2259, 1 Bevans 619, 205 Consol. T.S. 263, 3 *Martens Nouveau Recueil*

Given that it became a party to these laws in September 1935, that is, immediately before the Italian invasion on 3 October 1935, it could be the case that the accession was an attempt to mitigate the possible undesirable consequences of the war that was coming. It is indeed likely that this was a calculated move to notify the invading power to abide by the rules of IHL conventions,[29] notably as Italy was already a party to all of the conventions to which Ethiopia acceded.[30]

Yet, what was feared eventually happened. The 1935–36 Italo-Ethiopian war and the military occupation from 1937 until 1942 showed a total disregard for the rules of IHL by the Italian forces. This was evidenced through *inter alia* Italy's use of poisonous and mustard gas, bombing of Red Cross hospitals and ambulances, execution of captured prisoners without trial, massacres in Addis Ababa and Dabra Libnos, and shootings of 'witch-doctors'.[31] The horrors and

---

(ser. 3) 437, *entered into force* 26 January 1910; Hague Convention V – Rights and Duties of Neutral Powers and Persons in Case of War on Land: 18 October 1907, 36 Stat. 2310, 1 Bevans 654, 205 Consol. T.S. 299, 3 *Martens Nouveau Recueil* (ser. 3) 504, *entered into force* 26 January 1910; Protocol for the Prohibition of the Use of Asphyxiating, Poisonous or Other Gases, and of Bacteriological Methods of Warfare, Geneva, 94 L.N.T.S. 65, *entered into force* 08 February 1928.

29   See for example, Hague Convention IV, Article 2, 'the provisions contained in the Regulations referred to in Article 1, as well as in the present Convention, do not apply except between Contracting powers, and then only if all the belligerents are parties to the Convention'. This scope of application has changed with the adoption of the Geneva Conventions of 1949 where the Conventions remains applicable between the Contracting parties, even if the conflict is joined by a non-Contracting party. See International Committee of the Red Cross, *Commentary of 2016: Article 2*, paras 344–346, available at: <https://ihl-databases.icrc.org/applic/ihl/ihl.nsf/Comment.xsp?action=openDocument&documentId=BE2D518CF5DE54EAC1257F7D0036B518#_Toc452041593> accessed 29 September 2019. [Hereinafter: ICRC, *Commentary of 2016*].

30   For the list of IHL treaties to which Italy was a party before the outbreak of the Italo-Ethiopian war in 1935, see <https://ihl-databases.icrc.org/applic/ihl/ihl.nsf/vwTreatiesByCountrySelected.xsp?xp_countrySelected=IT> accessed 28 September 2019.

31   For some of the atrocities committed during the occupation, see I. Campbell, *The Addis Ababa Massacre: Italy's National Shame* (Oxford; Oxford University Press, 2017) 59–203; I. Campbell, *The Massacre of Debre Libanos: Ethiopia 1937: The Story of one of Fascism's Most Shocking Atrocities* (Addis Ababa: Addis Ababa University Press, 2014); R. Pankhurst, 'Italian Fascist War Crimes in Ethiopia: A History of Their Discussion, from the League of Nations to the United Nations (1936–1949)' (1999) 6(1–2) *Northeast African Studies* 83–140; Zewde, *A History of Modern Ethiopia*, *supra* note 1, 150–178; United Nations War Crimes Commission, The (Compilers), *History of the United Nations War Crimes Commission and the Development of the Laws of War* (London: His Majesty's Stationery Office, 1948) 51– 52. See also B. Bridle, 'Ethiopia 1935–36: Mustard gas and attacks on the Red Cross' *Le Temps* (13 August 2003), available at: <https://www.icrc.org/en/doc/resources/documents/article/other/5ruhgm.htm> accessed 5 August 2019; R. Baudendistel, 'Force versus law: The

indiscriminate nature of the war forced the Ethiopian Emperor into the exile that he said he took to save the people from extermination.[32]

In 1942, after the Italian military occupation had ended with the help of the British forces and following the return of the Emperor,[33] Ethiopia issued a declaration of war, siding with the Allies in their fight against the Axis Powers, which it described as 'the fight for the liberation of the world'.[34] In 1945, it adhered, as the eighth and the only African state, to the London Agreement for the Prosecution and Punishment of the Major War Criminals of the European Axis.[35] In doing so, it had hoped that the planned prosecution of the Axis Powers would include bringing Italy to justice for atrocities committed in Ethiopia. Regrettably, that never happened, notably because the Second Italo-Ethiopian war was considered 'another war', not part of the Second World War.[36] This same reason was invoked to justify the exclusion of Ethiopia from membership to the UN War Crimes Commission (UNWCC).[37] This 'other war' justification seems convincing, given that the IMT's temporal jurisdiction covered crimes committed following Germany's invasion of Poland on 1 September 1939, although this was in practice extended to cover certain crimes committed as early as 30 January 1933, the date Hitler was appointed Chancellor of Germany.[38]

International Committee of the Red Cross and chemical warfare in the Italo-Ethiopian war 1935–1936' (1998) 38(322) *International Review of the Red Cross* 81–104.

32 The exile of the Emperor in 1936 was allegedly meant to save the people from extermination by ceasing resistance and leaving the country. In a telegram sent to the League of Nations, the Emperor wrote on 10 May 1936, 'We have decided to bring to an end the most unequal, most unjust, most barbarous war of our age, and have chosen the road to exile in order that our people will not be exterminated...' See J. Dungan and L.D. Lafore, *Days of Emperor and Clown: The Italo-Ethiopian War, 1935–1936* (New York: Doubleday Books, 1973) 204.

33 For a brief account of the return of Emperor Haileselassie to Ethiopia with the help of the British army in East Africa, see A. Sbacchi, 'Haile Selassie and the Italians 1941–1943' (1979) 22(1) *African Studies Review* 25–42.

34 See The Declaration of War Proclamation, Proclamation No. 33/1942.

35 Agreement for the Prosecution and Punishment of the Major War Criminals of the European Axis, and Charter of the International Military Tribunal. London, 8 August 1945.

36 Ibid., 96–97. Although it is true that the 1935–36 Italo-Ethiopian war was a pre-Second World War conflict, Ethiopia also had a belligerent status during the Second World War. In 1942, soon after the Italian occupation of Ethiopia came to an end with the latter regaining its independence, Ethiopia declared that, in support of what it called 'the fight for the liberation of the world', a state of war existed between itself and the Axis powers. See The Declaration of War Proclamation, Proclamation No. 33/1942.

37 See Pankhurst, 'Italian Fascist War Crimes in Ethiopia', *supra* note 31, 96–98, 109–111.

38 See K.J. Heller, *The Nuremberg Military Tribunals and the Origins of International Criminal Law* (Oxford: Oxford University Press, 2011) 237–242. The fact that the prosecution of war

Not fully discouraged by the futility of its efforts to bring the Italians to justice internationally, Ethiopia issued Imperial Order No. 1784, which established the Ethiopian War Crimes Commission (EWCC) in 1946.[39] The EWCC was mandated to assemble evidence of war crimes and bring charges and criminal proceedings against Italian individuals.[40] 50 suspects were investigated and Ethiopia informed the UNWCC that it had gathered sufficient evidence to bring the Italian offenders to justice for crimes committed during the war and the occupation. Although the UNWCC refused to examine these cases,[41] Ethiopia maintained its effort to bring Italian nationals to justice. It is arguable that the prospect of securing extradition of Italian nationals for prosecution in Ethiopia was reflected in the Treaty of Peace with Italy, concluded in Paris in 1947,[42] whose Article 38 recognized 3 October 1935 (the date Italy invaded Ethiopia) as the start date with respect to all kinds of claims (which might have included criminal responsibility for the atrocities committed) Ethiopia had against Italy or Italian nationals. It read,

> the date from which the provisions of the present Treaty shall become applicable as regards *all measures and acts of any kind whatsoever* entailing the responsibility of Italy or of Italian nationals towards Ethiopia, shall be held to be October 3, 1935.[43]

Following the peace treaty and Ethiopia's statement that 'the charges would be limited in number and the suspects, if surrendered, would be tried by a court which would include European judges', the UNWCC agreed to review Ethiopia's request.[44] It received charges prepared by Ethiopia against ten selected Italians for consideration by Committee I, which examined the charges and placed

---

crimes committed during the Second World War was meant to include the period from 30 January 1933 was also implied in Control Council Law No.10, which stated that, 'in any trial or prosecution for a crime herein referred to, the accused shall not be entitled to the benefits of any statute of limitation in respect to the period from 30 January 1933 to 1 July 1945, nor shall any immunity, pardon or amnesty granted under the Nazi regime be admitted as a bar to trial or punishment'. See Control Council Law No. 10, Punishment of Persons Guilty of War Crimes, Crimes Against Peace and Against Humanity, 20 December 1945, 3 *Official Gazette Control Council for Germany* 50–55 (1946), Article 5.

39 Ethiopian Imperial Order No. 1784; FO 372/4385, T. 19415.
40 Pankhurst, 'Italian Fascist War Crimes in Ethiopia', *supra* note 31, 109.
41 Ibid., 124.
42 Treaty of Peace with Italy, Paris, 10 February 1947; 61 Stat.1245;T.I.A.S. 1648, *entered into force* 15 September 1947.
43 Ibid., Article 38. Emphasis added.
44 United Nations War Crimes Commission, *supra* note 31, 149.

the accused on the list of war criminals in 1947.⁴⁵ Nonetheless, Ethiopia did not succeed in executing its plan to institute criminal proceedings, because, in reality, extradition of Italian nationals to Ethiopia could not be obtained.⁴⁶

In 1949, when the British and the French withdrew their support to facilitate the extradition of Italians to Ethiopia, the hope to see justice for the atrocities perpetrated against Ethiopians vanished.⁴⁷ Consequently, what also simultaneously faded out was Ethiopia's proposal to institute an ahead-of-its-time hybrid criminal tribunal. Ultimately, the question of justice for Ethiopian victims came to a dead end when attempts to establish a Nuremberg-Tokyo-styled Italian tribunal also proved to be unattainable.⁴⁸

Besides, the failed prosecution attempt might have had an adverse effect on the development of war crimes law in Ethiopia. In particular, the absence of sufficient international cooperation on the matter might have created in Ethiopia a disinterest to embrace new developments in the field of IHL. This could be seen in relation to the Geneva Conventions of 12 August 1949, which were adopted around the same time Ethiopia became aware of the fact that the Italian Generals would not be extradited to it.⁴⁹ Although it signed the Geneva Conventions on the date of their adoption, Ethiopia did not ratify them until another 20 years passed, which was unprecedented given that the Genocide Convention was ratified less than a year after its adoption.⁵⁰ In fact, no other treaty signed by Ethiopia waited so long for a ratification by the Parliament.⁵¹ In that sense, the frustrating failure to prosecute Italians for war crimes could have, arguably, played a role in Ethiopia's delayed ratification of the Geneva Conventions of 1949.

Notwithstanding its efforts to prosecute Italian nationals for atrocities committed during the war and the occupation, Ethiopia did not have a domestic law providing for the criminalization and punishment of war crimes. Neither the 1930 Penal Code nor the 1953 Federal Crimes Act contained provisions

---

45 Ibid., 483.
46 For details, see Pankhurst, 'Italian Fascist War Crimes in Ethiopia', *supra* note 31, 136.
47 See L. Prosperi, 'The Missed Italian Nuremberg: The History of an Internationally-sponsored Amnesty' available at: <https://papers.ssrn.com/sol3/papers.cfm?abstract_id=2887267> accessed 29 September 2019, 20–21.
48 For details, see ibid.
49 Ibid., 21.
50 For details, see Chapter 5, section 5.2.
51 Next to the Geneva Conventions of 1949, the instrument that took a long time (nine years) to be ratified by the Ethiopian Parliament was the Convention for the Suppression of Unlawful Seizure of Aircraft [Hijacking Convention], 860 U.N.T.S. 105, *entered into force* 14 October 1971. This was signed in 1970 and ratified in 1979.

on war crimes. It was the Penal Code of 1957 that introduced war crimes into Ethiopian law.

Interestingly, when compared to war crimes laws in other national legal systems, it is arguable that the war crimes provisions of the Penal Code of 1957 were pioneering and represented the most comprehensive incorporation of the prohibition of war crimes into a municipal law.[52] In that regard, credit goes to the drafter of the Code, Swiss jurist Jean Graven, who used both The Hague Conventions *and* IHL conventions to which Ethiopia was not yet a party, i.e. the Geneva Conventions of 1949. As he put it in his essay *The Penal Code of the Empire of Ethiopia*, war crimes

> are infractions of the humanitarian conventions of The Hague and Geneva, laid down more systematically and completely than did the Swiss Military Penal Code revised by the law of 21 December, 1950, and the Yugoslav Military Penal Code revised on 27 February 1951, or again certain special laws like those of the Netherlands of July 1952 and May 1954, after the Diplomatic Conference at Geneva on the Red Cross Conventions in 1949. In this realm, the Ethiopian Code has really given an example which places it at the head of the laws of the World: these offences against international law are all regulated and punished in accordance with the ordinary principles of the law of the country.[53]

The war crimes provisions in the Penal Code of 1957 (Articles 282–295) were drafted in a manner that ensured their applicability irrespective of the international or internal nature of the armed conflict.[54] When the Penal Code was repealed and replaced by the Criminal Code in 2005 (FDRE Criminal Code), similar categories of war crimes were maintained under the new war crimes provisions (Articles 270–282). Nonetheless, two major differences between the two codes emerge – in addition to the difference in penalties, which will be discussed in Chapter 8. First, Article 270 of the Criminal Code, *war crimes against the civilian population*, expanded the list of acts prohibited under this

---

52 See R. van Elst, 'Implementing Universal Jurisdiction Over Grave Breaches of the Geneva Conventions' (2000) 13(1) *Leiden Journal of International Law* 815–854, 825–828.
53 J. Graven, 'The Penal Code of The Empire of Ethiopia' (1964) 1(2) *Journal of Ethiopian Law* 267–298, 295.
54 The war crimes provisions were listed under Article 282–295 of the Penal Code of 1957. See however section 7.3. below regarding the fact that some of the provisions do not constitute war crimes. For the discussion on the scope of the abolition of the distinction between international and internal armed conflicts, see section 7.4.

provision. While seven conducts were prohibited under Article 282 of the Penal Code of 1957,[55] Article 270 now lists 14 proscribed conducts.[56]

---

55   See the Penal Code of 1957, Article 282, which read: Article 282- War crimes against the Civilian Population. Whosoever, in time of war, armed conflict or occupation, organizes, orders or engages in, against the civilian population and in violation of the rules of public international law and of international humanitarian conventions: (a) killings, torture or inhuman treatment, including biological experiments, or any other acts involving dire suffering or bodily harm, or injury to mental or physical health; or (b) wilful reduction to starvation, destitution or general ruination through the depreciation, counterfeiting or systematic debasement of the currency; or (c) the compulsory movement or dispersion of the population, its systematic deportation, transfer or detention in concentration camps or forced labor camps; or (d) forcible enlistment in the enemy's armed forces, intelligence services or administration; or (e) denationalization or forcible religious conversion; or (f) compulsion to acts of prostitution, debauchery or rape; or (g) measures of intimidation or terror, the taking of hostages or the imposition of collective punishments or reprisals; or (h) the confiscation of estates, the destruction or appropriation of property, the imposition of unlawful or arbitrary taxes or levies, or of taxes or levies disproportionate to the requirements of strict military necessity, is punishable with rigorous imprisonment from five years to life, or, in cases of exceptional gravity, with death.

56   See FDRE Criminal Code, Article 270 (i)-(p), which reads:
     Article 270- War crimes against the Civilian Population.
     Whosoever, in time of war, armed conflict or occupation, organizes, orders or engages in, against the civilian population and in violation of the rules of public international law and of international humanitarian conventions:
     ...
     (i) the confiscation, destruction, removal, rendering useless or appropriation of property such as foodstuffs, agricultural areas for the production of foodstuffs, crops, livestock, drinking water installations and supplies and irrigation works, health centers, schools; or
     (j) the destruction, removal, attack, rendering useless or appropriation of the historical monuments, works of art, or places of worship or using them in support of military effort; or
     (k) withholding the provision of clothing, bedding, means of shelter, medical supplies and other supplies essential to the survival of the civilian population of the occupied territory; or
     (l) attacking, displacing, causing to disappear or mistreating persons who, before the beginning of hostilities, were considered as stateless persons or refugees under the relevant international instruments, or under the national legislation of the State of refuge or State of residence; or
     (m) recruiting children who have not attained the age of eighteen years as members of defense forces to take part in armed conflict; or
     (n) using any means or method of combat against the natural environment to cause widespread, long term and severe damage and thereby to prejudice the health or survival of the population; or (o) attacking dams, dykes, and nuclear electrical generating stations, if their attack causes the release of dangerous forces and consequent severe losses among the civilian population; or

Furthermore, Article 271 of the Criminal Code of 2005 proscribes a war crime that did not appear under the corresponding provision of the Penal Code of 1957, Article 283. The former added to its list of 'war crimes against wounded, sick shipwrecked persons or medical services' a crime referred to as compelling persons engaged in medical, religious and journalistic activities not to perform acts contrary to what is expected by their profession.[57] The legislator's willingness to incorporate new developments in the field of IHL, such as the adoption of the 1977 Protocols Additional to the Geneva Conventions,[58] was invoked as the reason for the expanded list of prohibited acts in the Criminal Code.[59]

Second, compared to the Penal Code of 1957, the Criminal Code of 2005 encapsulates a definition of protected persons, namely, the *'wounded'* and *'sick'*, and *'shipwrecked'*.[60] This is fairly surprising as the Criminal Code rarely provides for a definition of the terms or concepts it uses and it is unclear why these terms specifically are defined therein, notably as other groups of persons, such as *medical personnel, civilians, combatants,* or *prisoners of war,* are left undefined. Given that Ethiopian law requires that its war crimes provisions be interpreted in the light of international law and IHL treaties, as discussed below, this definitional endeavor might not have been necessary at all, in

---

       (p) passing of sentences and carrying out of executions without previous judgment pronounced by a regularly constituted Court which affords all the judicial guarantees, is punishable with rigorous imprisonment from five years to twenty-five years, or, in more serious cases, with life imprisonment or death.

57   See FDRE Criminal Code, Article 271(c).
58   See Protocol Additional to the Geneva Conventions of 12 August 1949, and Relating to the Protection of Victims of International Armed Conflicts (Protocol I), 1125 U.N.T.S. 3, *entered into force* 7 December 1978 [Hereinafter: AP I]; Protocol Additional to the Geneva Conventions of 12 August 1949, and Relating to the Protection of Victims of Non-International Armed Conflicts (Protocol II), 1125 U.N.T.S. 609, *entered into force* Dec. 7, 1978. [Hereinafter: AP II].
59   See FDRE Criminal Code, *Explanatory Notes,* Article 270.
60   See FDRE Criminal Code, Article 271 (2), which reads,
       for the purpose of sub-Article 1,
         a) 'wounded' and 'sick' means persons, whether military or civilian, who, because of trauma, disease or other physical or mental disorder or disability, are in need of medical assistance or care and who refrain from any act of hostility. These terms also cover maternity cases, newly born babies and other persons who may be in need of immediate medical assistance or care, such as the infirm or expectant mothers, and who refrain from any act of hostility.
         b) 'shipwrecked' means persons, whether military or civilian, who are in peril at sea or in other waters or in the air as a result of misfortune affecting them or the vessel or aircraft carrying them and who refrain from any act of hostility.

particular since the definitions included merely copy *verbatim* those in Article 8 of AP I.[61]

7.3 War Crimes Law in Ethiopia and the Serious Violations of IHL Yardstick

War crimes law establishes individual criminal responsibility for violations of rules of IHL. This is however not to say that all IHL violations constitute war crimes. In its influential *Tadić* interlocutory appeal decision, the ICTY Appeals Chamber affirmed that war crimes are *serious* violations of rules of IHL.[62] The following development uses these definitional conditions to analyze the Ethiopian law of war crimes and explore whether the conducts criminalized under domestic law violate a rule of IHL and satisfy the seriousness requirement.

7.3.1 Do the War Crimes Provisions in Ethiopia Satisfy the Violation of a Rule of IHL Requirement?

The FHC stated in *Legesse Asfaw et al.* that Ethiopian criminal law included 13 provisions (Articles 282–294 of the Penal Code of 1957 and Articles 270–283 of the Criminal Code of 2005) criminalizing war crimes.[63] This assertion apparently relied on the previously mentioned statement made by Jean Graven.[64] In a similar line, academic literature has generally referred to the existence of 13 war crimes provisions in Ethiopian law.[65] Yet, this is an inaccurate conclusion for two reasons.

Firstly, it should be pointed out that neither the Penal Code nor the Criminal Code contains a specific section exclusive to listing war crimes. The war crimes provisions are listed in Chapter I (Fundamental Crimes) of Title II (Crimes in Violation of International Law) of the Special Part of both Codes.[66] Yet, it is also

---

61 See AP I, Article 8(a) and (b).
62 See *Tadić*, (Decision on the defense motion for interlocutory appeal on jurisdiction), *supra* note 22, para. 94.
63 See *Legesse Asfaw et al.,* (Trial Judgment), *supra* note 16, 335.
64 See *supra* note 53.
65 For a literature stating the existence of 13 war crimes provisions in Ethiopian criminal law, see M.T. Tessema, *Prosecution of Politicide in Ethiopia: The Ethiopian Red-Terror Trials* (The Hague: T.M.C Asser Press, 2018) 107; T.S. Metekia, 'Punishing Core Crimes in Ethiopia: Analysis of the Domestic Practice in Light of and in Comparison, with Sentencing Practices at the UNICTs and the ICC' (2019) 19(1) *International Criminal Law Review* 160 -190, 166.
66 See also Chapter I, Title II of the Special Part of the FDRE Criminal Code.

possible that offences that may fall under the category of war crimes appear in other parts of the Codes. For instance, Article 315 (2) of the Criminal Code of 2005, in the military crimes section,[67] proscribes the improper use of enemy uniforms in time of war; an act prohibited by the 1907 Hague Regulations,[68] AP I,[69] and, as a war crime, by the ICC Statute.[70]

Secondly, a closer look at the 13 provisions reveals that not all of them actually deal with conduct that could amount to a war crime under international law. Some of these provisions – namely, Articles 274, 277, and 278 of the Criminal Code of 2005 –[71] are indeed not concerned with repressing a violation of a rule of IHL.

Article 274 criminalizes acts of 'provocation and preparation' to commit crimes provided in what it referred to as 'the preceding Articles',[72] namely: *i*) war crimes against the civilian population,[73] *ii*) war crimes against wounded, sick or shipwrecked persons or medical services,[74] *iii*) war crimes against prisoners and interned persons,[75] and *iv*) pillage, piracy and looting.[76] This provision deals with the proscription of acts such as incitement, conspiracy and plan to commit genocide and war crimes as separate offenses as opposed to modes of liability. Although the discrete criminalization of incitement and conspiracy to commit genocide is an approach consistent with Articles III and V of the Genocide Convention,[77] the legal basis for a similar form of criminalization with respect to war crimes is unavailable. The significance of a separate criminalization of these acts is also unclear, provided that persons engaged in acts of incitement, conspiracy, and planning the commission of war crimes could be punished pursuant to the application of rules of criminal participation enshrined in the general part of the Criminal Code.[78] Even more, there is

---

67   Military crimes are provided in the FDRE Criminal Code under Articles 284–322.
68   Hague Convention IV and its annex: Regulations Concerning the Laws and Customs of War on Land, The Hague 18 October 1907 [Hereinafter: 1907 Hague Regulations], Article 23(f).
69   See AP I, Article 39(2).
70   ICC Statute, Article 8(2)(b)(vii).
71   For the corresponding provisions in the Penal Code of 1957, see Articles 286, 289, and 290.
72   The expression 'preceding Articles' refers to provisions (Articles 269–273) in Chapter I (Fundamental Crimes) of Title II (Crimes in Violation of International Law) of the Special Part of the Criminal Code.
73   FDRE Criminal Code, Article 270.
74   Ibid., Article 271.
75   Ibid., Article 272.
76   Ibid., Article 273.
77   See FDRE Criminal Code, Articles 26–41.
78   See ibid., Article 277. The provision reads,
     Article 277- Breach of Armistice or Peace Treaty

no apparent reason why the provision criminalizes acts of 'provocation and preparation' in connection with certain war crimes only while it excludes other war crimes such as those listed under Articles 279–283 of the Criminal Code.

Article 277 of the Criminal Code of 2005 (Article 289 of the Penal Code of 1957) proscribes what is generally regarded as a domestic crime or as the international crime of aggression rather than a war crime, namely, the violation of an armistice or of a peace treaty duly concluded.[79] Since a peace treaty marks the permanent cessation of hostilities,[80] its breach may be regarded as the start of new war, which should be regulated by rules of international law on the use of force (*ius ad bellum*). On the contrary, war crimes occur as a result of a serious violation of *ius in bello*, irrespective of whether an armed conflict broke out in violation of *ius ad bellum* or not.[81] The application of *ius in bello* ends when 'a general conclusion of peace is reached; or in the case of internal conflicts, a peace settlement is achieved'[82] – provided that armed violence does not continue after such a settlement.[83]

An armistice, unlike a peace treaty, often suspends the conduct of hostilities.[84] Because the existence of an armistice does not amount to the restoration of peace or cessation of an armed conflict,[85] its breach may in itself constitute neither a violation of *ius ad bellum* nor of *ius in bello*. A breach of armistice may, however, constitute a crime in domestic law. Under Ethiopian law, continuing or resuming hostilities contrary to official orders may in fact fall under the military crime of insubordination.[86] As such, a crime under

---

Whoever, having been officially' informed of an armistice or peace treaty duly concluded and contrary to the orders given, continues hostilities, or in any other way knowingly infringes one of the agreed conditions,.is punishable with simple imprisonment, or, in more serious cases, with rigorous imprisonment not exceeding ten years.

79 Ibid.
80 For details on peace treaties marking the end of armed conflicts, see D. Akande, 'Classification of Armed Conflicts: Relevant legal Concepts' in E. Wilmshurst (ed.), *International Law and the Classification of Conflict* (Oxford: Oxford University Press, 2012) 171–274, 192–193.
81 In this regard, there is strict separation of jus *ius in bello* and *ius ad bellum*. See ICRC, *Commentary of 2016, supra* note 29, Common Article 2, paras 215–216.
82 *Tadić*, (Decision on the defense motion for interlocutory appeal on jurisdiction), *supra* note 22, para. 70.
83 ICTY, *Prosecutor* v. *Boškoski and Tarčulovski*, Trial Chamber, (Judgment), 10 July 2008, IT, 04-82-T, para. 293.
84 Nonetheless, state practice has been regarded as suggesting the use of armistice to permanently suspend hostilities. See Y. Dinstein, *War, Aggression and Self-Defence*, (5th ed, Cambridge: Cambridge University Press, 2005) 42–47.
85 See ICRC, *Commentary of 2016, supra* note 29, Common Article 2, para. 275.
86 See FDRE Criminal Code, Article 298.

Article 277 of the Criminal Code of 2005 does not constitute a war crime as it does not constitute a violation of a rule of IHL.

Article 278 of the Criminal Code of 2005 (Article 290 of the Penal Code of 1957 contains a crime named *franc-tireur*, a French word that often appears in connection to the Franco-Prussian war and apparently refers to non-combatants (such as priests, peasants and other classes of civilians) who engage in treacherous hostile acts against the enemy or occupying power.[87] The definition in Ethiopian criminal law is however different in the sense that a *franc-tireur* engages in activities hostile towards Ethiopia not towards the enemy. According to the provision in question, a *franc-tireur* is a person who is not a member or an auxiliary of armed forces recognized by the officials of the Ethiopian government and who engages during wartime in hostile acts against the Ethiopian defence force, its services, lines, or means of communications or transport.[88] The Amharic version of the Criminal Code gives a slight indication since it uses 'Fano' (ፋኖ) as the legal synonym for *franc-tireur*,[89] a term which in common usage refers to an 'outlaw, volunteer campaigner who fights on his own, not as part of an organization or group and not acknowledging any person as his leader'.[90]

It is not clear as to who exactly is a *franc-tireur*.[91] From the content of Article 278, a *franc-tireur* may be a national of any country including Ethiopia. Actions of Ethiopian nationals as 'Fano' (ፋኖ) that constitute violence against the Ethiopian defense forces during wartime could be regarded as a purely domestic crime. In fact, other provisions in the Criminal Code such as those dealing

---

87 See in general, F. van Langenhove, *The growth of a legend; A study based upon the German accounts of francs-tireurs and 'atrocities' in Belgium* (New York: G.P. Putnam's Sons, 1916).

88 FDRE Criminal Code, Article 278.

89 See FDRE Criminal Code, Article 278 (Amharic version).

90 See T.L. Kane, *Amharic-English Dictionary: Volume II* (Wiesbaden: Otto Harrassowitz, 1990) 2316.

91 Nonetheless, *francs-tireurs* should not be confused with mercenaries. From the contents of Article 278, *francs-tireurs*, unlike mercenaries, may engage in a hostile act against the defence force out of reasons not motivated by private or material gains. As defined by Article 47 of the AP I, a mercenary is a person who:

a) is specially recruited locally or abroad in order to fight in an armed conflict; b) does, in fact, take a direct part in the hostilities; c) is motivated to take part in the hostilities essentially by the desire for private gain and, in fact, is promised, by or on behalf of a Party to the conflict, material compensation substantially in excess of that promised or paid to combatants of similar ranks and functions in the armed forces of that Party; d) is neither a national of a Party to the conflict nor a resident of territory controlled by a Party to the conflict; e) is not a member of the armed forces of a Party to the conflict; and f) has not been sent by a State which is not a Party to the conflict on official duty as a member of its armed forces.

with crimes against the external security and defensive power of the State[92] and the military crime of sabotage[93] cover similar acts as those provided under Article 278 as acts of *francs-tireurs*. As far as IHL is concerned, it seems that *francs-tireurs* may enjoy the protections accorded to civilians, unless and for such a duration that, they take a direct part in hostilities,[94] the existence of which may be assessed on a case by case basis.[95]

Be that as it may, the rest of the Criminal Code's provisions on war crimes do not cast doubt as to whether they deal with violations of a rule of IHL.[96] In fact, most of these provisions contain an express reference to IHL conventions and public international law. As a result, the war crimes provisions in Ethiopian criminal law consider IHL as their legal basis, which should be consulted whenever a need for interpretation arises. As it will be discussed below, they also allow for the direct application of IHL before Ethiopian courts.[97]

7.3.2 *The Serious Breaches of IHL Requirement in Ethiopian War Crimes Provisions*

The *Tadić* Appeals Chamber stated that a violation of IHL that may be regarded to constitute a war crime must be 'serious'.[98] The requirement of 'seriousness' is adopted to determine war crimes that could fall under Common Article 3 as opposed to those that constitute grave breaches of the Geneva Conventions and other violations that are expressly regarded as war crimes in the relevant IHL treaties. As the meaning of 'seriousness' is not self-evident, the ICTY

---

92   See FDRE Criminal Code, in particular, Article 247(d) on impairment of the defensive power of the state and Article 248(a) on high treason.
93   See ibid., Article 327(1)(a) of the FDRE Criminal Code which reads, 'whoever intentionally destroys, damages or renders unfit for use installations, material, equipment or any other object used by the Defence Forces… is punishable with rigorous imprisonment not exceeding ten years'.
94   This is not to suggest that the civilian status of *francs-tireurs* is always clear. Nonetheless, they could be regarded as civilians even in case of doubt, pursuant to Article 50(1) of AP I, which states, 'in case of doubt whether a person is a civilian, that person shall be considered to be a civilian'. On the notion of civilians and civilians taking direct part in hostilities, see E. Crawford, 'Who is a Civilian? Membership of Opposing Groups and Direct Participation in Hostilities' in M. Lattimer and P. Sands (eds.), *The Gray Zone: Civilian Protection Between Human Rights and the Laws of War* (Oxford: Hart, 2018) 19–40.
95   See ICTR, *Prosecutor v. Rutaganda,* Trial Chamber, (Judgment), 6 December 1999, ICTR-96-3, para. 100; ICTY, *Prosecutor v. Strugar*, Appeals Chamber, (Judgment), 17 July 2008, para.178.
96   See FDRE Criminal Code, Articles 270, 271, 272, 273, 275, 276, 279, 280, 281, 283, and 315.
97   See section 7.5. below.
98   *Tadić*, (Decision on the defense motion for interlocutory appeal on jurisdiction), *supra* note 22, para. 94.

Appeals Chamber stated that a violation is serious when it constitutes a 'breach of a rule protecting important values'.[99] Besides, serious breaches are those that 'involve grave consequences for the victim'.[100] To that end, 'the fact of a combatant simply appropriating a loaf of bread in an occupied village' was mentioned by the Appeals Chamber as an example of an IHL violation that does not constitute a serious breach of IHL.[101]

In what appears to be incongruent with the requirement of seriousness, a person commits a war crime under Article 281(2) of the Criminal Code of 2005 if he or she *insults* a protected person.[102] This provision criminalizes as a war crime insulting a person belonging to, or a representative of, an international humanitarian organization as well as a person placed under the protection of such an organization.[103] Similarly, Article 283 of the Code proscribes insulting an enemy bearing a flag of truce, or an enemy negotiator, or any person accompanying him or her.[104]

Insulting a protected person may however not satisfy the conditions of seriousness set out in *Tadić*. One may argue that a mere insult does not seem to constitute a grave injury to the victim nor a violation of a rule protecting an important value. Furthermore, in Ethiopian law, insult is generally not a serious crime. An act of insult is punishable only upon complaint of the victim; a condition which in itself shows that insult is considered as an offense of lesser seriousness.[105] Other evidence relating to the level of seriousness compared to

---

99   Ibid.
100 Ibid.
101 Ibid. Such an act may still constitute a violation of IHL for 'falling foul of the basic principle laid down in Article 46, paragraph 1, of The Hague Regulations (and the corresponding rule of customary international law) whereby ' "private property must be respected" by any army occupying an enemy territory'. Ibid.
102 See also the Penal Code of 1957, Article 293(a).
103 See FDRE Criminal Code, Article 281, entitled 'Hostile Acts against International Humanitarian Organizations'. Paragraph 1(a) of this provision reads: 'Whoever, intentionally and in time of [war] indulges. in hostile acts against, or threats or insults to persons belonging to the International Red Cross or Red Crescent or to corresponding humanitarian relief organizations or to the representatives of those organizations or to persons placed under their protection is punishable the punishment shall be rigorous imprisonment from one year to five years'.
104 Article 283 of the Criminal Code, which proscribes 'hostile acts against the bearer of a flag of truce' reads:
     'whoever maltreats, threatens, *insults* or unjustifiably detains an enemy bearing a flag of truce, or an enemy negotiator, or any person accompanying him, is punishable with simple imprisonment'. Emphasis added.
105 See FDRE Criminal Code, Article 615. Exceptionally, the prosecution office may not need to wait for a complaint of the victim to institute a proceeding in special cases of insult such as those made against the honour of the state, a foreign state and inter-state

a (war) crime is the penalty it entails. As per Article 615, insult is punishable with simple imprisonment not exceeding three months, or a fine not exceeding 300 Birr (approximately ten dollars).[106] Even in the case of insult as war crimes, the prescribed penalty is simple imprisonment, except when the crime is committed as an act hostile against international humanitarian organizations. In such cases, the punishment is rigorous imprisonment from one to five years; a penalty which implies that if this particular type of insult is considered as serious, it still ranks among the lowest half on the scale of seriousness.[107]

In sum, war crimes provisions in Ethiopian Criminal do not appear to have been enacted with strict adherence to the requirement that only serious violations of rules of IHL could be considered war crimes. Nonetheless, this is arguably negligible, given that only two offenses of insult out of the whole list of war crimes appear to not be passing the seriousness test. An overview of the remaining war crimes provisions in Ethiopian criminal law indeed indicates that all the other offenses listed as war crimes in Ethiopian law are severe enough to pass the gravity threshold set up by IHL.

7.4 Neutrality of the Ethiopian War Crimes Provisions: The Abolition of the Distinction between Armed Conflicts

International humanitarian law emphasizes the distinction between international and non-international armed conflicts. As a result of such a distinction two sets of rules exist in IHL treaties: *i*) rules of IHL applying to international armed conflicts such as the 1907 Hague Regulations, the 1949 Geneva Conventions and AP I; and *ii*) rules of IHL applying to non-international armed conflicts, mainly Common Article 3 to the 1949 Geneva Conventions and AP II.[108] This implies the existence of different categories of war crimes depending on the nature of the armed conflict, although there exists no compelling justification for treating war crimes differently just because the context

---

institutions, a military superior and contempt of court. See ibid., Articles 618, 264, 266, 297, and 449.

106 In all the provision dealing with special cases of insult mentioned in the preceding footnote, an act of insult is punishable with simple imprisonment, a form of punishment limited to less serious offenses. For the concept of simple imprisonment. see Chapter 8 section 8.2.1.2.

107 See ibid.

108 See J.K. Kleffner, 'Scope of Application of International Humanitarian Law' in D. Fleck (ed.), *The Hand Book of International Humanitarian Law* (3rd. ed., Oxford: Oxford University Press, 2013) 43–78, 44.

of the armed conflict differs. Akande notes that the reason behind the persistence of the distinction between international and non-international armed conflicts relates to the erroneous consideration by states that 'equating non-international and international armed conflicts would undermine State sovereignty and, in particular, national unity and security'.[109]

Interestingly however, the distinction between war crimes in international and non-international armed conflicts has been gradually fading away due to developments in customary international law. Such a development was already noted a quarter of a century ago in *Tadić*, where the ICTY Appeals Chamber stated that *the general essence* of rules governing international armed conflict has become applicable in non-international armed conflict.[110] The Chamber added:

> it cannot be denied that customary rules have developed to govern internal strife. These rules, as specifically identified in the preceding discussion, cover such areas as protection of civilians from hostilities, in particular from indiscriminate attacks, protection of civilian objects, in particular cultural property, protection of all those who do not (or no longer) take active part in hostilities, as well as prohibition of means of warfare proscribed in international armed conflicts and ban of certain methods of conducting hostilities.[111]

The Rome Statute of the ICC could also be seen as symptomatic of the fact that the scope of the conflict-based division of war crimes is getting narrower, although the distinction between the two types of conflicts persists. As discussed further in section 7.5.3. below, amendments adopted in 2010 and in 2017 have allowed for the punishment of several war crimes irrespective of the type of armed conflict, although there still remain several acts which can only be prosecuted as war crimes before the ICC if committed only in the context of an international armed conflict.

In Ethiopian criminal law, war crimes could be 'committed in time of war, armed conflict, or occupation'.[112] Because these notions are not defined in the Criminal Code, Ethiopian courts may refer to 'public international law and

---

109 Akande, 'Classification of Armed Conflicts: Relevant legal Concepts', *supra* note 80, 182–185.
110 *Tadić*, (Decision on the defense motion for interlocutory appeal on jurisdiction), *supra* note 22, para. 126.
111 Ibid., para 127.
112 See FDRE Criminal Code, Article 270.

international humanitarian conventions' in order to examine whether a given situation could constitute a war,[113] or an armed conflict,[114] or occupation.[115]

---

113   In international law, *war* is a tricky concept to define. There are attempts to define it using its antonym, 'peace' – and war then refers to the absence of peace. See Akande, 'Classification of Armed Conflicts: Relevant legal Concepts', *supra* note 80, 186. Traditionally, the application of IHL required a formal declaration of belligerence to determine the existence of a state of war; a position that changed with the adoption of the Geneva Conventions of 1949, which rendered the requirement of the recognition of a state of war irrelevant. See Article 2 Common to Geneva Conventions of 1949, para. 1; ICRC, *Commentary of 2016*, *supra* note 29, Common Article 2, paras 203–209; Kleffner, 'Scope of Application of International Humanitarian Law' *supra* note 108, 44. The existence of a state of war does not need to be explicit in a manner that requires the existence of a formal declaration of war. As also stated by the Eritrea-Ethiopia Claims Commission (EECC): 'once the armed attack in the Badme area occurred and Ethiopia decided to act in self-defense, a war resulted that proved impossible to restrict to the areas where that initial attack was made'. See Reports of International Arbitral Awards, Eritrea-Ethiopia Claims Commission, *between Federal Democratic Republic of Ethiopia and the State of Eritrea* 'Partial Award: Jus Ad Bellum, Ethiopia's Claims 1–8', 19 December 2005, para. 19, available at: <https://pcacases.com/web/sendAttach/763> accessed 29 September 2019.

114   As for the meaning of an *armed conflict*, it could be difficult for an Ethiopian court to find help in IHL because the relevant treaties do not define it. As defined by the ICTY's Appeals Chamber in *Tadić* for the first time in 1995, the meaning and scope of the notion of armed conflict depends on the type of conflict: international or non-international. Accordingly, an international armed conflict 'exists whenever there is a resort to armed force between States' while a non-international armed conflict exists whenever there is 'protracted armed violence between governmental authorities and organized armed groups or between such groups within a State'. *Tadić*, (Decision on the defense motion for interlocutory appeal on jurisdiction), *supra* note 22, para. 70. See also ICTY, *Prosecutor v. Haradinaj*, Trial Chamber, (Judgment), 3 April 2008, IT-04-84-T, para. 60 Compared to a non-international armed conflict, the existence of an international armed conflict requires no intensity of violence: an international armed conflict will be qualified as such provided the use of force was not the result of an error. This definitional approach avoids the creation of a legal limbo due to the possible inapplicability of IHL while the parties assess whether the violence reached a certain level of threshold. See Akande, 'Classification of Armed Conflicts: Relevant legal Concepts' *supra* note 80, 191; ICRC, *Commentary of 2016*, *supra* note 29, Common Article 2, para. 239; J. Pictet (ed.), *Commentary on the Geneva Conventions of 12 August 1949, Vol. I-IV,* (ICRC,1952) Article 3, paras 49–50.

115   *Occupation* as defined in Article 42 of the 1907 Hague Regulations refers to the actual placement of a territory under the authority of the hostile army. The application of The Hague Regulations was limited to a situation of occupation resulting from the context of an international armed conflict. This scope of application remained unchanged, although – with the adoption of the Geneva Conventions – the focus of the rules of IHL governing occupation evolved from safeguarding 'the interest of the ousted regime' to safeguarding 'the protection of the population in the enemy's hands'. See E. Benvenisti, *The International Law of Occupation* (2nd ed., Oxford: Oxford University Press, 2013) 11–12. Common Article 2 to the Geneva Conventions explicitly included the fact that occupation

Nonetheless, the law does not classify war crimes based on the international or non-international nature of an armed conflict, although it has not expressly abolished the distinction. The implicit abolition of this distinction goes back to the Penal Code of 1957.[116] The exact same approach is retained in the Criminal Code of 2005, and its significance can be seen from two perspectives.

First, from a procedural point of view, Ethiopian courts do not need to undergo the often rigorous process of characterizing a certain conflict as internal or international, unlike the practice in the international arena, which, at times, has proved to be overly complex.[117] In practice, the FHC did not engage in detailed discussions of the types of armed conflicts, although it made a swift remark in *Legesse Asfaw et al.* that the armed conflict was of a non-international character and that the defendants did not dispute its character.[118] This characterization was not only unconvincing but also unnecessary. It was unconvincing because it was unsubstantiated. Given that in the 1980s several protracted armed conflicts took place in Ethiopia between government forces and different armed groups (liberation fronts) such as the EPLF, the TPLF, EDU, and EPLA in the northern regions, as well as the OLF (in the eastern and western regions),[119] any conclusion as to the existence of an internal armed conflict should offer a detailed analysis of the parties, places, and intensity of the conflict at the time of the events alleged in the indictment. The *Legesse Asfaw et al.* case was devoid of such analysis.

It was also unnecessary for the FHC to attempt to determine the type of armed conflict because this was not required under Ethiopian law. For an Ethiopian court, admittedly unlike for a foreign court adjudicating war crimes committed in Ethiopia,[120] a determination of whether a given situation constitutes

<blockquote>
may materialize in the absence of an armed resistance. The ICJ has also highlighted in the *Armed Activities Case* that the defining factors appears to be the absence of consent of the ousted government and the fact that the occupying power gained effective control of the territory and exercised its authority by replacing that of the occupied power. See ICJ, *Democratic Republic of the Congo v. Uganda*, Case Concerning Armed Activities on the Territory of the Congo, Judgment of 19 December 2005, para 173, available at: <https://www.icj-cij.org/files/case-related/116/116-20051219-JUD-01-00-EN.pdf> accessed 1 August 2019.
</blockquote>

116   See the Penal Code of 1957, Article 282.
117   For details, see R. Cryer *et al.*, *An Introduction to International Criminal Law and Procedure* (3rd ed., Cambridge: Cambridge University Press, 2014) 274–275.
118   *Legesse Asfaw et al.*, (Trial Judgment), *supra* note 16, 384.
119   See section 7.1. above.
120   The absence of the requirement of distinction of armed conflicts could put Ethiopian war crimes trials in a procedurally less burdensome position, compared to international trials and certain domestic trials. With respect to the latter, one could refer to the trial of Eshetu Alemu in the Netherlands where the District Court of The Hague had to make a

an armed conflict could be sufficient. This could have been achieved by making a determining the intensity of the armed conflict in order to clarify that the conflict was not just a case of internal disturbances and riots with respect to which the rules of IHL do not apply.[121] Such a determination could have been deduced from various factual circumstances, which, as summarized by Kleffner, include:

> the number, duration, and intensity of individual confrontations; the type of weapons and other military equipment used; the number and calibre of munitions fired; the number of persons and type of forces partaking in the fighting, the number of causalities; the extent of material destruction; the number of civilians fleeing combat zones ... involvement of UN Security Council.[122]

Second, from a substantive point of view, all acts expressly listed in Ethiopian domestic law as war crimes are punishable irrespective of the type of armed conflict in which they may be committed. This could be deemed a positive development, notably when seen in contrast with the most recent laws of war crimes such as the Rome Statute of the ICC, in which not all kinds of war crimes are punishable when committed in non-international armed conflicts. Indeed, the following war crimes are punishable by an Ethiopia court, but not by the ICC, when committed in non-international armed conflicts. These are:

1. Launching an attack in the knowledge that such attack will cause incidental loss of life or injury to civilians or damage to civilian objects or widespread, long-term, and severe damage to the natural environment which would be clearly excessive in relation to the concrete and direct overall military advantage anticipated;[123]

---

determination of the character of the conflict that took place in Ethiopia in the late 1970s. This was not an easy task, as it required the presentation and examination of various documentary evidence and testimonies of expert witnesses as to the history of Ethiopia and of the armed conflicts in the 1970s. *Eshetu Alemu*, (Judgment), *supra* note 17, section 7.

121   As a minimum threshold of conflicts, war crimes law does not concern itself with mere internal disturbances and riots, the distinction of which may appear significant in the context of armed conflicts of a non-international character. See ICC Statute, Article 8(2)(f).

122   See Kleffner, 'Scope of Application of International Humanitarian Law' *supra* note 108, 49–50. See also Akande, 'Classification of Armed Conflicts: Relevant legal Concepts' *supra* note 80, 191; ICRC, *Commentary of 2016, supra* note 29, Common Article 2, para. 239.

123   ICC Statute, Article 8(2)(b)(iv). Punishable in Ethiopia irrespective of the type of armed conflict pursuant to Article 270(o) and (h) of the Criminal Code.

2. Attacking or bombarding, by whatever means, towns, villages, dwellings, or buildings which are undefended and which are not military objectives;[124]
3. Killing or wounding a combatant who, having laid down his arms or no longer having a means of defence, has surrendered at discretion;[125]
4. Making improper use of a flag of truce, of the flag or of the military insignia and uniform of the enemy or of the United Nations, as well as of the distinctive emblems of the Geneva Conventions, resulting in death or serious personal injury;[126]

---

124   ICC Statute, Article 8(2)(b)(v). The prohibited 'attack' under this provision is essentially related to the fact that the towns, villages, dwellings or buildings are undefended and not military objectives. An attack against military objectives, that is, against defended towns, villages, dwellings or buildings, may constitute war crimes under Article 8(2)(b)(i), (ii), and (iv) of the ICC Statute. This provision's additional expressions such as 'bombarding' and 'by whatever means' are regarded redundant, given that 'attack' is broadly defined under Article 49 of AP I. See K. Dörmann, *Elements of War Crimes under the Rome Statute of the International Criminal Court: Sources and Commentary* (Cambridge: Cambridge University Press, 2003) 181–182; R. Arnold and S. Wehrenberg, 'Article 8: War Crimes-para. 2(b)(iv)' in O. Triffterer and K. Ambos (eds.), *The Rome Statute of the International Criminal Court: A Commentary* (3rd ed., München: C.H.Beck.Hart.Namos, 2016) 380.

Although there is no provision in Ethiopian law that directly and expressly prohibits the offense listed under Article 8(2)(b)(v) of the ICC Statute, the bombardment of villages and towns could be punished as war crimes on the basis of Article 270 (a) of the Criminal Code, which prohibits 'killings, torture or inhumane treatment ...or any other acts involving dire suffering or bodily harm, or injury to mental or physical health'. In practice, the same provision applies irrespective of whether the attack is against defended or undefended towns, villages, dwellings, or buildings. In *Legesse Asfaw et al.*, the SPO relied on Article 282(a) of the Penal Code (Article 270(a) of the Criminal Code) to prosecute persons responsible for: i) aerial bombardment of the town of Hawzein (on a market day and where no military activities were noticed) resulting in the death of approximately 5,000 civilians; ii) aerial bombardment of the town of Wukro killing 3,000 civilians, and iii) aerial bombardment of undefended locality in Chila, which resulted in the death of about 2,000 about civilians. See *Legesse Asfaw et al.,* (Trial Judgment), *supra* note 16, 282–283. For details see the discussion in section 7.7. below.

125   ICC Statute, Article 8(2)(b)(vi). Punishable in Ethiopia irrespective of the type of armed conflict pursuant to Article 275 (a) of the Criminal Code.

126   ICC Statute, Article 8(2)(b)(vii). Punishable in Ethiopia irrespective of the type of armed conflict pursuant to Articles 282 and 315 of the Criminal Code. Article 282 of the Criminal Code proscribes the abuse *per se* and does not require death or serious personal injury to result from it. It also does not cover the misuse of uniform of the United Nations. To the extent that the ICC Statute focuses on perfidious attack by improper use of the protected signs and emblems, as a prohibited method of warfare, such acts could fall under Article 276 of the Criminal Code. Nonetheless, this provision of the Criminal Code is applicable only in the context of international armed conflicts because this provision does not allow for the applicability of customary international law as discussed in section 7.5.3. below.

5. The transfer, directly or indirectly, by the occupying power of parts of its own civilian population into the territory it occupies, or the deportation or transfer of all or parts of the population of the occupied territory within or outside this territory;[127]
6. Declaring abolished, suspended, or inadmissible in a court of law, the rights and actions of the nationals of the hostile party;[128]
7. Compelling the nationals of the hostile party to take part in the operations of war directed against their own country, even if they were in the belligerent's service before the commencement of the war;[129]
8. Committing outrages upon personal dignity, in particular humiliating and degrading treatment;[130]
9. Using starvation of civilians as a method of warfare by depriving them of objects indispensable to their survival, including wilfully impeding relief supplies as provided for under the Geneva Conventions.[131]

Notwithstanding this pioneer and progressive development in abolishing the distinction between armed conflicts, one could point out, upon a closer look, that several war crimes which are punishable when committed in the context of international armed conflicts remain unpunishable in Ethiopian criminal law when committed in non-international armed conflicts. Such a regressive aspect occurs because, on the one hand, the Ethiopian Criminal Code implicitly abolished the type-of-conflict-based distinction of war crimes while, on

---

[127] ICC Statute Article 8(2)(b)(viii). Punishable in Ethiopia irrespective of the type of armed conflict pursuant to Article 270(c) of the Criminal Code. Nonetheless, the Criminal Code does not contain the phrase 'own civilians' or 'population of the occupied territory'. Instead, it only refers to 'the population'. It also criminalizes the detention of population in concentration camps or forced labour camps.

[128] ICC Statute, Article 8(2)(b)(xiv). Punishable in Ethiopia irrespective of the type of armed conflict pursuant to Article 280 of the Criminal Code.

[129] ICC Statute, Article 8(2)(b)(xv). Punishable in Ethiopia irrespective of the type of armed conflict pursuant to Articles 270(d) (civilian population) and 272(b) (PoWs or interned persons) of the Criminal Code.

[130] ICC Statute, Article 8(2)(b)(xxi). Punishable in Ethiopia irrespective of the type of armed conflict pursuant to Articles 275 and 279 of the Criminal Code. The prohibition under Article 275 of the Criminal Code is applicable only when the victim is a dead person while Article 279 covers maltreatment of 'sick or wounded person, or a prisoner of war or war internee'. The word 'person' under Article 8(2)(b)(xxi) of the ICC Statute may include dead persons, and, unlike the Ethiopian law, is not limited to sick, wounded or detained persons. See Dörmann, *Elements of War Crimes under the Rome Statute of the International Criminal Court*, supra note 124, 314–324.

[131] ICC Statute, (Article 8(2)(b)(xxv). Punishable in Ethiopia irrespective of the type of armed conflict pursuant to Articles 270(i) and (k) of the Criminal Code. For details see section 7.5.2.3. below.

the other, it allows only for the direct application of IHL treaties, thereby excluding the applicability of war crimes defined in customary international law. In effect, the law adopted a contradictory approach that defeats the whole purpose of abolishing the type-of-armed-conflict-based distinction insofar as, as it will be discussed in section 7.5.3 below, it is customary international law that serves as a legal basis to consider several war crimes as punishable when committed in the context of internal armed conflicts.

7.5 The Scope of War Crimes in Ethiopian Law: Interpretative and Direct Application of IHL

Most of the war crimes provision in Ethiopian criminal law contain an express reference to IHL conventions and public international law, with the exception of provisions discussed in section 7.3.1. above. The reference to IHL treaties and international law takes two forms. Some of the provisions mention IHL treaties and international law as the legal basis of the war crimes they expressly specify. Some others incorporate war crimes into the Ethiopian law by making a direct reference to IHL treaties. In doing so, the provisions treat international customary and treaty law differently, as detailed in the separate discussions provided in the following sections.

7.5.1 *IHL Treaties as the Interpretative Tool of Ethiopian War Crimes Provisions*

It is stated in the *chapeau* of Articles 270, 271, 272, and 275 of the Criminal Code of 2005 that the prohibited acts are punishable when committed 'contrary to public international law and humanitarian conventions'.[132] Each of these provisions carry an exhaustive list of prohibited acts.[133] Put differently, the *chapeau* explicitly positions IHL conventions and international (customary and treaty) law as the legal sources for the Code's war crimes provisions; a position which takes all its importance when interpretation is required.

In *Legesse Asfaw et al.*, the FHC extensively referred to IHL conventions in determining various complex issues. In particular, the Court undertook an interesting – even if often tediously repetitive – discussion on the key principles of IHL, such as those defining the status of victims and perpetrators of war crimes, proportionality of an attack, military necessity, the prohibition of

---

132 A similar approach was followed in the corresponding provisions of the Penal Code. See Penal Code of 1957, Articles 282, 283, 284, and 287.
133 For example, see FDRE Criminal Code, Article 270.

indiscriminate attack, all of which were fundamental to the case at hand.[134] Interestingly, the IHL treaties that Ethiopian courts may invoke for the purpose of interpretation do not need to be the ones to which Ethiopia is a party: neither the Penal Code nor the Criminal Code makes such a requirement. Thus, as was in fact the case in *Legesse Asfaw et al.,* Ethiopian courts may interpret Ethiopian war crimes provisions in the light of international instruments to which Ethiopia was not – and still is not – a party[135] when the domestic law was enacted,[136] or when the offense was committed,[137] or when the trials were being held.[138] Similarly, international conventions that post-date the enactment of the Ethiopian war crimes provisions may be consulted for interpretation.

What is more, due to the non-existence in Ethiopian law of the distinction between internal and international armed conflicts,[139] it appears that Ethiopian courts can apply IHL treaties applicable to international armed conflicts to situations of internal armed conflicts. In *Legesse Asfaw et al.,* the FHC qualified the conflict as an internal armed conflict to which rules governing non-international armed conflicts applied.[140] With no explanation, it however also applied rules of IHL conventions that are applicable to international

---

134 See section 7.5.2. below.
135 One of the documents to which the Court paid significant attention was the Declaration Renouncing the Use, in Time of War, of Explosive Projectiles Under 400 Grammes Weight. Saint Petersburg, 29 November–11 December 1868. Ethiopia is not a signatory to this declaration. Nonetheless, the Court invoked it to highlight that the objective of the laws of war is to mitigate the calamities of war, a concept enshrined in the preamble of the declaration. See *Legesse Asfaw et al.,* (Trial Judgment), *supra* note 16, 314.
136 In this regard, an example could be the reference made in *Legesse Asfaw et al.* to the 1949 Geneva Conventions, to which Ethiopia became a party long after it had promulgated the Penal Code. See *Legesse Asfaw et al.,* (Trial Judgment), *supra* note 16, 329–340.
137 See *Legesse Asfaw et al.,* (Trial Judgment), *supra* note 16, 329–340. In this case, the FHC interpreted war crimes provisions by heavily relying on an array of IHL instruments including those to which Ethiopia was not a party at the time the offenses being prosecuted were committed (1980), such as AP I and AP II, both of which Ethiopia ratified in 1994. See ibid. Nonetheless, the reference to AP I and AP II could be seen as a reference to the 1949 Geneva Conventions since the two Protocols were adopted to supplement the Conventions, not to modify the existing conditions of their application. See AP I, Article 1; AP II, Article 1.
138 For example, the Court made reference to the Resolutions of the Intergovernmental Conference on the Protection of Cultural Property in the Event of Armed Conflict, The Hague, 14 May 1954, to which Ethiopia acceded only in 2015. See *Legesse Asfaw et al.,* (Trial Judgment), *supra* note 16, 363.369.
139 See section 7.4.1. below.
140 See *Legesse Asfaw et al.,* (Trial Judgment), *supra* note 16, 335, 384.

armed conflicts, including Article 85 of AP I which deals with the repression of grave breaches.[141] In fact, as discussed above, the Court's attempt to characterize the armed conflict was uncalled for.[142]

7.5.2 Direct Application of IHL Treaties and the Legality Principle in Ethiopian Law

There is no requirement in Ethiopian criminal law that an *international crime* must be specified in domestic law to subject an alleged offender to prosecution. To the contrary, there are two instances under which Ethiopian law allows for the direct application of international treaties. The first one, which could apply to war crimes as well as to other international crimes, refers to situations where international crimes are committed abroad. This includes a case of universal jurisdiction where neither the perpetrators nor the victims are Ethiopians but the offense is an international crime not specified in the domestic law. Article 17 of the Criminal Code of 2005 states that Ethiopia has jurisdiction over

> any person who has committed outside Ethiopia a crime against international law or an international crime specified in Ethiopian legislation, or *an international treaty or a convention to which Ethiopia has adhered*.[143]

The second one is specifically related to war crimes, and more precisely to the war crimes of using *prohibited means and methods of warfare*. In relation to this category of war crimes, the role of IHL as a source of war crimes law in Ethiopia takes a whole different meaning as it changes from serving as an interpretative source to become a binding source with direct application. Article 276 of the Criminal Code of 2005 reads:

> whoever uses, or orders to be used, against the enemy any means or method of combat expressly forbidden by Ethiopian law or *international conventions to which Ethiopia is a party* is punishable with simple imprisonment for not less than three months; or, if the crime is grave,

---

141 While discussing war crimes committed in the context of an internal armed conflict, the FHC referred to the 1970 Hague regulations, the 1949 Geneva Conventions, and AP I, all of which were applicable to conflicts of an international nature. See *Legesse Asfaw et al.*, (Trial Judgment), *supra* note 16, 336–337, 384–385.

142 See section 7.4.1. below.

143 FDRE Criminal Code, Article 17(1). Emphasis added. See also the Penal Code of 1957, Article 17.

with rigorous imprisonment from five years to twenty-five years; or, in the gravest cases, with life imprisonment or death.

The reference to IHL conventions in this provision indicates that acts that are not expressly listed in the Criminal Code could still constitute war crimes in Ethiopian law as long as they constitute a violation of a rule of an IHL treaty to which Ethiopia is a party. In fact, neither prohibited weapons nor prohibited methods are itemized by Article 276. In short, IHL is the applicable law, and Article 276 could be considered as the single most important provision that allows the direct application of international law by Ethiopian courts. No other provision in the Criminal Code creates a criminal offense by the simple act of prescribing a penalty to prohibitions defined in international conventions.

This direct application of an international treaty by Ethiopian courts is subjected to a single requirement, which is whether Ethiopia is a party to the treaty in question. This condition did not exist under Article 285 of the Penal Code of 1957, which was broader in scope as it allowed for the direct application of *all known international treaties* (የታወቁ ኢንተርናሲዮናል ስምምነቶች).[144] The reason for a more restrictive approach adopted in the Criminal Code relates to the legislator's belief that 'Ethiopia has the obligation to recognize and apply only those treaties to which it is a party'.[145]

As much as it might be praised from the perspective of direct application of IHL in national courts, Article 276 should also be scrutinized from the perspective of the principle of *nullum crimen sine lege*. Whether international law prohibiting a certain conduct could be regarded as a direct source of criminal law depends on whether such a possibility is allowed under the principle of legality. According to Article 2 of the Criminal Code of 2005, Ethiopian courts are not allowed to 'treat as a crime and punish any act or omission which is not prohibited by *law*'.[146] The reference to 'law' in this provision includes the Criminal Code itself and other 'regulations and special laws of criminal nature'.[147] Nonetheless, there is no express prohibition in Ethiopian criminal law to include international treaties – such as those referred to in Article 276 – within the scope of Article 2's reference to 'law'.

Given that it is only for the prosecution of ordinary crimes that the law requires the existence in municipal law of a provision that expressly criminalizes a certain conduct,[148] it seems that international crimes are not subjected

---

144 See the Penal Code of 1957 (Amharic version), Article 285.
145 See FDRE Criminal Code, *Explanatory Notes*, Article 276.
146 See FDRE Criminal Code, Article 2(2). Emphasis added.
147 See Ibid., Article 3.
148 See FDRE Criminal Code, Article 18.

to such a condition. International treaties could thus also serve as a source of law for an international crime to be prosecuted and punished in Ethiopia even in the absence of domestic provisions to that effect.

A similar understanding could be deduced from the relevant provisions of the FDRE Constitution. Article 22 of the Constitution that lays down the prohibition of non-retroactivity of criminal law does not make any express reference to the body of law that could serve as a source of criminalization. It focuses on the substance of the criminal offense as opposed to its legal basis. It reads, 'no one shall be held guilty of any criminal offence on account of any act or omission which did not constitute a criminal offence at the time when it was committed'.[149] It could therefore be argued that for the purpose of this provision, the definition of a criminal offense can be found either in domestic law or in international law.

Another relevant provision in the FDRE Constitution is Article 28, which refers to international crimes using the expression 'crimes against humanity'.[150] It states that international crimes (that entail a criminal liability that could not be set aside by amnesty, pardon or barred by period of limitation) could be defined *by international agreements ratified by Ethiopia* and by other laws of Ethiopia.[151] International crimes referred to by Article 28 of the Constitution are genocide, torture, and war crimes.[152]

From the reading of Articles 22 and 28 of the Constitution and of Articles 2 and 17 of the Criminal Code enacted on the basis of the Constitution, it may be concluded that the principle of legality in Ethiopia is not a bar to the prosecution and punishment of a crime based on a definition provided solely in international law. The only limitation is that such prosecution and punishment must not be inconsistent with the principle of legality, which is specifically protected by Article 13 of the Constitution according to which fundamental rights and freedoms

> shall be interpreted in a manner conforming to the principles of the Universal Declaration of Human Rights, International Covenants on Human Rights and international instruments adopted by Ethiopia.[153]

---

149   The FDRE Constitution, Article 22(1).
150   See Chapter 5, section 5.3.2.
151   The FDRE Constitution, Article 228(1).
152   See the FDRE Constitution, *Explanatory Notes*, Article 28. See also FDRE Criminal Code, Article 44.
153   The FDRE Constitution, Article 13(2).

At this point, the significant question is whether the principle of legality as defined in international law allows for the prosecution of international crimes that are not defined by domestic law. If it does, it would mean that the same holds true for the principle of legality under the FDRE Constitution (as required by its Article 13). If it does not, there could be no legal basis for an Ethiopian court to directly apply IHL treaties in war crimes trials. To answer this question, the following development provides a detailed discussion of the *nullum crimen* and *nulla poena* aspects of the principle of legality as enshrined in international instruments to which Ethiopia is a party and as developed in the jurisprudence of regional and international courts and judicial bodies.

7.5.2.1   Nullum Crimen Sine Lege: International Treaties as Sources of War Crimes in Ethiopia

It is noteworthy that *nullum crimen sine lege* is generally regarded as one of the oldest and fundamental principles in criminal law.[154] In international law, the principle is formulated in reaction to the debates during the Nuremberg and Tokyo trials.[155] The principle has been enshrined in several treaties to which Ethiopia is a party. Article 11 of the Universal Declaration of Human Rights (UDHR) defines this principle in the following terms:

> no one shall be held guilty of any penal offence on account of any act or omission which did not constitute a penal offence, under national or *international* law, at the time when it was committed.[156]

---

154   The STL Appeals Chamber stated in 2011, 'it is warranted to hold that by now [the principle of legality] has the status of a peremptory norm (*jus cogens*), imposing its observance both within domestic legal orders and at the international level'. See STL, *Unnamed defendants v. The Prosecutor*, Appeals Chamber (Interlocutory Decision on the Applicable Law: Terrorism, Conspiracy, Homicide, Perpetration, Cumulative Charging) 16 February 2011, (STL- 11- 01/I), para. 76.

155   For a detailed discussion on the debates surrounding the principle of legality at Nuremberg, see K. S. Gallant, *The Principle of Legality in International and Comparative Criminal Law* (Cambridge: Cambridge University Press, 2009) 67–129. Traces of the principle of legality can be found in international law in the pre-Nuremberg and Tokyo era. *Nullum crimen* issues were raised in 1919 by the Commission on Responsibilities at the Paris Peace Conference, and in 1935 by the Permanent International Court of Justice. See W.A. Schabas, *Unimaginable Atrocities: Justice, Politics, and Rights at the War Crimes Tribunal* (Oxford: Oxford University Press, 2012) 48–49.

156   See Universal Declaration of Human Rights, G.A. res. 217A (III), U.N. Doc A/810 at 71 (1948), Article 11. Emphasis added. [Hereinafter: UDHR].

A similar formulation is included in the International Covenant on Civil and Political Rights (ICCPR).[157] The principle is also encapsulated in several regional human rights treaties including the African [Banjul] Charter on Human and Peoples' Rights[158] as well as in IHL treaties.[159] None of these instruments require for an international crime to already be codified in the domestic legal order at the time of its commission for it to be considered as such.

It is also established in the jurisprudence of both the HRC[160] and the ECtHR[161] that, from the perspective of the principle of legality, it is permissible to prosecute, convict, and punish those responsible for committing crimes, which, at the time when they were committed, were sufficiently defined in international law. The reference to international law also includes what is referred to under the ECHR and ICCPR as *general principles of law recognized by the civilized (community) of nations*.[162]

---

157   See International Covenant on Civil and Political Rights, G.A. res. 2200A (XXI), 21 U.N. GAOR Supp. (No. 16) at 52, U.N. Doc. A/6316 (1966), 999 U.N.T.S. 171, *entered into force* Mar. 23, 1976, Article 15 (1). [Hereinafter: ICCPR].

158   See African [Banjul] Charter on Human and Peoples' Rights, adopted June 27, 1981, OAU Doc. CAB/LEG/67/3 rev. 5, 21 I.L.M. 58 (1982), *entered into force* 21 October 1986, Article 7(2). [Hereinafter ACHPR].

159   See GC III, Article 99; GC IV, Articles 65–68; AP I, Article 75(4)(c); AP II, Article 6(2)(c).

160   HRC, *David Michael Nicholas v. Australia*, (Communication No. 1080/2002), 19 March 2004, U.N. Doc. CCPR/C/80/D/1080/2002(2004), para 7.5; HRC, *Klaus Dieter Baumgarten v. Germany*, (Communication No. 960/2000), 19 September 2003, U.N. Doc. CCPR/C/78/D/960/2000 (2003), para. 9.3.

161   It is generally understood that for the purpose of the principle of legality offenses that are defined in international law should, at the time when they were committed, be sufficiently accessible and foreseeable to the alleged defendant. See ECtHR, *Kononov v. Latvia*, Grand Chamber, (Judgment), 17 May 2010, Application No. 36376/04, para. 187; ECtHR, *Korbely v. Hungary*, Grand Chamber, (Judgment), 19 September 2008, Application No. 9174/02, para. 73–76; ECtHR, *Šimšić v. Bosnia and Herzegovina*, (Judgment), 10 April 2012, Application No. 51552/10, para. 25; ECtHR, *Streletz, Kessler and Krenz v. Germany*, (Judgment), 22 March 2001, Applications Nos. 34044/96, 35532/97 and 44801/98, para. 91.

162   The ECHR and the ICCPR both contain a separate second paragraph, Article 7(2) and Article 15(2) respectively, which appear to be allowing for the prosecution of crimes based on what is referred to as 'general principles of law recognized by civilized (community of) nations'. Instead of the ECHR's 'civilized of nations', Article 15(2) of the ICCPR uses 'community of nations', which, according to Nowak, was preferred by the ICCPR to make the provision less Eurocentric. See M. Nowak, *U.N. Covenant on Civil and Political Rights: CCPR Commentary* (Strasbourg: N.P. Engel, 1993) 281. However, the word 'civilized', as it also appears under Article 38 of the ICJ Statute, presumptively refers to all UN member states. See M.C. Bassiouni, 'A Functional Approach to General Principles of International Law' (1989–1990) 11(1) *Michigan Journal of International Law* 768–818. According to Grabenwarter, 'albeit worded as an exception, [Article 7(2)] has the same content as, and serves the same purpose as the reference to international law under

The fact that international criminalization is *per se* sufficient to prosecute offenders of international crimes does not make the principle of legality less significant; the prominence of the principle is in fact signified by its non-derogable status in international human rights law.[163] One of the purposes

---

paragraph 1'. See C. Grabenwarter, *European Convention on Human Rights: Commentary* (München: C.H.Beck.Hart.Namos, 2014) 178.

The jurisprudence of the ECtHR gives no precise indication as to what is meant by 'general principles of law', although the Court has largely alluded to the interpretation given by the European Commission on Human Rights in *X* v. *Belgium* and reiterated that the scope of Article 7(2) is confined to conducts criminalized in relation to WWII circumstances. See *Kononov* v. *Latvia, supra* note 161, para. 186. The only exception appears to be the decision reached by the ECtHR in *Kolk and Kislyiy* v. *Estonia*, where the Court stated that crimes against humanity were proscribed in 1949 pursuant to general principles of law. See ECtHR, *Kolk and Kislyiy* v. *Estonia*, (Decision on Admissibility), 17 January 2006, Application Nos. 23052/04 and 24018/04, 9–10. This decision was heavily criticized, notably by Cassese on several grounds, including that 'general principles of law' are just gap filling subsidiary sources of international law and that they did not exist in 1949 to proscribe crimes against humanity. A. Cassese, 'Balancing the Prosecution of Crimes against Humanity and Non-Retroactivity of Criminal Law: The Kolk and Kislyiy v. Estonia Case before the ECHR' (2006) 4(1) *Journal of International Criminal Justice* 410–418, 414–416.

In several subsequent cases involving the legality principle, the ECtHR has largely distanced itself from discussing Article 7(2) and limited its analysis to Article 7(1). For details, see W.A. Schabas, *The European Human Rights Convention: A Commentary* (Oxford: Oxford University Press, 2015) 354. At the same time, however, it has repeatedly underlined that paragraph 2 of Article 7 shall be read in concordance with the reference to 'international law' under paragraph 1. See *Kononov* v. *Latvia, supra* note 161, para 186; ECtHR, *Maktouf and Damjanović* v. *Bosnia and Herzegovina*, Grand Chamber, (Judgment), 18 July 2013, Applications Nos. 2312/08 and 34179/08, para. 72. ECtHR, *van Anraat* v. *the Netherlands* (Decision on Admissibility), 6 July 2010, Application No.65389/09, para. 186.

An express and firm rejection of Article 7 (2) in the ECtHR's jurisprudence is to be found in the more recent case of *Vasiliauskas* v. *Lithuania*, in which the Grand Chamber found a violation of Article 7(1) in relation to the domestic prosecution of 'political genocide' committed post-WWII. In this case, the Grand Chamber emphasized that a conviction that could not be justified under the first paragraph of Article 7 cannot be justified under its second paragraph either. See ECtHR, *Vasiliauskas* v. *Lithuania*, Grand Chamber, (Judgment), 20 October 2015, Application No. 35343/05, paras 186–190.

163 See ACHR, Article 27; The Revised ArCHR, Article 4; ECHR, Article 15(2); ICCPR, Article 4. Although the ACHPR contains no clause on non-derogability of human rights, the African Human Rights Commission took the position, in the *Chad Massive Violations* case, that derogations are not allowed even in a civil war situation. See African Commission Human and People's Rights, *Commission Nationale des Droits de l'Homme et des Libertés* v. *Chad*, Comm. No. 74/92 (1995), October 1995, para. 21. In other cases, the Commission interpreted the absence of derogation clause as an 'expression of the principle that the restriction of human rights is not a solution to national difficulties', and that 'limitations on the rights and freedoms enshrined in the Charter cannot be justified by emergencies or special circumstances'. See respectively, African Commission Human and People's Rights,

of the principle of legality is that it ensures, by demanding *accessibility and foreseeability* of the law, the availability of a reasonable notice concerning a prohibited conduct and its consequences, so that the public is effectively safeguarded against arbitrary prosecution, conviction, and punishment.[164] In this regard, the fact that core crimes are manifestly illegal satisfies, by and of itself, the accessibility and foreseeability criteria. Such an assertion is based on the assumption that, as the ECtHR repeatedly stated, 'even the most cursory reflection' by the defendant is sufficient to foresee that engaging in conducts that could constitute core crimes entails individual criminal responsibility.[165] In short, core crimes are too flagrant and shocking to the human conscience that they simply cannot not put perpetrators of such crimes on notice as to the existence of a corresponding criminal liability. In that regard, it is noteworthy that, unlike the ICC Statute which attaches the 'manifestly unlawful' label in connection to the defense of superior order only to genocide and crimes against humanity,[166] the ECtHR does not make such a distinction in relation to the principle of legality.

Irrespective of the international or domestic nature of an offense, the principle of legality operates on the basis of an assumption, since it is not concerned with the defendant's *actual* knowledge of what the criminal law prohibits or

---

Amnesty International and Others v. *Sudan*, Comm. No. 48/90, 50/91, 52/91, 89/93 (1999), 15 November 1999, para. 79; African Commission Human and People's Rights, *Constitutional Rights Project, Civil Liberties Organisation and Media Rights Agenda* v. *Nigeria*, Comm Nos. 140/94, 141/94, 145/95 (1999), 15 November 1999, para. 41. For a discussion on the non-derogability of human rights under the ACHPR, see F. Viljoen, *International Human Rights Law in Africa* (Oxford: Oxford University Press, 2007) 251–253; L. Sermet, 'The absence of a derogation clause from the African Charter on Human and Peoples' Rights: A critical discussion' (2007) 7(1) *African Human Rights Law Journal* 142–161.

164 Gallant, *The Principle of Legality in International and Comparative Criminal Law*, *supra* note 155, 20–23. See also *Kononov* v. *Latvia*, *supra* note 161, para. 185; *Streletz, Kessler and Krenz* v. *Germany*, *supra* note 161, para. 88; *Vasiliauskas* v. *Lithuania*, *supra* note 162, para. 153.

165 See *Kononov* v. *Latvia*, *supra* note 161, para. 238; *Korbely* v. *Hungary*, *supra* note 161, paras 73–76; *Šimšić* v *Bosnia and Herzegovina*, *supra* note 161, para. 24. For a detailed analysis of the role of 'manifest illegality of the core crimes' in fulfilling the accessibility and foreseeability of the principle of legality, see Ferdinandusse, *Direct Application of International Law in National Courts* (The Hague: T.M.C. Asser Press, 2006) 242–248; ICTY, *Prosecutor* v. *Hadžlhasanović*, Appeals Chamber, (Judgment), 22 April 2008, IT-01-47-AR72, para. 34; ICTY, *Prosecutor* v. *Milutinović et al.*, Appeals Chamber, (Decision on Dragoljub Ojdanić's Motion Challenging Jurisdiction – Joint Criminal Enterprise), 21 May 2003, IT-99-37-AR72, para. 42; *Unnamed defendants*, (Interlocutory Decision on the Applicable Law: Terrorism, Conspiracy, Homicide, Perpetration, Cumulative Charging), *supra* note 154, para. 134.

166 ICC Statute, Article 28.

not.¹⁶⁷ Theoretically, what matters most is not a reference to a specific provision, but the possibility that the defendant has the awareness that a particular conduct constitutes a crime. Even with respect to ordinary offenses, the absence of a written rule has not always been regarded as running counter to the principle of legality's foreseeability and accessibility criteria.¹⁶⁸ It can thus be correctly assumed that an ordinary soldier is aware of acts that constitute a war crime, even when there exists a state practice that tolerates or encourages a perpetration of similar crimes.¹⁶⁹

Overall, it does not constitute a violation of the principle of legality to prosecute and punish acts that are criminalized in international law, but not in domestic law, at the time of their commission. Therefore, the aforementioned conclusion that the legality provisions in the FDRE Constitution and the Criminal Code of 2005 recognized international treaties as sources of criminal offenses is in conformity with the UDHR and with the above discussed other treaties. This establishes the fact that war crimes proscribed by the relevant international treaties could indeed be regarded as criminal offenses in Ethiopian law without further parliamentary action. However, that does not *per se* ensure the direct application of international provisions by Ethiopian courts, for this has to depend on the *nulla poena* aspect of the principle of legality as discussed below.

7.5.2.2 Nulla Poena Sine Lege: Trying War Crimes Defined in International Treaties

The availability in international law of a definition of an international crime may not entail its direct application by municipal courts without further involvement of the Parliament, even after ratification or accession. As the STL noted, 'in criminal matters, international law cannot substitute itself for

---

167 As embodied in the notion of *ignorantia juris non excusta,* the principle of legality only requires the availability to the public of a notice as to what is prohibited by criminal law. See Gallant, *The Principle of Legality in International and Comparative Criminal Law, supra* note 155, 21–22. See also D. Luban, 'Fairness to Rightness: Jurisdiction, Legality, and the Legitimacy of International Criminal Law' in S. Besson & J. Tasioulas (eds.), *The Philosophy of International Law* (Oxford: Oxford University Press, 2010) 570–588, 584, according to whom the fair notice requirement in the principle of legality is a legal fiction.

168 See ECtHR, *Jorgic* v. *Germany*, (Judgment), 12 July 2007, Application No. 74613/01, paras 100–101; *Streletz, Kessler and Krenz* v. *Germany, supra* note 161, para. 50; ECtHR, *S.W.* v. *the United Kingdom*, (Judgment) 22 November 1995, Application No 20166/92, paras 34–36. See also Grabenwarter, *European Convention on Human Rights: Commentary supra* note162, 181.

169 See *Kononov* v. *Latvia, supra* note 161, para. 235; *Streletz, Kessler and Krenz* v. *Germany, supra* note 161, paras 77–79; *Vasiliauskas* v. *Lithuania, supra* note162, paras 157–158.

national legislation; in other words, international criminalisation alone is not sufficient for domestic legal orders to punish that conduct'.[170] This is because, as is the case in Ethiopia, the *nullum crimen* aspect of the principle of legality should also be accompanied with the *nullum poena* aspect of the principle,[171] which can only be fulfilled by a parliamentary act, except in those jurisdictions where judges may have the authority to apply penalties not sufficiently specified at the time of the commission of the crime.[172]

Accordingly, one could regard the above-mentioned Article 17 of the Criminal Code of 2005 as a mere prescription of universal jurisdiction over international crimes committed outside Ethiopia, except for those international crimes already listed in Ethiopian law. Ethiopian courts may thus exercise jurisdiction over 'international crimes specified in an international treaty or a convention to which Ethiopia has adhered'[173] but only after the Ethiopian Parliament enacts a legislation supplying a penalty clause to the alleged crime. In this regard, it could be debatable as to whether the Parliament may lawfully prescribe a penalty to an international crime after the crime has been committed.

There appears to be no clear prohibition in Ethiopian law of prescribing a penalty for a crime that post-dates the commission of the crime. In defining *nulla poena sine lege,* Article 2 of the Criminal Code of 2005 does not seem to be requiring that the penalty for a crime should be prescribed before the commission of the offense. It simply states that 'the Court may not impose penalties or measures other than those prescribed by law'.[174] Likewise, the FDRE Constitution does not expressly prohibit the imposition of a new penalty for an international crime that did not already have a penalty attached to it. Its Article 22 prohibits the retroactive imposition of a heavier penalty, not that of a new penalty.[175] If one could argue that a new penalty is by essence heavier than no penalty, and thus also in contravention of Article 22, one could however also argue that insofar as the Constitution allows for the punishment of

---

170   *Unnamed defendants,* (Interlocutory Decision on the Applicable Law: Terrorism, Conspiracy, Homicide, Perpetration, Cumulative Charging), *supra* note 154, para. 131.
171   FDRE Criminal Code, Article 2 (2).
172   For approaches regarding the application of penalties by the judiciary, see Ferdinandusse, *Direct Application of International Criminal Law in National Courts, supra* note 165, 248–256.
173   FDRE Criminal Code, Article 17 (1).
174   Ibid., Article 2(2).
175   See FDRE Constitution, Article 22(1), which reads '...nor shall a heavier penalty be imposed on any person than the one that was applicable at the time when the criminal offence was committed'.

crimes proscribed under international law, as discussed above, it must be the case that the Parliament may lawfully prescribe penalties to such crimes, be it before or after their commission.

In any event, it may be safely asserted that the *nullum poena* principle is satisfied when it comes to the war crimes of using prohibited means and methods of warfare. As noted above, Article 276 of the Criminal Code criminalizes acts defined in international treaties by referring to international conventions and contains a penalty clause. This provision thus sufficiently combines the *crimen* and *poena* aspects of the principle of legality, as a result of which Ethiopian courts can prosecute and punish alleged perpetrators by directly applying IHL treaties ratified by Ethiopia.

7.5.3 *Customary International Law and War Crimes in Ethiopia: The Regressive Aspect*

As explained in the above cited *Tadić* decision, a rule of IHL, the infringement of which could constitute war crimes, must belong to either *customary* or treaty law.[176] A violation of customary rules of IHL constitutes a war crime, provided that the requirement of seriousness is fulfilled.[177] The principle of legality, discussed above, does not distinguish between treaty or customary international law. This indicates that both can thus serve as a source of crimes for which prosecution can be carried out before domestic courts even in the absence of a domestic provision criminalizing the conduct.

Nonetheless, Ethiopian criminal law treats customary international law differently. In particular, there is no provision in Ethiopian law that allows for the direct application of customary international law in a similar manner that Article 276 allows for the applicability of IHL conventions in domestic trials. Although Article 22 of the FDRE Constitution does not refer to either domestic or international law, Article 28 defines international crimes in reference to international conventions only. According to Article 17 of the Criminal Code, Ethiopia's jurisdiction over international crimes committed abroad is limited to those offenses that are specified in Ethiopian legislation, or in *an international treaty or a convention* to which Ethiopia has adhered. As such, nowhere does the Ethiopian law recognize, for the purpose of prosecution in Ethiopia, an international crime defined only in customary international law.

The practical implication of the absence of a reference in Ethiopian law to customary rules of IHL becomes visible in connection to war crimes that are

---

176 *Tadić*, (Decision on the defense motion for interlocutory appeal on jurisdiction), *supra* note 22, para. 94.
177 On the requirements of seriousness, see the discussion in section 7.3.2 above.

proscribed neither in international treaties nor in Ethiopian law, but in customary international law. In this regard, conventional war crimes are now punishable when committed in non-international armed conflicts only because the developments in customary international law have arguably extended their applicability from international armed conflicts to non-international armed conflicts. For instance, some of the prohibited means of warfare mentioned in international conventions have become applicable to non-international armed conflicts due to the application of customary international law, as evidenced by the amendments made to Article 8 of the Rome Statute of the ICC in 2010[178] and 2017.[179]

Ethiopian law's failure to recognize customary international law as a legal basis for war crimes is a regressive development which is incongruent to its laudable move of abolishing the distinction between international and non-international armed conflicts already in 1957.[180] It could be seen as a significantly regressive aspect of the Ethiopian law of war crimes when put in

---

178   See Resolution on amendments to article 8 of the Rome Statute of the International Criminal Court, RC/Res.5, Depositary Notification C.N.651.2010 Treaties-6, dated 29 November 2010, available at: <http://treaties.un.org> accessed on 29 September 2019. The war crimes include: i) employing poison or poisoned weapons (ICC Statute, Article 8(2)(e) xiii); ii) employing asphyxiating, poisonous or other gases, and all analogous liquids, materials or devices (ICC Statute, Article 8(2)(e) xiv); and iii) employing bullets which expand or flatten easily in the human body, such as bullets with a hard envelope which does not entirely cover the core or is pierced with incisions (ICC Statute, Article 8(2)(e) xv). The reason for such expansion, as expressed in the 2010 Amendment, is to mirror the development in customary international law. See ibid. paras 8–9.

179   See Resolution on amendments to article 8 of the Rome Statute of the International Criminal Court, ICC-ASP/16/Res.4, adopted at the 12th plenary meeting on 14 December 2017, by consensus, ICC-ASP/16/20, available at: <https://asp.icc-cpi.int/iccdocs/asp_docs/Resolutions/ASP16/ICC-ASP-16-Res4-ENG.pdf> accessed on 29 September 209. The 'new' war crimes are: i) employing microbial, biological or toxin weapons (ICC Statute, Article 8(2)(b)(xxvii) and Article 8 (2) (e) (xvi)); ii) employing weapons that injure by fragments undetectable by X-rays (ICC Statute, Article 8(2)(b)(xxviii) and Article 8(2) (e) (xvii); and ii) employing laser blinding weapons (ICC Statute, Article 8(2)(b)(xxix) and Article 8 (2) (e) (xviii). Unlike the previous one, this amendment does not mention whether this extension results from a development in customary international law. Instead, it simply states that these crimes constitute 'serious violations of the laws applicable in international armed conflict and in armed conflict not of an international character'. See ibid., para. 7. Arguably, there is no requirement in the Rome Statute that newly added crimes need to have a legal basis in customary international law at the time of the amendment. See The Report of the Working Group on Amendments, ICC-ASP/16/22, 15 November 2017, paras 13–14, available at: <https://asp.icc-cpi.int/iccdocs/asp_docs/ASP16/ICC-ASP-16-22-ENG.pdf> accessed 30 July 2019.

180   See section 7.4. above.

parallel with the gradual disappearance of IHL's traditional divide between war crimes based on the type of armed conflicts in which they were perpetrated, as discussed above.[181] Practically speaking, this means that a range of war crimes that are now proscribed in non-international armed conflicts are not punishable in Ethiopia precisely because Article 276 does not allow for the direct application of customary international law. For instance, the following acts, while constituting war crimes in non-international armed conflicts punishable by the ICC, have no corresponding prohibition under Ethiopian law:

1. Utilizing the presence of a civilian or other protected person to render certain points, areas or military forces immune from military operations;[182]
2. Killing or wounding treacherously a combatant adversary;[183]
3. Employing poison or poisoned weapons;[184]
4. Employing bullets which expand or flatten easily in the human body, such as bullets with a hard envelope which does not entirely cover the core or is pierced with incisions.[185]

Even more, the exclusion of customary international law under Article 276 is not just something that could be seen as a major setback to the development of war crimes law in Ethiopia. As it stands now, the war crimes provisions in Ethiopian criminal law, in particular those dealing with means and methods of warfare, have allowed for the applicability of a 'preposterous' and 'inhumane' legal regime, to borrow the words of the ICTY Appeals Chamber in *Tadić*:

---

181 See section 7.4. above.

182 ICC Statute, Article 8(2)(b)(xxiii). The use of human shields has its legal bases in Geneva Convention III, Article 23(1); Geneva Convention IV, Articles 28, and AP I, Articles 51(7) and 58. According to the ICTY Appeals Chamber, the criminalization of 'human shields' under the ICC Statute and the Statute of the UN Special Court for East Timor (Article 6–6.1(b)(xxiii)) may indicate the emergence of a corresponding proscription under customary international law. See ICTY, *Prosecutor* v. *Blaskić*, Appeals Chamber, (Judgment), 29 July 2004, IT-95-14-A, para. 653, *fn.* 1366.

183 ICC Statute, Article 8(2)(e)(ix). The legal bases for this war crime are Article 23(b) of The Hague Regulations and Article 37(1) of AP I. Nonetheless these laws are not applicable in cases involving internal armed conflicts. The application of the prohibition of perfidy in non-international armed conflicts is the result of a prohibition in customary international law. *Tadić*, (Decision on the defense motion for interlocutory appeal on jurisdiction), *supra* note 22, para. 125.

184 ICC Statute, Article 8(2)(e)(xiii). Article 23 (a) of the 1907 Hague Regulation may be invoked as a legal basis for this war crime in IHL.

185 ICC Statute, Article 8(2)(e)(xv). Use of dum-dum bullets was prohibited in IHL by the Declaration on the Use of Bullets Which Expand or Flatten Easily in the Human Body of 29 July 1899.

elementary considerations of humanity and common sense make it preposterous that the use by States of weapons prohibited in armed conflicts between themselves be allowed when States try to put down rebellion by their own nationals on their own territory. What is inhumane, and consequently proscribed, in international wars, cannot but be inhumane and inadmissible in civil strife.[186]

7.6 Individual Acts of War Crimes: Ethiopian Law *vis-à-vis* the ICC Statute

Looking at the sub paragraphs of the war crimes provisions in the Criminal Code of 2005, there are now 35 individual acts of war crimes in Ethiopian law.[187] The Penal Code of 1957 had proscribed 26 individual acts of war crimes.[188] Neither Codes adopted a clear structure in listing the prohibited acts constitutive of war crimes. Unlike the approach followed in the ILC Draft Code, and later on by the ICTs and the ICC, war crimes in Ethiopia are not categorized on the basis of the type of armed conflicts within which the crimes were perpetrated since there is no armed-conflict based distinction in Ethiopian law.

Besides, Ethiopian law lacks a methodical classification of war crimes in the sense that some of the provisions appear unnecessarily fragmented or misplaced while some others mix different prohibitions under a single provision. For instance, the act of causing violence to a person rendered *hors de combat* appears as a criminal offense under two separate provisions for no apparent reason.[189] The provision on the use of illegal means of combat fails to distinguish prohibited means of warfare from prohibited methods of warfare. Several war crimes that could fall under the category of prohibited means and methods of warfare are listed under the Criminal Code's Article 270 (war

---

186 *Tadić*, (Decision on the defense motion for interlocutory appeal on jurisdiction), *supra* note 22, para. 119.

187 These are listed under Articles 270 (16 individual acts), 271 (three individual acts), 272 (two individual acts), 275 (four individual acts), 281(2) (two individual acts), 282 (two individual acts), and Articles 273, 276, 279, 280, 283, and 315 (one individual act each).

188 Article 282 of the Penal Code of 1957 listed eight individual acts instead of 16 under Article 270 of the Criminal Code of 2005. Article 284 of the former listed two acts while the latter's Article 271 contains three acts. For details, see section 7.2. above.

189 See the Penal Code of 1957, Articles 287 and 291; FDRE Criminal Code, Articles 275 and 279.

crimes against the civilian population) instead of Article 276 (unlawful methods and means of warfare).

Although some amount of comparison has already been made above,[190] this section fully summarizes the war crimes in the FDRE Criminal Code by comparison with the ICC Statute, which admittedly contains the most detailed list of war crimes in international criminal law.[191] The latter contains 53 individual acts of war crimes listed under Articles 8(2)(a)(i) to 8(2)(e)(xv), most of which are listed twice due to the applicability of the type-of-conflict-based distinction. By contrast, war crimes provisions in Ethiopian law are more general. At times, some of the provisions appear to be too general and a single provision in the Criminal Code contains war crimes listed under different provisions of the ICC Statute, as can be seen from Table 4 below, which compares the war crimes listed under the ICC Statute with those listed in the Ethiopian Criminal Code. The comparison in Table 4. is accompanied with brief explanations provided in footnotes whenever necessary, in particular, to point out significant differences between the two documents.[192]

TABLE 4   Brief comparison of war crimes in the ICC Statute and FDRE Criminal Code

ICC Statute		FDRE Criminal Code
Article 8(2)(a)	i	Article 270 (a)
Grave breaches of the Geneva	ii	Article 270 (a)
Conventions of 12 August 1949,	iii	Article 270 (a)
namely, any of the following acts	iv	Article 270 (h)
against persons or property protected	v	Articles 270 (d) & 272 (b)[193]
under the provisions of the relevant	vi	Articles 270 (p) & 280[194]
Geneva Convention:	vii	Article 270(c)
	viii	Article 270(g)

---

190   See sections 7.4 and 7.5.3 above.
191   The overly detailed nature of the list of war crimes in the ICC Statute may be problematic, see W.A. Schabas, *An Introduction to the International Criminal Court* (5th ed., Cambridge: Cambridge University Press, 2017) 114.
192   Some of the differences between the two laws which are already discussed in other parts of this chapter are not repeated here.
193   Article 270(d) applies when the victims are civilians while Article 272(b) covers prisoners of war and interned persons.
194   Article 270(p) of the Criminal Code includes the prohibition on passing of sentences and carrying out of executions without previous judgment.

TABLE 4   Brief comparison of war crimes in the ICC Statute and FDRE Criminal Code (*cont.*)

ICC Statute		FDRE Criminal Code
Article8(2)(b) Other serious violations of the laws and customs applicable in international armed conflict, within the established framework of international law, namely, any of the following acts:	i	Article 270(a)[195] and (g)
	ii	Article 270 (i)
	iii	Article 281(2) (b)
	iv	Article 270 (o) & (h)
	v	Articles 270(a) and (h)[196]
	vi	Article 275 (a)
	vii	Articles 276*, 282, & 315[197]
	viii	Article 270(c)[198]
	ix	Article 270(i) & (j)[199]
	x	Article 270(a)[200]
	xi	Article 276*[201]
	xii	Article 276*[202]
	xiii	Articles 270(h), (i) & 273
	xiv	Article 280[203]
	xv	Articles 270(d) & 272(b)[204]
	xvi	Article 273[205]

195   See below the discussion under section 7.7.2.1.
196   See *supra* note 124.
197   See *supra* note 126.
198   The Criminal Code does not make a distinction between 'own civilians' and 'civilians of the occupied territory'. It also proscribes the detention of civilians in concentration camps or forced labour camps.
199   Ethiopian law proscribes not only the attack but also the use of protected civilian objects 'in support of military effort'. (Article 270(j)).
200   The Criminal Code does not cover the prohibition of 'scientific and medical experiments'. It also does not specifically encompass acts of physical mutilation except when the victim is a dead person (Article 275(b)).
201   Punishable under Article 276 (prohibited methods of warfare) as Ethiopia is a party to the source convention, i.e. 1907 Hague Regulations, Article 23(b).
202   Punishable under Article 276 (prohibited methods of warfare) as Ethiopia is a party to the source convention i.e. 1907 Hague Regulations, Article 23(d).
203   Article 280 of the Criminal Code is broader in the sense that it covers both the right to fair trial and access to courts.
204   Article 270(d) of the Criminal Code protects civilians while Article 272(b) safeguards PoWs or interned persons.
205   The Criminal Code proscribes pillaging a property under Article 273 without making reference to a place or town. Unlike most of the provisions on war crimes, this article does not make reference to international law or IHL conventions. Nonetheless, the provision

TABLE 4   Brief comparison of war crimes in the ICC Statute and FDRE Criminal Code (*cont.*)

ICC Statute		FDRE Criminal Code
	xvii	Article 276*
	xviii	Article 276*
	xix	Article 276*
	xx	Article 276*
	xxi	Article 279
	xxii	Article 270 (f)[206]
	xxiii	Article 276*
	xxiv	Articles 281 and 283[207]
	xxv	Articles 276*, 270(i) &(k)[208]
	xxvi	Article 270(m)[209]

is broader than the corresponding provision in the ICC Statute as it expressly proscribes looting, piracy, economic spoliation or removal of property under the pretext of military necessity. The broader definition is in line with the developments in international criminal law. See Dörmann, *Elements of War Crimes under the Rome Statute of the International Criminal Court*, *supra* note 124, 275–277.

206   The Criminal Code does not prohibit acts such as forced pregnancy and enforced sterilization. In fact, the ICC Statute, Article 8(2)(b)(xxii) contains a non-exhaustive list of prohibited acts. See Schabas, *An Introduction to International Criminal Court*, *supra* note 119, 125.

207   The Criminal Code extends its protection to any person placed under the protection of international humanitarian organizations (Article 281) and the bearer of flag of truce (Article 283).

208   See the discussion below under section 7.5.2.3.

209   Instead of 'conscripting' and 'enlisting', the Criminal Code uses the word 'recruiting' as stated in Article 77(2) AP I. The minimum age for the war crime of recruiting children is set to18, instead of 15 in the ICC Statute and applicable rules of IHL. The provision may cover the prohibition of voluntary enlistment of children under the age of 18, given that this is also regarded as the minimum age for voluntary recruitment. Nonetheless, age verification could be difficult in practice since the majority of Ethiopians do not possess birth certificates. However, there were reports that children as young as 14 years of age were recruited into the military, in particular during and in the aftermath of the Ethio-Eritrean war. For instance, see Immigration and Refugee Board of Canada, *Ethiopia: Conscription since the May 1998 war with Eritrea, including the minimum age by law and in practice, and the treatment by the authorities of youth leaders who refuse to persuade others to volunteer or advise them not to be conscripted*, 23 June 2000, ETH34702.E, available at: <https://www.refworld.org/docid/3ae6ad5b34.html> accessed 28 September 2019.

TABLE 4 Brief comparison of war crimes in the ICC Statute and FDRE Criminal Code (*cont.*)

ICC Statute		FDRE Criminal Code
Article 8(2)(c) In the case of an armed conflict not of an international character, serious violations of article 3 common to the four Geneva Conventions of 12 August 1949, namely, any of the following acts committed against persons taking no active part in the hostilities, including members of armed forces who have laid down their arms and those placed hors de combat by sickness, wounds, detention or any other cause:	i	Article 270(a)
	ii	Article 279
	iii	Article 270(g)
	iv	Article 270(p)
Article 8(2)(e) Other serious violations of the laws and customs applicable in armed conflicts not of an international character, within the established framework of international law, namely, any of the following acts:	i	Articles 270(g), (l) & (n)[210]
	ii	Articles 281 & 283
	iii	Article 281[211]
	iv	Article 270(i) and (j)
	v	Article 273
	vi	Article 270(f)
	vii	Article 270(m)[212]
	viii	Article 270(c)
	ix	N/A
	x	Article 276*[213]

210 Article 270(l) of the Criminal Code expressly proscribes attacking persons considered refugees or stateless under relevant international instruments.
211 Despite Ethiopia's long history of participation in peacekeeping missions, attacks on UN personnel involved in peacekeeping missions is not proscribed in the Criminal Code. Even more, Ethiopia is not a party to the Convention on the Safety of United Nations and Associated Personnel, G.A. res. 49/59, 49 U.N. GAOR Supp. (No. 49) at 299, UN Doc. A/49/49 (1994).
212 See *supra* note 209. The English version of the Criminal Code refers to recruitment to 'a member of defense forces' – implying national defense force than 'armed forces or groups'. The Amharic version simply states 'recruiting to military services' to take part in armed conflict. As such the crime is punishable both in internal and non-internal armed conflicts.
213 The war crime of 'declaring that no quarter will be given' is punishable when committed in non-international armed conflicts pursuant to Article 276 of the Criminal Code, because Article 4(1) of AP II and Common Article 3 to the Geneva Conventions serve as its international legal basis.

TABLE 4   Brief comparison of war crimes in the ICC Statute and FDRE Criminal Code (*cont.*)

ICC Statute		FDRE Criminal Code
	xi	Article 270(a)
	xii	Articles 270(h), (i) & 273
	xiii	N/A
	xiv	N/A
	xv	N/A
N/A[214]		Article 270(e

* – Prohibited means or methods of warfare punishable through direct application of international treaties pursuant to Article 276 of the Criminal Code.
N/A – Offense 'Not Available' due to the inapplicability of customary international law under Article 276 of the Criminal Code.

7.7   War Crimes in Ethiopian Practice: The *Legesse Asfaw et al.* Case

As noted earlier, the case of SPO v. *Legesse Asfaw et al.*, is the only war crimes case the SPO brought against the *Dergue* for crimes committed between 1974 and 1991. In this case, the SPO brought four charges against 23 defendants, out of which only five were present at trial. All of the defendants were military officers ranking from Major to Brigadier General, most of whom were Air Force pilots trained to conduct air strikes.[215] Captain Legesse Asfaw, the lead defendant, was a decorated military Captain in charge of military operations in the northern part of the country, the then Tigray region.[216] He was also a permanent member of the *Dergue*, and, as the FHC noted, he had special powers that made him even superior to the Ministry of Defense as long as military operations in Tigray were concerned.[217]

Central to all of the charges was the aerial bombardment of undefended towns, villages and dwellings in three locations that were not military objectives. The first aerial bombardment mentioned in the case occurred in Chila town on a market day in February-March 1983, and resulted in the death of about 2,000 civilians.[218] The other two incidents occurred five years later. The second one was the

---

214   The war crimes of forcible religious conversion and denationalization under Article 270(e) of the Criminal Code do not appear in Article 8(2) of the ICC Statute.
215   *Legesse Asfaw et al.* (Trial Ruling), *supra* note 19, 90–96.
216   *Legesse Asfaw et al.*, (Trial Judgment), *supra* note 16, 315.
217   Ibid.
218   *Legesse Asfaw et al.* (Trial Ruling) *supra* note 19, 2.

bombardment of about 3,000 civilians who had gathered to receive a relief aid at the town of Wukro in March-April 1988.[219] The third aerial bombardment took place, similarly to the first one, on a market day in the town of Hawzien on 22 June 1988, killing about 5,000 civilians and gravely injuring over 1,000 others.[220]

Three of the four counts, counts 1–3, dealt with the killings generated by the three incidents according to the order of events.[221] The fourth count dealt with the offense of grave bodily injury related to the third incident.[222] No explanation is available as to why the war crime of bodily injury was not included in the indictment for the other two incidents (Chila and Wukro).

As the attacks were not connected to each other, it is not clear why all of them had to be dealt with in a single trial, although doing so was procedurally permitted.[223] The problematic aspect of the joinder of defendants and offenses can be seen from the fact that the discussion in this case overwhelmingly focused on the bombardment of the town of Hawzien, so much so that the other two attacks were not treated by the FHC separately. In terms of producing evidence, the SPO focused on the Hawzien incident in a manner that gave a marginal treatment to the other two events. Out of the three, it was only the Hawzien incident that was exposed to excavations by the Argentine Forensic Anthropology Team (EEAF), although the forensic evidence was not used at trial.[224] In fact, the case is commonly referred to as the *Hawzien Case*, including by the SPO, which in fact omits references to Chila and Wukro in its final report, the *Dem Yazele Dossie*.[225]

As to the applicable law, *Legesse Asfaw et al.* was conducted on the basis of the Penal Code of 1957, the law in force at the time the crimes were committed. As will be noted below, the Criminal Code of 2005 contains similar provisions and, as will be shown in Chapter 8, by application of the principle of *lex mitior*, the persons convicted in this case were punished on the basis of the later law.[226]

7.7.1 The Individual Acts of War Crimes Prosecuted in Legesse Asfaw et al.

As for the individual acts, the defendants in *Legesse Asfaw et al.* were charged with committing war crimes in violation of Article 282 (a) (b) and (C) of the Penal Code,[227] which reads:

---

219 Ibid.
220 Ibid., 3.
221 Ibid., 1–3.
222 Ibid.
223 See the Criminal Procedure Code of Ethiopia, Articles 16 and 17.
224 See T.S. Metekia, 'Violence Using and Against the Dead: Ethiopia's Dergue Cases' (2018) 4(1) *Journal of Human Remains and Violence* 76–92, 84–86.
225 *Dem Yazele Dossie*, supra note 15, 432–433.
226 See Chapter 8, section 8.3.
227 *Legesse Asfaw et al.* (Trial Ruling) supra note 19, 1.

Whosoever, in time of war, armed conflict or occupation, organizes, orders, or engages in, against the civilian population and in violation of the rules of international law or international humanitarian conventions:
a) killing, torture or inhuman treatment, including biological experiments, or any other acts involving dire sufferings or bodily harm, or injury to mental or physical health;
b) wilful reduction to starvation, destitution or general ruination through the, depreciation, counterfeiting or systematic debasement of the currency; or
c) the compulsory movement or dispersion of the population, its systematic deportation, transfer or detention in concentration camps or forced labour camps;

With regards to the crimes under Article 282(a), the SPO referred to acts of 'killings' and 'bodily harm'. It referred to 'starvation' under Article 282(b), without linking it to 'depreciation, counterfeiting or systematic debasement of the currency'.[228] The SPO did not mention how the crimes under Article 282(c) took place in the context of the bombardment of the said towns. In fact, this third category of crimes was never discussed in the case and was left out by the FHC with no explanation. In addition to the war crimes of killing, bodily injury, and starvation, the Court found that the defendants had committed acts that constituted war crimes of 'collective punishment and reprisals' (Article 283(g) of the Penal Code),[229] and damage to property (282(h) of the Penal Code),[230] which were not mentioned in the indictment. It however did not impose a punishment for these crimes. The following subsections provide a separate discussion of the crimes for which the defendants in *Legesse Asfaw et al.* were convicted and punished, to show how war crimes are interpreted in Ethiopian practice as compared to international jurisprudence.

7.7.1.1   Killing a Civilian

Killing as a war crime in Ethiopian law covers all cases of causing death of one or more civilian persons. It comprises acts referred to in the Statutes of the ICTs and the ICC as 'willful killing'[231] or 'murder',[232] which were consider

---

228   See section 7.5.2.3. below.
229   *Legesse Asfaw et al.,* (Trial Judgment), *supra* note 16, 385.
230   Ibid.
231   ICC Statute, Article 8(2)(a)(i), ICTY Statute, Article 2.
232   Ibid., Article 8(2)(c)(i); ICTY Statute, Article 3.

identical offenses by the ICTY in the Čelebić case.[233] For the crime of killing under Article 282(a) of the Penal Code (Article 270(a) of the Criminal Code), the victim may be a civilian who is not sick, wounded, or interned, as these group of civilians are covered under other provisions.[234] As such, killing under Article 282 (a) of the Penal Code appears to be narrower than the concept of murder in the above-mentioned Statutes of the ICTs and the ICC, which as stated by the ICTY, protect a broader category of victims, i.e. 'persons not taking direct part in hostilities' including combatants placed *hors de combat*.[235]

Virtually all kinds of deaths resulting from a violation of rules of IHL could constitute the war crime of killing under Ethiopian law, as long as they are not caused by negligence be it gross or ordinary – a category of *mens rea* that can be considered applicable in Ethiopian trials only when expressly provided by law.[236] Article 282(a) of the Penal Code of 1957 (Article 270(a) of the Criminal Code) covers cases where the death of a civilian is the result of an attack, irrespective of the means or nature of the attack. As long as a civilian death has occurred, this provision could be applied to punish those who have intentionally directed attacks against the civilian population as such or those who have intentionally launched an attack in the knowledge that such attack will cause incidental loss of life – a case of indirect intention.[237] In that respect, an attack that resulted in the death of a civilian could be carried out by whatever means, and the law's interest focuses more on the fact that civilian has been a victim of an attack rather than the nature of the attack itself.

As this is essentially the factual basis for the case at hand, the war crime of killing as mentioned in Ethiopian criminal law covers cases where the death of civilians occurred from attacking or bombarding, by whatever means, towns, villages, dwellings, or buildings which are undefended and which are not military objectives. Such a war crime has been expressly provided under the Statutes of the ICTY and the ICC with respect to international armed conflicts[238] and punishable as the war crime of attacks against a civilian population under Article 8(2)(e)(i) in situations of non-international armed conflicts. In fact, launching an attack is *per se* sufficient to establish individual criminal

---

233 See ICTY, *Prosecutor* v. *Delalić et al.*, Trial Chamber, (Judgment), 16 November 1998, IT-96-21, paras 422–423.
234 See FDRE Criminal Code, Articles 271(1)(a) and 272(a).
235 See ICTY, *Prosecutor* v. *kordić and Čerkez*, Trial Chamber, (Judgment), 26 February 2001, IT-95-14/2-T, para. 233.
236 See the Penal Code of 1957, Article 59; FDRE Criminal Code, Article 59.
237 *Legesse Asfaw et al.*, (Trial Judgment), *supra* note 16, 332–337.
238 See ICC Statute, Article 8(2)(b)(v); ICTY Statute, Article 3(c).

responsibility under the ICC statute.²³⁹ The reason behind IHL's rule prohibiting attacking undefended localities (Article 25 of the Hague Regulations) is that the use of military force could be automatically disproportionate due to the very fact that the localities are undefended.²⁴⁰ Although the discussion primarily focused on the war crime of killing civilians, the Court in *Legesse Asfaw et al.* also explained why attacking undefended localities is always prohibited. According to the Court, undefended localities with no military activity such as the three towns mentioned in the case at hand represent no military objective. In those circumstances, the FHC noted that one should not discuss whether the attack was justified by military necessity because 'military necessity does not exist in the absence of a military objective'.²⁴¹

The FHC's discussion in the war crimes case emphasized that the protection of civilians possesses a unique position in the laws of war. In doing so, the FHC stated that the actual presence of enemy soldiers in the attacked towns could not have changed the civilian status of the population.²⁴² Even in cases where an attack is directed against military objectives such as defended localities, the Court stated that 'military necessity should not be regarded as the overriding principle' capable of justifying the launching of the attack.²⁴³ Accordingly, the presence of civilians within the targeted military objectives must be regarded as a circumstance compelling either the cancellation of the attack in order to achieve intended military gain through other ways or postponement of a planned attack in order to take necessary precautionary measures to avoid civilian casualties.²⁴⁴ International jurisprudence has also highlighted the protection of civilians in a comparable manner. In *Kupreškić*, where the absolute illegality of the intentional bombardment of civilians was referred to as a universally recognized principle, the Trial Chamber stated that 'the protection of civilians in time of armed conflict, whether international or internal, is the bedrock of modern humanitarian law'.²⁴⁵

---

239   See G, Werle and F. Jessberger, *Principles of International Criminal Law* (3rd ed., Oxford: Oxford University Press, 2014) 477.
240   See ibid., 495.
241   Ibid., 359.
242   *Legesse Asfaw et al.,* (Trial Judgment), *supra* note 16, 359.
243   Ibid., 359.
244   Ibid. 358–359.
245   See ICTY, *Prosecutor* v. *Kupreškić*, Trial Chamber, (Judgment), 14 January 2000, IT-95-16, para. 521. See also the references in the judgment such as: League of Nations, Official Journal, Special Supplement no. 182, Records of the XIxth Ordinary Session of the Assembly, 15–17; Legality of the Threat or Use of Nuclear Weapons (Advisory Opinion), ICJ Reports 1996, 257 (para.78).

In *Legesse Asfaw* et al., the FHC further noted that the obligation to protect and spare civilian lives is an extremely stringent one, which cannot be circumvented by invoking a superior order, contrary to what the Defense had argued.[246] In explaining the responsibility of pilots undertaking military strikes, the Court stated that the fact that an order to strike a military target was given by a superior commander does not relieve the pilot from responsibility, in particular where the attack results in killing or harming the civilian population.[247] Irrespective of the existence of a superior order, a pilot must avert the strike by his or her own decision at the moment he or she becomes aware that civilians are present in the locality being or about to be bombarded.[248]

According to the Court, those pilots who participated in the bombardment of towns such as Hawzien for several hours on a market day could not have been unaware of the fact that most, if not all, of the victims were civilian market goers.[249] Air strikes were carried out while the military jets were flying low over roof tops, in such a way that a pilot could distinguish a civilian from an armed combatant as well as a human from a cattle.[250] Regardless, the attack resulted in the death of about 5,000 thousand people in Hawzien and many dead bodies were found all over the town and in the outskirts.[251] Accordingly, the Court concluded that the attacks constituted the war crime of killing in violation of Article 282(a) of the Penal Code.[252]

7.7.1.2 Bodily Injury

The third count in *Legesse Asfaw et al.* was concerned with the war crime of causing bodily injury resulting from the bombardment of the town of Hawzien. This crime appears under Article 282(a) of the Penal Code (Article 270(a) of the Criminal Code) as the war crime of 'causing dire sufferings or bodily harm [to], or injury to mental or physical health' of a civilian. Similar to the above discussion with respect to killing a civilian, the offense of bodily injury covers cases where the civilian population becomes victimized as a result of a deliberate targeting

---

246 See ibid., 316, 336. See also *Legesse Asfaw et al.*, (Sentencing Judgment), *supra* note 21, 405.
247 *Legesse Asfaw et al.*, (Trial Judgment), *supra* note 16, 359.
248 Ibid., 363.
249 Ibid.
250 See *Legesse Asfaw et al.* (Trial Ruling) *supra* note 19, 91–92.
251 Ibid. The fact that the dead bodies were not recovered was not regarded as a bar to enter a conviction for killing. A similar practice exists in in the international jurisprudence. See for instance, ICTY, *Prosecutor* v. *Krnojelac*, Trial Chamber, (Judgment), IT-97-25-T, para. 326.
252 *Legesse Asfaw et al.*, (Trial Judgment), *supra* note 16, 384–385.

of the civilian population, of an indiscriminate attack, or of an attack directed against military objectives.

In principle, as far as it causes dire sufferings or bodily harm, or injury to the mental or physical health of a civilian, any attack could be punished under this provision, irrespective of the type of the armed conflict. Thus, acts covered under the ICC Statute's Articles 8(2)(a)(iii),[253] 8(2)(b)(i), (iv), (v),[254] 8(2)(c)(i),[255] and 8(2)(e)(i)[256] could be punished in Ethiopia pursuant to Article 282(a) of the Criminal Code, as long as the victims of bodily injury are civilians who, at the time of the attack, were not sick, wounded, or detained.[257]

The FHC did not discuss the specific elements of the offenses of causing dire sufferings or bodily harm to, or of injury to the mental or physical health of, a civilian. It was simply stated that the aerial bombardment of Hawzien left over 1,000 civilians with severe bodily injury. This position is perhaps in line with international criminal law, under which the war crime of causing dire sufferings or bodily harm, or injury to mental or physical health covers acts that are not severe enough to constitute torture.[258]

7.7.1.3   Starvation of Civilians as a Method of Warfare

Starvation as a war crime was first mentioned in Ethiopian criminal law under Article 282(b) of the Penal Code of 1957. A closer look reveals a discrepancy between the Amharic and English versions of the Code. While the English version required starvation to result from acts of 'depreciation, counterfeiting or systematic debasement of the currency', the Amharic version seemed

---

253   ICC Statute, Article 8(2)(a)(iii): 'wilfully causing great suffering, or serious injury to body or health'.
254   ICC Statute, Article 8(2)(b)(i): 'intentionally directing attacks against the civilian population as such or against individual civilians not taking direct part in hostilities'; Article 8(2)(b)(iv): 'intentionally launching an attack in the knowledge that such attack will cause incidental loss of life or injury to civilians or damage to civilian objects or widespread, long-term and severe damage to the natural environment which would be clearly excessive in relation to the concrete and direct overall military advantage anticipated'; Article 8(2)(b)(v): 'attacking or bombarding, by whatever means, towns, villages, dwellings or buildings which are undefended and which are not military objectives'.
255   ICC Statute, Article 8(2)(c)(i): 'Violence to life and person, in particular murder of all kinds, mutilation, cruel treatment and torture'.
256   ICC Statute, Article 8(2)(e)(i): 'intentionally directing attacks against the civilian population as such or against individual civilians not taking direct part in hostilities'.
257   Similar to the case of killing, bodily injury to sick, wounded, or interned civilians is covered under Articles 271(1)(a) and 272(a) of the Criminal Code.
258   Dörmann, *Elements of War Crimes under the Rome Statute of the International Criminal Court*, supra note 124, 338.

to treat it as a separate offense. It reads, 'willful starvation of the population; depreciating, counterfeiting or systematic debasing of the currency to put the population in overall destitution or ruination of its life'.[259] Such a provision does not appear to have a specific basis in IHL. According to the ICRC's *Study on Practice Relating to Rule 53* (starvation as a method of warfare), Ethiopian law is the only one to expressly link starvation with acts of 'depreciation, counterfeiting or systematic debasement of the currency'.[260] In the international arena, this offense does not seem to have existed outside of the list of war crimes compiled by the Commission on Responsibilities established by the 1919 Preliminary Peace Conference of Paris to inquire into 'breaches of the laws and customs of war committed by forces of the German Empire and their Allies' during WWI.[261]

The Penal Code's discrepancy was rectified by the Criminal Code of 2005. According to the latter, the crime of starvation under Article 270(b) results from an attack on the currency. It reads, 'willful reduction to starvation, destitution or general ruination through the, depreciation, counterfeiting or systematic debasement of the currency'. Nonetheless, the Criminal Code created its own discrepancy between its two versions. Unlike the English version, the Amharic version does not limit the cause of starvation to the said methods of currency manipulation. It added the phrase, 'በማናቸውም ሁኔታ አስቦ' which could be translated to 'in whatever means calculated' to cause the starvation of the civilian population.[262]

Starvation as a method of warfare, as enshrined in the national laws of several countries,[263] the rules of IHL[264] and the ICC Statute (only with respect to international armed conflicts)[265] refers to a situation where civilians are

---

259 Translation by the author. The original(Amharic) version reads:
ሆነ ብሎ ሕዝብን ችጋር እንዲደርስበት ያደረገ ገንዘብ ዋጋ እንዳያገኝ ባለዋጋነቱን ዝቅ አድርጎ በማክሰር ሐሰተኛ ገንዘብ በማተም ወይም በተደራጀ ዐቅድ ገንዘብን በማውረድ ሕዝብን በጠቅላላ ችግር ላይ በመጣል ኑሮውን ያበላሽ እንደ ሆነ

260 See International Committee of the Red Cross, Customary IHL: Practice Relating to Rule 53 (Starvation as a Method of Warfare), Available at: <https://ihl-databases.icrc.org/customary-ihl/eng/docs/v2_rul_rule53> accessed 28 September 2019.

261 United Nations War Crimes Commission, *supra* note 3, 32–35.

262 See FDRE Criminal Code, Article 270(b). The Amharic version reads:
ገንዘብ ዋጋ እንዳያገኝ ዋጋዉን ዝቅ አድርጎ በማክሰር፣ ሐሰተኛ ገንዘብ በማተም፣ ወይም በተደራጀ ዐቅድ ገንዘብን በማዋረድ ወይም በማናቸውም ሁኔታ አስቦ ሕዝብን ሰረሀብ የዳረገ፣ በችግር ላይ የጣለ ወይም በአጠቃላይ የሕዝቡን ኑሮ ያናጋ እንደሆነ

263 See International Committee of the Red Cross, *Customary IHL: Practice Relating to Rule 53*, *supra* note 260.

264 See AP I, Article 54(1); AP II, Article 14.

265 See ICC Statute, Article 8(2)(b)(xxv).

deprived of objects indispensable to their survival, including willfully impending relief supplies. Ethiopian law also prohibits as war crimes acts that could constitute depriving civilians of objects indispensable to their survival. In particular, Article 270(k) proscribes 'withholding the provision of clothing, bedding, means of shelter, medical supplies and other supplies essential to the survival of the civilian population of *the occupied territory*'.[266] Although the commission of the prohibited acts may lead to the starvation of the civilian population, the prohibition does not require starvation to result in order for the crime to materialize. Furthermore, the prohibition enshrined in this provision is not limited to starvation as a method of warfare during armed conflict: Article 270(k) reads more like a general prohibition of starvation of the civilian population in occupied territory.

Under Article 270(i) of the Criminal Code, it is a war crime against the civilian population to engage in acts of 'confiscation, destruction, removal, rendering useless or appropriation of property such as foodstuffs, agricultural areas for the production of foodstuffs, crops, livestock, drinking water installations and supplies and irrigation works...'. However, the provision does not expressly require these acts to be carried out in order to cause the starvation of civilians or to be used as a method of warfare.

Overall, Ethiopian law does not appear to have expressly criminalized the war crime of using starvation as a method of warfare. An Ethiopian court may however punish the use of starvation as a method of war in two ways. The first option is to invoke the above provisions, Articles 270(b), 270(i), or 270(k) as the case may be, and interpret the prohibition of starvation in line with IHL so that these provisions are applicable when used as a method of warfare. The second option is to rely on Article 276 of the Criminal Code (Article 288 of the Penal Code) which proscribes the use of prohibited (illegal) methods of warfare (combat) defined in the international conventions to which Ethiopia is a party. The fact that the starvation of civilians as a method of warfare (combat) has already been prohibited in AP I and AP II[267] means that it is also punishable in Ethiopia irrespective of the type of conflict. In that sense, the war crime of using the starvation of civilians as a method of warfare has a binary existence in Ethiopian criminal law.

For some reason, the Court in *Legesse Asfaw et al.* did not invoke Article 288 of the Penal Code in finding the perpetrators guilty of committing the war crime of starvation of civilians as a method of combat. Without referring

---

266 FDRE Criminal Code, Article 270(k). Emphasis added.
267 See AP I, Article 54(1); AP II, Article 14.

to the specific law that was considered as violated, the relevant part of the judgment stated,

> their destruction of property not justified by military necessity [and] destruction of various supplies and foodstuffs essential to the survival of the civilian population ascertains that they violated *the law* that prohibits starvation as means of combat.[268]

It is some ten pages later that the Court listed the specific provisions that were found to be violated by the defendants and here mentioned Article 282(b) of the Penal Code.[269] As such, one could only conclude that the Court was referring to the Amharic version of Article 282(b) that proscribes the starvation of civilians when it referred to 'the law' in the above quoted text. Regardless, this finding could arguably be disputed from a point of law, because the Court did not explain how Article 282(b) could be interpreted as encompassing the use of starvation as a method of warfare. The Court stated that, under Article 282(b), starvation of civilians was criminalized as an independent crime whose existence is *per se* sufficient to establish criminal responsibility. In other words, starvation of civilians under this provision was not criminalized as a prohibited method of warfare, that is, as 'a weapon to annihilate or weaken the population' to win a war.[270]

The Court's finding could also be challenged from a point of fact. From that angle, the manner in which the defendants were found guilty of the crime of starvation of civilians under Article 282(b) seems unconvincing. Although the SPO accused the defendants of willful reduction to starvation of the civilian population, the issue was not framed and discussed by the Court. The dispute between the SPO and the defendants was essentially whether the towns were undefended or whether they were military objectives. In the end, the Court's assessment centered around such issues as: whether enemy combatants were present in the bombarded towns; whether the bombardment was justified by

---

268 *Legesse Asfaw et al.*, (Trial Judgment), *supra* note 16, 374. Emphasis added. Translation by the author. The original (Amharic) version reads:
ያለመታደራዊ አስፈላጊነት ንብረቶችን ማውደማቸው፣ ለሲቪል ህዝብ በሕይዎት መቀጠል አስፈላጊ የሆኑ የተለያዩ የሸቀጣ ሸቀጦችና እህል በማውደም ማስራብን እንደማከናወኛ መሳሪያ መጠቀምያ የሚከለክለውን ህግ መጣሳቸውን ያረጋግጣል፡፡

269 Ibid., 385.

270 See ICRC, *Commentary of 1987: Protection Of Objects Indispensable To The Survival Of The Civilian Population*, para. 2090, Available at: <https://ihl databases.icrc.org/applic/ihl/ihl.nsf/Comment.xsp?action=openDocument&documentId=6377CFD2C9D23F39C-12563CD00434C81> accessed 28 September 2019.

the defendants' assumption that enemy combatants had entered the attacked towns; whether the presence of enemy combatants in the town could have, or had, changed the civilian status of the dwellers.[271] It is thus out of the blue that the Court concluded on page 274 of its judgment that the defendants had violated the law prohibiting causing starvation to use it as a method of warfare.

Furthermore, no evidence was presented in support of the conclusion that the defendants had *aimed* at starving the civilian population as a method of warfare by destroying properties essential for its survival. The fact that the bombardment resulted in destroying civilian equipment and foodstuffs does not suggest that the defendants had the requisite *mens rea* to starve the population, let alone to use it as a method of warfare. The Penal Code's use of the word ሆን ብሎ (willfully or deliberately) indicates that *intention* is the requisite mental element for the war crime of starvation. Absent an express reference to negligence, Ethiopian criminal law imposes intention (direct or indirect) as a required mental element of an offense, as pointed out earlier.[272] The Court however did not mention what evidence established the defendants' intent to starve the civilian population in the bombarded localities nor did it specify which civilians were targeted or affected by the said starvation. Given that the Court concluded at one point that the bombardment was aimed to annihilate all civilians (including children, women, and elderly),[273] it could be unrealistic to deduce from the situation that the defendants had at the same time intended to starve the civilian population. The Court's finding, thus, amounted to stating that the defendants had aimed at starving the dead civilians, which seems highly unlikely.

7.7.2 Legesse Asfaw et al.: *Conviction without Discussing the Nexus Element*

A prohibited act constitutes a war crime only if its commission has a nexus to an armed conflict, and, therefore, not all crimes committed during war can be regarded as war crimes. As developed in the jurisprudence of the ICTY and the ICTR, a nexus between the prohibited act and the armed conflict can be established when the conduct is 'closely related to the conflict'.[274] According to the ICC Elements of Crimes, the nexus requirement is fulfilled when the conduct is committed 'in the context of and associated with' an armed conflict.[275]

---

271 See *Legesse Asfaw et al.,* (Trial Judgment), *supra* note 16, 345–3606; *Legesse Asfaw et al.* (Trial Ruling) *supra* note 19, 87–100.
272 See the Penal Code of 1957, Article 59(2); FDRE Criminal Code, Article 59(2).
273 *Legesse Asfaw et al.,* (Trial Judgment), *supra* note 16, 362.
274 Ibid., para. 70.
275 ICC Elements of Crimes, Article 8(2)(a)(i).

In *Legesse Asfaw et al.*, the nexus requirement was not discussed. At one point however, the Court stated, 'because the acts were committed *in connection* to the internal armed conflict that took place in the country, the Court examines them using rules applicable to non-international armed conflicts'.[276] The statement was not accompanied by any explanation and it is not very clear whether the Court was in fact attempting to establish a nexus between the conducts of the defendants and the armed conflict. In particular, the Court did not make a list of the acts committed by the defendants and examine each of them against a set of criteria of nexus, as is usually done by the international courts and tribunals. Nonetheless, this does not mean that the conducts in the case at hand could not have fulfilled the requirement of nexus to an armed conflict, as explained below.

All of the three aerial bombardments in Chila, Wukro, and Hawuzien, which resulted altogether in the death of about 10,000 civilians and in grave bodily injury of about 1,000 civilians, were carried out in the context of an armed conflict. The existence of the conflict played a substantial part in the decisions made to bombard undefended towns under the guise of the existence of military objective. Although there was no military activity in the targeted towns at the time of the attacks, the attacks were all carried out when an armed conflict existed between government forces and the forces of the TPLF and EPLF,[277] and the decisions to attack were reached under the assumption by the government forces that enemy soldiers had entered the said towns.[278] In addition, as established in the case at hand, the defendants acted in pursuance of a military campaign put in place by the *Dergue* to destroy the military capability of the armed groups.[279] As such, the existence of an armed conflict 'played a substantial part in the perpetrator's ability to commit it, his decision to commit it, the manner in which it was committed or the purpose for which it was committed'.[280]

The existence of a nexus could be explained further in reference to the specific criteria developed by the *Kunarac* Appeals Chamber, which include: 'the

---

276   *Legesse Asfaw et al.*, (Trial Judgment), *supra* note 16, 384. Emphasis added. Translation by the author. The original (Amharic) versiosn reads: 'የተፈጸመው ድርጊት በሀገር ውስጥ ከነበረው የትጥቅ ግጭት ጋር በተያያዘ ስለ ነበረ ዓለም አቀፍ በልሆኑ የትጥቅ ግጭት ላይ ተፈጻሚነት ከላቸው የሕግ ድንጋጌዎች አድራጎቱን ስንመዝነው።'.
277   However, it was not mentioned in the case whether it was EPLF or TPLF forces or both that were fighting the *Dergue* during the time relevant for the aerial bombardment of the towns.
278   *Legesse Asfaw et al.*, (Trial Judgment), *supra* note 16, 375.
279   Ibid., 318.
280   See *Kunarac et al.*, Appeals Chamber, (Judgment), *supra* note 23, para. 58.

fact that the perpetrator is a combatant; the fact that the victim is a non-combatant; the fact that the victim is a member of the opposing party; the fact that the act may be said to serve the ultimate goal of a military campaign; and the fact that the crime is committed as part of or in the context of the perpetrator's official duties'.[281]

First, the perpetrators were all members of the defense forces of the government and, therefore, had a combatant status during the armed conflict. Most of them were air force pilots on active duty and capable of launching airstrikes upon superior orders.[282] Legesse Asfaw, the main defendant, was at the time a military captain who was also the governor of the Tigray region and member of the *Dergue*'s central committee.[283] None of the defendants were sick, wounded, or detained by the enemy forces at the time of the conflict, and, thus, their status as combatants was not disputed.

Second, the victims in *Legesse Asfaw et al.* were civilians. The attacks in Chila and Hawzien were carried out against market goers from surrounding villages and dwellers of the towns while those attacked in Wukro town were civilians gathered from neighboring villages to collect a relief aid.[284] The allegation by the defendants that there were enemy soldiers in the attacked towns was found to lack evidentiary basis and the FHC rightly noted that this could not have changed the civilian status of the victims even if it were true.[285]

Third, the victims were civilians belonging to the opposing groups. The attacks were carried out against towns that were regarded to have fallen into the hands of liberation fronts. It was stated in the case that, at the time of the attacks, the opposing groups had gained control (although not permanently) over several towns and localities in the Tigray region, and that airstrikes were carried out routinely.[286] The victims were thus considered by the perpetrators as enemy civilians, based on the requirement of allegiance (not nationality) to the armed groups.

Fourth, the fact that the attacks were meant to serve a goal of military campaign could also be inferred from the use of extensive military forces and high-level decisions. In that respect, the aerial bombardments carried out using Mig-25 jets equipped with machine guns, bombs, and incendiary devices were a result of decisions reached based on coordinated military communiqués

---

281   Ibid. para. 59.
282   *Legesse Asfaw et al.,* (Trial Judgment), *supra* note 16, 314.
283   Ibid.
284   Ibid., 315.
285   Ibid., 359.
286   Ibid., 311.

from Asmara (the major military base in the northern part of the country), the Airforce base in Bishoftu, and the military headquarters in Addis Ababa.[287]

Finally, the involvement of high-ranking military officials shows that the crime was committed in the context of the perpetrators' official duties.[288] Accordingly, it is safe to conclude that the defendants acted in furtherance of, or under the guise of, the armed conflict; a conclusion which establishes a nexus between the attacks mentioned in *Legesse Asfaw et al.* and the armed conflict.

7.8 The Absence of More War Crimes Trials: Why Only *Legesse Asfaw Et al.*?

As discussed in Part 1 of this book, the SPO was only authorized to investigate war crimes committed by officials and members of the armed forces of the *Dergue*. Unsurprisingly therefore, other groups were not investigated, as explained in Chapter 4. Even as regards the *Dergue*, the SPO exhibited a frustrating performance as to the investigation and prosecution of war crimes. Out of the hundreds of SPO cases,[289] only one, the above discussed *SPO v. Legesse Asfaw et al.*, dealt with the prosecution of war crimes.

In explaining the reasons behind the absence of additional war crimes charges against the *Dergue*, the SPO mentioned a lack of reliable and sufficient evidence due to, *inter alia,* the highly mobile nature of the *Dergue*'s army; Eritrea's secession and the irretrievability of military communiqués from the *Dergue*'s military base in Asmara, the capital city of Eritrea; and the inability of eye witness testimonies to point out individual commanders and members of the army who had participated in committing acts that could constitute war crimes.[290]

The SPO's inability to prosecute many cases of war crimes ultimately raises doubts as to its interest in prosecuting war crimes in general. Given the existence of countless military operations marred with allegations of violations of the laws of war,[291] one may legitimately question why only Hawzien, Chila, and Wukro were judicially adjudicated. Was it because these crimes were

---

287 Ibid., 336.
288 For the status of the defendants see section 7.5.2. below.
289 The exact number of SPO cases has not been reported, although the SPO stated that it had investigated a total of 364 cases. See *Dem Yazele Dossie, supra* note 15, Annex 2.
290 See ibid., 432.
291 Ibid., 432.

committed in the home villages of those who were governing the country at the time?²⁹² Was it because the incidents were too noticeable and already politicized to the victor's advantage not to be referred to as war crimes? Was the SPO's failure to investigate into war crimes in general a deliberate abstention in order not to implicate the victors in the process?

It is generally difficult to provide an answer to these kinds of questions that are already filled with skepticism. However, it could also be overly simplistic to dismiss the doubts as unfounded. To the contrary, there is evidence showing that the SPO process neglected potential war crime cases.

The SPO's practice regarding war crimes was a considerable setback from what was initially planned and reported. In 1994, before the initial indictment was filed against Mengistu and 105 others, the SPO published a report entitled 'The Special Prosecution Process of War Criminals and Human Rights Violators in Ethiopia'.²⁹³ In the report, it was stated that the Office 'has ten times more evidence than needed to successfully prosecute several of the detained and many of the exiles for serious criminal offences'.²⁹⁴ Although there is no detailed and specific discussion of potential war crimes charges, the report was prepared in a manner that conveyed the impression that the Office was preparing to prosecute more than one case of war crimes.²⁹⁵ This was further demonstrated in an essay published in 1995 by T.S. Engelschiøn, a Norwegian special advisor to the SPO. The essay, which seems to be an elaborated version of the SPO's report, informs that the SPO established a 'war crimes team'²⁹⁶ dealing with 'hundreds and hundreds of examples of flagrant violations of international humanitarian law and Articles of the Penal Code of Ethiopia'.²⁹⁷

---

292   The TPLF-EPRDF leaders who controlled government powers by overthrowing the *Dergue* in 1991 were from the Tigray region. The same people had formed the Transitional Government of Ethiopia and had established the SPO in August 1992, as discussed in Part 1 of this book.

293   SPO, 'Report of the Office of the Special Prosecutor 1994: The Special Prosecution Process of War Criminals and Human Rights Violators in Ethiopia' in N.J. Kritz (ed.), *Transitional Justice: How emerging democracies reckon with former regimes; Laws, Rulings and Reports* (Washington DC: United States Institute of Peace Press, 1995) 559–574.

294   See ibid., 560.

295   Such an impression can be derived from the report's reference to the exiles as 'war criminals in exile', from discussions based on the Geneva Conventions for the purpose of extradition, and from the listing of the Penal Code of 1957's war crimes provisions as potential provisions on which the forthcoming charges were to be based. See ibid., 559, 567, 573.

296   See T.S. Engelschiøn, 'Ethiopia: War Crimes and Violations of Human Rights ' (1995) 34(9) *Military Law and Law of War Review* 9–32, 19.

297   Ibid., 14–15.

It can be construed from Engelschiøn's essay that, in those days, the SPO was satisfied with the availability and relevance of the evidence and that discussions were rather predominantly about legal issues such as the choice of applicable law and whether the SPO could directly apply IHL rules or whether it had to limit itself to the war crimes provisions of the Penal Code.[298] Furthermore, in a statement that casts doubt on the reliability of the SPO's claim regarding the insufficiency of relevant evidence for cases of war crimes, Engelschiøn wrote:

> I do not know about any other cases relevant to war crimes and violations of International Humanitarian Customary Law where you have such an amount of written materials as evidence.[299]

This point notwithstanding, it is possible that the documentary evidence in the SPO's possession had not been fully evaluated when Engelschiøn worked with the SPO. As such, it might be too hasty to use his report as irrevocable proof that sufficient evidence existed to support additional war crimes charges. Conversely, the same may be said with respect to the SPO's report. Adopting a more wholesome approach and looking at the other cases prosecuted by the SPO, it nonetheless appears that the SPO might have, notably in instances dealing with offenses committed and prosecuted in the eastern and northern parts of the country, preferred to use the qualifications of murder or grave willful injury in cases however best described as war crimes.

In the East, where armed activities took place between the government forces and the OLF, cases from the Supreme Court of the Harari Regional State (HSC) indicate that acts that could constitute war crimes were also prosecuted by the SPO as ordinary crimes of murder and grave willful injury. Notable examples included the execution of prisoners belonging to the OLF's Shiek Jarra Abba-Gada group at the Babille military camp,[300] acts of torture perpetrated against members of the OLF detained in the interrogation center of the 9th Army Division in Dire Dawa,[301] and public mass executions of

---

298 Ibid., 19–20.
299 Ibid., 26.
300 See HSC, SPO v. *Girma Sisay Mengesha et al.*, (Indictment), 23 December 1996, File No. 05/1990, 3.
301 HSC, SPO v. *Bekele Kassa Abbadima et al.*, (Revised Indictment), 3 October 2003, File No. 04/1995, 3–4.

alleged members and affiliates of the OLF in various towns across the now East Harargie parts of the Oromia region.[302]

In the North, the region that was, arguably, the epicenter of the armed conflict during the *Dergue* regime, a review of the cases adjudicated by the Supreme Court of the Tigray Regional State (TSC) reveals that the perpetration of several acts that could constitute war crimes were here again prosecuted as murder and grave bodily injury. In several instances, the SPO defendants were officials, members of the police, the militia, and the armed forces, while the victims were members and civilians with allegiance to armed groups such as the EPLF, the EPRA, and the TPLF. The crimes were perpetrated in public, in military camps, and in Red-Terror special detention centers across several towns such as Mekele, Adwa, Shire, Aksum, and Hawzien.[303]

In defense of the SPO, it is possible to argue that the absence of war crimes charges finds a justification in the extensive prosecution of genocide it conducted, assuming that it had deliberately chosen to prosecute genocide instead of war crimes. Genocide against political groups, as prosecuted by the SPO, covered crimes committed with the intent to destroy members of political groups in places where there was an armed conflict between the *Dergue* and the rebel groups. In that sense, prosecuting the *Dergue* for genocide instead of war crimes may symbolize and capture the SPO's allegation that the *Dergue* had the intent/plan to destroy members of political opposition groups (both in time of war and in time of peace).[304] Further, the term political groups, as discussed in Chapter 6, was understood in the *Dergue* trials not only as including non-armed groups such as the EPRP and the AESM but also armed groups such as the EPLF, the OLF, and the TPLF, thereby arguably overlapping with the notion of victimhood as embodied within the war crimes category.

Be that as it may, it remains unclear why the SPO did not use the qualification of war crimes, even if only in the alternative charges, notably for offenses perpetrated in the context of the armed conflicts. Given the sufficiency of evidence to prove the charges of murder and bodily injury, which, aside from

---

302 HSC, SPO v. *Solomon Negussie et al.,* (Revised Indictment), 3 December 1999, File No. 04/1990, 92–93: see in particular count 25. See also HSC, SPO v. *Hailu Iticha et al.,*(Revised Indictment), 30 January 2000, File No. 04/1993, 9–10.

303 TSC, SPO v. *Aseffa Belaye Gezahegn et al.,* (Indictment), 28 December 2000, File No. 06/1992, 13–16; TSC, SPO v. *Teferra Woldetensay et al.,* (Indictment), 28 December 2000, File No. 01/1992, 9–14; TSC, SPO v. *Tekleberehen Negash et al.,* (Indictment), 12 February 1998, File No. 01/1991, 5, 13.

304 For details, see Chapter 6, section 6.4.

being ordinary crimes, are also underlying offenses of war crimes, the SPO would only have had to establish the 'contextual element' to prove the perpetration of war crimes. Due to the apparent situation of armed conflict, not least in the northern and eastern parts of the country, evidencing the existence of an armed conflict and its nexus to the underlying offenses would surely not have been too difficult a task.

From the foregoing, it is safe to state that the SPO substituted potential war crimes charges with ordinary charges, thereby effectively avoiding any discussion of the armed conflict and of the parties involved. In that sense, it may be argued that both the law and the practice here created a firewall against any possibility of implicating the armed groups in the commission of international crimes during the armed conflicts.

The political landscape under which the SPO was made to operate might have also contributed to this choice of charges. The SPO was only established as a special office, not as an independent institution. It was an office accountable directly to a purely political organ, the Office of the Prime Minister, which was entirely composed of the leaders and members of the EPRDF.[305] The EPRDF was the victor and, as already discussed under Chapter 3, there is evidence showing that the decision to prosecute was reached to garner political legitimacy for the EPRDF.[306] It might well be that this same concern led the SPO into treating potential war crimes cases as ordinary murders or grave willful injuries. As also noted further in Chapter 3, the EPRDF was engaged in portraying the past as evil and the present as a savior, if not a victim, that did not participate in the atrocities perpetrated during the armed conflict.[307] The exclusion of war crimes cases might thus have been calculated to ensure political acceptability of the EPRDF leaders by ensuring that no shred of evidence would come to light to make the public doubt their alleged cleanness.

7.9 Conclusion

This chapter has discussed the law of war crimes as well as the only war crimes case in the *Dergue* trials, the State that was a pioneer in the international effort to prevent and punish the perpetration of war crimes. As also pointed out at

---

305   See SPO Proclamation, Article 2(2).
306   See Chapter 3, section 3.5.
307   See ibid.

the outset of this book, Ethiopia's commitment to prosecute war crimes could have led to some innovative developments which might have included the establishment of a hybrid war crimes tribunal, had it not failed due to a lack of sufficient cooperation by powerful states at the end of the Second World War.

Back in 1957, the Ethiopian law on war crimes could have been regarded as one of the most advanced war crimes laws, in particular for abolishing, though implicitly, the listing of war crimes based on the distinction between international and non-international armed conflicts. It could also have been applauded for providing direct application of IHL treaties involving the war crimes of using prohibited means and methods of warfare. Of all international crimes, only war crimes could be treated in such exceptional way in Ethiopian criminal law. Recent changes in Ethiopian criminal law – as endorsed with the entry into force of the Criminal Code of 2005 – have also been used to expand the list of war crimes under Ethiopian law in a manner that mirrors developments in IHL.

Yet, as progressive as it might be on certain aspects, the Ethiopian law of war crimes has also proved to be regressive on others, as shown in this chapter. The fact that some of the provisions that were traditionally considered war crimes provisions do not pass the *Tadić* test that requires war crimes to be serious violations of rules of IHL could be seen as a minor problem. Ethiopian law's major defect is rather that it does not allow for the direct application of customary international in the same way as it allows for the direct application of IHL treaties. This has led to rendering the abolition of the type-of-armed-conflict-based distinction of war crimes practically insignificant – a shortcoming that could really put Ethiopian law behind contemporary developments in international criminal law which is moving towards having a single set of war crimes irrespective of the type of armed conflict.

The war crimes trial by the FHC in *Legesse Asfaw et al.* case dealt with the most notorious cases of indiscriminate bombardments of undefended towns that killed and injured several thousands of civilians. The Prosecution appears to represent a case of selective prosecution of war crimes, as several other potential cases were not characterized as such for allegedly political reasons. The war crimes case however made an extensive reference to IHL treaties in a manner that never happened in other international crimes trials. Except for this apparently positive aspect, the case was handled by the FHC in a way that exhibited numerous shortcomings.

Firstly, the Court in *Legesse Asfaw et al.* did not adequately and separately analyze each of the three attacks based on which the SPO's charge was filed. Secondly, even with respect to the Hawzien attack, the Court did not explore one of the important elements of war crimes, i.e. the nexus to armed conflict requirement. Thirdly, the individual war crimes for which the defendants were convicted were not methodically examined by the Court. It did not provide a distinct discussion of the elements of crimes (*actus reus* and *mens rea*) for the war crimes of killing, of bodily injury, and of starvation. In fact, the Court's finding on the war crime of starvation was, as discussed in this chapter, indefensible from both a factual and a legal standpoint.

CHAPTER 8

Punishment and Sentencing of Core Crimes in Ethiopia

8.1   Introduction

In the four groups of trials examined in this book, 5,492 suspects have been prosecuted for core crimes.[1] In the *Dergue* trials, the SPO indicted 5,119 individuals.[2] The *Oromo-Gumuz* trials prosecuted 276 defendants[3] while the *Anuak-Nuwer* trials brought only nine persons to justice.[4] In the CUD cases, 88 individuals stood trial, all of whom were acquitted of genocide-related charges by the FHC on the ground that they lacked specific intent (plan) to destroy members of political or ethnic groups, as discussed in Chapter 6.[5] Instead, the CUD defendants were convicted and punished for treason, a crime which will not be discussed in this book.[6]

The *Anuak-Nuwer* trials found three of the nine defendants guilty.[7] In the *Oromo-Gumuz* trials, 174 out of 276 suspects were convicted.[8] The *Dergue* trials

---

[1]   This chapter is an elaborated and revised version of an article published in early 2019. See T.S. Metekia, 'Punishing Core Crimes in Ethiopia: Analysis of the Domestic Practice in Light of and in Comparison, with Sentencing Practices at the UNICTs and the ICC' (2019) 19(1) *International Criminal Law Review* 160–190.

[2]   Of the 5,119 defendants, 157 were women while the remaining 4,962 were men. 2,188 of the defendants were tried *in absentia*. See Special Prosecutor's Office, *Dem Yazele Dossie: Begizeyawi Wotaderawi Dergue Weyem Mengist Abalat Benetsuhan Zegoch Laye Yetefetsem Wenjel Zegeba* (Addis Ababa: Far-East Trading P.L.C., 2010), annex, table II.

[3]   See FHC, *Federal Prosecutor* v. *Aliyu Yesufe Ibrahim et al.,* (Indictment), 3 September 2008, File No.71000,1-8; FHC, *Federal Prosecutor* v. *Tadesse Jewannie Mengesha et al.,* (Indictment), 22 August 2008, 1–9; FHC, *Federal Prosecutor* v. *Tesfaye Neno Loya et al.,* (Indictment), 20 September 2008, File No. 74796, 1–4.

[4]   See FHC, *Federal Prosecutor* v. *Gure Uchala Ugira et al.,* (Indictment) 2 February 2004, File No. 31855, 1–2.

[5]   See Chapter 6, section 6.5.2. See also Chapter 4, section 4.2.1.

[6]   *See* FHC, *Federal Prosecutor* v. *Engineer Hailu Shawul et al.,* (Judgment), 30 March 2007, File No. 43246/97, 5; FHC, *Federal Prosecutor* v. *Berehene Kehassaye Woldeselassie et al.,* (Judgment), 19 April 2007, File No. 45671/98, .7; FHC, *Federal Prosecutor* v. *Kifle Tigeneh et al.,* (Ruling), 16 April 2007, File No. 44562, 23.

[7]   See *Federal Prosecutor* v. *Gure Uchala Ugiraet al.,* (Sentencing Judgment), 30 March 2005, File No. 31855, 1–3.

[8]   FHC, *Federal Prosecutor* v. *Aliyu Yesufe Ibrahim et al.,* (Sentencing Judgment), 5 September 2009, File No. 71000, 1–6; *Federal Prosecutor* v. *Tadesse Jewannie Mengesha*

TABLE 5 Summary of number of persons indicted, convicted, and acquitted on charges of genocide and war crimes

Trials	Persons indicted	Persons convicted	Persons acquitted	Persons convicted in absentia	Persons acquitted in absentia	Overall conviction rate
Dergue	5,119	3,583	1,536	1,308	880	69.9%
Anuak-Nuwer	9	3[9]	6	-	-	33.3%
CUD	88	0	88	0	2	0%
Oromo-Gumuz	276	174	102	2	-	63%
Total	5,492	3,760	1,732	1,310	882	68.46%

entered a guilty verdict for 3,583 of the 5,119 defendants.[10] On average, the conviction rate of the three trials stands at 69.5 percent, which means that 3,760 of the 5,404 suspects were convicted and punished.

These three trials can safely be regarded as trials of core crimes, namely, genocide and war crimes – crimes against humanity not even being, as discussed earlier, listed as criminal offenses under Ethiopian law.[11] The *Anuak-Nuwer* and the *Oromo-Gumuz* trials focused entirely on the prosecution of genocide against ethnic groups while the SPO's focus in the *Dergue* trials was on genocide against political groups, although in one instance it also prosecuted war crimes against the civilian population. Some of the SPO cases were also devoted to the prosecution of purely domestic crimes such as aggravated murder committed during the *Dergue* era[12] – a practice criticized by the FSC on the ground that the SPO law did not provide for the prosecution of purely

    et al., (Sentencing Judgment), 2 September 2009, File No. 70996, 1–4; *Federal Prosecutor v. Tesfaye Neno Loya et al.*, (Sentencing Judgment) 20 May 2009, File No. 74796, 1–3.

9   This figure represents convictions entered for genocide. Two more defendants were convicted of ordinary crimes.

10   *Dem Yazele Dossie*, *supra* note 2, 464.

11   See in particular, Chapter 5, section 5.3.2.

12   The two most notable SPO cases that dealt only with domestic crimes and ultimately resulted in the imposition of the death penalty are: OSC, *SPO v. Aman Gobena et al.*,

domestic crimes unless they were perpetrated within the context of abuse of power or genocide.[13]

With respect to the defendant-crime-ratio, only 20 of the 3,583 individuals convicted in the *Dergue* trials were found guilty of committing war crimes against the civilian population.[14] It is not fully clear how many of the remaining 3,564 defendants were punished for committing genocide against political groups, because this figure includes defendants convicted and punished for the ordinary crimes included in the alternative charges of the SPO indictments. In the *Anuak-Nuwer* trials, three of the five convictions were entered in relation to the commission of genocide against ethnic groups.[15] The other two defendants were found guilty of committing the ordinary crime of harboring and aiding in violation of Article 439 of the Penal Code; a conviction entered *in lieu* of the charge of complicity in genocide.[16] In the *Oromo-Gumuz* trials, 171 of the 174 convictions were entered in relation to the crime of genocide against members of ethnic groups. Of these, two defendants were convicted for committing rape in addition to genocide.[17] A conviction for arson and aggravated robbery was entered in relation to the remaining three defendants, whom the FHC found not guilty of the genocide charge.[18]

An overview of the Ethiopian cases shows that a wide variety of sentences, including the most severe penalties, were meted out to those found guilty of perpetrating core crimes. As abridged in the following table, the penalty imposed on perpetrators of core crimes varied from two years of *rigorous*[19] imprisonment to punishment by death. In the *Dergue* trials, 52 death sentences, 182 life sentences, and 921 sentences of rigorous imprisonment from 15 to 25 years were imposed. In the *Oromo-Gumuz* trials, the FHC sentenced seven individuals to death, eight individuals to life in prison, and 95 individuals to rigorous imprisonment from 15 to 25 years. The *Anuak-Nuwer* trials punished *génocidaires* with the maximum of 14 years of rigorous imprisonment.

(Sentencing Judgment), 23 April 2002, File No. 8/92; and FHC, SPO v. *Abdulekadir Mohammed Burka*, (Sentencing Judgment) 13 July 2004, File No. 17011.
13 See Chapter 2, section 2.3.3.
14 See FHC, SPO v. *Legesse Asfaw et al.*, (Sentencing Judgment), 4 April 2008, File No. 03116, 1–13. The total number of defendants prosecuted for war crimes in this case was 23, out of which two defendants were acquitted while the SPO dropped the charge against one accused. See FHC, SPO v. *Legesse Asfaw et al.*, (Trial Ruling), 10 January 2007, File No. 03116, 108.
15 See *Gure Uchala Ugiraet al.*, (Sentencing Judgment) *supra* note 7, 1–3.
16 Ibid.
17 See *Tadesse Jewannie Mengesha et al.*, (Sentencing Judgment) *supra* note 8, 13–14.
18 *Aliyu Yesufe Ibrahim et al.*, (Sentencing Judgment) *supra* note 8, 3–4.
19 Rigorous imprisonment is defined in section 8.2.2.2.1. below.

TABLE 6   Summary of sentences imposed for genocide and war crimes

Trials	Sentences imposed				
	Death	Life	15 to 25 years	≤ 15 years	Minimum Sentence
Dergue	52	182	921	2,028	2 years
Anuak-Nuwer	-	-	-	3	13 years
Oromo-Gumuz	7	8	95	66	5 years

However, not all of those condemned actually served their sentence, as over a third of the defendants were sentenced in their absence, as noted in Table 5. above.[20] Two of the convicts in the *Oromo-Gumuz* trials were sentenced *in absentia*. In the *Dergue* trials, 1,308 were sentenced *in absentia*.[21] Of these 1,308, 22 were the highest ranking *Dergue* officials, including Colonel Mengistu Hailemariam.[22] In the war crimes case, 15 of the 20 convicts were still at large at the time of the sentencing judgment.[23]

This chapter analyzes the manner in which these trials have punished core crimes. It examines the Ethiopian law and practice on sentencing in comparison with that of the UNICTS (ICTY and ICTR) and the ICC. In this respect, the justification for comparing the domestic and the international systems rests on the fact that both systems have functional equivalence in prosecuting and punishing core crimes.[24] To provide for a comprehensive analysis of the Ethiopian practice, the chapter juxtaposes, when relevant, the punishment of core crimes with that of domestic crimes.

In connection to the comparative analysis that this chapter undertakes, it should be noted that international law does not specify penalties applicable to core crimes. This is usually the case with international treaties due to

---

20 As discussed in Chapter 4, Ethiopian law and practice allows for the retrial of persons convicted and sentenced *in absentia*, and a new sentence could be passed by a court of retrial. See Chapter 4, section 4.3.
21 *Dem Yazele Dossie, supra* note 2, annex, table II.
22 FHC, SPO v. *Colonel Mengistu Hailemariam et al.,* (Sentencing Judgment), 10 January 2007, File No. 1/87, 1–4.
23 *Legesse Asfaw et al.,* (Sentencing Judgment), *supra* note 14, 1.
24 See Chapter 1, section 1.7.

state parties' divergent views on the issue of appropriate penalties for crimes in international law.[25] Although the Genocide Convention and the Geneva Conventions of 1949 require that state parties provide for, respectively 'effective penalty'[26] and 'effective penal sanctions',[27] this has been understood as not limiting states' discretion to punish core crimes by providing penalties they deem appropriate.[28] In that sense, forms and nature of penalties attached to core crimes may vary from jurisdiction to jurisdiction, and such divergence does not *per se* indicate the ineffectivness of a particular penal sanction.

Given that the expressions 'effective penalty' or 'effective penal sanctions' are not self explanatory, commentators have suggested that effectivness shall be seen with respect to both the kind of penalty and the purpose/rationale of punishment. As regards the former, the penalty provided for core crimes in national law is required to be sufficiently severe to reflect the gravity of these crimes.[29] It is also suggested that any form of punishmnent less than imprisonment may not be regarded as severe enough for this purpose.[30] As for the latter, commentators have also opined that punishment of core crimes in domestic law should be provided in a manner that is 'intended and designed to deter' the commission of core crimes.[31]

Nonetheless, these opinions should be approached with caution. For instance, measuring effectiveness by using 'deterrence' as the preferred purpose of punishmnent may not be entirely convincing, since there are significant justifications to punish core crimes on the basis of retributive rationales,

---

25 See B. Saul, 'The Implementation of the Genocide Convention at National Level' in P. Gaeta (ed.), *The UN Genocide Convention: A Commentary* (Oxford: Oxford University Press, 2009) 58–86, 73.

26 See Genocide Convention, Article v.

27 See Geneva Convention for the Amelioration of the Condition of the Wounded and Sick in Armed Forces in the Field, 75 U.N.T.S. 31, *entered into force* 21 October 1950, Article 49.

28 See C.J. Tams *et al.*, *Convention on the prevention and Punishment of the Crime of Genocide: A Commentary* (München: C.H.Beck. Hart.Nomos, 2014), 230–231; See also International Committee of the Red Cross, *Commentary of 2016: Article 49*, paras 2838–2846, available at: <https://ihl-databases.icrc.org/applic/ihl/ihl.nsf/Comment.xsp?action=openDocument&documentId=3ED0B7D33BF425F3C1257F7D00589C84#_Toc452054238> accessed 25 September 2019. [Hereinafter: ICRC, *Commentary of 2016*].

29 Tams *et al.*, *Convention on the Prevention and Punishment of the Crime of Genocide: A Commentary*, 230–231; ICRC, *Commentary of 2016*, paras 2838–2846.

30 Tams *et al.*, *Convention on the Prevention and Punishment of the Crime of Genocide: A Commentary*, 230–231; ICRC, *Commentary of 2016*, paras 2838–2846.

31 Tams *et al.*, *Convention on the Prevention and Punishment of the Crime of Genocide: A Commentary*, 230. See also A. La Rosa, 'Sanctions as a means of obtaining greater respect for humanitarian law: A review of their effectiveness', (2008) 90(1) *International Review of the Red Cross*, 221–247.

as discussed in section 8.4. below. As will be deduced from the overall discussion in this chapter, effectiveness of punishment depends more on whether the actual sentence takes into account the unique and specific nature of the manner in which core crimes are often committed. In that sense, the purpose of punishment is arguably more relevant than the form and kind of penalty prescribed in the law, which is usually, as was also shown in Chapter 2, not more severe than the penalty provided for domestic crimes.[32] Indeed, the gravity of core crimes does not systematically guarantee that national laws reserve the most severe penalties for these offenses. At the same time however, it is precisely the gravity of core crimes that implies that the municipal law may not proscribe them using penalties that are less severe than those prescribed for ordinary crimes.

Accordingly, this chapter comprises six sections. Section 8.2 explores the applicable laws and the available penalties. Section 8.3 discusses the issue of *lex mitior* to examine how Ethiopian courts have dealt with changes in the criminal law that affected penalties. Section 8.4 focuses on sentencing rationales invoked in the Ethiopian trials of core crimes and compares and contrasts them with the purposes of punishment in the international arena. Finally, section 8.5 makes a comparative analysis of aggravating and mitigating factors in sentencing and points out the similarities and differences that may exist between the sentencing practice in Ethiopia and the practice of international criminal courts and tribunals. Finally, Section 8.6 addresses the individualization of sentences and the totality principle in mass trial cases.

8.2 Applicable Penalties for Core Crimes under Ethiopian Law: Principal and Secondary

The prosecution and punishment of core crimes in Ethiopia were based solely on extant domestic criminal laws.[33] Although, as discussed in detail in Chapter 7, the direct application of international law is generally permissible, this is only valid with respect to the substantive elements of the crime, not to

---

32   See Chapter 2, sub-section 2.3.1.
33   The *Dergue* trials and the *Anuak-Nuwer* trials were conducted on the basis of the Penal Code of 1957, in force from 1958 to 2005; the first criminal law in Ethiopia to criminalize and punish core crimes. The FDRE Criminal Code, which entered into force in 2005 by repealing the Penal Code of 1957, served as the applicable law in the *Oromo-Gumuz* trials. For details, see Chapter 5, section 5.6.

the penalty.³⁴ In other words, under Ethiopian law, judges are not allowed to consider penalties that are not specifically prescribed by the legislator in the applicable domestic law.³⁵ Ethiopian criminal law (both the Penal Code of 1957 and the Criminal Code of 2005) divides available penalties into two categories: secondary and principal.

8.2.1 *Principal Penalties*

Principal penalties are more severe and punitive as compared to secondary penalties. Ethiopian law divides them into three: *i*) compulsory labor; *ii*) pecuniary penalties; and *iii*) penalties entailing loss of liberty (including loss of life). The first one, reserved for crimes of minor importance that are punishable with no more than six months of simple imprisonment, may apply to core crimes only when the convicted person fails to pay fines.³⁶ The last two penalties are applicable to core crimes in the manner discussed below. To briefly show the scope and the type of penalties provided for core crimes in Ethiopian law in the light of penalties provided in international criminal law, the following table draws a comparison of penalties applicable to these crimes under Ethiopian law and under the respective Statutes of the ICC and of the UNICTs.

Under Ethiopian law, any particular principal penalty is generally an independent penalty. It is also possible that, as it will be shown below, one form of principal penalty is imposed in conjunction with another form of principal penalty. A principal penalty may also be accompanied with secondary penalties, which have, as noted below, accessory application. In that respect, the laws' treatment of the penalty of confiscation of property as a principal penalty³⁷ is unconvincing, since this penalty is applicable almost always in addition to other principal penalties, and when expressly provided by law, as discussed below.

---

34 Nonetheless, no Ethiopian trial has prosecuted core crimes on the sole basis of international law. As discussed in Chapters 6 and 7, the trials were, however, not devoid of references to international criminal law, international humanitarian law, and international human rights law. One may identify two notable areas in which Ethiopian courts referred to international laws in their prosecution of core crimes: *i*) the applicability of the Genocide Convention with respect to genocide against political groups; and *ii*) the applicability of several conventions making up the laws of armed conflict to the non-international armed conflict that took place in Ethiopia during the *Dergue* regime. See Chapter 5, section 5.5; Chapter 7, section 7.3.1.1.
35 See Chapter 7, section 7.3.1.2.
36 FDRE Criminal Code, Article 103. See the discussion in section 8.2.2.1. below.
37 By providing for 'confiscation of property' under Article 97, the Penal Code of 1957 treated this as a principal penalty (Articles 88–119). See also, FDRE Criminal Code, Articles 90–120.

TABLE 7   Penalties applicable to core crimes: Ethiopian law *vis-à-vis* the Statutes of the ICC and UNICTs

Penalty	Ethiopian law	ICC Statute	ICTY Statute	ICTR Statute
Death	√	X	X	X
Life	√	√[38]	√	√
Prison terms	5–25 years[39]	30 years maximum	no limit	no limit
Fine	If committed with a motive of gain	√	X	X
Compulsory Labor	If the convict fails to pay fines	X	X	X
Confiscation and return of property	X	√	√	√
Secondary penalties	√	X	X	X

X: Not applicable √: Applicable

8.2.1.1   Pecuniary Penalties: Confiscation of Property and Fines

In relation to pecuniary penalties (fines and confiscation of property),[40] a significant point of departure between Ethiopian law and the laws of the ICC and the UNICTs concerns the confiscation and return of property acquired, directly or indirectly, through the commission of a crime.[41] This penalty is provided in

---

[38]   Exceptionally, when justified by 'the extreme gravity of the crime and the individual circumstances of the convicted person'. See ICC Statute, Article 77(1)(b).

[39]   The minimum prison term is not the absolute minimum since, as it will be discussed further, a court may not be bound by it.

[40]   *See* FDRE Criminal Code, Book II, Chapter II.

[41]   It is important that confiscation of a property derived from the commission of a crime is distinguished from confiscation of a property that is used to commit a crime. The latter is applicable to offenses, for instance, of falsification of goods and traffic in arms listed in the Criminal Code and to most of the telecom fraud offenses mentioned in a separate proclamation. See FDRE Criminal Code, Articles 391–395; Telecom Fraud Offence Proclamation, Proclamation No. 761/2012, *entered into force* 4 September 2012, Article 12.

the Statute of the ICC[42] and in those of the UNICTs,[43] although in the case of the latter it has not been applied, even when circumstances demanded it.[44] By contrast, Ethiopian law does not allow for the applicability of this penalty for core crimes. With respect to several domestic crimes however, the law allows for the confiscation of a property acquired, directly or indirectly, through the commission of a crime.[45]

The justification for the inapplicability of the penalty of confiscation of property for core crimes is missing. Article 98 of the Criminal Code, the provision that sets out the general principles for the imposition of confiscation of property, does not specify why this penalty is available for some crimes but not for others. Although the text of the relevant provisions indicates that this penalty is linked to crimes whose commission could involve a motive of gain,[46] it is not applicable with respect to several such crimes, including crimes against movable property.[47]

As for core crimes, one can mention a number of hypothetical scenarios in which a person may benefit, directly or indirectly, from their commission. Perpetrators of core crimes may succeed, partly or fully, in materializing their willingness to acquire property that belongs to the victims, as was evidenced in Ethiopian core crimes cases. In the *Oromo-Gumuz* cases, it was shown that perpetrators derived economic benefit from the genocidal campaign through the appropriation of several cattle, donkeys, household equipment, and harvests that belonged to the victims.[48] In the trials of the *Dergue* era genocide,

---

Also, confiscation of a proceed of a crime should not be confused with sequestration of a property, which the law prescribes exceptionally even if the property is neither a proceed of a crime nor used in the commission of a crime. This happens in the context of political crimes such as conspiring or engaging in hostile acts against the constitutional order or the internal and external security of the State, criminalized under Article 241 of the Criminal Code. See FDRE Criminal Code, Articles 99 and 260.

42 ICC Statute, Article 77(2)(b).
43 ICTR Statute, Article 23(3); ICTY Statute, Article 24(3).
44 See for details, G. Mettraux, *International Crimes and the Ad Hoc Tribunals* (Oxford: Oxford University Press, 2005) 358.
45 See the FDRE Criminal Code, Article 98. In contrast to the law of the ICC (Article 79) according to which confiscated property benefits the victims, in Ethiopia, such property, has, in principle, to be forfeited to the State. Nonetheless, an individual victim may claim the return of his or her property or its value within five years of the date of publication of notice regarding the recovery of the property.
46 See FDRE Criminal Code, Articles 346, 413, 419.
47 See for instance crimes against property (which include theft, robbery, looting, money laundering) in the FDRE Criminal Code, Articles 665–684.
48 *Tadesse Jewannie Mengesha et al.,* (Sentencing Judgment), *supra* note 8, 4; *Tesfaye Neno Loya et al.,* (Sentencing Judgment), *supra* note 8, 41.

overwhelmingly motivated by political gain, the defendants were accused of stealing the properties of their victims whom they detained, killed, and tortured. As the SPO alleged in *Mengistu et al.*, the *Dergue* officials had appropriated victims' property to the amount of 11,521,206.15 Ethiopian Birr (approximately 2,000,000 USD at the time the indictment was issued in 1994).[49]

The exclusion of a penalty of confiscation of property for core crimes is more striking when war crimes are involved, notably because some categories of war crimes are, by their very nature, predicated upon the existence of a motive of gain. These include: pillage, piracy, and looting committed on the pretext of military necessity,[50] confiscation or appropriation of a civilian estate or property,[51] the imposition of unlawful or arbitrary or disproportionate taxes or levies,[52] robbing or plundering a wounded sick or dead enemy on the battlefield.[53]

Yet, Ethiopian courts have refrained from entertaining the issue of confiscation and return of property, even when – as in in *Mengistu et al.* – it was proven that the perpetrators had acquired their victims' property. This might be a consequence of the application of the principle *nulla poena sine lege,* although the legacy of the jurisprudence of FSC CB – that is, the court of last resort for the interpretation of the law – is here one of uncertainty. In a 2012 case known as the *Witchcraft* case, the FSC CB held that confiscation of property shall be ordered in all circumstances as long as courts ascertain that the property in question is a direct or an indirect product of the commission of the crime.[54] Six months later, the FSC CB found in another case that it is a violation of *nulla poena sine lege* to confiscate property acquired through the commission of a crime unless such a penalty is expressly provided in the pertinent provision of the law.[55]

---

49   See FHC, SPO v. *Colonel Mengistu Hailemariam et al.,* (Revised Indictment), 28 November 1995, File No 1/87, Count 211, 275. For the applicable rate of exchange (USD to EthB), see Department of the Treasury, 'Treasury Reporting Rates of Exchange 1994' (10 March 1995), 2, available at: <https://www.gpo.gov/fdsys/pkg/GOVPUB-T63_100-d76dceb12c3da467a628389acb709b6b/pdf/GOVPUB-T63_100   d76dceb12c-3da467a628389acb709b6b.pdf> accessed 29 September 2019.
50   See FDRE Criminal Code, Article 273.
51   Ibid., Article 270 (h).
52   Ibid.
53   Ibid., Article 274.
54   See FSC-CB, *Tamerat Geleta et al* v. *Federal Prosecutor,* (Decision), 25 July 2012, File no. 66943, 4–5.
55   See FSC-CB, *Worku Fekadu and Shume Ararsso* v. *Prosecutor for Benishangul-Gumuz Regional State,* (Decision), 25 January 2013, File no. 75387, 2–3.

In contrast to the Statutes of the ICTY and ICTR, which exclude fines as a form of punishment,[56] Ethiopian law allows for the imposition of fines, in addition to imprisonment, in a manner that is more or less similar to the ICC Statute.[57] It is the commission of a crime with a motive of gain, irrespective of whether the gain is an essential element of the crime, that exceptionally justifies the imposition of fines under Ethiopian law.[58] Both the Ethiopian Criminal Code and the ICC Statute provide for the mandatory payment of fines. In case of default, Ethiopian courts may, as a last resort, order the convicted person to perform compulsory labour for the State for a maximum of two years[59] while the ICC can extend prison terms by up to five years.[60]

Nonetheless, none of the Ethiopian core crimes trials have imposed fines, even when the existence of a motive of gain was pointed out to be the motive behind the commission of genocide. For instance, in the *Oromo-Gumuz* trials, the motive behind the genocidal act of the *Gumuz* against the *Oromo* farmers living along the borders of the two regional states was to acquire disputed land occupied by the farmers.[61] Not only did the court fail to consider imposing fines in these cases, but it also did not qualify the existence of the motive of gain as an aggravating factor, which was however possible by application of Article 86 of the Criminal Code. This Ethiopian practice stands in stark contrast with the practice of the ICC, which has considered the imposition of fines in its sentencing decisions in *Katanga*[62] and in *Lubanga*,[63] although it actually did not impose any fine in either of these cases due to, respectively, the defendant's impecuniousness and absence of evidence of any assets.

---

56   See ICTR, *Prosecutor v. Kambanda*, Trial Chamber, (Judgment and Sentence), 4 September 1998, ICTR 97-23-S, para. 10.

57   ICC Statute, Article 77 (2)(a); ICC Rules of Procedure and Evidence, Rule 146. See also R. Young, 'Fines and Forfeiture in International Criminal Justice' in R. Mulgrew and D. Abels (eds.), *Research Handbook on the International Penal System* (Cambridge: Cambridge University Press, 2016) 109–111.

58   See FDRE Criminal Code, Article 92 (2).

59   This happens when the defendant, who cannot produce sureties and securities, has no property that can be seized and sold or is unwilling to perform some work for the State. See FDRE Criminal Code, Articles 93–96.

60   ICC Rules of Procedure and Evidence, Rule 46(5).

61   See *Tadesse Jewannie Mengesha et al.*, (Sentencing Judgment), *supra* note 8, 6–7; *Tesfaye Neno Loya et al.*, (Sentencing Judgment), *supra* note 8, 4.

62   ICC, *Prosecutor v. Germain Katanga*, Trial Chamber II, (Sentencing Judgment), 23 May 2014, CC-01/04-01/07-3484, para. 169.

63   See ICC, *Prosecutor v. Thomas Lubanga Dyilo*, Trial Chamber I (Decision on Sentence Pursuant to Article 76 of the Statute), 10 July 2012, ICC-01/04-01/06, para. 106.

8.2.1.2 Penalties Entailing Loss of Liberty and Life: From Incarceration to Punishment by Death

Penalties that entail temporary or permanent loss of liberty are the primary forms of punishment applicable to core crimes: Ethiopian law authorizes the imposition of prison terms which range from ten days to life in prison.[64] It also prescribes a penalty that has been abolished in international criminal justice, namely, the death penalty.[65] Genocide is punishable with a minimum of five years of rigorous imprisonment.[66] This minimum penalty is also prescribed for six of the 11 war crimes in the Criminal Code, as identified in Chapter 7.[67] The maximum sentence a court can impose for both categories of core crimes is the death sentence.[68] Inchoate crimes such as conspiracy and incitement to commit genocide or war crimes are punishable with rigorous imprisonment not exceeding five years.[69] The following section provides a separate discussion of penalties entailing loss of liberty with a particular focus on their applicability to the core crimes that were prosecuted in Ethiopia.

8.2.1.2.1 *Rigorous Imprisonment for Five to Twenty-Five Years*

Under Ethiopian law, there are two types of sentences of imprisonment: *simple* and *rigorous*. Simple imprisonment usually extends from a period of ten days to three years (exceptionally reaching five years when expressly provided by law), and is applicable to offenses referred to as 'not of serious nature', and when these offenses are committed by persons who are 'not a serious danger to a society'.[70] Rigorous imprisonment applies to *grave crimes* committed by criminals who are particularly dangerous to society.[71] This type of imprisonment ranges from a period of one year to life,[72] and it 'carries with it the

---

[64] FDRE Criminal Code, Article 108.
[65] W.A. Schabas, 'International Law and the Abolition of Death Penalty' (1998) 55(3) *Washington and Lee Law Review* 798–799.
[66] The Penal Code of 1957, Article 281; FDRE Criminal Code, Article 269.
[67] These are: *i*) war crimes against a civilian population; *ii*) war crimes against wounded sick or shipwrecked persons or medical services; *iii*) war crimes against prisoners and interned persons; *iv*) pillage, piracy and looting; *v*) dereliction of duty towards the enemy; *vi*) use of illegal means of combat. See FDRE Criminal Code, Articles 270, 271, 272, 723, 275, 276.
[68] Ibid.
[69] Ibid., Article 274.
[70] See the Penal Code of 1957, Article 105; FDRE Criminal Code, Article 106.
[71] See the Penal Code of 1957, Article 107; FDRE Criminal Code, Article 108. The Amharic version reads 'ከባድ ወንጀል'/grave crimes/ while the English versions of both codes use a different expression, namely, 'offenses of a very grave nature'. Translation by the author.
[72] See the Penal Code of 1957, Article 107; FDRE Criminal Code, Article 108.

deprivation of all civil rights'.[73] Furthermore, a sentence of rigorous imprisonment is not subject to suspension[74] and its execution is accompanied by 'more severe conditions' of imprisonment, as compared to simple imprisonment.[75] Although there is no guidance in the law as to what sort of conditions are to be considered severe enough for this purpose, the conditions of imprisonment must always respect the human dignity of the prisoner and comply with international human rights law – a constitutional promise that practice often fails to uphold.[76]

The Criminal Code prescribes a penalty of rigorous imprisonment for about 261 offenses – that is, for more than half of the total of 492 offenses it criminalizes, with the exception of petty offenses.[77] Some categories of war crimes such as denial of justice are however regarded as less grave and are punishable with simple imprisonment both in the Penal Code and in the Criminal Code.[78] Some other war crimes are punishable with a maximum of five years of rigorous imprisonment.[79] Compared to the Penal Code, the Criminal Code imposed

---

73 See the Penal Code of 1957, Article 122(2); FDRE Criminal Code, Article 124(2).
74 Article 191 of the Criminal Code provides for the conditional suspension of pronouncement of a sentence of simple imprisonment of not more than three years, provided that doing so is justified by the need to promote the reform and reinstatement of the criminal. Instead, the court may place the criminal on probation without entering a conviction.

   According to the Federal Supreme Court's Cassation decision, suspension of a penalty should not be seen as a privilege given to the convicted person or as something fully left to the discretion of the judges. Provided that the requirements of the law are fulfilled, a convicted person has the right to ask the court to suspend the penalties pronounced against him or her. See FSC CB, *Girma Desta v. Tigray Regional State Prosecutor*, (Decision), 21 May 2008, File No. 34280, 5–6.

   While the suspension of a penalty of simple imprisonment is mandatory, even a rigorous imprisonment of one year (the minimum available in the law) cannot be suspended. See FDRE Criminal Code, Article 191.
75 See Penal Code of 1957, Article 107(2); FDRE Criminal Code, Article 108(2).
76 Article 21 of the FDRE Constitution expressly conditions imprisonment to the due respect of the prisoner's dignity as a human being. It can also be deduced from Article 13(2) of the Constitution that relevant provisions of international human rights instruments apply to the treatment of prisoners in Ethiopia. Nonetheless, prison observation reports indicate the existence in Ethiopia of treatments in violation of international human rights law. See for instance, UN Committee Against Torture (CAT), *Concluding observations of the Committee against Torture: Ethiopia*, 20 January 2011, CAT/C/ETH/CO/1, paras 10, 26, 29, available at: <http://www.refworld.org/docid/4d6cca412.html> accessed 30 September 2019.
77 For the list of petty offenses, see FDRE Criminal Code, Articles 838–865.
78 See Penal Code of 292, Article 2; FDRE Criminal Code, Article 280.
79 These are war crimes involving maltreatment of, or dereliction of duty towards, wounded and sick or prisoners (Article 279 of the Criminal Code), hostile acts against international

a more severe minimum penalty for certain war crimes.[80] It also changed the Penal Code's penalty of simple imprisonment to one of rigorous imprisonment with respect to the war crime of maltreatment of, or dereliction of duty towards, wounded, sick, or prisoners.[81]

However, the five years of rigorous imprisonment prescribed as a minimum penalty for genocide and for the above-mentioned categories of war crimes has not always been seen as proportionate to the gravity of these crimes. For instance, an attempt was made in a Draft Criminal Code completed in 1989 to increase it to ten years of rigorous imprisonment.[82] This however never materialized. Yet, several other offenses which were punishable with a minimum penalty of five years under the Penal Code now carry a more severe minimum penalty, that is, ten years of rigorous imprisonment.[83]

The Criminal Code's failure to apply the same minimum penalty for core crimes resulted in practice in the application of a penalty scheme that one could qualify as absurd. To elucidate this, one needs to look at the crime of attack on the political or territorial integrity of the State, a crime punishable with a minimum of ten years of imprisonment.[84] This crime, as interpreted in *Federal Prosecutor v. Waltajji Begalo et al.,* comprises acts constituting a forcible transfer of people from one regional state to the other,[85] which can also be regarded as underlying offenses of genocide or war crimes.[86] Practically speaking, this means that, when committed with the intent to destroy a protected group in case of genocide or with a nexus to an armed conflict in the case of war crimes, these acts are punishable more leniently with five years of rigorous imprisonment instead of the minimum of ten years.

A similar contradiction exists when the offense of aggravated homicide, which carries a minimum sentence of rigorous imprisonment for life, is involved.[87] Paradoxically, when an aggravated homicide is committed as an

---

humanitarian organizations (Article 281 of the Criminal Code), and abuse of emblems and insignia of international humanitarian organizations (Article 282 of the Criminal Code). See also the Penal Code of 1957, Articles 291, 293, and 294.

80 For details, see Table 7. above
81 See the Penal Code of 1957, Article 2; FDRE Criminal Code, Article 279.
82 Draft Criminal Code of Peoples' Democratic Republic of Ethiopia, September 1989, Article 281.
83 See FDRE Criminal Code, Articles 240–241, 249, 407–408, 411, 413- 415, 512, 573, 596, 690.
84 Ibid., Article 241.
85 See FHC, *Federal Prosecutor v. Waltajji Begalo et al.,* (Trial Judgment), 26 February 2015, File No. 136639, 22.
86 See FDRE Criminal Code, Articles 269 (1) and 270 (1).
87 Ibid., Article 439.

underlying offense to genocide or war crimes, the penalty could be as lenient as five years of rigorous imprisonment instead of the minimum life imprisonment. The cases of *Aman Gobena et al.* and *Abdulkadir Mohammed Burka*, which dealt with aggravated homicide as a purely domestic crime, overwhelmingly show the absurdity of the sentencing scheme.[88] In both cases, the courts considered life sentence as the minimum penalty applicable, which they then aggravated into the death sentence.[89] In contrast, in several cases involving genocide and war crimes through the commission of aggravated homicide, the lower reference point for punishment was five years of rigorous imprisonment, and it took several levels and grounds of aggravation for a convict to be sentenced to life imprisonment, let alone to death.[90]

It should be pointed out here that the five years of imprisonment that the core crimes carry is not the absolute minimum. Courts may, pursuant to Article 180 of the Criminal Code, freely mitigate it to a prison term of as low as one year of rigorous imprisonment.[91] In practice, free mitigation was applied in the *Dergue* trials.[92] In *Mekonnen Gelan et al.*, the SNNPRS SC freely mitigated the punishment for genocide and sentenced several defendants to rigorous imprisonments ranging from two to four years.[93] Section 8.5.2.2. below critically explores this sentencing judgment.

In contrast, the maximum prison term of 25 years for core crimes is an absolute maximum, which judges are never allowed to exceed.[94] As such, core crimes are punishable in Ethiopia with a prison term that is lower than what the ICC Statute permits as the maximum, namely 30 years of

---

88 *Aman Gobena et al.*, (Sentencing Judgment), *supra* note 12, 7–9; SPO v. *Abdulkadir Mohammed Burka*, (Sentencing Judgment), *supra* note 12, 4.
89 Ibid.
90 See for instance, FHC, SPO v. *Negash Woldemichael et al.*, (Sentencing Judgment), 17 November 2006, File No. 03114, 4–6; FHC, SPO v. *Seleshi Mekuria et al.*, (Sentencing Judgment), 8 November 2000, File No.959/89, 1–3.
91 See section 4.2.1. below.
92 In contrast, the *Anuak-Nuwer* trials punished *génocidaires* with a minimum of 13 years imprisonment while the *Oromo-Gumuz* trials applied the minimum penalty prescribed under Article 269 of the Criminal Code, which is five years of rigorous imprisonment.
93 See SNNPRS SC, SPO v. *Mekonnen Gelan et al.*, (Sentencing Judgment), 4 June 2005, File No. 1338, 312–314. This information is based on the examination of the sentencing judgments collected for the purpose of this study. The book does not claim to have collected and studied all of the cases in the *Dergue* trials, due to inaccessibility of some of the cases, not to mention that there is no sufficient information as to the number of the cases actually prosecuted by the SPO.
94 FDRE Criminal Code, Article 108.

imprisonment.⁹⁵ Similarly, the ICTY and the ICTR, which are not bound by any specified limitation to prison terms, have in several cases punished perpetrators of core crimes with a fixed prison term that is way more than the maximum allowed in Ethiopia. In *Nyiramasuhuko et al.*⁹⁶ and *Krstić*,⁹⁷ the tribunals have imposed their longest prison terms to date, that is, respectively, 47 and 46 years of imprisonment, aside of course from the cases in which the defendants were condemned to life imprisonment.

8.2.1.2.2 *Life Imprisonment: With a Possibility of Early Release*

A life sentence, the maximum penalty in the systems of the international criminal courts and tribunals,⁹⁸ has always been one of the applicable penalties in Ethiopia since the enactment of the country's first penal code in 1930.⁹⁹ Currently, about 45 offenses in the Criminal Code of 2005 are punishable with a life sentence. This includes genocide and the seven war crimes mentioned above.¹⁰⁰ The Ethiopian core crimes trials have imposed a total of 190

---

95   ICC Statute, Article 77.
96   See ICTR, *Prosecutor* v. *Nyiramasuhuko et al.*, Appeals Chamber, (Judgment), 14 December 2015, ICTR-98-42-A, para. 3523. Other ICTR defendants punished with determinate sentences that are more than the maximum allowed for core crimes under Ethiopian law include: Kajelijeli (45 years), Gatete (40 years), Bagasora (35 years), Ngeze (35 years) and Barayagwiza (30 years). See, respectively, ICTR, *Prosecutor* v. *Kajelijeli*, Appeals Chamber, (Judgment), 23 May 2005, ICTR-98-441, para. 324; ICTR, *Prosecutor* v. *Gatete*, Appeals Chamber, (Judgment), 09 June October 2012, ICTR-00-61-A, para. 287; ICTR, *Prosecutor* v. *Bagasora et al.*, Appeals Chamber, (Judgment), 14 December 2011, ICTR-98-41-A, para. 741; ICTR, *Prosecutor* v. *Nahimana et al.*, Appeals Chamber, (Judgment), 28 November 2007, ICTR 99-52-A, para. 1074.
97   ICTY, *Prosecutor* v. *Krstić*, Trial Chamber, (Judgment) 2 August 2001, IT-98-33, para. 726. The Appeals Chamber then reduced Krstić's punishment to 35 years of imprisonment. See ICTY, *Prosecutor* v. *Krstić*, Appeals Chamber, (Judgment), 19 April 2004, Case No. IT-98-33-A, paras 5–38. In *Dragomir Milosević*, the ICTY Appeals Chamber reduced the 33 years of imprisonment imposed on the accused by the Trial Chamber to 29 years. See ICTY, *Prosecutor* v. *Dragomir Milosević*, Appeals Chamber, (Judgment) 12 November 2009, IT-98-29-11-A, para. 337.
98   See ICC Statute, Article 77 (1) (B); Rules of Procedure and Evidence, ICTY and ICTR, Rule 101(A). To date, the ICTY has imposed 11 life sentences. See http://www.icty.org/en/cases/judgement-list, accessed 30 September 2019.
99   Penal Code of Ethiopia, *entered into force* September 1930, Articles 161–190.
100   The domestic crimes that are punishable by life in prison fall under various categories such as crimes against the constitutional order and internal security of the state (FDRE Criminal Code, Articles 238, 240, 241, 246, 247, 248, 251, 252), military crimes (ibid., Articles 288, 298, 299, 303, 306, 311, 313, 314, 316, 312), crimes against the physical and economic interest of the State (ibid., Articles 379, and 381), aggravated forms of offenses against the freedom and security of communications (ibid., Articles 505–511, and 514), aggravated

life sentences, which is about 5.5 percent of the total of 3,670 punishments imposed.[101] In *Mengistu et al.*, the FHC's sentencing judgment is known to have imposed the highest number of life sentences in one single trial as it sentenced 46 convicts to life imprisonment.[102]

A life sentence in Ethiopia has a unique position in the sense that the law avoids any possible confusion between life sentence and fixed prison terms on the one hand and between a life sentence and the death penalty on the other. By limiting the maximum prison term to 25 years even in cases of concurrent crimes, the law avoids the addition of sentences to impose a prison term that may amount to life in prison or even go beyond, a problem witnessed in the case of UNICTS, as discussed below.

Life imprisonment under Ethiopian law does not amount to what some referred to as 'putting an individual in a waiting room until [his or her] death'.[103] Similar to the Rome Statute of the ICC that provides for life imprisonment with the possibility of parole,[104] Ethiopian law is compatible with the jurisprudence of regional human rights courts which considers irreducible life sentences as inhuman and degrading treatment.[105] According to the Criminal Code, the adoption of life imprisonment without depriving convicts of any hope of release indicates the major place it 'has allocated for the rehabilitation of offenders'.[106] Nonetheless, as a secondary effect, a sentence of life carries with itself a permanent deprivation of civil rights. A lifer loses all civil rights, including the right to vote and be elected, the right to be a witness or an expert witness, and the right to exercise paternal authority, a profession or engage in industry or commerce.[107] In this regard, the law significantly differentiates between being sentenced to life in prison and to the maximum term of imprisonment allowed in Ethiopian law (25 years of rigorous imprisonment) insofar

---

homicide (ibid., Article 539), and sexual outrages resulting in physical injury or death of the victim (ibid., Articles 620, 627, 631).

101 See Table 5 above.
102 *Colonel Mengistu Hailemariam et al.,* (Sentencing Judgment), *supra* note 22, 479–481.
103 G. de Beco 'Life Sentences and Human Dignity' (2005) 9(3) *The International Journal of Human Rights* 411–419, 414.
104 ICC Statute, Article 110 (3).
105 See ECtHR, *Kafkaris v. Cyprus*, Grand Chamber, (Judgment), 12 February 2008, Application No. 21906/04, paras 97–108; ECtHR, *Vinter and Others v. the United Kingdom*, Grand Chamber, (Judgment), 9 July 2013, Applications Nos. 66069/09, 130/10 and 3896/10, paras 119–122.
106 FDRE Criminal Code, Preface, IV.
107 Ibid., Articles 123 and 124.

as, in the case of the latter, the deprivation of civil rights is temporary and may last between six months to five years.[108]

Neither the Penal Code of 1957 nor the Criminal Code of 2005 provides a clear guidance for the judges as to when a court should or should not impose a life sentence. Ethiopian law does not contain a provision similar to Article 77 (1) (b) of the Rome Statute that restricts the imposition of life sentence to cases 'justified by the extreme gravity of the crime and the individual circumstances of the convicted person'. Nonetheless, a closer look at the text of the law and a thorough examination of offenses entailing life imprisonment reveal that *it is the circumstances of their commission that justifies the applicability of the sentence of life imprisonment.* In prescribing a life sentence, the criminal law often uses phrases such as 'in cases of exceptional gravity' to refer to the degree of gravity of the circumstances of the commission of a crime or to the extent of the consequences of the commission. For instance, as is the case with offenses such as rape, sexual assault upon infants, and crimes against the freedom and security of communications, life sentence is prescribed when the commission of the crime results in grave bodily injury or death of a victim.[109] For offenses against the internal security of the State, the existence of a war or of a danger of a war at the time of the commission of the crime constitutes a case of exceptional gravity.[110]

In deciding penalties for core crimes, circumstances of commission also seem to be relevant. They are referred to in the law using expressions such as 'more serious cases' (Articles 269 and 270), 'cases of exceptional gravity' (Articles 272, 278), and 'gravest cases' (Article 272). Yet, the assessment of these circumstances is left to the discretion of the court, as discussed in section 8.5.1.

Under Article 202 of the Criminal Code, a lifer is eligible for conditional release upon serving 20 years of the sentence. The Rome Statute is here more severe as this eligibility criterion is set at 25 years.[111] It is noteworthy that, on this particular issue, the practice of the ICTY and the ICTR has evolved. Up until the *Galić* early release decision in 2015, it had been regarded that it was the law of the State in which the convicted person was imprisoned that determined the lifer's eligibility for early release; a reality that raised concerns regarding the equal treatment of similarly-situated convicts. Since *Galić*, a sentence of life imprisonment has been considered as equivalent to a hypothetical

---

108   Ibid., Article 124 (1).
109   See ibid., Articles 505–512.
110   See FDRE Criminal Code, Articles 247 and 252.
111   ICC Statute, Article 110 (3).

sentence of at least 45 years, and a lifer may be released upon having served two-thirds of a life sentence, which is 'more than 30 years'.[112] For the sake of consistency, this criterion remained intact despite the jurisprudential change introduced by the *Nyiramasahuko* appeals judgment, which, on 14 December 2015, went beyond the hypothetical sentence of 'at least 45 years', and reduced a life sentence to 47 years.[113]

Upon granting early release, an Ethiopian court may require the prisoner to undergo a period of probation of five to seven years.[114] However, a persistent recidivist,[115] that is, a person who repeats the commission of a crime more than once, is not eligible for early release.[116] This exception is, perhaps, not relevant to core crimes, in relation to which recidivism appears to be not common, as highlighted in the jurisprudence of the UNICTs as well as in the sentencing decision of the ICC in *Al Mahdi*.[117]

8.2.1.2.3 The Death Penalty: Its Exceptionality and the Rarity of Executions

The death penalty has a basis in the Ethiopian Constitution and can be carried out as long as it is confirmed by the President[118] and as the convict has not been granted amnesty or pardon.[119] Yet, compared to the death penalty prescribed in relation to domestic crimes, the one attached to core crimes is different in the sense that it cannot be subjected to a full pardon or remitted by amnesty, as specified in Article 28 of the FDRE Constitution. Besides, while a death sentence can usually be commuted to any lesser penalty deemed necessary by the competent authority, a death penalty issued for core crimes can only be commuted to a sentence of rigorous imprisonment for life.[120] In

---

112   See MICT, *Prosecutor v. Stanislav Galić*, (Reasons for the President's Decision to Deny the Early Release of Stanislav *Galić* and Decision on Prosecution Motion), 23 June 2015, MICT-14-83-ES, public redacted version, paras 35 and 36.
113   MICT, *Prosecutor v. Stanislav Galić*, (Reasons for the President's Decision to Deny the Early Release of Stanislav *Galić*), 18 January 2017, MICT-14-83-ES, public redacted version, para. 21.
114   FDRE Criminal Code, Articles 204, 205, 208.
115   Ibid., Article 202 (2).
116   Ibid., Article 188.
117   See ICC, *Prosecutor v. Ahmad Al Faqi Al Mahdi*, Trial Chamber VIII, (Judgment and Sentence), 27 September 2016, ICC-01-12-01/15, para. 96.
118   The President is the head of the State with nominal and ceremonial powers, unlike the Prime Minister who is the head of the government with actual powers, including those of chief executive and of commander-in-chief of the armed forces.
119   FDRE Criminal Code, Article 117 (2).
120   FDRE Constitution, Article 28 (2).

that regard, it appears that international crimes and their punishment have a unique status in the Ethiopian criminal justice system.

As detailed below, the law conditions the imposition of death penalty. Once issued, it needs to be approved by the President. Once approved by the President, the death sentence should be enforced forthwith, except when the law requires the suspension of the execution owing to full or partial irresponsibility, serious illness, or the pregnancy of the person awaiting execution.[121] The President's silence does not amount to a disapproval of the death sentence. Besides, there is no time frame within which the President shall exercise his or her prerogative to approve the enforcement of the death sentence. At the same time, there is nothing in the law that guarantees the release or commutation of sentence of a prisoner awaiting execution in cases when the President does not consent to the execution.

A person condemned to death is required to await execution in prison under the same conditions as a prisoner serving rigorous imprisonment.[122] Article 224 of the Criminal Code provides that the prisoner may remain on death row for as long as 30 years – the expiry of which renders the death sentence unenforceable. This is no doubt a very long period to endure with, to borrow the ECtHR's expression in *Soering*, 'the anguish and mounting tension of living in the ever-present shadow of death'.[123] Given that the conditions of confinement in Ethiopia exhibit the presence of the death row phenomenon,[124] the law and practice may raise concerns regarding the existence of inhuman and degrading treatment of prisoners awaiting executions.

As mentioned, there are two cumulative requirements that the law puts in place for the imposition of the death penalty: *i*) express stipulation in the law; and *ii*) individual circumstances. The first requirement relates to the principle of legality in that the death penalty can only be imposed when the law specifically lays it down as a punishment for a crime. In that sense, it is the legislator, not the judge, who determines which offenses entail death penalty. As a principle, in prescribing death penalty, the legislator has emphasized the *completeness and gravity* of the offense.[125] Owing to the requirement of completeness, attempted offenses are not punishable by death. Nonetheless, in

---

121   FDRE Criminal Code, Article 119.
122   Ibid., Article 118.
123   ECtHR, *Soering* v. *United Kingdom*, (Judgment), 7 July 1989, Application No. 14038/88, para. 106.
124   UN Committee Against Torture (CAT), *Concluding observations of the Committee against Torture: Ethiopia, supra* note 76, para. 24.
125   FDRE Criminal Code, Article 117.

what constitutes a clear disregard of this rule, Ethiopian courts have imposed the death penalty for an attempted offense.[126]

With regards to gravity, the Penal Code and the FDRE Constitution state that the imposition of the death sentence is reserved, respectively, to 'grave crimes' or 'serious criminal offenses' both of which refer to the Amharic expression 'ከባድ ወንጀል'.[127] This expression is however dubious. As noted above, even offenses that are punishable with a lesser penalty, *i.e* rigorous imprisonment from one year to life can be regarded to be 'grave crimes'. The choice of a right expression to typify crimes that entail death penalty was therefore not meticulous. Looking back at the *travaux préparatoires* of the Constitution, members of the Constitutional Commission debated over choosing an adequate label for crimes that would entail death penalty and specifically over whether to use the Penal Code's expression 'grave crimes' or to prefer 'exceptionally grave crimes'.[128] The Commission finally adopted the phrase 'serious criminal offenses' which appears in the final version of the Constitution. Slightly differently, the Criminal Code states in its Amharic version that a death sentence shall be pronounced only in cases of 'እጅግ በጣም ከባድ', that is 'extremely grave' crimes.[129] The Code's *travaux préparatoires* are unfortunately silent on what this expression connotes and why it was preferred over the one used in both its predecessor and the Constitution.

The second requirement for the imposition of the death penalty relates to the individual circumstances of the convicted person. Accordingly, the death penalty can be imposed on exceptionally dangerous criminals. Besides, the death penalty shall not be imposed if the convict has not attained the age of 18 years at the time of the commission of the crime or if there is an extenuating circumstance.[130]

---

126 See for instance, the 2007's acid-attack case where two women victims survived an attempted murder: the FHC sentenced one of the convicts to death for attempted murder. FHC, *Federal Prosecutor v. Demisew Zerihun and Yacob Hailemariam*, (Sentencing Judgment), 7 November 2008, File No. 54027.
127 See FDRE Constitution, Article 15; Penal Code of 1957, Article 119.
128 This can be inferred from Article 15 of the FDRE Constitution, which deals with the right to life. The provision states that only *serious criminal offenses* entail death penalty. See 'The Minutes of the 84th Ordinary Session of the Constitutional Committee (24 February 1994)' in The Constitutional Commission, 'Minutes, Vol. II: Ordinary Sessions No 51- No 88 held from 2 November 1993 to 3 April 1994' (Addis Ababa: FDRE House of Federations, Unpublished) 197–198.
129 FDRE Criminal Code, Article 117.
130 Ibid., Article 117.

Absent any specifics in the law as to how to determine whether the convicted person is exceptionally dangerous, courts in the *Dergue* and in the *Oromo-Gumuz* trials have relied on the applicability of aggravating factors such as the manner of commission of the crime, the convict's desire to take life, and the number of dead victims.[131] The FSC's appeal decision on sentencing in *Melaku Teferra* confirmed the death sentence imposed by the FHC and justified it mainly on the exceptional dangerousness of the appellant which it established from several aggravating factors.[132] It notably stated:

> Melaku Teferra has persistently committed extremely grave crimes. By taking the life of 971 people, he is unrivalled in his extremely dangerous criminality. It is not necessary to spare the life of such a merciless and extremely dangerous criminal. This kind of criminal should not be allowed to re-join the society.[133]

One of the most controversial aspects of the sentencing practice involving the death penalty relates to the application of the third type of circumstances, namely the (un)availability of a mitigating factor. Although the law itself is clear that even the existence of a single mitigating factor is sufficient to bar the imposition of the death penalty, the practice is inconsistent and at times arbitrary. In *Mengistu et al.*, the FSC overturned the lower court's sentencing decision and converted 18 life sentences into death sentences.[134] It did so mainly by rejecting all of the mitigating factors identified by the FHC,[135] which, notwithstanding its finding that the defendants were exceptionally dangerous, had based its judgment on the availability of mitigating factors.[136] According to the FHC,

> it should be stressed that the death penalty, being at the last edge of all punishments and irreversible, is a unique form of punishment that cannot be pronounced except when all the requirements are fulfilled... The availability of several aggravating factors cannot be regarded *per se*

---

131 See section 8.5.2.4. below.
132 See FSC, *SPO v. Melaku Teferra*, (Appeals Judgment), 1 December 2006, File No. 23776, 5–8.
133 Ibid., 8. Translation by the author. The original (Amharic) version reads, 'እንዲህ አይነት ምህረት የለሽ እና አደገኛ ወንጀለኛ ከዚህ በኋላ በህይወት እንዲቆይ ማድረግ አስፈላጊ አይደለም። ከዚህ በኋላ እንዲህ አይነት ወንጀለኛ ወደ መህበረሰቡ መቀላቀል አይገባውም።'.
134 FSC, *SPO v. Colonel Mengistu Hailemariam et al.*, (Appeals Judgment), 26 May 2008, File No.30181, 85–99.
135 Ibid., 94. See also section 8.5.2.2.2. below.
136 Ibid., 95.

sufficient to impose the death penalty unless the absence of a mitigating factor is ascertained.[137]

The FHC arguably went the extra mile to avoid the imposition of the death penalty in *Mengistu et al.* and its sole focus on judicial mitigating factors, i.e. mitigating factors other than those expressly listed in the law, was challenged on appeal by the SPO.[138] Yet, this is not new. A similar approach had already been adopted by the OSC in *Aman Gobena et al.*, where the court mitigated two death sentences to sentences of life imprisonment using judicial mitigation.[139] In other cases, such as in *Abdulkadir Mohammed Burka*,[140] *Getachew Teke'aba*,[141] *Gesgese Gebremeskel Ateraga et al.*,[142] *Tesfaye Woldeselassie et al.*,[143] and *Zenebe Ayele et al.*,[144] courts have declined to consider comparable grounds of mitigation and punished several defendants by death. In these instances, the sentencing practice focused predominantly on the exceptional dangerousness of the convicts, and, in the process, disregarded the mitigating factors' unique relevance in death penalty cases.[145]

Overall, there is no doubt that, for comparable crimes, Ethiopian perpetrators have received a harsher punishment than those convicted by the UNICTs and the ICC, if only because the death penalty is not applicable in the practice of these international criminal courts and tribunals, unlike what was the case for the Nuremberg and the Tokyo Tribunals.[146] Nonetheless, this comparison should be approached with caution as the choice of penalties in national legal

---

137 See *Colonel Mengistu Hailemariam et al.*, (Sentencing Judgment), *supra* note 22, 8–9. Translation by the author. The original (Amharic) version reads:
እዚህ ላይ የሞት ቅጣት የመጨረሻዉ የቅጣቶች ሁሉ ደርቻ እና የማይመለስ ቅጣት በመሆኑ እንዲሁ ሁሉ ቅድመ ሁኔታዎች በሙሉ ካልተሟሉ በቀር ሊፈረድ የማይችል የተለየ ቅጣት መሆኑ ልብ ሊባል ይገባል፡፡ ... የቱንም ያህል የቅጣት ማክበጃ ቢኖርም የቅይጣት ማቅላያ ምክንያት አለመኖሩ ካልተረጋገጠ በቀር የሞት ቅጣት ለመፍረድ በቂ አይሆንም ፡፡
138 See section 8.5.2.2. below.
139 *Aman Gobena et al.*, (Sentencing Judgment), *supra* note 12, 108–110.
140 *Abdulekadir Mohammed Burka*, (Sentencing Judgment), *supra* note 12, 2–3.
141 FHC, SPO v. *Getachew Tek'eba*, (Sentencing Judgment), 9 November 1999, File no. 914/89, 3–5.
142 FHC, SPO v. *Gesgese Gebremeskel Ateraga et al.*, (Sentencing Judgment), 24 February 2006, File No.03099, 40–54.
143 FHC, SPO v. *Colonel Tesfaye Woldeselassie et al.*, (Sentencing Judgment), 4 August 2003, File No. 03101, 26–32.
144 FHC, SPO v. *Zenebe Ayele et al.*, (Sentencing Judgment), 3 June 2003, File no. 641/89, 109–112.
145 These cases are discussed further under section 8.5.2.2.2.
146 For a discussion on the earlier practice in international justice that favored the imposition of death penalty for international crimes, see W.A. Schabas, *Death Penalty in International*

systems is not required to mirror the international system, not least as far as the death penalty is concerned. As provided under Article 80 of the Rome Statute, even State Parties to the ICC are not under an obligation to abolish the death penalty as part of their membership to the Court.[147]

As shown in Table 6. above, Ethiopian courts have imposed 52 death sentences in the *Dergue* and the *Oromo-Gumuz* trials. None of these were executed. However, executions have occurred for persons found guilty of committing ordinary crimes, and outside the scope of core crimes trials. According to a study conducted in 2013 by Aseffa Kesito, former Minister of Justice who at the time of the study was a special advisor to the President, only three executions were carried out in Ethiopia since 1991.[148] There have since been no reported instances of execution. One may, of course, read a political motive into the enforcement of death sentences in Ethiopia. The three executions carried out were against prisoners convicted of committing offenses in which the victims were top-ranking military or government (Ethiopian or foreign) officials.[149] However, concluding that the death penalty has been abolished for non-political crimes might be too hasty: the reason behind the rarity of the enforcement of death sentences is far from clear and the required relevant information is inaccessible; this may relate, according to Amnesty International, to a general lack of governmental transparency.[150]

Law (3rd ed., Cambridge: Cambridge University Press, 2002) 235–241. With respect to the Nuremberg and Tokyo trials, the death penalty was considered one of the applicable penalties that was to be imposed when determined by the IMT to be just. See The Nuremberg Charter, Article 27; The Tokyo Charter, Article 16.

147 See for details, R. Mulgrew, *Towards the Development of the International Penal System* (Cambridge: Cambridge University Press, 2013) 13–14.

148 A. Kesito, 'Death Penalty in Ethiopia' (Adama, *conference paper*, September 2013) 20–25.

149 It was the assassination of Hayelom Araya, a Major General, and Kinfe Gebre-Medehin, the country's head of intelligence and security services that justified, respectively, the first and second executions. In the third case, three individuals were executed for killing two members of the Ethiopian security forces that intervened in a shootout to avert the assassination attempt carried out in 1995 against Hosni Mubarak, the then Egyptian President, in Addis Ababa. See ibid. In connection to the last execution, it should be pointed out that, contrary to what has been widely reported, the assassination attempt carried out against a foreign president could not have been the relevant factor for the imposition of death penalty in this case, because the death penalty is only applicable with respect to completed offenses. It is thus likely that the Court here considered such attempt as an aggravating factor warranting the detah penalty.See the FDRE Criminal Code, Article 119.

150 Amnesty International, 'Death Sentences and Executions in 2013' 26 March 2014, 43, available at: <http://www.amnestyusa.org/sites/default/files/act500012014en.pdf> accessed 15 August 2019.

There is no indication that Ethiopia intends to abolish the death penalty. It is among the countries that have consistently voted against UN General Assembly resolutions on a moratorium on the use of the death penalty.[151] Specifically to crimes, at the Rome Diplomatic Conference held from 15 June to 17 July 1998 to draft the Rome Statute of the ICC, Ethiopia expressed its preference to keep the death penalty.[152] It also endorsed the view that the 'death penalty is not a human rights issue'.[153] This rigidity notwithstanding, other applicable penalties under Ethiopian law underwent certain changes, as detailed in the next section.

8.2.2   Secondary Penalties

Secondary penalties are accessory penalties, which may be imposed mostly in addition to the principal penalties discussed above.[154] They include caution, reprimand, admonishment, apology, and deprivation of rights.[155] Military courts may order a secondary penalty of reduction in rank or of dismissal from the defense forces of a member convicted of committing a crime.[156] The coming into force of the Criminal Code in 2005 abolished physical punishment, in particular flogging, which had been prescribed as one of the secondary penalties under the Penal Code.[157]

As a matter of principle, secondary penalties may be imposed only in addition to the principal penalties, when deemed beneficial to the reform of the criminal and to society at large.[158] It is also possible for a court to only impose a secondary penalty, even for crimes punishable with rigorous imprisonment or with death, including core crimes.[159] This occurs, theoretically, where there are mitigating circumstances,[160] or where the law provides for a free mitigation of the punishment,[161] or still where the enforcement of a sentence is

---

151   FDRE Criminal Code, Article 119.
152   See Schabas, *Death Penalty in International Law*, supra note 146, 257–258.
153   Ibid., 258.
154   See the Penal Code of 1957, Article 120; FDRE Criminal Code, Article 123.
155   See FDRE Criminal Code, Articles 121–128.
156   Ibid., Article 127.
157   See the Penal Code of 1957, Article 121.
158   FDRE Criminal Code, Article 123.
159   Ibid., Article 122(2).
160   Extenuating circumstances are mentioned under Articles 82 and 83 of the Criminal Code. For details, see section 8.5.2.2. below.
161   Free mitigation of punishment is available where there are special mitigating factors that fall short of justifying the acquittal of the defendant. See FDRE Criminal Code, Article 180. For details, see the discussion under section 8.5.2.1. below.

postponed.¹⁶² However, none of the core crimes trials Ethiopia merely sentenced offenders to caution, reprimand, admonishment, and apology.

Secondary penalties are generally applicable to minor crimes and petty offenses, save the penalty of deprivation of rights which may be pronounced in relation to all categories of offenses. Unlike individuals convicted by international criminal courts and tribunals, Ethiopians found guilty of core crimes were often deprived of certain rights in addition to the principal penalties. This for example included barring an ex-police officer from resuming professional work as a detective for a certain number of years after serving a prison term for unlawful detention and torture (as genocide).¹⁶³

No other form of secondary penalty was imposed as an addition to the principal penalties, even if there might have been a missed opportunity with respect to apology. In their joint submission of sentencing opinion, the convicts in *Mengistu et al.* requested the FHC to take into account the fact that they had asked the government to create a forum for them so that they could officially apologize to the Ethiopian public for the crimes committed during their time in power.¹⁶⁴ In fact, the defendants had already raised this point at the beginning of the trial, requesting amnesty and reconciliation instead of prosecution.¹⁶⁵ Back then, the Court had rejected the claim on the grounds that it was not within its mandate to allow for amnesty or reconciliation and that the defendants' offer to apologize to the public could not discontinue an ongoing trial.¹⁶⁶ At the sentencing phase, the SPO reiterated its earlier stance on the matter and stated that the defendants were never truly remorseful.¹⁶⁷ The FHC however accepted the defendants' readiness to apologize as a mitigating factor, although it was skeptical as to their sincerity.¹⁶⁸ It still found that the request for an 'apology forum' could be seen 'as a good thing for the future; meaning, as a request aimed at bringing reconciliation'.¹⁶⁹

Yet, it is arguable that the Court could have done more with the defendants' readiness to apologize. It could have ordered the convicts to make

---

162   After convicting and sentencing, a court may suspend the enforcement of a sentence for a specified period of probation. See FDRE Criminal Code, Article 192.
163   See for instance, FHC, SPO v. *Gebremedehen Berga Barosa et al.*, (Sentencing Judgment), 11 April 2001, File no. 646/89, 7.
164   *Colonel Mengistu Hailemariam et al.*, (Sentencing Judgment), *supra* note 22, 10.
165   FHC, SPO v. *Colonel Mengistu Hailemariam et al.*, (Ruling on Preliminary Objections), 10 October 1995, File No. 1/87, 94.
166   Ibid.
167   *Colonel Mengistu Hailemariam et al.*, (Sentencing Judgment), *supra* note 22, 4. See also Chapter 3, section 3.4.
168   *Colonel Mengistu Hailemariam et al.*, (Sentencing Judgment), *supra* note 22, 14.
169   Ibid., 15.

a public apology and the relevant administration to create the requested apology-forum. Although it is not within its power to arrange for national reconciliation, which it noted at the beginning of the trial, the FHC could have ordered the defendants to 'apologize to the public' pursuant to Article 122(1) of the Penal Code.[170] Had it ordered an apology, in addition to the sentence of life imprisonment it pronounced against all of the defendants, the FHC could have used this as the start of the good thing it wanted to happen: reconciliation. Perhaps doing so would have dissuaded the SPO from taking the case on appeal to demand the death penalty against all of the convicts, which the FSC pronounced against 18 of them[171]

8.3 Changes in Applicable Penalties and the Principle of *Lex Mitior*

It was while the *Dergue* and the *Anuak-Nuwer* trials were still ongoing that the Penal Code of 1957, on the basis of which the prosecutions were being carried out, was repealed and replaced by the Criminal Code on 9 May 2005. At the time of the commencement of the *Anuak-Nuwer* trials in 2004, the Criminal Code was being submitted to Parliament for final approval. In 2005, when the Criminal Code came into force, several cases in the *Dergue* trials, including the high-profile ones, were already pending for 12 years – a process which was criticized by the African Commission on Human and Peoples' Rights (ACHPR) as involving a violation of the accused's right to be tried within a reasonable time.[172]

Although the principle of legality requires that the determination of guilt or innocence be made on the basis of the law in force at the time of the commission of the crimes, the same principle supports the application of *lex mitior*, that, with regards to punishment, the more lenient law should be applicable. This is enshrined under Article 22 (2) of the FDRE Constitution as well as in international instruments to which Ethiopia is a party.[173] As a result, it was imperative for the judges in the *Anuak-Nuwer* and the *Dergue* trials to consider the more lenient penalty provisions with respect to sentencing judgments reached after 9 May 2005. The question is, therefore, whether when compared to the Penal Code, the Criminal Code prescribes a less severe penalty.

---

170   See also FDRE Criminal Code, Article 122(1).
171   See the discussion under section 8.5.2.2.2. below.
172   See ACHPR, *Haregewoin Gabre-Selassie and IHRDA (on behalf of former Dergue officials) v. Ethiopia*, (Decision), 12 October 2013, Comm. No. 301/2005, para. 240.
173   For an elaborated discussion on principle of legality, see Chapter 7 sub-section 7.5.2.1.

As noted earlier, both the Penal Code and the Criminal Code punish most of the core crimes with a minimum penalty of five years of rigorous imprisonment and with a maximum penalty of death. Yet, if in both Codes the available penalties are divided into two ranges based on the gravity of the circumstances of the commission of the crimes, an important difference exists. As provided in Table 8. below, in the Penal Code, and under normal circumstances of commission, most core crimes[174] were punishable with penalties ranging from five years to life imprisonment. The death penalty was applicable when similar offenses were committed in circumstances referred to by law as 'gravest cases'.[175] According to the Criminal Code however, as shown in the Table, most core crimes are now punishable, under 'normal circumstances of commission', with penalties ranging from five years to 25 years imprisonment, and it is only in the 'more serious cases' that life imprisonment or death will be pronounced.[176]

TABLE 8   Penalties for Core Crimes under the Penal Code and the Criminal Code

Core Crimes		Applicable Penalties	
		The Penal Code of 1957	FDRE Criminal Code
Genocide		*NSC*: rigorous imprisonment from five years to life *GC*: death	*NSC*: rigorous imprisonment from five to 25 years *MSC*: life or death
War Crimes	against the civilian population	"	"
	against wounded, sick or shipwrecked persons or medical services	"	"
	against prisoners and interned persons	"	"
	of pillage, piracy and looting	"	"

---

174   This refers to the core crimes prosecuted in the Ethiopian trials (genocide and war crimes against the civilian population) as listed in Table 7.
175   The Penal Code of 1957, Articles 281–285.
176   FDRE Criminal Code, Articles 269–273.

TABLE 8   Penalties for Core Crimes under the Penal Code and the Criminal Code (*cont.*)

Core Crimes	Applicable Penalties	
	The Penal Code of 1957	FDRE Criminal Code
of dereliction of duty towards the Enemy	NSC: rigorous imprisonment GC: death	NSC: rigorous imprisonment CEG: life or death
of use of illegal means of combat	NSC: simple imprisonment for not less than three months G: three years to life GC: death	NSC: simple imprisonment for not less than three months G: five to 25 years GC: life or death
of maltreatment of, or dereliction of duty towards wounded, sick, or prisoners	NSC: simple imprisonment not exceeding five years	NSC: rigorous imprisonment not exceeding five years
of denial of justice	NSC: simple imprisonment	NSC: simple imprisonment from three to five years
of hostile acts against international humanitarian organizations	"	NSC: simple imprisonment CEG: with rigorous imprisonment not exceeding five years
of abuse of emblems and insignia of international humanitarian organizations	NSC: simple imprisonment CEG: with rigorous imprisonment not exceeding five years	"
of hostile acts against the bearer of a flag of truce	NSC: simple imprisonment	NSC: simple imprisonment

NSC – Normal Circumstances of Commission
MSC – More Serious Cases
" – same as above
CEG – Circumstances of Exceptional Gravity
G – Grave
GC – Gravest Cases

Compared to sentences stipulated by the Penal Code, the Criminal Code's provisions are less severe and provide for sentences: *i*) under 'normal circumstances of commission', of a maximum of 25 years instead of a rigorous life imprisonment; and *ii*) under more serious circumstances of commission, of rigorous life imprisonment or death (instead of solely providing for the death penalty). Under the Criminal Code, a court may thus choose between life sentence or death sentence and may still opt for the life sentence even where there is no mitigating factor. Under the Penal Code, only the existence of a mitigating factor compelled the court not to apply the death sentence. As a result, it is clear that the penalty provisions of the Criminal Code of 2005 are more advantageous for the convict.

Regardless, sentencing judgments in both the *Dergue* trials and the *Anuak-Nuwer* trials have mostly disregarded the principle of *lex mitior* and sentenced the convicts using the more severe law. Some of the courts did not even mention it as relevant. This was particularly striking in the sentencing judgments in *Mengistu et al.* in the *Dergue* trials and in *Gure Uchala et al.* in the *Anuak-Nuwer* trials. In these – and several other – cases, the issue remained seemingly unnoticed, and the courts acted as if the Penal Code's penalty clause had not been amended.

In some cases, courts discussed *lex mitior* because the defendants raised it in their sentencing opinion, arguing that they should not be punished on the basis of the Penal Code but on that of the Criminal Code. Yet, this did not amount to an application of the later law, more favorable to the defendant. In the case of *SPO v. Getaneh Jembere et al.*, the ASC retained the Penal Code's penalty and dismissed the defendants' argument on the ground that there was no difference between the two laws.[177] In *SPO v. Wubeshiet Zegeye et al.*, the FSC noted that there was a difference between the repealed law (Article 281 of the Penal Code) and the law in force (Article 269 of the Criminal Code) regarding punishment for genocide.[178] Perplexingly, the Court still punished the defendants on the basis of the repealed provision on the ground that the difference between the two laws was 'insignificant'.[179] The Court did not explain how, and why for that matter, any difference in the applicable penalties should be dismissed for insignificance. Let alone a change in the applicable penalty, even

---

177 See ASC, *SPO v. Getaneh Jembere et al.*, (Sentencing Judgment), 17 August 2005, File No.00764, 60.
178 See FSC, *SPO v. Wubeshiet Zegeye et al.*, (Appeals Judgment), 30 April 2007, File No.22340, 41.
179 Ibid.

an amendment to a sentencing guideline triggers the application of *lex mitior*, as decided by the Cassation Bench.[180] Further, one may argue that the difference was not insignificant at all. Under normal circumstances, the difference between the two laws involves the possibility of being punished either by a maximum of 25 years or by life imprisonment. In more serious circumstances of commission, the difference could be seen as a matter of life and death, i.e. as in being sent to prison for life – with, as discussed earlier, a possibility of early release –or in being executed.

In other cases, however, the Criminal Code's penalty provisions were applied for crimes committed before its entry into force – upholding the principle of *lex mitior* while at the same time manifesting the absence of uniformity and consistency in sentencing practices among Ethiopian courts. This inconsistency in sentencing resulted in an unequal treatment of persons found guilty of similar or comparable offenses. In the case of Captain Legesse Asfaw, it has even caused the same individual to be punished on the basis of the old law by one of the FHC's criminal bench and on the basis of the new one by another other bench of the same Court.[181]

8.4 Sentencing Rationales

The absence of clear guidance in relation to sentencing rationales in the founding documents of the UNICTs and the ICC, which has been considered one of the challenges in international sentencing practice, is, to a certain degree, not a problem in the Ethiopian legal system. Article 1 of the Criminal Code lays down the goals of criminal law and the rationales of punishment.[182] Nonetheless, as all available rationales of sentencing are meant to apply to all

---

180 In its recent decisions, the FSC CB stated that the coming into force of a new sentencing guideline that dictates a more favorable way of calculating mitigating and aggravating factors calls for the applicability of the principle of *lex mitior*. See FSC CB, *Federal Prosecutor v. Semir Ibrahim Hibu*, (Decision), 21 June 2013, File No. 95440, 5; FSC-CB, *SNN-PRS Prosecutor v. Solomon Dessalegn*, (Decision),10 June 2013 File No. 95438, 9.

181 Captain Legesse Asfaw, the lead defendant in the war crimes case, was also the seventh defendant in the genocide trial in *Mengistu et al*. He was punished, in the former, on the basis of the Criminal Code, and, in the latter, on the basis of the Penal Code, although both judgments were issued after the Criminal Code had entered into force. For the war crimes case, see *Legesse Asfaw et al.,* (Sentencing Judgment) *supra* note 14. 2. For the genocide cases, see *Colonel Mengistu Hailemariam et al.,* (Sentencing Judgement) *supra* note 22; *Colonel Mengistu Hailemariam et al.,*(Appeals Judgment), *supra* note 134.

182 This was also the case with the Penal Code of 1957.

types of crimes, it is up to a particular court to choose and apply the rationale it deems appropriate to punish core crimes. In practice, however, Ethiopian courts merely recite in general terms the rationales available in the law, as shown below. This is arguably also the case in international sentencing practice where courts often do not detail the impact a particular sentencing rationale has on the calculation of the actual sentence.[183]

The Penal Code of 1957 was both utilitarian and retributivist in its sentencing rationales. It aimed at 'providing for…the reform of offenders and measures to prevent the commission of further crimes', and was, therefore, utilitarian in purpose.[184] In referring to retribution, the Code stated its aim as 'providing for the punishment of offenders'.[185] The Criminal Code however appears to have implicitly excluded the latter by confining the aims of punishment to deterrence (specific and general), rehabilitation and incapacitation.[186]

Ethiopian courts themselves seem to have rejected retribution even before its official exclusion by the Criminal Code. It was not invoked as a rationale in the *Dergue* and the *Anuak-Nuwer* cases in which the sentences were pronounced on the basis of the Penal Code. This makes Ethiopian practice stand in marked contrast to the way the UNICTs and the ICC have invoked sentencing rationales, in which retribution has been regarded as the principal purpose of punishment.[187]

What makes the sentencing approach followed by Ethiopian courts different, if not problematic, is not the exclusion *per se* of retribution, but rather the reason for such an exclusion: it seems that retribution was seen as equivalent to vengeance. Some courts appeared to have based their sentencing decisions on a retributive rationale using expressions such as 'an

---

183 See S. D'Ascoli, *Sentencing in International Criminal Law: The UN ad hoc Tribunals and Future Perspectives for the ICC* (Oxford: Hart Publishing, 2011) 207.
184 See the Penal Code of 1957, (Amharic version), Article 1, which reads, 'የወንጀላኛ መቅጫ ሕግ... የወንጀለኞች መቅጫ ማረሚያ እንዲሁም ከፉትና ከወንጀል እንዲወገዱ ማድረጊያ ነው።'.
185 Ibid. See also J. Graven, 'The Penal Code of The Empire of Ethiopia' (1964) 1(2) *Journal of Ethiopian Law* 267–298, 292. See, however, P. Graven, *An Introduction to Ethiopian Penal Law: Arts. 1–84 Penal Code* (Addis Ababa-Nairobi: Faculty of Law Haile Selassie I University in association with Oxford University Press, 1965) 7–8.
186 FDRE Criminal Code, Article 1.
187 See ICTY, *Prosecutor* v. *Aleksovski*, Appeals Chamber, (Judgment), 24 March 2000, IT-95-14/1-A, para. 185; ICTY, *Prosecutor* v. *Kordić and Čerkez*, Appeals Chamber, (Judgment), 17 December 2004, IT-95-14/2-A, para. 1075; ICTR, *Prosecutor* v. *Rutaganira*, Trial Chamber, (Judgment), 14 March 2005, ICTR-95-3-T, paras 108–109; Germain Katanga, Trial Chamber II, (Sentencing Judgment), *supra* note 62, para. 38.

offender should be punished because he broke the law'.[188] Nonetheless, they often failed to drive the argument home for an apparent fear that such reasoning could easily be associated with, or mistaken for, an expression of vengeance.[189]

Given that both the defendants and some commentators have widely accused the *Dergue* trials of exercising victor's justice and vengeance, it is understandable that courts might have wanted to send a positive message as to the impartiality of the proceedings. Arguably, that is partly why in *Mengistu et al.* the FHC rejected the death penalty by stating that 'in the given circumstances imposing the death penalty serves no purpose other than vengeance'.[190] Nonetheless, while disavowing vengeance as the purpose of punishment is one thing, emphasizing the fact that retribution is not an expression of vengeance is another. That is apparently what the UNICTs and the ICC have been doing by persistently reiterating a disclaimer that retribution as a purpose of punishment is not an expression of vengeance, but an expression of the international community's condemnation of core crimes.[191]

Concerning deterrence (specific or general), Ethiopian courts have recited the Criminal Code's statement that 'punishment can deter wrongdoers from committing other crimes; it can also serve as a warning to prospective wrongdoers'.[192] Several courts have also attached significant importance to specific deterrence.[193] The UNICTs have, by contrast, treated specific deterrence as a less important sentencing rationale, because the commission of core crimes is seen as dependent upon the existence of a political context that goes well beyond the will of any particular individual.[194] Despite the Ethipian courts' insistence on specific deterrence, this context was also true in Ethiopia where

---

188 ASC, SPO v. *Sisay Balachew et al.*, (Sentencing judgment), 25 April 2002, File No. 9/92, 148; TSC, SPO v. *Yekuno Amelak et al.*, (Sentencing judgment), 3 March 2003, File No. 4/92, 1866.
189 Ibid.
190 See *Colonel Mengistu Hailemariam et al.*, supra note 22, 9. Translation by the author. The original (Amharic) version reads.
191 ICTY, *Prosecutor v. Momir Nikolić*, Trial Chamber, (Sentencing Judgment) 12 December 2003, ICTY- IT-02-60/1/S, paras 86–87; *Al Mahdi*, Trial Chamber VIII, (Judgment and Sentence), supra note 117, para. 67.
192 FDRE Criminal Code, Preface, IV.
193 See SNNPR SC, SPO v. *Aregaw Hailemariam et al.*, (Sentencing judgment), 14 July 2005, File No. 3647, 51; *Yekuno Amelak et al.*, (Sentencing judgment), supra note 188, 1866.
194 See ICTR, *Prosecutor v. Ntakirutimana et al.*, Trial Chamber, (Judgment and Sentence) 21 February 2003, ICTR-96-10, para. 882. See also W.A. Schabas, *The UN International*

core crimes could not have been committed without the participation of a large number of people in the orchestration and the implementation of the State and organizational plan or policy;[195] a reality which renders recidivism less likely. This should have arguably been reflected in the sentencing by putting more emphasis on general deterrence and less on specific deterrence.

As for rehabilitation, to which the law claims to be paying greater attention than any of its other aims,[196] case law has often mentioned it but without any explanation and always together with other purposes of punishment such as general and specific deterrence. As such, the role it played in determining and justifying specific sentences is not very clear. Due to this lack of transparency in sentencing, it is difficult to compare and contrast Ethiopian practice with its international counterparts, where rehabilitation is regarded as playing a marginal role, given the gravity of core crimes.[197]

Lastly, it is noteworthy that some courts have justified punishment using rationales that are not listed in the statutory law, namely 'healing victims' wounds',[198] 'preparing perpetrators for reconciliation',[199] and 'ensuring respect for the human rights of life and liberty'.[200] Likewise, the UNICTs have created justifications such as 'reconciliation' which do not belong to the traditional sentencing rationales.[201] In the international system, however, the new rationales do not appear to have served more than a nominal purpose, which was also the case in the Ethiopian trials. One may however point out the *Mengistu et al.* case as a significant exception, where *possible contribution to reconciliation* served as a purpose of punishment in the light of which the defendants' willingness to make a public apology was regarded as a mitigating factor. This has ultimately contributed, together with other mitigating factors, to the Court's decision to exclude the applicability of the death penalty against the defendants.[202]

      Criminal Tribunals: The Former Yugoslavia, Rwanda and Sierra Leone (Oxford: Oxford University Press, 2006) 557.

195 See for instance FHC, SPO v. *Colonel Mengistu Hailemariam et al.*, (Trial Judgment) 12 December 2006, File No. 401, 116.

196 See FDRE Criminal Code, Preface, IV.

197 See ICT, *Prosecutor* v. *Zejnil Delalić et al.*, Appeals Chamber, (Judgment), 20 February 2001, IT-96-21-A, para. 806.

198 See *Gesgese Gebremeskel Ateraga et al.*, (Sentencing Judgment) *supra* note 142, 4.

199 *Colonel Mengistu Hailemariam et al.*, (Sentencing Judgment), *supra* note 22, 16.

200 FHC, SPO v. *Eshetu Alemu*, (Sentencing Judgment), 8 May 2000, File No. 921/89, 3.

201 See ICTR, *Prosecutor* v. *Kamuhanda*, Trial Chamber, (Judgment), 22 January 2004, ICTR-95-54A-T, para. 754; ICTY, *Prosecutor* v. *Momir Nikolić*, Trial Chamber, (Judgment), 2 December 2003, IT-02-60/1-S, para. 93.

202 See section 8.2.1. above.

The practice of creating new rationales is unwarranted, because Ethiopian law does not give judges the discretion to do so. Even if courts have unfettered discretion to take into account mitigating and aggravating factors that are not listed in the law, this should be done within the realm of the purposes of punishment already laid out under Article 1 of the Criminal Code.[203] Furthermore, the newly identified sentencing rationales have, unlike the practice in international tribunals and courts, specific and momentary application due to the non-existence of precedent-rule in the Ethiopian legal system.

8.5 Factors in Sentence Determination: Aggravation and Mitigation

The determination of the appropriate penalty under Ethiopian law depends on the analysis of: *i*) the gravity of the crime and the circumstances of its commission, and *ii*) the degree of individual guilt.[204] The two factors may overlap. As a result, the law requires that courts need to distinguish between the two factors and treat them separately to avoid double-counting, i.e. using the same aggravating or mitigating factor twice.[205] As it will be seen, it could be safely submitted here that the sentencing practice by international criminal courts and tribunals is based on the examination of similar sentencing factors which are classified into *i*) gravity of the crime, and *ii*) individual circumstances of the convicted person.[206]

8.5.1 *Gravity of the Crime and the Circumstances of Its Commission: The Initial Penalty*

As discussed above in section 8.2, Ethiopian law prescribes the minimum and maximum penalties for each of the acts it proscribes based on whether they are minor, not serious, grave, or extremely grave. As such, it is within the power of the legislator, not the courts, to make a general determination as to whether a particular crime is graver than other crimes. In other words, there is no judicial heirarchy in Ethiopia between the gravity of genocide and that

---

203   See in particular the discussion under section 8.5.2.2.2. below.
204   See FDRE Criminal Code, Article 88 (2). See also FSC CB, *Bihonegn Demessie* v. *Tigray Regional State Prosecutor*, (Decision), 24 July 2013, File no. 88542, 3.
205   See FDRE Criminal Code, Articles 82(2) and 84(2).
206   See B. Holá et al., 'Consistency of International Sentencing: ICTY and ICTR Case Study' (2012) 9(5) *European Journal of Criminology* 539–552, 541.

of war crimes. Such a practice may result in the imposition of comparable penalties for different types of core crimes. Indeed, there is no difference in the type and severity of penalties imposed on persons convicted of genocide as compared to those imposed on war criminals. This may however not be true for the sentencing practice in international criminal courts and tribunals. As shown in empirical studies conducted by Holá and others on sentencing practices of the UNICTs, *génocidaires* were punished more severely than war criminals who themselves received longer sentences than those convicted of crimes against humanity.[207]

In fact, Ethiopian courts do not even establish a hierarchy between the gravity of core crimes and that of domestic crimes. However, one may point out rare examples of judicial attempts to demarcate the gravity of core crimes. In *Mengistu et al.*, for instance, the FSC stated, 'in Ethiopian criminal law *genocide is a big crime*. Thus, the death penalty is expressly stated in the special part of the law defining genocide'.[208] Nonetheless, it is not so clear what the Court was alleging, in particular, as to the gravity of genocide as compared to other crimes entailing death penalty.

This does not mean that courts do not determine the gravity of the specific offense under consideration for sentencing. In fact, a court has to determine the gravity of any particular crime for which the defendant is found guilty. Doing so is a prerequisite for the specification of the *initial penalty*, i.e. the specific penalty the court has to indicate by choosing from the minimum and maximum sentences set by the law. This has to be specified at the beginning of the sentencing stage as it serves as a preliminary or 'hypothetical'[209] penalty upon which the court bases itself to calculate mitigating or aggravating factors and pronounce the final sentence. The court's choice of the initial penalty usually depends on its assessment of the gravity of the crime committed that it has to establish from the *circumstances of its commission*.[210]

---

207 Ibid., 549; see also B. Holá *et al.*, 'International Sentencing Facts and Figures: Sentencing Practice at the ICTY and ICTR' (2011) 9(1) *Journal of International Criminal Justice* 411–439, 422–423.

208 *Colonel Mengist Hailemariam et al.*, (Appeals Judgment), *supra* note 144, 91. Translation by the author. The original (Amharic) version reads: 'በኢትዮጵያ የወንጀል ሕግ ዘር ማጥፋት ትልቅ ወንጀል ነው። ስለዚህ የዚር ማጥፋት ወንጀል በሚመለከተው የሕጉ ልዩ ክፍል በግልጽ የሞት ቅጣት ተደንግጎ ይገኛል።'.

209 See Graven, *An Introduction to Ethiopian Penal Law*, *supra* note 185, 268.

210 Ethiopian criminal law is not explicit as to how a court shall determine the gravity of the crime and specify the initial penalty. However, as can be seen from the sentencing judgment in *Legesse Asfaw et al.*, the assumption, as also envisaged later in the sentencing guideline of 2010, is that courts determine the gravity of a crime and specify the initial

In practice, the circumstances of the commission of a crime could also constitute aggravating or mitigating factors,[211] which are to be taken into consideration after the initial penalty has been determined.[212] The many sentencing judgments analyzed in this book indicate that, with the notable exception of the war crimes case,[213] Ethiopian courts have not specified in their sentencing judgments the gravity they attached to a particular crime and the initial penalty they chose. As a result, it is difficult to verify whether a specific sentencing judgment involved double-counting through the application of the same circumstances of commission to determine the gravity of the crime *and* to aggravate or mitigate the initial penalty.[214]

In contrast, as the international practice is more transparent, it avoids the occurrence of double-counting. In *Lubanga*, the ICC declined to consider the age of the children (Lubanga's victims) as an aggravating factor in order not to commit double aggravation.[215] It is also an established practice of the UNICTs that double-counting, if found to be significant, warrants reduction or addition of sentence by the Appeals Chamber.[216] Most importantly, to avoid

---

penalty based on the circumstances of the commission of the crime. See *Legesse Asfaw et al.*, (Sentencing Judgment), *supra* note 14, 12–13; See also FSC, Revised Sentencing Guideline, No. 2/2013 *entered into force* 12 October 2013, Articles 4(1), 4(4) and 19(5). See also FSC CB, *Fesseha Tadesse Mewucha v. Federal Prosecutor*, (Decision), 4 October 2014, File No. 80815, 6–8.

211 In this regard, it is worth noting that the Revised Sentencing Guideline stated that aggravating and mitigating factors cannot be taken into account to determine the gravity of the crime. Instead, it suggested that the gravity of a crime be determined based on factors including: the manner of the commission of the crime, the harm caused, the benefits acquired, the crime being committed intentionally or not, or the extent of negligence shown in committing the offense under consideration. See ibid., Articles 19(5) and (6). There is nothing in Ethiopian criminal law that excludes these factors from being regarded as aggravating or mitigating pursuant to Articles 82–86 of the Criminal Code. This is notably the case because mitigating and aggravating factors under Ethiopian law are, in reality, infinite, as discussed in section 8.5.2 below.

212 See FDRE Criminal Code, Articles 174–184; Revised Sentencing Guideline, Articles 19 and 26.

213 *Legesse Asfaw et al.*, (Sentencing Judgment), *supra* note 14, 12–13.

214 FDRE Criminal Code, Articles 82 (2) and 84 (2). See also, FSC CB, *Federal Prosecutor v. Berihun Fekadu*, (Decision), 10 June 2011, File No. 59356, 3; Graven, *An Introduction to Ethiopian Penal Law*, *supra* note 185, 268.

215 See *Thomas Lubanga Dyilo*, Trial Chamber I, (Decision on Sentence Pursuant to Article 76 of the Statute), *supra* note 63, para. 78; *Al Mahdi*, Trial Chamber VIII, (Judgment and Sentence), *supra* note 117, paras 87–88.

216 See ICTY, *Prosecutor v. Limaj et al.*, Appeals Chamber (Judgment), 27 September 2007, IT-03-66-A, paras 143–144; ICTY, *Prosecutor v. Momir Nikolić*, Appeals Chamber, (Judgment on Sentencing Appeal), 8 March 2006, IT-02-60/1-A, para. 58.

double-counting, the UNICTs' Trial Chambers shall 'consider and count all aspects and implications' of the sentencing factor they apply.[217]

A sentencing judgment's opacity has a different magnitude and effect in Ethiopia, as it becomes irremediable even on appeal. Firstly, as it is too difficult, if not impossible, to formulate specific grounds of appeal against an opaque judgment, most of the sentencing appeals carry a brief but general claim that a given sentence is unfair, i.e. too severe or too lenient.[218] Secondly, this reality has apparently forced the FSC (the Court of Appeal) to unconventionally approach sentencing appeals by framing the issue as broadly as 'whether the sentence imposed appears unfair in the eyes of the law'.[219] This has, ultimately, resulted in the appeals process being virtually a *fresh trial,* which has no basis in the text of Ethiopian law.[220] Similarly, such a practice was considered to have no basis in the jurisprudence of the UNICTs. As explained by the ICTY Appeals Chamber in *Nikolić,* 'sentencing appeals, as with all appeals to the Appeals Chamber from a judgement of a Trial Chamber, are appeals *stricto sensu.* They are not trials *de novo*'.[221]

Ironically, the FSC has not solved the opacity problem. The appeals judgments are as opaque as those of the trial courts. In particular, the FSC does not examine or criticize the lower courts' failure to specify the initial penalty. Rather, it focuses on superficial and enigmatic assessments of sentencing factors, and often abruptly concludes that the sentence imposed does not appear to be too severe or too lenient or that there is no ground to examine the trial court's sentencing judgment.[222]

---

217 See *Dragomir Milosević,* Appeals Chamber, (Judgment), *supra* note 97, para. 309.
218 See for instance, FSC, *Abera Afewerke* v. SPO, (Statement of Appeal), 1 October 2002, File No. 7559, 7.
219 See FSC, *Geremew Qenno* v. SPO, (Judgment), 29 June 2001, File No. 6659, 7; FSC, *Gizaw Tadesse et al.* v. SPO, (Appeal Judgment), 30 April 2002, File No. 6470, 12; FSC, *Haregewoine* v. SPO, (Appeals Judgment), 29 October 2002, File No. 7369, 12; FSC, *Maseresha Abebe* v. SPO, (Appeals Judgment), 2 July 2001, File No 6688, 12; FSC, *Teshome Kebede et al.,* v. SPO, (Appeals Judgment), 26 March 2002, File no. 6486, 8; FSC, *Ziyad Alemu* v. SPO, (Appeals Judgment), 13 March 2002, File No 7358, 4.
220 See Criminal Procedure Code of Ethiopia, Proclamation No. 185 of 1961, *entered into force* 2 February 1962, Article 194.
221 See ICTY, *Prosecutor* v. *Dragan Nikolić,* Appeals Chamber, (Judgment on Sentencing Appeal), 4 February 2005, IT-94-02-1, para. 8.
222 See FSC, *Colonel Mekonnen Semeneh et al.* v. SPO, (Appeals Judgement), 29 November 2002, File No. 6511, 28; FSC, *Colonel Nemera Disassa* v. SPO, (Appeals Judgment), 8 June 2001, File No 6508, 4; FSC, *Feyissa Saboka* v. SPO, (Appeals Judgment), 1 June 2001, File No. 6509, 11; FSC, SPO v. *Mergia Bededa,* (Appeals Judgment), 4 December 2006, File No. 21345, 32, 44–46; FSC, *Tolossa Waqoyya* v. SPO, (Appeals Judgment), 30 January 2003, File No. 7472, 10.

8.5.2 The Degree of Individual Guilt: Reviewing the Initial Penalty through Separate Treatment of Mitigating and Aggravating Factors

In invoking the degree of individual guilt as a sentencing factor, Ethiopian courts may rely on, *inter alia,* the criminal's dangerous disposition, antecedents, motives, purpose, personal circumstances, and standard of education.[223] These factors fall within the ambit of mitigating or aggravating circumstances.[224] There are a complex set of rules that govern aggravation and mitigation and delineate the judge's discretion in sentencing.

Similar to its international counterparts, Ethiopian criminal law recognizes two types of aggravating and mitigating factors: statutory (listed in the Code) and judicial (judge-made).[225] Ethiopian law further divides the statutory aggravating and mitigating factors into two: general and special.[226] General mitigating or aggravating factors imply ordinary mitigation or aggravation, that is, mitigation or aggravation within, respectively, the minimum and maximum bounds of the penalty specific to the crime under consideration.[227] Special mitigating and aggravating factors have a special effect – the so-called free mitigation or free aggravation. This special effect implies the power to go below the minimum or beyond the maximum limits of the penalty for a specific crime and to impose a sentence as low as the general minimum rigorous imprisonment (one year) or as high as the general maximum rigorous imprisonment (25 years).[228]

Interestingly, there is no difference in weight among general aggravating or mitigating factors, be them statutory or judicial; each of them carries equal weight. Accordingly, it is not within the discretion of the court to attach less weight to one sentencing factor and more to another, unlike what is the case

---

It was in a bid to mitigate this lack of transparency (and also inconsistency) in sentencing that the FSC issued the country's first sentencing guideline in May 2010, which was after the core crimes trials had completed. The guideline imposed on all courts an obligation to support their determination of gravity of the crime and the initial penalty with as much reason as possible. See The Federal Supreme Court Sentencing Guideline, No. 1/2010, *entered into force* 15 May 2010. The authority to issue such guideline was delegated to the FHC by the legislator in 2005, which implies that the need to make the sentencing process transparent and consistent was a long-felt one. See FDRE Criminal Code, Article 88(4).

223 See FDRE Criminal Code, Article 88 (2).
224 See *Fesseha Tadesse Mewucha,* (Decision), *supra* note 210, 8–11.
225 FDRE Criminal Code, Articles 84–85.
226 Ibid., Articles 82–85.
227 Ibid., Articles 179 and 183.
228 Ibid., Articles 184–188.

at the UNICTs and the ICC.²²⁹ The only difference of significance among the sentencing factors is the one that exists between the general and special ones.

In punishing core crimes, Ethiopian courts have considered all forms of extenuating and aggravating circumstances available in the law. As such, as opposed to international judges, Ethiopian judges did not 'stress that the gravity of the offence is the primary consideration in sentencing'.²³⁰ The international nature of these crimes did not affect the application of mitigating factors in sentencing the perpetrators; nor did their inherent heinousness served in itself as an aggravating factor. However, the sentencing practice lacks uniformity and consistency, which could be because the applicable law did not offer detailed guidelines on how to calculate the aggravating and mitigating factors in sentencing. To some extent, the same can be said of the UNICTs and the ICC.²³¹

8.5.2.1 Special Mitigating Factors

Generally, the special mitigating factors that justify free mitigation are family and affectionate relationships.²³² Apparently, this provision is a continuation of the 1930 Penal Code's approach adopted to give effect to the traditionally strong family relationships in Ethiopia.²³³ Besides, factors that fall short of exculpating criminal responsibility may instead qualify as special mitigating factors upon express stipulation in the law to that effect.²³⁴

Of the three Ethiopian trials that punished perpetrators of core crimes, only the *Dergue* trials have applied free mitigation to punish *génocidaires* with sentences below the minimum limit of five years of rigorous imprisonment. This was notably the case in *Mekonnen Gelan et al.*, which imposed two and four years of rigorous imprisonment on, respectively, 14 and nine defendants found guilty of genocide.²³⁵ To justify these sentences, the Court invoked: *i)* the young age of the defendants at the time of the commission of the crime (defendants being high school students), *ii)* the defendants' lack of education (defendants being peasants), and *iii)* the 'prevailing circumstances of the time', i.e. that there was a power struggle between the *Dergue* and the

---

229 See for instance, *Germain Katanga*, Trial Chamber II, (Sentencing Judgment), *supra* note 62, paras 143–144.
230 Holá *et al.*, 'Consistency of International Sentencing, *supra* note 206, 541.
231 See D'Ascoli, *Sentencing in International Criminal Law*, *supra* note 183, 216–218.
232 FDRE Criminal Code, Article 83; the Penal Code of 1957, Article 80.
233 Graven, *An Introduction to Ethiopian Penal Law*, *supra* note 185, 248–249. See also Penal Code of 1930, Article 236.
234 See FDRE Criminal Code, Articles 72, 74–77, 79, 81.
235 *Mekonnen Gelan et al.,* (Sentencing Judgment), *supra* note 93, 312–314.

victims (political opposition groups) and that the crimes were committed as a response to the multi-sided and intricate violence of the time.[236] This calls for a series of remarks insofar as the application of free mitigation in *Mekonnen Gelan et al.* is tricky. This is not only because the sentencing judgment is devoid of sufficient explanation but also because the grounds invoked by the Court were not expressly provided for in the law to justify free mitigation, as required under Article 180 of the Criminal Code.[237] On appeal, the FSC aggravated the two-year sentence to a five-year one with respect to four defendants against whom the SPO had lodged an appeal.[238] As the FSC rightly (but swiftly) noted, free mitigation based on a ground not expressly provided as a special mitigating factor is unjustified.[239]

Pursuant to Articles 48 and 49 of the Criminal Code, being of a young (or old) age may be invoked for the purpose of free mitigation. Nonetheless, it has to be clearly shown that age rendered the defendants 'incapable of understanding the nature and consequence of the act or regulating the conduct of their act according to such understanding'.[240] The Court in *Mekonnen Gelan et al.* did not clarify this.

Likewise, the law does not in any way consider as a special mitigating factor a lack of formal education *per se*. It may not even be regarded as a general statutory mitigating factor. It may come into the picture as a special mitigating factor only if it explains excess in self-defense[241] or mistake or ignorance of the law.[242] In practice, not all judges agreed to invoke it as a judicial mitigating factor. As can be inferred from *Gure Uchala et al.* of the *Anuak-Nuwer* trials, where

---

236   The first and the second factors were invoked cumulatively to justify free mitigation and impose two years of rigorous imprisonment on 14 defendants. These defendants were found to be young, i.e. 18 years and below. They were also considered as lacking education because they were, at the time of the commission of genocide, attending high school. The second and the third grounds were applied to freely mitigate punishment and impose four years of rigorous imprisonment on nine defendants, all of whom were peasants. Being peasants, according to the Court, they lacked formal education. Due to their lack of education, the peasants were unable to resist the 'prevailing circumstances of the time' and hence participated in the violence and perpetrated genocide against political groups. See ibid., 312–313.
237   See also the Penal Code of 1957, Article 185.
238   These are: Tsige Kassa, Gizaw Gerange, Zerihun Yelema, and Tewabech Genetu. It is not clear why the SPO did not appeal against the other ten defendants that were sentenced to two years of rigorous imprisonment. See *Mergia Bededa*, (Appeals Judgment), *supra* note 222, 36–38.
239   Ibid.
240   The FDRE Criminal Code, Article 48.
241   Ibid., Article 79 (1).
242   Ibid., Article 81 (1).

the perpetrators being peasants with no apparent education was considered to be a general mitigating factor by the majority, a dissenting opinion stated that everyone (educated or not) knows that killing another is a crime for 'this is always condemned in all cultures'.[243]

As for 'prevailing circumstances of the period' as a mitigating factor, nowhere does the law mention such a factor: it was created by judges and available only as a judicial mitigating factor. As noted above, however, the law does not grant the courts the discretion to create special mitigating factors and apply them in free mitigation.[244] Accordingly, the Court in *Mekonnen Gelan et al.* erred in law by holding that 'prevailing circumstances of the period' justified free mitigation – as it also did with the other factors mentioned in the foregoing paragraphs.

8.5.2.2 General Mitigating Factors

As pointed out above, Ethiopian criminal law allows for two types of general mitigating factors: statutory and judicial, which both have similar weight and effect. The following sub-sections discuss each category separately.

8.5.2.2.1 *Statutory Mitigating Factors*

There are five general statutory mitigating factors in Ethiopian law: good character; acting with honorable and disinterested motive; justified fear (including obedience to superior orders); expression of sincere remorse; and provocation or mental distress.[245] These factors are also available in the practice of the UNICTs and of the ICC.[246] An overview of the Ethiopian sentencing practice in core crimes cases indicates that each of the general statutory mitigating factors were applied in one way or another to mitigate the applicable penalties down to the minimum of five years of rigorous imprisonment.

The practice greatly disagreed on the issue of whether the perpetrator's lack of criminal record, which is commonly accepted as an indicative of a 'good character',[247] shall be taken into account, to, by and of itself, mitigate a sentence. While numerous sentencing judgments considered it a mitigating

---

243 See FHC, *Federal Prosecutor* v. *Gure uchala et al.,* (Sentencing Judgment: Dissenting Opinion of Judge Nuru Seid), 30 March 2005, File No. 31855, 7.
244 See also FDER Criminal Code, Article 86.
245 Ibid., Article 82.
246 See Mettraux, *International Crimes and the Ad Hoc Tribunals, supra* note 44, 351–352.
247 As stated in *Gure Uchala Ugiraet al.,* 'the fact that a criminal record cannot be shown against the defendants is symptomatic of her or his good character'. See *Gure Uchala Ugiraet al.,* (Sentencing Judgment), *supra* note 7, 3.

ground, even in cases where the accused was not present on trial,[248] the FSC however specified in *SPO v. Girma Demessie et al.* that it cannot warrant mitigation unless it is complemented with either the criminal's lack of thought, or lack of intelligence or ignorance, or simplicity of mind at the time of the commission of the crime.[249] If this decision is no doubt a correct reading of Article 82 (1) (a) of the Criminal Code, a recent decision of the Cassation Bench regarded the absence of criminal record as *per se* sufficient to justify ordinary mitigation.[250]

In contrast, the ICC does not consider the absence of prior criminal convictions as a mitigating factor, because, as the Court stated in *Al Mahdi*, it 'is a fairly common feature among individuals convicted by international tribunals'.[251] More equivocally, the UNICTs lacked clarity and uniformity in their application of absence of criminal record to mitigate the severity of a sentence. Several cases considered this factor as justifying mitigation of a sentence while several others have either disregarded it altogether or attached to it an insignificant mitigating weight.[252] Still, unlike the Ethiopian practice, international practice distinguishes between 'good character' and 'lack of prior criminal record'.[253] The former focuses on reputation, credibility, personality and social conduct of the accused, while the latter refers solely to whether the defendant was convicted of any other crime before the commission of the crime under consideration.[254]

The *Dergue* trials however were not cautious when considering the absence of a criminal record as a mitigating factor. In fact, they should have, in most cases, disregarded it altogether, because, from a factual point of view, the entire *Dergue* regime was a period of absolute impunity, in particular as far as politically motivated crimes were concerned. As is evident from the cases, several perpetrators had no criminal record, which was not because they did not commit crimes but because there was no functioning justice system that

---

[248] For instance, in *Aman Gobana et al.*, the OSC mitigated two death sentences to sentences of life imprisonment on the ground that the defendants had, among others, no criminal record. See *Aman Gobena et al.*, (Sentencing Judgment), *supra* note 12,110. See also SNNPR SC, *SPO v. Mezemer Abebe at al.*, (Sentencing Judgment), 5 March 2005, File No. 0457,122.
[249] FSC, *SPO v. Girma Demessie et al.*, (Appeals Judgment), 26 February 2002, File No. 5853, 2.
[250] See FSC CB, *Fesseha Abay and Hiwot Yeseraw v. Federal Prosecutor*, (Decision), 3 May 2010, File No. 53612, 3. See also FSC CB, *Abebayehu Samuel v. Oromia Justice Bureau*, (Decision), 4 October 2017, File No. 135787, 4.
[251] *Al Mahdi*, Trial Chamber VIII, (Judgment and Sentence), *supra* note 117, para. 97.
[252] See D'Ascoli, *Sentencing in International Criminal Law*, *supra* note 183, 193–194.
[253] Ibid., 191–194.
[254] Ibid., 191.

could have brought them to justice. Had there been such a system, it might have already interrupted the commission of the crimes for which they stood trial after the downfall of their regime. It could then be preposterous to mitigate sentences based on the lack of a criminal record with respect to a public official who has been found guilty by the court of participating in the commission of genocide from 1974 to 1991.[255] To do that is to engage in a self-defeating exercise, as it amounts to rewarding the criminal for establishing a system of impunity.

8.5.2.2.2 *Judicial Mitigating Factors: An Unfettered Judicial Discretion in Ethiopian Law and in ICL*

In addition to applying the statutory mitigating factors, Ethiopian courts have exercised their broad discretion to invoke numerous grounds of mitigation. In what represents the most controversial example of the use of mitigating factors, the majority in *Mengistu et al.* pronounced a life sentence instead of the death penalty after identifying eight grounds of mitigation.[256] These were: *i*) the prevailing circumstances at the time of the commission, *ii*) lack of education, *iii*) old age, *iv*) age-related sickness, *v*) lengthy trial, *vi*) contribution to the defense of the country and international peacekeeping missions, *vii*) reform during detention, and *viii*) signs of remorse and reconciliation.[257] The Presiding Judge, Medehen Kiros, dissented by predicating his argument on Article 182 of the Criminal Code, which he erroneously considered to have the effect of limiting the court's discretion in applying judicial mitigating factors.[258]

On appeal, the FSC rejected all of the FHC's mitigating factors and aggravated the penalties by changing 18 life sentences into death sentences.[259] The reasons that the FSC put forward to reject the FHC's mitigating factors are too brief to be convincing, except, arguably, for the eighth factor, in which it stated

---

255 For such an instance, see in general, FHC, SPO v. *Kassaye Aragaw et al.*, (Sentencing Judgment), 17 November 2005, File No. 03114, 2–8.
256 *Colonel Mengistu Hailemariam et al.*, (Sentencing Judgment), *supra* note 22, 8–20.
257 Ibid.,16–17.
258 See FHC, SPO v. *Colonel Mengistu Hailemarima et al.*, (Sentencing Judgment: Dissenting Opinion of Judge Medehen Kiros), 11 January 2007, File No. 1/87, 8. Article 182 of the Criminal Code governs exemption or waiver of penalty and states that a court cannot exempt a criminal from punishment or waive the penalty in whole or in part in cases where it is not expressly allowed by law. It is possible that the dissenting opinion misconstrued the law and the issue, because the sentencing judgment was not concerned with exemption and waiver of penalty, but with ordinary mitigation of penalty, which is, as stated above, governed by Articles 82 and 179 of the Criminal Code, not by Article 182.
259 See *Mengistu Hailemariam et al.*, (Appeals Judgment), *supra* note 134, 95.

that the mere sign of remorse is not sufficient to mitigate a sentence.[260] Even then, it seems the FCS misread the FHC's reasoning. As noted in section 8.2.1., the FHC did not invoke *remorse* within the context of Article 79(1)(e) of the Penal Code, where sincerity of repentance is required.[261] Signs of remorse shown by the defendants in *Mengistu et al.*, the sincerity of which was already doubted by the FHC itself, were taken into account within the context of the defendants' readiness to apologize and its potential contribution to reconciliation in Ethiopia.[262]

Furthermore, in rejecting the FHC's mitigating factors, the FSC ran into a contradiction not only with judgments issued by several other courts but also with its own decisions in comparable cases.[263] For instance, unlike its conclusion in this case that being of old age and a victim of age-associated diseases is by no measurement a mitigating ground,[264] the FSC had argued oppositely in *SPO v. Tiruneh Habteselassie*, where it mitigated a death sentence to life imprisonment on the sole basis of the appellant's sickness.[265]

Secondly, the FSC unwarrantedly intervened with the trial court's broad discretion to create as many judicial mitigating factors as it may deem necessary, which the FHC emphasized when it decided to invoke the mitigating factors.[266] In this respect, it should be noted that Ethiopian trial judges enjoy a

---

260   Ibid., 93.
261   See the Penal Code of 1957, Article 79 (1) (e):
      General Extenuating Circumstances.
         (1) The Court may reduce the penalty, within the limits allowed by law (Art. 184), in the following cases: ...
         e) when he manifested a sincere repentance for his acts after the crime, in particular by affording succour to his victim; recognizing his fault or giving himself up to the-authorities, or by repairing, as far as possible, the injury caused by his crime.
      The Criminal Code added to this list that the admission of all the ingredients of the crime stated in the criminal charge could be considered as an act showing sincere remorse. See FDRE Criminal Code, Article 82(1)(e).
262   See section 8.2.1. above.
263   Regarding reform during detention, see FHC, SPO v. *Tsegaye Mamo et al.*, (Sentencing Judgment), 3 August 2003, File No. 631/89, 6. As for 'prevailing circumstances of the period', see HSC, SPO v. *Denbi Disassa et al.*, (Sentencing Judgment), 23 April 2004, File No. 3/95, 178; HSC, SPO v. *Tadesse Tegegne et al.*, (Sentencing Judgment), 23 July 2004, File No. 5/95, 83.
264   See *Colonel Mengistu Hailemariam et al.*, (Appeals Judgment), *supra* note 134, 95.
265   See FSC, SPO v. *Tiruneh Habteselassie*, (Appeals Judgment), 1 December 2006, File No. 21163, 21. For similar judgments by other courts, see TSC, SPO v. *Aseffa Belay et al.*, (Trial Judgment), 11 December 2003, File No.5/90, 815.
266   *Colonel Mengistu Hailemariam et al.*, (Sentencing Judgment), *supra* note 22, 13.

comparable degree of 'unfettered discretion' than that of international judges, in particular as far as creating mitigating or aggravating factors is concerned.[267]

Nevertheless, in revising the FHC's sentencing judgment, the FSC did not show that the FHC had exercised its discretion to create judicial mitigating factors beyond what is permitted by law. Its rejection was based on an unexplained and unsubstantiated conclusion that mitigating factors applied by the FHC were not *adequate* and *sufficient* (ተገቢና በቂ ያልሆኑ). These conditions do not appear to have any legal basis since the relevant law only requires that the court shall motivate its decision:

> the Court shall give reasons for applying extenuating or aggravating circumstances not expressly provided for in this Code and shall state clearly its reasons for taking *this exceptional course*.[268]

The only obvious limitation to this unfettered discretion, which the FSC did not explore, appears to be whether the mitigating (or aggravating) factors that are invoked by the judges reflect the purposes of punishment (sentencing rationales) enshrined in the law. As clearly stated in both Codes, 'the penalties and measures provided by this Code must be applied in accordance with the spirit of this Code and so as to achieve the purpose it has in view (Article 1)'.[269] As a result, the FSC's judgment amounts to an unwarranted intrusion into the discretion of the trial court.[270] Such an exercise of appellate power is also not permissible in international practice.[271]

It is arguable that the FSC's sentencing decision in *Mengistu et al.* reflected the intention of the Court to emphasize the gravity of the crimes and the extreme dangerousness of the convicts in order to impose the death penalty.[272] The same could be said in relation to the dissenting opinion.[273] This implicit

---

[267] Regarding the discretionary power of international judges, see ICTR, *Prosecutor v. Ruggiu*, Trial Chamber I, (Judgment and Sentence), 1 June 2000, ICTR-97-32-I, para. 34.

[268] See the Penal Code of 1957, Article 83. Emphasis added. Under the criminal code, it appears that the application of judicial mitigating and aggravating factors is no longer treated as an 'exceptional course'. See FDRE Criminal Code, Article 86.

[269] See the Penal Code of 1957, Article 85; FDRE Criminal Code, Article 87.

[270] See the Criminal Procedure Code, Article 194.

[271] See ICTR, *Prosecutor v. Kayishema and Ruzindana*, Appeals Chamber, (Judgment), 4 December 2001, ICTR-95-1-A, para. 337.

[272] See *Colonel Mengistu Hailemariam et al.*, (Appeals Judgment), *supra* note 134, 91–94.

[273] See *Colonel Mengistu Hailemariam et al.*, (Sentencing Judgment: Dissenting Opinion of Judge Medehen Kiros), *supra* note 241, 7–9.

  A closer look at the dissenting opinion further reveals that Judge Kiros's view has more to do with the gravity of the crime than with the existence or absence of judicial

tendency to relegate mitigating factors does not seem to be limited to the FSC, in particular when aggravating factors have an overwhelming presence. The FHC itself overlooked mitigating factors in *Abdulkadir Mohammed Burka*,[274] *Gesgese Gebremeskel et al.*,[275] *Tesfaye Woldeselassie et al.*,[276] and *Zenebe Ayele et al.*[277] In *Getachew Tek'eba*, the first of the SPO cases to pronounce the death penalty, the FHC ignored a possible mitigating factor, namely the 'absence of a criminal record', unconventionally brought to the attention of the court by the SPO itself.[278] The FHC here also pronounced the death penalty while the SPO was requesting life sentence.[279]

The view that considers an aggravating factor capable of rendering a mitigating factor insignificant, if not inapplicable, finds support in international sentencing practice. For instance, the ICTY Appeals Chamber in *Popović et al.*

---

mitigating factors. As he argued, 'the use of a judicial mitigating factor should be weighed against the gravity of the crime under consideration and can only be applied if it comes out as sufficiently clear to the extent of concluding that the legislator should not have failed to list it as a mitigating factor'. See ibid., 8. Translation by the author. The original (Amharic) version reads:

ፍርድ ቤቱ ባዚህ የሕግ አንቀጽ መሠረት የሚቀበለው የቅጣት ማቅለያ ምክንያት ከተፈጸመው የወንጀል ድርጊት ክብደት ጋር ተገናዝቦ በቂነቱ በጉልህ የሚታይና ሕግ አውጪው በፍጹም ሊዘነጋው አይገባም ነበር የሚባልበት ምክያትነት ያለው መሆን ይኖርበታል።

This argument is unconvincing. Firstly, it adds a further qualification to the requirement that a single mitigating factor is sufficient to render the death sentence inapplicable. The argument calls for according a lesser or insignificant weight to judicial mitigating factors. Attaching such a proviso to the application of judicial mitigating factors amounts to treating these factors as having lesser effect relative to statutory mitigating factors, which does not have any basis in the law. The judges' discretion to create judicial mitigating factors does not include treating them as less (or more) significant than statutory mitigating factors. Secondly, the dissenting opinion proposed that, in recognizing a circumstance not listed in the law as a mitigating factor, a judge should check whether the legislator could have allowed for mitigation based on the same factor if placed in a similar situation. This too does not reflect the essence of the law. In judicially creating a mitigating factor, it is simply sufficient for the court to justify why it deems that it is necessary to consider a mitigating factor not listed in the law. Anything more amounts to setting the bar unreasonably high based on an erroneous assumption that the legislator had a checklist of every possible mitigating factor.

274   *Abdulekadir Mohammed Burka*, (Sentencing Judgment), *supra* note 12, 2–3.
275   See *Gesgese Gebremeskel Ateraga et al.*, (Sentencing Judgment), *supra* note 142, 40–54.
276   *Colonel Tesfaye Woldeselassie et al.*, (Sentencing Judgment), *supra* note 143, 26–32.
277   *Zenebe Ayele et al.*, (Sentencing Judgment), *supra* note 154, 109–112.
278   *Getachew Tek'eba*, (Sentencing Judgment), *supra* note 141,1-3. This case is one of the few exceptions in which the Prosecution raised a factor that could potentially mitigate the sentence. For similar instances, see FHC, SPO v. *Kidanemariam Berehanu Gemta*, (Sentencing judgment), 7 February 2000, File no. 642/89, 4.
279   *Getachew Tek'eba*, (Sentencing Judgment), *supra* note 141, 3.

stated, in relation to the imposition of a life sentence, that, 'the existence of mitigating circumstances does not automatically result in a reduction of sentence or preclude the imposition of a sentence of life imprisonment where the gravity of the offence so requires'.[280] In reaching this conclusion, the Appeals Chamber in *Popović* relied on the appeals judgments of the ICTR in *Nizeyimana,*[281] *Ntabakuze,*[282] and *Niyitegeka,*[283] and, thereby, presented the point as an established practice of the UNICTs. Similarly, as noted in *Blaškić et al.* in connection to the defendant's position of power, an aggravating factor may either significantly increase the sentence or 'at least lead the Trial Chamber to *give less weight to the mitigating circumstances*'.[284]

Nonetheless, the law in Ethiopia is unequivocally different in the sense that neither a multiplicity nor the perceived weightiness of aggravating factors affects the application of mitigating factors. In fact, a single mitigating factor should result in an automatic reduction of a sentence, including the ultimate penalty. There should be a mandatory assessment of both aggravating and mitigating factors. Moreover, the courts should first aggravate the penalty on the basis of any aggravating factors and then mitigate the sentence by applying mitigating factors.[285] The crux of the matter is that there is a rule of separate treatment of mitigation and aggravation; and, as Philip Graven put it, the factors 'do not exclude each other'.[286]

8.5.2.3   Special Aggravating Factors

The special aggravating factors that generate free aggravation are concurrence of crimes and recidivism.[287] The concurrence of crimes is the only special aggravating factor that has been used in Ethiopian trials of core crimes. It occurs when a person commits two or more successive crimes; when the same criminal act simultaneously contravenes several criminal provisions; or

---

280   See ICTY, *Prosecutor* v. *Popović et al.,* Appeals Chamber, (Judgment), 30 January 2015, IT-05-88-A, para. 2053.
281   ICTR, *Prosecutor* v. *Nizeyimana*, Appeals Chamber, (Judgment), 29 September 2014, ICTR-00-55C-A, para. 445.
282   ICTR, *Prosecutor* v. *Ntabakuze*, Appeals Chamber, (Judgment), 8 May 2012, ICTR-98-41A-A, paras 267, 280.
283   ICTR, *Prosecutor* v. *Niyitegeka*, Appeals Chamber, (Judgment), 9 July 2004, ICTR-96-14-A, para. 267.
284   ICTY, *Prosecutor* v. *Blaškić*, Trial Chamber, (Judgment), 3 March 2000, IT-95–14-T, para. 789 (emphasis added).
285   FDRE Criminal Code, Article 189(1).
286   Graven, *An Introduction to Ethiopian Penal Law, supra* note 185, 269.
287   See the Penal Code of 1957, Article 82; FDRE Criminal Code, Article 85.

when the commission of a single crime harms the interests of more than one person.[288] The vast majority of the *Dergue* trials and the *Oromo-Gumuz* trials used the multiplicity of convictions as special aggravating factors. Defendants were found to have committed a domestic crime (murder, grave bodily injury or rape) in addition to a core crime (genocide or war crime). No single defendant was found guilty of both genocide and war crimes at the same time by the same court.

Pronouncing multiple sentences on a single criminal found guilty of multiple offenses is not permissible under Ethiopian law. The court may determine separate sentences for each of the concurrent crimes knowing that at the end they will become a single sentence either by way of absorption or by way of addition.[289] The absorption rule applies to death sentences and life sentences. Once the death sentence is determined for one of the concurrent crimes, it may be taken as final for it absorbs any other penalty the court might impose for the other crimes. The same rule applies where the maximum penalty imposed for one of the concurrent crimes is a life sentence.[290] The addition rule works with sentences of fixed prison terms. Accordingly, the court may add sentences imposed for each of the concurrent crimes and determine the final sentence, without exceeding the general maximum, namely, 25 years of rigorous imprisonment.[291]

Accordingly, Ethiopian law provides for a mandatory single sentence for multiple convictions. In that, it differs from the UNICTs, where a trial chamber enjoys the discretion to impose a single penalty when the accused has been found guilty of multiple crimes that are linked together.[292] Further, the existence of a single sentence rule in Ethiopia renders irrelevant such issues as consecutive or simultaneous enforcement of multiple sentences that international practice however has to deal with. The absorption and addition rules apply even to sentences passed on the same individual by different courts and at different times, as was the case with respect to defendants in the *Dergue* trials such as Melaku Teferra, Eshetu Alemu, Kebede Kiberet, Getachew Teke'abe, and Legesse Asfaw.[293] To avoid any possibility of duplication of sentences

---

288 FDRE Criminal Code, Article 66.
289 Ibid., Articles 184–188.
290 Ibid., Article 184.
291 Ibid., Articles 184–188.
292 See *Nahimana et al.*, Appeals Chamber, (Judgment), *supra* note 96, paras 1040–1043; *Blaškić*, Trial Chamber, (Judgment), *supra* note 284, para. 807.
293 On the application of absorption or addition in such cases, see FSC CB, *Mekonnen Welelaw v. Federal Ethics and Anti-Corruption Commission Prosecutor*, (Decision), 26 June 2014, File No. 96503, 2–4.

against a convict, Ethiopian courts have often postponed sentencing a convict who was being tried for another crime by another chamber or court.[294]

8.5.2.4   General Aggravating Factors

As is the case with general mitigating factors, Ethiopian criminal law divides the general aggravating factors into two categories: statutory and judicial. Just like the mitigating factors, they both have similar weight and effect, at least in theory. The following sub-sections discuss each of them separately.

8.5.2.4.1   *Statutory Aggravating Factors*

Similar to the number of general statutory mitigating factors, the Criminal Code identifies five general statutory aggravating factors, namely, reprehensible motives, abuse of a position of power, vulnerability of victims, vicious circumstances of the commission and participation in a criminal agreement.[295] International practice has also taken similar factors of aggravation into account.[296] The sentencing practice shows that Ethiopian trials have applied all of these grounds as well as other judge-made ones.

With respect to reprehensible motives, the law requires aggravation of penalty 'when the criminal acted with treachery, with perfidy, with a base motive (such as envy, hatred and greed), with a deliberate intent to injure or do wrong, or with special perversity or cruelty'.[297] In the *Dergue* trials, these elements were referred to using expressions such as 'absolute desire to take life and commit genocide' (ነብስ ለማጥፋትና ዘር ለማጥፋት ሙሉ ፍላጎት), as stated with respect to Eshetu Shenkutie[298] and Colonel Tiruneh Habtesellassie,[299] and 'addiction to killing'(የመግደል ሱስ), as highlighted in *Gesgese Gebremesekel Ateraga et al.*[300] and *Melaku Teferra*.[301]

Abuse of a position of power was frequently mentioned as an aggravating factor in the *Dergue* trials. In pronouncing the 18 death sentences in *Mengistu et al.*, the FSC highlighted the abuse of a position of power in the sense that the defendants were members of the *Dergue's* Standing Committee, the regime's

---

294   See FHC, SPO v. *Eshetu Shenkutie et al.*, (Sentencing Judgment), 2 October 2000, File No. 940/89, 36; *Legesse Asfaw et al.*, (Sentencing Judgment), *supra* note 14, 2.
295   See the Penal Code of 1957, Article 81; FDRE Criminal Code, Article 84.
296   See Mettraux, *International Crimes and the Ad Hoc Tribunals*, *supra* note 44, 350–351.
297   FDRE Criminal Code, Article 84 (1) (a).
298   *Eshetu Shenkutie et al.*, (Sentencing Judgment), *supra* note 294, 34.
299   See FHC, SPO v. *Petros Gebre et al.*, (Sentencing Judgment), 28 February 2005, File No. 1459/92, 2.
300   See *Gesgese Gebremeskel Ateraga et al.*, (Sentencing Judgment), *supra* note 142, 40–54.
301   See *Melaku Teferra*, (Appeals Judgment), *supra* note 132, 5–8.

highest executive organ.³⁰² A closer look at the practice further reveals that being the highest ranking or a low-ranking officer in the general military hierarchy or civilian structure did not make a difference for the assessment of the abuse of a position of power. It operated on the assumption that as any position of authority carries with it a duty to serve and protect others, the perpetrator must be subjected to a harsher sentence as long as he or she had a position of authority at the time of the commission of the crime.³⁰³ The Ethiopian courts, unlike the UNICTs, did not take a clear approach that punishment may increase as the position of authority increases in rank.³⁰⁴

In fact, the position of authority as an aggravating factor can be set aside if it is shown that the perpetrator did not abuse his or her position of power. Judges may disregard the position of authority and instead mitigate the sentence on grounds such as obedience to a superior order, as was done by the FSC in *Teshome Kebede et al.*,³⁰⁵ and by the Amhara Supreme Court (ASC) in *Demetse Gebremedehen et al.*³⁰⁶ Obedience to superior orders can however not be inferred solely from the existence of a superior and subordinate relationship. As highlighted in *Legesse Asfaw et al.*, there should be a proof that there was a superior order and that the subordinate acted pursuant to that order.³⁰⁷ Interestingly, according to the judgment of the OSC in *Teshome Gobenea et al.*, even a regional governor can successfully invoke obedience to superior order – in the case of a justified fear – as a mitigating factor.³⁰⁸ In this regard, Ethiopian practice appears to be more or less similar to the practice of the UNICTs and of the ICC where the emphasis is not on the position of authority *per se* but on the abuse of that position.³⁰⁹

---

302   See *Colonel Mengistu Hailemariam et al.*, (Appeals Judgment) *supra* note 134, 95.
303   *Aliyu Yesufe Ibrahim et al.*, (Sentencing Judgment), *supra* note 8, 5. See also *Gizaw Tadesse et al.*, (Appeals Judgment), *supra* note 219,11.
304   For the relevant practice in the UNICTs, see Holá *et al.*, 'International Sentencing Facts and Figures, *supra* note 207, 418–419.
305   *Teshome Kebede et al.*, (Appeals Judgment), *supra* note 219, 6.
306   ASC, SPO v. *Demetse Gebremedehen et al.*, (Sentencing Judgment), 16 August 2005, File No. 1310, 7.
307   See *Legesse Asfaw et al.*, (Sentencing Judgment), *supra* note 14, 3.
308   *Aman Gobena et al.*, (Sentencing Judgment), *supra* note 12, 7–9.
309   See ICTY, *Prosecutor v. Babić*, Appeals Chamber, (Judgment on Sentencing Appeal), 18 July 2005, IT-03-72-A, para. 80; ICTR, *Prosecutor v. Ndinddabahizi*, Appeals Chamber, (Judgment) 16 January 2007, ICTR-01-71-A, para. 136. See also ICC, *Prosecutor v. Thomas Lubanga Dyilo*, Appeals Chamber, (Judgment on the appeals of the Prosecutor and Mr. Thomas Lubanga Dyilo against the 'Decision on Sentence Pursuant to Article 76 of the Statute'), 1 December 2014, ICC-01/04-01/06 A4A6, para. 82.

As for aggravation based on the vulnerable status of the victims, Ethiopian trials contain interesting examples. In the *Anuak-Nuwer* trials, the Court considered the refugee status of the victims as an aggravating factor.[310] According to the Court, perpetrators should have given 'special protection' to the victims.[311] In this case, and in line with the text of the law,[312] the vulnerability of the victims was considered to be, by and of itself, an aggravating factor. In other cases, however, courts considered the vulnerability of the victims as an aggravating factor but only together with other circumstances such as the special cruelty of the perpetrator or the vicious circumstances of the commission of the crime. In the *Oromo-Gumuz* trials, the fact that the perpetrators were not willing to spare children, women, and the elderly from their genocidal campaign was regarded as showing the vicious circumstances of the commission.[313] In the *Dergue* trials, the courts considered the infliction of acts of torture on the elderly as implying extreme cruelty on the part of the perpetrators.[314]

In condemning convicts to death, the judges in the *Dergue* trials relied on the existence of vicious circumstances surrounding the commission of the crimes such as violence against the dead, in which the dead were denied a proper burial, hauled across or dumped on the streets, thrown into mass graves or abysses, and fed to beasts.[315] The judges in the *Oromo-Gumuz* trials followed a similar approach in relation to convicts who were found to have eaten the organs (kidneys and livers), drunk the blood, and butchered the genitals and elbows of their victims as a sign of superiority and victory.[316] Likewise, the UNICTs have also noted that vicious circumstances of the commission constitute 'a decisive aggravating circumstance'.[317]

---

310   See *Gure Uchala Ugiraet al.*, (Sentencing Judgment), *supra* note 7, 3.
311   Ibid.
312   See FDRE Criminal Code, Article 84(1)(e).
313   *Tadesse Jewannie Mengesha et al.*, (Sentencing Judgment), *supra* note 8, 1–4.
314   See TSC, SPO v. *Tekleberehane Negash et al.*, (Sentencing Judgment), 23 April 2002, File No. 1/91, 695.
315   See for instance, FHC, SPO v. *Debela Dinsa Wege et al.*, (Sentencing Judgment), 10 August 2005, File No.912/89, 3–5. For details, see T.S. Metekia, 'Violence against and using the Dead: Ethiopia's Dergue Cases' (2018) 4(1) *Journal of Human Remains and Violence* 86–87. Usually, denial of proper burial and mourning for the victims was considered by Ethiopian courts as an aggravating factor in sentencing. See for instance, FHC, SPO v. *Getahun Zenebe Woldeselassie et al.*, (Sentencing Judgment) 09 November 2003, File No. 962/89, 2–3.
316   See *Aliyu Yesufe Ibrahim et al.*, (Sentencing Judgment), *supra* note 8, 6–7; *Tadesse Jewannie Mengesha et al.*, (Sentencing Judgment), *supra* note 8, 8.
317   See *Blaškić*, Trial Chamber, (Judgment), *supra* note 284, para. 783. See also ICTR, *Prosecutor* v. *Kayishema and Ruzindana*, Trial Chamber, (Sentencing Judgment), 21 May 1999, ICTR-95-1-T, para. 18.

8.5.2.4.2 Judicial Aggravating Factors

In punishing core crimes, Ethiopian courts have developed aggravating factors that do not exactly fit into any of the general statutory aggravating factors discussed above. An analysis of the relevant case law allowed to identify three such factors: absence from trial; relatively higher education; and high number of victims.

Several Ethiopian courts have regarded the absence of the accused as an aggravating factor.[318] Insofar as trials *in absentia* are not permitted before the UNICTs and the ICC,[319] such aggravating factor simply does not exist before these institutions and could be seen as typical of the Ethiopian core crimes trials. Yet, if Ethiopian law permits trials *in absentia* as last resort proceedings in relation to crimes punishable with rigorous imprisonment of 12 years and above,[320] it does not discriminate against a fugitive offender. The absence of the accused as an aggravating factor is, therefore, a purely judicial creation, most probably prompted by the need to respond to the unprecedented proliferation of absence in the *Dergue* trials.[321] Perhaps going further, the judges in the war crimes case considered presence at trial as a mitigating factor: applying a proportionality principle to sentencing, the judges opined that it would be unfair to punish the present and the absent alike.[322]

This particular scenario aside, the aggravation or mitigation of sentences on account of situation-specific factors is not unique to Ethiopian trials. Similarly, the UNICTs have taken into account factors that have a particular relevance to the situation in which they have been operating. For instance, voluntary surrender has been regarded by the ICTY as a mitigating factor owing to the challenges the Tribunal faced in relation to state cooperation.[323] In a similar

---

318   See FHC, SPO v. *Elias Tsegaye et al.*, (Sentencing Judgment), 4 May 2001, File No. 632/89, 6; FSC, SPO v. *Tafa Gurmu*, (Judgment), 19 April 2001, File No. 4896, 3; *Legesse Asfaw et al.*, (Sentencing Judgment), *supra* note 14, 7.

319   For details regarding the (in)applicability of trials *in absentia* in international criminal justice, see P. Gaeta, 'Trial In Absentia Before the Special Tribunal for Lebanon' in A. Alamuddin *et al.* (eds.), *The Special Tribunal for Lebanon: Law and Practice* (Oxford: Oxford University Press, 2014) 232–238; W.A. Schabas, 'In Absentia Proceedings before International Criminal Courts' in G. Sluiter and S. Vasiliev (eds.), *International Criminal Procedure: Towards a Coherent Body of Law* (London: Cameron May, 2009) 336–342.

320   See Criminal Procedure Code, Article 161.

321   See Chapter 4, Section 4.3.

322   See *Legesse Asfaw et al.*, (Sentencing Judgment), *supra* note 14, 7.

323   See ICTY, *Prosecutor v. Milan Simić*, Trial Chamber II, (Sentencing Judgment),17 October 2002, IT-95–9/2-S, para. 107.

vein, Ethiopian courts have mitigated sentences for convicts who voluntarily decided to remain in prison despite opportunities to escape.[324]

The defendants' relatively higher level of education is regarded as a typical form of aggravating factor. In *Hailu Burrayu et al.*, the FSC reversed the lower courts' sentencing judgment and increased penalties on the ground that the defendant was a high school teacher at the time he committed a crime.[325] While aggravating the sentence on the ground that the defendant was a fifth year law student when he participated in the commission of genocide, the FHC stated in *Elias Tsegaye et al.* that 'at that level of education the defendant should have been aware of the inviolability of the human right to life'.[326] In the war crimes case, the fact that the defendants had relevant military training was considered as an aggravating factor and the Court highlighted that it is part of basic military training to avoid indiscriminate attack.[327]

Such practice is not limited to the Ethiopian trials and the UNICTs have also considered as an aggravating factor the perpetrator's high level of education. This was for instance the case before the ICTR which regarded the higher and relevant education of defendants as an aggravating circumstance and notably excluded mitigating factors with respect to Ntakirutimana, a medical doctor,[328] and Barayagwiza, a lawyer by training.[329]

If Ethiopian courts have generally considered the existence of a *high number of victims* to be an aggravating factor, the practice reveals significant disparity, maybe because the legal system has not developed sentencing guidelines for cases where a single perpetrator can be responsible for the death of hundreds of victims. It was straightforward to emphasize the number of victims in *Melaku Teferra*, where the accused was responsible for the death of 971 people and no mitigating circumstance was accepted.[330] In the *Oromo-Gumuz* trials, the Court emphasized the number of victims in imposing the death penalty on

---

324   See FHC, SPO v. *Abebe Melaku et al.*, (Sentencing Judgment), 10 October 2003, File No. 277/93, 13.
325   See FSC, SPO v. *Hailu Burrayu et al.*, (Appeals Judgment), 18 July 2007, File No.22983, 38.
326   See *Elias Tsegaye et al.*, (Sentencing Judgment), *supra* note 318, 7.
327   See *Legesse Asfaw et al.*, (Sentencing Judgment), *supra* note 14, 12.
328   Pointing out the expertise of the defendant as an aggravating factor, the ICTR stated, 'it is particularly egregious that, as a medical doctor, he took lives instead of saving them'. See *Ntakirutimana et al.*, Trial Chamber, (Judgment and Sentence), *supra* note 194, para. 910.
329   See ICTR, *Prosecutor* v. *Nahimana et al.*, Trial Chamber, (Judgment and Sentence), 3 December 2003, ICTR-99-52-T, para. 1100.
330   See FHC, SPO v. *Melaku Teferra*, (Judgment and Sentence), 8 December 2005, File No. 03112, 40.

defendants who killed ten and more victims.³³¹ In *Teshome Bayyu*, a defendant found guilty of killing 123 people was sentenced to life in prison.³³²

It is true that there is no mathematical formula that determines punishment in proportion to the number of victims, and sentencing is a process that takes into account several aggravating and mitigating factors before determining the final penalty. As such, the number of victims may not be regarded as the most significant factor in sentencing. Yet, Ethiopian courts have at times tried to vary sentencing based on the number of victims. In SPO v. *Zegeye Teferra*, where the FSC quashed the lower court's judgment with respect to five killings, it stated that the penalty shall be reduced in proportion to the number of murders for which the accused was acquitted.³³³ The Court then reduced a life sentence imposed by the FHC to 22 years of rigorous imprisonment.³³⁴

8.6 Multiplicity of Convicts and the Problem of Individualization of Punishment

Core crimes trials in Ethiopia have often been mass trials, with the exception of the *Anuak-Nuwer* trials where there were only nine defendants. 5,119 defendants were tried in the *Dergue* cases, while 276 defendants stood trial in the *Oromo-Gumuz* cases. It is possible that no other core crimes trial in history has prosecuted a comparable number of defendants as those prosecuted in Ethiopia, save for the case of Rwandan national courts and the *Gacaca* courts for genocide-related cases.³³⁵ As of September 2019, the ICTY and ICTR have tried and punished, respectively, 90 and 62 individuals³³⁶ and the ICC has convicted eight defendants (including a conviction for contempt of court).³³⁷

Most importantly, there was rarely a trial of one single defendant in Ethiopia's core crime cases. By way of illustration, it can be noted that the main genocide trial, *Mengistu et al.*, had, initially, 106 co-defendants while 23 defendants stood trial in the war crimes case. *Mekonnen Gelan et al.* stands out as

---

331 *Tadesse Jewannie Mengesha et al.*, (Sentencing Judgment), *supra* note 8, 6.
332 FHC, SPO v. *Teshome Bayyu et al.*, (Sentencing Judgment), 22 January 2009, File No. 07415, 15.
333 FSC, SPO v. *Zegeye Teferra et al.*, (Appeals Judgment), 15 May 2003, File No. 23192, 6.
334 Ibid.
335 1,958,634 cases were tried through *Gacaca* courts. See http://gacaca.rw/about/achievements/, accessed 19 February 2018.
336 On the ICTY, see http://www.icty.org/sid/24, accessed 20 February 2018; on the ICTR, *see* http://unictr.unmict.org/en/tribunal, accessed 20 February 2018.
337 See https://www.icc-cpi.int/Pages/defendants-wip.aspx, accessed 31 August 2018.

the single trial with the highest number of co-defendants, that is, 237. In the *Oromo Gumuz* trials, *Tadesse Jewannie et al.* and *Aliyu Yesufe et al.* had, respectively, 137 and 127 co-defendants.

At times, the multiplicity of defendants created issues concerning the accused's right to defend oneself. In *Mengistu et al.*, the FHC rejected the defendants' preliminary objection requesting a separate trial and asserted that the joinder of the defendants was justified as the manner of the commission of the crime involved all of them.[338] The ultimate effect of the multiplicity of defendants was felt at the sentencing stage where it tested the judges' willingness and ability to uphold the Criminal Code's principle of individualization of sentences and non-transmissibility of personal circumstances (Article 41) as well as the totality principle (Article 88(2)).

Several sentencing judgments failed to individualize the penalty by attributing personal circumstances collectively to several defendants. In *Mengistu et al.*, for instance, mitigating factors such as illness, old age, service in peacekeeping missions, were applied by the FHC collectively to all defendants.[339] In *Mekonnen Gelan et al.*, several defendants were sentenced to identical penalties because they were either young students or uneducated peasants.[340] In these and several other cases, the courts neither considered the personal circumstances of the defendants separately nor discussed the level of participation of each convict.

In other cases, personal circumstances were ignored altogether as sentencing judgments were limited to only mentioning the convicts' participation in the commission of the crime, although not even explicitly stating its actual gravity and its implication for the determination of the sentences.[341] In *Aliyu Yesufe et al.*, 17 convicts were each condemned to 15 years of rigorous imprisonment on the ground that they all participated in the killing of four individuals.[342] In *Tadesse Jewannie et al.*, 27 defendants were sentenced to 20 years because, according to the court, 'they killed one person each'.[343] In *Brigadier General Tedla Desta et al.*, 11 defendants were sentenced to nine years of rigorous imprisonment based on the common ground that they all participated in the unlawful arrest of several young persons.[344]

---

338   See *Colonel Mengistu Hailemariam et al.*, (Ruling on Preliminary Objections), *supra* note 165, 101.
339   Ibid.
340   *Mekonnen Gelan et al.*, (Sentencing Judgment), *supra* note 93, 312–314.
341   See section 8.5.1. above.
342   *Aliyu Yesufe Ibrahim et al.*, (Sentencing Judgment), *supra* note 8, 3–4.
343   *Tadesse Jewannie Mengesha et al.*, (Sentencing Judgment), *supra* note 8, 1–14.
344   OSC, SPO v. *Brigadier General Tedla Desta et al.*, (Judgment), 13 May 2001, File No. 24/92, 144.

These remarks notwithstanding, Ethiopian courts have, like their international counterparts,[345] often highlighted the need to individualize sentences and respect the totality principle. In that regard, virtually all sentencing judgments in Ethiopia state that the sentence shall be calculated in compliance with Articles 41 and 88 of the Criminal Code. At times, the FSC reversed the lower courts' sentencing judgments by invoking that the convict should be punished to the extent of his or her participation.[346] It thus appears that the core crimes' trials simply involved too many defendants per trial to treat each and one of them separately and methodically. One might, therefore, need to consider the unique challenge that Ethiopian courts faced when comparing them to the UNICTs and the ICC where, so far, the maximum number of defendants in one single case was seven and five respectively.[347]

8.7 Conclusion

This chapter has discussed the general and significant rules governing sentencing determination in Ethiopia in the context of genocide and war crimes trials. It has analyzed Ethiopian law and practice in comparison to the law and practice of the UNICTs and the ICC. It has also discussed the punishment of core crimes in comparison with that of domestic crimes, not least regarding applicable penalties and sentencing rationales.

The chapter has revealed the absence in Ethiopian law of a penalty scheme that takes into account the nature and gravity of core crimes, because of which some domestic crimes are punishable, paradoxically, more severely than core crimes. It has also pointed out several differences in the applicable penalties available in Ethiopian law, the Statutes of the UNICTs, and the Statute of the ICC. The applicability of the death penalty in Ethiopia represents the most significant difference. Some of the differences are understandable in the sense that municipal laws (including those of states parties to the ICC) are not required to apply international penalties,[348] although international law strives

---

345 For the UNICTs' practice concerning the totality principle and the individualization of sentences, see Mettraux, *International Crimes and the Ad Hoc Tribunals*, supra note 44, 355–357.
346 See for instance, *Feyissa Saboka* (Appeals Judgment), supra note 222, 5.
347 See ICTY, *Prosecutor v. Popović et al.*, Trial Chamber II, (Judgment) 10 June 2010, IT-05-88-T; ICC, *Prosecutor v. Bemba et al.*, Trial Chamber VII, (Judgment), 22 March 2017, ICC-01/05-01/13.
348 See Mulgrew, *Towards the Development of the International Penal System*, supra note 147, 13–14.

to minimize the difference by employing approaches such as the progressive abolition of the death penalty.[349]

According to this chapter's findings, nowhere in their judgments have the Ethiopian courts explained and analyzed the sentencing rationales they invoked. While the UNICTs and the ICC have attempted to justify the punishment of core crimes by giving due regard to their distinct nature, Ethiopian courts, by contrast, have employed sentencing rationales in a manner that is typical to the punishment of domestic crimes. This deficit may find an explanation in the fact that Ethiopian judges lack expertise in the evolving field of international criminal law; a problem that has been identified as one of the shortcomings of national prosecutions of core crimes in general.[350]

The chapter has found that both Ethiopian and international sentencing practices lack transparency. To a certain degree, the exercise of broad judicial discretion by both international and domestic courts has contributed to such a problem. However, the opacity of Ethiopian sentencing judgments has created further difficulties for verifying double counting errors. As shown in this chapter, the difference in the scope of discretion between international and Ethiopian judges explains most of the differences between the two sentencing systems, in particular with regards to the application of aggravating and mitigating factors. Nonetheless, there are also cases in which Ethiopian courts have imposed more severe, or to the contrary more lenient, penalties by misapplying aggravating and mitigating factors. In so doing, the practice of Ethiopian courts has failed to comply with Article 86 (2) of the Ethiopian Criminal Code that requires providing an explanation in order to invoke new mitigating or aggravating grounds.

Finally, the chapter has shown that there is *in principle* no noticeable difference between the Ethiopian and the international systems as to the need to individualize sentences and comply with the totality principle. Ethiopian practice is however significantly deficient in this regard. This could be because Ethiopian courts had to deal with the unique challenge of punishing, in several instances, an unmanageable number of defendants in one single trial.

---

349 See for details C. Heyns and others 'The Right to Life and the Progressive Abolition of the Death Penalty', in M. deGuzman and D. Amann (eds.), *Arcs of Global Justice: Essays in Honour of William A. Schabas* (Oxford University Press, Oxford, 2018) 127–134.

350 See A. Cassese, 'The Italian Court of Cassation Misapprehends the Notion of War Crimes: The Lozano Case' (2008) 6(1) *Journal of International Criminal Justice* 1084–1087; R. Cryer et al., *Introduction to International Criminal Law and Procedure* (2nd ed., Cambridge: Cambridge University Press, 2010) 35.

CHAPTER 9

Conclusion

Trying Core Crimes with Political Ambition and Judicial Ineptness

This book has investigated the prosecution of core crimes in Ethiopia, using as a comparative yardstick the substantive and procedural standards of international criminal law (ICL). This approach finds its rationale in the fact that, as laid out in Chapter 1, core crimes, whether prosecuted by international or municipal courts, have their legal basis in international (criminal) law. This assertion – firmly rooted in in the international doctrine and jurisprudence – accepts that, even with respect to national prosecutions of core crimes, the law that governs the prohibition of core crimes does not usually emanate from the prosecuting state's own legal system, but from international treaties and custom. Interestingly for the purposes of this book, this was exactly the conclusion reached by the FSC in *Mengistu et al.*, with respect to genocide, and by the FHC in *Legesse Asfaw et al.*, concerning war crimes.[1]

That being said, states are gradually integrating the – international – prohibition of core crimes into their own legal system; an integration which means that the enforcement of ICL also very much depends on the prosecution of core crimes at the national level. Municipal courts are not only allowed but also, sometimes, required by international law to prosecute persons accused of having perpetrated core crimes.[2] International criminal justice is not a *domaine réservé* of international institutions;[3] it is also made up of national enforcement mechanisms in which the jurisdiction over the prosecution of core crimes belongs to municipal courts. This is more strongly evidenced in the idea that the ICC is merely complementary to national courts. Accordingly, national and international courts have similar and equivalent functions as to the prosecution of core crimes. This state of affairs constituted the basis for the comparative analysis adopted in this book to examine the following questions:

---

1   See Chapters 5 and 7.
2   See Chapter 2, section 3.2.
3   As Jessberger rightly puts it, 'the popular equation of international justice with prosecution by international criminal courts is foreshortened, and may be misleading'. See F. Jessberger, 'International v. National Prosecution of International Crimes' in A. Cassese (ed.) *The Oxford Companion to International Criminal Justice* (Oxford: Oxford University Press, 2009) 208.

i) how does the Ethiopian criminal justice system provide for the prosecution of core crimes?
ii) were prosecutions of core crimes in Ethiopia in line with standards of ICL? If not, which deviations and/or deficits exist (both in law and in practice) in comparison with ICL standards?

To methodically examine these questions, the book was structured into two parts consisting of a total of eight chapters. The structural approach followed in this book results from, and reflects, the fact that national prosecutions of core crimes involve two interrelated stages. As explained in Chapter 1, these stages may be referred to as the stage of *setting into motion of a prosecution of core crimes* (the first stage) and the stage of *actual prosecutions or trials* (the second stage). The book has thoroughly examined the whole process of national prosecution of core crimes in Ethiopia, exploring in detail both stages, to assess whether it was carried out in compliance with relevant international standards. Part 1 examined how Ethiopia set the prosecutions in motion, with a particular emphasis in the discussion on the *Dergue* trials, due to their pioneering and large scale nature. Part 2 discussed the trials, both in terms of the applicable laws used and of the manner in which Ethiopian courts interpreted the elements of core crimes and imposed punishment on those persons found guilty of committing these crimes.

9.1 Findings in Part 1 Prosecuting Core Crimes through Political Emphasis and Indifference

In Part 1, the focus of this book was the actual decision taken by Ethiopia to, on four distinct occasions, prosecute international crimes committed by Ethiopians against Ethiopians on Ethiopian territory. Although the discussion explored the choices made by Ethiopia in the context of the country's transition from the dictatorial *Dergue* regime to a new political order, the interest of the discussion was not *per se* on transitional justice but rather on the content and context of the decision(s) to prosecute core crimes.

The discussion conducted in Part 1, in particular in Chapters 2 and 3, was aimed at delineating the contents and scope of the initial decision to prosecute the *Dergue*. In that sense, the book was not interested on whether the choice to prosecute the *Dergue* and exclude amnesty was desirable from the perspective of reconstructing Ethiopia, which could nonetheless be a point of interest from the perspective of transitional justice. Instead, the discussion was guided by whether the decision to prosecute was in line with international standards relevant to prosecuting core crimes. As a compliance yardstick for

CONCLUSION   433

this particular issue, it was stated in Chapter 1 that a mere decision to prosecute is not sufficient as national prosecutions of international crimes require the putting in place of a series of measures that ensure the compliance of the ensuing prosecutions to ICL standards. In that respect, the putting in place of compliance ensuring measures at the first stage of the national prosecution of core crimes highly determines the compliance of its second stage to ICL standards.

Essentially, compliance ensuring measures that should accompany a decision to prosecute are those involving the removal of all impediments that could either bar the prosecutions from kicking off or only allow for incomplete trial processes, as discussed in Chapter 1. Such measures may include the removal of legal impediments to prosecuting core crimes such as amnesty laws, statute of limitations, immunities, and the *ne bis in idem* principle. Adopting compliance ensuring measures also involves ensuring that prosecutions will not be hindered by either procedural laws limiting jurisdiction or substantive laws not reflecting the international definition of these core crimes as expressed in international criminal law. The adoption of such measures not only reinforces the state's decision to prosecute, it may also evidence its genuine willingness to do so.

9.1.1   *Politically Motivated Foundations of the Ethiopian Core Crimes Trials*

The first main finding in Part 1 of this book was that the first decision to prosecute core crimes committed during the *Dergue* regime (1974–1991) that was reached by the TGE on 2 August 1992, through the establishment of the SPO, was predominantly political. Except for stating that the decision is essential, the SPO Proclamation did not specify why the TGE chose to respond to the past injustices with prosecution. The political nature of the decision to prosecute can be inferred from three factors: *i*) the lack of popular participation in the making of the decision (Chapter 2), *ii*) the TGE's intention to use prosecutions for political recognition (Chapter 3), and *iii*) the unjustified selectivity of alleged offenders (Chapter 4).

The decision to prosecute the *Dergue* was, as discussed in Chapter 2, reached by the TPLF/EPRDF leaders behind closed doors after the TGE had practically disintegrated due to the OLF's departure. Disregarding recommendations to prosecute only the 'big fish', the TPLF/EPRDF reached the decision to bring to trial all members and affiliates of the *Dergue*. Albeit allegations that this decision was reached on the basis of a public demand, this book concluded that there was no evidence of the existence of any meaningful participation of the victims and of the families of the victims in any discussion on what was to be the most appropriate response to the crimes committed during the *Dergue* regime. Rather than aiming for prosecutions, survivors and families of the victims were engaged in mourning gatherings that were focused on identifying bodies of the deceased and other issues concerning memory and remembrance.

The initial decision to prosecute in the *Dergue* case resulted neither from discussions between victims and the new rulers nor from the unapologetic attitude of the alleged perpetrators, as claimed by the TGE. There was no forum for dialogue between the survivors/families of the victims and alleged perpetrators that could have shaped in one way or another the State's response to past crimes. Although briefly proposed during the failed London Talks of May 1991, the decision to prosecute was not a result of negotiations, because no substantive peace talks were held while the *Dergue* was still in power and, at the time it was forcefully overthrown, it had left with no bargaining power to negotiate or demand amnesty. The question of how to respond to past abuses was not raised and discussed in the Addis Ababa Conference of July 1991 that was attended by several military and civilian groups nor were clear directions suggested in the 1991 Transitional Charter that established the TGE.

The examination of the possible motives for the TGE's decision to prosecute the *Dergue*, undertaken in Chapter 3, indicated that a genuine will to prosecute core crimes was in reality missing. Notwithstanding the TGE's and SPO's attempts to retrospectively explain that the decision to bring the *Dergue* to trial was reached to uphold the international duty to prosecute, no such duty under international or national laws was actually applicable to the core crimes that fell under the jurisdiction of the SPO, namely, genocide against political groups and war crimes committed in the context of a non-international armed conflict.

The primary motive behind the TGE's decision to hold the *Dergue* accountable seems to have been its intention to use the prosecutions to garner political legitimacy, which the TPLF/EPRDF was lacking both internally and internationally due to the undemocratic nature of its ascendancy to power. In addition to this, the fact that the alleged perpetrators were portrayed as not possessing any sense of remorse and repentance, which is commonly deemed as a prerequisite for forgiveness, might have played in favor of reaching the decision to prosecute. Yet, there is no evidence showing that the perpetrators were given the opportunity to show remorse and ask for forgiveness. To the contrary, the *Dergue* defendants have repeatedly requested Ethiopian courts for the creation of an apology forum, an issue that was a point of contention between the FHC and the FSC, as noted in Chapter 7.

The political nature of the decision to prosecute the *Dergue* is further evidenced by its contents, in particular regarding the scope of personal jurisdiction envisaged in the decision. The decision, as laid out in the SPO Proclamation, aimed at bringing to justice the vanquished, and the vanquished *only*. In that sense, the decision to prosecute was a political verdict that found the vanquished guilty and the victors innocent, despite the availability of evidence that the latter had also participated in the commission of atrocities. A similar approach was adopted by the Ethiopian government in 2005, when it reached the decision to only prosecute the CUD and its affiliates for post-election violence, while in fact the vast majority of the crimes were perpetrated by its own forces.

Both the *Dergue* era and the 2005 post-election conflicts ended in a manner that clearly established the victor and vanquished status of the parties to the conflict. In both instances, the vanquished had no real or perceived bargaining power that they could have used to influence the politically motivated choices made by the victors. The decisions to prosecute thus seemed clear examples of victor's justice.

9.1.2 Unremoved Impediments: Our Judges, Our Laws

The second main finding in Part 1 of the book was that the political nature of the initial decision to prosecute the *Dergue* had adverse effects on the process of setting the prosecution of core crimes in motion. As it was driven by the aforementioned political motives, the decision was abrupt in the sense that it lacked adequate planning and preparation. The hastiness of the decision to prosecute the *Dergue* was, as discussed in Chapter 2, further expressed in the vagueness of the notion *'heinous and horrendous crimes'*, as employed in the SPO Proclamation to describe the crimes that were to be prosecuted. It was not clear from this expression whether the focus of the decision to prosecute was on core crimes or on all types of crimes that were regarded as grave pursuant to the extant domestic criminal law. Although later on it was decided by the FSC that the SPO's mandate was limited to genocide and abuse of power, this did not stop the SPO from prosecuting domestic crimes, since the FSC decision, unlike that of its Cassation Bench, has no binding legal force and since the doctrine of legal precedent is not applicable in the Ethiopian legal system.

The reason behind the vagueness of the SPO Proclamation in describing the nature of the crimes envisaged for prosecution may be found in the fact that Ethiopia's decision to prosecute the *Dergue* was not accompanied with preliminary investigations into the scale and nature of the atrocities committed during the *Dergue* regime. Such an investigation could have been carried out through the establishment of an impartial Commission of Inquiry. By disregarding this option, the Ethiopian process did not only deviate from the country's past experience, but also stood in contrast to relevant international practices, as identified in Chapter 2. Without a Commission of Inquiry, the Ethiopian process could still have produced a comprehensive legislation on the prosecution of core crimes, had the decision and drafting process of the SPO law involved international criminal justice experts; an approach adopted by certain special and hybrid criminal courts such as the Iraqi High Tribunal.[4]

One of the significant flaws in the TGE's decision to bring the *Dergue* to trial was that it did not examine and determine the applicable law based on which core crimes would be prosecuted. The determination of the law which was to be used in the prosecution of core crimes was left to the SPO, which ultimately decided to try the perpetrators for genocide against political groups, i.e. politicide, and war crimes based on the existing criminal law. In the process, not only international law was disregarded as an applicable law, but also the deficits in the municipal law, pointed out in Chapters 5 and 7, were not rectified; a rectification which could have been possible had the decision to prosecute involved a thorough examination, and possible revision, of the applicable law. The reason for the SPO's reliance on the domestic law was linked to the principle of legality, as noted in Chapter 5. Nonetheless, as discussed in detail, in particular in Chapter 7, the principle of legality in Ethiopian law does not prohibit the prosecution of core crimes on the basis of international law.

It was also identified in this book that the decision to prosecute the *Dergue* was reached at a point when the judicial system was at its lowest capacity in terms of numbers of judges and legal practitioners specifically trained in ICL. There was no effort to mitigate this infrastructural deficit before the commencement of the trials, which is why most of the judgments issued by Ethiopian courts were superficial, as examined in Part 2 of the book. The TGE could have mitigated this problem by creating possibilities for the establishment of a tribunal composed of international and Ethiopian judges and lawyers, an approach that was not foreign to Ethiopia, as evidenced by the establishment of special courts[5] and as could be inferred from the failed attempt to establish the EWCC in 1946–1949.[6] Although international experts were involved in assisting the SPO during the initial stage of the process, this was brief and largely based on informal arrangements between international donors and the Ethiopian government. As such, a more formal arrangement

---

4   See Chapter 2, section 2.3.
5   See Chapter 3, section 3.1.
6   See Chapter 7, section 7.2.

that would have included international experts as an integral part of the mechanism established to prosecute core crimes in Ethiopia was not explored.

In fact, the decision to prosecute the *Dergue* was not motivated by the need to fight impunity for core crimes. Such an interest could have been manifested through adopting measures intended to ensure that the Ethiopian trials comply with standards of ICL, not least through removing impediments that could hinder subsequent prosecutions. A typical example of such an impediment which could and should have been removed is the immunity of head of state. By failing to stipulate that the head of state could not rely on immunity, the SPO Proclamation very much appears as a mere piece of legislation enacted to announce a political statement rather than a comprehensive document laying out a firm legal basis for the envisaged prosecutions. Such an impediment to prosecution should not have been overlooked as the decision to prosecute was notably aimed at bringing to justice the entire leadership and affiliates of the ousted government. Indeed, the discussion in Chapter 2 explained how the issue of immunity of head of state was one of the contentious issues during the trial, which Ethiopian courts have rejected in a legally indefensible ruling.

Yet, the positive development as regards removing impediments to prosecution was the SPO Proclamation's removal of statutory limitations even if, as discussed in Chapter 2, this had nothing to do with the international nature of the crimes that were prosecuted. Firstly, the crimes were, as noted above, vaguely referred to as heinous and horrendous, which implies that the correct qualification of the crimes was not known at the time the decision to prosecute was reached. Secondly, the provision had no bearing in practice as courts relied on the Penal Code of 1957, which already allowed for the prosecution of core crimes until 25 years after the date of their commission. Thirdly, Ethiopia's lack of a specific commitment to remove statutory limitations for core crimes was apparent from the fact that it made no attempt to ratify the Convention on the Non-Applicability of Statutory Limitations to War Crimes and Crimes Against Humanity.[7]

As examined in Part 1 of the book, the political motivations behind the decision to prosecute the *Dergue* resulted in using the prosecutions as a symbolic gesture of the government's commitment to establish the rule of law and serve justice. Symptomatically, the government lacked any interest in locating fugitive offenders and secure their extradition. About half of the defendants in the *Dergue* trials, that is 2,188, were tried *in absentia* – which included the

---

7 Convention on the Non-Applicability of Statutory Limitations to War Crimes and Crimes Against Humanity, G.A. res. 2391 (XXIII), annex, 23 U.N. GAOR Supp. (No. 18) at 40, U.N. Doc. A/7218 (1968), *entered into force* 11 November 1970.

lead defendant in *Mengistu et al*, i.e. Colonel Mengistu Hailemariam. Although trial *in absentia* is permissible in Ethiopian law, unlike what is predominantly the case in international criminal justice, the State still has a two-fold obligation to search for defendants and to request the extradition of those who were located. This obligation implies that the national prosecution of core crimes may require the making of arrangements necessary to achieve successful mutual cooperation in criminal matters. Ethiopia seems to have failed in this regard too, since the poor human rights records of its government and its inadequate legal system have been invoked as a reason why it could not have extradition treaties with countries such as the U.S., where large number of Ethiopian fugitives were allegedly located. Consequently, the Ethiopian core crimes trials have treated trials *in absentia* as regular proceedings, although, as discussed in Chapter 4, the law requires them to be considered as exceptional proceedings that should be adopted as a last resort.

The extent to which the deeply political nature of the initial decision to prosecute the *Dergue* affected the actual prosecutions may also be seen from the discussions in Chapters 4 and 7 with respect to war crimes. As noted in these chapters, the need to serve the political interests of the ruling party, the TPLF/EPRDF, might be the reason why war crimes prosecutions were limited to just one single case, *Legesse Asfaw et al.* Contrary to the reasons mentioned by the SPO, such as lack of sufficient evidence to prosecute more war crimes cases, it was established in this book that several potential cases of war crimes were actually prosecuted as ordinary crimes.

In sum, the decision to prosecute the *Dergue* was not motivated by the need to fight impunity for core crimes. Instead, the entire process was driven by political interests. As such, it was concerned less with ensuring the effectiveness of the prosecutions and more with celebrating the domestic effort, which the SPO referred to as 'our national effort' and 'our own laws'; expressions meant to highlight that Ethiopia prosecuted members of the entire defunct regime for both international and ordinary crimes without significant external support and using only its existing domestic laws.[8]

9.1.3 *The Hidden Trials: Governmental Indifference to the Prosecution of Core Crimes*

The *Anuak-Nuwer* and the *Oromo-Gumuz* trials may not be characterized as trials resulting from overt political reasons, because the relevant situations did not involve the forces and officials of the federal government, as discussed in

---

8 *Dem Yazele Dossie*, 438–439.

CONCLUSION   439

Chapter 4. As a result, neither the defendants nor the crimes were subjected to selective prosecution. The manner in which the trials kicked off however remains unknown. Although these cases marked the only instances of genocide committed against groups protected by the Genocide Convention, there was no specific decision or announcement as to either the start or the end of the trials, which might have dwarfed their significance, including using them to warn potential offenders.

In Chapter 3, it was noted that Ethiopia was under both an international obligation, emanating from the Genocide Convention, and a national obligation, enshrined in Article 28 of the FDRE Constitution, to prosecute acts of genocide committed in the *Anuak-Nuwer* and *Oromo-Gumuz* situations. Nonetheless, the question whether the prosecutions were indeed carried out to uphold such a duty may not be convincingly answered in the positive. This is not only because of the already mentioned hidden nature of the trials but also because there were several notable allegations of widespread perpetration of core crimes with respect to which the alleged perpetrators were not brought to trial – a situation that showed the State's continued disregard for the obligation to prosecute such crimes.

In a bid to elucidate the overall position of Ethiopia towards the repression and prosecution of core crimes, the book also looked beyond the four instances of core crimes' prosecution it closely examined. The conclusion is that in instances where general amnesties were granted for political purposes, no prior determination was made as to whether the commission of core crimes were implicated. This shows a lack of sufficient attention for the repression and prosecution of core crimes. Further, Ethiopia has so far failed to precisely define and criminalize crimes against humanity, although the need to do so was already highlighted during the drafting of the FDRE Constitution and in the debates during the early stages of the *Dergue* trials, as discussed in Chapters 3 and 5. Such instances are symptomatic of Ethiopia's indifference to the prosecution of core crimes when it was devoid of discernable political interest. As such, the *Anuak-Nuer* and *Oromo-Gumuz* trials did not offer any indication as to whether Ethiopia treats the prosecution of core crimes any differently from that of ordinary domestic crimes.

9.2 Findings in Part 2 Duality of the Applicable Law and Singularity of the Jurisprudence

In Part 2 of the book, the Ethiopian trials were examined in comparison with the text of ICL and the developments in international case law. It was noted in Chapters 6 and 7 that the Ethiopian trials of, respectively, genocide and war crimes did not refer to the developments in international criminal courts and tribunals that were dealing with the prosecution of similar crimes at the international level at around the same time. In fact, Ethiopian courts have not shown any interest in referring to international case law even when the SPO attempted to argue some issues based on developments in international criminal courts and tribunals. Such a lack of interest may be explained by the general nature of the Ethiopian legal system that does not allow room for the doctrine of *stare decisis*. Conversely, international criminal courts and tribunals have not referred to the Ethiopian laws or case law, which may have to do with the inaccessibility of the domestic legal system and case law, as pointed out in Chapter 1.

If international case law thus remained absent from the Ethiopian courtrooms and judgments, such was not the case when it came to the texts of international law such as treaties and statutes. Ethiopian courts took relevant international laws, which they rightly highlighted as sources of the domestic provisions on core crimes, into account. As such, as noted in Chapters 5 and 7, Ethiopian trials have recognized the availability of a dual set of laws that could be applicable to prosecute core crimes, the only – yet noticeable – exception being the laws on punishment and sentencing.

9.2.1 *Ethiopian Core Crimes Trials and Dualism of the Applicable Law*

Since 1957, Ethiopian law criminalizes the crime of genocide and several war crimes. These crimes were incorporated with the help of a foreign jurist whose task was to draft the Penal Code of 1957. This was initially done in French and translated into Amharic and English. Several discrepancies exist between the authoritative Amharic version and the English version of the Code, in particular in relation to the crime of genocide. Most of the discrepancies have not been fully rectified, despite the fact that a new criminal code was promulgated in 2005 and entirely repealed the Penal Code of 1957. In particular, Ethiopian law never succeeded in incorporating a *verbatim* copy of the crime of genocide as defined in Article II of the 1948 Genocide Convention, although an attempt to that effect was made in 1989. As a result, each and every constitutive element of the crime of genocide is defined differently under Ethiopian criminal law as compared to the Genocide Convention. The main cause for the many discrepancies between the domestic and the international laws is the fact that Ethiopian law has not clearly distinguished between crimes against humanity and the crime of genocide, whereas these are distinct concepts in international criminal law.

On the positive side, the Criminal Code of 2005 mirrors the definition in the Convention of genocidal *mens rea* by using *intent to destroy* instead of

CONCLUSION   441

its predecessor's ambiguous Amharic phrase, የማጥፋት ዕቅድ (intent/plan to destroy). At the same time, it has also significantly broadened the existing differences between Ethiopian criminal law and the Genocide Convention, in particular in relation to the list of protected groups. Although it now regards ethnic and national groups as protected groups, the Criminal Code of 2005 contains twice the number of groups protected by the Genocide Convention. Specifically, the inclusion of political groups within the Ethiopian definition of genocide was regarded as a move to remedy the Convention's shortcoming. Another significant discrepancy between the Ethiopian law and the Genocide Convention might have resulted from the ambiguity of the Convention itself, in particular as regards the words 'as such', which do not have corresponding terms in the Ethiopian definition, as shown in Chapter 6.

It was also established in Chapter 5 that, in addressing the discrepancies between the domestic and international definitions of the crime of genocide, Ethiopian courts have followed two approaches: permissibility of expanding domestic laws and impermissibility of conflicting domestic laws. The former, which emphasizes that the Genocide Convention does not prohibit the protection of more groups, finds support in other international case law, such as that of the ECtHR. The latter was invoked in a manner that not only established the duality of laws governing the crime of genocide in Ethiopia but also that positioned the Genocide Convention above Ethiopian criminal laws, perhaps even including its Constitution.

The hierarchical superiority of the Genocide Convention also opened the possibility of its direct applicability in Ethiopian trials with respect to certain issues. Nonetheless, the practice seems to have misconstrued the scope of the duality of genocide laws where, for instance, the Convention was invoked by courts to adjudicate issues that fall outside of the conventional scope, a noticeable example being genocide against political groups, as was discussed in Chapters 3 (obligation to prosecute), 4 (immunity of heads of state), and 5 (the question of repealed laws).

With respect to war crimes, the duality of applicable laws was from the outset expressly provided for in the domestic law. The fact that war crimes in Ethiopian law constitute serious violations of rules of IHL was, as discussed in Chapter 7, self-evident from the criminal law's express reference to IHL treaties and international law. In prosecuting war crimes, Ethiopian courts are indeed required by law to interpret war crimes provisions in line with international law in general and with IHL treaties in particular.

Most importantly, Ethiopian law has provided for the direct applicability of IHL rules on prohibited means and methods of warfare. Accordingly, a conduct that has been proscribed as a prohibited means and method of warfare constitutes a crime even if no such crime has been expressly specified in domestic law. Further, an Ethiopian court can enter a conviction for a conduct not expressly prohibited in domestic law as long as it constitutes a prohibited means and method of warfare under IHL. Such an approach, as discussed in detail in Chapter 7, violates neither the domestic nor the international formulation of *nullum crimen sine lege*. By prescribing penalties for crimes that would be prosecuted through the direct application of IHL treaties, Ethiopian criminal law has already removed a potential procedural impediment to the prosecution of crimes that are exclusively defined in international law, i.e. the *nulla poena sine lege* aspect of the principle of legality.

Yet, what could arguably be described as the most significant defect of the Ethiopian war crimes law is the fact that the relevant provisions do not allow for the direct applicability of customary international law, the application of which is, therefore, limited to serving as an interpretative tool for existing domestic war crimes provisions. The magnitude of this defect is considerable as it limits the significance of the most advanced and pioneer aspects of the Ethiopian law of war crimes, namely, the abolition of the IHL traditional approach that distinguishes between war crimes based on the international or non-international nature of the armed conflict. As a result, several war crimes involving the use of prohibited means and methods of warfare that are punishable when committed in non-international armed conflicts due to the application of customary international law are punishable in Ethiopia only when committed in the context of international armed conflicts. Due to its refusal to provide for the direct applicability of customary international law, Ethiopian law lags behind contemporary developments in international criminal law that have shown an evolution towards having a single set of war crimes irrespective of the type of armed conflict.

9.2.2   *The Singularity of the Ethiopian Core Crimes Jurisprudence: The Undiscussed Crimes*

The duality of the applicable law disappeared during the trials, and even more so in the genocide cases, where discussions on the substantive elements of the crimes were limited to a brief examination of the extant domestic provisions. As a result, the jurisprudence of Ethiopian courts remains isolated in the sense that it contains no meaningful reference to the Genocide Convention. Paradoxically, even the FHC and the FSC, the same courts that highlighted the Convention's status as the source of the Ethiopian provisions on genocide, failed to invoke it when examining the elements of the crime. Systematic analyses of the elements of genocide, that have so far been commonly the case in international trials, did not occur in the Ethiopian trials.

CONCLUSION 443

Given that the domestic definition listed elements that were not mentioned in the international definition and that the Genocide Convention was recognized by the courts as superior to the domestic law, it may have been imperative to solve discrepancies based on the analysis of the Convention's definition. The ambiguity of the domestic law on genocide, such as that of the Penal Code of 1957 with respect to genocidal *mens rea*, could have been clarified based on the corresponding provisions in the Genocide Convention. Recognizing the duality of the applicable law should have been considered as entailing a duty for the judges to familiarize themselves with the Convention's definition of genocide. Yet, no single reference to the Convention's *travaux préparatoires* were made by Ethiopian courts. The Ethiopian genocide trials were also devoid of any reference to the international doctrine on genocide, which could have helped the courts in explaining their – mostly unsubstantiated – rulings and verdicts.

Let alone the Genocide Convention, Ethiopian courts have also failed to methodically discuss the domestic laws they applied. Although some of the acquittals, such as the one rendered by the FHC in the CUD's *Shawul et al.*, provided sound explanations of the notion of intent to destroy and of the fact that it should be distinguished from discriminatory intent, a similar explanation did not appear in other cases. In the *Dergue* trials, the proof that the perpetrators had a *plan* to destroy was considered *per se* sufficient to constitute genocidal *mens rea*, without however explaining whether this was also a legal requirement. In the *Oromo-Gumuz* cases, rather inexplicably, the judgment considered the *plan* to destroy as an element of genocidal *mens rea* while the applicable law, the Criminal Code of 2005, expressly refers to 'intent to destroy'.

In what appears to have resulted from a lack of full engagement with the applicable law, Ethiopian courts have, unlike their international counterparts, excessively relied on the victims' membership to a protected group in a manner that equated any attack on a protected group with a genocidal attack. At times, it is not clear from the case law whether, in the courts' understanding, it is members of the group or the group itself that are protected by the law criminalizing genocide. Even then, Ethiopian courts did not attempt to determine and define whether an alleged targeted group was indeed a protected group in the eyes of the law of genocide. This was notably striking in those trials that dealt with genocide against ethnic groups, where no definitional parameter was provided to characterize such groups.

Furthermore, Ethiopian courts have often failed to draw a clear connection between the *actus reus* elements of genocide and the genocide itself. In most instances, proof of *actus reus* was considered *per se* sufficient to prove the commission of genocide. In the process, the Ethiopian case law overlooked the importance of linking the *actus reus* to the genocidal *mens rea*, as a result of which defendants were convicted on the sole bases that they had committed the prohibited acts and that the victim belonged to a protected group, as alleged by the prosecutor. In a fairly safe exercise of judicial extrapolation, it can be asserted that, before international criminal courts and tribunals applying standards of ICL, such convictions would have been for crimes against humanity and not for genocide.

Rarely has the Ethiopian jurisprudence reflected a consensus on a particular element of genocide. Such instance was noted in particular in connection to the irrelevance of substantiality of the number of victims, regarding which the international practice stands divided. Nonetheless, in such and other instances where Ethiopian jurisprudence seems to have reflected the text of ICL, it still remains difficult to ascertain whether this was the result of a well-thought-out interpretation of the law, simply because the judgments are usually undiscussed and unsubstantiated.

Overall, the Ethiopian genocide trials have prosecuted an international crime without referring to international law, even if such reference was not only possible but also required. As such, the trials have trivialized an international crime and equated the prosecution of core crimes with that of domestic crimes. Moreover, the fact that the judgments have failed to carefully consider each and every aspect of the crime before reaching a verdict has resulted in what can be characterized as undiscussed convictions, and, thus, in undiscussed genocides.

To a large extent, war crimes were prosecuted in Ethiopia in a progressive trial that made extensive reference to IHL treaties, in the same way a municipal court would refer to its own domestic laws. The FHC reference to IHL conventions was aimed at coming to a decision on various complex issues in war crimes trials. As noted in Chapter 7, doing so enabled the Ethiopian trial to reach an understanding of war crimes that is similar to that reached in international trials on issues such as the status of victims and perpetrators, the proportionality of an attack, military necessity, and the prohibition of indiscriminate attacks.

Be that as it may, the *Legesse Asfaw et al.* case was also a reminder that a court's reliance on international law does not guarantee the soundness of its overall findings. Evidently, the Court in *Legesse Asfaw et al.* did not provide for an adequate and separate examination of each of the attacks based on which the SPO's charge was filed, as detailed in Chapter 7. The individual war crimes for which the defendants were convicted were not methodically explored by the Court, which also failed to provide a separate and legally defensible

CONCLUSION 445

discussion of the elements of crimes (*actus reus* and *mens rea*). Most significantly, the FHC entered a conviction for war crimes without establishing one of its *sine qua non* elements, i.e. the nexus to armed conflict requirement.

Such a regression in a relatively progressive trial appears to have resulted from the fact that the Court's reference to international law did not go beyond discussing the letter of the law. Indeed, the FHC's analysis of IHL treaties was neither detailed nor structured; this could have been greatly improved had the court consulted preparatory works, legal commentaries, international jurisprudence, and other scholarly writings, none of which were in fact available in Amharic, the Ethiopian language of core crimes trials. As also pointed out in Chapter 7, the Ethiopian war crimes trial did not only differ from the practice of international war crimes trials but also stood in stark contrast with domestic war crimes prosecutions of Ethiopian crimes, such as the *Eshetu Alemu* case in the Netherlands, in which the District Court of The Hague heavily relied on the jurisprudence of the ICTY, ICTR, and ICC to determine many of the issues raised.[9]

9.2.3 *Punishing Core Crimes as Ordinary Crimes: Ineffectiveness in Law and Practice*

Finally, Chapter 8 of the book discussed an aspect of core crimes trials that lacks a strong common legal basis between national and international prosecutions: sentencing and punishment. Unlike the case of substantive provisions on elements of crimes, ICL does not contain a detailed list of penalties that states may prescribe for core crimes. As noted in the chapter, the general

---

9 For a similar approach taken in other decisions of Dutch courts, see R.A. Kok, 'National Adjudication of International Crimes: 'A Dutch Approach' in E.V. Sliedregt and S. Vasilliev (eds.), *Pluralism in International Law* (Oxford: Oxford University Press, 2014) 220–224. Most interestingly, recent developments indicate that certain national courts are required by their domestic laws to refer to decisions of international criminal tribunals for the purpose of prosecuting core crimes, although international law does not impose such a requirement. See W. Ferdinandusse, 'The Interaction of National and International Approaches in the Repression of International Crimes' (2004) 15(5) *The European Journal of International Law* 1041–1053, 1051. Even more, national courts have in practice prosecuted core crimes by referring to cases in other domestic jurisdictions, as well as to decisions of international courts and tribunals. With regards to referring horizontally to the laws and decisions of other states, the experience of the Australian High Court, in particular in *Polyukhovich*, could be seen as an interesting practical illustration. The Australian High Court made references in particular to cases and laws in Israel, Canada, Netherlands, the U.K., and the U.S. See *Polyukhovich v. The Commonwealth of Australia and Another* (1991) 172 CLR 501 F.C. 91/026. See further H. Burmester 'The determination of customary international law in Australian courts' (2004) 4(1) *Non-State Actors and International Law* 39–47.

requirement in ICL instruments that the domestic law shall prescribe 'effective penalty/penal sanctions' for genocide and war crimes does not imply the existence of specific and binding suggestions as to the form and nature of penalties.[10] As a result, the availability in Ethiopian law of the death penalty for core crimes is not *per se* a point of strict contention between contemporary international law and the domestic law, although the former encourages its abolition. Yet, in treating core crimes as capital offenses, Ethiopian criminal law does not consider them to be graver than ordinary crimes, several of which are also punishable by death.

The fact that core crimes in Ethiopian law are not graver than ordinary crimes is not controversial, despite its admittedly absurd consequences. The sentencing law and practice have in fact proved to be paradoxical as they have allowed for the imposition of more severe penalties on ordinary crimes than on core crimes, even when the latter comprise the former as their underlying offenses. This is symptomatic of how the Ethiopian legal system has not accorded any special attention to international crimes in a manner that appreciates and encapsulates the unique intricacies behind their commission and repression.

The ineffective penalty scheme that treats core crimes as punishable less severely than domestic crimes such as murder could have been remedied at the sentencing stage by invoking sentencing rationales that could better reflect the nature and context of core crimes. However, this did not happen. To the contrary, the Ethiopian practice has effectively treated core crimes as ordinary crimes by subjecting them to the application of sentencing rationales that are more relevant to justify the punishment of ordinary crimes. The international practice is in this regards more precise and convincing. It notes that sentencing rationales are required to mirror the interest of the international community (retribution) and that the commission of core crimes is dependent upon the existence of a political context that goes well beyond the will of any particular individual (general deterrence).

Still, both Ethiopian and international courts have developed new sentencing rationales such as the sentences' *relevance to reconciliation*, which appears to be an indirect attempt to complement retributive justice with restorative justice. Although such a rationale may help mitigate the often devastating effects the commission of core crimes has on social cohesion, neither international courts nor Ethiopian courts have explained this rationale in any meaningful way. This is particularly regrettable on the part of Ethiopian courts, given

---

10   See Chapter 8, section 8.1.

that the law allows for the imposition of a secondary penalty of apology in which a court may order perpetrators to apologize to the victims for the crimes they have committed. If it were espoused, such an approach could have, arguably, assisted in opening a dialogue between the perpetrators and the victims towards national reconciliation, which was regarded as missing in Ethiopia, as pointed out in Chapters 3 and 8.

Although the discussion on the available penalties and sentencing rationales was not indicative of the treatment of core crimes as different from ordinary crimes, Chapter 8 also examined the manner in which Ethiopian trials have determined sentences for persons found guilty of committing core crimes. This was carried out with the aim of identifying whether Ethiopian courts emphasized the gravity of core crimes during the process of sentencing determination. Nonetheless, unlike the practice in international courts and tribunals, Ethiopian courts did not make any determination as to whether a core crime (genocide or war crime) was of a particular gravity demanding a severer sentence. The application of aggravating and mitigating factors was also not affected by the international nature of genocide or war crimes. In other words, the international practice, which, due to the gravity of international crimes, considers aggravating factors weightier than mitigating factors was not reflected in the Ethiopian trials. Irrespective of the international or domestic nature of a given crime, aggravating and mitigating factors were treated both in law and practice as mutually exclusive determinants. Overall, the sentencing law and practice in Ethiopia did not distinguish between core crimes and ordinary crimes in any way whatsoever.

In fact, Ethiopian practice shows that the sentences were often determined through an opaque assessment of the gravity of the crimes and of the individual circumstances of the convicts; a problem to which international practice is also not immune. In defense of the Ethiopian courts, one could invoke the fact that they had to deal with the unique challenge of punishing, in several instances, an unmanageable number of defendants in one single trial. Nonetheless, such a reality also indicates that the trials were not systematically organized.

9.3   Final Remarks: Legacy of Trials That Did Not Mirror ICL Standards

From the foregoing, the simplest and most straightforward answer to the first question of the book is that the Ethiopian criminal justice system provides for the prosecution of core crimes, just like it does for that of ordinary crimes. Decisions and announcements made in the early 1990s as to the prosecution of the *Dergue* might have created the impression that Ethiopia paid some kind of special attention to the prosecution of core crimes. Such was however not the case. As was also the case with the CUD trials, the government was not interested in the international nature of the crimes being prosecuted, but rather in using the prosecutions for its own political benefit. The same may also be said of the *Anuak-Nuwer* and *Oromo-Gumuz* trials, which, due to their – perceived and admittedly real – lack of political significance, considered core crimes as any other ordinary crimes. Perhaps in a more visible fashion, core crimes were deliberately treated as ordinary crimes when doing so allowed to shelter the government from popular discontentment, as was the case with the war crimes trial. In sum, the national legal system was not revised and/or prepared in a manner that could have enabled it to undertake the prosecution of core crimes in line with the standards of ICL.

As regards the second question, the book concluded that the Ethiopian core crimes trials were, in most aspects, not compliant with ICL standards. Despite its pioneering role in incorporating the crime of genocide, Ethiopian law contains several discrepancies when compared to the international definition provided by the Genocide Convention. These discrepancies were not rectified in practice through judicial interpretation. As for the law on war crimes, if it does proscribe most of the acts criminalized as such in IHL treaties, it however excludes customary international law as a source of war crimes; an exclusion which constitutes a significant deviation from the contemporary trend in the international proscription of war crimes. The analysis of the judicial practice also reveals a fundamental deficit, namely, war crimes' convictions without prior establishment of the nexus between the alleged conduct and an armed conflict. The shortcomings of the Ethiopian core crimes trials were further evidenced by deficient punishments, as neither the law nor the practice linked specific penalties or sentencing rationales to the nature and gravity of core crimes. Overall, the Ethiopian trials did not mirror ICL standards probably because *they were not meant to do so*. They were designed for political reasons, and the actual trials were troubled by judicial ineptness.

Overall, one may question the importance, if any, of the Ethiopian core crimes trials in the global effort to fight impunity for core crimes by both national and international courts. With regards to national prosecutions of international crimes in general, the Ethiopian experience could serve as solid evidence that a mere decision to prosecute core crimes does not guarantee that the ensuing trials will comply with ICL standards. It may also serve as further substantiation of why, under the complementarity scheme, the ICC should continue to only consider states as willing to prosecute when their announcement to prosecute is accompanied by the putting in place of necessary measures to remove

CONCLUSION

all impediments to the prosecution of core crimes, as noted in Chapter 1. Indeed, trials such as those conducted in Ethiopia were flawed from the start and could have neither guaranteed nor resulted in a process that could be regarded, under the ICC Statute, as an 'effective prosecution'.[11]

At the national level, it is doubtful that the core crimes trials left behind an inspiring legacy and, admittedly, the Ethiopian public barely considers that justice has been served – a reality that was already noted by the Ethiopian government in relation to the *Dergue* trials.[12] Yet, some positive contributions of the Ethiopian core crimes trials may still be pointed out. First, it is because of its decision to prosecute the *Dergue* and of the subsequent trials that Ethiopia now has the obligation to prosecute core crimes enshrined in its Constitution. This obligation is significant in the sense that it covers crimes for which international law does not, arguably, impose a similar obligation such as war crimes committed in non-international armed conflicts and crimes against humanity, as discussed in Chapter 3. The fact that such an obligation is expressly stated in the Constitution could also mean that some recent amnesties could be revoked in the future on grounds of unconstitutionality.

Second, and in connection with this obligation to prosecute, it is again because of the decisions and trials discussed in this book that the Ethiopian Constitution now provides for the inapplicability of statutory limitations to the prosecution of core crimes. This too is a significant development given that Ethiopia is, as noted above, not a state party to the Convention on the Non-Applicability of Statutory Limitations to War Crimes and Crimes Against Humanity, which also includes genocide. As a result of this development, perpetrators of core crimes will not be able to circumvent liability indefinitely, since prosecutions could be initiated when the required political will emerges. When it does, Ethiopia will need to review its legal system to ensure that all institutional and legal impediments are removed so that future prosecutions of core crimes will not be as deficient as those of the past.

11 ICC Statute, Preamble, para. 4.
12 See K. Tronvoll, 'The Quest for Justice or the Construction of Political Legitimacy: The Political Anatomy for the Red Terror Trials' in K. Tronvoll *et al.* (eds.), *The Ethiopian Red Terror Trials: Transitional Justice Challenged* (Martlesham: James Currey, 2009) 84–95.

List of Cases

National Jurisdictions

Ethiopia

ASC, SPO v. *Abera Ayalew et al.*, (Indictment), 24 September 1999, File No.22/90.

ASC, SPO v. *Abera Ayalew et al.*, (Trial Judgment), 4 December 2006, File No. 16170.

ASC, SPO v. *Brigadier General Girma Neway et al.*, (Indictment), 23 December 1997, File No. 24/90.

ASC, SPO v. *Dagnenet Ayalew et al.*, (Indictment), 23 December 1997, File No. 13/90,

ASC, SPO v. *Dagnenet Ayalew et al.*, (Trial Judgment), 26 January 2004, File No. 13/90.

ASC, SPO v. *Demetse Gebremedehen et al.* (Ruling on Preliminary Objection), 11 October 2000, File No. 25/90.

ASC, SPO v. *Demetse Gebremedehen et al.*, (Sentencing Judgment), 16 August 2005, File No. 25/90.

ASC, SPO v. *Getaneh Jembere et al.*, (Sentencing Judgment), 17 August 2005, File No.00764.

ASC, SPO v. *Sisay Balachew et al.*, (Sentencing judgment), 25 April 2002, File No. 9/92.

FHC, *Federal Anti-Corruption and Ethics Commission v. Asmare Abate et al.*, (Ruling on Prosecutor's Request for by Defualt Proceeding), 20 December 2004, File No. 35044.

FHC, *Federal Prosecutor v. Aliyu Yusufe Ibrahim et al.*, (Trial Judgment), 6 September 2009, File No. 7100/2000.

FHC, *Federal Prosecutor v. Berehene Kehassaye Woldeselassie et al.*, (Trial Judgment),19 April 2007, File No. 45671/98.

FHC, *Federal Prosecutor v. Berehene Kehassaye Woldeselassie et al.*, (Indictment),15 December 2006, File No. FHC 45671/98.

FHC, *Federal Prosecutor v. Demisew Zerihun and Yacob Hailemariam*, (Sentencing Judgment), 7 November 2008, File No. 54027.

FHC, *Federal Prosecutor v. Engineer Hailu Shawul et al.*, (Indictment), 15 December 2006, File No. 43246/97.

FHC, *Federal Prosecutor v. Engineer Hailu Shawul et al.*, (Trial Ruling), 3 May 2007, File No. 43246/97.

FHC, *Federal Prosecutor v. Getachew Aseffa et al.*, (Indictment), 7 May 2019, File No. 238040.

LIST OF CASES 451

FHC, *Federal Prosecutor* v. *Gure Uchala Ugira et al.*, (Indictment) 4 January 2004, File No. 586/96.

FHC, *Federal Prosecutor* v. *Gure uchala Ugira et al.*, (Sentencing Judgment), 30 March 2005, File No. 586/96.

FHC, *Federal Prosecutor* v. *Gure Uchala Ugira et al.*, (Trial Judgment), 25 March 2005, File No. 586/96.

FHC, *Federal Prosecutor* v. *Kifle Tigeneh et al.*, (Indictment), 30 June 2006, File No. 44562.

FHC, *Federal Prosecutor* v. *Kifle Tigeneh et al.*, (Trial Ruling), 16 April 2007, File No. 44562/99.

FHC, *Federal Prosecutor* v. *Tadesse Jewanie Mengesha et al.*, (Indictment), 22 August 2008, File No. 70996/2000.

FHC, *Federal Prosecutor* v. *Tadesse Jewanie Mengesha et al.*, (Trial Judgment) 24 August 2009, File No. 70996/2000.

FHC, *Federal Prosecutor* v. *Tesfaye Neno Loya et al.*, (Trial Judgment), 30 April 2009, File No. 74796/2000.

FHC, *Federal Prosecutor* v. *Waltajji Begalo et al.*, (Trial Judgment), 26 February 2015, File No. 136639,

FHC, SPO v. *Abdulekadir Mohammed Burka*, (Sentencing Judgment),13 July 2004, File No. 17011.

FHC, SPO v. *Abdulekadir Mohammed Burka*, (Trial Judgment), 8 July 2004, File No. 17011.

FHC, SPO v. *Abebe Melaku et al.*, (Sentencing Judgment), 10 October 2003, File No. 277/93.

FHC, SPO v. *Ademasu Amare et al.*, (Revised Indictment), 7 July 1998, File No. 654/1989.

FHC, SPO v. *Ali Musa et al.*, (Trial Judgment), 9 May 2001, File No. 925/89.

FHC, SPO v. *Asazenew Bayyisa et al.*, (Abebe Mohammed Hassen's Preliminary Objection on the Indictment), 14 December 1997, File No. 643/1989.

FHC, SPO v. *Asazenew Bayyisa et al.*, (Indictment), 23 December 1996, File No. 643/1989.

FHC, SPO v. *Asazenew Bayyisa et al.*, (Ruling on Preliminary Objections), 22 May 1998, File No. 643/1989.

FHC, SPO v. *Asazenew Bayyisa et al.*, (SPO's Response to the Defendant's Preliminary Objection on the Indictment), 01 April 1998, File No. 643/1989.

FHC, SPO v. *Basha Bekele Fasil and Abera Lemma*, (Trial Ruling), 3 June 1999, File No. 263/1989.

FHC, SPO v. *Colonel Mengistu Hailemariam et al.*, (Indictment), 25 October 1994, File No. 1/87.

FHC, SPO v. *Colonel Mengistu Hailemariam et al.*, (Revised Indictment), 28 November 1995, File No. 1/87.

FHC, SPO v. *Colonel Mengistu Hailemariam et al.*, (Ruling on Preliminary Objections), 10 October 1995, File No. 1/87.

FHC, SPO v. *Colonel Mengistu Hailemariam et al.*, (Sentencing Judgment), 11 January 2007, File No. 1/87.

FHC, SPO v. *Colonel Mengistu Hailemariam et al.*, (Trial Judgment), 12 December 2006, File No. 1/87.

FHC, SPO v. *Colonel Mengistu Hailemariam et al.*, (Trial Ruling), 23 January 2003, File No.1/87.

FHC, SPO v. *Colonel Tesfaye Woldeselassie Eshete et al.*, (Revised Indictment), 09 November 2000, File No. 03101.

FHC, SPO v. *Colonel Tesfaye Woldeselassie Eshete et al.*, (Sentencing Judgment), 4 August 2003, File No. 03101.

FHC, SPO v. *Debela Dinsa Wege et al.*, (Indictment), 8 November 2000, File No.912/89.

FHC, SPO v. *Debela Dinsa Wege et al.*, (Sentencing Judgment), 10 August 2007, File No.912/89.

FHC, SPO v. *Demissie Weldemariam et al.* (Initial Indictment), 23 December 1996, File No. 963/1989.

FHC, SPO v. *Elias Tsegaye et al.*, (Sentencing Judgment), 4 May 2001, File No. 632/89.

FHC, SPO v. *Eshetu Alemu*, (Sentencing Judgment), 8 May 2000, File No. 921/89.

FHC, SPO v. *Eshetu Alemu*, (Trial Judgment), 8 May 2000, File No. 921/89.

FHC, SPO v. *Eshetu Shenkutie et al.*, (Sentencing Judgment), 2 October 2000, File No. 940/89.

FHC, SPO v. *Feyyisa Seboka et al.*, (Trial Judgment), 20 November 2000, File No. 934/89.

FHC, SPO v. *Gebremedehen Berga Barosa et al.*, (Sentencing Judgment),11 April 2001, File No. 646/89.

FHC, SPO v. *Geremew Debele*, (Trial Judgement), 8 February 1999, File No. 952/89.

FHC, SPO v. *Geremew Debele*, (Indictment), 23 December 1997, File No. 952/89.

FHC, SPO v. *Geremew Debele*, (Ruling on Preliminary Objections), 13 April 1998, File No. 952/89.

FHC, SPO v. *Geremew Debele*, (Trial Ruling), 8 February 1999), File No. 952/89.

FHC, SPO v. *Gesegesse Gebremeskel Aterega et al.*, (Indictment), 23 December 1996, File No. 03099/1989.

FHC, SPO v. *Gesgese Gebremeskel Ateraga et al.*, (Sentencing Judgment), 24 February 2006, File No.03099.

LIST OF CASES 453

FHC, SPO v. *Getachew Tek'eba*, (Sentencing Judgment), 9 November 1999, File no. 914/89.

FHC, SPO v. *Getachew Tekeba* (Indictment), 23 November 1996, File No. 914/89.

FHC, SPO v. *Getahun Zenebe Woldeselassie et al.*, (Revised Indictment) 16 June 1999, File No. 962/89

FHC, SPO v. *Getahun Zenebe Woldeselassie et al.*, (Sentencing Judgment) 09 November 2003, File No. 962/89.

FHC, SPO v. *Hailu Burayu Sima et al.*, (Trial Ruling), 13 June 2003, File No. 428/92.

FHC, SPO v. *Hailu Burrayyu Sima et al.*, (Trial Judgment), 31 October 205, File No. 428/92.

FHC, SPO v. *Kalbessa Negewo*, (Indictment), 13 January 2008, File No. 62185.

FHC, SPO v. *Kalbessa Negawo*, (Trial Ruling), 14 January 2009, File No. 62185.

FHC, SPO v. *Kassaye Aragaw et al.*, (Sentencing Judgment),17 November 2005, File No.03114.

FHC, SPO v. *Kidanemariam Berehanu Gemta*, (Sentencing judgment), 7 February 2000, File No. 642/89.

FHC, SPO v. *Legesse Asfaw et al.*, (Sentencing Judgment), 4 April 2008, File No. 03116.

FHC, SPO v. *Legesse Asfaw et al.*, (Trial Judgment), 4 March 2008, File No. 03116.

FHC, SPO v. *Melaku Teferra* (Indictment), 23 November 1996, File No. 03112.

FHC, SPO v. *Melaku Teferra*, (Judgment and Sentence), 8 December 2005, File No. 03112.

FHC, SPO v. *Negash Woldemichael et al.*, (Sentencing Judgment), 17 November 2006, File No. 03114.

FHC, SPO v. *Petros Gebre et al.*, (Sentencing Judgment), 28 February 2005, File No. 1459/92.

FHC, SPO v. *Seleshi Mekuria et al.*, (Sentencing Judgment), 8 November 2000, File No. 959/89.

FHC, SPO v. *Tesfaye Belayeneh* et al., (Indictment), 23 December 1997, File No. 934/89.

FHC, SPO v. *Teshome Ashenie*, (Indictment), 29 June 2000, File No. 1937/1992.

FHC, SPO v. *Teshome Bayyu et al.*, (Indictment), 15 May 2001, File No. 07415.

FHC, SPO v. *Teshome Bayyu et al.*, (Sentencing Judgment), 22 January 2009, File No. 07415.

FHC, SPO v. *Teshome Bayyu et al.*, (Trial Judgment), 15 January 2009, File No. 07415.

FHC, SPO v. *Teshome Kebede* et al., (Indictment), 23 December 1997, File No. 931/89.

FHC, SPO v. *Tsegaye Mamo et al.,* (Sentencing Judgment), 3 August 2003, File No. 631/89.

FHC, SPO v. *Zenebe Ayele et al.,* (Indictment), 23 December 1997, File No 641/89.

FHC, SPO v. *Zenebe Ayele et al.,* (Sentencing Judgment), 28 July 2003, File No. 641/89.

FSC CB, *Abebayehu Samuel* v. *Oromia Justice Bureau,* (Decision), 4 October 2017, File No. 135787.

FSC CB, *Bihonegn Demessie* v. *Tigray Regional State Prosecutor,* (Decision), 24 July 2013, File No. 88542.

FSC CB, *Federal Prosecutor v Semir Ibrahim Hibu,* (Decision), 21 June 2013, File No. 95440.

FSC CB, *Federal Prosecutor* v. *Berihun Fekadu,* (Decision), 10 June 2011, File No. 59356.

FSC CB, *Fesseha Abay and Hiwot Yeseraw* v. *Federal Prosecutor,* (Decision), 3 May 2010, File No. 53612.

FSC CB, *Fesseha Tadesse Mewucha* v. *Federal Prosecutor,* (Decision), 4 October 2014, File No. 80815.

FSC CB, *Girma Desta* v. *Tigray Regional State Prosecutor,* (Decision), 21 May 2008, File No. 34280.

FSC CB, *Mekonnen Welelaw* v. *Federal Ethics and Anti-Corruption Commission Prosecutor,* (Decision), 26 June 2014, File No. 96503.

FSC CB, *Prosecutor* v. *Ennat Hanacho et al.,* (Decision),15 November 2011, File No. 75980.

FSC CB, *Prosecutor* v. *Semachew Lengereh Alemu* (Decision) 15 November 2011, File No. 75980.

FSC CB, *Prosecutor* v. *Woldu Gebrezgi et al.,* (Decision), 29 August 2014, File No.94070.

FSC CB, SNNPRS *Prosecutor v Solomon Dessalegn,* (Decision),10 June 2013 File No. 95438.

FSC CB, *Tamerat Geleta et al* v. *Federal Prosecutor,* (Decision), 25 July 2012, File no. 66943.

FSC CB, *Worku Fekadu and Shume Ararsso* v. *Prosecutor for Benishangul-Gumuz Regional State,* (Decision), 25 January 2013, File No. 75387.

FSC CB, *Zewedu Tesfaye Semegne* v. *Tigray State Bureau of Justice,* (Decisions), 1 December 2014, File No. 93577

FSC, *Abera Afewerke* v. SPO, (Statement of Appeal), 1 October 2002, File No. 7559.

FSC, *Colonel Mekonnen Semeneh et al.* v. SPO (Appeals Judgement), 29 November 2002, File No. 6511.

FSC, *Colonel Nemera Disassa* v. SPO, (Appeals Judgment), 8 June 2001, File No 6508.

FSC, *Federal Anti-Corruption and Ethics Commission* v. *Asmare Abate* and *Kebede Kiros,* (Appeals Judgment), 24 May 2006, File No. 18127

FSC, *Federal Prosecutor* v. *Ikok Abuna Abong,* (Decision), 18 July 2005, File No. 19523/97.

FSC, *Feyissa Saboka* v. *SPO,* (Appeals Judgment), 1 June 2001, File No. 6509.

FSC, *Geremew Qenno* v. *SPO,* (Appeals Judgment), 29 June 2001, File No. 6659.

FSC, *Gizaw Tadesse et al.* v. *SPO,* (Appeals Judgment), 30 April 2002, File No. 6470.

FSC, *Haregewoine* v. *SPO,* (Appeals Judgment), 29 October 2002, File No. 7369.

FSC, *Maseresha Abebe* v. *SPO,* (Appeals Judgment), 2 July 2001, File No 6688.

FSC, *Melaku Rufael* v. *SPO,* (Appeals Judgment), 2 August 2004, File No. 13241.

FSC, *Jarmosa Ayansa Jamato* v. *Federal Prosecutor,* (Appeals Decision), 07 April 2010, File No. 53594.

FSC, *SPO* v. *Basha Bekele Fasil and Abera Lemma,* (Appeals Judgment), 26 October 1999, File No. 4166/92.

FSC, *SPO* v. *Colonel Mengistu Hailemariam et al.,* (Appeal Judgment), 26 May 2008, File No. 30181.

FSC, *SPO* v. *Girma Demessie et al.,* (Appeals Judgment), 26 February 2002, File No. 5853, 2.

FSC, *SPO* v. *Gizaw Tadesse et al.*, (Appeals Judgement), 30 April 2002, File No. 6471.

FSC, *SPO* v. *Hailu Burrayu Sima et al.,* (Appeals Judgment), 18 July 2007, File No.22983.

FSC, *SPO* v. *Melaku Teferra,* (Appeal Judgment), 1 December 2006, File No. 23776.

FSC, *SPO* v. *Mergia Bededa,* (Appeals Judgment), 4 December 2006, File No. 21345.

FSC, *SPO* v. *Selashi Tessema et al.,* (Appeals Judgment), 7 June 2002, File No. 6/89.

FSC, *SPO* v. *Tafa Gurmu,* (Appeals Judgment), 22 March 2001, File No.4896.

FSC, *SPO* v. *Teshome Kebede,* (Appeals Judgment), 26 March 2002, File No. 6486.

FSC, *SPO* v. *Tiruneh Habteselassie,* (Appeals Judgment), 1 December 2006, File No. 21163.

FSC, *SPO* v. *Wubeshiet Zegeye et al.,* (Appeals Judgment), 30 April 2007, File No.22340.

FSC, *SPO* v. *Zegeye Teferra et al.,* (Appeals Judgment), 15 May 2003, File No. 23192, 6.

FSC, *Teshome Kebede et al.,* v. *SPO,* (Appeal Judgment), 26 March 2002, File no. 6486.

FSC, *The Federal Anti-Corruption Commission* v. *Alemetsehaye Wondemu,* (Appeal Judgment, 16 June 2006), File No. 2093.

FSC, *Tolossa Waqoyya* v. SPO, (Appeals Judgment), 30 January 2003, File No. 7472.

FSC, *Ziyad Alemu* v. SPO, (Appeals Judgment), 13 March 2002, File No 7358, 4.

HSC, SPO v. *Amanshoa Gebrewolde et al.,* (Trial Judgment), 2 February 2004, File No.4/90/1.

HSC, SPO v. *Amanshoa Gebrewolde et al.,* (Trial Ruling), 5 August 2003, File No. 4/90/1/(00021).

HSC, SPO v. *Bekele Kassa Abbadima et al.,* (Revised Indictment), 3 October 2003, File No. HSC 04/1995.

HSC, SPO v. *Bekele Kassa Abbadima et al.,* (Trial Judgment), 26 April 2004, File No. 4/95(00254).

HSC, SPO v. *Colonel Zelleke Beyene et al.,* (Trial Judgment), 5 May 2004, File No. 2/95 (00252).

HSC, SPO v. *Denbi Disassa et al.,* (Indictment), 3 October 2002, File No. HSC 3/95.

HSC, SPO v. *Denbi Disassa et al.,* (Sentencing Judgment), 23 April 2004, File No. 3/95.

HSC, SPO v. *General Solomon Negussie et al.* (SPO responses to the Defendants preliminary objection to the indictment), 03 December 1999, File No. 04/1990.

HSC, SPO v. *General Solomon Negussie et al.,* (Defendants preliminary objection to the indictment), 3 December 1999, File No. 04/1990.

HSC, SPO v. *General Solomon Negussie et al.,* (Revised Indictment) 3 December 1999, File No. 04/1990.

HSC, SPO v. *General Solomon Negussie et al.,* (SPO Response to Preliminary Objections), 24 May 1999, File No. 4/91.

HSC, SPO v. *Girma Sisay Mengesha et al.,* (Indictment) 23 December 1996, File No. 05/1990,

HSC, SPO v. *Hailu Iticha et al.,* (Revised Indictment), 30 January 2000, File No. 04/1993.

HSC, SPO v. *Tadesse Tegegne et al.,* (Sentencing Judgment), 23 July 2004, File No. 5/95.

OSC, SPO v. *Aman Gobena et al.,* (Sentencing Judgment), 23 April 2002, File No. 8/92.

OSC, SPO v. *Aman Gobena et al.,* (Trial Judgment), 11 April 2000, File No. 8/92.

OSC, SPO v. *Brigadier General Tedela Desta et al.,* (Initial Indictment), 20 September 1999, File No. 28/85.

OSC, SPO v. *Brigadier General Tedela Desta et al.,* (Revised Indictment), 10 October 1999, File No. 1/1989.

OSC, SPO v. *Brigadier General Tedla Desta et al.,* (Trial Judgment), 13 May 2001, File No. 24/92.

OSC, SPO v. *Colonel Debeb Hurrissie et al.,* (Indictment), 16 November 1999, File No. 463/92.

OSC, SPO v. *Colonel Sahile Barie et al.,* (Indictment), 16 November 1999, File No. 7/92.

SNNPRS SC, SPO v. *Aregaw Hailemariam et al.,* (Sentencing judgment), 14 July 2005, File No. 3647.

SNNPRS SC, SPO v. *Mezemer Abebe at al.,* (Sentencing Judgment), 5 March 2005, File No. 0457.

SNNPRS SC, SPO v. *Mekonnen Gelan et al.,* (Revised Indictment), 22 May 2001, File No. 1338/97.

SNNPRS SC, SPO v. *Mekonnen Gelan et al.,* (Sentencing Judgment), 4 June 2005, File No. 1338.

SNNPRS SC, SPO v. *Mezemer Abebe et al.,* (Trial Ruling), 16 November 2003, File No. 0457.

TSC, SPO v. *Aseffa Belay Gezahegn et al.,* (Trial Judgment), 11 December 2003, File No. 06/1992.

TSC, SPO v. *Aseffa Belaye Gezahegn et al.,* (Indictment), 28 December 2000, File No. 06/1992.

TSC, SPO v. *Colonel Ayanaw Mengistie et al.,* (Ruling on Preliminary Objections), 23 November 1999, File No. 3/90.

TSC, SPO v. *Colonel Ayenaw Mengistie et al.,* (Indictment), 30 September 1999, File No. 3/90.

TSC, SPO v. *Teferra Woldetensay et al.,* (Indictment), 28 December 2000, File No. 01/1992.

TSC, SPO v. *Tekleberehane Negash et al.,* (Sentencing Judgment), 23 April 2002, File No. 1/91.

TSC, SPO v. *Tekleberehen Negash et al.,* (Indictment), 12 February 1998, File No. 01/1991.

TSC, SPO v. *Yekuno Amelak et al.,* (sentencing judgment), 3 March 2003, File No. 4/92.

Other National Jurisdictions

Australia
Kruger v. *The Commonwealth* (1997) 190 CLR 1.
Polyukhovich v. *The Commonwealth of Australia and Another* (1991) 172 CLR 501 F.C. 91/026.
Canada
Regina v. *Finta*, 1 S.C.R. 701 (Canada Sup. Ct. 24 March 1994).

France
Fédération Nationale de Déportés et Internés Résistants et Patriotes And Others v. Barbie, 78 International Law Reports 125, 130 (Cass. crim.1983).
Israel
District Court of Jerusalem, *Attorney General v. Adolf Eichmann*, Criminal Case No. 40/61, Judgment, 11 December 1961.
South Africa
Azanian People's Organization (AZAPO) and Others v. President of the Republic of South Africa and Others (CCT17/96) [1996] ZACC 16; 1996 (8) BCLR 1015; 1996 (4) SA 672, 25 July 1996.
Spain
Audiencia Nacional, Auto de la Sala de lo Penal de la Audiencia Nacional confirmando la jurisdicción de España para conocer de los crímenes de genocidio y terrorismo cometidos durante la dictadura chilena, (5 November 1998), Case 173/98.
The Netherlands
District Court of The Hague, *Prosecutor v. Eshetu Alemu*, Judgment, 15 December 2017, (ECLI:NL:RBDHA:2017:14782).
United States of America
Abebe-Jiri v. Negewo, 519 U.S. 830, 117 S.Ct. 96 (Mem), 136 L.Ed.2d 51, 65 USLW 3258.
District Court for the District of Colorado, *United States v. Worku*, (27 May 2014) D.C. No. 1:12-CR-00346-JLK-1.
United States Court of Appeal, (Eleventh Circuit, Judgment, 10 January 1996), Case No. 93–9133, *Abebe-Jiri v. Negewo*.
United States District Court, *Abebe-Jiri v. Negewo*, Case No. 1:90-CV-2010-GET, N.D. Georgia, Atlanta Division, 20 August 1993 (1993 WL 814304).
United States District Court, *Negewo v. Chertoff*, (S.D. Alabama, Northern Division, 5 January 2007) Civil Action No. 06-00631-WS-C (2007 WL 38336).

International Criminal Courts and Tribunals

Extraordinary Chambers in the Courts of Cambodian
Prosecutor v. Nuon Chea and Khieu Samphan, Trial Chamber, (Judgment), 16 November 2018, Case File/Dossier No. 002/19-09-2007/ECCC/TC.
International Criminal Court
Prosecutor v. Ahmad Al Faqi Al Mahdi, Trial Chamber VIII, (Judgment and sentence), 27 September 2016, ICC-01-12-01/15.

Prosecutor v. Bemba et al., Trial Chamber VII, (Judgment), 22 March 2017, ICC-01/05-01/13.

Prosecutor v. Germain Katanga, Trial Chamber II, (Sentencing Judgment) 23 May 2014, CC-01/04-01/07-3484.

Prosecutor v. Jean-Pierre Bemba Gombo et al., Trial Chamber, (Judgment), 19 October 2016, ICC-01/05-02/13.

Prosecutor v. Lubanga, Pre-Trial Chamber I, (Decision on the Confirmation of Charges), 29 January 2007, ICC-01/04-01/06.

Prosecutor v. Omar Hassan Ahmad Al Bashir, Pre-Trial Chamber I, (*Warrant* of Arrest for Omar Hassan Ahmad Al Bashir), 4 March 2009, ICC-02/05-01/09-1.

Prosecutor v. Omar Hassan Ahmad Al Bashir, Pre-Trial Chamber I, (*Second Warrant* of Arrest for Omar Hassan Ahmad Al Bashir) 11 July 2010, ICC-02/05-01/09-1.

Prosecutor v. Thomas Lubanga Dyilo, Appeals Chamber, (Judgment on the appeals of the Prosecutor and Mr. Thomas Lubanga Dyilo against the 'Decision on Sentence Pursuant to Article 76 of the Statute), 1 December 2014, ICC-01/04-01/06 A4A6.

Prosecutor v. Thomas Lubanga Dyilo, Trial Chamber I (Decision on Sentence Pursuant to Article 76 of the Statute), 10 July 2012, ICC-01/04-01/06.

International Criminal Tribunal for the Former Yugoslavia

Prosecutor v. Aleksovski, Appeals Chamber, (Judgment), 24 March 2000, IT-95-14/1-A.

Prosecutor v. Babić, Appeals Chamber, (Judgment on Sentencing Appeal), 18 July 2005, IT-03-72-A.

Prosecutor v. Blagojević and Jokić, Trial Chamber, (Judgment), 17 January 2005, IT-02-60-T.

Prosecutor v. Blaškić, Trial Chamber, (Judgment),3 March 2000, IT-95–14-T.

Prosecutor v. Blaskić, Appeals Chamber, (Judgment) 29 July 2004, IT-95-14-A.

Prosecutor v. Boškoski and Tarčulovski, Trial Chamber, (Judgment) 10 July 2008, IT, 04-82-T.

Prosecutor v. Brđanin, Trial Chamber, (Judgment), 1 September 2004, IT-99-36.

Prosecutor v. Delalić et al., Appeals Chamber, (Judgment), 20 February 2001, IT-96-21-A.

Prosecutor v. Dragan Nikolić, Appeals Chamber, (Judgment on Sentencing Appeal), 4 February 2005, IT-94-02.

Prosecutor v. Dragomir Milošević, Appeals Chamber, (Judgment) 12 November 2009, IT-98-29-11.

Prosecutor v. Hadžihasanović, Appeals Chamber, (Judgment), 22 April 2008, IT-01-47-AR72.

Prosecutor v. *Hadžihasanović*, Trial Chamber, (Judgment), 15 March 2006, IT-01-47-AR72.

Prosecutor v. *Haradinaj*, Trial Chamber, (Judgment), 3 April 2008, IT-04-84-T.

Prosecutor v. *Jelisić*, Appeals Chamber, (Judgment), 5 July 2001, IT-95-10-A.

Prosecutor v. *Jelisić*, Trial Chamber, (Judgment), 14 December 1999, IT-95-10-T.

Prosecutor v. *Kordić and Čerkez*, Appeals Chamber, (Judgment), 17 December 2004, IT-95-14/2-A.

Prosecutor v. *Krnojelac*, Trial Chamber, (Judgment), 15 March 2002, IT-97-25-T.

Prosecutor v. *Krstić*, Appeals Chamber (Judgment), 19 April 2004, Case No. IT-98-33-A.

Prosecutor v. *Krstić*, Trial Chamber, (Judgment) 2 August 2001, IT-98-33.

Prosecutor v. *Kunarac et al.*, Appeals Chamber, (Judgment), 12 July 2002, IT-96-23/1-A.

Prosecutor v. *Kupreškić*, Trial Chamber, (Judgment), 14 January 2000, IT-95-16.

Prosecutor v. *Limaj et al.*, Appeals Chamber, (Judgment) 27 September 2007, IT-03-66-A.

Prosecutor v. *Milutinović et al.*, Appeals Chamber, (Decision on Dragoljub Ojdanić's Motion Challenging Jurisdiction – Joint Criminal Enterprise), 21 May 2003, IT-99-37-AR72.

Prosecutor v. *Mladić*, Trial Chamber I, (Judgment), 22 November 2017, IT-O9-92-T.

Prosecutor v. *Nikolić*, Appeals Chamber, (Judgment on Sentencing), 8 March 2006, IT-02-60/1-A.

Prosecutor v. *Nikolić*, Trial Chamber, (Judgment), 2 December 2003, IT-02-60/1-S.

Prosecutor v. *Nikolić*, Trial Chamber, (Sentencing Judgment),12 December 2003, IT-02-60/1/S.

Prosecutor v. *Popović et al.*, Appeals Chamber, (Judgment),30 January 2015, IT-05-88-A.

Prosecutor v. *Popović et al.*, Trial Chamber, (Judgment), 10 June 2010, IT-05-88-T.

Prosecutor v. *Sikirica et al.*, Trial Chamber, (Judgment on Defense Motions to Acquit), 3 September 2001, IT-95-8-T.

Prosecutor v. *Simić*, Trial Chamber II, (Sentencing Judgment),17 October 2002, IT-95-9/2-S.

Prosecutor v. *Solobodan Milošević*, (Trial Decision on Motion for Judgment of Acquittal of 16 June 2004), IT-02-54-T.

Prosecutor v. *Stakić*, Appeals Chamber, (Judgment), 22 March 2006), IT-97-24-A.

Prosecutor v. *Stakić*, Trial Chamber, (Judgment), 31 July 2003, IT-97-24-T.

Prosecutor v. *Strugar*, Appeals Chamber, (Judgment), 17 July 2008, IT-01-42-A.

LIST OF CASES 461

Prosecutor v. *Tadić*, Appeals Chamber, (Decision on the defense motion for interlocutory appeal on jurisdiction), 2 October 1995, IT-94-1-AR72.

Prosecutor v. *Tadić*, Trial Chamber, (Judgment), 7 May 1997, IT-94-1-T.

Prosecutor v. *Tolimir*, Trial Chamber II, (Judgment), 12 December 2012, IT-05-88.

International Criminal Tribunal for Rwanda

Prosecutor v. *Akayesu,* Trial Chamber, (Judgment), 2 September 1998, ICTR-96-4-T.

Prosecutor v. *Bagaragaza,* Appeals Chamber, (Decision on Rule 11*bis* Appeal), 30 August 2006, Case No. ICTR-05-86-AR11bis.

Prosecutor v. *Bagasora et al.*, Appeals Chamber, (Judgment), 14 December 2011, ICTR-98-41-A.

Prosecutor v. *Bagilishema,* Trial Chamber, (Judgment), 7 June 2001, ICTR-95-1A-T.

Prosecutor v. *Elizaphan and Ntakirutimana,* Trial Chamber, (Judgment and Sentence), 21 February 2003, ICTR-96-10 & ICTR-96-17-T.

Prosecutor v. *Gacumbitsi,* Trial Chamber, (Judgment), 17 June 2004, ICTR-2001-64-T.

Prosecutor v. *Gatete,* Appeals Chamber, (Judgment), 09 June October 2012, ICTR-00-61-A.

Prosecutor v. *Kajelijeli,* Appeals Chamber, (Judgment), 23 May 2005, ICTR-98–441.

Prosecutor v. *Kajelijeli,* Trial Chamber, (Judgment), 1 December 2003, ICTR-98-44A-T.

Prosecutor v. *Kambanda,* Trial Chamber, (Judgment and Sentence), 4 September 1998, ICTR 97-23-S.

Prosecutor v. *Kamuhanda,* Trial Chamber, (Judgment), 22 January 2004, ICTR-95-54A-T.

Prosecutor v. *Kayishema and Ruzindana,* Appeals Chamber, (Judgment), 1 June 2001, ICTR-95-1-A.

Prosecutor v. *Kayishema and Ruzindana,* Trial Chamber, (Judgment) 21 May 1999, ICTR-95-1-T.

Prosecutor v. *Kayishema and Ruzindana,* Trial Chamber, (Sentencing Judgment), 21 May 1999, ICTR-95-1-T.

Prosecutor v. *Mpampara,* Trial Chamber, (Judgment), 11 September 2006, ICTR-01-65-T.

Prosecutor v. *Musema,* Trial Chamber, (Judgment), 27 January 2000, ICTR-96-13-T.

Prosecutor v. *Muvunyi,* Trial Chamber, (Judgment), 15 September 2006, ICTR-2000-55A-T.

Prosecutor v. *Nahimana et al.*, Appeals Chamber, (Judgment), 28 November 2007, ICTR 99-52-A.

Prosecutor v. *Nahimana et al.*, Trial Chamber, (Judgment and Sentence), 3 December 2003, ICTR-99-52-T.

Prosecutor v. *Ndinddabahizi,* Appeals Chamber, (Judgment) 16 January 2007, ICTR-01-71-A.

Prosecutor v. *Niyitegeka,* Appeals Chamber, (Judgment), 9 July 2004, ICTR-96-14-A.

Prosecutor v. *Nizeyimana,* Appeals Chamber, (Judgment), 29 September 2014, ICTR-00-55C-A.

Prosecutor v. *Ntabakuze,* Appeals Chamber, (Judgment), 8 May 2012, ICTR-98-41A-A.

Prosecutor v. *Ntakirutimana et al.*, Trial Chamber, (Judgment) 21 February 2003, ICTR-96-10.

Prosecutor v. *Nyiramasuhuko et al.*, Appeals Chamber, (Judgment), 14 December 2015, ICTR-98-42-A.

Prosecutor v. *Ruggiu,* Trial Chamber, (Judgment and Sentence), 1 June 2000, ICTR-97-32-I.

Prosecutor v. *Rutaganda,* Appeals Chamber, (Judgment), 26 May 2003, ICTR-96-3-A.

Prosecutor v. *Rutaganda,* Trial Chamber (Judgment), 6 December 1999, ICTR-96-3-T.

Prosecutor v. *Rutaganira,* Trial Chamber, (Judgment), 14 March 2005, ICTR-95-3-T.

Prosecutor v. *Semanza,* Appeals Chamber, (Judgment), 20 May 2005, ICTR-97-20-A.

Prosecutor v. *Semanza,* Trial Chamber, (Judgment), 15 May 2003, ICTR-97-20-T.

Prosecutor v. *Seromba,* Trial Chamber, (Judgment), 13 December 2006, ICTR-2001-66-T.

Prosecutor v. *Simba,* Appeals Chamber, (Judgment), 27 November 2007, ICTR-01-76-A.

Mechanism for International Criminal Tribunals

Prosecutor v. *Stanislav Galić,* (Reasons for the President's Decision to Deny the Early Release of Stanislav *Galić* and Decision on Prosecution Motion), 23 June 2015, MICT-14-83-ES.

Prosecutor v. *Stanislav Galić,* (Reasons for the President's Decision to Deny the Early Release of Stanislav *Galić*), 18 January 2017, MICT-14-83-ES.

Special Court of Serra Leone

Prosecutor v. *Brima et al.,* Trial Chamber, (Judgment), 20 June 2007, SCL-04-16-T.

LIST OF CASES 463

Prosecutor v. *Fofana et al.*, Trial Chamber, (Judgment), 2 August 2007, SCSL-04-14-T.
Special Tribunal for Lebanon
Prosecutor v. *Ayyash et al*, Appeals Chamber, (Judgment), 1 November 2012, STL-11-01/PT/AC/AR126.1.
Unnamed defendants v. *the Prosecutor*, Appeals Chamber, (Interlocutory Decision on the Applicable Law: Terrorism, Conspiracy, Homicide, Perpetration, Cumulative Charging), 16 February 2011, STL- 11- 01/I.

Other International and Regional Courts and Bodies

African Commission on Human and People's Rights
Noah Kazingachire, John Chitsenga, Elias Chemvura and Batanai Hadzisi (represented by Zimbabwe Human Rights NGO Forum) v. *Zimbabwe*, (Decision), May 2012, Communication 295/042.
Commission Nationale des Droits de l'Homme et des Libertés v. *Chad*, October 1995, (Comm. No. 74/92 (1995)).
Amnesty International and Others v. *Sudan*, 15 November 1999, (Comm. No. 48/90, 50/91, 52/91, 89/93 (1999).
Constitutional Rights Project, Civil Liberties Organisation and Media Rights Agenda v. *Nigeria*, 15 November 1999, (Comm Nos. 140/94, 141/94, 145/95 (1999).
Haregewoin Gabre-Selassie and IHRDA (on behalf of former Dergue officials) v. *Ethiopia*, (Decision), 12 October 2013, Comm. No. 301/2005.
Economic Community of West African States Court of Justice
Hissein Habré v. *Republic of Senegal*, Judgment No: ECW/CCJ /Jud/06/10, 18 November 2010, General Role No. ECW/CCJ/App/07/08.
European Court of Human Rights
Colozza v. *Italy*, (Judgment), 12 February 1985, Application, No. 9024/80.
Jorgic v. *Germany*, (Judgment), 12 July 2007, Application No. 74613/0.
Kafkaris v. *Cyprus*, Grand Chamber, (Judgment), 12 February 2008, Application No. 21906/04.
Kolk and Kislyiy v. *Estonia*, (Decision on Admissibility), 17 January 2006, Application Nos. 23052/04 and 24018/04.
Kononov v. *Latvia*, Grand Chamber, (Judgment), 17 May 2010, Application No. 36376/04.
Korbely v. *Hungary*, Grand Chamber, (Judgment) 19 September 2008, Application No. 9174/02.

Kuznetsov v. *Ukraine*, (Judgment, Merits and Just Satisfaction), 29 April 2003, Application No. 39042/97.

M.C. v. *Bulgaria*, (Judgment), 4 December 2003, Application No. 39272/98.

Maktouf and Damjanović v. *Bosnia and Herzegovina*, Grand Chamber, (Judgment), 18 July 2013, Applications Nos. 2312/08 and 34179/08.

Nachova and others v. *Bulgaria*, (Judgment), 6 July 2005, Applications Nos. 43577/98 and 43579/98.

S.W. v. the United Kingdom, (Judgment), 22 November 1995, Application No 20166/92.

Sejdovic v. *Italy*, (Judgment), 1 March 2006, Application No. 56581/00.

Šimšić v. *Bosnia and Herzegovina*, (Judgment), 10 April 2012, Application No. 51552/10.

Soering v. *United Kingdom*, (Judgment), 7 July 1989, Application No. 14038/88.

Streletz, Kessler and Krenz v. *Germany*, (Judgment), 22 March 2001 Applications Nos. 34044/96, 35532/97 and 44801/9.

Tepe v. *Turkey*, (Judgment, Merits and Just Satisfaction), 9 May 2003, Application No. 27244/95.

Timurtas v. *Turkey*, (Judgment, Merits and Just Satisfaction), 13 June 2000, Application No. 23531/94.

van Anraat v. *the Netherlands* (Decision on Admissibility), 6 July 2010, Application No.65389/09.

Vasiliauskas v. *Lithuania*, Grand Chamber, (Judgment), 20 October 2015, Application No. 35343/05

Vinter and Others v. *the United Kingdom*, Grand Chamber, (Judgment), 9 July 2013, Applications Nos. 66069/09, 130/10 and 3896/10.

Human Rights Committee

David Michael Nicholas v. *Australia*, Communication No. 1080/2002, U.N. Doc. CCPR/C/80/D/1080/2002 (2004).

Klaus Dieter Baumgarten v. *Germany*, Communication No. 960/2000, U.N. Doc. CCPR/C/78/D/960/2000 (2003).

Inter-American Court of Human Rights

Luis Alfredo Almonacid Arellano et al. v. *Chile*, (Judgment, Preliminary Objections, Merits, Reparations and Costs), 26 September 2006, Report No. 44/02, Case No. 12.057.

Cantoral-Benavides v. *Peru*, (Judgment, Reparations and Costs), 3 December 2001, Series. C No.88.

Cesti Hurtado v. *Peru*, (Judgment, Reparation and Costs), 31 May 2001, Series. C No. 86.

Villagrán-Morales et al. (The Street Children) v. *Guatemala*, (Judgment, Reparations and Costs), 26 May 2001, Series. C No. 63.

Trujillo-Oroza v. *Bolivia*, (Judgment, Reparations and Costs), 27 February 2002, Series C No. 92.

Myrna Mack Chang v. *Guatemala*, (Judgment (Merits, Reparations and Costs) of 25 November 2003, Series C No. 101.

Baldeón-García v. *Perú*, (Judgment (Merits, Reparations, and Costs of 6 April 2006), Series C No. 147.

Blanco-Romero et al. v. *Venezuela*, (Judgment, Merits, Reparations and Costs), 28 November 2005, Series C No. 138.

Ituango Massacres v. *Colombia*, (Judgment, Preliminary Objections, Merits, Reparations and Costs), 1 July 2006, Series C No. 148.

Mapiripán Massacre v. Colombia, (Judgment, Merits, Reparations, and Costs), 15 September 2005, Series C No. 134.

The Massacres of El Mozote and Nearby Places v. *El Salvador*, (Judgment, Merits, Reparations, and Costs), 25 October 2012), Series C No. 252.

Velásquez-Rodríguez v. *Honduras*, (Judgment), 29 July 1988, Series C No. 4.

El Amparo v. *Venezuela*, (Judgment, Reparations), 14 September 1996, Series C No. 28.

International Court of Arbitration

Reports of International Arbitral Awards, Eritrea-Ethiopia Claims Commission, between *Federal Democratic Republic of Ethiopia and the State of Eritrea* 'Partial Award: Jus Ad Bellum, Ethiopia's Claims 1–8', 19 December 2005.

International Court of Justice

United Kingdom v. *Iran,* Anglo-Iranian Oil Co, (Judgment), 22 July 1952.

Bosnia and Herzegovina v. *Serbia and Montenegro*, (Judgment), 26 February 2007, ICJ Reports 20076.

Bosnia and Herzegovina v. *Serbia and Montenegro*, (Judgment of 26 February 2007) ICJ Reports 20076, 122, 179.

Legality of the Threat or Use of Nuclear Weapons (Advisory Opinion), ICJ Reports 1996, 257.

Democratic Republic of the Congo v. *Uganda*, Case Concerning Armed Activities on the Territory of the Congo, (Judgment), 19 December 2005.

Case Concerning the Arrest Warrant of 11 April 2000, *Democratic Republic of the Congo* v. *Belgium*, Judgment, 14 February 2002.

South West Africa Cases: *Ethiopia* v. *South Africa* and *Liberia* v. *South Africa*, Second Phase, 1966.

List of Laws

Ethiopian Laws

1955 Revised Constitution of Ethiopia, *entered in to force* 2 November 1955

A Proclamation to Provide for the Establishment of a Special Court: Proclamation No.215/1981.

A proclamation to provide for the granting of amnesty to outlaws who have committed homicide and other offences, Proclamation No.29/1975, *entered into force* 4 February 1975)

Administration of Justice Proclamation, Proclamation 1/1942,

Commission of Inquiry Establishment Proclamation, Proclamation No. 326 of 1974, *entered into force* 12 July 1974.

Criminal Procedure Code of Ethiopia, Proclamation No. 185 of 1961, *entered into force* 2 February 1962.

Defense Forces (Amendment) Proclamation, Proclamation No. 123/1998, *entered into force* 30 June 1998, Article 38(1).

Definitions of Power of Provisional Military Administration Council and of its Chairman, Proclamation No.2 /1974, *entered into force* 15 September 1974.

Draft Criminal Code of Peoples Democratic Republic of Ethiopia, September 1989.

Ethiopian Imperial Order No. 1784; FO 372/4385, T. 19415.

Extradition Treaty between the Transitional Government of Ethiopia and the Republic of Djibouti, signed in Djibouti on 28 April 1994.

Extradition Treaty between the Transitional Government of Ethiopia and the Republic of Djibouti Ratification Proclamation, Proclamation No. 104/1994, *entered into force* 28 September 1994.

Federal Courts Proclamation Re-amendment Proclamation, Proclamation No.454/2005, *entered into force* 14 June 2005,

Federal Crimes Proclamation, Proclamation No. 138 of 1953, *entered into force* 25 September 1953.

Federal Negarit Gazeta Establishment Proclamation, Proclamation No. 3/1995

FSC, Revised Sentencing Guideline, No. 2/2013 *entered into force* 12 October 2013.

Government Ownership and Control of the Means of Production Proclamation, Proclamation No. 26 of 1974, *entered into force,* 7 February 1975.

Government Ownership of Urban Lands and Extra Houses Proclamation: Proclamation No. 47/1975, *entered into force,* 7 August 1975

High Commissioner for the Implementation of the National Peace Call Establishment Decree, Council of State Special Decree No.8/1989, *entered into force* 25 February 1989.

National Revolutionary Operation Command Proclamation, Proclamation No. 129 of 1977, *entered into force*, 27 August 1977.

Peoples Organizing Provisional Office Establishment Proclamation, Proclamation No.91 of 1976, *entered into force*, 21 April 1976.

Proclamation Establishing the Office of the Special Prosecutor: Proclamation No. 22/1991, *entered into force* 8 August 1992.

Proclamation for Repatriation of Ethiopian Refugees in the Republic of Djibouti, Proclamation No. 183/1980,

Proclamation to Provide for the Establishment of an Inquiry Commission to investigate the conflict occurred in Gambella Regional State on 13 December 2003, Proclamation No 398/2004.

Provisional Military Government Establishment Proclamation, Proclamation No. 1 of 1974, *entered into force*, 12 September 1974.

Provisional Military Government Establishment Proclamation, Proclamation No.1 of 1974, *entered into force* 12 September 1974.

Provisional National Advisory Commission Establishment Proclamation, Proclamation No.12 of 1974, *entered into force*, 16 December 1974.

Public Ownership of Rural Lands Proclamation, Proclamation No. 31 of 1975, *entered into force*, 4 March 1975.

Redefinition of Powers and Responsibilities of the Provisional Military Administration Council and the Council of Ministers Proclamation, proclamation No. 110 of 1977, *entered into force*, 11 February 1977.

Seera Yakkaa Rippaabiliika Dimokiraatawaa Federaalawaa Itoophiyaa 1997, Keewwata 269, available at: <http://ethcriminalawnetwork.com/system/files/FDRE%20Criminal%20Code%20-%20Afan%20Oromo.pdf> accessed 4 May 2019.

Special Courts-Martial Establishment Proclamation, Proclamation No. 7/1974, *entered into force* 19 October 1974.

Telecom Fraud Offence Proclamation, Proclamation No. 761/2012, *entered into force* 4 September 2012,

The Criminal Code of the Federal Democratic Republic of Ethiopia, Proclamation No. 414/2004 *entered into force* 9 May 2005.

The Declaration of the Establishmnet of the People's Democratic Republic of Ethiopia, Proclamation No. 2/1987.

The Declaration of War Proclamation, Proclamation No. 33/1942.

The Memorial of the Korean War, Establishment Decree of 1952, Decree No. 12/1952.

The Penal Code of 1957, French Version (Code Penal De L'Empire D'Ethiopie).

The Penal Code of the Empire of Ethiopia of 1957, Proclamation No. 158/1957, Extraordinary Issue No. 1, of 1957 of the Negarit Gazeta, 23 July 1957, *entered into force* 5 May 1958.

The Revised Special Penal Code, Proclamation No 241/1981 *entered into force* 8 September 1981.

Transitional Period Charter of Ethiopia: Proclamation No.1/1991, *entered into force on* 22 July 1991.

Other National Jursidictions

Andora
Nouveau Code Pénal Andorre.

Angola
Constitution of Angola 2010, Article 129(e), available at: <https://www.constituteproject.org/constitution/Angola_2010?lang=en> accessed 28 September 2019.

Argentina
Decree No. 187/83, 15 December 1983 (Decreto 187, 15 diciembre 1983), reprinted in Anales de Legislación Argentina (1984), Tomo XLIV-A, LA LEY, 137–138.

Australia
Australia's Genocide Convention Act No. 27, 1949.

Belgium
Criminal Code of the Republic of Belgium (1867, as of 2016).

Brazil
Brazil's Constitution of 1988 with Amendments through 2014, section XLIII. available at: <https://www.constituteproject.org/constitution/Brazil_2014.pdf> accessed 28 September 2019.

Constituição Da República Federativa Do Brasil De 1988 Incluindo Reformas De 1992, 1993, 1994, 1995, 1996,

Brasil – Lei N°2.889, De 1° de Outubro de1956 – Genocidio.

Burkina-Faso
Loi n° 25–2018/AN Portant Code Penal Burkina-Faso

Canada
Code Criminel. S.R., ch. C-34, Article 318(2).

Chile
Supreme Decree No.355 (Chile): Creation of the Commission on Truth and Reconciliation, (Santiago, 25 April 1990) available at: <http://www.usip.org/sites/default/files/file/resources/collections/commissions/Chile90-Charter.pdf> accessed 28 September 2019.

The Juvenile Justice (Care and Protection of children) Act of India, 2015.

Decree Law 2.191 of April 1978.

LIST OF LAWS 469

Colombia

Colombia's Constitution of 1991 with Amendments through 2005, Transitory Article 30, available at: <https://www.constituteproject.org/constitution/Colombia_2005.pdf> accessed 28 September 2019.

Côte d'Ivoire

Loi n° 1981-640 du 31 juillet 1981, instituant le Code pénal (modifiée par la loi n° 1995-522 du 6 juillet 1995).

Ecuador

The Constitution of the Republic of Ecuador 2008 (Rev.2011), available at: <https://www.constituteproject.org/search?lang=en&q=Ecuador> accessed 28 September 2019.

France

Code Pénal France (1994).

Iraq

The Statute of the Iraqi Special Tribunal, issued 10 December 2003, available at: <https://www.legal-tools.org/uploads/tx_ltpdb/Iraq_IST_Statute__2003__E__01_03.pdf> accessed 28 September 2019.

Israeli

Israeli Law No. 5710-1950 on the Prevention and Punishment of Genocide

Luxemburg

Code pénal, En vigueur Dans Le Grand-Duché De Luxembourg (Législation: Jusqu'au 10 Juillet 2016).

Mali

Loi N° 01-079 Du 20 Août 2001 Portant Code Pénal.

Pakistan

Pakistan 1973 (reinst. 2002, rev. 2015) available at: <https://www.constituteproject.org/constitution/Pakistan_2015?lang=en> accessed 11 January 2019.

Paraguay

The Constitution of Paraguay 1992 (rev. 2011) available at: <https://www.constituteproject.org/search?lang=en&q=Paraguay> accessed 20 March 2019. Note, however, that the Constitution does not make a precise reference to crimes against humanity.

Sierra Leone

Agreement between the Government of the Republic of Sierra Leone and the Revolutionary United Front of Sierra Leone (RUF/SL), done in Abidjan on 30 November 1996, available at: <http://www.sierra-leone.org/abidjanaccord.html> accessed 22 March 2019.

Peace Agreement between the Government of Sierra Leone and the Revolutionary United Front of Sierra Leone, issued in Lomé, 3 June 1999, Article XXVI. Available at: <http://www.sierra-leone.org/lomeaccord.html> accessed 20 March 2019.

Switzerland
Code pénal suisse du 21 décembre 1937 (Etat au 1er septembre 2017).
Swiss Criminal Code of 21 December 1937 (Status as of 1 January 2017) English version,
Venezuela
The Constitution of Venezuela (Bolivarian Republic of) 1999 (rev. 2009), available at: <https://www.constituteproject.org/search?lang=en&q=venezuela> accessed 28 September 2019.

Laws of International Criminal Courts and Tribunals

Law on the Establishment of the Extraordinary Chambers in the Courts of Cambodia, with inclusion of amendments as promulgated on 27 October 2004 (NS/RKM/1004/006), available at: <https://www.eccc.gov.kh/sites/default/files/legal-documents/KR_Law_as_amended_27_Oct_2004_Eng.pdf> accessed 30 September 2019.

Resolution on amendments to article 8 of the Rome Statute of the International Criminal Court, RC/Res.5, Depositary Notification C.N.651.2010 Treaties-6, dated 29 November 2010, available at<http://treaties.un.org> accessed 30 September 2019.

Resolution on amendments to article 8 of the Rome Statute of the International Criminal Court, ICC-ASP/16/Res.4, adopted at the 12th plenary meeting on 14 December 2017, by consensus, ICC-ASP/16/20, available at: <https://asp.icc-cpi.int/iccdocs/asp_docs/Resolutions/ASP16/ICC-ASP-16-Res4-ENG.pdf> accessed 30 July 2019.

Rome Statute of the International Criminal Court U.N. Doc. 2187 U.N.T.S. 90, *entered into force* 1 July 2002.

Statute of the Extraordinary African Chambers within Senegalese judicial system for the prosecution of international crimes committed on the territory of the Republic of Chad during the period from 7 June 1982 to 1 December 1990, available at: <http://legal.au.int/en/sites/default/files/Agreement%20AU-Senegal%20establish ing%20AEC-english_0.pdf> accessed 30 September 2019.

Statute of the International Tribunal for Rwanda, adopted by S.C. Res. 955, U.N. SCOR, 49th Sess., 3453d mtg. at 3, U.N. Doc. S/RES/955 (1994), 33 I.L.M. 1598, 1600 (1994).

Statute of the International Tribunal for the Prosecution of Persons Responsible for Serious Violations of International Humanitarian Law Committed in the Territory of the Former Yugoslavia since 1991, U.N. Doc. S/25704 at 36, annex

(1993) and S/25704/Add.1 (1993), adopted by Security Council on 25 May 1993, U.N. Doc. S/RES/827 (1993),

The Statute of the Iraqi Special Tribunal, issued 10 December 2003, available at: <https://www.legal-tools.org/uploads/tx_ltpdb/Iraq_IST_Statute__2003__E__01_03.pdf> accessed 30 September 2019.

UN Security Council, Statute of the Special Court for Sierra Leone, 16 January 2002, available at: <http://www.refworld.org/docid/3dda29f94.html> accessed 30 September 2019.

United Nations, Agreement for the prosecution and punishment of the major war criminals of the European Axis (London Agreement), 82 U.N.T.C. 280, *entered into force* 8 August 1945.

UNTAET Regulation No. 2000/15 on the Establishment of Panels with Exclusive Jurisdiction over Serious Criminal Offences, available at: <https://www.legal-tools.org/doc/c082f8/> accessed 30 September 2019.

International Treaties, Agreements, and Declarations

African [Banjul] Charter on Human and Peoples' Rights, adopted June 27, 1981, OAU Doc. CAB/LEG/67/3 rev. 5, 21 I.L.M. 58 (1982), *entered into force* 21 October 1986.

American Convention on Human Rights, O.A.S. Treaty Series No. 36, 1144 U.N.T.S. 123, *entered into force* July 18, 1978, *reprinted in* Basic Documents Pertaining to Human Rights in the Inter-American System, OEA/Ser.L.V/II.82 doc.6 rev.1 at 25 (1992).

Control Council Law No. 10, Punishment of Persons Guilty of War Crimes, Crimes Against Peace and Against Humanity, December 20, 1945, 3 Official Gazette Control Council for Germany 50–55 (1946).

Convention against Torture and Other Cruel, Inhuman or Degrading Treatment or Punishment, G.A. res. 39/46, [annex, 39 U.N. GAOR Supp. (No. 51) at 197, U.N. Doc`. A/39/51 (1984)], *entered into force* 26 June 1987.

Convention for the Protection of Human Rights and Fundamental Freedoms, 213 U.N.T.S. 222, *entered into force* Sept. 3, 1953, *as amended by* Protocols Nos 3, 5, 8, and 11 *which entered into force* on 21 September 1970, 20 December 1971, 1 January 1990, and 1 November 1998 respectively.

Convention on the Non-Applicability of Statutory Limitations to War Crimes and CrimesAgainst Humanity, G.A. res. 2391 (XXIII), annex, 23 U.N. GAOR Supp. (No. 18) at 40, U.N. Doc. A/7218 (1968), *entered into force* 11 November 1970.

Convention on the Prevention and Punishment of the Crime of Genocide, 78 U.N.T.S. 277, *entered into force* 12 January 1951.

Convention on the Safety of United Nations and Associated Personnel, G.A. res. 49/59, 49 U.N. GAOR Supp. (No. 49) at 299, U.N. Doc. A/49/49 (1994).

Declaration (XIV) Prohibiting the Discharge of Projectiles and Explosives from Balloons. The Hague, 18 October 1907, *entered into force* 27 November 1909.

Geneva Convention for the Amelioration of the Condition of the Wounded and Sick in Armed Forces in the Field, 75 U.N.T.S. 31, *entered into force* 21 October 1950.

Geneva Convention for the Amelioration of the Condition of Wounded, Sick and Shipwrecked Members of Armed Forces at Sea, 75 U.N.T.S. 85, *entered into force* 21 October 1950.

Geneva Convention relative to the Protection of Civilian Persons in Time of War, 75 U.N.T.S. 287, *entered into force* 21 October 1950.

Geneva Convention relative to the Treatment of Prisoners of War, 75 U.N.T.S. 135, *entered into force* 21 October 1950.

Hague Convention III- Opening of Hostilities: 18 October 1907, 36 Stat. 2259, 1 Bevans 619, 205 Consol. T.S. 263, 3 Martens Nouveau Recueil (ser. 3) 437, *entered into force* 26 January 1910;

Hague Convention IV – Laws and Customs of War on Land: 18 October 1907, 36 Stat. 2277, 1 Bevans 631, 205 Consol. T.S. 277, 3 Martens Nouveau Recueil (ser. 3) 461, *entered into force* 26 January 1910.

Hague Convention IV and its annex: Regulations Concerning the Laws and Customs of War on Land, The Hague 18 October 1907.

Hague Convention IX concerning Bombardment by Naval Forces in Time of War, 3 Martens Nouveau Recueil (ser. 3) 604, 205 Consol. T.S. 345, *entered into force* 26 January 1910;

Hague Convention V – Rights and Duties of Neutral Powers and Persons in Case of War on Land: 18 October 1907, 36 Stat. 2310, 1 Bevans 654, 205 Consol. T.S. 299, 3 Martens Nouveau Recueil (ser. 3) 504, *entered into force* Jan 26 January 1910;

Hague Convention VI – Status of Enemy Merchant Ships at the Outbreak of Hostilities: 18 October 1907, 205 Consol. T.S. 305, 3 Martens Nouveau Recueil (ser. 3) 533, *entered into force* 26 January 1910;

Hague Convention VII relative to the Conversion of Merchant Ships into War-Ships, 3 Martens Nouveau Recueil (ser. 3) 557, 205 Consol. T.S. 319, *entered into force* 26 January 1910;

Hague Convention VIII relative to the Laying of Automatic Submarine Contact Mines, 3 Martens Nouveau Recueil (ser. 3) 580, 205 Consol. T.S. 331, *entered into force* 26 January 1910.

Hague Convention XI – Restrictions With Regard to the Exercise of the Right of Capture in Naval War: 18 October 1907, 36 Stat. 2396, 1 Bevans 711, 205 Consol. T.S. 367, 3 Martens Nouveau Recueil (ser. 3) 663, *entered into force* 26 January 1910.

Hague Convention XIII -Rights and Duties of Neutral Powers in Naval War: 18 October 1907, 36 Stat. 2415, 1 Bevans 723, 205 Consol. T.S. 395, 3 Martens Nouveau Recueil 713 (ser. 3), *entered into force* 26 January 1910.

Hague IV, Declaration II- Concerning the Prohibition of the Use of Projectiles Diffusing Asphyxiating Gases, July 29, 1899, 26 Martens Nouveau Recueil (ser. 2) 998, 187 Consol. T.S. 453, *entered into force* 4 September 1900;

Hague IV, Declaration III- Concerning the Prohibition of the Use of Expanding Bullets, July 29, 1899, 26 Martens Nouveau Recueil (ser. 2) 1002, 187 Consol. T.S. 459, *entered into force* 4 September 1900;

International Convention for the Protection of All Persons from Enforced Disappearance, Human Rights Council, Report to the General Assembly on the First Session of the Human Rights Council, at 32, U.N. Doc. A/HRC/1/L.10 (2006).

International Convention on the Protection of the Rights of All Migrant Workers and Members of Their Families, G.A. res. 45/158, annex, 45 U.N. GAOR Supp. (No. 49A) at 262, U.N. Doc. A/45/49 (1990), *entered into force* 1 July 2003.

International Covenant on Civil and Political Rights, G.A. res. 2200A (XXI), 21 U.N. GAOR Supp. (No. 16) at 52, U.N. Doc. A/6316 (1966), 999 U.N.T.S. 171, *entered into force* 23 March 1976.

Model Treaty on Extradition, Adopted by General Assembly resolution 45/116, subsequently amended by General Assembly resolution 52/88, A/RES/45/116, 68th plenary meeting, 14 December 1990.

Nuremberg Rules, in Agreement for the Prosecution and Punishment of the Major War Criminals of the European Axis, 82 U.N.T.S. 279, *entered into force* Aug. 8, 1945.

Peace Agreement between the Government of Sierra Leone and the Revolutionary United Front of Sierra Leone, issued in Lomé, 3 June 1999, Article XXVI. Available at: <http://www.sierra-leone.org/lomeaccord.html> accessed 20 March 2019.

Protocol Additional to the Geneva Conventions of 12 August 1949, and Relating to the Protection of Victims of International Armed Conflicts (Protocol I), 1125 U.N.T.S. 3, *entered into force* Dec. 7, 1978.

Protocol Additional to the Geneva Conventions of 12 August 1949, and Relating to the Protection of Victims of Non-International Armed Conflicts (Protocol II), 1125 U.N.T.S. 609, *entered into force* Dec. 7, 1978

Conflicts (Protocol II), 1125 U.N.T.S. 609, *entered into force* 7 December 1978.

Protocol for the Prohibition of the Use of Asphyxiating, Poisonous or Other Gases, and of Bacteriological Methods of Warfare, Geneva, 94 L.N.T.S. 65, *entered into force* 08 February 1928.

Slavery, Servitude, Forced Labor and Similar Institutions and Practices Convention of 1926 (Slavery Convention of 1926), 60 L.N.T.S. 253, *entered into force* 9 March 1927.

Treaty of Peace with Italy, Paris, 10 February 1947; 61 Stat.1245;T.I.A.S. 1648, *entered into force* 15 September 1947.

Treaty of Wuchale: Italy-Ethiopia [1889]' available at: <https://www.britannica.com/event/Treaty-of-Wichale> accessed 30 September 2019.

Universal Declaration of Human Rights, G.A. res. 217A (III), U.N. Doc A/810 at 71 (1948).

Vienna Declaration and Program of Action, Adopted by the World Conference on Human Rights in Vienna on 25 June 1993, available at: <http://www.ohchr.org/EN/ProfessionalInterest/Pages/Vienna.aspx> accessed 30 September 2019.

Bibliography

Articles and Book Chapters

Abbink J., 'The impact of violence: The Ethiopian 'Red Terror' as a Social Phenomenon' in P.J. Bräunlein and A. Lauser (eds.), *Kriegund Frieden: Ethnologische Perspektiven* (Bremen: Kea-Edition, 1995) 129–145.

Abbink J., 'The Ethiopian Revolution after 40 Years (1974–2014): Plan B in Progress?' (2015) 31(3) *Journal of Developing Societies* 333–357.

Abebe A.K., 'Human Rights under the Ethiopian Constitution: A Descriptive Overview' (2011) 5(1) *Mizan Law Review* 41–71.

Aguilar M., 'The Nagaa Boorana: Contemporary Discussions on Ritual and Political Diversity' (2008) 15(1) *Journal of Oromo Studies* 181–202.

Akande D., 'Sources of International Criminal Law' in A. Cassese, (ed.) *The Oxford Companion to International Criminal Justice*' (Oxford: Oxford University Press, 2009) 41–53.

Akande D., 'Classification of Armed Conflict: Relevant Legal Concepts' in E. Wilmshurst (ed.), *International Law and the Classification of Conflicts* (Oxford: Oxford University Press, 2012) 171–274.

Akhavan P., 'The Crime of Genocide in the ICTR Jurisprudence' (2005) 3(1) *Journal of International Criminal Justice* 989–1006.

Akhavan P., 'Universal Repression of Crimes Against Humanity' in L.N. Sadat (ed.,) *Forging a Convention for Crimes Against Humanity* (Cambridge: Cambridge University Press, 2011) 28–42.

Alie J., 'Reconciliation and traditional justice: Tradition-based practices of the Kpaa Mende in Sierra Leone' in L. Huyse and M. Salter (eds.), *Traditional Justice and Reconciliation after Violent Conflict: Learning from African Experiences* (Stockholm: International IDEA, 2008) 123–147.

Allen P. and Keller A., 'The Concept of a Just Peace, or Achieving Peace Through Recognition, Renouncement, and Rule' in P. Allen and A. Keller (eds.), *What Is Just Peace?* (Oxford: Oxford University Press, 2006) 197–215.

Allo A and Tesfaye B, 'Spectacles of illegality: mapping Ethiopia's show trials' (2015) 13(1) *African Identities* 279–296.

Aneme G.A., 'Apology and s: The Case of the Red-Terror Trials in Ethiopia' (2006) 6(1) *African Human Rights Law Journal* 64–84.

Asgedom M., 'The Place of Crimes against Humanity under the Ethiopian Legal System: A Reflection' (2013) 3(2) *Bahir Dar University Journal of Law* 401–415.

Bakker CH.A.E, 'A Full Stop to Amnesty in Argentina: The Simón Case' 2005 (3) *Journal of International Criminal Justice* 1106–1120.

Bassiouni M.C., 'A Functional Approach to General Principles of International Law' (1989–1990) 11(1) *Michigan Journal of International Law* 768–818.

Bassiouni M.C., 'Human Rights in the Context of Criminal Justice: Identifying International Procedural Protections and Equivalent Protections in National Constitutions' (1993) (3)1 *Duke Journal of Comparative & International Law* 235–298.

Bassiouni M.C., 'International Crimes: Jus Cogens and Obligatio Erga Omnes' (1996) 59(4) *Law and Contemporary Problems* 63–74.

Bassiouni M.C., 'The Discipline of international Criminal Law' in M.C. Bassiouni (ed.), *International Criminal Law, Vol I: Sources, Subjects, and Contents* (3rd ed., Leiden: Martinus Nijhoff Publishers, 2008) 1–17.

Baudendistel R., 'Force versus law: The International Committee of the Red Cross and chemical warfare in the Italo-Ethiopian war 1935–1936' (1998)38(322) *International Review of the Red Cross* 81–104.

Berster L., 'Article II' in C.J. Tams *et al., Convention on the Prevention and Punishment of the Crime of Genocide: A Commentary* (München: C.H.Beck.Hart.Nomos, 2014), 79–156.

Bothe M., 'War Crimes' in Cassese and others (eds.), *The Rome Statute of the International Criminal Court: A Commentary* (Oxford: Oxford University Press, 2002) 417–424.

Briottet R., 'French, English, Amharic: the law in Ethiopia' (2009) 9(2) *Journal of Romance Studies* 1–9.

Bulcha M., 'Genocidal Violence in the Making of Nation and State in Ethiopia' (2005) 9(2) *African Sociological Review* 1–54.

Bulto T.S., 'The Monist-Dualist Divide and the Supremacy Clause: Revisiting the Status of Human Rights treaties in Ethiopia' (2009) 23(1) *Journal of Ethiopian Law* 132–160.

Burmester H., 'The determination of customary international law in Australian courts' (2004) 4(1) *Non-State Actors and International Law* 39–47.

Cassese A., 'Reflections on International Criminal Justice' (1998) 61(1) *Modern Law Review* 1–10.

Cassese A., 'The Statute of the International Criminal Court: Some Preliminary Reflections' (1999) 10(1) *European Journal of International Law* 144–171.

Cassese A., 'The ICTY: A Living and Vital Reality' (2004) 2(1) *Journal of International Criminal Justice* 585–597.

Cassese A., 'The Italian Court of Cassation Misapprehends the Notion of War Crimes: The Lozano Case' (2008) 6(1) *Journal of International Criminal Justice* 1084–1087.

Cassese A., 'Balancing the Prosecution of Crimes against Humanity and Non-Retroactivity of Criminal Law: The Kolk and Kislyiy v. Estonia Case before the ECHR' (2006) 4(1) *Journal of International Criminal Justice* 410–418.

Cassese A., 'Is Genocidal Policy a Requirement for the Crime of Genocide?' in P. Gaeta (ed.), *The UN Genocide Convention: A Commentary* (Oxford: Oxford University Press, 2009) 128–136.

Clapham C., 'Re-writing Ethiopian History' (2002) 18(1) *Annales d'Éthiopie* 37–54.

Cohen S., 'State crimes of previous regimes: knowledge, accountability, and the policing of the past, Law and Social Inquiry' (1995) 20(1) *Law and Social Inquiry* 7–50.

Crawford E., 'Who is a Civilian? Membership of Opposing Groups and Direct Participation in Hostilities' in M. Lattimer and P. Sands (eds.), *The Gray Zone: Civilian Protection Between Human Rights and the Laws of War* (Oxford: Hart, 2018) 19–40.

Cryer R., 'The Doctrinal Foundations of International Criminal Law' in M.C. Bassiouni (ed.), *International Criminal Law, Vol I: Sources, Subjects, and Contents* (3rd ed., Leiden: Martinus Nijhoff Publishers, 2008) 107–128.

Davies T.E., 'How the Rome Statute Weakens the International Prohibition on Incitement to Genocide' (2009) 22 (2) *Harvard Human Rights Journal* 245–270.

de Beco G., 'Life Sentences and Human Dignity' (2005) 9(3) *The International Journal of Human Rights* 411–419.

Degan V.D., 'On the Sources of International Criminal Law' (2005) 4(1) *Chinese Journal of International Law* 45–83.

Deguzman M.M., 'Article 21: Applicable Law' in O. Triffterer and K. Ambos (eds.), *The Rome Statute of the International Criminal Court: A Commentary* (3rd. ed., Munich: C.H. Beck – Hart – Nomos, 2015) 932–948.

del Ponte C., 'Prosecuting the Individuals Bearing the Highest Level of Responsibility', (2004) 2(1) *Journal of International Criminal Justice* 516–519.

Dörmann K., 'War crimes under the Rome Statute of the International Criminal Court, with a Special Focus on the Negotiations on the Elements of Crimes' (2003) 7(1) *Max Planck Yearbook of United Nations Law* 342–407.

Dörmann K. and Geiß R., 'The Implementation of Grave Breaches into Domestic Legal Orders' (2009) 7(1) *Journal of International Criminal Justice* 703–716.

Dowding K.M. and Kimber R., 'The Meaning and Use of 'Political Stability'' (1983) 11(1) *European Journal of Political Research* 229–243.

Elgesem F. and Aneme G.A., 'The Rights of the Accused: A Human Rights Appraisal', in K. Tronvoll et al. (eds.), *The Ethiopian Red Terror Trials: Transitional Justice Challenged* (Suffolk: James Curry, 2009) 33–50.

Engelschøin T.S., 'Ethiopia: War Crimes and Violations of Human Rights' [1995] 34(9) *Military Law and Law of War Review* 9–32.

Engstrom P. and Pereira G., 'From Amnesty to Accountability: Ebb and Flow in the Search for Justice in Argentina' in F. Lessa and L.A. Payne (eds.), *Amnesty in the Age of Human Rights Accountability: Comparative and International Perspectives* (Cambridge: Cambridge University Press, 2012) 97–122.

Enyew E.L., 'Ethiopian customary dispute resolution mechanisms: forms of restorative justice?' (2014) 14(1) *African Journal on Conflict Resolution* 125–154.

Ferdinandusse W., 'The Interaction of National and International Approaches in the Repression of International Crimes' (2004) 15(5) *The European Journal of International Law* 1041–1053.

Ferdinandusse W., 'The Prosecution of Grave Breaches in National Courts' (2009) 7(1) *Journal of International Criminal Justice* 723–74.

Fournet C., 'Reflection on the Separation of Powers: The Law of Genocide and the Symptomatic French Paradox' in R. Henham and P. Behrens (eds.), *The Criminal Law of Genocide: International, Comparative and Contextual Aspects* (Farnham: Ashgate, 2007) 211–222.

Fournet C., 'The Actus Reus of Genocide' in P. Behrens and R. Henham (eds.), *Elements of Genocide* (Abingdon: Routledge, 2012) 53–69.

Fournet C. and Pégorier C., 'Only One Step Away From Genocide: the Crime of Persecution in International Criminal Law' (2010) 10(5) *International Criminal Law Review* 713–738.

Gade C.B.N., 'Restorative Justice and the South African Truth and Reconciliation Process' (2013) 32(1) *South African Journal of Philosophy* 11–35.

Gaeta P., 'Grave Breaches of the Geneva Conventions' in A. Clapham *et al.* (eds.), *The 1949 Geneva Conventions: A Commentary* (Oxford: Oxford University Press, 2014) 615–646.

Gaeta P., 'Trial In Absentia Before the Special Tribunal for Lebanon' in A. Alamuddin *et al.* (eds.), *The Special Tribunal for Lebanon: Law and Practice* (Oxford: Oxford University Press, 2014) 229–250.

Gebrehiwot M. and Haftetsion F., 'The Politics in Naming the Ethiopian Federation' (2015) 48 *Journal of Ethiopian Studies* 89–117.

Geiger R., 'The German Border Guard Cases and International Human Rights' (2009) 9(1) *European Journal of International Law* 540–549.

Gibson J.L., 'The Truth about Truth and Reconciliation in South Africa' (2005) 26(4) *International Political Science Review* 341–36.

Gibson J.L., 'Overcoming apartheid: can truth reconcile a divided nation?' (2010) 31(2) *South African Journal of Political Studies* 129–155.

Gorove S., 'The Problem of Mental Harm in the Genocide Convention' (1951) 2(2) *Washington University Law Review* 174–187.

Graven J., 'The Penal Code of The Empire of Ethiopia' (1964) 1(2) *Journal of Ethiopian Law* 267–298.

Graybill L.S., 'Pursuit of Truth and Reconciliation in South Africa' (1998) 45(1) *Africa Today* 103–133.

Gudina M., 'Elections and democratization in Ethiopia,1991–2010' (2011) 5(4) *Journal of Eastern African Studies* 664–680.

Hailemariam Y., 'The Quest for Justice and Reconciliation: The International Criminal Tribunal for Rwanda and the Ethiopian High Court' (1999) 22(1) *Hastings International and Comparative Law Review* 667–745.

Harbeson J., 'A Bureaucratic Authoritarian Regime: Is Ethiopia Democratic?' (1998) 9(4) *Journal of Democracy* 62–69.

Harff B. and Gurr T.R., 'Victims of the State: Genocides, Politicides and Group Repression since 1945' (1989) 1(1) *International Review of Victimology* 23–41.

Hayner P., 'Past Truths, Present Dangers: The Role of Official Truth Seeking in Conflict Resolution and Prevention' in P. Stern and D. Druckman (eds.), *International conflict resolution after the Cold War* (Washington DC.: National Academy Press, 2000) 338–382.

Henrard K., 'The Viability of National Amnesties in View of the Increasing Recognition of Individual Criminal Responsibility at International Law' (1999) 8(1) *Michigan State University-DCL Journal of International Law* 595–650.

Heyns C. et al., 'The Right to Life and the Progressive Abolition of the Death Penalty', in M. deGuzman and D. Amann (eds.), *Arcs of Global Justice: Essays in Honour of William A. Schabas* (Oxford University Press, Oxford, 2018) 127–134.

Holá B., Bijleveld C. and Smeulers A., 'Consistency of International Sentencing: ICTY and ICTR Case Study' (2011) 9(5) *European Journal of Criminology* 539–552.

Holá B., Smeulers A. and Bijleveld C., 'International Sentencing Facts and Figures: Sentencing Practice at the ICTY and ICTR' (2011) 9(1) *Journal of International Criminal Justice* 411–439.

Holcomb B.K., 'Contending Democracies: US-Sponsored Democracy Encounters Indigenous Oromo Democratic Forms' in A. Jalata (ed.), *State Crisis, Globalisation, and National Movements in North-East Africa* (London: Routledge, 2004) 122–164.

Huyssteen E.V., 'Building State & Nation Justice, Reconciliation & Democratization in Ethiopia & South Africa' in Tronvoll K. et al. (eds.), *The Ethiopian Red Terror Trials: Transitional Justice Challenged* (Martlesham: James Currey, 2009) 98–115.

i Linares S.S., 'Francoism Facing Justice: Enforced Disappearances before Spanish Courts' (2013) 11(1) *Journal of International Criminal Justice* 463–483.

Idris I., 'The Place of International Human Rights Conventions in the 1994 Federal Democratic Republic of Ethiopia (FDRE) Constitution' (2000) 20(1) *Journal of Ethiopian Law* 113–138.

Jembere A., 'Treaty Making Power and Supremacy of Treaty in Ethiopia' (1970) 7(2) *Journal of Ethiopian Law* 409–434.

Jesman C., 'The Egyptian Invasion of Ethiopia' (1959) 58(230) *African Affairs* 75–81.

Jessberger F., 'International v. National Prosecution of International Crimes' in A. Cassese (ed.) *The Oxford Companion to International Criminal Justice* (Oxford: Oxford University Press, 2009) 208–216.

Jessberger F., 'The Definition of and the Elements of the Crime of Genocide' in P. Gaeta (ed.), *The UN Genocide Convention: A Commentary* (Oxford: Oxford University Press, 2009) 87–111.

Kebede A., 'The Social Origins of Military Dictatorship in Ethiopia' 2010 (26)(3) *Journal of Developing Societies* 295–327.

Kebede M., 'The Civilian left and the Radicalization of the *Dergue*' (2008) 24(2) *Journal of Developing Societies* 159–182.

Keller E.J., 'Government and Politics' in T.P. Ofcansky and L. Berry (eds.), *Ethiopia: A Country Study* (Washington, D.C.: Federal Research Division Library of Congress, 1991) 207–266.

Keneni T., 'Exploring Gumaa as an Indispensable Psycho-Social Method of Conflict Resolution and Justice Administration' (2013) 13(1) *African Journal on Conflict Resolution* 37–58.

Kidane W.L., 'The Ethiopia 'Red Terror Trials'' in M.C. Bassiouni (ed.), *Post-Conflict Justice* (Ardsley: Transnational Publishers, 2001) 667–694.

Kissi E., 'Rwanda, Ethiopia and Cambodia: links, fault lines and complexities in a comparative study of genocide' (2004) 6(1) *Journal of Genocide Research* 115–133.

Kissi E., 'Remembering Ethiopia's 'Red Terror': History of a Private Effort to Preserve a Public Memory' in ERTDRC, *Documenting the Red Terror: Bearing Witness to Ethiopia's Lost Generations* (Ottawa: ertdrc North America Inc, 2012) 9–23.

Kok R.A., 'National Adjudication of International Crimes: 'A Dutch Approach'' in E.V. Sliedregt and S. Vasilliev (eds.), *Pluralism in International Law* (Oxford: Oxford University Press, 2014) 220–224.

Kreß C., 'The Crime of Genocide Under International Law' (2006) 6(4) *International Criminal Law Review* 461–502.

Kreß C. and Prost K., 'Article 87' in O. Triffterer and K. Ambos (eds), *The Rome Statute of the International Criminal Court: A Commentary* (3rd ed., München: C.H.Beck.Hart.Namos, 2016) 2014–2045.

Kwakwa E., 'Governance, Development and Population displacement in Africa: A call for Action' (1995) 3(1) *African Yearbook of International Law* 17–52.

La Rosa A., 'Sanctions as a means of obtaining greater respect for humanitarian law: a review of their effectiveness', (2008) 90(1) *International Review of the Red Cross* 221–247.

Luban D., 'Fairness to Rightness: Jurisdiction, Legality, and the Legitimacy of International Criminal Law' in S. Besson & J. Tasioulas (eds.), *The Philosophy of International Law* (Oxford: Oxford University Press, 2010) 570–588.

Lyons T., 'The Transition in Ethiopia' (1991) 127(1) *CSIS Africa Notes* 1–8.

Mallinder L., 'Exploring the Practice of States in Introducing Amnesties, Study submitted for the International Conference 'Building a Future on Peace and Justice', (Nuremberg, 25–27 June 2007).

Maogoto J.N., 'Reading the Shadows of History: The Turkish and Ethiopian 'Internationalized' Domestic Crime Trials' in K.J. Heller and G. Simpson (eds.), *The Hidden Histories of War Crimes Trials* (Oxford: Oxford University Press, 2013) 290–305.

Mayfield J.V., 'The Prosecution of War Crimes and Respect for Human Rights: Ethiopia's Balancing Act' (1995) 9(1) *Emory International Law Journal* 553–594.

Mengesha A.D., Yesuf, S.S. and Gebre, T., 'Indigenous Conflict Resolution Mechanisms among the Kembata Society' (2015) 3(2) *American Journal of Educational Research* 225–242.

Metekia T.S., 'Violence Against and Using the Dead: Ethiopian Dergue Cases' (2018) 4(1) *Human Remains and Violence* 76–92.

Metekia T.S., 'Punishing Core Crimes in Ethiopia: Analysis of the Domestic Practice in Light of and in Comparison, with Sentencing Practices at the UNICTs and the ICC' (2019) 19(1) *International Criminal Law Review* 160–190.

Micheau A.P., 'The 1991 Transitional Charter of Ethiopia: A New Application of the Self-Determination Principle' (1996) 28 (2) *Case Western Reserve Journal of International Law* 367–394.

Milkias P., 'Mengistu Haile Mariam: Profile of a Dictator' (1994) 4(1) *Ethiopian Review* 57–59.

Mundorff K., 'Other People's Children: A Textual Contextual Interpretation of the Genocide Convention, Article 2(e)' 2009 (50)1 *Harvard International Law Journal* 61–129.

Myers L.J. and Shinn D.H., 'Appreciating Traditional forms of Healing Conflict in Africa' (2010) 2(1) *Black Diaspora Review* 2–13.

Newton M.A., 'The Iraqi High Criminal Court: Controversy and Contributions' (2006) 88 (862) *International Review of the Red Cross* 399–425.

Ofcansky T.P., 'National Security' in T.P. Ofcansky and L. Berry (eds.), *Ethiopia: A Country Study* (Washington, D.C.: Federal Research Division Library of Congress, 1991) 267–325.

Ongen T. and Wyngaert C., 'Ne bis in idem Principle, Including the Issue of Amnesty' in A. Cassese *et al.* (eds.), *The Rome Statute of the International Criminal Court, Volume I: A Commentary* (Oxford: Oxford University Press, 2002) 705–729.

Orentlicher D.F., 'The Duty to Prosecute Human Rights Violations of a Prior Regime' (1991) 100(8) *The Yale Law Journal Company* 2537–2615.

Ottway M., 'Eritrea and Ethiopia: negotiations in a transitional conflict' in W. Zartman (ed.), *Elusive Peace: negotiating an end to civil wars*, (Washington DC: Brookings Institution Press, 1995) 103–120.

Pankhurst R., 'Italian Fascist War Crimes in Ethiopia: A history of Their Discussion, from the League of Nations to the United Nations (1936–1949)' 1999 (6)(1–2) *Northeast African Studies* 83–140.

Plaut M., 'Ethiopia's Oromo Liberation Front' (2006) 33(109) *Review of African Political Economy* 587–593.

Prouveze R. and Brenaz N., 'International and domestic prosecutions' in M.C. Bassiouni (ed.), *The Pursuit of International criminal justice, Vol. I: A World Study on Conflicts, Victimization, and Post-Conflict Justice* (Antwerp: Intersentia, 2010) 386–387.

Prunier G., 'The Ethiopian Revolution and the Derg Regime' in G. Prunier and E. Ficquet, (eds.), *Understanding Contemporary Ethiopia: Monarchy, Revolution and the Legacy of Meles Zenawi* (Oxford: Oxford University Press, 2015), 209–232.

Ratner S., 'The United Nations Group of Experts for Cambodia' (1991) 93(4) *The American Journal of International Law* 948–953.

Reda K.T., 'Conflict and alternative dispute resolution among the Afar pastoralists of Ethiopia' (2011) 3(3) *African Journal of History and Culture* 38–47.

Redae M., 'The Ethiopian Genocide Trial' (2002) 1(1) *Ethiopian Law Review* 1–26, 18–26.

Santamaria Y., 'Afro communism: Ethiopia, Angola, and Mozambique' in M. Kramer (ed.), *The Black Book of Communism: Crimes, Terror, Repression* (Cambridge: Harvard University Press, 1999) 683–704.

Sarkin J., 'Transitional Justice and the Prosecution Model: The Experience of Ethiopia' (1999) 2(1) *Journal of Law, Democracy and Development* 253–266.

Saul B., 'The Implementation of the Genocide Convention at the National Level' in P. Gaeta (ed.), *The UN Genocide Convention: A Commentary* (Oxford: Oxford University Press, 2009) 58–86.

Sbacchi A., 'Haile Selassie and the Italians 1941–1943' (1979) 22(1) *African Studies Review* 25–42.

Schabas W.A., 'International Law and the Abolition of Death Penalty' (1998) 55(3) *Washington and Lee Law Review* 798–799.

Schabas W.A., 'In Absentia Proceedings before International Criminal Courts' in G. Sluiter and S. Vasiliev (eds.), *International Criminal Procedure: Towards a Coherent Body of Law* (London: Cameron May, 2009) 336–342.

Schabas W.A., 'Victor's Justice: Selecting Situations at the International Criminal Court' (2009–2010) 43(1) *John Marshall Law Review* 535–552.

Schabas W.A., 'Article 6: Genocide' in O. Triffterer and K. Ambos (eds), *The Rome Statute of the International Criminal Court: A Commentary* (3rd ed., München: C.H.Beck. Hart.Namos, 2016) 127–143.

Schabas W.A. and El Zeidy M.M., 'Article 17: Issues of Admissibility' in O.Triffterer and K. Ambos (eds.), *The Rome Statute of the International Criminal Court: A Commentary* (3rd. ed., Munich: C.H. Beck – Hart – Nomos, 2015) 781–831.

Schaefer C., 'The Red Terror Trials Versus Traditions of Restorative Justice' in K. Tronvoll *et al.* (eds.), *The Ethiopian Red Terror Trials: Transitional Justice Challenged* (Martlesham: James Currey, 2009) 68–83.

Selassie A.G., 'Ethiopia: Problems and Prospects for Democracy' 1992 (1)1 *William and Mary Bill of Rights Journal* 205–226.

Sermet L., 'The absence of a derogation clause from the African Charter on Human and Peoples' Rights: A critical discussion' (2007) 7(1) *African Human Rights Law Journal* 142–161.

Shany Y., 'The Road to the Genocide Convention and Beyond' in P. Gaeta (ed.), *The UN Genocide Convention: A Commentary* (Oxford: Oxford University Press, 2009) 3–26.

Shimeles B., 'Ye 1966tu Mermari Komisiyon Anesase, Kenewune ena Keziya Yekesemenew' 2009 (5)2 *Wonber- Alemayehu Haile Memorial Foundations Periodical* 3–24.

Spiga V., 'Non-retroactivity of Criminal Law: A New Chapter in the Hissène Habré Saga' (2011) 9(1) *Journal of International Criminal Justice* 5–23.

Starygin S. and Selth J., 'Cambodia and the Right to be Present: Trials in absentia in the Draft Criminal Procedure Code' (2005) 1(1) *Singapore Journal of Legal Studies* 170–188.

Strauss P.L., 'On Interpreting the Ethiopian Penal Code' 1968 5(2) *Journal of Ethiopian Law* 375–377.

Taye B.A., 'Ethnic Cleansing in Ethiopia' (2018) 50(1) *Journal of Peace Research* 77–104.

Tegegn M., 'Mengistu Red Terror' (2012) 10(13) *African Identities* 249–263.

Tereke G., The Red Terror in Ethiopia: A Historical Aberration, (2008) 24(2) *Journal of Developing Societies* 183–206.

Tiba F.K., 'The Mengistu Genocide Trial in Ethiopia' (2007) 5 (1) *Journal of International Criminal Justice* 513–526.

Tiba F.K, 'The Trial of Mengistu and other Derg Members for Genocide, Torture and Summary Executions in Ethiopia' in C. Murungu and B. Japhet (eds.), *Prosecuting International Crimes in Africa* (Pretoria: Pretoria University Law Press, 2011) 168–184.

Tiba F.K., 'Mass Trials and Modes of Criminal Responsibility for International Crimes: The Case of Ethiopia' in K.J. Heller and G. Simpson (eds.), *The Hidden Histories of War Crimes Trials* (Oxford: Oxford University Press, 2013) 306–326.

Toggia P., 'The Revolutionary Endgame of Political Power: The Genealogy of 'Red Terror' in Ethiopia' (2012) 10(3) *African Identities* 265–280.

Tronvoll K., 'The Quest for Justice or the Construction of Political Legitimacy: The Political Anatomy for the Red Terror Trials' in K. Tronvoll *et al.* (eds.), *The Ethiopian Red Terror Trials: Transitional Justice Challenged* (Martlesham: James Currey, 2009) 84–95.

Tusso H., 'Indigenous Processes of Conflict Resolution in Oromo Society' in I.W. Zartman (ed.) *Traditional Cures for Modern Conflicts: African Conflict 'Medicine'* (London: Lynne Rienner Publishers, 2000) 79–93.

Van Dyke J., 'The Fundamental Human Right to Prosecution and Compensation' (2000–2001) 29 *Denver Journal of International Law and Policy* 77–100.

van Elst R., 'Implementing Universal Jurisdiction Over Grave Breaches of the Geneva Conventions' (2000) 13(1) *Leiden Journal of International Law* 815–828.

van Huyssteen E., 'Building State & Nation: Justice, Reconciliation & Democratization in Ethiopia & South Africa' in K. Tronvoll *et al.* (eds.), *The Ethiopian Red Terror Trials: Transitional Justice Challenged* (Martlesham: James Currey, 2009) 98–115.

Vanderlinden J., 'An Introduction to the Sources of Ethiopian Law from the 13th to the 20th Century' (1966) 3 *Journal of Ethiopian Law* 227–302.

Vaughan S., 'The Role of the Special Prosecutor's Office' in K. Tronvoll et al. (eds.), *The Ethiopian Red Terror Trials: Transitional Justice Challenged* (Suffolk: James Curry, 2009) 51–67.

Vestal T.M., 'Reflections on the Battle of Adwa and its Significance for Today' in P. Milkias and G. Metaferia (eds.), *The Battle of Adwa: Reflections on Ethiopia's Historic Against European Colonialism* (New York: Algora Publishing, 2005) 21–36.

Wiebel J., 'The State of Scholarship on the Ethiopian Red Terror' in ERTDRC, *Documenting the Red Terror: Bearing Witness to Ethiopia's Lost Generations* (Ottawa: ERTDRC North America Inc, 2012) 89–96.

Wiebel J., 'Let the Red Terror Intensify' Let the Red Terror intensify": political violence, governance and society in urban Ethiopia, 1976–78'., (2015) 48(1) *International journal of African Historical Studies* 13–30.

Woldemariam G.A., 'The Place of International Law in the Ethiopian Legal System' (2016) 1(1) *Ethiopian Yearbook of International Law* 61–93.

Wright Q., 'The Test of Aggression in the Italo-Ethiopian War' (1936) 30(1) *The American Journal of International Law* 50–55.

Young R., 'Fines and Forfeiture in International Criminal Justice' in R. Mulgrew and D. Abels (eds.), *Research Handbook on the International Penal System* (Cambridge: Cambridge University Press, 2016) 109–111.

Zewd B., 'The history of the Red Terror: Contexts and Consequences' in K. Tronvoll et al. (eds.), *The Ethiopian Red Terror Trials: Transitional Justice Challenged* (Martlesham: James Currey, 2009) 17–32.

Books and Dissertations

Abebe B. et Ficquet É., *Dictionnaire Français Amharique* (Addis Abeba: Shama Books, 2003).

Abtahi H. and Webb P., *The Genocide Convention: the Travaux Préparatoires* (Vol.II, Leiden: Martinus Nijhoff Publishers, 2008).

Akande D., *Classification of Armed Conflicts: Relevant Legal Concepts* (Oxford: Oxford University Press, 2011).

Ambos K., *Treatise on International Criminal Law, Vol I: Foundations and General Part* (Oxford: Oxford University Press, 2013).

Ambos K, *Treatise on International Criminal Law: Vol II, The Crimes and Sentencing* (Oxford, Oxford University Press, 2014.

Bassiouni M.C., *International Criminal Law: International Enforcement* (3rd ed., Leiden: Martinus Nijhoff Publishers, 2008).

Bassiouni M.C., *Crimes Against Humanity: Historical Evolution and Contemporary Application* (Cambridge: Cambridge University Press, 2011).

Bassiouni M.C., *Crimes Against Humanity: Historical Evolution and Contemporary Application* (Cambridge: Cambridge University Press, 2011).

Benvenisti E., *The International Law of Occupation* (2nd ed., Oxford: Oxford University Press, 2013).

Berhe A., *A Political History of the Tigray People's Liberation Front (1975–1991): Revolt, Ideology and Mobilisation in Ethiopia* (PhD Dissertation, Vrijie Universiteit Amsterdam, 2009).

Broomhall B., *International Justice and the International Criminal Court: Between Sovereignty and the Rule of Law* (Oxford: Oxford University Press, 2003).

Campbell I., *The Massacre of Debre Libanos: Ethiopia 1937: The Story of one of Fascism's Most Shocking Atrocities* (Addis Ababa: Addis Ababa University Press, 2014).

Campbell I., *The Addis Ababa Massacre: Italy's National Shame* (Oxford: Oxford University Press, 2017).

Cassese A., Gaeta P., Baig L., Fan M., Gosnell C. and Whiting A., *Cassese's International Criminal Law* (Oxford: Oxford University Press, 2013).

Chigara B., *Amnesty in International Law: The Legality under International Law of National Amnesty Laws*, (London: Longman, 2002).

Clapham A., Gaeta P. and Sassòli, M. (eds.), *The 1949 Geneva Conventions: A Commentary* (Oxford: Oxford University Press, 2014).

Clapham C., *Transformation and Continuality in Revolutionary Ethiopia* (Cambridge: Cambridge University Press, 1989).

Cohen J., *Intervening in Africa: Superpower Peacemaking in a Troubled Continent* (New York: St. Martin's Press LL.C., 2000).

Conley B., *Memory from the Margins: Ethiopia's Red Terror Martyrs Memorial Museum* (Gewerbestrasse: Palgrave Macmillan, 2019).

Corréard M.H. and Grundy V. (eds.), *The Oxford-Hachette French Dictionary* (2nd edn., Oxford: Oxford University Press, 1997).

Cryer R., *Prosecuting International Crimes: Selectivity and the International Criminal Law Regime* (Cambridge: Cambridge University Press, 2005).

Cryer R., Friman H., Robinson D. and Wilmshurst, E., *An Introduction to International Criminal Law and Procedure* (3rd ed., Cambridge: Cambridge University Press, 2014).

D'Ascoli S., *Sentencing and International Criminal Law; The UN ad hoc and Future perspectives for the ICC* (Oxford: Hurt Publishing, 2011).

Desta F., *Abiyotuna Tizitaye [my Reminiscences of the Revolution]* (Los Angeles: Tsehai Publishers, 2015).

Dinka T., *Ethiopia during the Derg Years: An Inside Account* (Los Angeles: Tsehai Publishers, 2016).

Dinstein Y., *War, Aggression and Self-Defence*, (5th ed, Cambridge: Cambridge University Press, 2005).

Dörmann K., *Elements of War Crimes under the Rome Statute of the International Criminal Court: Sources and Commentary* (Cambridge: Cambridge University Press, 2003).

Dungan J. and Lafore L.D., *Days of Emperor and Clown: The Italo-Ethiopian War, 1935–1936* (New York: Doubleday Books, 1973).

Ferdinandusse W., *Direct Application of International Law in National Courts* (The Hague: T.M.C. Asser Press, 2006).

Fisher S.Z., *Ethiopian Criminal Procedure: A Source Book* (Addis Ababa: Faculty of Law of Haile Selassie I University, 1969).

Fournet C., *The Crime of Destruction and the Law of Genocide: Their Impact on Collective Memory* (Aldershot: Ashget Publishing Limited, 2007).

Fournet C., *Genocide and Crimes Against Humanity: Misconception and Confusion in French Law and Practice* (Oxford: Hart Publishing, 2013).

Freeman M., *Necessary Evils: Amnesties and the Search for Justice* (Cambridge: Cambridge University Press, 2009).

Gallant K.S., *The Principle of Legality in International and Comparative Criminal Law* (Cambridge: Cambridge University Press, 2009).

Gemechu D., 'Conflict and Conflict Resolution among Waliso Oromo of Eastern Macha: The Case of the Guma' (PhD Dissertation, Addis Ababa University, 2007).

Grabenwarter C., *European Convention on Human Rights: Commentary* (München: C.H.Beck.Hart.Namos, 2014).

Graven P., *An Introduction to Ethiopian Penal Law: Arts.1–84 Penal Code* (Addis Ababa: Faculty of Law of Haile Selassie University I, 1965).

Haile D., *Accountability for Crimes of the Past and the Challenges of Criminal Prosecution: The Case of Ethiopia* (Leuven: Leuven University Press, 2000).

Haile-Selassie T., *The Ethiopian Revolution 1974–1991: From a Monarchical Autocracy to a Military Oligarchy* (London: Kegan Paul International, 1997).

Halliday F. and Maxine M., *The Ethiopian Revolution* (London: NLB, 1981).

Heller K.J., *The Nuremberg Military Tribunals and the Origins of International Criminal Law* (Oxford: Oxford University Press, 2011).

Henze P.B., *Layers of Time: A history of Ethiopia* (New York: Palgrave, 2000).

Jembere A., *An Introduction to the Legal History of Ethiopia: 1434–1974* (Lit Verslag: Münster, 2000).

Junod S.S., 'Commentary on Protocol II' in Sandoz and others (eds.), *Commentary on the Additional Protocols of 8 June 1977 to the Geneva Conventions of 12 August 1949* (Leiden: Martinus Nijhoff Publishers, 1987).

Kane T.L., *Amharic-English Dictionary: Volume II* (Wiesbaden: Otto Harrassowitz, 1990).

Kefale A., *Federalism and Ethnic Conflict in Ethiopia: A Comparative Regional Study* (New York: Routledge, 2013).

Kiros S., *Criminal Procedure Law: Principles, Rules and Practices* (Bloomington: Xlbris, 2010).

Kissi E., *Revolution and Genocide in Ethiopia and Cambodia*, (Lanham: Lexington Books, 2006).

Klabbers J., *International Law* (Cambridge: Cambridge University Press, 2013).

Kleffner J.K., 'Scope of Application of International Humanitarian Law' in D. Fleck (ed.), *The Hand Book of International Humanitarian Law* (3rd. ed., Oxford: Oxford University Press, 2013).

Lemkin R., *Axis Rule in Occupied Europe: Laws of Occupation, Analysis of Government, Proposals for Redress* (Washington: Carnegie Endowment for World Peace, 1944).

Leslau W., *English-Amharic Context Dictionary* (Wiesbaden: Otto Harrassowitz, 1973).

Lessa F. and Payne L. (eds.), *Amnesty in the Age of Human Rights Accountability: Comparative and International Perspectives* (Cambridge: Cambridge University Press, 2012).

Leta L., *The Ethiopian State at the Crossroads: Decolonization and Democratization or Disintegration* (Lawrenceville: Red Sea Press, 1999).

Mallinder L., *Amnesty, Human Rights and Political Transitions: Bridging the Peace and Justice Divide* (Portland: Hart Publishing, 2008).

Markakis J. and Nega A., *Class and Revolution in Ethiopia* (Nottingham: Spokesman Books, 1978).

Markham C.R., *A History of the Abyssinian Expedition* (London: Macmillan and Co., 1869).

Matsuoka A. and Sorenson J., *Ghosts and Shadows: Construction of Identity and Community in an African Diaspora* (Toronto: University of Toronto Press, 2001).

Metaferia G., *Ethiopia and the United States: History, Diplomacy, and Analysis* (New York: Algora Publishing, 2009).

Mettraux G., *International Crimes and The Ad Hoc Tribunals* (Oxford: Oxford University Press, 2005).

Mikaberidze A., *Atrocities, Massacres, and War Crimes, Vol I: an Encyclopedia* (Santa Barbara: ABC-CLIO, 2013).

Minear R.H., *Victors' Justice: The Tokyo War Crimes Trial* (Princeton: Princeton University Press, 1971).

Mulgrew R., *Towards the Development of the International Penal System* (Cambridge: Cambridge University Press, 2013).

Murray R., *The African Charter on Human and People's Rights: A Commentary* (Oxford: Oxford University Press, 2019).

Neave A., *On Trial at Nuremberg* (Boston: Little, Brown and Company, 1978).

Nersessian D.L., *Genocide and Political Groups* (Oxford: Oxford University Press, 2010).

Novak A., *Comparative Executive Clemency: The Constitutional Pardon Power and the Prerogative of Mercy in Global Perspective* (New York: Routledge, 2016).

Nowak M., *U.N. Covenant on Civil and Political Rights: CCPR Commentary* (Strasbourg: N.P. Engel, 1993).

Nowak M. and McArthur E., *The United Nations Convention against Torture: A Commentary* (Oxford: Oxford University Press, 2008).

Ntoubandi F.Z., *Amnesty for Crimes against Humanity under International Law* (Leiden: Martinus Nijhoff Publishers 2007).

O'Keefe R., *International Criminal Law* (Oxford: Oxford University Press, 2015).

Overy R., *A History of War in 100 Battles* (New York: William Collins, 2014).

Pankhurst R., *The History of Famine and Epidemics in Ethiopia prior to the Twentieth Century* (Addis Ababa: Relief and Rehabilitation Commission, 1985/1986).

Pausewang S., Tronvoll K. and Aalen L. (eds.), *Ethiopia Since the Derg: A decade of Democratic Pretension and Performance* (London: Zed Books Ltd, 2002).

Peterson M.J., *Recognition of Governments: Legal Doctrine and State Practice, 1815–1995* (London: Palgrave Macmillan UK, 1997).

Pictet J. (ed.), *Commentary on the Geneva Conventions of 12 August 1949, Vol. I-IV*, (Geneva: ICRC, 1952).

Quigle J.B., *The Genocide Convention: an International Law Analysis* (Aldershot: Ashgate Publishing Limited, 2006).

Rainey B., Wicks E. and Ovey, C., *The European Convention on Human Rights* (6th edn., Oxford: Oxford University Press, 2014).

Raymond J., *The Battle of Adwa: African History in the Age of Empire* (Cambridge: Harvard University Press, 2011).

Reta D.S., 'National Prosecution and Transitional Justice: the case of Ethiopia, (PhD Dissertation, University of Warwick School of Law, 2014).

Robinson N., *The Genocide Convention: A Commentary* (New York: Institute of Jewish Affairs, 1960).

Rosa A.M.L., *Preventing and Repressing International Crimes: Towards an "Integrated" Approach Based on Domestic Practice: Report of the Third Universal Meeting of National Committees for the Implementation of International Humanitarian Law, Volume I* (Geneva: International Committee of the Red Cross, 2014).

Sarbo D.N., *Contested Legitimacy: Coercion and the State in Ethiopia* (PhD Dissertation, University of Tennessee, 2009).

Schabas W.A., *Death Penalty in International Law* (3rd ed., Cambridge: Cambridge University Press, 2002).

Schabas W.A., *The UN International Criminal Tribunals: The Former Yugoslavia, Rwanda and Sierra Leone* (Oxford: Oxford University Press, 2006).

Schabas W.A, *Genocide in International Law: The Crime of Crimes* (2nd ed., Cambridge: Cambridge University Press, 2009).

Schabas W.A., *The European Human Rights Convention: A Commentary* (Oxford: Oxford University Press, 2015).

Schabas W.A., *Unimaginable Atrocities: Justice, Politics, and Rights at the War Crimes Tribunal* (Oxford: Oxford University Press, 2012).

Schabas W.A., *An Introduction to the International Criminal Court* (5th ed., Cambridge: Cambridge University Press, 2017).

Scholler H., *The Special Court of Ethiopia:1922–1935* (Stuttgart: F. Steiner Verlag Wiesbaden, 1985).

Shaw M.N., *International Law* (6th ed., Cambridge: Cambridge University Press, 2008).

Shifaw D., *The Diary of Terror: Ethiopia 1974–1991* (Bloomington: Trafford Publishing, 2012).

Shinn D.H. and Ofcansky T.P., *Historical Dictionary of Ethiopia* (Lanham: Scarecrow Press, 2013).

Smeulers A. and Grünfeld A., *International Crimes and other Gross Human Rights Violations: A Multi- and Interdisciplinary Textbook* (Leiden: Martinus Nijhoff Publishers, 2011).

Stan L. and Nedelsky N. (eds.), *Encyclopaedia of Transitional Justice: Volume II.* (Cambridge: Cambridge University Press, 2013).

Staub E., *The Roots of Evil: The Origins of Genocide and Other Group Violence* (Cambridge: Cambridge University Press, 1989).

C.J., Berster L. and Schiffbauer B. (eds.), *Convention on the Prevention and Punishment of the Crime of Genocide: A Commentary* (München: Verlag C.H. Beck oHG, 2014).

Teffera H., *Tower in the Sky* (Addis Ababa: Addis Ababa University Press, 2012).

Tereke G., *The Ethiopian Revolution: War in the Horn of Africa* (New Haven: Yale University Press, 2009).

Tesfaye A., *Political Power and Ethnic Federalism: The struggle for Democracy in Ethiopia* (Lanham: University Press of America, 2002).

Tessema M.T., *Prosecution of Politicide in Ethiopia: The Red-Terror Trials* (The Hague: Asser Printing Press, 2018).

Thirlway H., *The Sources of International Law* (Oxford: Oxford University Press, 2014).

Tiruneh A., *The Ethiopian Revolution, 1974–1987: A transformation from aristocratic to a totalitarian autocracy* (Cambridge: Cambridge University Press, 1993).

Tola B., *To kill the Generation: The Red Terror in Ethiopia* (2nd ed., Washington DC: Free Ethiopian Press, 1989).

Triffterer O. and Ambos K. (eds.), *The Rome Statute of the International Criminal Court: A Commentary* (3rd ed., München: C.H.Beck.Hart.Namos, 2016).

Tronvoll K., Schaefer C. and Aneme G.A. (eds.), *The Ethiopian Red Terror Trials: Transitional Justice Challenged* (Martlesham: James Currey, 2009).

United Nations War Crimes Commission, The (Compilers), *History of the United Nations War Crimes Commission and the Development of the Laws of War* (London: His Majesty's Stationery Office, 1948).

van Langenhove F., *The growth of a legend; a study based upon the German accounts of francs-tireurs and 'atrocities' in Belgium* (New York: G.P. Putnam's Sons, 1916).

Vestal T.M., *Ethiopia: A Post-Cold War African State* (Westport: Preager Publishers, 1999).

Viljoen F., *International Human Rights Law in Africa* (Oxford: Oxford University Press, 2007). Werle G. and Jessberger F., *Principles of International Criminal Law* (3rd ed., Oxford: Oxford University Press, 2014).

Whitebread C. and Slobogin C., *Criminal Procedure: An Analysis of Cases and Concept*, (3rd edn, New York: The Foundation Press, 1993).

Wilson R.A., *The politics of truth and reconciliation in South Africa – legitimizing the Post-Apartheid State* (Cambridge: Cambridge University Press, 2001).

Wittmann R., *Beyond Justice: The Auschwitz Trial* (Cambridge: Harvard University Press, 2005) 15–53.

Wogederes F., *Egnana Abiyotu [We and the Revolution]* (Los Angeles: Tsehai Publishers, 2014).

Woldegiorgis D., *Red Tears: War, Famine and Revolution in Ethiopia* (Trenton, The Red Sea Press, 1989).

Young J., *Peasant Revolution in Ethiopia: The Tigray People's Liberation Front, 1975–1991* (Cambridge: Cambridge University Press, 1997).

Zahara A. and Sluiter G., *International Criminal Law* (Oxford: Oxford University Press, 2008).

Zewde B., *A History of Modern Ethiopia: 1855–1991* (2nd edn., Oxford: James Currey Ltd, 2001).

Zewde B., *The Quest for Socialist Utopia: The Ethiopian Student Movement, c. 1960–1974* (Oxford: James Currey Ltd, 2014).

Other Documents

'Giving Peace a Chance' (1990) (13)3 *Quarterly Yekatit*.

'The Search for Lasting Peace' (1990)13(4) *Quarterly Yekatit*.

Bridle B., 'Ethiopia 1935–36: Mustard gas and attacks on the Red Cross' *Le Temps* (13 August 2003), available at <https://www.icrc.org/en/doc/resources/documents/article/other/5ruhgm.htm> accessed 27 September 2019.

Central Statistical Agency of Ethiopia, 'Census 2007 Report: National Statistical', 72–73, available at <http://www.csa.gov.et/census-report/complete-report/census-2007> accessed 27 September 2019.

Department of State, 'Country Reports on Human Rights Practices for 1990', available at: <https://archive.org/details/countryreportson1990unit> accessed 27 September 2019.

Ethiopian News Agency, 'Peace Talks Resume' 1989 (13) (2) *Quarterly Yekatit*.

BIBLIOGRAPHY   491

European Parliament Resolution on the Situation in Ethiopia and the New Border Conflict (P6_TA(2005)0535), adopted 15 December 2005, para. 5, available at: <http://www.europarl.europa.eu/sides/getDoc.do?type=TA&reference=P6-TA-2005-0535&language=EN> accessed 27 September 2019.

Hamber B. and Kibble S., *From Truth to Transformation: The Truth and Reconciliation Commission in South Africa,* Catholic Institute for International Relations, February 1999, available at: <http://www.csvr.org.za/publications/1714-from-truth-to-transformation-the-truth-and-reconciliation-commission-in-south-africa> accessed 27 September 2019.

Immigration and Refugee Board of Canada, *Ethiopia: Conscription since the May 1998 war with Eritrea, including the minimum age by law and in practice, and the treatment by the authorities of youth leaders who refuse to persuade others to volunteer or advise them not to be conscripted,* 23 June 2000, ETH34702.E, available at: <https://www.refworld.org/docid/3ae6ad5b34.html> accessed 27 September 2019.

Kesito A., 'Death Penalty in Ethiopia' (Adama, *Conference Paper,* September 2013) 20–25.

Lata L., 'The Making and Un-making of Ethiopia's Transitional Charter', Paper presented on the thirty-seventh annual meeting of the African Studies Association (No.1994:105, Toronto: November 1994) 1–23.

Colletta N. et al., 'Case Studies in War-to-Peace Transition: the Demobilization and Reintegration of Ex-Combatants in Ethiopia, Namibia, and Uganda' The World Bank (Washington, D.C.: 30 June 1996) 27, available at: <http://documents.worldbank.org/curated/en/1996/06/696461/case-studies-war-to-peace-transition-demobilization-reintegration-ex-combatants-ethiopia-namibia-uganda> accessed 27 September 2019..

Office of the Prosecutor, *The principle of complementarity in practice* (informal expert paper), available at: <https://www.icc-cpi.int/NR/rdonlyres/20BB4494-70F9-4698-8E30-907F631453ED/281984/complementarity.pdf> accessed 27 September 2019.

Prosperi L., 'The Missed Italian Nuremberg: The History of an Internationally-sponsored Amnesty' available at <https://papers.ssrn.com/sol3/papers.cfm?abstract_id=2887267> accessed 27 September 2019.

Report of Truth and Reconciliation Commission of South Africa, V. IV (1998), para. 48, available at <http://www.justice.gov.za/trc/report/finalreport/Volume%204.pdf> accessed 26 May 2019.

Shaw R., 'Rethinking Truth and Reconciliation Commissions: Lessons from Sierra Leone' (United States Institute for Peace Special Reports, Washington DC, 2005) 7 available at: <https://www.usip.org/publications/2005/02/rethinking-truth-and-reconciliation-commissions-lessons-sierra-leone> accessed 27 September 2019.

South Africa,'Report of The Truth and Reconciliation Commission: Minority Position' (TRC, Vol 5, 29 October 1998) 443–444 available at:<http://www.justice.gov.za/trc/report/finalreport/Volume5.pdf> accessed 27 September 2019.

Special Prosecutor's Office, *Dem Yazele Dossie: Begizeyawi Wetaderawi Dergue Weyem Mengist Abalat Benetsuhan Zegoch Laye Yetefetseme Wenjel Zegeba* (Addis Ababa: Far-East Trading P.L.C., 2010).

SPO, 'Report of the Office of the Special Prosecutor 1994: The Special Prosecution Process of War Criminals and Human Rights Violation in Ethiopia' in N.J. Kritz (ed.), *Transitional Justice: How emerging democracies reckon with former regimes; Laws, Rulings and Reports* (Washington DC: United States Institute of Peace Press, 1995) 559–575.

The Carter Center, 'Observing the 2005 Ethiopian National Elections: Carter Center Final Report' December 2009, Available at: <https://www.cartercenter.org/resources/pdfs/news/peace_publications/election_reports/ethiopia-2005-finalrpt.pdf> accessed 27 September 2019.

The Foreign Secretary, Letter to the Foreign and Common Wealth Office (London SW1A 2AH), 10 January 1986, 2 available at: <https://discovery.nationalarchives.gov.uk/details/r/C14568616#imageViewerLink> accessed 27 September 2019.

The Observatory, 'Ethiopia: The Situation of Human Rights from Bad to Worse' (FIDH-OMCT Report of International Mission of Judicial Observation, No.463, 2 December 2006), 12–15, available at: <http://www.omct.org/files/2006/12/3823/ethiopia_obs4632_1106_eng.pdf> accessed 27 September 2019.

Trial Observation and Information Project (TOIP), *Ethiopia's Red Terror Trials: Africa's First War Tribunal* (Consolidated Summary and Reports from Trial Observations made from 1996–1999, Compiled by NIHR's Project, 2000).

Tsadik H., 'Prosecuting the past- affecting the future: the Ethiopian Transitional Justice Trials' (A SIDA Minor Field Study, Department of Peace and Conflict Research Uppsala University, 2007), 16 available at: <https://www.pcr.uu.se/digitalAssets/654/c_654492-l_1-k_mfs_tsadic.pdf> accessed 27 September 2019.

Tsegaw E., 'Luba Basa & Harma Hodha: Traditional Mechanisms of Conflict Resolution in Metekkel, Ethiopia' (Asien-Afrika-Institut, Universität Hamburg, Germany, 2004) available at: <http://www.justiciarestaurativa.org/mount/www.restorative-justice.org/Articlesdb/Articles/4657> accessed 27 September 2019.

U.S. Department of State, '2005 Country Reports on Human Rights Practices: Ethiopia' (Bureau of Democracy, Human Rights, and Labor, 8 March 2006), Section 1(a), available at: <https://www.state.gov/j/drl/rls/hrrpt/2005/61569.htm> accessed 27 September 2019.

U.S. Department of State, '2006 Country Reports on Human Rights Practices: Ethiopia' (Bureau of Democracy, Human Rights, and Labor, 6 March 2007), available at: <https://www.state.gov/j/drl/rls/hrrpt/2006/78734.htm> accessed 27 September 2019.

U.S. Department of State, 'Ethiopia Human Rights Practices, 1993' (U.S. State Department, 31 January 1994), available at: <https://www.refworld.org/docid/3ae6aa4d10.html> accessed 27 September 2019.

U.S. Department of State, Bureau of Democracy, Human Rights, and Labor, *2006 Country Reports on Human Rights Practices: Ethiopia* (6 March 2006), available at <https://www.state.gov/j/drl/rls/hrrpt/2006/78734.htm> accessed 27 September 2019.

Vaughan S., 'The Addis Ababa Transitional Conference of July 1991: Its Origins, History and Significance' (1994) 54(1) *Occasional Papers, Edinburgh University Centre of African Studies* 1–79.

Warner R., 'The Workers' Party of Ethiopia' (A report Prepared by the Federal Research Division of the Library of Congress under an Interagency Agreement, Washington DC, 12 October 1984), available at: <http://oai.dtic.mil/oai/oai?verb=getRecord&metadataPrefix=html&identifier=ADA303418> accessed 27 September 2019.

Wijkman A., 'European Parliament Delegation to Observe Federal and Regional Parliamentary Elections in Ethiopia: A Report, 12–17 May 2005' (June 2005), Annex C, 1. available at: <http://www.europarl.europa.eu/intcoop/election_observation/missions/2004–2009/20051505_ethiopia.pdf> accessed 27 September 2019.

General Comments, Reports, and Resolutions

Committee Against Torture (CAT), *Concluding observations of the Committee against Torture: Ethiopia*, 20 January 2011, CAT/C/ETH/CO/1, paras. 10, 26, 29, available at<http://www.refworld.org/docid/4d6cca412.html> accessed 27 September 2019.

G.A. Res. 96 (I), UN Doc. N231, (11 December 1946).

Human Rights Committee, General Comment 31, Nature of the General Legal Obligation on States Parties to the Covenant, U.N. Doc. CCPR/C/21/Rev.1/Add.13 (2004).

Report of the International Commission of Inquiry on Darfur to the Secretary General, pursuant to Security Council Resolution SC Res. 1564, 18 September 2004, Annex to Letter dated 31 January 2005 from the Secretary-General addressed to the President of the Security Council, S/2005/60, 1 February 2005.

Resolution Adopted by the General Assembly [on the report of the Third Committee (A/52/644/Add.2)] Resolution 52/135, Situation of Human Rights in Cambodia, adopted on 27 February 1998, A/RES/52/135, available at: <http://www.unakrt-online.org/content/resolution-52135-adopted-general-assembly> accessed 30 September 2019.

Security Council, Resolution 780(1992) Adopted by the Security Council at its 3119th meeting on 6 October 1991, S/RES/780(1992), available at: <http://www.un.org/en/ga/search/view_doc.asp?symbol=S/RES/780(1992)> accessed 30 September 2019.

Security Council, Resolution 935(1994) Adopted by the Security Council at its 3400th meeting on 1 July 1994, S/RES/935(1994), available at: <https://www.refworld.org/docid/3b00f16034.html> accessed 30 September 2019.

UN Security Council Resolution 1593 (31 March 2005) UN Doc S/RES/1593.

UN Security Council, Security Council Resolution 1595 (2005) on Lebanon, adopted by the Security Council at its 5160th meeting on 7 April 2005, S/RES/1595 (2005) available at: <https://unispal.un.org/DPA/DPR/unispal.nsf/0/AAF6AAC927E83BEE85256FDD0050FCFA> accessed 30 September 2019.

United Nations High Commissioner for Human Rights, Situation of human rights in East Timor: Commission on Human Rights resolution 1999/S-4/1(adopted at its fourth special session), 27 September 1999, available at: <http://www.unhchr.ch/Huridocda/Huridoca.nsf/(Symbol)/E.CN.4.RES.1999.S-4.1.En?Opendocument> accessed 30 September 2019.

Electronic Sources

'Ethiopian President Asks for Cease-Fire', *The Stanford Daily*, 23 May 1991, available at: <http://stanforddailyarchive.com/cgi-bin/stanford?a=d&d=stanford19910523-01.2.16> accessed 27 September 2019.

'President Mulatu Grants Amnesty to TPDM members' (Ethiopian Brodacatsting Service, 26 October 2015), available at<http://www.ebc.et/web/ennews/-/president-mulatu-grants-amnesty-to-tpdm-members> accessed 28 October 2015.

Ethiopian rebels pledge democratic rule', *The Stanford Daily* (London, 29 May 1991), available at:<http://stanforddailyarchive.com/cgi-bin/stanford?a=d&d=stanford19910529-01.2.19&e=-------en-20--1--txt-txIN-------> accessed 27 September 2019.

Targeting the *Anuak*, Human Rights Watch, available at: <http://www.hrw.org /reports /2005/03/23/targeting-*Anuak*> accessed 27 September 2019.

Addis Ababa University School of Law: An Overview, available at: <http://www.aau.edu.et/clgs/academics/school-of-law/overview/> accessed 27 September 2019.

African Watch, 'Ethiopia, Waiting for Justice: Shortcomings in Establishing the Rule of Law' (Human Rights Watch, 8 May 1992), available at: <http://www.refworld.org/docid/45cc5f472.html> accessed 27 September 2019.

Aljazeera News, 'Andargachew Tsige Pardoned by Ethiopia' available at: <https://www.aljazeera.com/news/2018/05/andargachew-tsige-pardoned-ethiopia-180526163642586.html> accessed 27 September 2019.

Amnesty International, 'Amnesty International Report 2006: Ethiopia', 23 May 2006, available at: <https://www.refworld.org/docid/447ff7a62f.html> accessed 27 September 2019.

Amnesty International, 'Because I am *Oromo*: Sweeping repression in the Oromia region of Ethiopia' (Amnesty International Report, 27 October 2014), available at: <https://www.amnesty.org/en/documents/afr25/006/2014/en/> accessed 27 September 2019.

BIBLIOGRAPHY

Amnesty International, 'Death Sentences and Executions in 2013' 26 March 2014, available at: <http://www.amnestyusa.org/sites/default/files/act500012014en.pdf> accessed 27 September 2019.

Amnesty International, 'Ethiopia: End of an Era of Brutal Repression – A New Chance for Human Rights' (Amnesty International, 18 June 1991), available at: <https://www.amnesty.org/en/documents/afr25/005/1991/en/> accessed 20 March 2019.

Amnesty International, 'Ethiopia: Report of 1994' (Amnesty International, January 1994), available at: <http://www.refworld.org/docid/3ae6a9f512.html> accessed 27 September 2019.

Amnesty International, 'Ethiopian Activist at Risk of Torture: Andargachew Tsige', 4 July 2014, Index number: AFR 25/003/2014, available at: <https://www.amnesty.org/en/documents/afr25/003/2014/en/> accessed 27 September 2019.

Amnesty International, 'Justice Under Fire: Trials of opposition leaders, journalists and human rights defenders in Ethiopia' (Amnesty International Report, 29 July 2011), available at: <https://www.amnesty.org/en/documents/AFR25/002/2011/en/> accessed 27 September 2019.

BBC News, 'Ethiopia to Host Africa Union Summit after Omar al-Bashir Malawi Row' (12 June 2012), available at: <http://www.bbc.co.uk/news/world-africa-18407396> accessed 27 September 2019.

BBC News, 'US admits helping Mengistu escape' (The BBC, 22 December 1991), available at: <http://news.bbc.co.uk/2/hi/africa/575405.stm> accessed 27 September 2019.

European Parliament Resolution on Ethiopia (P6-TA(2006)0501) *adopted 16 November 2006*, para B, available at: <http://www.europarl.europa.eu/sides/getDoc.do?pubRef=-//EP//TEXT+TA+P6-TA-2006-0501+0+DOC+XML+V0//EN> accessed 27 September 2019.

European Parliament Resolution on the Situation in Ethiopia (P6_TA(2005)0383), adopted 13 October 2005, available at: <http://www.europarl.europa.eu/sides/getDoc.do?type=TA&reference=P6-TA-2005-0383&language=BG&ring=B6-2005-0541> accessed 27 September 2019.

Harden B., 'Rebel leaders Pledges Coalition Government, then Free Elections' The Washington Post (Washington DC, 29 May 1991), available at: <https://www.washingtonpost.com/archive/politics/1991/05/29/rebel-leader-pledges-coalition-government-then-free-elections/a5818143-9397-470d-a1b2-b44e28e9e98d/> accessed 27 September 2019.

Human Rights Watch, 'Ethiopia: Crackdown Spreads Beyond Capital, as Arbitrary Arrests Continue, Detainees Face Torture and Ill-Treatment' 15 June 2005, available at: <https://www.hrw.org/news/2005/06/15/ethiopia-crackdown-spreads-beyond-capital> accessed 27 September 2019.

Human Rights Watch, 'Ethiopia: Events of 2018' available at: <https://www.hrw.org/world-report/2019/country-chapters/ethiopia> accessed 27 September 2019.

Human Rights Watch, 'Ethiopia: Reckoning under the Law' (Human rights Watch, 1 December), available at: <https://www.hrw.org/report/1994/12/01/ethiopia-reckoning-under-law> accessed 27 September 2019.

Human Rights Watch, 'Evil Days: 30 Years of War and Famine in Ethiopia' (Report of African Watch, September 1991), available at <https://www.hrw.org/sites/default/files/reports/Ethiopia919.pdf> accessed 27 September 2019.

Human Rights Watch, 'War Crimes in Bosnia Herzegovina' (Report of Helsinki Watch, August 1992), available at: <https://www.hrw.org/reports/pdfs/y/yugoslav/yugo.928/yugo928full.pdf> accessed 27 September 2019.

Human Rights Watch, 'World Report 2006: Ethiopia, Events of 2005', available at: <https://www.hrw.org/world-report/2006/country-chapters/ethiopia> accessed 27 September 2019.

Human Rights Watch, 'World Report 2016: Ethiopia, Events of 2015', available at: <https://www.hrw.org/world-report/2016/country-chapters/ethiopia> accessed 27 September 2019.

Human Rights Watch, Collective Punishment: War Crimes and Crimes against Humanity in the Ogaden area of Ethiopia's Somali Region, 13 June 2008, available at: <http://www.hrw.org/node/62176> accessed 27 September 2019.

Human Rights Watch, *Ethiopia: Waiting For Justice: Shortcomings in Establishing the Rule of Law*, 8 May 1992, available at: <https://www.refworld.org/docid/45cc5f472.html> accessed 27 September 2019.

Human Rights Watch's Submission to the Committee against Torture on Ethiopia September 2010', available at: <http://tbinternet.ohchr.org/Treaties/CAT/Shared%20Documents/ETH/INT_CAT_NGO_ETH_45_8752_E.pdf> accessed 27 September 2019.

Kiley S., 'A pointless, savage war is finally over' *CNN* (18 September 2018), available at <https://edition.cnn.com/2018/09/18/opinions/ethiopia-eritrea-war-comes-to-an-end-kiley-opinion-intl/index.html> accessed 27 September 2019.

Krauss C., 'Ethiopia's Dictator Flees: Officials Seeking U.S. Help', *The New York Times*, 22 May 1991, available at: <<http://www.nytimes.com/1991/05/22/world/ethiopia-s-dictator-flees-officials-seeking-us-help.html?pagewanted=all> accessed 27 September 2019.

Lewthwaite G.A., 'Rebels pledge democracy in Ethiopia: U.S.-brokered talks end in agreement after fall of capital' The Baltimore Sun (London, 29 May 1991), available at: <http://Articles.baltimoresun.com/1991-05-29/news/1991149072_1_addis-ababa-ethiopians-eprdf> accessed 27 September 2019.

Maasho A. and E., 'Africans Tell ICC: Heads of State Should not be Tried' (Reuters, World News, 11 October 2013) available at: <http://www.reuters.com/article/us-africa-icc-idUSBRE99A0YT20131011> accessed 27 September 2019.

Prime Minister Abiy Ahmed Speech to the Parliament, 1 July 2018, available at<https://www.youtube.com/watch?v=wJnC2aX4jP8&t=8079s> accessed 27 September 2019.

The Associated Press, 'Inquiry Says Ethiopian Troops Killed 193 in Ballot Protests in '05', *The New York Times*, 19 October 2006, available at: <http://www.nytimes.com/2006/10/19/world/africa/19ethiopia.html> accessed 27 September 2019.

Trial International. 'Martin Bormann' available at <'https://trialinternational.org/latest-post/martin-bormann/> accessed 27 September 2019.

Index

1930 Penal Code   107, 108n73, 194–195, 317–318
59 Senior officials   59
a rule of IHL, violations of   321, 323–324, 325
a year zero for democracy   122–123

Abera Ayalew et al   257n118
Abiy Ahmed   136
Absorption and addition rules   421–422
Abuse of power   6–7n28, 71–72, 71–72n150, 74n163, 137, 175, 266, 374–375, 435
Addis Ababa Conference   53–55, 57, 88
African Human Rights Commission   341–342n163
aggravated homicide   73n157, 74n166, 77n176, 177, 229nn206–209, 229–231, 229nn206–209, 230nn210–212, 253, 253n97, 253–254n95, 254n99, 386–387nn85–87, 386–387nn85–87
Aggravated property damage   6–7n28, 71–72
Aggravating Factors   257–258, 394–395, 394n129, 407, 408, 409n208, 411, 417–418, 419, 418–419n265, 420–421, 422, 425, 447
Aliyu Yusuf Ibrahim et al   285, 286, 288, 373–374n8, 421, 428n339
All Ethiopian Socialist Movement   48n27, 54
American Bar Association   20–22n87
Amhara Supreme Court   152–153, 423
Amnesty   38, 159
　Amnesty laws 36, 43–44n2
　Blanket amnesty 64
　De facto amnesty 93, 136, 137
　Self-proclaimed amnesty 137
　Not subjected to amnesty 169, 203
another war, see also Second Italo-Ethiopian war,   315
anti-people   228nn197–198, 246–247n50
anti-revolutionary   228n198, 277–278n222
anti-unity   227–228, 279n239
Anuak-Nuwer   9–10, 9–10n35, 14, 24–25, 28, 44, 44–45n10, 45, 50, 129, 130, 131, 140–141, 170, 237, 248, 249, 253, 272–273, 286, 288, 299–300n355, 373–374, 375, 378–379n32, 387–388n89

Apology   8–9, 16–17n65, 94, 96–97n24, 98n29, 100–101n42, 117, 118n129, 119–122, 136, 254n100, 397–399, 406, 434, 446–447
AP I   320–321, 335–336
AP II   103
Applicable law   38n146, 40, 63–64n104, 76–77, 76–77n174, 106–107n66, 107–108, 189–190, 208, 232, 233n222, 441, 442, 443
Article 38, ICJ Statute   340n162
As such   191, 200–201, 207–208, 214, 216, 219, 224–225, 226–227, 229–230, 239–240, 242, 248, 259–261n133, 265–266, 271–272, 277–278n219
AZAPO judgment   56, 61n96

Bargaining power   58, 110, 112
Begashaw Gurmessa   291–292
Big-Fish   93, 143–144, 273–274
Bodily Harm   100–101n41, 210, 217, 256–258
Bodily injury   211, 215, 216, 229, 251, 256–257, 258–259n123, 259–262, 296–297, 303–304, 354, 355, 358–359, 359–360n235, 364, 369–370, 371–372
Bosnia and Herzegovina v. *Serbia and Montenegro*   239–240n14, 245–246n47, 300–301n363

campaigns of violence   276n214
Cantoral-Benavides v. *Peru*   34n135
Central Revolutionary Investigation Department   268, 280–282, 292
Cherif Bassiouni   69–70, 232–233
Chila   102, 332n124, 354
Circular situation of inter-dependence   287
Civilized Nations   230–231, 340n162
Coalition for Unity and Democracy   10–11
Coalition of Democratic Ethiopia Forces (CODEF)   48n27, 54
Codification Commission   207–208, 213
Cohen, Herman   49, 50, 51, 126–127
Commission of inquiry   60, 66–68n123, 68–70, 69nn133-134, 130, 133–134, 163–164, 239–240n14, 247n55, 249, 288–289n291, 435–436

INDEX

499

Common Article 3   325–326, 327–328
Compliance ensuring measures   432–433
Compulsory Movement   214, 216
Conflicting domestic laws, impermissibility   441
Constitutions of Ethiopia
  1931 Constitution43–44n189, 81–82, 170–171n144, 193, 193n20
  1955 Revised Constitution43–44, 81–82n191, 82, 82n200, 85, 107–108, 107–108n71, 170–171n144, 193n21
  1989 PDRE Constitution6n33, 87, 210–211, 219–220
  1995 FDRE Constitution, *see also* FDRE Constitution,6–7n 26, 165–166, 249–250
  Constitutional Interpretation171–172n 144, 221n 159
  Ephemeral Constitutions106, 218–219
Constitutions
  of Angola63–64n120, 65, 132
  of Brazil63–64n117, 132
  of Colombia63 65, 132
  of Ecuador132
  of Pakistan63–64n119
  of Philippines63–64n116
  of Venezuela132
Convention Against Torture   75, 222, 259–261n133
Convention on the Non-Applicability of Statutory Limitations to War Crimes and Crimes   77, 77n175, 437, 437n7, 449
Convention on the Prevention and Punishment of the Crime of Genocide   2–3, 20–22n88, 96–97, 98, 99, 100, 191, 239n14
  Article V194–195, 209, 219–220, 376–377n25
  Article II201, 204, 214, 216, 238
  Article III187–88, 96–97, 194–195n22, 209, 236
Core crimes   1–2, 1–2n1, 6–7, 11–12, 14–15, 18, 19, 20–22, 23, 24–25
Crime without a name   195n29
Crimes against Humanity   20–22n 87, 20–22n88, 71, 72, 78, 137, 169, 223, 262–263,
  Not trials for crimes againts humanity75–76
  Duty to prosecute crimes against himanity104–105, 131
  Genocide as crimes against humanity,197, 198, 200–201
  Humanity195, 243
Crimes in Violation of International Law   321–322
Criminal Procedure Code 1960   24–25n96,
  Article 160174nn169-170, 177nn184-185
  Article 161176, 177–178
CUD trials (Cases)   10–11, 14, 28, 130, 135
Customary International Law
  On the ambit of genocide99–100
  On rules of IHL232
  On non-international armed conflict328 345–347
  On direct application of371, 442
  Effective Penalty/ Penal Snactions

Dagnenet Ayalew et al   292n316, 301n366
Darfur situation   57
Darfur Commission/ report   247, 288–289
David Michael Nicholas v. *Australia*   36–37n141, 340n160
Death Penalty (Capital Punishment)   64, 391–393, 394–395
Debela Dinsa Wege et al.   250n117
Dem Yazele Dossie   8–9n33, 61–62, 61–62n99, 85–86nn226-227, 96n22, 97n27, 102n48, 104n58, 114n109, 145n21, 146–149n36, 149n41, 152n54, 155n74, 156, 156n49, 156n80, 339n121
Democratic Republic of Congo v. Belgium   83–84n209
Democratic Republic of the Congo v. Uganda   328–330n115
Dergue   5–6n19
Dergue regime   5–6n20, 6–7
Dessein   205, 206
Deterrence   377–378, 404, 405–406
Direct Application of IHL   87, 312, 325, 333–334, 337, 343, 345, 371
direct application of IHL   312, 325, 337
direct involvement of state officials   276n214
disappeared deceased   141–142
discretion to create judicial mitigating factors   418, 418–419n270

Domestic crimes 6–7n28, 8–9n33, 20–22n87, 32–33, 32–33n125, 44n10, 62, 63, 71–72, 73–74, 131–132, 161–162, 168–169, 310, 374–375, 374–375n11, 376, 377–378, 380–381, 388–389n97, 391–392, 408, 429–430, 435, 439, 444, 446
Double Counting 407, 409–410, 430
Draft Criminal Code of 1989 215, 242, 386
Dual judicial structue, 6–7n26

early release 390–391, 402–403
Enforced Disappearance 36–37n140, 255, 269, 270–271
Eritrea 46n15, 49, 51n42, 54–55
Eritrean Liberation Front 47, 309–310
Eritrean Penal Code of 2015 266–267n162
Eshetu Alemu 31–32, 310–311, 421–422n290, 445n9
Eshetu Alemu 31–32, 310–311, 328–330n120, 421–422
establishment of institutions of violence 276n214, 278
Ethiopia
 Armed conflicts 308–310
 International criminal justice 1–2n2, 2–3
 International treaties ratified 2–3nn5-10, 313–314nn 27-29
 Origins and history of 1–2, 4nn13-15
 Peae keeping operations 1–2n4
Ethiopian Criminal Law Network 28–29
Ethiopian Democratic Union 97, 309–310
Ethiopian Jews 48, 50–51n42
Ethiopian People's Revolutionary Party (EPRP) 9–10n 33, 16–17n 64, 48n27, 61, 151, 152n55, 156, 245, 298
Ethiopian Peoples' Revolutionary Army 154, 310
Ethiopian Peoples' Revolutionary Democratic Front (EPRDF) 10–11, 46–47, 53–54, 91, 111, 116, 124, 125–127, 293–294
Ethiopian Television 97–98n27
Ethiopian Trials 15, 19–20, 140, 190, 406, 422, 425–426, 441, 448
Ethiopian War Crimes Commission 316
Ethnic groups 234–235, 240–241, 242, 248, 272–273

European Convention on Human Rights 98, 100
European Parliament 123–124n158, 127–128, 163n107, 168–169n132
Extradition 177–178
Extradition, obligation to request 177

Federal Anti-Corruption and Ethics Commission v. Asmare Abate et al 175
Federal Prosecutor v. Engineer Hailu Shawul et al, 27, 161–162, 162–163n101, 286, 287, 289, 292–293, 294
Federal Prosecutor v. Gure uchala et al 141
Fédération Nationale de Déportés et Internés Résistants et Patriotes And Others v. *Barbie* C1.P31 n88
FDRE Constitution
 Article 13 166, 220, 234–235, 338, 339
 Article 15 64n111, 165–166n118, 393n124
 Article 22 234, 338, 344–345, 399
 Article 28 78, 80, 95, 131, 133–134, 169, 203–204, 338, 345, 391–392
FDRE Criminal Code
 Article 270 202n66, 318–319, 348–349, 358–359, 360n212, 360, 360–361n244, 361
 Article 269 10–11, 197n40, 202, 208n111, 217–218, 218n147, 253n87, 256, 258, 270, 285, 399
 Article 276 336–337, 345, 347–349, 361
 Article 316 64–65n112
Federal Crimes Act of 1953
Fournet 259, 287
franc-tireur 324–325
Functional equivalence 20–22, 282, 376

General Comment 31 35n136, 181n208
general mens rea 252nn83-84, 252–253
Genocide through Rape-Trauma Syndrome (RTS-genocide) 263–264
Gereb 119–120
German Border Guard case 231n216
Gesgese Gebremeskel Ateraga et al 395, 422
Getachew Teke'aba 395
Grave willful injury 6–7n28, 71–72, 75, 203–204, 259–262, 259–261n133, 368–369
Group is central to 242

INDEX

Gudegambela 119–120n132
Guma, 119–120n133

Hailu Burrayu et al. 381–382
Harma Hodha 119–120n134
Hawzien 102, 353–354
Heinous crimes 65, 132
Hissène Habré 36–37n140
Historically unjust relationships 130
House of Federation 6–7n26, 81–82n196, 141

ICC Statute
  Article 7(2)f262–263
  Article 8(2)312
  Elements of Crimes266, 284–285, 363
ICTR Statute 66n122, 202–203, 380–381
ICTY Statute 66n122, 202–203
In Absentia 6–7, 11–12n46, 140, 170, 170–171n141, 171–172, 172–173nn 153-157, 173, 173n161, 186, 285, 310–311, 373–374n2, 374, 376, 376–377n19, 425, 425–426n315, 437–438
In part 90n2, 98n29, 131, 210, 211, 215, 217, 241, 251–252, 261–263, 267, 271–272, 275, 294–295, 296, 297–299, 299–300nn 355-356, 302, 416–417n 255
In whole 98n29, 131, 210, 211, 215, 217, 241, 251–252, 261–263, 267, 271–273, 275, 294–295, 297–299
Individual circumstances 392–393, 447
Individualization 378, 428, 429–430n342
Initial Penalty 408, 409n 207, 409, 410, 411n219
Inquiry commission 69n132, 133–134nn187-188, 135, 163–164n109, 164, 164n111, 165n115, 168, 169nn136-137, 249n66
Institutions of Violence 146–149n39, 276, 279–280
Intent 204, 204–205n84, 206–208, 213, 214, 215, 251–252, 251–252n80, 252–253nn 85-86, 254n97, 263–264, 271–274, 275, 276, 277, 278, 282, 284–285, 286, 287–289, 290, 292–293, 297, 298, 302, 303, 304, 306, 363, 369, 440–441
Inter-American Court of Human Rights 23
Inter-dependence 287, 287n285
Internal Health 211–212, 251, 256, 296–297

International case law 23, 305, 311–312, 439–440, 441
International comparative analysis 20
International Convention for the Protection of All Persons from Enforced Disappearance 270–271n 181
International Covenant on Civil and Political Rights 98, 171–172n151, 235n227
  Article 14170–171
  Article 15234–235, 340n157, 340n162
International crimes, locus of the criminal prohibition 20–22n87
International Criminal Court 2–3, 2–3n6, 20–22n87, 34n132, 44–45n7
International Criminal Law 14–15, 18, 19, 20, 23, 24–25, 38, 76, 88–89, 95, 169, 239, 296, 431, 432–433, 439–440, 444, 448
International Criminal Tribunal for Former Yugoslavia 23
International Criminal Tribunal for Rwanda 18, 18n72, 91–92n7
International Humanitarian Law 2–3n5, 23, 66–68n122, 93–94n12, 100–101, 218–219, 232, 233n222, 311–312, 327–328, 328–330n108, 331n122, 367, 379n33
International Law Commission 200–201n54
International Law Commission 200–201n54, 301n365
International Military Tribunal 172–173n157, 199–200n51
Ituango Massacres v. Colombia 35n137

Jean Graven 2–3n12, 206–207, 209–210, 209–210n120, 318, 321
Judge Medehen Kiros 416, 418–419n270
Judge Nuru 422–423, 424–425, 426
judge-made 411, 422
judicial aggravating factors 425
Judicial System 93, 436–437

Kalbessa Negawo 30.185
Kayishema and Ruzindana 263–264n150
Killing a civilian 358–359
Klaus Dieter Baumgarten v. Germany 36–37n141, 340n160
Kononov v. Latvia 36–37n142, 340nn161-162, 341–342nn164-165, 342–343n169

Korbely v. Hungary 36–37n142, 340n161, 341–342n165

Lack of Remorse 94, 118, 119–120
Lata, Leenco 57
Legality 13n47, 36–37, 105, 232, 233, 234, 312, 337, 338, 339, 340, 341–343, 342–343nn 164-165, 343–344n 167, 345, 392–393, 399, 400n169, 436
  Accessibility 20–22n85, 29, 183–184, 341–342, 342–343n165
  Foreseeability 341–343, 342–343n165
  Lex mitior 233, 234, 354, 378, 399, 402–403
  Manifestly unlawful 312
  Nulla Poena Sine Lege 344–345, 382, 441–442
  Nullum Crimen Sine Lege 100, 337, 339, 441–442
Legesse Asfaw et al 155, 310–312, 321, 330, 334–336, 353, 354–355, 356–357, 358–359, 364, 365, 371, 423, 431, 438, 444–445
lex posterior 219–220n153, 228–229
life sentence 176, 375, 427
Luba basa 119–120n134
Luis Alfredo Almonacid Arellano et al. v. Chile 34n133, 35n137, 36–37n143

M.C. v. Bulgaria 34n127
Membership to political group 242, 246, 247, 290–291
Means of warfare 313–314n28, 328, 345–346, 348–349
Mekonnen Gelan et al. 145–146n22, 386, 387, 414, 427–428
Meles Zenawi 6–7n 29, 91, 110–111
Mengistu Hailemariam 6–7n29, 49, 52n 48, 111, 151, 157, 178, 277–278n225, 278n 228, 279–280n 235
Mengistu et al 8–9n34, 24–25, 79, 84, 99, 178, 198–199, 223, 242, 246–247, 275, 394–395
Mental Harm 211–212, 214, 256–261, 269, 282, 305, 381–382, 388–389, 398
Mens Rea
  general 251–253
  Genocidal *mens rea* 253, 254, 263, 267, 272
Methods of warfare 314–315n29, 336–337, 345, 347–349, 361, 371, 441–442

Michu, 119–120n135
Mitigating factors 378, 394–395, 398n158, 406, 409, 411–412
motive 253–254, 381, 382n47, 383, 396, 414, 434
Model Treaty on Extradition 181
Multiplicity 259, 296–297, 318–319n55, 332n124, 355, 358–359, 420–421, 428n114

Ne bis in idem 36
Necessary measures against 227–228
Nexus to an armed conflict 311, 363, 364, 371–372, 386, 444–445
Non-retroactivity 36–37n140, 36–37n143, 105, 338

Obligation to prosecute 29–30, 35, 133-134, 36–37n137, 93–94, 95, 96, 97, 103, 136–137, 201–202, 439, 441, 449
official commands 276n214
Ogaden National Liberation Front 48n27
Ordinary penal provisions 20–22n87
Oromia Supreme Court 183–184
Oromo Liberation Front 48, 154, 309–310
Oromo-Gumuz 11, 11–12n44, 14, 24–25, 44, 45, 94, 129, 131, 139, 140–142, 170, 175, 233, 236, 253, 287, 373, 374–375, 381–382, 438–439, 443

Peace
  Absence of peace 328–330n113
  Anti-peace activities 136
  International peace 73
  Just peace 57
  Lasting peace 56, 130
  Peace Agreement 56nn 69-71
  Peace and Democracy transitional conference 53–54
  Peace and Stability 55
  Peace call 108–109nn 82-83
  Peace talks 48, 49, 50–51
  Peace Treaty 316–317, 323
  Traditional philosophies to peace and 120–121
  Unjust peace 57, 58
Pecuniary Penalties 379, 380–381
Penal Code of 1957 2–3,

INDEX

Article 281 9–10, 71, 75, 97–98, 104–105, 197, 198–199, 201, 203–204, 207, 208–209, 210–212, 214, 215, 218–219, 222, 224–225, 226–227, 228–230, 239–240, 243, 253, 256, 262, 266–267, 270, 326, 384n63, 386n79, 402–403
Article 282 71n143, 79, 100–101n41, 102n47, 102n48, 155, 310n16, 354–355nn205-206, 355–356nn212-213, 358n230, 358–360, 362n247
Article 240 107
Article 119 108
Article 522 64–65n147, 74n166, 229–230, 230–231n213
Peoples' Democratic Republic of Ethiopia 48, 386–387n 79
Personal Jurisdiction 38, 143–144, 149, 154–155
Petty offenses 65–66, 81, 385–386, 385–386n74, 398
Plan 16–17n64, 52, 73, 88–89, 97, 136, 161, 163, 204, 205, 206, 207, 207–208n 106, 216, 217–218, 253, 254n97, 272–273n187, 272–273
Political groups 19, 71, 97, 98, 99–100, 135–136n191, 157–158, 162–163, 173n163, 195, 211–212, 213, 214, 221, 222, 229, 241, 242, 243, 245–246, 273–274, 275, 283, 291–292, 369, 374–375, 434, 436, 441
Political Legitimacy 91–92n3, 93–94, 123, 125–126, 137, 370, 434
Politicide 19, 71, 97–98, 99, 100, 229, 435
Politicide 19, 71, 98, 99, 100, 225, 228–229
presumptive mens rea 251–252n82
Prevent Propagation 262
Principal Penalties 379, 397, 398
Principle of opportunity 105
Progeny 210, 211, 251, 262
Progressive abolition of the death penalty 429–430
pronouncements, and campaigns of violence; 276n214
Prosecutor v. *Ahmad Al Faqi Al Mahdi* 391, 415
Prosecutor v. *Akayesu* 24–25n94, 237–238n8
Prosecutor v. *Brima et al.,* 24–25n100
Prosecutor v. *Fofana et al* 24–25n100
Prosecutor v. Jelisić 271–272n187

Prosecutor v. Krstić 287–288n 288, 289–290, 294, 392
Prosecutor v. Kupreškić 292–293n318, 357
Prosecutor v. *Lubanga* 24–25n101
Prosecutor v. *Tadić* 24–25n103, 102n49, 311n22
Protected Groups 97, 98, 99–100, 131, 195, 204, 214, 217–218, 221, 222–223, 240–241, 243–244, 248, 292–293, 295, 301, 440–441
Provisional Military Government 5–6n20, 79n1787, 113n104, 225n185
Public Security Protection Committee 279

R. v. *Finta* 20–22n88
Rape 4n28, 11n 44, 154–155, 259–261, 262–263, 264, 268–269, 318–319n 55, 375, 390
Rape 6–7n28, 11n44, 71–72, 100–101n41, 154–155, 202–203n70, 257–258n119, 259–261, 262–264, 268–269, 318–319n55, 375, 390, 420–421
Rape Trauma Syndrome 263
recidivism 391, 405–406
Reconciliation 16–17, 49–50, 56, 57, 90, 113, 116–117, 116–117n117, 118
Red-Terror 150, 151, 152
   Let the Red-Terror intensify277
   Red-Terror camaign54, 146–149n 34, 152
   Red-Terror committee115
   Red-Terror Trials8–9, 8–9n33, 19
redundant 262, 264, 304–305
Regular Public Prosecutor 38, 78
relatively small 295
restructuring institutions of violence 276n214
retaliatory genocide 268n169
retaliatory genocide 141–142
Retribution 404–406
Revised Special Penal Code of 1981 63–64n107, 108–109n79, 109–110n83, 159–160n94, 215
Revolutionary Information Unit 277–278, 279
Rigorous Imprisonment 63, 375, 384–386

Schabas 99–100, 210
SCSL Statute 66n122, 93–94n12

Second Italo-Ethiopian war   192, 308–309, 315
Serious criminal offenses   64, 64n111, 393, 393n125
seriousness of an injury   261–262
service in peacekeeping missions   428
Shimglena   119–120n136
Simple Imprisonment   63, 326–327
Sixth Committee, UNGA   191, 242
slow death genocide   268–269n170
Southern Nations Nationalities and Peoples' Regional State Supreme Court (SNNPR SC)   255, 387
special aggravating factors   420–421
Special Court   108–109n76, 108–109n78, 159–160
Special Court for Sierra Leone   61n97
special mitigating factors   397–398n158, 412, 414
Special Penal Code   108–109, 159–160, 175, 215
special prosecution office   160
Special Prosecutor's Office (SPO)   5–6, 60, 61–62, 160
specificity of the crime of genocide   259
SPO Proclamation   46–47, 62, 66, 69–70, 70n139, 73, 73n157, 76, 76n174, 77–78,
  Article 6   70, 73, 74, 143, 146, 149, 199
  Article 9   160
SPO v. Abdulekadir Mohammed Burka   74, 74nn165-166, 374–375n11, 386–387n85
SPO v. Aman Gobena et al.   74, 74n164, 74n166, 374–375n11
SPO v. Basha Bekele Fasil and Abera Lemma   73, 73nn157-158
SPO v. General Solomon Negussie et al.   72, 72n154
SPO v. Geremew Debele   221, 237–238, 274–275
SPO v. Geremew Debele C1.P35 n95, C5.P96 n159, C6.P4 n7, C6.P92 n206, C6.P93 nn207–208
SPO v. Kassaye Aragaw et al   415–416n252
SPO v. Melaku Teferra   179nn195-196, 257–258n119, 394, 422, 426–427
Srebrenica   293–294n327, 295n337
Stable and permanent   247n150
Starvation   333, 355, 359–361, 362–363
Subject Matter Jurisdiction   62, 65–66, 70, 71, 73–74
substantiality requirement   295, 299n335

Summary execution   18, 59, 60–61, 69, 75n168, 78, 131–132, 157–158, 197, 201–202, 242, 259–261n133

Tadesse Jewannie Mengesha et al   28n 112, 141–142, 170, 286
Tepe v. Turkey   34n131, 43–44n8
Tesfaye Nenno Loya et al   141–142, 253n88, 254, 255–256n104, 255–257, 286, 303–304n379, 427n58
Tesfaye Woldeselassie et al   395, 418–419
Teshome Bayyu et al.   292 425
the Anglo-Iranian Oil Co. case   236
the dead is dead   117
the Dergue interrogators   268n169
Thomas Lubanga Dyilo   383
Tigray Peoples' Liberation Front (TPLF)   110–111, 125, 129, 309–310
Tigray Peoples' Democratic Movement   135–136
Torture   75, 257, 259–261n133, 368–369, 398, 424
Transitional Government of Ethiopia   5–6, 45n12
Truth
  Historical truth 61
  Judicial truth 61–62
  Tell the full truth 118
  Truth and Reconciliation Commission 56–57n71, 57, 118, 120–121n137
  Truth telling 118, 119–120
  whole truth 60–61

Unfettered Discretion   407, 417–418n264, 418
United Nations War Crimes Commission   314–315n31, 316–317n44, 361n239
Uniqueness of genocide   20–22n89
Universal Declaration of Human Rights   59n86, 87, 171–172n149, 220, 235, 338, 339, 339n156
Unlawful arrest or detention   6–7n28, 71–72
Unnamed defendants v. the Prosecutor   36–37n146, 339n154
Utilitarian   404

Velásquez-Rodríguez v. Honduras   34
Victor's Justice   140–141, 140n5, 142–143, 149, 151n49, 152–153, 154, 156–159, 156n78, 161, 405, 435

INDEX

Violence   161, 163–164, 165–166, 165n114, 167, 168–169, 168–169n134, 173, 186, 245n46, 248, 255n104, 259–261, 266, 276

Waltajji Begalo   386, 386n82
White-Terror   150, 150–151n46, 151, 153, 157–158, 245, 309–310n14
willingness to apologize   121–122

Wofelala   259–261, 259–261n132
Wukro   102, 102n50, 332n124, 353–354, 364, 365, 366–367

Yosef Kiros   29, 161n95, 178n190

Zimbabwe, a safe haven   52, 178

Printed in the United States
By Bookmasters